W9-DIM-490

Anxiety and Depression

Distinctive and Overlapping Features

This is a volume in
PERSONALITY, PSYCHOPATHOLOGY, AND PSYCHOTHERAPY
A Series of Monographs, Texts, and Treatises
Under the Editorship of David T. Lykken and Philip C. Kendall

Anxiety and Depression

Distinctive and Overlapping Features

Edited by

Philip C. Kendall
Department of Psychology
Temple University
Philadelphia, Pennsylvania

David Watson
Department of Psychology
Southern Methodist University
Dallas, Texas

Academic Press, Inc.
Harcourt Brace Jovanovich, Publishers
San Diego New York Berkeley Boston London Sydney Tokyo Toronto

ACADEMIC PRESS, INC.
San Diego, California 92101

United Kingdom Edition published by
ACADEMIC PRESS LIMITED
24-28 Oval Road, London NW1 7DX

Library of Congress Cataloging-in-Publication Data

Anxiety and depression : distinctive and overlapping features /
[edited by] Philip C. Kendall and David Watson.
p. cm. — (Personality, psychopathology, and psychotherapy)
Includes bibliographies and index.
ISBN 0-12-404170-1 (alk. paper)
1. Anxiety. 2. Depression, Mental. I. Kendall, Philip C.
II. Watson, David, Date. III. Series
[DNLM: 1. Anxiety Disorders. 2. Depressive Disorders. WM 172
A63612]
RC531.A56 1989
616.85′223—dc19
DNLM/DLC
for Library of Congress 88-7813
CIP

PRINTED IN THE UNITED STATES OF AMERICA
89 90 91 92 9 8 7 6 5 4 3 2 1

To our children
MARK, REED, BART, and ERICA

Contents

Contributors xiii
Preface xv

Part I
Theoretical Perspectives

1. Understanding Anxiety and Depression: Their Relation to Negative and Positive Affective States

David Watson and Philip C. Kendall

I. Introduction 3
II. The Relation between Anxiety and Depression 4
III. Anxiety and Depression as Affective States 6
IV. Relation of Anxiety and Depression to Negative and Positive Affectivity 9
V. Directions for Future Research: Positive Affect's Relation to Endogenous Depression 19
VI. Implications and Conclusions 20
References 22

2. Cognitive-Behavioral Perspectives: Theory and Research on Depression and Anxiety

Philip C. Kendall and Rick E. Ingram

I. Introduction 27
II. Empirical Research on Cognitive Constructs 31
III. Methodological Issues and Strategies in Examining Cognitive Specificity 38
IV. Theoretical Perspectives 41
V. Summary and Conclusions 48
References 49

3. **Behavioral Models of Anxiety and Depression**
Lynn P. Rehm

I. Introduction 55
II. General Assumptions 57
III. Theories of Anxiety 64
IV. Theories of Depression 68
V. Summary and Conclusions 75
References 76

Part II
Assessment Issues

4. **The Anxiety and Depressive Disorders: Descriptive Psychopathology and Differential Diagnosis**
Lee Anna Clark

I. Introduction 83
II. Clinical Studies of Depression and Anxiety 92
III. Summary and Conclusions 121
References 123

5. **Self-Report Assessment of Depression and Anxiety**
Ian H. Gotlib and Douglas B. Cane

I. Introduction 131
II. Diagnostic Criteria 132
III. Psychometric Issues 136
IV. Self-Report Measures of Depression 137
V. Self-Report Measures of Anxiety 142
VI. Scales Measuring Both Depression and Anxiety 146
VII. Discriminant Validity 150
VIII. The Relationship among Self-Report Measures of Depression and Anxiety: Possible Explanations 155
IX. Conclusions 160
References 163

6. **Anxiety and Depression in Children and Adolescents: Negative Affectivity or Separate Constructs?**
A. J. Finch, Jr., Julie A. Lipovsky, and Charles D. Casat

I. Introduction 171
II. Diagnostic Definitions 172

III. Methods of Assessment 177
IV. Assessment Research Evidence 183
V. Biological Correlates of Depression and Anxiety 188
VI. Conclusions and Implications 193
References 196

Part III
Precursors and Concomitants

7. Major Life Events in Anxiety and Depression

Timothy W. Smith and Kenneth D. Allred

I. Introduction 205
II. Approaches to the Measurement of Life Stress 207
III. The Role of Life Events in Depression 209
IV. Life Events in Anxiety 212
V. Studies of Anxiety and Depression 213
VI. Considerations for Future Research 215
VII. Summary and Conclusions 218
References 219

8. The Effects of Daily Life Events on Negative Affective States

Alex J. Zautra, Charles A. Guarnaccia, and John W. Reich

I. Introduction 225
II. Why Small Events Are Important 227
III. Development of the Inventory of Small Life Events (ISLE) 229
IV. Daily Events and Negative Affects 231
V. Attributions about Daily Events: Their Effects on Anxiety and Depression 233
VI. Small Events, Negative Mood, and Cognitions across Days 234
VII. Study of High-Risk Groups: Life Events and Aging Project (LEAP) 237
VIII. Summary 247
References 249

9. Affect and the Social Environment: The Role of Social Support in Depression and Anxiety

Joseph P. Stokes and David J. McKirnan

I. Introduction 253
II. The Nature of Social Support 254
III. Social Support and Depression 259
IV. Social Support and Anxiety 275
V. Conclusions and Future Directions 277
References 279

10. Social Problem Solving and Negative Affective Conditions

Arthur M. Nezu and Thomas J. D'Zurilla

I. Introduction 285
II. The Concept of Stress 286
III. A Transactional/Problem-Solving Model of Stress 289
IV. Problem Solving and Depression 297
V. Problem Solving and Anxiety 305
VI. Problem Solving, Depression, and Anxiety: The Specificity Question 307
References 310

11. An Epidemiological Perspective on the Anxiety and Depressive Disorders

Carolyn L. Williams and James Poling

I. Introduction 317
II. Overview of the Epidemiology of Mental Disorders 318
III. Concerns Relevant to Mental Disorders 323
IV. Distribution of Anxiety and Depressive Disorders 326
V. Risk Factors for Anxiety and Depressive Disorders 330
VI. Preventive Efforts for Anxiety and Depressive Disorders 335
VII. Summary and Conclusions 336
References 337

12. Anxiety and Depression in Seasonal Affective Disorders

Siegfried Kasper and Norman E. Rosenthal

I. Introduction 341
II. Seasonal Affective Disorder (SAD) 343
III. Seasonality as a Dimension in Normals and SAD Patients 347
IV. Relevance to SAD of Seasonal Rhythms in Animals 349
V. Phototherapy for SAD 352
VI. Practical Aspects of Phototherapy 359
VII. Psychobiology of SAD and the Physiological Effects of Phototherapy 363
VIII. Conclusions 368
References 369

Part IV
Treatment

13. Cognitive Theory and Therapy of Anxiety and Depression

David A. Clark and Aaron T. Beck

I. Introduction 379
II. Anxiety and Depression: Toward an Integrated Theory of Information Processing 380

III. Cognitive Therapy of Anxiety and Depression 396
IV. Empirical Status of Cognitive Therapy of Anxiety and Depression 400
V. Conclusions 404
References 405

14. Behavioral Treatments for Anxiety and Depression

Edna B. Foa, Barbara Olasov Rothbaum, and Michael J. Kozak

I. Introduction 413
II. Anxiety Disorders 414
III. Treatment of Anxiety Disorders 419
IV. The Behavioral Treatment of Depression 433
V. Similarities and Differences in Treatments of Anxiety and Depression 441
References 443

15. The Treatment of Anxiety and Depression: The Process of Affective Change

Jeremy D. Safran and Leslie S. Greenberg

I. Introduction 455
II. Information Processing and Biological Adaptation 458
III. Emotion 460
IV. Anxiety 464
V. Depression 474
VI. Conclusion 485
References 486

Part V
Summary and Conclusions

16. Common and Differentiating Features of Anxiety and Depression: Current Findings and Future Directions

David Watson and Philip C. Kendall

I. Introduction 493
II. Common (Nonspecific) Features 494
III. Critical, Differentiating Features 497
IV. Implications of the Findings and Directions for Future Research 501
V. Concluding Remarks 507
References 507

Index 509
List of Previous Volumes 517

Contributors

Numbers in parentheses indicate the pages on which the authors' contributions begin.

Kenneth D. Allred (205), Department of Psychology, University of Utah, Salt Lake City, Utah 84112

Aaron T. Beck (379), Center for Cognitive Therapy, University of Pennsylvania, Philadelphia, Pennsylvania 19104

Douglas B. Cane (131), Department of Psychology, University of Western Ontario, London, Ontario, Canada N6A 5C2

Charles D. Casat (171), Department of Psychiatry and Behavioral Sciences, Medical University of South Carolina, Charleston, South Carolina 29425

David A. Clark (379), Department of Psychology, University of New Brunswick, Fredericton, New Brunswick, Canada E3B 6E4

Lee Anna Clark (83), Department of Psychology, Southern Methodist University, Dallas, Texas 75275

Thomas J. D'Zurilla (285), Department of Psychology, State University of New York at Stony Brook, Stony Brook, New York 11794

A. J. Finch, Jr. (171), Department of Psychology and Behavioral Sciences, Medical University of South Carolina, Charleston, South Carolina 29425

Edna B. Foa (413), Medical College of Pennsylvania at Eastern Pennsylvania Psychiatric Institute, Philadelphia, Pennsylvania 19129

Ian H. Gotlib (131), Department of Psychology, University of Western Ontario, London, Ontario, Canada N6A 5C2

Leslie S. Greenberg (455), Department of Psychology, York University, North York, Ontario, Canada M3J 1P3

Charles A. Guarnaccia (225), Department of Psychology, Arizona State University, Tempe, Arizona 85287-1104

Rick E. Ingram (27), Department of Psychology, San Diego State University, San Diego, California 92182

Siegfried Kasper[1] (341), Clinical Psychobiology Branch, National Institute of Mental Health, Bethesda, Maryland 20892

Philip C. Kendall (3, 27, 493), Department of Psychology, Temple University, Philadelphia, Pennsylvania 19122

Michael J. Kozak (413), Department of Psychiatry, Medical College of Pennsylvania at Eastern Pennsylvania Psychiatric Institute, Philadelphia, Pennsylvania 19129

Julie A. Lipovsky (171), Department of Psychiatry and Behavioral Sciences, Medical University of South Carolina, Charleston, South Carolina 29425

David J. McKirnan (253), Department of Psychology, The University of Illinois at Chicago, Chicago, Illinois 60680

Arthur M. Nezu (285), Department of Psychiatry, Beth Israel Medical Center/Mount Sinai School of Medicine, New York, New York 10003

James Poling (317), Department of Psychology, Temple University, Philadelphia, Pennsylvania 19122

Lynn P. Rehm (55), Department of Psychology, University of Houston, Houston, Texas 77204-5341

John W. Reich (225), Department of Psychology, Arizona State University, Tempe, Arizona 85287-1104

Norman E. Rosenthal (341), Clinical Psychobiology Branch, National Institute of Mental Health, Bethesda, Maryland 20892

Barbara Olasov Rothbaum (413), Medical College of Pennsylvania at Eastern Pennsylvania Psychiatric Institute, Philadelphia, Pennsylvania 19129

Jeremy D. Safran (455), Clarke Institute of Psychiatry and University of Toronto, Toronto, Ontario, Canada M5T 1R8

Timothy W. Smith (205), Department of Psychology, University of Utah, Salt Lake City, Utah 84112

Joseph P. Stokes (253), Department of Psychology, The University of Illinois at Chicago, Chicago, Illinois 60680

David Watson (3, 493), Department of Psychology, Southern Methodist University, Dallas, Texas 75275

Carolyn L. Williams (317), Division of Epidemiology, School of Public Health, University of Minnesota, Minneapolis, Minnesota 55455

Alex J. Zautra (225), Department of Psychology, Arizona State University, Tempe, Arizona 85287-1104

[1]Present address: Psychiatrische Universitätsklinik, D-6900 Heidelberg, Voßtraße 4, Federal Republic of Germany.

Preface

During the decades of the 1970s and 1980s, mental health professionals have focused a great deal of attention on the depressive and anxiety disorders. In the study of depression, several notable developments have been of marked benefit for psychotherapy practice and research. Of particular interest to behavioral scientists have been such advances as (1) the emergence of behavioral treatments for depression, (2) the integration of cognitive and behavioral treatment strategies, and (3) research documentation that these and other psychologically based treatments are not only effective but in fact produce outcomes comparable to pharmacotherapy. Anxiety, too, has remained centrally important to the treatment-evaluation literature. Studies of the anxiety disorders have addressed such issues as the development and treatment of specific phobias, the relation between panic disorder and agoraphobia, the underlying causes of obsessive–compulsive symptomatology, and the role of anxiety and stress in the development, maintenance, and/or exacerbation of health problems.

Why then, we asked, has so much less attention been paid to the relation between anxiety and depression? Why has there been relatively little concern over the apparent overlap between these constructs? We have no ready explanation for this past neglect, but we offer this volume as a systematic attempt to address these issues. Its purpose is to explore directly the similarities and differences between anxiety and depression. The respective authors have been asked to identify the shared and distinctive aspects of these disorders, and to consider the implications for the theory, assessment, diagnosis, and treatment of anxiety and depression.

Theoretical models for anxiety and depression are typically formulated without concern for discriminant validity; that is, underlying structures and processes are proposed without regard for whether or not they characterize the other disorder as well. In contrast, contributors to the present volume confront this overlap directly. The initial chapters examine basic theoretical issues. First, Watson and Kendall explore the emotional underpinnings of anxiety and depression, examining them as basic affective states that reflect substantial dispositional differences in temperament. They discuss these disorders in the context of a two-dimensional structure of experienced mood and demonstrate important similarities and differences between them. Next, Kendall and Ingram, using cognitive content, attributional style, and information-processing style as examples of cognitive-behavioral theory, identify both distinctive and overlapping features of the two disorders. Finally, Rehm examines various behavioral models for anxiety and depression, noting the adaptive, evolutionary significance of each disorder.

The next part examines assessment issues. In her chapter, Clark considers both the symptomatology and diagnosis of the anxiety and depressive disorders. She notes, for example, that clinicians' ratings of anxiety and depression are more independent when they are generated as part of a diagnostic process; what effect this has on the validity of the ratings is, however, unclear. Next, Gotlib and Cane provide a careful examination of the major self-report scales in the area. Self-report assessment has received the greatest attention from both researchers and clinicians, and not unreasonably so—after all, the target constructs involve dysphoric emotional status, and self-reports are prime sources of such data. However, Gotlib and Cane show that a large proportion of the items on widely used anxiety and depression scales actually measure aspects or symptoms common to both disorders, with a subsequent loss of discriminant validity. Finch, Lipovsky, and Casat reach similar conclusions in their review of anxiety and depression measures that are used to study children and adolescents.

The third part of the book concerns the precursors and concomitants of anxiety and depression. Much recent research has investigated the psychological sequelae of both major and minor life events. Smith and Allred's review indicates that major life changes are associated with significant levels of emotional distress. However, researchers in this area have focused mainly on depression, to the relative neglect of anxiety. Thus, connections between particular classes of events and specific types of emotional distress remain to be established. Similarly, Zautra, Guarnaccia, and Reich review the data regarding more routine life events. They report that such events have important effects on subjective well-being, but more specific affect–event relations remain unclear.

Considerable evidence indicates that social support systems foster good adjustment; conversely, a lack of social supports has been strongly implicated in emotional distress. Stokes and McKirnan are quick to point out, however, that the direction of causality is not clear in these studies.

While the sudden loss of social support might plausibly lead to anxiety and/or depression, undesirable personality/social interactional characteristics associated with anxiety and depressive disorders may also weaken one's social support systems. The authors argue for a cognitive view of social support; that is, they emphasize the importance of support as it is subjectively perceived by the individual, rather than as an objective aspect of the person's environment. Next, Nezu and D'Zurilla analyze the literature on social problem solving. They suggest that anxiety and depression are likely to occur when efforts at social problem solving are ineffective and lead to negative outcomes. Although this model would seem to suggest an underlying similarity in the etiologies of anxiety and depression, the authors maintain that individuals' perceptions, expectations, and beliefs about their problems—and their perceived ability to solve these problems—may serve to separate the two disorders.

Williams and Poling provide a basic epidemiological analysis of the anxiety and depressive disorders. Above all, their review provides a strong empirical documentation of the substantial level of co-occurrence in these two disorders. Finally, Kasper and Rosenthal close Part III with an examination of seasonal variations in mood and mood disorders. Most of this research has focused on systematic, seasonal fluctuations in depression in a highly susceptible subset of the population. The authors explore some evolutionary and biological explanations for these phenomena and describe a unique new treatment—phototherapy—for ameliorating these fall and winter depressions. Interestingly, anxious mood is also a common symptom in this disorder, but seasonal fluctuations in anxiety have not yet been systematically investigated.

The fourth part of the book examines the treatment of anxiety and depression. Using the features of cognition described by Kendall and Ingram, Clark and Beck suggest that the depressive and anxious disorders can be distinguished by the content of their respective schemata. The subjective world of the depressive is dominated by an overwhelmingly negative view of the self, the world, and the future. In contrast, the anxious individual overestimates the possibility of harm or danger in the environment, while minimizing his or her ability to cope with this threat. Clark and Beck review the assumptions of cognitive-behavioral treatments for depression and anxiety and suggest differing therapeutic strategies for the two disorders. Foa, Rothbaum, and Kozak reach similar conclusions in their review of behavioral treatments in this area. Behavioral theories of depression emphasize a deficiency in the availability of positive reinforcement. Accordingly, behavioral treatments seek to increase reward-seeking behavior and, in addition, to increase the client's perception that rewards are being received. In contrast, treatments for anxiety seek to correct misperceptions about the imminence of danger, and to reduce the autonomic manifestations of anxiety or panic. However, behavioral treatments for the two disorders also show important similarities. For example, both involve procedures designed to reduce subjective distress, and both aim at altering the client's perceptions of action/outcome contingencies. Next, Safran and Greenberg emphasize that emotions are adaptive responses that should be experienced and expressed. They argue that the blocking of emotional experience results in various negative consequences, including both anxiety and depression. Accordingly, they offer treatment techniques designed to help clients experience and express their emotions more fully. The fifth and final part of the volume is devoted to Watson and Kendall's summary, conclusions, and recommendations for future research.

Reasoned analyses of theory, measurement, and treatment can identify key similarities and differences in anxiety and depression. Given the generally separate foci of their respective literatures, there has been a need for a comprehensive treatment of the relation between these two disorders. The present volume, conceived broadly to cover the domains of clinical psychology, psychiatry, personality, and basic affect research, is designed to fill this void. The editors express their gratitude to their respective staffs, colleagues, and students who cooperated in various portions of the production of this book. Some of the preparation of this work was facilitated by a Biomedical Research Grant from Temple University to Philip C. Kendall. We wish to acknowledge the assistance of the staff at Academic Press, and we also thank each of the authors for being a part of this venture.

Theoretical Perspectives

questions their validity as specific measures of "anxiety" or "depression." In fact, analyses have generally shown that anxiety and depression scales are as highly correlated with each other as they are among themselves, and factor analyses have suggested that they tap a single undifferentiated factor (e.g., Dobson, 1985; Gotlib, 1984; Mendels et al., 1972; Tanaka-Matsumi & Kameoka, 1986). However, the problem is even more pervasive: Anxiety and depression scales are also highly correlated with measures of anger, hostility, neuroticism, pessimism, general maladjustment, and (negatively) with ego strength. These findings indicate that subjective distress is dominated by a large general factor that has variously been called *neuroticism, general psychological distress,* or, most recently, *negative affectivity* (Gotlib, 1984; Watson & Clark, 1984; Zurawski & Smith, 1987).

B. Symptom and Diagnostic Data

It would be a mistake to conclude that these poor discriminant findings simply reflect the limitations of self-report assessment, because the same problem can be seen in other types of data as well. For example, clinicians' and teachers' ratings of anxiety and depression are also strongly related (e.g., Deluty et al., 1986; Foa et al., 1983; Lipman, Rickels, Covi, Derogatis, & Uhlenhuth, 1969; Wolfe et al., 1987; Zuckerman et al., 1967). Moreover, anxious and depressive symptoms tend to co-occur in patients, so that many patients who report one type of symptom also experience the other (Derogatis, Klerman, & Lipman, 1972; Kellner et al., 1972; Roth, Gurney, Garside, & Kerr, 1972; for discussions of symptom overlap, see Breier et al., 1985; Gersh & Fowles, 1979).

Substantial overlap can also be seen at the diagnostic level. For example, Woodruff, Guze, and Clayton (1972) reported that half of their anxiety neurotic subjects were also diagnosed as having secondary depression. Similarly, Breier, Charney, and Heninger (1986) found that 70% of their patients with an anxiety disorder (agoraphobia and/or panic disorder) had experienced at least one major depressive episode. Finally, both symptom and diagnostic data indicate that there is a large group of mixed anxious–depressed patients who must be distinguished from those with purer forms of anxiety or depression (Akiskal, 1985; Gersh & Fowles, 1979).

C. Biological and Genetic Evidence

Drug, family, and twin studies suggest that at least some forms of anxiety and depression may share a common diathesis. For example, the evidence linking panic disorder and depression is strong: There is considerable evidence that antidepressant drugs significantly reduce panic attacks and other anxiety-related symptoms, and that noradrenergic hyperactivity is involved in both panic disorder and certain subtypes of depression (e.g., Breier et al., 1985; Kahn et al., 1986). Moreover, while some inconsistencies in the data remain unexplained (see Clark, this volume), a number of family and twin studies suggest that depression and anxiety share a common genetic diathesis (e.g., Kendler, Heath, Martin, & Eaves, 1987; Leckman, Weissman, Merikangas, Pauls, & Prusoff, 1983; Munjack & Moss, 1981).

Taken together, these data provide evidence of a substantial degree of overlap between anxiety and depression. The association between them is strong enough to suggest to some researchers that they are simply variants of a single disorder (see Breier et al., 1985, for a discussion of this issue). Most clinicians and researchers in the field, however, continue to believe that the basic distinction is valid and should be maintained (e.g., Akiskal, 1985; Foa & Foa, 1982). They point to distinct subgroups of patients within each class, and to subjective and physiological correlates that are unique to each type of disorder (e.g., the REM sleep disturbance that is found in depression, but not anxiety; see Akiskal, 1985; Kupfer et al., 1983). Some researchers have noted essential differences in the psychological therapies developed for anxiety and depression, while others (e.g., Ingram, Kendall, Smith, Donnell, & Ronan, 1987) have reported cognitive processing features that distinguish them. Across the board, it is agreed that there is need for further research and better theoretical models to improve the differentiation of anxiety and depression. In the remainder of this chapter we present a model that we believe represents a step in this direction.

III. Anxiety and Depression as Affective States

A. Relation to the Primary Emotions

In order to understand the relationship between anxiety and depression, it is useful to consider the basic affective states that underlie them. Several prominent theories of human emotion have been proposed in recent years, including those of Ekman (Ekman, 1982; Ekman, Friesen, & Ellsworth, 1972), Izard (1972, 1977), Plutchik (1962, 1980), and Tomkins (1962, 1963). Although these models differ in their particulars, they share many essential features. All posit a relatively small number of discrete emotions, generally ranging between 7 and 10, with a core set that is common to every model—joy, interest/excitement, surprise, fear, anger, sadness/anguish, contempt, and/or disgust. Each emotion is thought to have its own characteristic pattern of autonomic activity, and there is some evidence to indicate that this is true (Ekman, Levenson, & Friesen, 1983). Each emotion also has its own prototypic facial expression; for example, joy is accompanied by a smile, and anger, by a frown or glare (Ekman, 1982; Ekman et al., 1972; Izard, 1971, 1977). Finally, each basic affect reflects a different set of precipitating circumstances and gives rise to a characteristic range of adaptive behavior; for example, fear motivates escape from a threatening situation, whereas interest/excitement generates novel and exploratory behavior.

We will focus here on Izard's (1972, 1977) Differential Emotions Theory, because he has dealt most extensively with the affective basis of anxiety and depression. Izard argues for 10 basic emotions: 7 are negative (anger, fear, sadness/distress, contempt, disgust, guilt, and shame/shyness), 2 are positive (joy and interest/excitement), and 1 is relatively neutral (surprise). In this model, anxiety and depression are not themselves basic emotions, but instead reflect complex combinations of these fundamental affects (Blumberg & Izard, 1986; Izard, 1972, 1977). Specifically, fear is the dominant emotion in anxiety, but it interacts with variable combinations of the other emotions (especially anger, shame, guilt, sadness, and interest/excitement) to produce the overall experience. Izard argues that fear is always the central emotion in the experience of anxiety; the other emotions may or may not be important, depending upon the context of the anxiety reaction. In contrast, depression centers on the experience of sadness (also called distress or anguish), with other emotions (particularly disgust, contempt, anger, and to a lesser extent fear and guilt) involved in varying degrees, depending upon the situation.

Izard's theory thus proposes a clear differentiation between anxiety and depression at the basic emotional level: Anxiety is an experience that is dominated by fear, whereas depression centers on sadness. This model makes intuitive sense and, moreover, has been supported in several studies involving both adults and children (Blumberg & Izard, 1986; Izard, 1972, 1977).

B. Relations among the Negative Emotions

The notions that emerge from emotion theory (and the related data) make it all the more suprising that anxiety and depression are so difficult to separate empirically. Fear and sadness are conceptually distinct emotions that have different expressive patterns and that arise from different precipitating circumstances: Fear is a response to threat or danger, whereas sadness stems from separation, loss, or failure. If this is so—

and if fear and sadness centrally define anxiety and depression, respectively—then why are anxiety and depression so strongly related in both self-report and clinical data? To answer this question, we must consider the actual experience of affect—that is, mood as it is experienced and reported by the individual.

Self-reported mood yields a picture that is different from that seen in other types of data. In self-report the discrete conceptual categories break down to a considerable extent, and the basic emotions are not clearly distinguishable from one another; rather, self-rated mood is dominated by the overall hedonic tone of the affective experience. To illustrate the centrality of hedonic tone in self-report, we created mood scales that assess six of Izard's basic negative emotions. These scales are composed of synonym triads that were identified through a factor analysis of a larger set of mood descriptors (Zevon & Tellegen, 1982). The constructed scales measure fear (*afraid, frightened, scared*), sadness (*blue, downhearted, sad*), guilt (*ashamed, blameworthy, guilty*), anger (*angry, hostile, irritable*), contempt (*contemptuous, disdainful, scornful*), and disgust (*disgusted, loathing, revulsion*). The fear and sadness scales are, of course, most relevant to our examination of anxiety and depression.

These emotion scales were given to two large college student samples. The subjects were asked to rate the extent to which they had experienced each mood state on a 5-point Likert scale ranging from "very slightly or not at all" to "very much." Two different temporal instructions were used. Subjects rated how they felt either (1) "during the past few days" (n = 1005) or (2) "in general, that is, on the average" (n = 725). Note that the former instruction provides information about the subjects' recent or *state* mood, whereas the latter yields long-term or *trait* data.

Correlations among the six negative emotion scales in both samples are shown in Table 1.1. Several aspects of the table are noteworthy. First, the two sets of ratings clearly produced very similar results, indicating that the findings are relevant to both state and trait emotionality. Second, the fear and sadness scales are strongly related; they correlate .55 in the state data and .62 in the trait ratings. As noted previously, at the basic emotional level, anxiety is most strongly characterized by fear, whereas depression centers on sadness. Table 1.1 demonstrates that these primary emotions are themselves highly correlated in self-report and that they strongly co-occur in individuals. In other words, a person who experiences fear is very likely to report feeling sad as well. These results indicate that anxious and depressed moods are strongly confounded, even at the most basic affective level; this, in turn, helps to explain why anxiety and depression are so difficult to separate in scale or clinical data.

Table 1.1
Correlations among the Negative Emotion Scales[a]

Emotion scale	1	2	3	4	5	6
1. Sadness	—	.62	.67	.60	.52	.60
2. Fear	.55	—	.62	.57	.46	.53
3. Guilt	.37	.39	—	.55	.53	.58
4. Anger	.52	.41	.40	—	.65	.69
5. Contempt	.43	.38	.41	.56	—	.71
6. Disgust	.47	.39	.45	.60	.67	—

[a] Correlations for the trait ratings ($n = 725$) are shown above the diagonal, while those for the state ratings ($n = 1005$) are displayed below the diagonal. All coefficients are significant at the $p < .001$ level.

Third, all of the negative emotions are moderately to strongly related with one another. In the state data, the coefficients range from .37 to .66, with a median correlation of .43; similarly, in the trait data, the correlations range from .46 to .71 (median $r = .60$). The magnitude of these correlations is especially impressive given the modest reliability of three-item scales. Thus, we see that although these basic emotions can be distinguished in expressive and physiological data, they are nevertheless substantially related in self-report. These data demonstrate the dominant influence exerted by hedonic tone in emotional experience.

IV. Relation of Anxiety and Depression to Negative and Positive Affectivity

A. Analyses of Mood Descriptors

Thus far we have considered only the negative emotions, and our discussion may have implied that self-report is dominated by a single general distress factor. Actually, extensive evidence indicates that self-rated mood is characterized by two dominant dimensions (Watson, 1988b; Watson, Clark, & Tellegen, 1984; Watson & Tellegen, 1985). Specifically, the negative emotions combine to form a broad distress factor called *Negative Affect* (NA), while the positive mood states jointly comprise *Positive Affect* (PA).

NA is the general factor of subjective distress and dissatisfaction implied in the previous discussion. High NA is composed of terms reflecting a wide range of negative affective states, including *fear, nervousness, anger, guilt, contempt, disgust, sadness, loneliness,* and *self-dissatis-*

faction. Low NA is best defined by terms such as *calm* and *relaxed*. The existence of a general NA factor again indicates that negative mood states strongly co-occur with one another. Thus, an individual who reports feeling fearful is also likely to experience substantial amounts of anger, guilt, and sadness as well.

In terms of our present discussion, it is especially noteworthy that mood descriptors reflecting both anxious (e.g., *scared, afraid, anxious, worried, tense*) and depressed affect (e.g., *sad, blue, depressed, gloomy, downhearted*) are consistently strong markers of high NA (Tellegen, 1985; Watson & Clark, 1984; Watson & Tellegen, 1985). These findings help to illustrate why it is so difficult to separate anxious from depressive states—both states strongly reflect the influence of this general NA factor.

In contrast, PA reflects one's level of pleasurable engagement with the environment. High PA is composed of terms reflecting enthusiasm (e.g., *excited, enthusiastic*), joy (*delighted, joyful*), high energy (e.g., *active, energetic*), mental interest and alertness (e.g., *attentive, alert, interested*), and determination (e.g., *strong, determined*). However, low PA is more interesting for our purposes: It is best defined by descriptors reflecting fatigue (e.g., *sleepy, sluggish*) and depression (*sad, depressed*). In addition, it is noteworthy that anxiety-related mood terms (*anxious, worried, fearful*) are not significantly related to (low) PA. In other words, depression—but not anxiety—is related to the experience and/or reporting of low PA.

These mood data thus present a very interesting pattern. Anxiety can be viewed as a more or less pure state of high NA, with no significant secondary PA component. That is, an anxious individual is necessarily high on NA, but can be high, low, or anywhere in between on PA. In contrast, depression is a more complex combination of high NA and low PA. Thus, NA is a confounding influence that is common to both anxiety and depression, and is a major factor in producing the strong correlation found between them. However, the data also suggest that the loss of pleasurable engagement (i.e., low PA) is a significant and largely unique aspect of depression. Consequently, PA may be an important factor in the differentiation between depression and anxiety (Tellegen, 1985; Watson, 1988b; Watson & Tellegen, 1985).

To illustrate this pattern, we analyzed mood ratings obtained from a sample of 331 college students. Subjects rated the frequency with which they had experienced each of 35 affective states during the past few weeks. The ratings were made on a 4-point Likert scale; the options were: "little or none of the time," "some of the time," "a good part of the time," and "most of the time." The mood descriptors used in this analysis were selected to (1) assess a broad range of mood states and (2) include several terms directly relevant to the experience of both depressed and anxious affect.

These mood ratings were subjected to a principal factor analysis with squared multiple correlations as the communality estimates. Two large factors emerged, which together accounted for 80.4% of the common variance. These factors were then rotated to orthogonal simple structure using the varimax criterion.

The resulting factor loadings are displayed in Table 1.2 and are very consistent with previous research in this area. First, NA and PA again emerge as the two dominant dimensions of mood. The first factor includes terms reflecting fear, sadness, anger, guilt, contempt, disgust, and other negative affective states, and can clearly be identified as NA. The second factor, in turn, corresponds closely to the PA dimension that has been identified in numerous studies (Watson, 1988b; Watson & Tellegen, 1985). More importantly, these data also replicate previous findings concerning anxiety and depression. Both types of descriptors have strong positive loadings on NA, but only depression terms have

Table 1.2
Varimax-Rotated Factor Loadings of Selected Mood Terms[a]

Mood descriptor	Loading on: Factor 1 (Negative Affect)	Loading on: Factor 2 (Positive Affect)	Mood descriptor	Loading on: Factor 1 (Negative Affect)	Loading on: Factor 2 (Positive Affect)
Sad	.77	−.32	Scared	.54	−.03
Blue	.75	−.32	Ashamed	.48	−.10
Upset	.74	−.28	Contemptuous	.43	−.02
Depressed	.73	−.38	Guilty	.40	.07
Unhappy	.72	−.42	Jittery	.38	.11
Distressed	.69	−.21	Enthusiastic	−.15	.75
Miserable	.69	−.38	Excited	−.19	.72
Worried	.66	−.11	Happy	−.38	.71
Hostile	.64	−.24	Proud	−.05	.67
Gloomy	.63	−.35	Active	−.17	.65
Afraid	.63	−.02	Interested	−.06	.64
Angry	.62	−.21	Determined	.02	.63
Irritable	.62	−.21	Satisfied	−.34	.61
Revulsion	.62	−.06	Inspired	−.07	.58
Scornful	.56	−.11	Alert	−.12	.57
Disgusted	.56	−.22	Content	−.38	.57
Nervous	.54	−.02	Strong	−.09	.56
			Attentive	−.02	.48

[a] $n = 331$.

significant secondary loadings on PA. For example, *afraid* has NA and PA loadings of .63 and −.02, respectively, indicating that it is a pure marker of high NA. Similarly, *worried* loads .66 on NA, but only −.11 on PA. In contrast, terms such as *depressed, sad, blue, and unhappy* not only have strong loadings on NA but also have notable secondary loadings on PA; for example, *depressed* has NA and PA loadings of .73 and −.38, respectively.

These relationships can be viewed more simply when separate terms are combined at the scale level. We created anxiety and depression scales by summing relevant mood descriptors included in the sample. The resulting 5-item anxiety measure consisted of *worried, afraid, scared, nervous,* and *jittery,* while the six-item depression scale included *sad, blue, depressed, gloomy, unhappy,* and *miserable.* Consistent with previous findings, these scales correlated .54 with each other. These measures were then correlated with NA and PA factor scores, which were computed using the factor scoring weights generated by the varimax solution (for a general discussion of the calculation and use of factor scores, see Gorsuch, 1983, Chapter 12). As expected, the anxiety scale correlated .76 with NA but only −.04 with PA, again demonstrating that anxiety represents a more or less pure state of high NA. In contrast, the depression scale was strongly related to both factors, although more so with NA (.84 with NA, −.46 with PA).

In summary, extensive mood data indicate that NA and PA have important implications for the relationship between anxiety and depression. NA is a very broad dimension of subjective distress that subsumes, to a considerable extent, both anxious and depressed affect. Its common underlying influence helps to explain the strong correlations found between the two types of disorders. In contrast, low PA appears to be a unique component of depression. The mood data therefore suggest that PA may be a critical factor in distinguishing depression from anxiety.

B. Scale and Item Data

NA and PA can be examined in relation to items and commonly used scales of anxiety and depression. These data are highly convergent with the mood ratings, and again highlight the role of PA in distinguishing anxiety and depression. Tellegen (1985) constructed anxiety and depression scales using affect descriptors culled from several widely used self-report measures, including the BDI, State–Trait Anxiety Inventory (STAI) State Anxiety Scale (Spielberger, Gorsuch, & Lushene, 1970), and the Multiple Affect Adjective Check List (Zuckerman & Lubin, 1965). He also created state NA and PA scales using known markers from factor analytic studies of self-rated mood (summarized in Watson & Tellegen, 1985). Congruent with the data just presented, the anxiety and depression scales were highly interrelated ($r = .83$) and both were strong markers of high NA; however, only the depression scale was strongly (negatively) related to PA.

Similarly, Blumberg and Izard (1986) used several self-report emotion scales to predict anxiety and depression in children. Depression was measured using the Children's Depression Inventory (CDI; Kovacs & Beck, 1977) and anxiety was assessed with the State–Trait Anxiety Inventory for Children (STAIC; Spielberger, 1973). These two scales correlated .58 with one another, a typical finding for such measures (see Finch et al., this volume). Multiple regression analyses indicated that a Fear scale was the best single predictor of the STAIC, with various other negative emotions (Guilt, Sadness, and Shame) also making lesser contributions. As expected, the positive affect scales did not significantly add to the prediction of anxiety. In contrast, CDI scores were best predicted by Sadness; other negative affect scales (Hostility, Anger, Fear) also made modest contributions. Most importantly, and consistent with the model outlined above, the positive affect scales (Joy and Interest) contributed significantly to the prediction of the CDI.

In order to examine the relation between mood and self-rated clinical symptoms, we analyzed scores on various NA and PA scales, together with ratings on the Hopkins Symptom Checklist (HSCL; Derogatis, Lipman, Rickels, Uhlenhuth, & Covi, 1974), in a sample of 391 undergraduates. The HSCL and a subsequent 90-item version, the SCL-90 (Derogatis, Rickels, & Rock, 1976), have been used frequently as measures of clinical symptomatology in both normal and patient populations (e.g., Gotlib, 1984; Green, Gleser, Stone, & Seifert, 1975; Rickels, Lipman, Garcia, & Fisher, 1972; Uhlenhuth, Lipman, Balter, & Stern, 1974). The HSCL consists of a series of symptoms and complaints; subjects rate, on a 5-point Likert scale, how intensely they have experienced each problem during the past week.

The HSCL has four subscales that are pertinent to the present discussion. As its name suggests, the 11-item Depression subscale contains symptom complaints related to the depressive disorders (e.g., poor appetite, loss of interest, feelings of hopelessness). Three other subscales tap anxious symptomatology. The Anxiety subscale contains 7 items assessing anxious mood (e.g., feeling tense, fearful), autonomic symptoms (heart pounding or racing), and phobic behavior (avoiding places out of fear).The 12-item Somatization subscale consists of various anxiety-related physiological symptoms, including many related to panic disorder (e.g., feeling faint, dizzy; hot/cold flashes; chest pains). Finally, the Obsessive–Compulsive subscale contains 8 items assessing ruminative thinking (e.g., difficulty making decisions; worried about sloppiness or carelessness) and compulsive behavior (e.g., checking).

Item and total scores on these subscales were correlated with two sets of NA and PA measures, one assessing trait affect and the other assessing state affect. Trait affect was measured using the 14-item Negative Emotionality (NEM) Scale and 11-item Positive Emotionality (PEM) Scale from the Multidimensional Personality Questionnaire (MPQ; Tellegen, in press), a general true–false personality inventory. NEM and PEM have been extensively validated as measures of trait NA and PA (Watson, 1988b; Watson & Pennebaker, in press). They are both homogeneous (coefficient alpha for NEM = .82, PEM = .80) and appropriately stable over time (12-week retest = .72 for NEM, .77 for PEM; see Watson & Pennebaker, in press).

State affect was assessed using the NA and PA scales from the Positive and Negative Affect Schedule (PANAS; Watson, Clark, & Tellegen, 1988). Each scale consists of 10 items selected, on the basis of factor analyses, as relatively pure markers of either high NA or high PA. Watson, Clark, and Tellegen (1988) present extensive evidence demonstrating that the PANAS scales are highly reliable and valid measures of the underlying NA and PA mood factors. The PANAS scales can be used with various time instructions; in this analysis subjects rated (on a 5-point scale) the extent to which they had felt each mood state during the past few weeks.

Correlations between the mood scales and the anxiety-related symptoms and scores are presented in Table 1.3. Corresponding correlations

Table 1.3
Correlations between NA, PA, and Anxiety Symptoms and Scores[a]

Scale/item	Correlations with Negative Affect (NA)		Correlations with Positive Affect (PA)	
	NEM	PANAS NA	PEM	PANAS PA
Anxiety subscale items				
Trembling	.19*	.32*	.03	.04
Feeling tense or keyed up	.35*	.49*	−.06	−.04
Feeling fearful	.22*	.53*	−.06	−.08
Nervousness or shakiness inside	.36*	.57*	−.08	−.10
Having to avoid certain places or activities because of fear	.24*	.41*	−.09	−.18*
Suddenly scared for no reason	.16*	.28*	.01	−.05

Table 1.3 *(Continued)*

	Correlations with Negative Affect (NA)		Correlations with Positive Affect (PA)	
Scale/item	**NEM**	**PANAS NA**	**PEM**	**PANAS PA**
Heart pounding or racing	.21*	.38*	−.05	.06
Total anxiety subscale score	.40*	.68*	−.08	−.08
Somatization subscale items				
Headaches	.17*	.16*	−.08	−.09
Muscle soreness	.13	.14*	−.02	−.02
Trouble getting breath	.12	.20*	−.07	.01
Pains in the heart or chest	.19*	.28*	−.02	−.07
Faintness or dizziness	.14*	.20*	−.01	−.11
Lump in throat	.12	.31*	.02	−.08
Weakness in parts of body	.18*	.36*	−.06	−.08
Hot or cold spells	.27*	.39*	−.03	−.05
Feeling low in energy or slowed down	.32*	.47*	−.17*	−.24*
Lower back pains	.14*	.17*	−.04	.03
Numbness or tingling in parts of body	.14*	.34*	−.11	−.09
Heavy feelings in arms or legs	.17*	.32*	−.09	−.10
Total somatization subscale score	.34*	.52*	−.12	−.15*
Obsessive–Compulsive subscale items				
Having to do things very slowly to make sure they are right	.24*	.39*	−.14*	−.01
Having to check or double check	.26*	.42*	−.04	−.03
Trouble remembering things	.19*	.22*	−.17*	−.16*
Difficulty making decisions	.33*	.43*	−.14*	−.11
Mind going blank	.21*	.36*	−.06	−.07
Trouble concentrating	.35*	.46*	−.24*	−.24*
Worried about sloppiness or carelessness	.12	.23*	−.03	.13
Feeling blocked or stymied	.28*	.41*	−.18*	−.10
Total obsessive–compulsive score	.38*	.56*	−.19*	−.12

[a] $n = 391$. NEM, Negative Emotionality; PANAS, Positive and Negative Affect Schedule; PEM, Positive Emotionality.
*$p < .01$.

with depression are shown in Table 1.4. Because of the number of correlations involved, a stringent $p < .01$ criterion was used to determine significance.

Based on the results already reviewed, one would predict that NA would be significantly related to both anxiety and depression, but that PA would be correlated only with the latter. The data in Tables 1.3 and 1.4 strongly support these predictions. Both NA measures are related to a very broad array of complaints, including most symptoms of both anxiety and depression. NEM is significantly correlated with 23 of the 27 anxiety-related symptoms (85%) and to all 11 depressive complaints. It is also significantly related to all four subscale scores, with coefficients ranging from .34 to .46. The PANAS NA scale has an even stronger and more general association with the HSCL (this is not surprising given that the HSCL and PANAS NA scale both assess current functioning, whereas NEM measures long-term trait characteristics). The state NA scale is significantly related to all 38 items; moreover, many of these correlations are as high as can reasonably be expected (in the range .30 to .60), given the limited reliability of single items. State NA is also significantly relat-

Table 1.4
Correlations between NA, PA, and Depressive Symptoms and Scores[a]

	Correlations with Negative Affect (NA)		Correlations with Positive Affect (PA)	
Scale/item	NEM	PANAS NA	PEM	PANAS PA
Depression subscale items				
Feeling no interest in things	.23*	.36*	−.26*	−.23*
Feeling hopless about future	.29*	.45*	−.34*	−.22*
Feeling lonely	.26*	.45*	−.33*	−.21*
Feeling blue	.32*	.57*	−.29*	−.28*
Worrying or stewing about things	.40*	.49*	−.18*	−.15*
Crying easily	.26*	.37*	−.04	−.15*
Self-blame	.31*	.45*	−.20*	−.13
Thoughts of ending life	.19*	.26*	−.27*	−.11
Feeling trapped or caught	.27*	.54*	−.09	−.17*
Loss of sexual interest or pleasure	.17*	.27*	−.08	−.04
Poor appetite	.16*	.20*	−.06	−.02
Total depression subscale score	.46*	.71*	−.34*	−.28*

[a] $n = 391$. NEM, Negative Emotionality; PANAS, Positive and Negative Affect Schedule; PEM, Positive Emotionality.
*$p < .01$.

ed to all four subscale scores, with coefficients ranging from .52 to .71. We again see strong evidence that NA represents a very broad dimension of subjective distress that subsumes both anxious and depressive complaints.

As predicted, however, PA is more strongly and consistently related to depression than anxiety. Both PA measures are significantly correlated with 7 of the 11 depression symptoms (64%). In contrast, PEM is related to only 6 (22%)—and the PANAS PA scale to only 4 (15%)—of the 27 anxiety complaints. It is also noteworthy that only three anxiety symptoms are significantly correlated with both PA measures. A similar pattern can be seen at the scale level: Both PA measures are significantly related to the Depression subscale, but each is only related to one of the three anxiety scores, and, again, these relationships are not consistent across PA measures. These item and scale data yield the same general conclusion as did the mood ratings. NA is strongly correlated with both anxious and depressive symptomatology, whereas PA is consistently associated only with depression.

C. Clinical Data

Thus far we have not examined how NA and PA relate to clinical manifestations of anxiety and depression, and it is obviously important to do so. The clinical data on this point are not extensive, but the available evidence is generally consistent with the research already considered. The earliest relevant study was conducted by Hall (1977), who obtained diagnostic data and clinicians' ratings of anxiety and depression on a sample of male outpatients. Hall found that ratings and diagnoses of anxiety were significantly correlated with NA but not with PA, whereas ratings and diagnoses of depression were more highly related to (low) PA than to NA. These results reaffirm the crucial role of low PA in differentiating anxiety from depression.

Bouman and Louteijn (1986) examined the association between NA, PA, and depression in three groups of psychiatric patients: (1) major depressives, who met the corresponding criteria in the *Diagnostic and Statistical Manual of Mental Disorders* (DSM-III; American Psychiatric Association, 1980), (2) dysphoric patients who were significantly depressed, but who did not meet full DSM-III criteria for major depression (e.g., dysthymics), and (3) nondepressives. The patients' scores on a number of mood and personality scales were factor analyzed and two factors were extracted, which Bouman and Luteijn interpreted as NA and PA. Consistent with our model, the major depressives had significantly lower PA scores than did the dysphoric patients, who, in turn, were lower on PA than was the nondepressed group. Based on these results, Bouman and Luteijn concluded that depression is a complex affective state that reflects both high NA and low PA. These data are very encouraging; however, a limitation of Bouman and Luteijn's study for the present purposes is that it does not permit a direct comparison between anxiety and depression.

Data that are directly relevant to this issue were reported by Watson, Clark, and Carey (1988). They studied the relation between NA, PA, anxiety, and depression in a sample of 150 psychiatric patients (90 inpatient probands and 60 clinically diagnosed cotwins). Trait NA and PA were again measured by the NEM and PEM scales, respectively. Anxious and depressed symptomatology were assessed using relevant sections of the Diagnostic Interview Schedule (DIS; Robins, Helzer, Croughan, & Ratcliff, 1981). The DIS is a highly structured interview that elicits information about the frequency, severity, and co-occurrence of psychiatric symptoms over time. These symptom data can then be used to create computer-generated DSM-III diagnoses. The DIS has been widely used as a diagnostic measure in studies of psychiatric epidemiology, and research has generally supported its reliability and validity in this regard (Helzer et al., 1985; Robins, 1985; Robins, Helzer, Ratcliff, & Seyfried, 1982; Wittchen, Semler, & von Zerssen, 1985).

Watson, Clark, and Carey (1988) related the NEM and PEM scales to DIS responses at both the symptom and diagnostic level. Five DSM-III diagnoses were examined, three from the anxiety disorders (panic disorder, simple phobia, social phobia) and two from the depressive spectrum (major depression, dysthymic disorder). The symptom and diagnostic results both strongly corroborate earlier findings. As expected, PEM was related to most depressive complaints, but to relatively few anxiety symptoms. Moreover, it was significantly correlated with both depressive diagnoses, but with only one anxiety disorder (i.e., social phobia). This significant correlation is consistent with the general finding that social parameters are more strongly related to PA than to NA (see Watson, Clark, & Carey, 1988).

In contrast, NEM was related to a broad array of complaints, including most symptoms of both anxiety and depression. Overall, it was significantly correlated with 70% of the individual symptoms. NEM was also significantly correlated with all five DSM-III diagnoses. These data reaffirm that NA is a very general dimension of subjective distress. Clearly, the DIS—like other psychometric instruments of anxiety and depression—substantially reflects the influence of this broad and pervasive factor.

D. General Summary of Empirical Data

We have considered a wide array of evidence regarding the relationship between anxiety and depression. These diverse data offer a remarkably clear and consistent pattern: NA is strongly related to both anxiety and depression (whether at the basic mood, scale, or clinical level), whereas PA is associated only with depression. Thus, the data indicate that the loss of pleasurable engagement (i.e., low PA) is an important and largely unique aspect of depression and suggest that PA is a crucial factor in distinguishing depression from anxiety.

V. Directions for Future Research: Positive Affect's Relation to Endogenous Depression

An important and related topic for future research concerns PA's relation to the two basic subsyndromes of major depression. One subtype has been variously called *reactive, neurotic, exogenous,* or *psychological* depression (Akiskal, Bitar, Puzantian, Rosenthal, & Walker, 1978); it corresponds to "major depression without melancholia" in DSM-III. The second subtype has been termed *endogenous, autonomous, psychotic, vital,* or *endogenomorphic* depression, and is called "major depression with melancholia" in DSM-III. In the following discussion we will use the terms *neurotic* and *endogenous* depression.

Researchers disagree concerning the precise nature of these subsyndromes, but there is general agreement regarding some basic differences. Specifically, endogenous depression is viewed as the more severe disorder and is considered to have a stronger genetic and biological etiology. Endogenous depressives are also expected to show better premorbid personality functioning and to have fewer psychosocial stressors in their lives. Conversely, neurotic depressives are thought to exhibit poorer premorbid functioning and to have a stronger environmental/stress reactive basis to their disorder (Avery, Wilson, & Dunner, 1983; Fowles & Gersh, 1979; Klein, 1974; Mendels & Cochrane, 1968; Zimmerman, Coryell, Pfohl, & Stangl, 1986).

No study has directly examined PA's relationship with these subsyndromes. However, the available evidence—both theoretical and empirical—suggests that low PA might be a more prominent feature in endogenous than in neurotic depression. For example, in Klein's (1974) concept of "endogenomorphic depression," the loss of pleasurable experience, or anhedonia, is the defining characteristic. Klein argues that this subtype is characterized by a "pervasive impairment in the ability to experience pleasure or to respond affectively to the anticipation of pleasure. This key inhibition of the pleasure mechanism results in a profound lack of interest and investment in the environment" (p. 449).

Klein (1974) summarizes extensive clinical and biological data in support of his view. Akiskal et al. (1978) also report data generally supportive of this model. If this model is correct, the loss of PA would seem to be a central, defining feature of endogenous depression.

Numerous studies have compared the symptom patterns of neurotic and endogenous depressives. The findings vary across studies, but generally indicate that low-PA symptoms are more characteristic of endogenous depression. Nelson and Charney (1981) reviewed the results of 21 factor and cluster analytic studies; among the symptoms that best differentiated the two subsyndromes were the inability to experience pleasure and a loss of interest in normal activities, both of which were more common among endogenous patients. Based on their review, Nelson and Charney concluded that the inability to experience pleasure is "a major necessary symptom" (p. 11) of endogenous depression. It is also noteworthy that symptoms such as the inability to experience pleasure, decreased interest in work and activities, and decreased energy predicted tricyclic response in a sample of endogenous depressives (Nelson, Mazure, Quinlan, and Jatlow, 1984). Finally, endogenous depression shows a stronger pattern of diurnal variation (with the depression worse in the morning; see Nelson & Charney, 1981). Interestingly, PA—but not NA—shows a similar diurnal pattern (Clark, Watson, & Leeka, 1988).

Given these data, it seems plausible to suggest that low PA may be an especially prominent factor in endogenous depression. If this is so, then PA may not only play a useful role in distinguishing depression from anxiety, but may also help to differentiate endogenous from neurotic depression.

VI. Implications and Conclusions

A. The Role of NA and PA in the Assessment of Anxiety and Depression

The data we have reviewed are remarkably consistent and have clear implications for the assessment and treatment of anxiety and depression. We have seen that NA is a very general dimension of subjective distress that is correlated with a broad range of psychological complaints, including both anxious and depressive symptomatology. These data, together with earlier results (Watson & Clark, 1984), demonstrate that NA is an important general predictor of psychiatric disorder. However, the very pervasiveness of its relationship to psychiatric complaints indicates that NA is not very useful in differential diagnosis. That is, NA is a diffuse measure of psychological distress and poor functioning that differentiates most clinical groups from normals, but it will not effectively distinguish specific types of psychiatric disorder from one another (see Watson & Clark, 1984).

In contrast, low PA is differentially prominent in depression, indicating that PA may be a critical factor in distinguishing depression from anxiety and other disorders. Thus, the clinical and psychometric assessment of depression might both be improved if this PA component were weighted more heavily. Most self-report depression scales primarily measure NA, but also include a more modest PA component (as in Table 1.4; see also Tellegen, 1985; Watson & Clark, 1984; Watson, Clark, & Carey, 1988). In a convergent validity sense, this seems a reasonable strategy: As we have seen, depression is an affectively complex combination of high NA and low PA. However, this high-NA component is also prominent in many other psychological disorders, and so will generate high correlations among various measures of psychopathology. Because low PA appears to be more specific to depression, strengthening its contribution should improve the discriminant validity of depression measures and enhance the differential diagnosis of depression from anxiety and other disorders.

Data corroborating this point are reported by Kendall, Howard, and Hays (1987), who studied the predictive utility of the Automatic Thoughts Questionnaire (ATQ; Hollon & Kendall, 1980) with regard to depression. The ATQ normally consists of 30 negatively toned items; however, Kendall et al. found that adding 15 positively toned items significantly improved the prediction and identification of depressed cases.

B. Issues in the Assessment of Positive Affect

It is useful to consider how this PA component is best assessed. Psychiatric research has traditionally emphasized dichotomous assessment; for example, a given symptom such as anhedonia was simply recorded as present or absent. However, extensive evidence indicates that PA is a normally distributed dimension of both inter- and intraindividual differences (e.g., Clark & Watson, 1988; Watson, 1988a; Watson, Clark, & Tellegen, 1988; Watson & Tellegen, 1985). That is, people differ greatly in their characteristic PA levels, and a given individual's PA fluctuates widely from day to day and from moment to moment. Rather than simply assessing the presence or absence of pleasurable emotional experiences, it seems preferable to identify and examine these finer gradations. In particular, the dimensional approach seems better suited to the study of factors (both biological and environmental) that influence positive emotionality.

It might also be useful to focus more on the measurement of high PA. Studies of self-rated mood indicate that there are many more descriptors of high than of low PA, and, furthermore, that the high-PA terms tend to be purer markers of the underlying factor (e.g., Watson, Clark, & Tellegen, 1988; Watson & Tellegen, 1985). Thus, the optimal measurement approach may be to assess the degree to which individuals report various high-PA states, and then to infer depressive symptomatology from the relative absence of such experiences. This strategy avoids the pitfalls inherent in assessing low PA that were noted above, while minimizing the risk of producing yet another high-NA measure.

References

Akiskal, H. S. (1985).Anxiety: Definition, relationship to depression, and proposal for an integrative model. In A. H. Tuma & J. D. Maser (Eds.), *Anxiety and the anxiety disorders* (pp. 787–797). Hillsdale, NJ: Erlbaum.

Akiskal, H. S., Bitar, A. H., Puzantian, V. R., Rosenthal, T. L., & Walker, P. W. (1978). The nosological status of neurotic depression. *Archives of General Psychiatry, 35*, 756–766.

American Psychiatric Association. (1980). *Diagnostic and statistical manual of mental disorders* (3rd ed.). Washington, DC: Author.

Avery, D. H., Wilson, L. G., & Dunner, D. L. (1983). Diagnostic subtypes of depression as predictors of therapeutic response. In P. J. Clayton & J. E. Barrett (Eds.), *Treatment of depression: Old controversies and new approaches* (pp. 193–204). New York: Raven Press.

Beck, A. T. (1967). *Depression: Clinical, experimental, and theoretical aspects.* New York: Harper & Row.

Beck, A. T., Ward, C. H., Mendelson, M., Mock, J., & Erbaugh, J. (1961). An inventory for measuring depression. *Archives of General Psychiatry, 4*, 561–571.

Blumberg, S. H., & Izard, C. E. (1986). Discriminating patterns of emotions in 10- and 11-year-old children's anxiety and depression. *Journal of Personality and Social Psychology, 51*, 852–857.

Bouman, T. K., & Luteijn, F. (1986). Relations between the Pleasant Events Schedule, depression, and other aspects of psychopathology. *Journal of Abnormal Psychology, 95*, 373–377.

Breier, A., Charney, D. S., & Heninger, G. R. (1985). The diagnostic validity of anxiety disorders and their relationship to depressive illness. *American Journal of Psychiatry, 142*, 787–797.

Breier, A., Charney, D. S., & Heninger, G. R. (1986). Agoraphobia with panic attacks: Development, diagnostic stability, and cause of illness. *Archives of General Psychiatry, 43*, 1029–1036.

Clark, L. A., & Watson, D. (1988). Mood and the mundane: Relations between daily life events and self-reported mood. *Journal of Personality and Social Psychology, 54*, 296–308.

Clark, L. A., Watson, D., & Leeka, J. (1988). *Diurnal variation in positive affect: A robust psychobiological phenomenon.* Manuscript submitted for publication.
Deluty, B. M., Deluty, R. H., & Carver, C. S. (1986). Concordance between clinicians' and patients' ratings of anxiety and depression as mediated by private self-consciousness. *Journal of Personality Assessment, 50,* 93–106.
Derogatis, L. R., Klerman, G. L., & Lipman, R. S. (1972). Anxiety states and depressive neuroses. *Journal of Nervous and Mental Disease, 55,* 392–403.
Derogatis, L. R., Lipman, R. S., Rickels, K., Uhlenhuth, E. H., & Covi, L. (1974). The Hopkins Symptom Checklist (HSCL): A self-report symptom inventory. *Behavioral Science, 19,* 1–15.
Derogatis, L. R. Rickels, K., & Rock, A. (1976). The SCL-90 and the MMPI: A step in the validation of a new self-report scale. *British Journal of Psychiatry, 128,* 280–289.
Dinning, W. D., & Evans, R. G. (1977). Discriminant and convergent validity of the SCL-90 in psychiatric inpatients. *Journal of Personality Assessment, 41,* 304–310.
Dobson, K. S. (1985). An analysis of anxiety and depression scales. *Journal of Personality Assessment, 49,* 522–527.
Ekman, P. (Ed.). (1982). *Emotion in the human face* (2nd ed.). New York: Cambridge University Press.
Ekman, P., Friesen, W. V., & Ellsworth, P. (1972). *Emotion in the human face.* Elmsford, NY: Pergamon Press.
Ekman, P., Levenson, R., & Friesen, W. V. (1983). Autonomic nervous system activity distinguishes between emotions. *Science, 221,* 1208–1210.
Foa, E. B., & Foa, U. G. (1982). Differentiating depression and anxiety: Is it possible? Is it useful? *Psychopharmacology Bulletin, 18,* 62–68.
Foa, E. B., Grayson, J. B., Steketee, G. S., Doppelt, H. G., Turner, R. M., & Latimer, P. R. (1983). Success and failure in the behavioral treatment of obsessive–compulsives. *Journal of Consulting and Clinical Psychology, 51,* 287–297.
Fowles, D. C., & Gersh, F. (1979). Neurotic depression: The endogenous-neurotic distinction. In R. A. Depue (Ed.), *The psychobiology of the depressive disorders: Implications for the effects of stress* (pp. 55–80). New York: Academic Press.
Gersh, F. S., & Fowles, D. C. (1979). Neurotic depression: The concept of anxious depression. In R. A. Depue (Ed.), *The psychobiology of the depressive disorders: Implications for the effects of stress* (pp. 81–104). New York: Academic Press.
Gorsuch, R. L. (1983). *Factor analysis* (2nd ed.). Hillsdale, NJ: Erlbaum.
Gotlib, I. H. (1984). Depression and general psychopathology in university students. *Journal of Abnormal Psychology, 93,* 19–30.
Green, B. L., Gleser, G. C., Stone, W. N., & Seifert, R. F. (1975). Relationships among diverse measures of psychotherapy outcome. *Journal of Consulting and Clinical Psychology, 43,* 689–699.
Hall, C. A. (1977). *Differential relationships of pleasure and distress with depression and anxiety over a past, present and future time framework.* Unpublished doctoral dissertation, University of Minnesota, Minneapolis.
Helzer, J. E., Robins, L. N., McEvoy, L. T., Spitznagel, E. L., Stoltzman, R. K., Farmer, A., & Brockington, I. F. (1985). A comparison of clinical and Diagnostic Interview Schedule diagnoses. *Archives of General Psychiatry, 42,* 657–666.
Hollon, S. D., & Kendall, P. C. (1980). Cognitive self-statements in depression: Development of an Automatic Thoughts Questionnaire. *Cognitive Therapy and Research, 4,* 383–395.
Ingram, R. E., Kendall, P. C., Smith, T. W., Donnell, C., & Ronan, K. (1987). Cognitive specificity in emotional distress. *Journal of Personality and Social Psychology, 53,* 734–742.
Izard, C. E. (1971). *The face of emotion.* New York: Appleton-Century-Crofts.

Izard, C. E. (1972). *Patterns of emotions: A new analysis of anxiety and depression.* New York: Academic Press.

Izard, C. E. (1977). *Human emotions.* New York: Plenum.

Kahn, R. J., McNair, D. M., Lipman, R. S., Covi, L., Rickels, K., Downing, R., Fisher, S., & Frankenthaler, L. M. (1986). Imipramine and chlordiazepoxide in depressive and anxiety disorders. II. Efficacy in anxious outpatients. *Archives of General Psychiatry, 43,* 79–85.

Kellner, R., Simpson, G. M., & Winslow, W. W. (1972). The relationship of depressive neurosis to anxiety and somatic symptoms. *Psychosomatics, 13,* 358–362.

Kendall, P. C., Howard, B. L., & Hays, R. (1987). Self-referent speech and psychopathology. In R. M. Schwartz (Chair), *Cognitive–affective balance in anxiety, depression and hypomania.* Symposium conducted at the 95th Annual Convention of the American Psychological Association, New York.

Kendler, K. S., Heath, A. C., Martin, N. G., & Eaves, L. J. (1987). Symptoms of anxiety and symptoms of depression: Same genes, different environment? *Archives of General Psychiatry, 44,* 451–457.

Klein, D. F. (1974). Endogenomorphic depression: A conceptual and terminological revision. *Archives of General Psychiatry, 31,* 447–454.

Kovacs, M., & Beck, A. T. (1977). An empirical clinical approach towards a definition of childhood depression. In J. G. Schulterbrandt & A. Raskin (Eds.), *Depression in children: Diagnosis, treatment and conceptual models* (pp. 1–25). New York: Raven Press.

Kupfer, D. J.,Spiker, D. G., Rossi, A., Coble, P. A., Ulrich, R., & Shaw, D. (1983). Recent diagnostic and treatment advances in REM sleep and depression. In P. J. Clayton & J. E. Barrett (Eds.), *Treatment of depression: Old controversies and new approaches* (pp. 31–51). New York: Raven Press.

Leckman, J. F., Weissman, M. M., Merikangas, K. R., Pauls, D. L., & Prusoff, B. A. (1983). Panic disorder and major depression: Increased risk of depression, alcoholism, panic, and phobic disorders in families of depressed probands with panic disorder. *Archives of General Psychiatry, 40,* 1055–1060.

Lipman, R. S., Rickels, K., Covi, L., Derogatis, L. R., & Uhlenhuth, E. H. (1969). Factors of symptom distress: Doctor ratings of anxious neurotic outpatients. *Archives of General Psychiatry, 21,* 328–338.

Mendels, J., & Cochrane, C. (1968). The nosology of depression: The endogenous-reactive concept. *American Journal of Psychiatry, 124,* 1–11.

Mendels, J., Weinstein, N., & Cochrane, C. (1972). The relationship between depression and anxiety. *Archives of General Psychiatry, 27,* 649–653.

Munjack, D. J., & Moss, H. B. (1981). Affective disorder and alcoholism in families of agoraphobics. *Archives of General Psychiatry, 38,* 869–871.

Nelson, J. C., & Charney, D. S. (1981). The symptoms of major depressive illness. *American Journal of Psychiatry, 138,* 1–13.

Nelson, J. C., Mazure, C., Quinlan, D. M., & Jatlow, P. I. (1984). Drug-responsive symptoms in melancholia. *Archives of General Psychiatry, 41,* 663–668.

Nezu, A. M., Nezu, C. M., & Nezu, V. A. (1986). Depression, general distress, and causal attributions among university students. *Journal of Abnormal Psychology, 95,* 184–186.

Orme, J. G., Reis, J., & Herz, E. J. (1986). Factorial and discriminant validity of the Center for Epidemiological Studies Depression (CES-D) Scale. *Journal of Clinical Psychology, 42,* 28–33.

Plutchik, R. (1962). *The emotions: Facts, theories, and a new model.* New York: Random House.

Plutchik, R. (1980). *Emotion: A psychoevolutionary synthesis.* New York: Harper & Row.

Rickels, K., Lipman, R. S., Garcia, C. R., & Fisher, E. (1972). Evaluating clinical improvement in anxious outpatients. *American Journal of Psychiatry, 128,* 119–123.

Robins, L. N. (1985). Epidemiology: Reflections on testing the validity of psychiatric interviews. *Archives of General Psychiatry, 42,* 918–924.

Robins, L. N., Helzer, J.E., Croughan, I., & Ratcliff, K. S. (1981). The NIMH Diagnostic Interview Schedule: Its history, characteristics, and validity. *Archives of General Psychiatry, 38,* 381–389.
Robins, L. N., Helzer, J. E., Ratcliff, K. S., & Seyfried, W. (1982). Validity of the Diagnostic Interview Schedule, Version II: *DSM-III* diagnoses. *Psychological Medicine, 12,* 855–870.
Roth, M., Gurney, C., Garside, R. F., & Kerr, T. A. (1972). Studies in the classification of affective disorders—the relationship between anxiety states and depressive illnesses. *British Journal of Psychiatry, 121,* 147–161.
Spielberger, C. D. (1973). *Preliminary manual for the State-Trait Anxiety Inventory for Children.* Palo Alto, CA: Consulting Psychologists Press.
Spielberger, C. D., Gorsuch, R. L., & Lushene, R. E. (1970). *Manual for the State-Trait Anxiety Inventory.* Palo Alto, CA: Consulting Psychologists Press.
Tanaka-Matsumi, J., & Kameoka, V. A. (1986). Reliabilities and concurrent validities of popular self-report measures of depression, anxiety, and social desirability. *Journal of Consulting and Clinical Psychology, 54,* 328–333.
Tellegen, A. (1985). Structures of mood and personality and their relevance to assessing anxiety, with an emphasis on self-report. In A. H. Tuma & J. D. Maser (Eds.), *Anxiety and the anxiety disorders* (pp. 681–706). Hillsdale, NJ: Erlbaum.
Tellegen, A. (in press). *Multidimensional Personality Questionnaire.* Minneapolis: University of Minnesota Press.
Tomkins, S. S. (1962). *Affect, imagery, and consciousness: Vol. 1. The positive affects.* New York: Springer.
Tomkins, S. S. (1963). *Affect, imagery, and consciousness: Vol. 2. The negative affects.* New York: Springer.
Uhlenhuth, E. H., Lipman, R. S., Balter, M. B., & Stern, M. (1974). Symptom intensity and life stress in the city. *Archives of General Psychiatry, 31,* 759–764.
Watson, D. (1988a). Intraindividual and interindividual analyses of Positive and Negative Affect: Their relation to health complaints, perceived stress, and daily activities. *Journal of Personality and Social Psychology, 54,* 1020–1030.
Watson, D. (1988b). The vicissitudes of mood measurement: Effects of varying descriptors, time frames, and response formats on measures of Positive and Negative Affect. *Journal of Personality and Social Psychology, 55,* 128–141.
Watson, D., & Clark, L. A. (1984). Negative Affectivity: The disposition to experience aversive emotional states. *Psychological Bulletin, 96,* 465–490.
Watson, D., Clark, L. A., & Carey, G. (1988). Positive and Negative Affectivity and their relation to anxiety and depressive disorders. *Journal of Abnormal Psychology, 97,* 346–353.
Watson, D., Clark, L. A., & Tellegen, A. (1984). Cross-cultural convergence in the structure of mood: A Japanese replication and a comparison with U.S. findings. *Journal of Personality and Social Psychology, 47,* 127–144.
Watson, D., Clark, L. A., & Tellegen, A. (1988). Development and validation of brief measures of Positive and Negative Affect: The PANAS Scales. *Journal of Personality and Social Psychology, 54,* 1063–1070.
Watson, D., & Pennebaker, J. W. (in press). Health complaints, stress, and distress: Exploring the central role of Negative Affectivity. *Psychological Review.*
Watson, D., & Tellegen, A. (1985). Toward a consensual structure of mood. *Psychological Bulletin, 98,* 219–235.
Wittchen, H.-U., Semler, G., & von Zerssen, D. (1985). A comparison of two diagnostic methods: Clinical ICD diagnoses versus *DSM-III* and Research Diagnostic Criteria using the Diagnostic Interview Schedule (Version 2). *Archives of General Psychiatry, 42,* 677–684.
Wolfe, V. V., Finch, A. J., Jr., Saylor, C. F., Blount, R. L., Pallmeyer, T. P., & Carek, D. J. (1987). Negative Affectivity in children: A multitrait-multimethod investigation. *Journal of Consulting and Clinical Psychology, 55,* 245–250.

Woodruff, R. A., Jr., Guze, S. B., & Clayton, P. J. (1972). Anxiety neurosis among psychiatric outpatients. *Comprehensive Psychiatry, 13,* 165–170.
Zevon, M. A., & Tellegen, A. (1982). The structure of mood change: An idiographic/nomothetic analysis. *Journal of Personality and Social Psychology, 43,* 111–122.
Zimmerman, M., Coryell, W., Pfohl, B., & Stangl, D. (1986). The validity of four concepts of endogenous depression. *Archives of General Psychiatry, 43,* 234–244.
Zuckerman, M., & Lubin, B. (1965). *Manual for the Multiple Affect Adjective Check List.* San Diego: Educational and Industrial Testing Service.
Zuckerman, M., Persky, H., Eckman, K., & Hopkins, T. (1967). A multitrait multimethod measurement approach to the traits (or states) of anxiety, depression, and hostility. *Journal of Projective Techniques and Personality Assessment, 31,* 39–48.
Zurawski, R. M., & Smith, T. W. (1987). Assessing irrational beliefs and emotional distress: Evidence and implications of limited discriminant validity. *Journal of Counseling Psychology, 34,* 224–227.

Cognitive-Behavioral Perspectives: Theory and Research on Depression and Anxiety

Philip C. Kendall
Rick E. Ingram

I. Introduction

The study of depressive and anxious disorders has occupied a central role in clinical psychology and psychiatry, and current cognitive-behavioral research efforts exemplify this emphasis. The overwhelming majority of clinical research efforts, however, have examined either depression or anxiety, with less than sufficient reference to potential relationships between the two states. Indeed, the bulk of this research dealing with emotional disorders has proceeded in parallel with the implicit assumption that these disorders represent relatively discrete entities with rela-

Anxiety and Depression

tively distinct cognitive mechanisms. However, this assumption of distinctiveness must be questioned in light of research showing that (1) depression and anxiety are highly correlated and (2) many of the cognitive mechanisms empirically examined within these "different" disorders are strikingly similar. Implicit assumptions of distinctiveness are not tenable without explicit data; investigative inquiries regarding depression and anxiety can no longer proceed in theoretical and methodological isolation from each other. The major intent of this chapter is to examine issues regarding the distinctive and overlapping features between depression and anxiety as they pertain to cognitive-behavioral theory and research.

A. A Brief Historical Perspective

Cognitive-clinical constructs initially evolved from radical behaviorism in the form of "covert behaviors." These early views on cognition were followed later by cognitive social learning theory, and most recently by information-processing approaches. Clinical behaviorism was characterized by many features, some of which (e.g., an emphasis upon empirical investigation) have been retained by current cognitive approaches. One particularly notable behavioristic feature was a rejection of diagnostic classes and formulations in favor of an idiographic approach to treatment. This approach focused on functional behavioral analyses aimed at determining specific behavioral problems and the variables maintaining these problems. Hence, depression and anxiety as nosological entities were considerably less important than was a precise analysis of the specific behavioral deficits and behaviors emitted by the individual.

Initially, cognitive approaches were concerned primarily with treatment (rather than theory) with a behaviorist emphasis on precise problem formulation, only this time with an emphasis on the cognitive factors maintaining the dysfunctional behavior. The cognitive remediation of these specific behavioral deficits was understandably of central importance—more important than was the nature of the dysfunction, at least in terms of broader descriptive and nosological features. While current cognitive-behavioral approaches continue to stress functional analyses of both cognitive and behavioral variables, targeting specific problems to be treated, and empirically verifying treatment outcomes, recent efforts have more on broader theoretical conceptualizations of the role of cognition in specified disorders. In line with trends in descriptive psychopathology toward understanding classes of dysfunction, and along with the now widespread acceptance of diagnostic systems such as the *Diagnostic and Statistical Manual of Mental Disorders* (DSM) series, cognitive-behavioral research efforts have become more committed to relating cognitive variables to specific disorders such as depression and anxiety. This trend is evident in cognitive theoretical proposals specifically formulated to account for depression (Beck, 1976; Ingram, 1984; Kuiper, Olinger, & MacDonald, 1988; Peterson & Seligman, 1984; see also Alloy, 1988) and anxiety (Barlow, 1988; Beck, 1976; Beck & Emery, 1985; Ingram & Kendall, 1987; Kendall & Ingram, 1987; Michelson & Ascher, 1987), as well as the numerous empirical investigations appearing that have sought to examine cognitive variables related to these two disorders. This concern is not just theoretical, however. A broader understanding of the variation due to certain classes of psychopathology provides a context within which to assess and treat individuals' psychological problems idiographically. An excellent example is cognitive therapy for depression (Beck, Rush, Shaw, & Emery, 1979). Based on a theoretical understanding of this disorder, this approach employs a set of general therapeutic methods that are individually tailored to the patient's specific problem within the framework of his or her depression. The empirical data have consistently documented the efficacy of this approach (e.g., Clark & Beck, this volume).

B. Theoretical and Methodological Issues in Current Work

Given the large body of cognitive-behavioral theory and research directed toward depression and anxiety, both clinicians and researchers should have a relatively good grasp on the cognitive variables that characterize these two dysfunctional emotional states. However, for both theoretical and methodological reasons, this desirable situation is not necessarily true. From a theoretical standpoint, conceptualizations of depression and anxiety typically offer little "theoretical specificity." That is, while theoretical formulations typically propose that certain processes characterize a given disorder, rarely do they specify that these processes do *not* characterize other disorders. In some instances theoretical models of different disorders are built upon highly similar key constructs. A case in point are models emphasizing self-focused attention. Defined generally as attention directed inwardly toward salient self-aspects as opposed to outwardly toward the environment (see Carver & Scheier, 1981), elaborate theoretical proposals describing the critical role of heightened self-focused attention in depression have been developed (e.g., Pyszczynski & Greenberg, 1987). Similarly, several models of anxiety have proposed a central role for such inwardly directed attention (Sarason, 1975, 1986; Wine, 1982). Although the labels differ somewhat, the similarity of the actual constructs to explain both depressive and anxious disorders is striking. In fact, evidence suggests that heightened self-focused attention may characterize not only depression and anxiety, but other disorders as well (Ingram, 1988a).

Methodologically, there have also been difficulties in establishing the variables that characterize depression and anxiety. While there has been no shortage of studies assessing cognition in each of these disorders, a preponderance of studies have not taken into account the correlation between depressive and anxious affect. For example, a variety of investigators have reported strong positive correlations between measures of these states (e.g., Craighead, 1981; Dobson, 1985; Gotlib, 1984; Hollon & Kendall, 1980; Zuckerman & Lubin, 1965, 1985). Additionally, researchers have found it quite difficult to establish "purely" depressed or anxious groups of individuals for cognitive research. In this vein, studies reported by Craighead, Hickey, and DeMonbreun (1979) and M. S. Greenberg and Alloy (1988) were unable to locate subjects who were depressed but not anxious. Employing test anxiety as a model of an anxiety state, Ingram, Kendall, Smith, Donnell, and Ronan (1987) were able to locate a group of depressed and not anxious subjects, but only after screening over 2000 potential subjects. Hence, with only several exceptions, studies thought to be investigating depression *or* anxiety have more likely been studies of depression *and* anxiety. Clearly, conceptual and empirical associations between depression and anxiety must be clarified before the meaningfulness of cognitive research on these states can be determined.

Our view is that although depressive and anxious states are indeed correlated, and may thus share some common mechanisms, the fact that the correlation is less than perfect indicates that there are features unique to each disorder as well. Further, the existence of unique mechanisms implies that there are in fact important differences between depression and anxiety. Within cognitive research, both conceptually and empirically establishing these differences is not simply an exercise in academic curiosity; such differences have important and direct theoretical, methodological, empirical, assessment, and treatment implications. From a theoretical standpoint, for instance, it is necessary to identify how extant cognitive constructs account for the shared and common features of depression and anxiety. Methodologically, it is important to separate depression from anxiety so that potential cognitive differences and similarities can be examined in an unconfounded fashion. Such an approach allows empirical data to reflect the operation of presumably different cognitive processes for different depressive and anxious features. Cognitive assessment likewise will need to be refined to discriminate the critical features that differentiate depression and anxiety. Finally, if the precision of conceptualizing and assessing depression and anxiety can be enhanced, then efforts to specify and target treatment plans and strategies to fit the critical aspects of each state will benefit enormously.

In addressing the issues raised by the covariance between depressive and anxious states, in this chapter we review cognitive theory and research relevant to the commonalities and differences between the two states. In particular, we briefly review the empirical research on comparable cognitive variables in depression and anxiety and then review research that appears to differentiate depressed and anxious states. After discussing salient methodological issues, we then describe a conceptual framework intended to facilitate an understanding of the unique and shared cognitive variance in depression and anxiety.

II. Empirical Research on Cognitive Constructs

A. Scope of Variables Studied

The number and diversity of cognitive variables studied in depression and anxiety are truly remarkable. The following list of variables represents only a sample of cognitive features empirically examined in these disorders. For depression, the cognitive factors thought to be important include cognitive bias (Krantz & Hammen, 1979), cognitive distortion (Hammen, 1978; Hammen & Krantz, 1976), underestimates of reinforcements (Hammen & Glas, 1975; Nelson & Craighead, 1977; Roth & Rehm, 1980), negative automatic thoughts (Hollon & Kendall, 1980; Harrell & Ryon, 1983; Dobson & Breiter, 1983), negative response bias (Rabin, 1985; Zuroff, Colussy, & Wielgus, 1983), task-distracting cognitions (Vredenburg & Krames, 1983), task recall deficiencies (Johnson, Petzel, Hartney, & Morgan, 1983), overestimates of negative event frequency (Kuiper & MacDonald, 1983), negative content information processing (Derry & Kuiper, 1981; Kuiper & Derry, 1982), stability of negative schematic processing (Dobson & Shaw, 1987; Ingram, Smith, & Brehm, 1983), self-schema consistency (Kuiper et al., 1988; Ross & Mueller, 1983), overestimates of depressive parameters (Kuiper et al., 1988), dysfunctional thoughts (Lam, Brewin, Woods, & Bebbington, 1987), negative inaccuracies in interpersonal feedback recall (Gotlib, 1983), negative construct accessibility (Gotlib & McCann, 1984; Gotlib & Cane, 1987), and irrational beliefs (Cook & Peterson, 1986).

For anxiety disorders, the list includes distorted cognition (Gormally, Sipps, Raphael, Edwin, & Varvil-Weld, 1981), negative attributional patterns (Alden, 1987), negative information processing (Mueller & Thompson, 1984), negative self-statements (Dodge, Heimberg, Hope,

& Becker, 1986), increased other-referent information processing (Smith, Ingram, & Brehm, 1983), enhanced encoding of anxiety information (McNally, Foa, & Donnell, 1988), irrational beliefs (Deffenbacher, 1986; Mizes, Landold-Fritsche, & Grossman-McKee, 1987), dysfunctional interpretations of ambiguous information (McNally & Foa, 1987), overestimates of risk judgments (Butler & Mathews, 1983, 1987), and increased environmental vigilance (MacLeod, Mathews, & Tata, 1986).

While the number of constructs investigated in these disorders is impressive, it is also obvious that many of these constructs are quite similar across depression and anxiety. There are some important differences, however. Anxiety research, for example, has typically employed a state–trait distinction (Kendall, 1978; Spielberger, 1975) that has not usually been incorporated in studies of depressive cognition. Nevertheless, the truly salient feature of the cognitive depression and anxiety research literature is their theoretical and empirical similarity.

B. Cognitive Specificity Studies of Depression and Anxiety

The majority of cognitive depression and anxiety studies are most likely confounded given that depressed individuals are usually also quite high in anxiety and vice versa. While some studies have assessed more "pure" depression or anxiety by ensuring that subjects are only depressed or anxious (i.e., no evidence of other disorders), these studies in and of themselves provide limited information as to specificity because the processes under study may also characterize nonstudied populations. Investigation of cognitive specificity in depression and anxiety therefore requires a comparative methodological approach that separates these states in the same study. To date, only a handful of studies have achieved this. The current section will briefly review those studies that have attempted to assess cognition simultaneously in both depression and anxiety. Variables investigated by these studies have generally included thought content, attributions, and information processing.

1. Thought Content

In line with much of the current emphasis in cognitive-clinical research, several studies have examined the content of depressed and anxious individuals' characteristic thinking patterns. In general, these studies have employed the Automatic Thoughts Questionnaire (ATQ; Hollon & Kendall, 1980), a widely used measure designed to assess the frequency of negative self-referent thoughts in depression. For example, Ingram, Kendall, Smith, Donnell, and Ronan, (1987) compared individuals selected for elevated depression to those selected for a specific kind of anxiety (test anxiety) on several cognitive measures, including the ATQ. Four groups of subjects were studied: one composed of individuals with high depression and low test anxiety, one of individuals with high test anxiety and low depression, one of individuals high in both depression and test anxiety, and, finally, a control group of individuals with neither high depression nor test anxiety. For this as well other studies described subsequently in this section, subjects with high depression and low anxiety will be referred to as *depressed* and subjects with high anxiety and low depression will be referred to as *anxious*.

Two forms of the ATQ were administered in the study by Ingram, Kendall, Smith, Donnell, and Ronan, (1987); one assessed thoughts during the past week and the second assessed frequency of thoughts during the experiment. A third measure of thought content, the Cognitive Interference Questionnaire (CIQ; Sarason, 1980), was also administered. Unlike the ATQ, the CIQ evaluates the frequency of task-irrelevant, distracting cognitions. Designed specifically to assess thought content in anxiety (Sarason, 1980), the CIQ was not intended necessarily to reflect negative self-referent thinking but to reflect instead the occurrence of task-irrelevant cognitions.

Comparison of "past week" ATQ means found that depressed subjects had scores significantly higher than the control group, but no significant differences were found between the control and anxiety groups. This same pattern was found for automatic thoughts during the experiment. For CIQ scores, on the other hand, an opposite pattern was found—anxious, but not depressed, subjects had scores significantly higher than the control group. Thus, anxious rather than depressed individuals reported more irrelevant cognition whereas depressed rather than anxious subjects reported more cognition that was negative and self-relevant in nature. However, for all three measures, subjects who were depressed *and* anxious had significantly higher scores than any of the other groups, suggesting that the combination of negative affective states may potentiate the frequency of several kinds of dysfunctional cognition.

An additional ATQ study conducted by Ingram (1988b) compared depressed and socially anxious subjects on negative self-referent automatic thoughts. Again, four groups were selected, this time representing the various combinations of depression and social anxiety. Socially anxious subjects had ATQ scores somewhat higher than control subjects, and depressed subjects had scores significantly higher than socially anxious subjects. Scores for depressed and socially anxious subjects, however, were not significantly greater than those for the depressed group. In another study employing depression and generalized anxiety, Ingram (1988c) also assessed automatic thinking. Again, depressed subjects had significantly higher scores than control subjects.

In this study, however, anxious subjects had scores comparable to depressed subjects while depressed and anxious subjects reported significantly more negative self-referent thoughts than any other group.

In two out of these three studies, depressed and anxious subjects evidenced significantly more negative automatic thoughts than did either depressed or anxious subjects. These findings held despite the fact that the respective depression and anxiety scores for subjects with both depression and anxiety were no higher than the same scores for the subjects experiencing only depression or only anxiety. Several possible conclusions are suggested. First, the generality or specificity of the particular anxiety state may be associated with different thought content features. That is, somewhat different patterns were found depending upon whether the anxiety state was specific (i.e., test or social) versus more generalized. For example, generally anxious subjects were found to report levels of negative automatic thoughts that were roughly equivalent to depressed subjects, whereas socially anxious and test-anxious subjects reported less. Hence, anxiety that is general across different situations may be characterized by a more dysfunctional thought pattern than is anxiety limited to certain situational contexts. Alternatively, these differences may be a function of the situational activation determinants of anxious states. While individuals reporting generalized anxiety are probably actively experiencing anxious affect at the time of experimental assessment, subjects selected for situational anxiety may not evidence dysfunctional cognition until they encounter the situations that are anxiety provoking for them. The differential anxiety pattern versus differential anxious affect hypothesis deserves further investigation. This different pattern of results does point to the need to consider potential cognitive differences in the *kind* or class of anxiety under investigation (Kendall, 1978; Smith et al., 1983). It is all too frequently the case that researchers refer to *anxiety* without specific reference to the kind of anxiety considered relevant. As these data suggest, all anxiety-based disorders may not be cognitively equal.

Another possible conclusion is that depression and at least some kinds of anxiety states may interact in ways that are uniquely different than either state alone, a situation that is analogous to the way that two main effects in an ANOVA might interact to produce results that are different than either effect alone. The mechanisms involved in such interactions are as yet unclear.

A recurrent finding throughout much of the cognitive-clinical literature is that the larger the net cast by the theoretical construct, the more likely it is to characterize dysfunction in general. The concept of automatic thoughts, for example, while proposed to capture the essence of cognition in depression, is sufficiently broad to apply to many dysfunctional states. Hence, the cognitive differentiation of depression and anxiety may require the assessment of different *kinds* of dysfunctional thought content. Recently, Beck, Brown, Steer, Eidelson, and Riskind (1987) have developed a scale to assess thought content in depression and anxiety. Employing subjects diagnosed with either depressive or anxiety disorders, Beck et al. (1987) extracted a sample of characteristic thoughts from therapy records for each group. These thoughts were then put into a self-statement inventory format. Subjects were asked to rate the frequency of each thought in four specific situations (e.g., "attending a social occasion"). Subject diagnostic groups were then used to select items that differentiated depression from anxiety. Following a refinement of the scale based on these subject responses, a final list of self-statements was developed, one relevant to depression and one relevant to anxiety. Depressive items reflected themes of failure and personal degradation while anxious items reflected themes of danger and harm. A cross-validation study with a different group of depressed and anxious patients confirmed that depressed subjects reported experiencing more frequent depression-relevant thoughts and anxious subjects reported more anxiety-relevant thoughts.

Kendall and Hollon (1988) have developed an Anxious Self-Statement Questionnaire (ASSQ) that reliably separates psychometrically defined highly anxious from normally anxious subjects. The ASSQ, like the ATQ, was cross-validated on a second sample. The items found to be discriminating were self-statements reflecting a sense of (1) the future, (2) uncertainty, and (3) questioning. The fact that the depressotypic ATQ items, as compared to the ASSQ items, were not suggestive of a questioning of the uncertainty of the future prompted a concern for evaluation of any potential distinctions between anxiety and depression based on the mode or form of characteristic automatic thoughts. In addition to thought content per se, the mode or form of thoughts may also distinguish depressive from anxious cognitions. In the Beck et al. (1987) study, frequently reported thoughts among depressed subjects were more absolutistic and past oriented, whereas anxious thoughts were more relevant to questions of uncertainty and to a future orientation. This "format" difference in depressive and anxious self-statements is consistent with proposals by Kendall (1985) and Kendall and Ingram (1987) that anxious individuals are characterized less by automatic "thinking" and more by automatic "questioning."

One other study, reported by Clark (1986), is relevant to the specific thought content of depressed and anxious individuals. Clark (1986) combined items from several measures (e.g., the ATQ) to develop a

Distressing Thoughts Questionnaire (DTQ). Assessing dysphoric emotion in a sample of 104 subjects, Clark found that subjects experiencing more depressive affect were likely to report thoughts of loss and failure, whereas individuals experiencing more anxiety were likely to report thoughts of harm and danger.

Taken together, the data from studies of depressive and anxious thought content present a relatively clear picture; depressive affect seems most closely associated with self-referent, definitive, past-oriented cognitions of sadness, failure, degradation, and loss. Conversely, anxiety appears most closely associated with future-oriented "questioning" cognitions (Kendall & Ingram, 1987) of broadly defined danger and harm. Some evidence for task-irrelevant, distracting cognitions in test anxiety also exists.

2. Causal Attribution Patterns

Another cognitive variable examined by Ingram, Kendall, Smith, Donnell, and Ronan (1987) was general attributional tendencies as operationalized by the Attributional Style Questionnaire (ASQ; Seligman, Abramson, Semmel, & von Baeyer, 1979). In this study, only main effects were found for the depression-independent variable, suggesting that typical styles of attributing causes for events are associated with depressive affect but not test anxiety. In particular, depressed but not test-anxious subjects showed a characteristic pattern of internal, stable, and global attributions for negative events and external, unstable, and specific attributions for positive events. This pattern of specificity was further supported in a study by Heimberg, Vermilyea, Dodge, Becker, and Barlow (1987), where dysthymic patients were compared on the ASQ to moderately depressed and nondepressed groups of anxiety disorder patients. While the negative attributional pattern was again found for dysthymic patients, only anxiety patients who were also moderately depressed evidenced this pattern. Heimberg et al. (1987) reported somewhat different results in a second study, which showed that social phobic and agoraphobic patients displayed a pattern of attributions similar to dysthymic patients. Covariance analyses examining subject depression scores suggested that although depressive affect was clearly related to attributional patterns, anxiety level also contributed somewhat to negative attributions. Finally, analyses reported by Anderson (Anderson & Arnoult, 1985; Anderson, Horowitz, & French, 1983) have indicated that different attributional patterns for different situations characterize depression, loneliness, and shyness. To the extent that shyness represents social anxiety, these data support different attributional parameters for depressive and anxious states.

3. Information Processing

Self-Referent Information Processing. Most studies of psychopathological information processing have sought to examine the self-schemata of depressed or anxious individuals. Employing the depth-of-processing incidental recall paradigm (Craik and Tulving, 1975; Rogers, Kuiper, & Kirker, 1977) to test self-schematic processes, M. S. Greenberg and Alloy (1988) selected subjects who were depressed, anxious but not depressed, and nondepressed–nonanxious. Anxiety scores for the "depressed" group were as high as those for the "anxious but not depressed" group and thus these subjects are probably most appropriately referred to as "depressed–anxious." In addition, although the depression scores of the subjects selected for anxiety were significantly lower than the depression scores of the depressed subjects, they were also higher than depression scores for control subjects.

Subjects in the M. S. Greenberg and Alloy (1988) study performed the depth-of-processing task using both the positive and negative depression-relevant stimuli and the positive and negative anxiety-relevant stimuli. In addition to rating the self-descriptiveness of the stimuli, as is typically the case in this paradigm, subjects were also asked to rate how each word described another person, a method of testing the processing of other-referent information. Consistent with a number of other studies of depressive information processing (e.g., Kuiper & Derry, 1982), results suggested that depressed–anxious subjects recalled a roughly equal mix of positive and negative depression-relevant words. Given the strong correlation between depressed and anxious states, this consistency across studies is not surprising inasmuch as previous studies of "depressed" subjects most likely actually employed subjects who were depressed and anxious. Anxious but not depressed subjects were also more likely to recall anxiety-relevant content whereas nondepressed–nonanxious subjects recalled primarily positive content. Further, differences were limited to self-rated material, suggesting that depressive or anxious information processing by depressed and anxious individuals is largely confined to self-relevant as opposed to other-relevant stimuli.

The study by Ingram, Kendall, Smith, Donnell, and Ronan (1987) also reported data on self-referent information processing. Employing a similar depth-of-processing paradigm with depressive, anxious, and nondepressed–nonanxious content stimuli, results suggested that depressed subjects recalled significantly more depressive content whereas anxious subjects recalled significantly more anxious content. Interestingly, subjects who were both depressed and anxious recalled both depressive and anxious information at levels that were somewhat below levels found in depressed or anxious subjects, but that were above levels found in control subjects. Apparently, these individuals may be cognitive primed to pick up both kinds of information relatively equally.

Considered together, the studies by Beck et al. (1987), M. S. Greenberg and Alloy (1988), and Ingram, Lumry, Cruet, and Sieber (1987) support the content-specificity hypothesis (Beck, 1976; Beck & Emery, 1985). This hypothesis argues that individuals with particular disorders are more likely to process information consistent with their disorders, which helps to maintain the disorder. More specifically, these data support the presence of different schema structures in depression and anxiety that are primed to facilitate the processing of depressive- or anxious-relevant information.

Environmentally Vigilant Information Processing. MacLeod et al. (1986) have reported an innovative experiment examining potential attention biases in anxiety. Specifically, they developed a paradigm for assessing the direction of attention and how that direction may be influenced by certain stimuli. Anxiety-producing situations typically fall into one of two classes: evaluations of the self and of physical danger threats. In the Macleod et al. (1986) study, both socially threatening (e.g., "criticized," "inferior") and physically threatening (e.g., "injury," "cancer") stimulus words were presented on a computer screen and were accompanied by a secondary stimulus probe. The subjects' task was to react to the stimulus probe by pushing a button at its onset. To the extent that subjects were focusing their attentional processing resources on the stimulus words, reaction times to the probe should be slowed accordingly. As expected, anxiety disorder patients performing this task had reaction times significantly longer than nonanxious control subjects. To test the specificity of these findings, a depressed patients group was also run through the paradigm. No evidence for an attentional bias toward the threatening stimuli was found for these subjects, however. Thus, an enhanced processing of threatening stimuli, at least as operationalized by the words employed by MacLeod et al. (1986), appears to be characteristic of anxiety but not depression.

III. Methodological Issues and Strategies in Examining Cognitive Specificity

Issues of cognitive specificity present some unique challenges for research. Accordingly, there are several recommendations and strategies for empirical research examining this specificity. These can be grouped according to either *general* or *unique* strategies. General strategies refer to those that, while relevant for cognitive specificity investigations, are also pertinent to broader aspects of descriptive psychopathology. Conversely, unique strategies are those that are primarily relevant to questions concerning cognitive specificity.

A. General Strategies

1. Multiple Assessment Periods

Levels of depression and anxiety can covary with a number of variables over time. For example, the depression level of an individual selected as depressed on one occasion may moderate significantly even over the usually short time interval between initial selection and subsequent experimental testing. Similarly, anxiety levels may moderate after selection, or, alternatively, in the case of situation-specific anxiety, may not be elevated at testing unless the appropriate situational context is present. Except in cases where initial selection and experimental testing are concurrent, which are relatively infrequent in cognitive-behavioral research efforts, multiple assessments of the emotional state are necessary: initially at selection and again at testing. Subjects that no longer meet study criteria are then eliminated from the experiment.

In addition to multiple assessment periods, the use of multiple assessment methods are also desirable (i.e., two different measures of depression or anxiety). The multitime, multimethod assessment strategy has several interrelated benefits. First, it decreases the probability that subject selection is measure dependent; that is, that subjects may be classified into a particular category because a given measure generates too many false positives (oversensitive) or too many false negatives (undersensitive). Hence, classification *reliability* is enhanced. Although measure-dependent classification errors may still occur even with two measures, the probability is decreased substantially. Second, confidence is increased that the state actually exists if subjects score above the cutoff on two different measures at two different times. Multitime and multimeasure assessment therefore also bolsters the *validity* of subject classification. Third, this method helps to ensure the stability of subjects' emotional states. Subjects classified as depressed or anxious on both occasions are thus more likely to exhibit the affect over some period of time, if even a short period. Such subjects may generally be more appropriate targets of research than are subjects whose affect level normalizes more quickly. Finally, this method increases confidence that the negative affect is present at the actual time of testing and, therefore, allows for adequate tests of hypotheses concerning the affect.

2. Psychopathological Control Groups

A general and useful strategy in descriptive psychopathology research is the use of comparison groups, typically composed of various psychiatric diagnoses. Such control groups are of more limited use in investigations of cognitive specificity because their heterogeneous nature may obscure the specific operation of some variables. Consider, for example, in a study of depression a control group composed of diagnoses of schizophrenia, psychopathy, alcoholism, anxiety, and various personality disorders. If the variable under investigation in depression also characterized anxiety (and not other disorders), but there were only 2 anxiety patients among 20 control group members, the data might well be interpreted to suggest that the variable was specific to depression.

Such groups are, however, useful in examining the factors that are common to disorders (rather than those that are critical or unique; see below for an extended discussion of these concepts). Hence, if significant differences are found between the target subjects and psychopathology control subjects on a given variable, it is reasonable to conclude that the variable is *not* a general feature of psychopathology. Similarly, findings that the variable does characterize the psychopathology control group suggest a common rather than specific variable.

3. Normal Controls

A relatively common methodological practice in creating normal control groups is to select individuals with very low levels of the target variable. Using the BDI in the case of a depression study, for example, researchers may select individuals with high scores to comprise their experimental group and individuals scoring very low (e.g., 0s and 1s) to make up their control group. Hammen (1983) has noted, however, that such procedures, which select for a complete absence of depression rather than for average or typical levels of depression, may actually select for individuals high in other psychopathological states, such as psychopathy and hypomania. Kendall, Hollon, Beck, Hammen, and Ingram (1987) therefore recommend that control groups be made up of individuals at the mean on measures of the construct, or possibly that three groups be selected: those who are high, average, and low on the measure.

B. Unique Strategies

1. Assessment of Multiple States

Perhaps the easiest strategy for assessing questions of specificity is to assess multiple dysfunctional states and then statistically control for nontarget states. In the case of depression and anxiety, for instance, if the focus is on depression, researchers would be well advised to assess anxiety as well. With data on subjects' depression and anxiety levels, statistical methods such as analysis of covariance or multiple regression can be employed to examine the specific effects of depression, unconfounded by anxiety level. While this may not be the optimal strategy because individuals with heightened levels of both depression and anxiety (who would be the majority of subjects represented in such a design) may differ from either "pure" depressed or "pure" anxious (Ingram, Kendall, Smith, Donnell, & Ronan, 1987), it is an improvement over designs that only assess the target affective group.

2. Experimental Selection of Nonoverlapping States

Undoubtedly the best, and unfortunately also the most difficult, tactic is to define subject groups orthogonally based on depression and anxiety levels. This strategy generally leads to a 2 × 2 design with respective cells of depressed and anxious subjects, depressed-only subjects, anxious-only subjects, and average-depressed/average-anxious (control) subjects. Although difficult, this strategy allows for direct tests of the specificity and generality of variables in depression and anxiety, both singularly and in combination.

A word of caution is in order regarding the analysis of data from such designs. Given that subject groups are formed on the basis of a 2 × 2 design, an ordinarily appropriate statistical analysis would be a 2 × 2 analysis of variance. Results of such analyses, however, can be misleading. For example, a main effect due to one variable (say anxiety) does not tell the complete story because this independent variable is not unconfounded; a main effect for anxiety is composed of two cells, one of anxiety-only subjects but also one of anxiety and depressed subjects. Similarly, the interaction term may be misleading in that it depends on the overall pattern of the four cells; in this design, however, the true measure of the interactive effects of the two variables is represented by *only* the single cell of subjects with both depression and anxiety. A more appropriate analysis is to consider each cell a level in a one-way design with the control group as a normal baseline from which to make subsequent mean comparisons. This allows for an evaluation of differences between controls and depressed, anxious, and depressed–anxious subjects, as well as for differences among these latter three groups.

IV. Theoretical Perspectives

A. The Meta-Construct Model of Psychopathology

As is apparent from this review, as well as from several of the other chapters in this volume (e.g., Clark & Beck), the number and diversity of cognitive constructs invoked to describe various aspects of depressive or anxious functioning are remarkable. Moreover, these constructs have received fairly solid empirical support as elements of depression and anxiety. At the same time, however, the data garnered in support of each of the proposed constructs merit several theoretical considerations.

At present, it is not clear which of the many constructs, or set of constructs, capture the essential elements of each of the disorders. Extant concepts of cognitive factors span a wide range of different "types" of cognition and levels of cognitive analysis. In depression, for example, depressed–nondepressed differences have been found in cognitive variables ranging from specific information retrieval to generalized dysfunctional beliefs. Similarly, cognitive differences in anxiety have been noted in variables as diverse as detailed attentional difficulties and broadly defined irrationality. Advances in our understanding of negative affective states require an integration of these different cognitive variables.

A correlated concern has to do with how these diverse constructs are differentially related to depression *or* anxiety, or, alternatively, how they may be jointly associated with depression *and* anxiety. As we have noted, many cognitive variables have been explored in parallel in depression and anxiety. A good number of these variables are conceptually quite similar (e.g., self-focused attention), whereas others tend to be more distinct (e.g., respective depressive and anxious self-referent information processing). Relatively few of these variables, however, have been explored with distinctly depressed (and not anxious) or distinctly anxious (and not depressed) individuals in sufficient detail to be able to draw any but the most preliminary conclusions about which factors are unique to depression or anxiety and which are nonspecific across both (and perhaps other) disorders. Efforts to address these concerns can have implications for the broader importance of cognitive approaches in understanding psychological disorders.

Ultimately the resolution to such conceptual issues lies in empirical research that examines separately the cognitive characteristics of depressive and anxious affective states and depressive and anxious disorders. Also needed are conceptual frameworks that are capable of integrating both similar and distinct depressive and anxious variables in a comprehensive fashion. The framework we will describe, called the *meta-construct model of psychopathology* (Ingram, 1988a; Ingram & Wisnicki, in press), is a generalized model of psychology aimed at describing and classifying various levels of cognitive analysis. The model incorporates two theoretical approaches to the description of different psychological functioning: a *cognitive taxonomy* that denotes various categories of cognitive constructs proposed to describe maladaptive functioning (Ingram, 1983; Ingram & Kendall, 1986, 1987; Kendall, 1985; see also Goldfried & Robins, 1983; Hammen, 1981; Hollon & Kriss, 1984; Marzillier, 1980; Turk & Speers, 1983), and a *components model of psychopathology* that seeks to examine the cognitive features that are unique to a particular disorder as well as those that appear to be generalized across disorders (Ingram & Kendall, 1987; Kendall & Ingram, 1987). The metaconstruct model proposes a structure for organizing both the taxonomy and the components model into broad conceptual categories that encompass both similar and different psychopathological features.

1. Cognitive Taxonomy Elements

In an effort to organize the numerous kinds of cognitive constructs that have been proposed to characterize depression and anxiety, we have suggested a cognitive taxonomy to describe the general categories into which these constructs fall. These categories consist of cognitive *structural, propositional* (stored content), *operational* (processes), and *product* variables. While these categories are proposed to be distinct in a conceptual sense, we suggest that constructs within each category operate jointly to produce what is typically referred to as cognition.

Cognitive Structural Constructs. Structural concepts refer broadly to the "architecture" of the cognitive system in that these variables describe mechanisms encompassing how information is stored and organized. Concepts such as short- and long-term memory are noteworthy examples of variables that focus upon the structural aspects of information processing.

Cognitive Propositional Constructs. Propositions refer to the content of information that is stored and organized within a structure. Episodic and semantic knowledge represent illustrations of propositional variables. Because this category describes the stored content of the cognitive system, it could easily be labeled as cognitive content. Since *content* is used in different ways to describe different phenomena (e.g., the content of self-statements and the content of beliefs), the term *propositions* was chosen to decrease ambiguity between classes of cognitive variables.

Cognitive Operational Constructs. Operations consist of the processes by which the system works. Some examples of cognitive operational variables include information encoding, retrieval, and attentional processes. Cognitive operations could also be referred to a cognitive processes. As with *content,* however—because *processes* have been used to describe cognitive variables spanning across all four categories—the term *operations* was chosen instead.

Cognitive Product Constructs. Products are defined as the end result of the operation of the cognitive system to process information; these are the cognitions or thoughts that the individual experiences as a result of the interaction of incoming information with cognitive structures, propositions, and operations. Examples include constructs such as attributions. Because an attribution is an individual's causal explanation of a prior behavioral event, it results from (is a product of) cognitive processing of related content.

2. Component Model of Psychopathology Elements

Partitioning the Variance in Psychopathology. It is unrealistic to assume that all or most cognitive variables are unique to a particular psychological disorder. We suggest that a useful metaphor for understanding how these variables relate to different disorders is to employ a model that views the variance in psychopathology in a manner analogous to the manner in which variance is conceptualized in experimental research. Specifically, we propose that the variance in psychopathology can be conceptually "partitioned" in much the same way that experimental variance is partitioned by an ANOVA. Hence, the ultimate symptomatic expression of a disorder is a function of several converging and identifiable sources of variance. For example, a two-way ANOVA would partition an experimental result into components represented as: Effect $= A + B + AB + E$, where A equals the unique variance due to the first factor, B equals the unique variance due to the second factor, AB equals the common or shared variance resulting from the interaction of the factors, and E represents the error variance. In a similar fashion, the expression of a particular psychopathology can be conceptualized as the result of the confluence of "critical psychopathological features," "common psychopathological features," and unpredictable error variance.

Critical Features. These features represent variance that is uniquely characteristic of a particular disorder and thus describe variables specific to a given psychopathology. Hence, these features are defined as those which not only differentiate disorder from nondisorder, but also differentiate one disorder from another.

Common Features. In contrast to critical psychopathological features, common features are those that are generally characteristic of all or most disorders and are therefore conceptualized as common or shared psychopathological variance. While these features do not differentiate particular disorders, however, they are defined as differentiating disorder from nondisorder. That is, although common features are not unique to a given disorder, they are "unique" to psychopathology in general and thus broadly separate adaptive from maladaptive functioning.

Error Variance. Finally, error variance represents the unpredictable variance in psychopathology that is due to nonsystematic factors. While the majority of variance in the expression of psychopathology can most likely be accounted for by critical and common features, the precise symptoms and characteristics of the disorder will also be influenced to some degree by the factors unique to the particular person involved. However, because error variance is by definition unpredictable, it will not be discussed further.

Interactions. In a two-way (or higher) ANOVA model, interactions are possible between independent variables. At present we have not included an interaction term in the meta-construct model. Such interactions are theoretically possible in that certain combinations of psychopathological states may produce cognitive characteristics that are sufficiently different from either state alone. For example, some data were reviewed in a previous section to suggest that the combination of depression and anxiety is associated with significantly more negative automatic thoughts than either depression or anxiety individually (Ingram, 1988c; Ingram, Lumry, Cruet, & Sieber, 1987). At present, however, there are insufficient empirical data to speculate on how various interactions of depression and anxiety differ from either disorder alone.

It is also important to note that the ANOVA metaphor should not be taken too literally by suggesting that all components of the ANOVA must be represented in the corresponding psychopathology conceptual model (such as interactions). That is, the ANOVA model is simply a useful analogy for thinking about how psychopathological variance can be broken down into specific and nonspecific aspects. Any other statistical procedure partitioning sources of variance (e.g., multiple regression, factor analysis) would serve just as well as a model for separating elements of psychopathology into conceptually interesting segments.

B. Meta-Construct Model of Depression and Anxiety

Given meta-construct conceptualizations of cognition in depression and anxiety, the following sections will summarize the cognitive data according to the various components of the model. Specifically, data pertaining to the structural, propositional, operational, and product dimensions of common features will first be reviewed. Next these same categories will be reviewed within the context of critical features.

1. Common Features

Structural/Propositional. Although cognitive schemata are usually referred to as structures, they are typically defined in terms of content rather than structure (Ingram & Kendall, 1986). Structures in and of themselves cannot be considered negative. However, the negative self-schema, as frequently conceptualized, encompasses both structural and propositional elements (Ingram & Kendall, 1986) and appears to be a feature common to psychological disorders. Distinguishing the negative self-schema as a common feature may partially be due to the broadness of its definition; that is, the term *negative* is virtually by definition a feature of dysfunctional states. Indeed, as we have noted, the more precise the conceptualization of a given construct, the more likely it is to fit only a given disorder. Nevertheless, even though *negative* is quite broad in scope, it does capture an essential element that is apparent in virtually all psychological disorders.

Operational. As with the negative self-schema, we proposed that negative information processing (e.g., overestimates of negative events, underestimates of rewards and positive events) is characteristic of many disorders. Although the conceptualization of *negative* is very broad, such information processing does seem adequate to describe dysfunction in general.

A large body of research has examined the association between exacerbated self-focused attention and both subclinical (Ingram & Smith, 1984; J. Greenberg & Pyszcynski, 1986; Smith & Greenberg, 1981) and clinical (Ingram, Lumry, Cruet, & Sieber, 1987) depression. Although approached from a somewhat different perspective, research has also found associations between self-focused attention and a variety of forms of anxiety (see Wine; Sarason). Indeed, increased self-focused attention may characterize disorders as diverse as hypomania, psychopathy, schizophrenia, and alcoholism (Ingram, 1988a). Hence, heightened self-focused attention seems most appropriately classified as an operation that is common to dysfunction but not critical to either depression or anxiety.

Products. Automatic thoughts are conceptualized as products in the sense that they refer to the cognitions that an individual experiences. Presumably the basis for these thoughts lies in propositional dimensions (i.e., the individual's beliefs while depressed or anxious that give rise to specific automatic cognitions).

The data are somewhat mixed with regard to automatic thoughts of the kind assessed by the ATQ. Some studies have suggested that they are relatively specific to depression (Ingram, Lumry, Cruet, & Sieber, 1987; Ingram, 1988c), while others have suggested an association with at least some kinds of anxiety (e.g., Ingram, 1988b). Moreover, the fact that individuals who are both depressed and anxious report more automatic thoughts further suggests that anxiety contributes some variance to this relationship. The "generic" concept of automatic thinking therefore appears to be more common than critical at the present time.

The data are clear-cut with regard to whether dysfunctional attitudes or irrational beliefs are present in depression. A variety of studies (e.g., Dobson & Shaw, 1986; Eaves & Rush, 1984; Giles & Rush 1984; Hamilton & Abramson, 1983; Reda, 1987; Simons, Garfield, & Murphy, 1987) have indicated that depressed individuals are more likely to endorse such attitudes on the Dysfunctional Attitudes Scale (DAS; Weissman & Beck, 1978). Less research has been done on dysfunctional attitudes in anxiety but the available data do suggest a similar presence (e.g., Deffenbacher, 1986). We thus suspect that such attitudes, to the extent that they have been defined in such a general fashion, are most likely common psychopathological features of depression and anxiety.

2. Critical Features

Structural/Propositional. Although self-schemata in depression and anxiety can both be described as negative or dysfunctional, the propositional nature of the schema differentiates the disorders. At the broadest level, the schematic/propositional structures of depressed individuals can be described as depression specific. That is, the content of prepotent information-processing structures in individuals, when they are depressed, seems to be characterized by themes of personal sadness and self-degradation.

The counterpart to the depressive self-schema is the anxious self-schema. Instead of self-degradation and sadness-related themes, however, the schemata of individuals describing themselves as anxious are better described by themes of danger and harm to the self.

Operational. The data suggest that depressive mood specifically impacts those processes that facilitate the encoding and retrieval of information, consistent with the depressive self-schema. In contrast, anxious individuals appear primed to encode and retrieve information, consistent with an anxious self-schema. Indeed, such schematic processes apparently serve as the structural/propositional basis for subsequent information-processing activities, such as the processing of external information (encoding processes) and the cognitions that individuals experience (retrieval processes).

One additional operational dimension appears to characterize anxiety. As the study by MacLeod et al. (1986) demonstrates, anxious individuals may be more environmentally hypervigilant for signs of threat. This hypervigilance might be a function of the anxious self-schema and it is possible that depressed individuals may be environmentally hypervigilant for data relevant to their active self-schemata as well (e.g., signs of social rejection). Studies have not yet addressed this specific possibility.

Products. In line with depressive self-schematic information processing, depressive cognitions seem specifically dominated by self-statements consisting of sad and self-degrading cognitions that are in a declarative form and are primarily past oriented. Anxious individuals' thoughts are more likely to revolve around themes of harm and danger and appear to be more future oriented. The data also suggest that these thoughts tend to be of a more questioning nature.

While there are some mixed results, the majority of data also indicate that negative attributional styles for both positive and negative event outcomes tend to be specific to depression. This is not to suggest, of course, that there are no particular attributional dimensions characteristic of anxiety, but rather that those examined thus far appear most relevant to depression.

V. Summary and Conclusions

In the present chapter we have attempted to elucidate the issues relevant to the cognitive specificity of depressive and anxious states. While there has been no shortage of studies examining cognition in depression or anxiety, the same cannot be said of specific and comparative cognitive investigations of these two states. Moreover, the array of cognitive constructs investigated is impressive in scope but is ultimately confusing in terms of understanding the different elements of the cognitive systems that underlie depression and anxiety. Albeit many of these constructs may represent only different labels or slightly different operationalizations (e.g., self-focused attention versus self-preoccupation), others genuinely reflect the operation of different levels of cognition. We have reviewed the extant research on various levels of cognition as they pertain to specificity and have attempted to point out the relevant issues, both methodological and theoretical, that are important for understanding depression and anxiety states. We have also described a model for classifying the various cognitive components of depression and anxiety, and based on available data and theory have speculated as to where the components fit.

The preliminary nature of our speculations is quite obvious in that data and theory have only recently begun to examine cognitive specificity issues. We are optimistic about the recent progress and anticipate that these are the beginning steps toward understanding how both specific and common psychopathological features are crucial elements of depression and anxiety.

References

Alden, L. (1987). Attributional responses of anxious individuals to different patterns of social feedback: Nothing succeeds like improvement. *Journal of Personality and Social Psychology, 52,* 100–106.

Alloy, L. B. (Ed.). (1988). *Cognitive processes in depression.* New York: Guilford Press.

Anderson, C. A., & Arnoult, L. H. (1985). Attributional style in everyday problems in living: Depression, loneliness, and shyness. *Social Cognition, 3,* 16–35.

Anderson, C. A., Horowitz, L. M., & French, R. (1983). Attributional style of lonely and depressed people. *Journal of Personality and Social Psychology, 45,* 127–136.

Barlow, D. (1988). *Anxiety and its disorders: The nature and treatment of anxiety and panic.* New York: Guilford.

Beck, A. T. (1976). *Cognitive Therapy and the emotional disorders.* New York: International Universities Press.

Beck, A. T., Brown, G., Steer, R. A., Eidelson, J. I., & Riskind, J. H. (1987). Differentiating anxiety and depression: A test of the cognitive specificity hypothesis. *Journal of Abnormal Psychology, 96,* 179–183.

Beck, A. T., & Emery, G. (1985). *Anxiety and phobias: A cognitive perspective.* New York: Basic Books.

Beck, A. T., Rush, A. J., Shaw, B. F., & Emery, G. (1979). *Cognitive therapy of depression.* New York: Guilford Press.

Butler, G., & Mathews, A. (1983).Cognitive processes in anxiety. *Advances in Behavior Research and Therapy 5,* 51–62.

Butler, G., & Mathews, A. (1987). Anticipatory anxiety and risk perception. *Cognitive Therapy and Research, 11,* 551–566.

Carver, C. S., & Scheier, M. F. (1981). *Attention and self-regulation: A control-theory approach to human behavior.* Berlin: Springer-Verlag.

Clark, D. A. (1986). Cognitive–affective interaction: A test of the " specificity" and "generality" hypotheses. *Cognitive Therapy and Research, 10,* 607–624.

Cook, M. L., & Peterson, C. (1986). Depressive irrationality. *Cognitive Therapy and Research, 10,* 293–298.

Craighead, W. E. (1981). Issues resulting from treatment studies. In L. Y. Rehm (Ed.), *Behavior therapy for depression: Present status and future directions* (pp. 73–95). New York: Academic Press.

Craighead, W. E., Hickey, K. S., & DeMonbreun, B. G. (1979). Distortion of perception and recall of neutral feedback in depression. *Cognitive Therapy and Research, 3,* 291–298.

Craik, F. I. M., & Tulving, E. (1975). Depth of processing and the retention of words in episodic memory. *Journal of Experimental Psychology, 104,* 268–294.

Deffenbacher, J. L. (1986). Cognitive and physiological components of test anxiety in real life exams. *Cognitive Therapy and Research, 10,* 635–644.

Derry, P.A., & Kuiper, N. A. (1981). Schematic processing and self-reference in clinical depression. *Journal of Abnormal Psychology, 90,* 286–297.

Dobson, K. S. (1985). Relationship between anxiety and depression. *Clinical Psychology Review, 5,* 305–324.

Dobson, K. S., & Breiter, H. J. (1983). Cognitive assessment of depression: Rehability and validity of three measures. *Journal of Abnormal Psychology, 92,* 107–109.

Dobson, K. S., & Shaw, B. F. (1986). Cognitive assessment of major depressive disorder. *Cognitive Therapy and Research, 10,* 13–29.

Dobson, K.S., & Shaw, B. F. (1987). Specificity and stability of self-referent encoding in clinical depression. *Journal of Abnormal Psychology, 96,* 34–40.

Dodge, C. S., & Heimberg, R. G., Hope, D. A., & Becker, R. E. (1986). *Evaluation of the social interaction self-statement test of social phobia patients.* Paper presented at the meeting of the Association for the Advancement of Behavior Therapy, Chicago.

Eaves, G., & Rush, A. J. (1984). Cognitive patterns in symptomatic and remitted unipolar major depression. *Journal of Abnormal Psychology, 93,* 31–40.

Giles, D. E., & Rush, A. J. (1984). *Biological and cognitive vulnerability markers to define populations at risk.* Paper presented at the meeting of the Association for the Advancement of Behavior Therapy.

Goldfried, M. R., & Robins, C. (1983). Self-schema, cognitive bias, and the processing of therapeutic experiences. In P. C. Kendall (Ed.), *Advances in cognitive-behavioral research and therapy* (Vol. 2, pp. 33–80). New York: Academic Press.

Gormally, J., Sipps, G., Raphael, R., Edwin, D., & Varvil-Weld, D. (1981). The relationship between maladaptive cognitions and social anxiety. *Journal of Consulting and Clinical Psychology, 49,* 300–301.

Gotlib, I. H. (1983). Perception and recall of interpersonal feedback: Negative bias in depression. *Cognitive Therapy and Research, 7,* 399–412.

Gotlib, I. H. (1984). Depression and general psychopathology in university students. *Journal of Abnormal Psychology, 93,* 19–30.

Gotlib, I. H., & Cane, D. B. (1987). Construct accessibility and clinical depression: A longitudinal investigation. *Journal of Abnormal Psychology, 96,* 199–204.

Gotlib, I. H., & McCann, C. D. (1984). Construct accessibility and depression: An examination of cognitive and affective factors. *Journal of Personality and Social Psychology, 47,* 427–439.

Greenberg, J., & Pyszcynski, T. (1986). Persistant high self-focus after failure and low self-focus after success. The depressive self-focusing style. *Journal of Personality and Social Psychology, 50,* 1039–1044.

Greenberg, M. S., & Alloy, L. B. (1988). *Depression versus anxiety: Schematic processing of self- and other-reterent information.* Manuscript submitted for publication.

Hamilton, E. W., & Abramson, L. Y. (1983). Cognition patterns and major depressive disorder: A longitudinal study in a hospital setting. *Journal of Abnormal Psychology, 92,* 173–187.

Hammen, C. L. (1978). Depression, distortion, and life stress in college students. *Cognitive Therapy and Research, 2,* 189–192.

Hammen, C. L. (1981). Assessment: A clinical and cognitive emphasis. In L. P. Rehm (Ed.), *Behavior therapy for depression: Present status and future direction* (pp. 255–277). Orlando, FL: Academic Press.

Hammen, C. L. (1983). Cognitive and social processes in bipolar effective disorder: A neglected topic. In C. L. Hammen (Chair), *Research issues and opportunities in bipolar affective disorder.* Symposium conducted at the meeting of the American Psychological Association, Anaheim, CA.

Hammen, C. L., & Glas, D. R. (1975). Depression, activity, and evaluation of reinforcement. *Journal of Abnormal Psychology, 84,* 718–721.

Hammen, C. L., & Krantz, S. (1976). Effect of success and failure on depressive cognitions. *Journal of Abnormal Psychology, 85,* 577–586.

Harrell, T. H., & Ryon, N. B. (1983). Cognitive-behavioral assessment of depression: Clinical validation of the automatic thoughts questionnaire. *Journal of Consulting and Clinical Psychology, 51,* 721–725.

Heimberg, R. G., Vermilyea, J. A., Dodge, C. S., Becker, R. E., & Barlow, D. H. (1987). Attributional style, depression, and anxiety: An evaluation of the specificity of depressive attributions. *Cognitive Therapy and Research, 11,* 537–550.

Hollon, S. D., & Kendall, P. C. (1980). Cognitive self-statements in depression: Development of an automatic thoughts questionnaire. *Cognitive Therapy and Research, 4,* 383–395.

Hollon, S. D., & Kriss, M. (1984). Cognitive factors in clinical research and practice. *Clinical Psychology Review, 4,* 35–76.

Ingram, R. E. (1983). Content and process distinctions in depressive self-schemata. In L. B. Alloy (Chair), *Depression and schemata.* Symposium conducted at the meeting of the American Psychological Association, Anaheim, CA.

Ingram, R. E. (1984). Toward an information processing analysis of depression. *Cognitive Therapy and Research, 8,* 443–478.

Ingram, R. E. (1988a). *Self-focused attention in clinical disorders: Review and a conceptual model.* Manuscript submitted for publication.

Ingram, R. E. (1988b). *Differentiation of cognitive variables in depression and social anxiety.* Manuscript in preparation.

Ingram, R. E. (1988c). *Cognitive specificity in depression and generalized anxious affect.* Manuscript submitted for publication.

Ingram, R. E., & Kendall, P. C. (1986). Cognitive clinical psychology: Implications of an information processing perspective. In R. E. Ingram (Ed.), *Information processing approaches to clinical psychology* (pp. 3–21). Orlando, FL: Academic Press.

Ingram, R. E., & Kendall, P. C. (1987). The cognitive side of anxiety. *Cognitive Therapy and Research, 11,* 523–536.

Ingram, R. E., Kendall, P. C., Smith, T. W., Donnell, C., & Ronan, K. (1987). Cognitive specificity in emotional distress. *Journal of Personality and Social Psychology, 53,* 734–742.

Ingram, R. E., Lumry, A., Cruet, D., & Sieber, W. (1987). Attentional processes in depressive disorders. *Cognitive Therapy and Research, 11,* 351–360.

Ingram, R. E., & Smith, T. W. (1984). Depression and internal versus external focus of attention. *Cognitive Therapy and Research, 8,* 139–152.

Ingram, R. E., Smith, T. W., & Brehm, S. S. (1983). Depression and information processing: Self-schemata and the encoding of self-referent information. *Journal of Personality and Social Psychology, 45,* 412–420.

Ingram, R. E., & Wisnicki, K. S. (in press). Cognition in depression. In P. Magaro & M. Johnson (Eds.), *Annual Review of Psychopathology.* Greenwich, CT: JAI Press.

Johnson, J. E., Petzel, T. P., Hartney, L. M., & Morgan, R. A. (1983). Recall of importance ratings of completed and uncompleted tasks as a function of depression. *Cognitive Therapy and Research, 7,* 51–56.

Kendall, P. C. (1978). Anxiety: States, traits—situations? *Journal of Consulting and Clinical Psychology, 46,* 280–287.

Kendall, P. C. (1985). Toward a cognitive-behavioral model of child psychopathology and a critique of related interventions. *Journal of Abnormal Child Psychology, 13,* 357–373.

Kendall, P. C., & Hollon, S. D. (in press). Anxious self-talk: Development of the Anxious Self-Statement Questionnaire. *Cognitive Therapy and Research.*

Kendall, P. C., Hollon, S. D., Beck, A. T., Hammen, C. L., & Ingram, R. E. (1987). Issues and recommendations regarding use of the Beck Depression Inventory. *Cognitive Therapy and Research, 11,* 289–299.

Kendall, P. C., & Ingram, R. E. (1987). The future for cognitive assessment of anxiety: Let's get specific. In L. Michelson & L. M. Ascher (Eds.), *Anxiety and stress disorders: Cognitive–behavioral assessment and treatment* (pp. 89–104). New York: Guilford Press.

Krantz, S., & Hammen, C. (1979). Assessment of cognitive bias in depression. *Journal of Abnormal Psychology, 88,* 611–619.

Kuiper, N. A., & Derry, P. A. (1982). Depressed and nondepressed content self-reference in mild depressives. *Journal of Personality, 50,* 67–80.

Kuiper, N. A., & MacDonald, M. R. (1983). Schematic processing in depression: The self-based consensus bias. *Cognitive Therapy and Research, 7,* 469–484.

Kuiper, N. A., Olinger, L. J., & MacDonald, M. (1988). Vulnerability and episodic cognitions in a self-worth contingency model of depression. In L. B. Alloy (Ed.), *Cognitive process in depression* (pp. 289–309). New York: Guilford Press.

Lam, D. H., Brewin, C. R., Woods, R. T., & Bebbington, P. E. (1987). Cognition and social adversity in the depressed elderly. *Journal of Abnormal Psychology, 96,* 23–26.

MacLeod, C., Mathews, A., & Tata, P. (1986). Attentional bias in emotional disorders. *Journal of Abnormal Psychology, 95,* 15–20.

Marzillier, J. S. (1980). Cognitive therapy and behavioural practice. *Behaviour Research and Therapy, 18,* 249–288.

McNally, R. J., & Foa, E. B. (1987). Cognition and agoraphobia: Bias in the interpretation of threat. *Cognitive Therapy and Research, 11,* 567–582.

McNally, R. J., Foa, E. B., & Donnell, C. D. (1988). *Memory bias for anxiety information in patients with paic disorder.* Manuscript submitted for publication.

Michelson, L., & Ascher, L. M. (Eds.). (1987).*Anxiety and stress disorders: Cognitive-behavioral assessment and treatment.* New York: Guilford Press.

Mizes, J. S., Landold-Fritsche, B., & Grossman-McKee, D. (1987). Patterns of distorted cognitions in phobic disorders An investigation of clinically severe simple phobics, social phobics, and agoraphobics. *Cognitive Therapy and Research, 11,* 583–592.

Mueller, J. H., & Thompson, W. B. (1984). Test anxiety and distinctiveness of personal information. In H. M. van der Ploeg, R. Schwarzer, & C. D. Spielberger (Eds.), *Advances in test anxiety research* (Vol. 3, pp. 21–37). Hillsdale, NJ: Erlbaum.

Nelson, R. E., & Craighead, W. E. (1977). Selective recall of positive and negative feedback, self-control behaviors, and depression. *Journal of Abnormal Psychology, 86,* 379–388.

Peterson, C., & Seligman, M. E. P. (1984). Causal explanations as a risk factor for depression: Theory and evidence. *Psychological Review, 91,* 347–364.

Pyszcynski, T., & Greenberg, J. (1987). Self-regulatory pseveration and the depressive self-focusing style: A self-awareness theory of reaction depression. *Psychological Bulletin, 102,* 122–138.

Rabin, A. S. (1985). *Selective memory in depression: Memory deficits or response bias?* Paper presented at the meeting of the Association for the Advancement of Behavior Therapy, Houston, TX.

Reda, M. A. (1987). Cognitive organization and antidepressants: Attitude modification during amitriptyline treatment in severely depressed individuals. In M. A. Reda & M. J. Mahoney (Eds.), *Cognitive psychotherapies* (pp. 119–149). Cambridge, MA: Ballinger.

Rogers, T. B., Kuiper, N. A., & Kirker, W. S. (1977). Self-reference and the encoding of personal information. *Journal of Personality and Social Psychology, 35,* 677–688.

Ross, M. J., & Mueller, J. H. (1983). *Consistency of the self-schema in depression.* Paper presented at the meeting of the Midwestern Psychological Association, Chicago.

Roth, D., & Rehm, L. P. (1980). Relationships among self-monitoring processes, memory and depression. *Cognitive Therapy and Research, 4,* 149–157.

Sarason, I. G. (1975). Anxiety and self-preoccupation. In I. G. Sarason & C. D. Spielberger (Eds.), *Stress and anxiety* (Vol. 2). New York: Hemisphere.

Sarason, I. G. (1980). Introduction to the study of test anxiety. In I. G. Sarason (Ed.), *Test anxiety: Theory, research, and applications* (pp. 3–14). Hillsdale, NJ: Erlbaum.

Sarason, I. G. (1986). Test anxiety, worry, and cognitive interference. In R. Schwarzer (Ed.), *Self-related cognitions in anxiety and motivation* (pp. 19–33). Hillsdale, NJ: Erlbaum.

Seligman, M. E. P., Abramson, L. Y., Semmel, A., & von Baeyer, C. (1979). Depressive attributional style. *Journal of Abnormal Psychology, 88,* 242–247.

Simons, A. D., Garfield, S. L., & Murphy, G. E. (1987). The process of change in cognitive therapy and pharmacotherapy of depression: changes in mood and cognition. *Archives of General Psychiatry, 41,* 45–51.

Smith, T. W., & Greenberg, J. (1981). Depression and self-focused attention. *Motivation and Emotion, 5,* 323–331.

Smith, T. W., Ingram, R. E., & Brehm, S. S. (1983). Social anxiety, anxious self-preoccupation, and recall of self-relevant information. *Journal of Personality and Social Psychology, 44,* 1276–1283.

Spielberger, C. D. (1975). The measurement of state and trait anxiety: Conceptual and methodolical issues. In L. Levi (Ed.), *Emotions: Their parameters and measurement.* New York: Raven Press.

Turk, D. C., & Speers, M. A. (1983). Cognitive schemata and cognitive processes in cognitive behavioral interventions: Going beyond the information given. In P. C. Kendall (Ed.), *Advances in cognitive-behavioral research and therapy* (Vol. 2, pp. 1–32). New York: Academic Press.

Vredenburg, K., & Krames, L. (1983). *Memory scanning in depression: The disruptive effects of cognitive schemas.* Paper presented at the meeting of the American Psychological Association, Anaheim, CA.

Weissman, A. N., & Beck, A. T. (1978). *Development and validation of the Dysfunctional Attitude Scale: A preliminary investigation.* Paper presented at the annual convention of the American Educational Research Association, Toronto.

Wine, J. D. (1982). Evaluation anxiety. A cognitive-attentional construct. In H. W. Krohne & L. Laux (Eds.), *Achievement, stress, and anxiety* (pp. 207–219). Washington, DC: Hemisphere.

Zuckerman, M., & Lubin, B. (1965). *Manual for the Multiple Affect Adjective Checklist.* San Diego: Educational and Industrial Testing Service.

Zuckerman, M., & Lubin, B. (1985). *Manual for the MAACL-R.* San Diego: Educational and Industrial Testing Service.

Zuroff, D. C., Colussy, S. A., & Wielgus, M. S. (1983). Selective memory and depression: A cautionary note concerning response bias. *Cognitive Therapy and Research, 7,* 223–232.

Behavioral Models of Anxiety and Depression

Lynn P. Rehm

I. Introduction

What is a behavioral model? Definitions of a behavioral approach to human problems vary considerably, whether the term used is behavior therapy, behavior modification, or behavioral analysis. Some definitions stress the application of learning-theory models to human problems, while some stress psychological laboratory methodology in application. Yet another theme is to stress analysis of individual problems at a low level of inference, identifying relationships among observables.

Behavioral approaches have derived constructs from many basic theories of learning. These theories have spanned a number of paradigms in psychology, including radical behavioral, neobehavioral, social learning, and cognitive approaches (Wilson, 1978). The defining limits of what is "behavioral" have become blurred. Applications are derived from a broad array of theories. Similarly, methods within behavioral approaches to therapy have expanded to include a range of techniques and strategies that overlap with those that derive from other theoretical paradigms. Behavioral clinicians have become more interested in categories of problems, classification, and structured programs for groups of

Anxiety and Depression

individuals, so that the individual analysis of problems is less of a defining characteristic of behavioral approaches than it used to be.

For the purposes of this chapter, I take the position that the essence of a behavioral approach is a functional analysis of behavior. A behavioral approach involves an examination of how the individual interacts with the environment. Behavior is a response to the environment, it changes the environment, and it is affected by the environmental consequences. In this chapter I try to differentiate and contrast anxiety and depression in terms of their functions as responses to and effects on the environment.

Taking this functional perspective, three kinds of questions can be asked about anxiety and depression. First, what is the value of the emotions of anxiety and depression in adapting to the environment? Presumably all people have the capacity to experience emotional states of anxiety or depression. Fear and sadness are part of the human repertory of responses. What value do they have in adaptation on a day-to-day basis, and what distinguishes the value of one from the other? Second, if these emotions are "hard wired" in human beings, how did this come to be from the standpoint of evolution? What is the adaptive value of these affects over the course of human history? While any answer to this type of question is necessarily speculative, it can be an instructive test of a conceptual approach to emotion to ask whether it makes sense from the standpoint of evolution. Can anxiety and depression be distinguished from the point of view of evolutionary function? Third, when and how do these affects become maladaptive or dysfunctional? Assuming some form of continuity between normal emotions and psychopathological disorders of emotion, is there an identifiable point at which adaptive function is lost? Do the disorders of anxiety and depression have any current or evolutionary function or are they adaptive emotions simply gone awry? Can they be differentiated in this respect?

These questions can be asked in two contexts. First, they can be asked of traditional psychological conceptions of anxiety and depression. Many general assumptions about the nature of anxiety are shared by behavioral approaches. Traditional diagnostic distinctions are among these assumptions. Looking at these general ideas will provide a starting point for examining functional significance. Second, current behavioral and cognitive-behavioral theories of anxiety and depression will be selectively reviewed to look at their stated and implied assumptions about the functions of anxiety and depression as emotions and as disorders. Again the goal will be to abstract themes and to contrast the two conditions.

II. General Assumptions

A. Psychiatric Diagnosis

It is a general premise of behavioral approaches that anxiety and depression as emotions are basic elemental capacities of all human beings. Individual differences may exist in the biological paramenters of emotion in terms of the intensity and response and pattern of recovery and adaptation (Lacey, 1967). Biological variables in turn will interact with experience to produce learning of emotional responses in new situations. A second basic premise is that learning is a basic set of processes that underlie acquisition of emotional responses whether within the normal or abnormal range. Behavioral approaches generally assume a continuity between normal and abnormal responses.

Traditional diagnoses have conceptualized abnormal anxiety and depression as discrete, discontinuous categories of dysfunction. In the area of anxiety disorders, phobias, panic disorder, generalized anxiety disorder, posttraumatic stress disorder, and obsessive–compulsive disorder are the clinical syndromes defined by the American Psychiatric Association's *Diagnostic and Statistical Manual of Mental Disorders* (revised third edition, DSM-III-R; American Psychiatric Association, 1987).

From the behavioral perspective, there are some functional differences among these categories, and it will be important to remember that abnormal anxiety may take these various forms. The issue with panic is the origin of the initial panic attacks. Some argue that panic attacks are of biological origin, representing an organic disregulation (Barlow et al., 1985). Few would disagree, however, that conditioning processes may occur which may lead to agoraphobia. The attention of this chapter is on the importance and functional significance of this conditioning process. The phobias are generally considered to be conditioned responses from a behavioral perspective, but again it will be important to distinguish among different patterns of stimulus and response among the specific phobias.

Generalized anxiety disorder has traditionally been defined in terms of the relative *absence* of clear stimulus response relationships, and in DSM-III-R has become something of a residual category for excessive anxiety when no other set of operational anxiety disorder criteria is met (Frances, Widiger, & Fyer, 1987). Modern behavioral criteria for the disorder (Barlow, Blanchard, Vermilyea, Vermilyea, & DiNardo, 1986; DiNardo, O'Brien, Barlow, Waddell, & Blanchard, 1983) define it in terms of two or more domains of stimuli to which the individual responds with anxiety. Posttraumatic stress disorder is defined in terms of the intensity of the initial conditioning situations and the pattern of responses that the individual uses to react to the conditioned anxiety. Obsessive–compulsive disorder similarly is characterized by anxiety responses and a pattern of behavior with which the individual attempts to cope with the anxiety responses.

A discussion of DSM-III-R anxiety diagnoses needs to include mention also of Axis II anxiety diagnoses. DSM-III-R recognizes the unreliability of subsets of the specific personality disorders and groups them by clusters of empirically related disorders. Cluster C includes two diagnoses that are closely related to anxiety. These are avoidant and obsessive–compulsive personality. In general, the behavioral approach to personality disorders is to analyze them in terms of more specific behaviors or less abstract classes of responses. A behavioral view of continuity would assume that the Axis II disorders are expressions of the same learning processes that are evident in the Axis I diagnoses. Avoidant personality corresponds generally to the problem behaviors of social phobia, and obsessive–compulsive personality has direct correspondence with the anxiety disorder of the same name. The emphasis in this chapter will be on general processes that apply to all categories of anxiety disorder but differentiations among diagnostic problem types will be important at a number of points in discussing functional analyses of the disorders.

The depression diagnoses raise another issue. The most notable distinction made in DSM-III-R is between bipolar and unipolar disorders. Bipolar disorders include significant episodes of mania or hypomania along with episodes of depression. Evidence suggests that the bipolar disorders have a strong genetic component and may represent a largely biological disregulation of emotion. While this assumption has had the unfortunate effect of decreasing interest in psychological approaches to the problem, this chapter will accept this convention and focus entirely on unipolar disorders.

Unipolar depression diagnoses differentiate between single and recurrent episodes. Within major depression the additional factor of melancholia can be diagnosed as present or absent. Both recurrent and melancholic concepts have a history in the idea of endogenous depression of presumed biological origin (e.g., Mendels, 1975). A biologically caused depression would have the severe somatic symptoms of melancholia and would produce multiple episodes. For the purposes of this chapter, melancholia and recurrent depressions will be considered patterns of depressive behavior varying also in intensity. Along these same lines, dysthymia, or neurotic depression, formerly considered a personality disorder, can be thought of as a chronic pattern of mild depression.

Biological, environmental, and psychological factors are all important in the etiology of depression. Biological vulnerability may increase responsivity to stressors, and some forms of depression may have heavier biological loadings, such as the melancholic subtype. Environmental stress may also vary in intensity and some forms of depression may be more heavily reactive to the environment, for example, normal bereavement. Most of the psychological theories posit psychological risk factors that predispose individuals to depression, and these factors are likely to vary in importance across different disorders. Again, some forms of depression may have a stronger psychological component. Dysthymia or a subset of the dysthymias may be an example. Dysthymia might represent the constant expression of a learned repertory, including a generalized pessimism and low self-esteem, for dealing with situations.

Most depressions should probably be considered a combined result of all three factors—biological, environmental, and psychological. In other words, these etiologies should be thought of as interacting to produce any given depression. Most theories focus on one etiological factor with varying degrees of acknowledgment of interactions with other factors. For the purposes of this chapter, the functional relationships that exist within normal and pathological depression will be examined with recognition of interactions among all three sets of etiological factors.

B. Response Components of Anxiety

A first discussion of the functional distinction between anxiety and depression from a behavioral perspective can come from a review of the simple response components generally accepted as making up anxiety and depression. Anxiety has traditionally been thought of as a mechanism for fight or flight, that is, a response to danger or the possibility of danger that prepares us for physical or active avoidance. This idea of the evolutionary significance of anxiety goes back to Darwin (1872/1979). From a behavioral perspective the symptoms of anxiety (and later depression) can be analyzed in terms of the three modalities of observable behavior (Lang, 1968): physiological, overt-motor, and verbal-cognitive.

The physiological components of anxiety involve arousal of the sympathetic nervous system. Increases in heart rate, blood pressure, respiration rate, and other changes prepare the body for strenuous fight or flight activity. These changes are functionally adaptive for dealing with the temporary physical dangers that our distant ancestors were likely to have encountered. Today, dangers are often less physical and more social. Dangers to self-esteem and social status are not likely to require sudden physical response. Thus the adaptive arousal mechanism becomes maladaptive when the dangers are symbolic and psychological. Sustained arousal produced by persistent perception of danger may interfere with adaptive behavior and be distressing to the individual. Prolonged arousal may lead to physiological breakdown and psychosomatic disorder (Selye, 1956).

Amplitude and pattern of physiological response is an individual difference factor. Lacey (1967) posits a stability–lability dimension that determines susceptibility to arousal by a variety of stimuli. Eysenck (1947) argues for a genetic factor in physiological responsivity. The anxiety response also functions as an aversive stimulus that is reduced by escape or avoidance.

The list of over-behavioral signs of anxiety begins with behavioral avoidance of a feared object, situation, person, or other stimulus. The "flight" function is served for realistic fears but maladaptive avoidance may restrict normal life activity. For example, the agoraphobic's avoidance of crowded places may restrict her ability to go out for social or business purposes.

The overt signs of anxiety, such as fearful demeanor and trembling hands, are thought also to serve a communication value in conveying fear to others. This might serve an evolutionary function in validating an inferior position in a social dominance hierarchy. Zajonc (1985) has recently argued against this idea, and has suggested that the patterns of facial musculature indicative of individual emotions may serve primarily to regulate blood pressure and temperature.

The classic studies of the relationship between anxiety and performance have recognized that the relationship changes for tasks of varying levels of complexity (e.g., Sarason, 1961). Essentially, the findings are that increasing levels of anxiety/arousal facilitate performance for simple tasks. Such tasks are the sort that would be involved in fight or flight. For tasks of medium complexity, low levels of anxiety/arousal facilitate performance but high levels may decrease performance. For very complex tasks anxiety/arousal may increasingly interfere with effective performance.This is a trade-off, in which the evolutionary value of facilitating simple responses becomes dysfunctional for the more complex tasks of modern society.

The cognitive parallel of the performance–anxiety relationship can be described in terms of information processing. Anxiety takes up short-term store processing capacity either as arousal per se (H. C. Ellis & Ashbrook, 1987) or as interfering internal speech (Wine, 1971). Thus, anxiety interferes with performance by interfering with complex or effortful processing.

Other cognitive-behavioral approaches focus on the content of the person's processes in perceiving danger and in making fight or flight decisions. For example, A. Ellis (1962) suggests that anxiety is the product of basic irrational beliefs that lead to perceptions of danger in many ordinary situations. The irrational belief that one must be competent and perfect in all activities in order to be a worthy person in the eyes of others would lead to the perception of danger of loss of positive evaluation by others in any situation in which one is not experienced and skilled. Other models to be reviewed below (e.g., Bandura, 1977; Lazarus, 1974) suggest that estimations of possible outcomes and assessments of resources to carry out potential actions are involved in perceptions of danger. The implication is that people develop generalized bases of knowledge and beliefs about the world and themselves that produce perceptions and mediate responses to danger. These may also be considered cognitive components of anxiety.

C. Response Components of Depression

There is less agreement on the evolutionary significance and function of depression than is the case for anxiety. Depression is viewed as a response to loss or to perceived or anticipated loss. Beck (1972), for example, from his cognitive perspective, differentiates depression from anxiety on the basis of perceived loss versus perceived danger. The response to loss is sometimes seen as a loss of generalized motivation; that is, a loss of motivation generalized across all response domains, including behavioral (e.g., activity decrease), somatic (e.g., loss of appetite), and cognitive (e.g., loss of interest) components.

Klerman (1974) has put the idea of depression as decreased general motivation into an evolutionary context. He suggests that conservation of energy is the evolutionary significance of depression. The prehistoric scenario he envisions focuses on a child who might become accidently lost and separated from his social group. The first response of active protest (crying out for help) is followed by passive despair and depression. This sequence is posited as an innate childhood model of grief and depression by such authorities as Bowlby (1960) and Spitz (1946). Depression is posed as functional in minimizing energy expenditure and thus in maximizing survival time until rescued by the social group. From Klerman's perspective, psychopathological depression represents failure in attempts at adaptation. Modern depression represents an adaptive mechanism that has become dysfunctional on both behavioral and biochemical levels.

The symptomatology of depression as it is traditionally conceptualized is quite broad and varied (Levitt & Lubin, 1975; Rehm, 1987, 1988). Even the quality of affect associated with depression is not a simple matter. While depression is often described as an "affective" disorder, the nature of that affect is variable. For example, persistent sadness or depressed mood was considered a necessary criterion symptom in DSM-III (APA, 1980), but in the new DSM-III-R (APA, 1987), either persistent sadness or persistent apathy is a sufficient emotional criterion. Apathy or anhedonia, the inability to experience positive affect, is an important symptom that is seen in some contexts as the feature that differentiates sad from anxious affect (cf. Tellegen, 1985; Watson & Tellegen, 1985). Irritability or hostility is as often listed as a symptom of depression as is anxiety. Some experts feel that subtypes of depression can be usefully determined by separating out depressions with different primary emotions (Overall, 1962; Overall & Hollister, 1980). The coexistence of anxiety and depression and the "comorbidity" of these diagnoses will be addressed later.

Traditional psychiatric views of depression stress "neurovegetative" signs as major symptoms. The classical symptoms of depressive disorder are seen as individual symptoms from a psychiatric perspective, but a behavioral approach would tend to distinguish among behavioral, somatic, and cognitive components (Rehm, 1987). Weight loss or gain (a somatic change) is accompanied by loss of appetite (a subjective cognitive change) and is presumably mediated by a reduction in eating (a change in overt behavior). Insomnia or hypersomnia represents a behavior change that has physiological and biochemical correlates. DSM-III-R notes that the symptom of agitation or retardation must be observable (overt behavior) and not just a subjective feeling (cognitive). Fatigue or loss of energy, presumably by self-report (therefore subjective/ cognitive with possible somatic correlates), is listed as a separate symptom. While not listed separately in DSM-III-R, an often-cited symptom is "loss of libido," which translates to decreased sexual activity and a concomitant loss of sexual interest or pleasure.

It is notable that depression contrasts with anxiety in the relative lack of physiological symptomatology. Autonomic arousal does not characterize depression, with the possible exception of anxious depression. However, physiological correlates of depression have been identified in a couple of areas. First, facial electromyogram (EMG) patterns have been found to differentiate emotional states (Schwartz, Fair, Salt, Mandel, & Klerman, 1976). Induced sadness, anxiety, or happiness produce distinct patterns of muscle tension. Individuals who score high on depression or anxiety trait measures show patterns parallel to those for induced mood. Second, sleep electroencephalogram (EEG) patterns of clinically depressed individuals have been shown to produce abnormal patterns (Kupfer & Foster, 1972; Kupfer, Foster, Reich, Thompson, & Weiss, 1976). Several patterns have been investigated. As an example, after falling asleep, depressed persons have been found to evidence abnormally short latencies for rapid eye movement sleep. By and large these findings have been seen as epiphenomena that may nevertheless have utility in clinical assessment applications.

DSM-III-R lists three other symptoms that are primarily cognitive: feelings of worthlessness or guilt, inability to concentrate and indecisiveness, and thoughts of death or suicide. Beck (1972) identifies three major cognitive factors as definitive of depression and refers to them as the cognitive triad: negative view of the self, negative view of the world, and negative view of the future. A negative view of self (worthlessness, guilt, low self-esteem, and helplessness) along with negative judgments about the world and the future (pessimism and hopelessness) may lead to suicidal ideation. Somewhat separate are the complaints of diminished cognitive functioning. This is, in part, a subjective complaint deriving from low self-esteem and helplessness, but may also have a veridical component as demonstrated by some recent research on memory, information processing, and problem solving in depression.

D. Summary

Traditional views of anxiety and depression as emotions, as diagnostic entities, and as clinical descriptions of symptomatology suggest ways in which the two conditions can be functionally described and differentiated. Anxiety serves the functions of fight or flight from danger. The various diagnostic categories reflect perceived sources of danger. Symptoms generally reflect arousal in the aid of fight or flight. The object of fear is usually identifiable and arousal occurs in its presence, but this arousal may become dysfunctional for dealing with modern complex problems. The processing of problem evaluation becomes very important, because dysfunctional anxiety arises from unrealistic perceptions of danger. The acquisition and maintenance mechanisms of these responses need to be explained by theory.

In contrast, the symptomatology of depression is heterogeneous and not as easy to summarize in functional terms. Depression may, in general, represent a response to loss or separation from important external objects, with a resulting loss of motivation that may serve to conserve energy until restoration of external support. Decrease in many types of basic behavior and a subjective loss in the pleasurableness or reinforcement value of behavior can be seen as reflecting the loss of motivation that results from loss of an externally motivating object. The problem is the overgeneralization of the decreased behavior. Why should loss of a job lead to loss of appetite and diminished interest in sex? This response overgeneralization is consistent with Klerman's (1974) idea of conservation of energy. Negative views of self, world, and future are also problematic. Is there any way in which this might serve any adaptive function in either a current functional analysis or in an evolutionary sense? These questions can be addressed to the specific theories of depression.

III. Theories of Anxiety

A. Anxiety as Conditioned Emotional Response

A basic theoretical assumption central to behavioral approaches to anxiety is the idea that anxiety can be thought of as a conditioned emotional response (Wolpe, 1958). The assumption holds that classical conditioning processes could explain the pairing of previously neutral stimuli with the elicitation of an unconditioned fear response by an unconditioned stimulus to produce anxiety. The functional value of this process is quite evident. The danger in many objects (being burned by fire, being bitten by an animal, being attacked by a person, etc.) may not be readily evident, but aversive experience in one incident should adaptively arouse the person in repeated or similar circumstances. The adaptive value of anxiety as facilitating fight or flight is enhanced by being conditionable and thus anticipatory. It is useful in anticipating danger and thus avoiding a repetition of injury or pain. Such anxiety is clearly associated with the presence or anticipation of a stimulus or situation.

Increasing anxiety is associated with a gradient of increasing thematic similarity to the original stimulus (e.g., worms might elicit some of the same anxiety as snakes), or of increasing proximity to the stimulus in time (e.g., anxiety increases as the hour of the important examination approaches) or space (e.g., increased anxiety as one approaches the snake; Wolpe, 1958). Thus, the primitive individual who was bitten by a particular type of snake would be anxiously aroused on the next encounter with a like snake and would stay at a comfortable distance. It would also be adaptive to avoid places where snakes are likely to be encountered and it might even be adaptive to avoid all snakes until the harmless ones could be distinguished from the dangerous.

Phobias are thus seen as conditioned anxiety responses based on untoward pairing of aversive experience and a neutral stimulus. The pairing may be arbitrary and not related to true danger. Failure to make appropriate discriminations among dangerous and nondangerous stimuli and stimulus and response overgeneralizations may also make the phobia unrealistic and maladaptive. A person who has been in an automobile accident might develop a maladaptive fear of driving and of cars generally, and might even be anxious hearing a traffic report on the radio. Counterconditioning approaches, such as systematic desensitization (Wolpe, 1958), are premised on the idea that phobic anxiety is conditioned and conditionable.

The anticipatory nature of anxiety leads to the notion of avoidance learning in phobias. Situations are avoided repeatedly despite no actual contact and no aversive experience, presumably because anticipatory anxiety is reduced, which negatively reinforces the avoidance. Again, the adaptive value of harm avoidance leads to modern phobic avoidance that is highly resistant to extinction. Agoraphobia and obsessive–compulsive disorder show particularly clear elements of avoidance. Exposure treatment procedures are based on this conceptualization of phobia.

The assumption that phobias are conditioned, however, does not hold up well to empirical test. Rachman (1977) cites six difficulties with the assumption that all phobias are acquired, conditioned anxiety responses. (1) People fail to acquire phobias under predicted conditions. (2) The phenomenon is difficult to produce in the lab. (3) The assumption of equipotentiality is untenable. That is, the idea that any stimulus can equally be the conditioned object of a phobia does not hold. (4) The distribution of human phobias is not consistent with this theory in that the feared objects are not proportional to aversive experience. (5) The history of many phobias is inconsistent with a conditioning origin. And, (6) indirect or vicarious acquisition clearly does occur. With regard to the latter two points Öst and Hugdahl (1983) found that of 80 phobic patients, 81% reported conditioning experiences but 9% reported vicarious acquisition and 10% no specific circumstance. Also, 46% reported a rapid onset of the phobia, 36% a gradual onset, and 18% a slow onset. Traumatic conditioning should be associated with rapid onset.

A partial answer lies in the consideration of other forms of learning. Vicarious learning is implicated in many phobias. Anxiety may be conditioned by observation of the aversive experience of a model or by being told of the aversive consequences of approaching some stimulus and being instructed to avoid it. Parents may often model phobic behavior to children and tell them of the dangers of some object or situation. Fear behavior may also be directly reinforced by parents or by other people in the phobic individual's social environment. Phobic behavior may be shaped in this way or it may be maintained by reinforcing consequences. The adaptive value of these processes is that realistic and adaptive harm avoidance can be conveyed from one human being to another in an efficient and effective manner. Conversely, unrealistic and maladaptive phobias can similarly be conveyed.

B. Preparedness

A second answer to the problem of lack of fit of clinical phobias with a pure conditioning model has been offered by Seligman (1971) in the idea of preparedness. He suggests that some stimulus–response pairings are more amenable to association because of their survival value. Evolution thus prepares us to make certain kinds of associations more readily than others. Such associations would have particular adaptive value, for example, novel taste associated with later nausea, or small, quick animals associated with danger of painful attacks. Such pairings would be characterized as occurring easily and quickly, being highly resistent to extinction, and broad in generalization.

The nature of these prepared types of conditioning often does not match modern experience and the reality of danger in a modern world. For example, children often develop fears of dogs after being frightened by them, but they seldom develop fears of doors after more painfully pinching their fingers. Fears of threatening animals are presumed to be more prepared.

An interesting extension of this concept has been developed by Öhman, Dimberg, and Öst (1985), who argue that different forms of phobias have different origins in evolution. Simple phobias are related to situations that call for caution (e.g., heights) or to potentially dangerous types of animals (e.g., small, fast-moving reptiles). These phobias are likely to be very stimulus bound. They should be expected to be frequent in early childhood and the child should ordinarily grow out of them as experience and skill allow discrimination of real danger from false. Social phobias are assumed to be based on dominance relationships. Certain kinds of interpersonal situations associated with dominance (e.g., eating situations, dealing with authority figures, heterosexual situations) would have special evolutionary significance. Such fears should originate in adolescence and should be more anticipatory in nature.

The nature of phobias generally fit these posited evolutionary origins. The essential idea is that the structure of phobias may reflect different evolutionary functions for fear behaviors. Specifically, physical harm avoidance and the maintenance of social dominance structures may produce functionally different patterns of anxious behavior.

C. Bioinformational Theory

Lang (1979, 1983) has moved from a strictly behavioral stance to a more cognitive position which he refers to as the bioinformational theory of emotion. From this perspective a phobia (which he argues provides a useful model for considering anxiety and emotion generally) can be seen as an organized set of propositions stored in memory. When the propositional network is activated in whole or in part, the person experiences anxiety, which like any emotion has the components of valence, arousal, and dominance or control. Anxiety is characterized by negative valence, high arousal, and low dominance or control. Presumably depression would differ primarily in that it would be characterized by negative valence, low or neutral arousal, and low dominance or control.

As employed in Lang's model, propositions consist of a subject, a relationship (verb), and object. He distinguishes stimulus, response, and meaning propositions. Stimulus propositions refer to the nature of the object of the fear; response propositions refer to the qualities of the response to the object; and meaning propositions refer to inferences about and implications of the object. Stimulus propositions would reflect the dimensions of the stimulus configuration to which the person would respond with anxiety. These representations of the stimulus could be realistic or not. They might include inaccurate information about the phobic object, for example, the erroneous belief that snakes are slimy. Response propositions represent the encoding of an individual's pattern of verbal, physiological, and behavioral anxiety response tendencies. Meaning responses are of interest because they represent the inferences, implications, and judgments that are associated with a phobia. These might include beliefs about the condition of having a phobia, e.g., what it means to be a fearful and phobic person.

D. Stress and Coping Models

One way to consider the functional significance of cognitive components of anxiety is to examine theories of coping with stress. These more general models have clear implications for a discussion of anxiety. For example, Bandura (1977), in his efficacy theory, makes a distinction between outcome and efficacy expectations. Outcome expectations involve beliefs about probable outcomes in specific situations given a particular performance. These beliefs are about contingency rules that operate in the world. In contrast, efficacy expectations have to do with people's conviction that they are capable of producing the particular performance. Thus, a person might know that it would not produce injury to pick up a harmless snake, but they might not feel capable of carrying out that simple act. Efficacy expectations are influenced by prior performance accomplishments, vicarious experiences, persuasive verbal communications, and current physiological state. Bandura argues that efficacy expectations are accurate predictors of anxious behavior. Efficacy expectations are specific to situations, including fearful situations.

The work of Lazarus (1966, 1974, 1981) on coping with stress adds another perspective on the functions of cognition in producing anxiety. Lazarus (1974) distinguishes between primary and secondary appraisals of situations. Primary appraisal assesses the danger in the situation in terms of what is at stake and what resources are available. The outcome of a primary appraisal is (1) acceptance of the situation, (2) a decision to act, or (3) a decision that more information is needed. Secondary appraisal concerns assessments of the ways of coping with the situation. Coping involves action coping, including attempts to change the situation (i.e., fight it or flee from it). It might also involve emotional coping; that is, ways of dealing with the affect elicited by the situation. Emotional coping would include such tactics as denial, distortion, not thinking about it, or seeking emotional support from another person.

The importance of these models is that perception of danger may vary as a function of measurable beliefs and typical styles of evaluating situations. Assessments of ability to cope may moderate perceived danger. Fight or flight depends upon accurate perceptions of the dangers involved in a situation and decisions about the resources and action repertory available to the individual. Complex learning and generalized response sets intervene between a situation and a behavioral response. It is notable that these models suggest that generalized conclusions about personal power and worth may be involved. The latter suggest connections and similarities between the cognitive processes of anxiety and depression. The following review of theories of depression will aid in making comparisons and contrasts.

IV. Theories of Depression

A. Ferster's Behavioral Analysis

One of the early behavioral analyses of depression was offered by Ferster (1973). Ferster asserted a number of propositions for the functional analysis of depression. He argued that the primary datum of depression is a reduced frequency of response. He also emphasized the response–reinforcement relationship. The individual's entire repertory of responses is affected. He suggests that depression is primarily a verbal phenomenon wherein verbal behavior is under control of inner states rather than external stimulus relationships. The depressed person is constantly vigilant in attempting to avoid aversive stimuli to the exclusion of responding that will produce positive reinforcement. The result is ratio strain; that is, a great amount of effort is expended for relatively little contingent reward. Depressed affect in such a situation would be a motive to cease responding or possibly to conserve energy. In either case the functional value would be to motivate the individual to seek alternative sources of reinforcement.

This overall analysis suggests that depression is indeed a reduction in motivated behavior, but that the significant factor is that behavior is misdirected toward avoidance of aversive outcomes rather than toward positive goals. The avoidance component suggests a functional overlap with anxiety. In addition, depression may be a motive to seek new sources of positive reinforcement.

B. Lewinsohn's Behavioral Theory

Lewinsohn (1974, 1976) developed a behavioral theory of depression based on a clinical and research program. Lewinsohn (1974) posited that depression could be seen as a type of extinction phenomenon. Depression is a response to a loss or lack of response-contingent reinforcement. This condition can result from one of three circumstances: (1) an environment that does not provide sufficient reinforcement due to loss or lack of sources of reinforcement, (2) a lack of social skill requisite to produce reinforcement in an important domain, and (3) an inability to experience pleasure in response to available reinforcement, presumed to be due to interfering social anxiety. Each of these causes of depression leads logically to a different therapy strategy: (1) activity increase to produce new sources of reinforcement, (2) social skill training to produce reinforcement, and (3) desensitization to eliminate interfering anxiety.

Lewinsohn and his colleagues have developed assessment instruments for measuring rewards and punishments in daily life—the Pleasant Events Schedule (MacPhillamy & Lewinsohn, 1982) and the Unpleasant Events Schedule (Lewinsohn & Talkington, 1979). Each schedule is a list of possible events that are presumed to approximate contingent reinforcements. Events are assessed either retrospectively over the past month or they are self-monitored on a daily basis. In either case, results suggest (MacPhillamy & Lewinsohn, 1982; Lewinsohn & Talkington, 1979; Rehm, 1978) that daily mood correlates positively with pleasant events and negatively with unpleasant events. An interesting implication of Lewinsohn's analysis is that mood is a function of the relative amounts of positive and negative reinforcement received. This could be contrasted with Ferster's idea of ratio strain that suggests that mood is a function of the ratio between effort expended and reinforcement received. Either suggests that mood is a gauge of success of current functioning and a possible aversive motive for change when success rates are low. Again, the implication is an impetus to redirect behavior.

Lewinsohn (1974) offers an alternative analysis for the functional significance of depressed behavior. He argues that the positive signs of depression (e.g., sad demeanor, weeping, and head hanging) are powerful elicitors of succorance from the social group. Following a loss of response-contingent reinforcement, such behavior elicits immediate social reinforcement from others. This immediate reinforcement serves adaptively to motivate the depressed person until new sources of immediate and delayed reinforcement can be established to maintain ordinary levels of behavior. The social environment may act to shape the depressed individual's behavior toward alternative sources of reinforcement. Presumably this effect has an evolutionary basis that is involved in the meaning communicated by depressive emotional behavior. By implication, it is adaptive for the social group for people to be influenced by sadness in another person and to try to eleviate this distress. Such behavior would maintain and enhance the social group.

Lewinsohn's analysis goes on to say that depression becomes dysfunctional when the immediate reinforcement by others serves to reinforce and maintain depressive behavior rather than to promote new efforts at adaptive behavior on the part of the depressed person. As the reinforced depressive behavior persists, it becomes aversive to others to continue to be in contact with the depressed person (i.e., the other person is not rewarded by change in the behavior or mood of the depressed person). Contact with the depressed person is avoided and thus the schedule of reinforcement is thinned. The thinner schedule further induces depression and strengthens formerly successful depressive behavior in a vicious cycle.

C. Helplessness Theory

Seligman's learned helplessness theory of depression has gone through a process of revision from its original animal model form (Seligman, 1974, 1975), to its attributional reformulation (Abramson, Seligman, & Teasdale, 1978), to more recent refinements (e.g., Alloy, Clements, & Kolden, 1985). In its original form the theory posited that depression results from experience with uncontrollable aversive experiences. What is learned is an overgeneralized sense of helplessness to control aversive stimuli in new situations where control is possible.

The attributional reformulation (Abramson et al., 1978) stated that helplessness results from the interaction of an aversive event with a negative attributional style. This depressive attributional style involves habitually attributing negative events to internal, stable, global causes ("It's because of me. It's because of something constant about me, and it's because of something that is true of me in all domains"). Similarly, the person with a depressive attributional style attributes positive events to external, unstable, and specific causes. In the theory's most recent form (Alloy et al., 1985), a depressive attributional style acts as a contributory vulnerability factor that may influence the attribution made about an aversive event. This negative attribution in turn leads to helplessness and hopelessness, which then is sufficient to bring on certain reactive depressions.

Two points are of interest here for the functional analysis of depression. First, it is clearly adaptive to make accurate attributions of success and failure. Attributions of causality guide decision-making processes and problem solving (e.g., "Can I accomplish my goal with additional effort or do I lack the skill?"). An adaptive attributional style would differentiate domains of activity (e.g., "I am generally skilled in math, but I have little ability in art and succeed only with great effort"), and would take into account all relevant situational information. It would still be of utility to make generalizations within domains of experience and thus to be able to make decisions in relatively novel circumstances. With an adaptive attributional style, a person would become sad in relatively limited circumstances when truly uncontrollable events leave the person helpless to accomplish major goals. For example, the sudden death of a spouse might truly preclude achieving previous life goals, which might need to be given up. An attributional style that is negative, inflexible, and overgeneralized is clearly maladaptive.

Second, it is notable that this theory contrasts with the two prior behavioral theories in that it stresses control of reinforcement rather than the quantity or quality of reinforcement. In essence it says that mood is a function of the differential ratio of contingent-to-noncontingent reinforcement. The control issue echoes the theme of Bandura and Lazarus in their discussion of efficacy and coping ability in dealing with stress, which was discussed earlier in the context of anxiety. Anxiety is mediated by perceived ability to cope with particular dangers or to avoid specific aversive stimuli. Depression is the perception of lack of control or inability to obtain important sources of positive reinforcement. Lazarus (1981) found that in dealing with real life stresses, depressed persons expressed a greater need for more information, a greater sense that a stressful situation must be accepted, more use of wishful thinking, and greater seeking of help and support from others.

D. Self-Control Theory

My own self-control or self-management model of depression (Rehm, 1977) was an attempt to integrate the factors identified by Lewinsohn, Seligman, and Beck (see below) into a broader self-regulatory framework. Using Kanfer's (1970) analysis of self-control, it was posited that the self-management behavior of depression-prone individuals was marked by six deficits: (1) depression-prone individuals attend selectively to negative events; (2) depression-prone individuals attend selectively to the immediate as opposed to the delayed effects of their behavior; (3) they set stringent self-evaluative standards; (4) they make depressive attributions of causation consistent with a negative image of themselves; (5) they administer insufficient contingent self-reward to motivate their behavior toward long-term goals; and (6) they administer excessive self-punishment, which interferes with effective exploration, problem solving, and persistence.

Self-management deals with the ways in which people organize their behavior in order to accomplish long-term, delayed goals. Depression occurs when these efforts are disrupted or are unsuccessful. Lack of positive self-management skills leads to an inability to reorganize behavior and restore effective goal-oriented behavior. While encorporating features from the other models, the self-control model emphasizes the importance of adaptation in the sense of striving toward long-term goals. It is not just immediate external rewards that influence human depression, but also more distant, delayed, and symbolic goals that may be very important in organizing the person's behavior. Loss of a goal could occur with little actual observable change in the immediate environment.

E. Cognitive Theory

Beck's (1972) cognitive theory of depression stresses negativity of cognition rather than perceptions of control. Beck makes the functional distinction between anxiety and depression, that anxiety has to do with perceptions of danger and harm, whereas depression has to do with perceptions of loss. The essential features of depression from Beck's perspective is the negative triad of a negative view of the self, negative view of the world, and negative view of the future. The depressed person is seen as distorting perceptions of the world, self, and future in a negative direction.

In Beck's view, experience is filtered through cognitive schemata. Schemata are cognitive structures that both store information in organized relationships and act as prototypes or rule relationships against which new experience is compared and interpreted. When people become depressed they engage negative schemata that produce negative distortions of experience. Beck describes specific forms of distortion such as selective abstraction and arbitrary inference. In selective abstraction, the person selectively focuses on minor negative aspects of situations to the relative exclusion of more positive information. In arbitrary inference, people arbitrarily assume that they are to blame for any negative event in their lives. Schemata operate without conscious effort and produce what Beck refers to as "automatic thoughts." These thoughts mediate perceptions of loss and thus sad affect. The depressed person uses negative schemata and produces frequent negative automatic thoughts, which in turn produce depressive affect. Beck's cognitive therapy uses various techniques to help the depressed person identify automatic thoughts, to demonstrate their distorting nature, and to change the irrational assumptions that underlie the thoughts.

Dysfunctional depressive schemata are acquired in childhood and may develop via early experiences of loss. They remain in existence in the individual's cognitive structures but are "latent" and come into use only when the person experiences another major loss.

Recent research has demonstrated an effect that closely corresponds to this concept of accessing "latent" schemata. Mood-congruent recall refers to the phenomenon where current affective state influences retrieval such that similarly toned memories are more likely to be accessed (Bower, 1981, 1983; Teasdale, 1983a, 1983b). In effect, mood acts as a cue or context that facilitates access to information that may have been stored with similar affect as a component. If one is in a sad mood, it will be easier to recall sad events from last week (Bower, 1981) or from childhood (Teasdale & Fogarty, 1979). If one is asked to recall a happy childhood event, it will take longer when in a current sad mood. The effect can be demonstrated with various pairs of contrasting emotions. Contrasting moods have been induced by hypnosis (Bower, 1981), recalling emotional past experiences (Leight & Ellis, 1981), or by reading lists of emotional sentences (Teasdale & Fogarty, 1979). Naturally occurring moods have also been used, including clinical depression, variations in clinical depression in individuals with diurnal variation in mood (Clark & Teasdale, 1982), and rapid-cycling manic depressives who learned lists in their manic and depressed states (Weingartner, Miller, & Murphy, 1977). All of these findings are consistent with the idea that emotion is a factor in the storage and retrieval of information. Depressed mood activates depressive schemata which might not be accessed during normal mood states.

Rehm and Naus (in press) have argued that these phenomena can be considered the central focus of a memory model of emotion that sees depression as affect-congruent information processing. The strong affective state induced by significant loss leads to accessing negative schemata, especially about oneself. These schemata affect ongoing processing of experience. This process underlies negative bias in selection of information, negative bias in inferences about self (low self-evaluation, guilt, negative attributions of causality, helplessness, hopelessness, etc.), and negative coping behavior (overestimation of threat, underestimation of resources, low efficacy, etc.).

From the functional perspective of this chapter, the question raised by Beck's concept of latent depressive schemata or by Rehm and Naus's affective memory model is whether this process has an adaptive value. As a speculative response to this question I suggest that mood-congruent recall may provide an efficient means of memory storage and retrieval. There is potential adaptive utility to a memory system that is partially organized by affective features. As Öhman et al. (1985) speculated as to the classes of dangers that might elicit adaptive anxiety, one could speculate as to what classes of losses might be likely to occur to prehistoric humans. Major areas might include interpersonal losses (separation, dominance conflicts, sexual competition, death, injury, and illness) and natural disasters (drought, flood, and famine). In the first instance sad mood may also serve to motivate and reinforce maintenance of social order. That is, avoidance of or escape from loss and thus avoidance of or escape from sad mood may be a motive toward maintaining positive relationships with others (Izard, 1977). In either case, a problem is presented involving necessary reorganization of behavior to regain optimal social functioning, for example, establishing new interpersonal interaction patterns or finding new food or water sources. Such problem solving or coping involves a relatively complex task needing to be solved over an extended period of time. To problem solve in such a situation, it would be advantageous to recall maximally all former or related problem situations and how people coped with them. If such memories were encoded with mood as a prominent feature, then they could be effectively accessed. The sad person could recall prior circumstances of loss and personal or group responses for coping with loss. An adaptive coping response would result. Coping responses would almost universally involve the social group and adjustments within the social group.

The evolutionary value of such a system is lost in a modern world, where losses are much more frequently personal losses in interpersonal contexts that are not as intimately supportive and involving. Loss of social status or loss of important objects focuses much more on personal responsibility and competence. Similarly, the sadness of current loss is likely to facilitate access to memories of past personal failures and incompetence. The primary difference is the personal focus and the fact that the affect is likely to be associated with the sense of personal inadequacy.

From this point of view, depression differs from anxiety in that anxiety and any highly arousing emotional state would restrict recall, last for short, intense periods of time, and focus attention on simple, immediate responses (e.g., fearful escape and avoidance). Depression would enhance a maximum range of similarly toned recall, last for an extended period, and dwell on dealing with past and present problems.

V. Summary and Conclusions

From the behavioral perspective of a functional analysis, anxiety and depression have many distinct and differentiating functions. Anxiety has traditionally been seen as serving the evolutionary function of enabling fight or flight from dangerous objects or situations. Escape and avoidance, that is, flight, are the primary overt behaviors associated with anxiety. Fighting and attack are more commonly associated with anger and hostility. Anxiety is characterized by physiological arousal, which serves the adaptive function of facilitating simple response repertories typical of escape and avoidance. Arousal is adaptive for maximum output over very short periods of effort. Anxiety is situation or stimulus bound. It arises in response to some specific stimulus, although the stimulus could be anticipatory or of internal, self-generated origin. Anxiety is highly conditionable although this is constrained by evolutionary differences in ease of conditioning for types of pairings.

Anxiety can be maladaptive and dysfunctional because of this conditionability. Unrealistic fears may be established by arbitrary conditioning. Modeling, instruction, and reinforcement of unrealistic fear may also be involved. Highly conditionable associations prepared by evolution may not be realistic or adaptive in modern society. Classes of situations for which evolution may have prepared us to be fearful may explain the most common types and groupings of fears. Modern dangers are more likely to be symbolic and enduring and, therefore, may require different, more complex, long-term coping and problem solving.

There is less commonality of agreement about the functions of depression. It is generally seen as a response to loss or to anticipation of loss. It involves decreases of behavior across virtually all response domains. Depression is relatively unrelated to specific situations or stimuli and it is an enduring emotion. Decreased motivation is a generally descriptive term. Behavior that had formerly been organized around achieving long-term goals deteriorates following the loss of the objective. The adaptive task is reorganization of response repertories toward new adopted goals. Three functions of depression have been suggested toward this end. First, depression may represent a decrease in behavior in order to conserve energy and endure a difficult and deprived period of readjustment. Second, depression may serve to elicit immediate social caregiving and social support in reorganization efforts. This phenomenon would be adaptive for the individual and for the social group. Third, depression may facilitate access to memories of adaptive coping and problem-solving strategies.

Each of these three functions may lead to maladaptive depressive disorder. Conservation of energy may be dysfunctional when readaptation requires effortful problem solving. Social support of the depressed person may reinforce and maintain depressive behavior in a vicious cycle. Facilitation of recall of memories with similar emotional features may result in dwelling on personal failure and incompetence rather than adaptive problem solving. Negative perceptions of self, world, and future are typical of the sad person's cognitive processing of experience. This may be facilitated by depression in a modern era in which there is an emphasis of individual responsibility for success and failure and for personal life progress.

Anxiety and depression overlap in several ways. First, many situations and experiences may involve both danger and loss, i.e., aversive stimuli and loss of positive stimuli. Responses to these mixed or combined situations ought to involve both the adaptive and maladaptive repertories of anxiety and depression. Second, many of the behaviors involved in anxious and depressive responses are topographically similar even though they may have different functional histories. For example, staying home from work could reflect avoidant anxiety or unmotivated depression. Third, in the cognitive realm both anxiety and depression in the modern world involve complex coping and problem-solving tasks that overlap considerably in terms of evaluations of situations, evaluations of personal and external resources, and assessments of coping skill and ability. It is in this latter area that anxiety and depression may overlap in the most inextricable ways.

References

Abramson, L. Y., Seligman, M. E. P., & Teasdale, J. D. (1978). Learned helplessness in humans: Critique and reformulation. *Journal of Abnormal Psychology, 87*, 49–74.

Alloy, L. B., Clements, C., & Kolden, G. (1985). The cognitive diathesis-stress theories of depression: Therapeutic implications. In S. Reiss & R. R. Bootzin (Eds.), *Theoretical issues in behavior therapy* (pp. 379–410). Orlando, FL: Academic Press.

American Psychiatric Association. (1980). *Diagnostic and statistical manual of mental disorders* (3rd ed.). Washington, DC: Author.

American Psychiatric Association. (1987). *Diagnostic and statistical manual of mental disorders* (3rd ed., rev.). Washington, DC: Author.

Bandura, A. (1977). Self-efficacy: Toward a unifying theory of behavior change. *Psychological Review, 84*, 191–215.

Barlow, D. H., Blanchard, E. B., Vermilyea, J. A., Vermilyea, B. B., & DiNardo, P. A.

(1986). Generalized anxiety and generalized anxiety disorder: Description and reconceptualization. *American Journal of Psychiatry, 143,* 40–44.

Barlow, D. H., Vermilyea, J., Blanchard, E. B., Vermilyea, B. B., DiNardo, R. A., & Cerny, J. A. (1985). The phenomenon of panic. *Journal of Abnormal Psychology, 94,* 320–328.

Beck, A. T. (1972). *Depression: Causes and treatment.* Philadelphia: University of Pennsylvania Press.

Bower, G. H. (1981). Mood and memory. *American Psychologist, 36,* 129–147.

Bower, G. H. (1983). Affect and cognition. *Philosophic Transactions of the Royal Society of London, B302,* 387–402.

Bowlby, J. (1960). Grief and mourning in infancy and early childhood. *Psychoanalytic Study of Children, 15,* 9–52.

Clark, D. M., & Teasdale, J. D. (1982). Diurnal variation in clinical depression and accessibility of memories of positive and negative experiences. *Journal of Abnormal Psychology, 91,* 87–95.

Darwin, C. (1979). *The expression of emotions in man and animals.* New York: St. Martin's Press. (Originally published, London: J. Murray, 1872)

DiNardo, P.A., O'Brien, G. T., Barlow, D. H., Waddell, M. T., & Blanchard, E. B. (1983). Reliability of DSM-III anxiety disorder categories using a new structured interview. *Archives of General Psychiatry, 40,* 1071–1075.

Ellis, A. (1962). *Reason and emotion in psychotherapy.* New York: Lyle Stuart.

Ellis, H. C., & Ashbrook, P. W. (1987). Resource allocation model of depressed mood states on memory. In K. Fiedler & J. Forgas (Eds.), *Affect, cognition and social behavior.* Toronto: Hagrefe.

Eysenck, A. J. (1947). *Dimensions of personality.* London: Routledge & Kegan Paul.

Ferster, C. B. (1973). A functional analysis of depression. *American Psychologist, 28,* 857–870.

Frances, A., Widiger, T., & Fyer, M. (1987, September). *The influence of classification methods on comorbidity.* Paper presented at the NIMH Conference, *Symptom comorbidity in anxiety and depressive disorders,* Tuxedo, NY.

Izard, C. E. (1977). *Human emotions.* New York: Plenum.

Kanfer, F. H. (1970). Self-regulation: Research issues and speculations. In C. Neuringer & J. L. Michael (Eds.), *Behavior modification in clinical psychology.* New York: Appleton-Century-Crofts.

Klerman, G. L. (1974). Depression and adoption. In R. J. Friedman & M. M. Katz (Eds.), *The psychology of depression: Contemporary theory and research.* Washington, DC: Winston & Wiley.

Kupfer, D. J., & Foster, F. G. (1972). Interval between onset of sleep and rapid eye movement sleep as an indicator of depression. *Lancet, ii,* 684–686.

Kupfer, D. J., Foster, F. G., Reich, L., Thompson, K. S., & Weiss, B. (1976). EEG sleep changes as predictors in depression. *American Journal of Psychiatry, 133,* 622–626.

Lacey, J. I. (1967). Somatic response patterning and stress: Some revisions of activation theory. In M. Appleby & R. Trumball (Eds.), *Psychological stress* (pp. 14–37). New York: Appleton-Century-Crofts.

Lang, P. J. (1968). Fear reduction and fear behavior: Problems in treating a construct. In J. M. Shlien (Ed.), *Research in psychotherapy* (Vol. 3, pp. 90–102). Washington, DC: American Psychological Association.

Lang, P. J. (1979). A bio-informational theory of emotional imagery. *Psychophysiology, 16,* 495–512.

Lang, P. J. (1983). Cognition in emotion: Concept and action. In C. Izard, J. Kagan, & R. Zajonc (Eds.), *Emotion, cognition, and behavior* (pp. 192–226). New York: Cambridge University Press.

Lazarus, R. S. (1966). *Psychological stress and the coping process.* New York: McGraw-Hill.

Lazarus, R. S. (1974). Psychological stress and coping in adaptation and illness. *International Journal of Psychiatry in Medicine, 5,* 321–333.
Lazarus, R. S. (1981). The stress and coping paradigm. In C. Eisdorfer, D. Cohen, A. Kleinman, & P. Maxim (Eds.), *Models for clinical psychopathology.* New York: Spectrum.
Leight, K. A., & Ellis, H. C. (1981). Emotional mood states, strategies and state-dependency in memory. *Journal of Verbal Learning and Verbal Behavior, 20,* 251–266.
Levitt, E. E., & Lubin, B. (1975). *Depression: Concepts, controversies and some new facts.* New York: Springer.
Lewinsohn, P. M. (1974). Clinical and theoretical aspects of depression. In K. S. Calhoun, H. E. Adams, & K. M. Mitchell (Eds.), *Innovative treatment methods of psychopathology.* New York: Wiley.
Lewinsohn, P. M. (1976). Activity schedules in treatment of depression. In J. D. Krumboltz & C. E. Thoresen (Eds.), *Counseling methods* (pp. 74–82). New York: Holt, Rinehart & Winston.
Lewinsohn, P. M., & Talkington, J. (1979). Studies on the measurement of unpleasant events and relations with depression. *Applied Psychological Measurement, 3,* 83–101.
MacPhillamy, D. J., & Lewinsohn, P. M. (1982). The Pleasant Events Schedule: Studies on reliability, validity, and scale intercorrelation. *Journal of Consulting and Clinical Psychology, 50,* 363–380.
Mendels, J. (1975). *The psychobiology of depression.* New York: Spectrum.
Öhman, A., Dimberg, U., & Öst, L. G. (1985). Animal and social phobias: Biological constraints on learned fear responses. In S. Reiss & R. R. Bootzin (Eds.), *Theoretical issues in behavior therapy* (pp. 123–175). Orlando, FL: Academic Press.
Öst, L. G., & Hugdahl, K. (1983). Acquisition of agoraphobia, mode of onset and anxiety response patterns. *Behaviour Research and Therapy, 21,* 623–631.
Overall, J. E. (1962). Dimensions of manifest depression. *Psychiatric Research, 1,* 239–245.
Overall, J. E., & Hollister, L. E. (1980). Phenomenological classification of depressive disorders. *Journal of Clinical Psychology, 36,* 372–377.
Rachman, S. (1977). The conditioning theory of fear acquisition: A critical examination. *Behaviour Research and Therapy, 15,* 375–387.
Rehm, L. P. (1977). A self-control model of depression. *Behavior Therapy, 8,* 787–804.
Rehm, L. P. (1978). Mood, pleasant events and unpleasant events: Two pilot studies. *Journal of Consulting and Clinical Psychology, 46,* 849–853.
Rehm, L. P. (1987). The measurement of behavioral aspects of depression. In A. J. Marsella, R. Hirschfeld, & M. Katz (Eds), *The measurement of depression: Clinical, biological, psychological and psychosocial perspectives.*New York: Guilford Press.
Rehm, L. P. (1988). Assessment of depression. In M. Hersen & A. S. Bellack (Eds.), *Behavioral assessment: A practical handbook* (3rd ed., pp. 313–364). New York: Pergamon Press.
Rehm, L. P., & Naus, M. J. (in press). A memory model of emotion. In R. E. Ingram (Eds.), *Contemporary approaches to depression: Treatment, research and therapy.* New York: Plenum.
Roth, D., Rehm, L. P., & Rozensky, R. A. (1980). Self-reward, self-punishment and depression. *Psychological Reports, 47,* 3–7.
Rozensky, R. A., Rehm, L. P., Pry, G., & Roth, D. (1977). Depression and self-reinforcement behavior in hospital patients. *Journal of Behavior Therapy and Experimental Psychiatry, 8,* 35–38.
Sarason, I. G. (1961). The effects of anxiety and threat on the solution of a difficult task. *Journal of Abnormal and Social Psychology, 62,* 165–168.
Schwartz, G. E., Fair, P. L., Salt, P., Mandel, M. R., & Klerman, G. L. (1976). Facial muscle patterning to affective imagery in depressed and nondepressed subjects. *Science, 192,* 489–491.

Seligman, M. E. (1971). Phobias and preparedness. *Behavior Therapy, 2,* 307–320.
Seligman, M. E. P. (1974). Depression and learned helplessness. In R. J. Friedman & M. M. Katz (Eds.), *The psychology of depression: Contemporary theory and research.* New York: Winston-Wiley.
Seligman, M. E. P. (1975). *Helplessness: On depression, development, and death.* San Francisco: W. H. Freeman.
Selye, H. (1956). *The stress of life.* New York: McGraw-Hill.
Shrauger, J. S., & Terbovic, M. L. (1976). Self-evaluations and assessments of performance by self and others. *Journal of Consulting and Clinical Psychology, 44,* 564–572.
Spitz, R. A. (1946). Anaclitic depression: An inquiry into the genesis of psychiatric conditions in early childhood. *Psychoanalytic Study of Childhood, 2,* 313–342.
Teasdale, J. D. (1983a). Affect and accessibility. *Philosophical Transactions of the Royal Society of London, B302,* 403–412.
Teasdale, J. D. (1983b). Negative thinking in depression: Cause, effect, or reciprocal relationship? *Advances in Behaviour Research and Therapy, 5,* 27–49.
Teasdale, J. D., & Fogarty, S. J. (1979). Differential effects of induced mood on retrieval of pleasant and unpleasant events from episodic memory. *Journal of Abnormal Psychology, 88,* 248–257.
Tellegen, A. (1985). Structures of mood and personality and their relevance to assessing anxiety, with an emphasis on self-report. In A. H. Tuma & J. D. Maser (Eds.), *Anxiety and the anxiety disorders.* Hillsdale, NJ: Erlbaum.
Watson, D., & Tellegen, A. (1985). Toward a consensual structure of mood. *Psychological Bulletin, 98,* 219–235.
Weingartner, H., Miller, H., & Murphy, D. L. (1977). Mood-state-dependent retrieval of verbal associations. *Journal of Abnormal Psychology, 86,* 276–284.
Wilson, G. T. (1978). Cognitive behavior therapy: Paradigm shift or passing phase? In J. P. Foreyt & D. P. Rathjen (Eds.), *Cognitive behavior therapy: Research and application* (pp. 7–32). New York: Plenum.
Wine, J. (1971). Test anxiety and direction of attention. *Psychological Bulletin, 76,* 92–104.
Wolpe, J. (1958). *Psychotherapy by reciprocal inhibition.* Stanford, CA: Stanford University Press.
Zajonc, R. B. (1985). Emotion and facial efference: A theory reclaimed. *Science, 228,* 15–21.

Assessment Issues

The Anxiety and Depressive Disorders: Descriptive Psychopathology and Differential Diagnosis

Lee Anna Clark

I. Introduction

Although long a concern of both clinicians and researchers, the precise nature of the relation between depression and anxiety remains a puzzle. The solutions offered have included viewing them as (1) different points along a single continuum; (2) sharing a common underlying diathesis, which manifests itself in different ways depending on other unknown factors; (3) phenomenologically distinct but temporally associated, with initial anxiety turning to depression when relief is not forthcoming; (4) heterogeneous within themselves, such that some subtypes are more differentiable than others; and (5) conceptually and empirically distin-

Anxiety and Depression

guishable on the basis of course, family history, associated symptoms, and so on. (For discussions regarding the history of the problem, see Breier, Charney, & Heninger, 1985; Derogatis, Klerman, & Lipman, 1972; Klerman, 1977; Roth & Mountjoy, 1982.) As can be seen from even this partial listing, some (although clearly not all) of the complexity of the controversy is due to there being multiple levels of meaning for the terms *anxiety* and *depression*. That is, some writers are primarily refering to mood states (view 3), others to clinical symptoms or syndromes (views 2 and 4), and still others to diagnostic entities (view 5). Clearly, conclusions drawn about anxiety and depression at one level of meaning may or may not be relevant when another is considered, and yet, to understand the phenomenon completely, relationships among the different meanings of anxiety and depression must ultimately be clarified.

Unfortunately, there is little standardization in the definition of anxiety and depression, even at the same level of meaning. For example, relevant symptoms or syndromes are assessed using a wide variety of patient self-report measures and clinical rating scales, not to mention unstructured clinical observation. Many of these anxiety and depression scales correlate in the .60 to .70 range with other measures of the same construct, and coefficients of this magnitude are generally regarded as evidence for good convergent validity. However, even at this level of relation, although patients identified using one measure are likely to be similar to those defined using a different measure, they clearly are not identical. Moreover, many of these measures correlate in the .40 to .60 range with measures of the *other* construct; that is, in some cases the discriminant correlations are as high as the convergent ones (see Gotlib & Cane, this volume). Surprisingly little attention has been given to determining the comparability of patients labeled anxious or depressed by these various means.

Similarly, diagnoses may be made using unstructured or highly structured interviews, and may or may not follow specified criteria. Even when the method and criteria for diagnosis are well defined, there is marked divergence in the composition of patient samples from study to study, precluding direct comparison of results. For example, a sample of anxious patients may be suffering primarily from panic disorder or agoraphobia, from generalized anxiety disorder (GAD), or from some (often unspecified) mixture of these disorders. Exclusion and inclusion criteria also differ across studies: Some researchers include any patient who meets the diagnostic criteria for a depressive or anxiety disorder, while others include only those patients for whom the depression or anxiety disorder is clearly primary. Systematic investigation of the effect of such differences within a single study would add greatly to our understanding of the phenomena, but, unfortunately, such research is rare. Furthermore, diagnostic practice has changed with time, so early researchers, compared to more recent ones, necessarily defined somewhat different diagnostic groups. Thus, while replicated findings suggest truly robust phenomena, the meaning of nonsignificant or divergent results is unclear.

More optimistically, many workers in the field are now aware of these problems, and concern for the reliability and construct validity of measures has increased. Moreover, specification of diagnostic criteria in the *Diagnostic and Statistical Manual of Mental Disorders* (DSM-III; American Psychiatric Association, 1980) has led to greater comparability of samples. Several multisite studies with large samples, careful diagnostic procedures, multiple self-report and clinicians' measures, and sophisticated designs and analytic techniques are ongoing or have recently been completed. Examples of such studies are found in three NIMH-sponsored projects: the Collaborative Program on the Psychobiology of Depression (e.g., Coryell, Endicott, Andreasen, & Keller, 1985), the Epidemiological Catchment Area Program (e.g., Regier et al., 1984), and the Center for Epidemiological Research (e.g., Leckman, Weissman, Merikangas, Pauls, & Prusoff, 1983b; Radloff, 1977).

This chapter is most centrally concerned with the depressive and anxiety disorders as clinical syndromes or diagnoses. The emphasis will be on elucidating both the overlapping and the differentiable aspects of the syndromes/disorders as currently defined in DSM-III and its recent revision (American Psychiatric Association, 1980, 1987). In this context, I will focus on clinicians' judgments regarding the relevant moods, symptoms, and syndromes. Of course, in making their ratings, clinicians depend a great deal on what their patients tell them, so self-report data clearly cannot be entirely ignored; however, because self-report is the focus of another chapter in this volume (Gotlib & Cane), its role will be minimized here. I also consider some data regarding the course, prevalence, familiality, treatment, and so on, of these syndromes, but I only speculate briefly about the underlying causal processes or disease entities.

A. Primary Diagnostic Categories of the Anxiety and Depressive Disorders

Before the advent of published standardized criteria for psychiatric diagnosis [e.g., Feighner et al., 1972; Research Diagnostic Criteria (RDC), Spitzer, Endicott, & Robins, 1978; DSM-III, APA, 1980], researchers interested in differentiating anxiety from depressive disorders either developed their own specifications or relied on clinical judgment. It is a tribute to the astuteness of early researchers (and perhaps to the robustness of the phenomena) that much of what they reported can still be brought to bear on more modern studies. In order to do so, however, it is necessary to "translate" their categories into those of DSM-III. What follows is a brief description of the DSM-III system, noting correspondences between it, DSM-II, and DSM-III-R.

1. Affective Disorders

Within the affective disorders, the primary diagnosis of interest is major depression. This disorder is marked by prominent and persistent depressed mood and/or loss of interest and pleasure in usual activities. Concurrent with the depressed mood/loss of interest, patients must exhibit at least four out of eight additional symptoms (e.g., sleep and/or appetite disturbance, retardation or agitation, decreased concentration, and suicidal ideation). One may further specify "with psychotic features," but the psychotic features must not be present in the absence of the mood disturbance (which would indicate schizophrenia or schizoaffective disorder). Finally, major depression can be diagnosed "with melancholia" if a particular pattern of symptoms is present (e.g., marked retardation, early morning awakening, and a distinctly different quality of depressed mood). Melancholia, often called "endogenous depression," is thought to represent a particularly severe, yet episodic, form of the disorder.

Two other diagnoses sometimes included in research are subjects with dysthymia, a milder but chronic form of affective (depressive) disorder, and adjustment disorder (with anxious and/or depressed mood), which is a transient maladaptive reaction to an external stressor. Since the publication of DSM-III, these categories have generally been excluded from research samples, presumably because investigators wish to assure clear-cut diagnostic groups, and because these disorders are more likely to be difficult to distinguish from normal-range reactions or personality. However, they are thought to be common (APA, 1987) and may account for a significant percentage of "normal" subjects who report significant levels of distress on self-report measures of anxiety and depression. Furthermore, there is evidence that dysthymia is more common in the first-degree relatives of people with major depression than in the general population (APA, 1987), so future researchers may wish to include these patients, as a separate group, in order to study the full range of depressive symptomatology. Finally, clear cases of bipolar and cyclothymic disorder (i.e., with one or more manic/hypomanic episodes) are generally not included in studies of anxiety and depression, perhaps because evidence suggests that the unipolar/bipolar distinction has etiological significance (Gershon et al., 1982).

Relation to Earlier Classification Schemes. Major depression corresponds to three different DSM-II diagnoses: manic-depressive illness, depressed type (if "with melancholia" is specified), depressive neurosis (if "without melancholia" is specified), and psychotic depressive reaction (if a precipitating stressor can be identified and "with psychotic features" is specified). Depressive neurosis also encompasses dysthymia and adjustment disorders, so early samples of patients with depressive neurosis were undoubtedly quite heterogeneous. Besides the official nomenclature, other terminology was commonly used; in particular, many studies distinguished endogenous versus reactive (or psychotic vs. neurotic) depression. The various terms used to subdivide depression are not completely synonymous, and many articles have been devoted clarifying the basic underlying distinction (for reviews, see Fowles & Gersh, 1982; Kendell, 1977). I will return to these dichotomies, but at this point it can suffice to say that they correspond most closely to major depression with melancholia versus major depression without melancholia or dysthymia.

2. Anxiety Disorders

Within the anxiety disorders, the primary diagnoses of interest are agoraphobia with and without panic attacks, panic disorder, and generalized anxiety disorder. The essential feature of agoraphobia is a marked fear of places or situations from which escape might be difficult (in the event of incapacitation due to anxiety), to the point that the individual's life is severely restricted or dominated by avoidance behavior. This disorder often develops in response to recurrent panic attacks, which are characterized by sudden intense fear without apparent provocation, accompanied by a number of physical symptoms or sensations (e.g., difficulty breathing, dizziness, sweating, and shaking). Interestingly, in DSM-III-R, the hierarchical order of these diagnoses has been changed, in large part because of the very small number of patients having agoraphobia without panic attacks. Currently, panic disorder has been made the primary diagnosis, with or without agoraphobia. Another major change in DSM-III-R concerns the relation with major depression. In DSM-III, panic disorder was not to be diagnosed if it developed subsequent to a major depressive episode, but this hierarchical relation has been eliminated in DSM-III-R, so that a patient may receive both diagnoses.

In generalized anxiety disorder (GAD), the prominent feature is chronic psychic and somatic anxiety in the absence of any clear precipitant. In DSM-III-R, the criteria for this diagnosis were made significantly more stringent: the duration requirement was changed from 1 to 6 months, and the number of symptoms required was increased from three to six. Thus, most studies of GAD using DSM-III criteria likely include many patients who would be diagnosed in DSM-III-R as having an adjustment disorder with anxious mood. The hierarchical status of GAD has also been revised: In DSM-III, GAD was a residual category that was only diagnosed in the absence of other anxiety disorders and depression, whereas in DSM-III-R, comorbidity with these disorders is recognized, as long as the generalized anxiety is not simply limited to its association with them.

Anxiety disorders that are usually excluded from studies of anxiety and depression include the simple and social phobias and obsessive–compulsive disorder. However, severe cases of the former are sometimes included under agoraphobia, and cases of the latter may be included if the anxious mood is more prominent than the obsessive–compulsive rituals.

Relation to Earlier Classification Schemes. In DSM-II terms, agoraphobia corresponds to phobic neurosis, which also encompassed the simple and social phobias, while anxiety neurosis included both panic disorder and GAD. Actual research practice, however, seems to have corresponded more closely to the DSM-III-R organization. That is, in early research, subjects were most commonly described as suffering from disorders that descriptively match panic disorder, agoraphobia, and severe GAD. Simple and social phobics were usually excluded, even though they were officially grouped with agoraphobia.

Given this diagnostic variation, one can from the outset anticipate difficulties in comparing results across studies, especially those done in different eras. As mentioned before, inconsistencies are therefore less informative than congruences, which suggest robust phenomena.

B. Reliability of Clinical Ratings and Diagnoses

For many years, the question of the reliability of clinical ratings and diagnoses was woefully neglected. When it was examined, the results were not encouraging, with the one exception that good reliabilities were often found for global severity ratings. For example, in a review of diagnostic reliability studies, Spitzer and Fleiss (1974) computed kappa coefficients[1] of .26 for neurotic depression and .45 for anxiety reaction, whereas correlations of .80 to .90 between clinicians' global ratings of

[1]Kappa is a statistic of interrater reliability developed by Cohen (1960) that corrects for chance agreement; .70 or higher indicates good reliability.

anxiety and depression were not uncommon (e.g., Beck, Ward, Mendelson, Mock, & Erbaugh, 1962; Lauterbach, 1958). Understandably, those writers in the 1960s and early 1970s who addressed the issue at all were generally pessimistic: "Ratings notoriously have only modest reliability . . . it was found that psychiatrists did not agree very well with one another" (Grinker & Nunnally, 1965, p. 252).

However, with the development of specific diagnostic criteria, structured interviews, and standardized rating scales, the situation changed dramatically. By the end of the 1970s, clinical researchers were more optimistic: "For most of the classes, the reliability for both interview situations is quite good" (Spitzer, Forman, & Nee, 1979, p. 817), and some were even boastful: "Clinician-to-clinician diagnoses have now attained remarkably high levels of reliability" (Matarazzo, 1983, p. 103). In the DSM-III field trials, for example, the phase-two kappa reliabilities for major affective and anxiety disorders were .80 and .72, respectively (APA, 1980).

At this point it is important to distinguish between ratings of syndromes and diagnoses—the former being scaled, the latter dichotomous. The best known of the syndromic rating scales are perhaps the Hamilton Rating Scales for Anxiety (HRSA; Hamilton, 1959) and Depression (HSRD; Hamilton, 1960), although many others with similar characteristics have been developed. For such scales, various aspects of the depressive or anxiety syndrome—mood, sleep disturbance, autonomic symptoms, and so on—are each rated; these are then summed to obtain an overall index of severity of the depressive or anxiety syndrome.

For diagnostic ratings, two structured interviews are notable. First, the Schedule for Affective Disorder and Schizophrenia (SADS; Endicott & Spitzer, 1978) is a semistructured clinical interview that yields clinical diagnoses—including subtypes—of affective disorders and schizophrenia when used in conjunction with the Research Diagnostic Criteria (Spitzer et al., 1978). Summary scale scores for several dimensions of psychopathology can also be scored. However, coverage of the anxiety disorders is limited with this instrument. Its successor, the Structured Clinical Interview for DSM-III (SCID; Spitzer & Williams, 1983), corrects this deficiency, but data on this instrument are still limited. Second, the Diagnostic Interview Schedule (DIS; Robins, Helzer, Croughan, & Ratcliff, 1981) is a highly structured interview designed for use by lay interviewers that is now being used by clinicians as well. It assesses symptoms of about 30 DSM-III diagnoses and can be computer-scored for these diagnoses. The Anxiety Diagnostic Interview Schedule (ADIS; DiNardo, O'Brien, Barlow, Waddell, & Blanchard, 1983) is modeled after the DIS and covers the anxiety disorders more extensively.

In addition to the original reliability/validation studies given above, published reviews or further studies of the reliability of these instruments are available (HRSD; Hedlung & Vieweg, 1979; Zimmerman, Coryell, Wilson, & Corenthal, 1986; SADS: Matarazzo, 1983; DIS: Breslau & Davis, 1985; Hesselbrock, Stabenau, Hesselbrock, Mirkin, & Meyer, 1982). The interested reader is referred elsewhere for detailed discussion of these instruments, but I will use some of these data to discuss a few key issues here. First, the reliability of a measure is not a fixed quantity, but varies systematically with a number of factors, especially differences in how information is obtained and interpreted. The highest reliabilities are found when ratings are made on heterogeneous populations by highly trained interviewers with similar backgrounds, and are based on exactly the same information (joint interviews, live observation, videotapes, and audiotapes have all been used). Under these conditions, both total score and diagnostic reliabilities (correlations/intraclass coefficients or kappa coefficients, respectively) are quite high, typically ranging from .70 to .90. Item reliabilities are lower, but still acceptable (mean intraclass coefficients tend to be around .70, with ranges from .40 to .90). If any of these conditions are altered, reliabilities suffer predictably. For example, Cicchetti and Prusoff (1983) demonstrated the effect of sample diversity in a 16-week study of treatment efficacy. They found an increase in HRSD reliability from .46 at intake, when variability was limited due to high levels of depression in most patients, to .82 at end point, when some patients had largely recovered but others were still quite ill.

When patients are interviewed independently, reliability is nearly always lower for a variety of reasons. One of the most important of these is the length of time between interviews, because this confounds rater and/or patient unreliability with actual status change. Thus, when investigating clinicians' reliability, only very short time intervals should be considered, and the ratings to be compared should certainly be made within a week of one another. Using longer time intervals to assess the stability of reported symptomatology is also important, but this is a different issue that should be researched separately. A second major source of unreliability across separate interviews is raters obtaining different information on which to base their judgments. In a study of the routine clinical intake diagnostic process, two-thirds of the cases of major disagreement stemmed at least partially from informational differences (Spitzer, Skodol, Williams, Gibbon, & Kass, 1982). This problem appears to be more severe if unstructured clinical interviews are used and/or raters have different background training (e.g., psychiatrists vs. psychologists), although little systematic research has been done on this point. Even under the best of circumstances, however, patients may remember or report events differently on two separate occasions, even within several hours. Thus, informational differences can be minimized, but not eliminated, when raters with similar training use structured interviews.

Reported values for short-timespan test–retest/interrater reliabilities on the above-named instruments thus vary widely, ranging from .46 (for HRSD total score, based on unstructured interviews by MD versus PhD/MA pairs; Cicchetti & Prusoff, 1983) to .90 (for a SADS/RDC diagnosis of major depression made by "pairs of research assistants who had considerable on-the-job training and many years of experience in interviewing psychiatric patients"; Spitzer et al., 1978, p. 779). More typical values for both ratings and diagnosis of depression by separate interview are in the .60 to .80 range. Interestingly, even with structured interviews, reliabilities for the anxiety disorders are more variable, ranging from lows in the .40s to a high of .85 (for agoraphobia with panic; DiNardo et al., 1983). Clearly, our understanding of the diagnosis of anxiety lags behind that for depression.

Differences in interpretation are most problematic when raters with different background training use unstructured interviews, whether or not simultaneous interviews are conducted. For example, nearly half the major disagreements in the study of the intake diagnostic process were at least partially due to interpretational differences (Spitzer et al., 1982). However, when structured interviews are used, or when the raters are highly skilled clinicians of similar background (as in the DSM-III field trials), interpretational differences are minimal. Ironically, a total lack of such differences may actually be suggestive of another problem. Studies of naturalistic observation have identified a phenomenon called *observer drift*, in which raters working together over time develop idiosyncratic rules for interpreting their observations, which results in ratings with high reliability but indeterminate accuracy (e.g., Foster & Cone, 1986). It is possible for pairs of raters to get to know each other's interpretations so well that they make similar judgments even when an outside observer would disagree. Interestingly, the solution to this problem is similar to that for unreliability: frequent regrouping and retraining of raters, and periodic review of the underlying concepts to be measured (Kendall & Norton-Ford, 1982). This may prove necessary even with semistructured interviews, although no studies have investigated this issue.

In summarizing the reliability data, the importance of using structured interviews and raters well trained in both the instrument and the underlying concepts cannot be overemphasized. If these guidelines are followed, results are likely to be highly reliable; if they are not (and there are many such studies, not to mention standard clinical practice), the replicability of the findings must be considered questionable. Finally, further research is needed into factors affecting the test–retest reliability of ratings, including the influence of raters' background training.

II. Clinical Studies of Depression and Anxiety

A. Mood and Syndrome Rating Scales

Although there are many correlational studies of anxiety and depression in self-report, there are surprisingly few that have investigated the relation between clinical measures of the constructs. Furthermore, only a small number of studies have directly compared subjects with depressive and anxiety disorders on rating scales, and the majority of these have also used self-ratings rather than clinician ratings. Generally speaking, the results are striking in that clear and consistent differentiation between measures of these constructs or between the two types of patients is rarely achieved with either type of rating. I discuss here only the findings regarding clinical ratings; for a review of the use of self-rating scales, the interested reader is referred elsewhere (Clark & Watson, in press; Gotlib & Cane, this volume).

1. Correlational Analyses

Very few studies that have used clinical rating scales of both anxiety and depression have included the same two measures, so the replicability of the findings is largely unknown. However, strong correlations have been reported between the two Hamilton scales, ranging from .53 in a sample of 240 neurotic outpatients (Johnstone et al., 1980) to .89 in a heterogeneous inpatient sample (Deluty, Deluty, & Carver, 1986). In the latter sample the scales may reflect general differences between neurotic and psychotic patients—that is, neurotic patients may score considerably higher on both scales than psychotic patients—and this would serve to increase the correlation between them.

The Hamilton scales were developed to assess syndromic severity and were expressly not intended for use in differential diagnosis. Thus, they were developed without regard to symptoms that overlap between the syndromes (such as insomnia and even depressed and anxious mood), so that the correlation between them is due partly to overlapping content. However, the HRSD correlated .60 with the summary Anxiety scale of the SADS in a sample of 48 depressed inpatients (Endicott, Cohen, Nee, Fleiss, & Sarantakos, 1981), and in the same study the SADS Anxiety and Depressive Syndrome scales also correlated .58. The similar level of these correlations suggests that the overlap is not unique to the Hamilton scales. Similarly, in an earlier study of 150 inpatients (Endicott & Spitzer, 1978), the SADS Anxiety scale correlated .47 and .39, respectively, with scales of Depressive-Associated Features and Depressive Mood and Ideation ($r = .74$ between the two depression scales), indicating that a relation between anxiety and depression can be found across the various facets of the syndromes.

In addition to research on these widely used measures, several studies have derived sets of depression and anxiety scales using factor or cluster techniques (Fleiss, Gurland, & Cooper, 1971; Lipman, Rickels, Covi, Derogatis, & Uhlenhuth, 1969) or simply by carefully delineating the symptoms to be rated for each syndrome (Foa & Foa, 1982; Zuckerman, Persky, Eckman, & Hopkins, 1967). Despite these differences in (1) method of derivation, (2) the resulting complexity of the scales, and (3) the patient samples rated, the correlations between scale pairs show a good deal of consistency (median = .46; range = .38–.67). It is noteworthy that these values are quite comparable to those reported above using the Hamilton and SADS scales. Thus, the correlation found between ratings of syndromic anxiety and depression appears to reflect truly shared variance that cannot be eliminated even by using sophisticated analytic techniques.

Two recent studies, however, have reported greater discrimination between anxiety and depression. One study investigated a small sample of patients with various anxiety and depressive disorders ($n = 16$ each), using the Covi Anxiety and Raskin Depression scales (Lipman, 1982), as well as 9-point global measures of anxiety and depression (Vye, 1986). Anxiety and depression were not significantly related using either set of ratings ($r = -.25$ for the Covi and Raskin scales; $r = -.04$ for the two global measures). Similarly, Riskind, Beck, Brown, and Steer (1987) reconstructed the Hamilton scales on the basis of factor and discriminant analyses, removing nine items and reassigning seven items to the other scale. In a cross-validation sample of 38 patients with major depressive disorder and 33 with generalized anxiety disorder, the original scales correlated .62, whereas the revised scales correlated only .15. Moreover, the hit rate for correct assignment of patients to their respective diagnostic groups was considerably higher with the revised scales.

How can we explain the discrepancy between these findings and the results of previous research? A careful review of the methods of each study reveals that these two are the only studies reviewed in this section in which the clinical ratings were made in direct connection with the diagnostic process. This suggests that when clinicians focus on making a differential diagnosis, a contrast effect regarding anxiety and depression may function (perhaps correctly or perhaps inappropriately) to magnify their distinction. I return to this point in a later section.

Summarizing the correlational studies, various clinical rating scales of anxiety and depression appear to be only moderately independent in neurotic samples; in more heterogeneous samples they are even less independent and may function largely as nonspecific measures of neurosis versus psychosis. If the focus of assessment is on differential diagnosis, however, the relative level of depression versus anxiety may be more salient to the rater, which increases the independence of the ratings but has unknown effects on their validity.

2. Factor Analytic Studies

A number of studies have factor analyzed clinical ratings of psychiatric symptoms. The number and range of symptoms included vary widely from study to study, as do the number of factors extracted and method of rotation, so a detailed analysis of these studies is beyond the scope of this chapter, but an overview of the findings will be presented and discussed.

Studies that have included a broad range of affective, anxious, and schizophrenic symptomatology have tended to find a unitary neurotic factor encompassing both depressive and anxious symptoms, and sometimes a separate retarded depression factor (see Costello, 1970, for a review). In contrast, those that have focused specifically on depressive and anxiety symptoms have generally reported either a bipolar anxiety versus depression factor when the unrotated principal components were examined (e.g., Roth, Gurney, Garside, & Kerr, 1972) or, more commonly with varimax rotation, separate anxiety and depression factors (Clark, Watson, & Carey, 1987b; Derogatis, Lipman, Covi, Rickels, & Uhlenhuth, 1970; Fleiss et al., 1971; Hamilton, 1967; Lipman et al., 1969). When a broad range of somatic items (including those considered related to anxiety) were rated individually, those items formed their own factor (Lipman et al., 1969).

Comparing the factors in studies that have found unitary versus bipolar or separate factors, qualitative differences can be seen. In studies finding unitary factors, mood disturbance items and/or symptoms common to anxiety and depression (e.g., insomnia, excessive worry) predominate, and the resulting factor resembles the pervasive personality dimension negative affectivity (NA; Watson and Clark, 1984), which is similar to neuroticism or emotionality (Eysenck & Eysenck, 1968, 1975). In contrast, in studies finding bipolar or separate factors, the anxiety pole (or factor) is usually fairly well defined and is best described as panic/agoraphobia, while the depression pole (or factor) is often more broad or, if specific, has a strongly endogenous flavor, centering on such core symptoms as loss of pleasure, hopelessness, and suicidal tendencies, in addition to depressed mood. Thus, the results of the various studies are not contradictory, but reflect the particular items and patient groups rated. In fact, in several studies—some using clinically rated items (Mountjoy & Roth, 1982b; Mowbray, 1972; Schapira, Roth, Kerr, & Gurney, 1972) and one using clinical and self-report rating scales (Roth & Mountjoy, 1982)—principal components analysis revealed both a general neurotic or severity factor and a second endogenous depression versus panic/anxiety factor. These results suggest that distinguishing dysthymia (neurotic depression) from anxiety (GAD) will likely prove quite difficult, if not impossible, and will require fine-grained analyses on large numbers of carefully assessed patients.

3. Group Comparisons

Several studies have directly compared patients with anxiety versus depressive disorders via rating scales. Fleiss et al. (1971) compared patients with anxiety neurosis and depressive neurosis on factor-analytically derived scales.The 45-item Depression scale contained items pertaining to depressed mood, loss of interest and appetite, low energy, and so on, but not items measuring endogenous or psychotic features (e.g., early morning wakening, depressive delusions). The 21-item Phobic Anxiety scale included primarily somatic and agoraphobic items; notably absent were two items describing anxious mood, which correlated more highly with the depression scale than with the anxiety scale. Thus, the scales might be better labeled "General Neurotic Reaction" (especially since the length of the Depression scale indicates that it encompasses a broad range of neurotic symptomatology) and "Panic/Agoraphobia." They found no difference on their Depression scale, but the anxiety neurotics scored significantly higher on the Phobic Anxiety scale. These results support the proposed reinterpretation of these scales. They also provide further evidence that if anxiety is to be distinguished from depression, it will not likely be by delineating subtle differences in the general mood or symptom patterns, but rather will result from focusing on the more distinctive syndromes of panic and major (especially endogenous) depression.

Three studies (Riskind et al., 1987; Lipman, 1982; Mountjoy & Roth, 1982a) have found differences in the predicted direction on both of the Hamilton scales, and two (Lipman, 1982; Vye, 1986) have found expected differences on the Covi Anxiety and Raskin Depression scales. Although it is heartening to find evidence of discriminant validity for anxiety and depression, given the moderately high correlations between these rating scales that were discussed earlier, a closer scrutiny of the results seems warranted. As noted above, in both the Riskind et al. and Vye studies—which found that anxiety and depression could be discriminated—the ratings were made by clinicians in the course of diagnosis. Is this true in the other studies as well? It turns out that this is indeed the case.

In the Mountjoy and Roth study, patients were initially selected through a screening of their intake notes. If they were judged to be suffering from an affective disorder (depressive or anxious), they were given a full clinical interview. On this basis, diagnostic assignments were made using research criteria and the various rating scales were completed. Thus, the ratings were made in direct connection with the diagnostic process, and it is not unlikely that the interviewers were especially sensitive to the relative weights of anxiety versus depressive symptoms in making diagnostic decisions. Finally, in the Lipman study, the Covi and Raskin scales were actually part of the criteria for inclusion in the study, and the Hamilton ratings were made at the same initial intake interview. The reliability of diagnosis was evaluated through independent ratings at a 1-week interval and was found to be at the low end of acceptability (kappa = .62; Downing et al., 1981).

Certainly, evidence supporting the discriminant validity of measures collected under these conditions must be considered questionable. At the same time, it is important to emphasize that these studies all possess a certain degree of ecological validity, in the sense that these researchers were carefully studying the symptom rating and diagnostic process much as it occurs in day-to-day clinical practice. It is highly likely that clinicians *do* pay attention to the relative weight of anxiety and depression symptoms in assigning diagnoses. A study by Downing and Rickels (1974) addresses this question directly.

Treating physicians rated 271 "neurotic outpatients with a diagnosis of mixed anxiety–depression" (p. 312) on 7-point global anxiety and depression rating scales, and also assigned them to treatment with either antianxiety (n = 122) or antidepressant (n = 149) medication. The groups could not be differentiated on the basis of their absolute level of anxiety, but did differ significantly in the predicted direction on their level of depression. Of particular interest here is that the two groups also differed in the *relative* levels of anxiety and depression. That is, although patients assigned to antianxiety treatment were rated as no more anxious than those assigned to antidepressant treatment, they were rated as relatively more anxious than depressed. Similarly, patients assigned to antidepressant treatment were relatively more depressed than anxious, as well as being rated more depressed in absolute terms. The difference between the two ratings was more marked in the anxious patients, who were rated as less severely disturbed overall. Although Vye (1986) did not report relative anxiety/depression scores, he also found that a global anxiety measure failed to differentiate his two groups, whereas the patients with depressive diagnoses were rated as significantly more depressed and as more severely disturbed overall. Thus, the "depressed" patients were just as anxious as the "anxious" patients, but were even more depressed, leading the clinicians to assign them a depressive rather than anxiety diagnosis. Again, it appears that the relative level of mood disturbance may have been more critical than the absolute level in determining diagnosis.

A study of 60 outpatients who met criteria for DSM-III panic disorder (92% were also agoraphobic) provides a different comparative perspective (Breier, Charney, & Heninger, 1984). Ignoring the DSM-III hierarchical criteria (which prohibit diagnosis of panic disorder if it is "due to" major depression), they determined that 68% of their sample met RDC criteria for definite major depression (lifetime). Researchers blind to the diagnostic interview data rated the patients on a number of clinical indices, including both Hamilton scales. Not surprisingly, patients with current or previous history of depression had significantly higher HRSD scores than those without, but they were also rated as significantly higher on the HRSA. The correlation between the two Hamilton scales was not reported, but they had very similar correlations with a measure of magnitude of depression (total number of months depressed; $r = .44$ for HRSA, .38 for HRSD).

Combining the results from the correlational and comparative studies, it is reasonable to conclude that at the level of global assessment or symptom rating scales, anxiety and depression are judged to be moderately correlated under circumstances where their distinction is not an issue or when the assessment is made blind to diagnostic information. However, if differentiation of the two is salient, as in the diagnostic process, clinicians may seek to contrast anxiety and depression, focusing on their relative levels and on features that distinguish them from each other. In terms of the "true" relation between anxiety and depression, this contrast effect artificially lowers the judged correlation between them, but it remains an empirical question whether this clinical bias is diagnostically valid. That is, the relative (as opposed to absolute) levels of anxiety or depression may, in fact, be the more useful determinant of primary diagnostic category. This assumes, of course, that the diagnoses themselves can, and should be, distinguished. It also implies that diagnoses should be hierarchically arranged, so that if a patient has both types of disorders, primary and secondary diagnoses can be meaningfully assigned. These issues have been the subject of debate for some time, and will be addressed further below.

4. Mood and Syndrome Overlap

The correlational, factor analytic, and group comparison studies reviewed indicate that anxiety and depressive moods and syndromes co-occur, but do not fully inform us regarding the nature of these relations. Is the co-occurrence equally divided between depressed patients who have anxiety symptoms and anxiety patients who show depression, or is there a directionality to the overlap? Two studies investigated depression and tension (both episodic and persistent) at one or more levels of severity in depressed versus anxious patients; both found considerable overlap (Mountjoy & Roth, 1982b; Roth et al., 1972). All depressed patients in both studies were rated as having severe depression, with 60–65% of these showing persistent depression. In contrast, only 21–23% of the anxiety disorder patients were rated as having persistent depression. The reverse pattern was seen for mild or episodic depression, with anxious patients showing more than depressed patients. Thus, the two groups could be distinguished not by the existence of depression per se, but by the level and persistence of the depressed mood.

No comparable pattern was seen for tension, however. In both studies, severe persistent tension was reported somewhat more frequently by anxious patients (33 and 31%) than by depressed patients (22 and 16%), but in the Mountjoy and Roth study the difference (33 vs. 22%) was not significant. For marked episodic tension, the two studies showed different levels overall, but a similar pattern: About 70% of patients (with either type of disorder) of Roth et al. had episodic tension, while approximately 40% of Mountjoy and Roth's patients (again with either type of disorder) did so. The reason for this inconsistency across studies is not clear, but the important point here is that each study was internally consistent—patients with both types of disorders reported episodic tension with equivalent frequency. Thus, with regard to the question of directionality in the reporting of depressive versus anxious symptoms, these studies suggest that depressed patients report persistent severe depression significantly more frequently, but that there is less or no difference in the frequency of reports of anxiety in the two types of patients.

Turning to global ratings of anxiety and depression, about half (48%) of the obsessive–compulsive patients studied by Foa and Foa (1982) had equal levels, 39% had more severe anxiety than depression, while only 13% had more severe depressive symptomatology. In contrast, Prusoff and Weissman (1981) found the opposite pattern in a sample of 323 depressed patients who were rated on 7-point global measures of depressed mood and psychic anxiety. Only about one-third of their patients had equal levels of anxiety and depression, a considerable number (44%) had higher levels of depression than anxiety, and relatively fewer (22%) had more anxiety than depression. The latter asymmetries are similar to those reported in the study of mixed anxiety–depression patients (Downing & Rickels, 1974), where the concern was assignment to either an antianxiety or an antidepressant medication group. In a study in which ratings of anxiety and depression in neurotic outpatients were made without regard to diagnosis, however, no asymmetry was found (Johnstone et al., 1980). Under these independent rating conditions, 42% of the patients were seen as having equivalent observed depression and anxiety and the remaining patients were equally divided: 30% had more depression than anxiety, and 28% had more anxiety than depression.

These data lend further support to the notion that the diagnostic process biases clinicians' ratings, and may be summarized as follows: (1) Many patients diagnosed as having an anxiety or depressive disorder show equal overall levels of the two moods; (2) if one of the two moods predominates, patients are more likely to be diagnosed with that syndrome, but (3) a sizable minority are diagnosed with the syndrome they show less severely; (4) this group is larger for those receiving depressive diagnoses than it is for anxiety diagnoses, but (5) if diagnosis is not an issue, the number of patients showing one or the other mood/syndrome more severely may be more equal.

B. Specific Symptoms

1. Description of Studies

A number of studies have compared patients with depressive and anxiety diagnosis on specific clinician-rated symptoms (Clark, Watson, & Carey, 1987a; Downing & Rickels, 1974; Mountjoy & Roth, 1982b; Roth et al., 1972; Torgersen, 1985). Two studies (Lipman, 1982; Prusoff & Klerman, 1974) examined self-reported rather than clinician-rated symptoms. These will also be included in this section, because at the level of specific symptoms the similarities and differences in self-report versus clinical report may provide valuable information for diagnosis. The methodologies of studies not already described will be discussed briefly here. Table 4.1 presents a synopsis of the patient populations, each study's criteria for inclusion/exclusion, and probable DSM-III equivalents.

As mentioned, the 271 patients studied by Downing and Rickels (1974) all received a "neurotic" diagnosis of mixed anxiety–depression. Based on their predominant symptomatology, they were assigned to clinical trials of either antianxiety agents or antidepressants.

Mountjoy and Roth's (1982b) subjects were a mixed group of inpatients and outpatients who had sought treatment, whereas subjects of Roth et al. (1972) were entirely inpatients. In both studies, patients with a hospital or clinic diagnosis of affective disorder (including anxiety) were given a structured clinical interview (for which Roth et al. reported an item reliability of .86 for two independent raters of a joint interview; $n = 29$). Patients were then included in the study if they met specified inclusion (see Tables 4.1 and 4.2) and exclusion criteria (e.g., mood

Table 4.1
Studies Comparing the Occurrence of Symptoms in Patients with Depression versus Anxiety Disorders

Study[a]	**Patients**	*n*	**Study criteria and/or diagnosis**	**Probable DSM-III equivalent**[b]
			Anxiety patients	
Clark et al. (1987)[c]	Inpatient	37	DIS diagnoses plus interview	Any DSM-III anxiety disorder
Downing & Rickels (1974)	Outpatient volunteers	122	Predominantly anxious	Any anxiety-relevant disorder
Lipman (1982)[d]	Outpatient volunteers	240	97% anxiety neurosis, 3% phobic neurosis	97% panic disorder/GAD, 3% agoraphobic
Mountjoy & Roth (1982b)	60% inpatient, 40% outpatient	73	59% anxiety neurosis, 41% phobic neurosis	59% panic disorder/GAD, 41% agoraphobic
Prusoff & Klerman (1974)[e]	Neurotic outpatients	364	Anxiety as primary feature	Any anxiety disorder
Roth et al. (1972)	Inpatient	68	Anxiety states, with tension, panic, and autonomic symptoms	Mixed GAD, agoraphobia, panic disorder, or panic attacks
Torgersen (1985)	Inpatients and outpatients	76	Anxiety neurosis	Panic disorder/GAD

			Depressed patients	
Clark et al. (1987a)[c]	Inpatient	52	DIS diagnoses plus interview	85% major depression, 15% minor depression (e.g., dysthymia)
Downing & Rickels (1974)	Outpatient volunteers	149	Predominantly depressed	Any nonpsychotic depression
Lipman (1982)[d]	Outpatient volunteers	424	Depressive neurosis	Any nonpsychotic depression
Mountjoy & Roth (1982b)	96% inpatient, 4% outpatient	43	Depressive neurosis, excluded endogenous depression	Primarily major depression without melancholia
Prusoff & Klerman (1974)[e]	Neurotic outpatients	364	Score of 7+ on Raskin Depression, excluded secondary depression	Any nonpsychotic depression
Roth et al. (1972)	Inpatient	62	Depressive illness, with pessimism and loss of energy and enthusiasm	Primarily major depression with and without melancholia
Torgersen (1985)	Inpatients and outpatients	74	Depressive neurosis	Any nonpsychotic depression

[a] Raters were clinicians unless otherwise noted.
[b] GAD, generalized anxiety disorder.
[c] Raters were trained lay interviewers.
[d] Both clinican and self-ratings were obtained.
[e] Self-ratings only.

disturbance was secondary to another disorder). Roth et al. included both endogenous and reactive depressives (Kerr, Schapira, Roth, & Garside, 1970), whereas Mountjoy and Roth explicitly excluded patients with endogenous or psychotic features.

Torgersen (1985) reported on a subset of 299 pairs of same-sexed twins, at least one of whom was seen as either an inpatient or outpatient and had received a research diagnosis of either anxiety neurosis or neurotic depression. At least two out of three independent judges initially agreed on the diagnosis of 94% of the anxiety neurotics and 87% of the depressives. The diagnosis of the remaining subjects was agreed upon after discussion. All subjects were interviewed with the Present State Examination (PSE; Wing, Cooper, & Sartorius, 1974) for lifetime symptoms. Unfortunately, Torgersen did not report on the full list of symptoms from the PSE, but presented only those symptoms that most discriminated the two groups. Thus, no disconfirming evidence is available, except for his one comment that both groups were high in depressed mood.

The final sample to be included (Clark et al., 1987a) is from a larger study of the heritability of psychiatric features and disorders. Subjects were twins admitted as psychiatric inpatients into the Washington University Medical Center and their cotwins, who by July, 1984, had both completed a battery of self-report inventories and been interviewed with the DIS (n = 150). Using both the DIS and other information, a team of clinical researchers diagnosed 69 of these patients as having an anxiety disorder (n = 17), a depressive disorder (n = 32), or both (n = 20); subjects with primary schizophrenia, alcoholism, or bipolar disorder were excluded.

Turning to the studies that used self-ratings, Lipman (1982) studied symptomatic volunteers who were recruited for a large-scale drug study comparing the efficacy of antianxiety and antidepressant medication. Subjects completed an 80-item Symptom Check List [SCL, originally developed by Prusoff, Kelman, and Frank (1954)] in which the patients rate the severity of each symptom on a 4-point scale. Lipman also did not report on the full list of symptoms, presenting only the most discriminating items for each group. The subjects used by Prusoff and Klerman (1974) were a heterogeneous group of "neurotic outpatients"; patients with primary psychosis, alcoholism, sociopathy, or organic impairment were excluded. Patients rated themselves on a 58-item version of the SCL used in the Lipman study (Derogatis, Lipman, Rickels, Uhlenhuth, & Covi, 1974).

2. Symptom Comparisons

In comparing patients diagnosed as having anxious or depressive disorders based on specific symptoms, it is useful to divide the symptoms into those that are diagnostic of (unique to) either the anxiety or depressive disorders, and those that are common to both types of disorders. The latter, of course, should not be expected to differentiate the two groups, whereas the former might be expected to show different rates of prevalence in patients with anxious versus depressive disorders. It is important to note that "differentiation" in these studies depends only on the rather weak test of a significant group difference in the prevalence of a given symptom, and says nothing about the absolute level of symptom reporting in either group. Thus, both common and rare symptoms may be noted as "significant" if a *relative* difference appeared. Unfortunately, studies comparing the frequency of symptom reporting are few and are too varied in methodology and population studied to investigate or compare adequately the absolute prevalence levels of symptoms.

Table 4.2 presents data comparing anxious and depressed patient groups on various symptoms of the anxiety disorders, Table 4.3 does the same for depressive symptoms, while Table 4.4 shows those symptoms that appear in both types of disorders. Some symptoms diagnostic of an anxiety or depressive disorder (e.g., dry mouth, easily startled/edgy, distinct quality of depressed mood, and depression worse in the morning) do not appear in the tables because they were not reported in any study. Because a variety of rating forms or checklists were used, it was not always possible to compare only identically worded symptoms across studies, and a moderate level of inference was often required. For example, one study might refer to loss of enjoyment, another to loss of pleasure, and yet a third to loss of interest. Such similar items are listed as one symptom in the tables. However, if a symptom was unique to a particular study, and could not be combined with other similar items, it is reported individually, even if used in only a single study. Thus, the tables represent a compromise between grouping conceptually similar symptoms for ease of presentation and interpretation, and respecting the complexity of the original item data.

Looking first at the "Clinical" columns of Table 4.2, one can see that the only symptoms consistently differentiating patient groups across studies are panic attacks, agoraphobic avoidance, and autonomic symptoms in general. When autonomic symptoms are examined individually, the data are sparse and no clear pattern emerges; only dizziness was found to be significant in more than one study. Other symptoms characteristic of anxiety disorders yielded more mixed results, or else were rated in only one study.

Similarly, in the self-ratings, no strong differentiation appears. In fact, Prusoff and Klerman's depressed patients rated themselves higher on several symptoms of anxiety. Moreover, Lipman notes that, except for the few exceptions shown in the table, his depressed patients rated

Table 4.2
Comparisons of Symptom Prevalence, by Type of Rating, on Criteria Unique to the Anxiety Disorders in Patients with Depressive versus Anxiety Disorders[a]

		Significant		NS	
Diagnosis	**Symptom**	**Clinical**	**Self**	**Clinical**	**Self**
Nonspecific	Anxious, tense	R, T	—	D, C	P[b]
	Autonomic symptoms, general	M, R, T	—	—	—
	Shortness of breath, choking	—	L	C	P
	Dizziness	R, C	—	—	P
	Heart racing	C	L, P	—	—
	Sweating	—	—	C	P[b]
	Nausea	—	—	—	P
	Abdominal upset	—	—	—	P[b]
	Hot/cold	—	L	C	P
Panic disorder	Panic attacks	C, M, R, T	L	—	P[b]
	Trembling, shaking	C	—	—	P
	Tingling	—	L	C	P
	Chest pain	C	P	—	—
	Derealization	R	—	C, M	—
	Fear of dying	—	—	C	—
Agoraphobia	Fear and avoidance of being in places[c]	M, R, T	L	—	P[b]
GAD[d]	Muscle tension or aches	T	—	—	P
	Trouble swallowing, lump in throat	—	L	—	P
	Irritability	—	—	D	P

[a] Studies included are those that found significant or nonsignificant (NS) differences in the frequency of symptom reporting between patients diagnosed as having depressive versus anxiety disorders. Key to studies: C, Clark et al. (1987a); D, Downing & Rickels (1974); L, Lipman (1982); M, Mountjoy & Roth (1982b); P, Prusoff & Klerman (1974); R, Roth et al. (1972); T, Torgersen (1985).
[b] Depressed patients rated themselves as signficantly higher.
[c] Places or situations from which escape might be difficult or in which help might not be available in the event of a panic attack.
[d] Generalized anxiety disorder.

themselves as higher than his anxiety patients on all 80 symptoms, including many symptoms of anxiety disorders. (They are not shown in the table because, as mentioned, he did not report significance levels for all symptoms.)

Apparently, patients with depressive disorders often experience and report that they have many symptoms considered diagnostic of anxiety disorders, including both of the general symptom classes of psychic and somatic anxiety. If the symptoms of anxiety disorders can meaningfully differentiate them from depression, it is probably not at the atomistic level of the individual symptom. Rather, it is more likely to be at a higher order or configural level, such as that defined by "panic attacks," which requires a co-occurring complex of psychological and physiological symptoms. These data also support the assumption of DSM-III that one cannot specify exactly which of a dozen autonomic symptoms will occur in anxiety/panic attacks; rather, it is the presence of any combination of a number of symptoms that is diagnostic of an anxiety disorder.

Turning to the symptoms of depressive disorders (Table 4.3), a somewhat more discriminant picture emerges. Depressed mood, loss of interest/pleasure, suicidal behavior, psychomotor retardation, early-morning wakening, and pessimism all differentiated the groups in at least two of three studies, and reasonable explanations for the nonconsistent findings are available in four cases. In the case of early-morning wakening and loss of interest/pleasure, it is possible that the explicit exclusion of endogenous patients from the Mountjoy and Roth sample was a factor in finding a nonsignificant difference. As for the lack of differentiation in depressed mood in Torgersen's data, recall that lifetime symptoms were assessed. It is likely that the anxious patients experienced significant depression during some periods in their lives, resulting in a nonsignificance difference overall. This is similar to the report of Roth et al. that "persistent depression" was seen more frequently in their depressed group, but that "episodic depression" was not. Furthermore, "depression worse than anxiety" *did* significantly differentiate between Torgersen's two groups. As noted before, the relative level of the two moods may be more discriminative than the absolute level.

Suicidal behavior was higher in the depressed patients of Clark et al. (41 vs. 24%), but the difference failed to reach significance. Finally, the reasons why single studies failed to find significant differences for psychomotor retardation and pessimism are not clear, but, in general, it appears that the symptoms most successful in discriminating the two types of disorders are either directly related to the mood disturbance (e.g., loss of interest) or are associated with more severe depression (e.g., suicidal behavior). Conversely, several items commonly consid-

Table 4.3
Comparisons of Symptom Prevalence, by Type of Rating, on Criteria Unique to the Depressive Disorders in Patients with Depressive versus Anxiety Disorders[a]

Diagnosis	Symptom	Significant		NS	
		Clinical	Self	Clinical	Self
Nonspecific	Depressed mood	C, D, M	L, P	T	—
	Loss of interest/pleasure[b]	C, T	L, P	M	—
	Loss of sexual interest	—	L, P	C, M	—
	Loss of appetite/weight loss	—	L, P	C, D, M	—
	Overeating/weight gain	—	—	C	—
	Increased sleep	—	—	C	—
	Suicidal gestures/behavior	R, M, T	—	C	—
	Suicidal ideation	M	L, P	C, R	—
Major depression	Psychomotor retardation	R, T	—	C	—
	Feelings of worthlessness or guilt	T	L, P	C, R	—
Melancholia	Early morning awakening	R, T	—	M	—
Dysthymia	Pessimism, brooding, self-pity	C, M, T	L, P	R	—

[a] Studies included are those that found significant or nonsignificant (NS) differences in the frequency of symptom reporting between patients diagnosed as having depressive versus anxiety disorders. Key to studies: C, Clark et al. (1987a); D, Downing & Rickels (1974); L, Lipman (1982); M, Mountjoy & Roth (1982b); P, Prusoff & Klerman (1974); R, Roth et al. (1972); T, Torgersen (1985).
[b] This symptom was "judged to have predominated" in the depressed patients of Roth et al., but its frequency was not reported in the anxiety patients for comparison.

ered symptomatic of depression are not good discriminators (loss of appetite and sexual interest) or give inconsistent results (suicidal ideation, feelings of worthlessness or guilt). As for the self-report data, they are strikingly clear. Depressed patients rate themselves as more disturbed on a wide variety of depressive symptoms.

Finally, the clinicians' data in Table 4.4 strongly confirm that symptoms shared across anxiety and depressive disorders do not generally differentiate between them when rated by clinicians. However, in the self-report data, it is interesting to note that depressed patients rate themselves higher than anxious patients on several of these symptoms. From this one might conclude that the nonreporting of these symptoms may suggest the presence of an anxiety rather than a depressive disorder, if the decision is between the two. This hypothesis deserves further research.

There is an extensive literature regarding the endogenous (also called *melancholic, psychotic,* or *endogenomorphic*) versus neurotic (*reactive, secondary*) distinction in depression (e.g., Fowles & Gersh, 1982; Kendell, 1977; Mendels & Cochrane, 1968), but there is a notable lack of data investigating this distinction in relation to the anxiety disorders. The data presented here indicate that such research could yield important information about the extensive "neurotic" border region between anxiety and depression. That is, symptoms less related to the "core" of depression or anxiety are perhaps those most likely to be seen in both neurotic depression and in anxiety (especially GAD), whereas symptoms specifically diagnostic of endogenous depression or panic/agoraphobia are also those most likely to differentiate the depressive from anxiety disorders. These data are quite congruent with the factor analytic results described earlier in which a general neurotic factor with symptoms of both anxiety and depression was often identified, but when separate or bipolar factors emerged they had characteristics of endogenous depression and/or panic/agoraphobia.

Given the degree of inconsistency both between and within the clinician- and self-rated studies, consideration of alternative explanations to the findings is warranted. In the two self-report studies, the depressed patients generally rated themselves as more symptomatic than did the anxious patients, and this was reflected in their ratings of some anxiety symptoms as well as those of depression. In contrast, in the Roth et al. and Mountjoy and Roth studies, more of the significant findings involved greater anxiety reported by anxiety neurotics, with the depressive symptoms fairly equally divided between significant and nonsignificant results. Thus, it is possible that the relative severity of illness of the two groups of patients compared in each study was the most salient factor in determining the results—that is, the depressed

Table 4.4
Comparisons of Symptom Prevalence, by Type of Rating, on Criteria Common to the Depressive and Anxiety Disorders in Patients with Depressive versus Anxiety Disorders[a]

	D > A[b]		A > D[c]		NS[d]	
Symptom	Clinical	Self	Clinical	Self	Clinical	Self
Restlessness, agitation	—	—	—	—	C, M, R	—
Fatigability, loss of energy	—	P	—	—	C, M	—
Difficulty concentrating	—	L, P	—	—	C, M, R	—
Insomnia	T	L, P	—	—	C, D, M, R	—

[a] Key to studies: C, Clark et al. (1987a); D, Downing & Rickels (1974); M, Mountjoy & Roth (1982b); P, Prusoff & Klerman (1974); R, Roth et al. (1972); T, Torgersen (1985).
[b] Studies in which depressed patients showed this symptom more frequently.
[c] Studies in which anxious patients showed this symptom more frequently.
[d] Studies in which no significant (NS) difference in symptom frequency was found between patients with depressive versus anxiety disorders.

patients in the two self-report studies were perhaps more severely ill than the anxiety patients, and vice versa for the two clinician-rated studies. However, we can reasonably eliminate a severity explanation for the Lipman study, because he reports clinicians' ratings for the two groups, and they are quite comparable. Because both the self-report studies used very similar methodologies—large samples of patients volunteering for drug research and exclusion of patients who did not meet similar severity criteria for their respective disorders—it is also reasonable to assume that there was no actual difference between the Prusoff and Klerman groups either. This suggests that rather than actual differences in severity, there may be a systematic bias in the self-report of anxious versus depressed patients, such that depressed patients experience their illness as more severe and as encompassing a wider range of symptomatology than do patients with anxiety of equal severity. This hypothesis deserves further research.

Turning to the patients of Mountjoy and Roth, there was no difference in the duration of illness, nor did the Mausley Personality Inventory contribute to a discriminant function of the two groups (Mountjoy & Roth, 1982a). Relatively more of the depressed patients were inpatients, but, given the results of the study, this fact runs counter to the severity hypothesis. A severity explanation can therefore reasonably be excluded for this sample also. In contrast, other data on the Roth et al. patients, including a follow-up study, show their anxious patients to be more severely ill both in terms of premorbid personality and prognosis (Gurney, Roth, Garside, Kerr, & Shapira, 1972), so a severity explanation cannot be excluded in this case. Thus, while it is not likely to be a strong or consistent factor, severity as a potential confound should be examined in future research comparing anxious with depressed patients.

C. Diagnostic Overlap

We have seen that anxiety and depression are moderately related at the mood, symptom, and syndromal levels. We have also seen that it is most difficult to distinguish "neurotic" depression from anxiety across these levels, and that the symptom picture presented by patients with these disorders resembles that of persons high in the personality trait negative affectivity (Watson & Clark, 1984) or neuroticism/emotionality (Eysenck & Eysenck, 1968, 1975). Finally, we have seen that the greatest differentiation is obtained when endogenous depression/melancholia is contrasted with panic disorder/agoraphobia. Ideally, we would now proceed to demonstrate the independence of these two or even three disorders through epidemiological, clinical, and family studies, pharmacological and other biological studies, and so on. Unfortunately, when we turn to these data, we find that the clarity we sensed to be glimmering in the distance was but a mirage, and that we remain in the real world of fuzzy boundaries.

1. Epidemiological Studies

Two large epidemiological studies present data relevant to the overlap between depressive and anxiety disorders (Boyd et al., 1984; Murphy, Sobol, Olivier, & Leighton, 1984). In the Murphy et al. study, five diagnoses (severe and moderate depression, severe and moderate anxiety, and a mild mixed affective disorder) were recorded and organized hierarchically, so it is not possible to examine the diagnostic overlap completely. However, the authors note that "most of the episodes diagnosed as depression also involved anxiety (72% in 1952 and 75% in 1970)" (p. 994).

Boyd et al. (1984) examined the co-occurence of various DSM-III diagnoses without regard to existing hierarchical rules. They argue that the rationale for these exclusion criteria has not been clearly set forth, and there is little empirical research investigating their use. Using the entire Epidemiological Catchment Area data set (ECA; Regier et al., 1984), they report "odds ratios" for the coexistence of a number of anxiety disorders with major depression: Having major depression increased the odds of having panic disorder by 19, agoraphobia by 15, simple phobia by 9, and obsessive–compulsive disorder by 11. For comparison's sake, it must be noted that having major depression also increased the odds of having schizophrenia by 29, and, more generally, that the presence of any disorder increased the odds of having almost any other disorder. Thus, the mere fact of overlap cannot address the question of the validity of exclusion criteria. More important will be longitudinal studies of co-occurrence, risk factors, genetics, and treatment outcome.

2. Clinical Studies

A number of studies have examined the overlap between the anxiety and depressive diagnoses in clinical samples. These are summarized in Tables 4.5 and 4.6 (the epidemiological data discussed above are also included). Although there is inevitable sample variation, the data are quite orderly. Table 4.5 shows a progression from a high degree of depression in patients with agoraphobia or panic disorder to a lower percentage of depression in those with GAD or simple/social phobias. Moreover, the overall weighted mean for heterogeneous groups of anxious patients is the same as the mean across all the other studies (53 vs. 56%), suggesting that if the mixed groups were broken down into more homogeneous subtypes, differing rates of depression would emerge.

Table 4.5
The Co-occurrence of Anxiety with Various Depressive Disorders

Study	Presenting diagnosis	*n*	Diagnostic criteria	Percentage overlap
Bowen & Kohout (1979)	Agoraphobia	55	Feighner	91% major depression
Harris et al. (1983)	Agoraphobia	20	DSM-III	60% secondary depression
Munjack & Moss (1981)	Agoraphobia	59	Study/RDC[a]	41% major depression
Sheehan & Sheehan (1982)	Panic/agoraphobia	100	DSM-III	92% dysthymia
Cloninger et al. (1981)	Panic/agoraphobia	32	Feighner	69% any depression
Breier et al. (1984)	Panic/agoraphobia	60	RDC	68% major depression
Gardos (1981)	Panic/agoraphobia	23	RDC[b]	52% any depression
Raskin et al. (1982)	Panic disorder	17	DSM-III	88% major depression
Boyd et al. (1984)	Panic disorder	67	DIS	45% major depression
Dealy et al. (1981)	Panic attacks[c]	38	DSM-III	53% major depression
Pariser et al. (1979)	Panic attacks	17	RDC	59% major depression
Weighted mean for panic/agoraphobia		488	—	67% depression
Clancy et al. (1978)	Anxiety neurosis[c]	112	Study	44% secondary depression
Woodruff et al. (1972)	Anxiety neurosis[c]	62	Study	50% secondary depression
Cloninger et al. (1981)	Any anxiety disorder	66	Feighner	70% any depression
Weissman et al. (1984)[d]	Any anxiety disorder	13	DSM-III	62% major depression
Clark et al. (1987a)	Any anxiety disorder	37	DSM-III	49% major depression
Gardos (1981)	Any anxiety disorder[e]	14	RDC[b]	64% any depression
Weighted mean for mixed anxiety disorders		304	—	53% depression
Breslau & Davis (1985)	GAD[f]: DSM-III-R	30	DIS	73% major depression
Cloninger et al. (1981)	GAD[g]	10	Feighner	60% any depression
Breslau (1985)	GAD: DSM-III	20	DIS	40% major depression
Raskin et al. (1982)	GAD	16	DSM-III	44% major depression

(*continued*)

Table 4.5 (*Continued*)

Study	Presenting diagnosis	*n*	Diagnostic criteria	Percentage overlap
Breslau & Davis (1985)	GAD: DSM-III	129	DIS	35% major depression
Dealy et al. (1981)	GAD	55	DSM-III	20% major depression
Weighted mean across DSM-III GAD		260	—	38% major depression
Munjack & Moss (1981)	Social/other phobias[h]	34	Study/RDC[a]	29% major depression

[a] Study criteria were used for the anxiety disorders; RDC criteria were used for depression.
[b] Restrospective chart review.
[c] Includes generalized anxiety disorder and panic disorder.
[d] Studied children.
[e] Excluding panic and agoraphobia.
[f] Generalized anxiety disorder.
[g] Anxiety neurosis without panic attacks.
[h] Included some subjects with panic attacks.

Several of the studies presented in this table applied hierarchical criteria in their selection of patients; that is, patients with primary depression were excluded even if they met the criteria for an anxiety disorder. However, Breier et al. (1984) reported that for approximately half of their patients with both types of disorder, at least one depressive episode occurred before the onset of the anxiety disorder. Thus, the data in the table are likely to underestimate the simple overlap between the two types of disorders, and to overestimate their co-occurrence if exclusion criteria were uniformly applied. As mentioned above, other data are needed to resolve the question of whether diagnoses ought to be arranged hierarchically.

One factor influencing the amount of depression seen in patients with anxiety disorders may be the severity of illness. For example, the panic/agoraphobic group is further divisible into patients with agoraphobia, who may be more severely disturbed, and those without, that is, with simple panic disorder or panic attacks; this subdivision results in rates of depression of 72 and 54%, respectively. Similarly, there is a sharp increase in the percentage of patients with depression when the more restrictive DSM-III-R criteria are used to diagnose GAD, with the new criteria selecting a more severely disordered sample. It remains an empirical question, therefore, whether the rate of co-occurrence of depression is a function of the type of anxiety disorder or its severity. These two parameters are, of course, not completely independent.

Similarly, the anxiety disorders are found with varying frequency in depressed patients (Table 4.6). Agoraphobia is the least prevalent, with panic, phobias, and GAD being progressively more common. As would be expected, when these are combined so that patients with any anxiety disorder are considered, the frequency of co-occurrence is the highest. This progression may be explained in part by reference to the base rates of the various anxiety disorders. The ECA studies (Robins et al., 1984) found a lifetime prevalence rate of 6% for agoraphobia (with or without panic attacks), 12% for all other phobias, and 1.4% for panic disorder (without agoraphobia). Other estimates of the lifetime prevalence for panic disorder range from 2 to 5% (Crowe, Noyes, Pauls, & Slymen, 1983; Crowe, Pauls, Slymen, & Noyes, 1980; Marks & Lader, 1973). GAD was not investigated in the ECA studies, but Breslau (1985) found the extremely high lifetime prevalence rate of 56%. Breslau and Davis (1985) also report a lifetime prevalence rate of 45% for GAD, but note that when DSM-III-R criteria are used, this rate drops to a more plausible 9%. Although these base rates do not perfectly parallel the overlap data, they do suggest that the more common anxiety disorders (phobias and GAD) will, not surprisingly, be found with greater frequency than the less common ones (agoraphobia and panic) in patients with depression.

Table 4.6
The Co-occurrence of Depression with Various Anxiety Disorders

Study	Presenting diagnosis	*n*	Diagnostic criteria	Percentage overlap
Schapira et al. (1970)	Depressive states	45	Study	22% agoraphobia
Leckman et al. (1983b)	Major depression	133	RDC	8% agoraphobia[a]
Weighted mean for agoraphobia		178	—	12%
Price et al. (1987)	Major depression	71	RDC	39% panic disorder
Leckman et al. (1983b)	Major depression	133	RDC	17% panic disorder[b]
Boyd et al. (1984)	Major depression	266	DIS	11% panic disorder
Cassidy et al. (1957)	MDI[c]	100	Study	33% anxiety attacks
Fawcett & Kratvitz (1983)	Major depression	200	RDC	29% panic attacks
Weighted means for panic disorder/attacks		770	—	22%

Schapira et al. (1970)	Depressive states	45	Study	31% mixed phobias[d]
Breslau (1985)	Major depression	16	DIS	50% GAD[e]
Leckman et al. (1983b)	Major depression	133	RDC	34% GAD
Weighted mean for GAD		149	—	36%
Murphy et al. (1984)	Depression	114	DPAX[f]	74% anxiety
Leckman et al. (1983a)[g]	Major depression	133	RDC	61% any anxiety
Weissman et al. (1984)[h]	Major depression	17	DSM-III	47% any anxiety disorder
Clark et al. (1987a)	Any depression	52	DSM-III	38% any anxiety disorder
Gardos (1981)	Any depression	20	RDC[i]	0% any anxiety disorder
Weighted means for any anxiety disorder		336	—	57%[j]

[a] Includes cases with additional panic disorder and generalized anxiety disorder.
[b] Includes cases with additional generalized anxiety disorder.
[c] Manic depressive Illness.
[d] Social, animal, and other phobias.
[e] Generalized anxiety disorder.
[f] Computer scoring of structured interview based on RDC and DSM-III.
[g] The same patients as Leckman et al. (1983b).
[h] Studied children.
[i] Retrospective chart review.
[j] Excluding Gardos (1981), 61%.

Schapira, Kerr, and Roth (1970) report the percentage of patients for whom the anxiety disorder preceded the onset of the depression. In one-half the patients with agoraphobia (11% of the total) the anxiety was primary, whereas the anxiety disorder preceded the depression in nearly three-fourths of those with specific phobias (23% of the total). Thus, even if one applies the DSM-III exclusion criteria and considers those patients with "secondary" anxiety not to have an anxiety disorder (because it is "due to" the depression), a sizable minority still meet the criteria for both types of disorders. (Note that the exclusion criteria for anxiety and depression are unidirectional.) Similarly, Leckman, Merikangas, Pauls, Prusoff, and Weissman (1983a) further subdivided their patients with both types of disorders into those whose anxiety always co-occurred with their depression (38% of the total) and those for whom at least some of the episodes were temporally separate (23% of the total). Again we see that many of the co-occurring anxiety disorders cannot be explained as "due to" the depression. More importantly, the rates of both depression and anxiety were elevated in the relatives of patients with both types of disorders, regardless of when the anxiety occurred. These data anticipate the family data discussed in the next section.

Longitudinal follow-up studies provide another type of information that bears on the question of the relation between the anxiety and depressive disorders. From 5 to 10 years after original contact, Cloninger, Martin, Clayton, and Guze (1981) reinterviewed 95% of 500 outpatients. The concordance between specific index and follow-up diagnoses for 66 patients who received a final follow-up diagnosis of an anxiety disorder was unimpressive (agreement ranged from 30 to 53%). However, the concordance for the simpler decision of whether or not a subject had significant anxiety symptoms was quite high, ranging from 80 to 92%. This is noteworthy because much of the unreliability was due to instability in whether the primary diagnosis was thought to be a depressive or an anxiety disorder. Thus, if hierarchical criteria were ignored, the reliability of diagnosis was considerably higher. In contrast, another follow-up study of 154 patients with anxiety states or depressive illnesses reported little cross-over in diagnosis despite a high degree of overlap in symptomatology (Roth et al., 1972; Schapira et al., 1972).

Three studies investigated factors predicting outcome in anxiety and depression, and concluded that significant anxiety symptoms were more strongly associated with poor prognosis than was depressive symptomatology (Coryell, Noyes, & Clancy, 1983; Kerr, Roth, Schapira, & Gurney, 1972; Schapira et al., 1972). The recovery rate for panic disorder was particularly poor—from 9 to 26% depending on length of follow-up (Coryell et al., 1983)—whereas that for mixed anxiety disorders was moderate, ranging from 41 to 59% (Noyes & Clancy, 1976; Schapira et al., 1972), and that for depression was considered good (48 to 75%; Coryell et al., 1983; Schapira et al., 1972). A shorter prior duration of illness was associated with a more positive outcome in all studies; however, there were conflicting results regarding the effects of age and sex. Furthermore, none of these studies considered diagnostic overlap in relation to prognosis.

3. Family and Genetic Studies

A number of family and other genetic studies have been carried out for anxiety and depression at various levels. Because several reviews have been published in recent years (Breier et al., 1985; Carey & Gottesman, 1981; Weissman, 1985), these data will only be summarized here. Although there are as yet unexplained inconsistencies in the literature that render it impossible to calculate precise estimates of heritabilities or to determine mode of transmission, the data are clear in generally supporting a genetic hypothesis for both major depression and for panic disorder/agoraphobia. While there does not appear to be familial transmission of GAD per se (Breier et al., 1985), the data have consistently shown significant heritability for the personality dimension negative affectivity/neuroticism (Carey & Gottesman, 1981; Kendler, Heath, Martin, & Eaves, 1987). This trait represents a very general factor of subjective distress and subsumes a broad range of negative mood states, including both anxiety and depression (Watson & Clark, 1984; Watson, Clark, & Carey, 1988). It may thus provide the link between the two types of disorders, as well as between normal mood and its pathological variants.

Family and genetic studies of the relation between depressive and anxiety disorders provide somewhat less consistent data. A number of studies, especially those which have ignored diagnostic exclusion criteria, have shown a familial relation between panic disorder and major depression (Bowen & Kohout, 1979; Leckman, Weissman, Merikangas, Pauls, & Prusoff, 1983b; Munjack & Moss, 1981; Price, Kidd, & Weissman, 1987; Weissman, Leckman, Merikangas, Gammon, & Prusoff, 1984). Others, which have relied on the family history method (Dealy, Ishiki, Avery, Wilson, & Dunner, 1981) or which have applied hierarchical criteria (Cloninger et al., 1981; Crowe et al., 1980, 1983; Harris, Noyes, Crowe, & Chaudhry, 1983; Noyes, Clancy, Crowe, Hoenk, & Slymen,1978), have not found this relationship. However, in two of these studies (Cloninger et al., 1981; Crowe et al., 1983), sufficient data were presented to recalculate the rate of depression in the relatives of anxious probands so as to include secondary depressive disorders, in which case an increased rate can be found: About 11 and 9%, respectively, of the relatives had depression, compared to 6.5% in the relatives of controls (Crowe et al., 1983). Cloninger et al. did not provide a comparison figure, but 11% is certainly higher than the population base rate (Robins et al., 1984). Thus, the discrepancies can largely be accounted for by differing diagnostic practices, and in general one must conclude that there is a familial relation between panic disorder and major depression. Further genetic studies with twins and adoptees are now needed to clarify this relation.

4. Psychopharmacological Studies

There is a large literature on the efficacy of various pharmacological agents in anxiety and depression, and review of these data is beyond the scope of this chapter. The interested reader is referred elsewhere for recent developments in this area (Breier et al., 1985; Klein, 1981; Tuma & Maser, 1985). Suffice it to say that there is strong evidence for a positive effect of tricyclic antidepressants and monoamine oxidase inhibitors in the treatment of both panic disorder and major depression, although neither of these drug classes is effective in treating GAD. In contrast, classical low-potency benzodiazepines are effective for GAD but not for panic or major depression. On the other hand, there is some evidence that the newer high-potency benzodiazepines are effective for all three disorders, although the data regarding depression must be considered preliminary.

Given the high frequency of depression in panic patients, some researchers have speculated that antidepressants were effective in this population because they alleviated this depression. However, it is becoming increasingly clear that the effectiveness of the antidepressants in treating panic is not simply due to their antidepressant effect, but that they may have an independent antipanic property as well. Thus, while drug studies have again pointed to a relation between panic and depression, they have not yet shed any further light on its precise nature. Furthermore, together with genetic studies, they indicate that GAD may not share the underlying diathesis that has been suggested for panic and major depression, although it may have links with each through the trait of negative affectivity.

5. Anxiety Plus Depression: A Different Animal?

The data presented in Tables 4.2 through 4.4. contrast patients with an anxiety disorder versus those with a depressive disorder, regardless of whether they had both. It is also possible to contrast patients who had both types of disorders with those who had only one type. In our data (Clark et al., 1987a), the depressive diagnosis was considered primary in the majority (70%) of patients with both types of diagnoses; nearly all of these (90%) had a major depression, and over half (55%) received both acute and chronic depressive diagnoses—so-called "double depression" (Keller & Shapiro, 1981). Of those patients for whom the anxiety diagnosis was considered more prominent, half had a major depression, while for the other half the depression was minor. None had a double depression.

Analysis of the frequency of symptom reporting in these three groups (depression only, anxiety only, anxiety and depression) revealed no significant differences among them for symptoms primarily associated with anxiety. Patients with only depression did report more depressive symptoms than those with only anxiety ($x = 8.0$ vs. 5.5), but those with both types of disorders reported an even greater number of depressive symptoms ($x = 10.1$). Furthermore, an interesting pattern of symptom reporting was found for certain depressive symptoms in these three groups of patients. Primary diagnosis per se did not affect the frequency of reporting these symptoms, but patients who had both an anxiety and a depressive diagnosis showed a significantly increased tendency to report them, compared to those who had only one type of disorder. In the case of one symptom (depressed mood), the increase of frequency was simply additive and paralleled the findings for the number of depressive symptoms: Depression-only patients more frequently reported depressed mood than did purely anxious patients (84 vs. 53%), while those with both types of disorders had the highest prevalence of depressive affect (95%). For these additive phenomena, the increased prevalence in patients with both types of disorders may be explained in terms of severity. That is, those who have an anxiety disorder in addition to a depressive disorder are generally those who are more severely ill. Thus, they are more likely to report depressed mood and experience more depressive symptoms in general.

For a number of other symptoms, however, there was a synergistic relation, such that having both disorders markedly increased the likelihood of showing a symptom over having either disorder alone (see Table 4.7). More specifically, in the depression-only or anxiety-only patients these symptoms were relatively infrequently reported (median, 25%; range, 0–53%), whereas when both disorders were present they were generally prevalent (median, 60%; range, 20–80%).

For these synergistic symptoms, a severity explanation seems inadequate. There is an emergent quality in the symptom cluster that is reminiscent of the "distinct quality" of the depressed mood in melancholia, like "being in a dark cage" (Hamilton, 1982, p. 4), although one symptom (increased sleep) is usually associated with atypical depression. These data thus suggest intriguing possibilities regarding the interactive

Table 4.7
Symptoms More Frequently Reported by Patients with Both Anxiety and Depression[a]

	Patients reporting the symptom (%)		
Symptom	**Anxiety only (n = 17)**	**Anxiety and depression (n = 20)**	**Depression only (n = 32)**
Fear of dying	6	25	0
Decreased libido	24	60	25
Increased sleep	12	55	25
Tired all the time	41	80	53
Poor concentration	47	75	34
Thoughts slowed	35	70	19
Checking compulsions	0	20	3

[a] Based on Clark et al. (1987a). $p < .025$ (corrected by Bonferroni for multiple comparisons).

nature of anxiety and depression, but they must be considered preliminary and require replication.

One other study has compared symptom frequency (as well as a number of other types of data) in groups of patients with pure panic or depression versus those with both disorders, who were further subdivided into those with primary panic versus primary depression (VanValkenburg, Akiskal, Puzantian, & Rosenthal, 1984). Chronic depression, agitation, and poor psychosocial outcome were more common in both mixed groups than in either pure group, while guilt feelings, delusions, amphetamine abuse, and a family history of alcoholism were more frequently seen in patients with depression plus secondary panic attacks. Predictable main effects were also found for depression (e.g., loss of interest, suicidal behavior) and, to a lesser extent, anxiety (e.g., hypochondriacal).

A number of studies of depressive subtypes have reported an anxious depression group, while others have investigated anxious patients with and without secondary depression. Diverse evidence suggests that these patients are more severely disordered, show a more chronic course, and are less responsive to treatment than those who manifest only anxious or depressive symptoms (for reviews, see Gersh & Fowles, 1982; VanValkenburg et al., 1984). Thus, the diagnosis of mixed anxiety–depression or anxious depression might be fruitfully added to the nosology. As Akiskal (1985) has speculated, "it is likely that anxiety and depression coexist in a subtype of nonretarded affective disorder which is qualitatively different from retarded (typically endogenous and often bipolar) conditions" (p. 793).

On the other hand, two studies present data suggesting that endogenous depression is frequently accompanied by anxiety. Recall that Breier et al. (1984) found 68% of their panic/agoraphobic subjects to meet RDC criteria for definite (lifetime) major depression. In about half of these patients, the first episode of depression preceded the anxiety, whereas one-third experienced only secondary depression and the remainder had both primary and secondary episodes. About 80% of these met RDC criteria for endogenous depression, with no difference in rate between those with primary versus secondary depression. The patients with a current or previous history of depression were more severely disordered on a number of measures compared to those without such a history, but again there were no differences based on when they experienced their depression. Fawcett and Kravitz (1983) investigated the incidence of anxiety (psychic and somatic anxiety, worry, phobic symptoms, and panic attacks) in patients with RDC major depression, both endogenous and nonendogenous. They found a much higher incidence of anxiety of all types in the subgroup with endogenous depression, and speculated that the endogenous subtype is not simply a more severe form of depressive illness, but may represent "an affective syndrome with more biological features or etiologic factors" (p. 10).

At this stage, therefore, we can only conclude that there appears to be both a quantitative and a qualitative interaction between anxiety and depression, such that the presence of one increases vulnerability to the other and also affects the way in which the depression is manifest. The precise nature of this interaction, however, remains unclear.

III. Summary and Conclusions

At every level from mood state to diagnostic entity, substantial overlap exists between anxiety and depression. The data presented are summarized as follows:

1. Mood and syndrome rating scales generally correlate from .40 to .50, although values as high as .89 and as low as −.25 have been reported.
2. Factor analytic studies of a broad range of symptoms frequently find a general anxious–depressed factor.
3. When syndrome ratings are made blind to diagnosis, patients with each type of disorder tend to be rated as having equal levels of the two syndromes.
4. Even when syndrome ratings are made as part of the diagnostic process, patients with anxiety or depressive disorders

are frequently rated as showing symptoms of the other syndrome.

5. A number of symptoms are shared by depressive and anxiety diagnoses (e.g., insomnia, loss of energy); moreover, for many symptoms that are unique to one type of diagnosis (e.g., anxious mood, specific autonomic symptoms, loss of appetite, feelings of worthlessness), no prevalence differences are found between anxious and depressed patients.
6. Although exact figures vary with the specific anxiety disorder, approximately half of all patients diagnosed with an anxiety disorder also meet criteria for a depressive disorder, and vice versa, if hierarchical criteria are ignored.
7. Family studies indicate that there is a familial relation between panic disorder and major depression. There is also evidence for the heritability of the personality trait of negative affectivity, a general disposition to experience aversive emotional states, including both anxiety and depression.
8. Pharmacological studies provide strong evidence that certain drug classes are effective in the treatment of both panic disorder and major depression.

Despite the overall consistency of these data in suggesting a strong relation between anxiety and depression, other data indicate that some meaningful distinctions can be made:

1. The typical anxiety–depression correlations in the .40 to .50 range may be viewed as evidence of quasi-independence as well as of overlap—the classic half-full/half-empty glass.
2. Factor analytic studies that have focused specifically on depressive and anxiety symptoms have frequently found separate endogenous depression and panic factors, or a bipolar factor with these syndromes as opposite poles.
3. Patients diagnosed as depressed tend to be rated as more depressed than those diagnosed as anxious (and vice versa). These differences may stem, in part, from clinicians' focusing on the relative rather than absolute level of the two syndromes, but the clinical validity of this "bias" remains an open question.
4. A significant minority of patients show a mixed anxious–depressed pattern, but in the majority of patients one or the other syndrome is clearly dominant.
5. Symptoms that do distinguish patients with depression from those with anxiety are those that describe the core syndromes of panic/agoraphobia (panic attacks, multiple autonomic symp-

toms, and avoidance behavior) or endogenous depression (loss of interest, suicidal behavior, psychomotor retardation, early-morning wakening, and pessimism).
6. Only about one-third of patients with phobias (other than agoraphobia) or GAD (as diagnosed in DSM-III) manifest major depression. Conversely, only 10–20% of the patients with major depression also meet criteria for agoraphobia or panic, although one-third to one-half have DSM-III GAD.
7. A genetic relation between depression and anxiety disorders other than panic has not been established.
8. Drugs that are useful in treating depression (and panic) are not effective in GAD, nor vice versa.

Ironically, in the descriptive rating data, the two syndromes that are most clearly differentiable are panic disorder and endogenous depression, whereas diagnostic, family, and pharmacological studies suggest that the *strongest* relation is between these same two disorders. Taken as a whole, the evidence supports the validity of the diagnostic revisions made in DSM-III-R—particularly the primacy of panic disorder (with agoraphobia as a complication), the more stringent requirements for GAD, and the further specification of melancholia (endogenous depression within major depression). The findings additionally suggest that more attention should be paid to a subgroup of patients who exhibit symptoms of both types of disorders. These patients are more chronically and severely disturbed than their counterparts with purer syndromes, and the quality of their depression appears distinctive as well. It might be fruitful to recognize a "generalized affective disorder"—an area of overlap among GAD, dysthymic disorder, atypical depression, and even certain personality disorders, such as avoidant or self-defeating—that may represent the extreme form of the personality trait negative affectivity/neuroticism. As people high in negative affectivity have also been shown to present with multiple physical complaints (Watson & Pennebaker, in press), such a diagnosis might also encompass patients who do not meet the extensive criteria for somatization disorder but whose clinical picture includes somatic as well as emotional distress. This disorder would be symptomatologically reminiscent of the officially defunct neuroses, but need not carry their theoretical or etiological implications.

References

Akiskal, H. S. (1985). Anxiety: Definition, relationship to depression, and proposal for an integrative model. In A. H. Tuma & J. D. Maser (Eds.), *Anxiety and the anxiety disorders* (pp. 787–797). Hillsdale, NJ: Erlbaum.

American Psychiatric Association. (1980). *Diagnostic and statistical manual of mental disorders* (3rd ed.). Washington, DC: Author.
American Psychiatric Association. (1987). *Diagnostic and statistical manual of mental disorders* (3rd ed., rev.). Washington, DC: Author.
Beck, A. T., Ward, C. H., Mendelson, M., Mock, J. E., & Erbaugh, J. K. (1961). An inventory for measuring depression. *Archives of General Psychiatry, 4,* 561–571.
Beck, A. T., Ward, C. H., Mendelson, M., Mock, J. E., & Erbaugh, J. K. (1962). Reliability of psychiatric diagnosis: 2. A study of consistency of clinical judgments and ratings. *American Journal of Psychiatry, 119,* 351–357.
Bowen, R. C., & Kohout, J. (1979). The relationship between agoraphobia and primary affective disorders. *Canadian Journal of Psychiatry, 24,* 317–322.
Boyd, J. H., Burke, J. D., Gruenberg, E., Holzer, C. E., Rae, D. S., George, L. K., Karno, M., Stoltzman, R., McEvoy, L., & Nestadt, G. (1984). Exclusion criteria of DSM-III. *Archives of General Psychiatry, 41,* 983–989.
Breier, A., Charney, D. S., & Heninger, G. R. (1984). Major depression in patients with agoraphobia and panic disorder. *Archives of General Psychiatry, 41,* 1129–1135.
Breier, A., Charney, D. S., & Heninger, G. R. (1985). The diagnostic validity of anxiety disorders and their relationship to depressive illness. *American Journal of Psychiatry, 142,* 787–797.
Breslau, N. (1985). Depressive symptoms, major depression, and generalized anxiety: A comparison of self-reports on CES-D and results from diagnostic interview. *Psychiatry Research, 15,* 219–229.
Breslau, N., & Davis, G. C. (1985). DSM-III generalized anxiety disorder: An empirical investigation of more stringent criteria. *Psychiatry Research, 15,* 231–238.
Carey, G., & Gottesman, I. I. (1981). Twin and family studies of anxiety, phobic, and obsessive disorders. In D. F. Klein & J. Raskin (Eds.), *Anxiety: New research and changing concept* (pp. 117–136). New York: Raven Press.
Cassidy, W. L., Flanigan, N. B., Spellman, M., & Cohen, M. E. (1957). Clinical observations in manic depressive disease: A quantitative study of one hundred manic depressive patients and fifty medically sick controls. *Journal of the American Medical Association, 164,* 1535–1546.
Cicchetti, D. V., & Prusoff, B. A. (1983). Reliability of depression and associated clinical symptoms. *Archives of General Psychiatry, 40,* 987–990.
Clancy, J., Noyes, R., Hoenk, P. R., & Slymen, D. J. (1978). Secondary depression in anxiety neurosis. *Journal of Nervous and Mental Diseases, 166,* 846–850.
Clark, L. A., & Watson, D. (in press). Theoretical and empirical issues in differentiating anxiety from depression. In J. Becker & A. Kleinman (Eds.), *Advances in mood disorders.* Hillsdale, NJ: Erlbaum.
Clark, L. A., Watson, D., & Carey, G. (1987a). *Discrimination of patients with depressive and/or anxiety disorders through symptom ratings.* Unpublished raw data.
Clark, L. A., Watson, D., & Carey, G. (1987b). *Factors of symptom ratings in patients with depressive and/or anxiety disorders.* Unpublished raw data.
Cloninger, C. R., Martin, R. L., Clayton, P., & Guze, S. B. (1981). A blind follow-up and family study of anxiety neurosis: Preliminary analysis of the St. Louis 500. In D. F. Klein & J. Rabkin (Eds.), *Anxiety: New research and changing concepts* (pp. 137–154). New York: Raven Press.
Cohen, J. (1960). A coefficient of agreement for nominal scales. *Educational Psychological Measurement, 20,* 37–46.
Cooper, J. E., Kendell, R. E., Gurland, B. J., Sharpe, L., Copeland, J. R. M., & Simon, R. (1972). *Psychiatric diagnosis in New York and London.* London: Oxford University Press.
Coryell, W., Endicott, J., Andreasen, N., & Keller, M. (1985). Bipolar I, bipolar II, and non-

bipolar major depression among the relatives of affectively ill probands. *American Journal of Psychiatry, 142,* 817–821.

Coryell, W., Noyes, R., & Clancy, J. (1983). Panic disorder and primary unipolar depression: A comparison of background and outcome. *Journal of Affective Disorders, 5,* 311–317.

Costello, C. G. (1970). Classification and psychopathology. In C. G. Costello (Ed.), *Symptoms of psychopathology* (pp. 1–26). New York: Wiley.

Crowe, R. R., Noyes, R., Pauls, D. L., & Slymen, D. J. (1983). A family study of panic disorder. *Archives of General Psychiatry, 40,* 1065–1069.

Crowe, R. R., Pauls, D. L., Slymen, D. J., & Noyes, R. (1980). A family study of anxiety neurosis: Morbidity in families of patients with and without mitral valve prolapse. *Archives of General Psychiatry, 37,* 77–79.

Dealy, R. S., Ishiki, D. M., Avery, D. H., Wilson, L. G., & Dunner, D. L. (1981). Secondary depression in anxiety disorders. *Comprehensive Psychiatry, 22,* 612–618.

Deluty, B. M., Deluty, R. H., & Carver, C. S. (1986). Concordance between clinicians' and patients' ratings of anxiety and depression as mediated by private self-consciosness. *Journal of Personality Assessment, 50,* 93–106.

Derogatis, L. R., Klerman, G. L., & Lipman, R. S. (1972). Anxiety states and depressive neurosis. *Journal of Nervous and Mental Disease, 155,* 392–403.

Derogatis, L. R., Lipman, R. S., Rickels, K., Uhlenhuth, E. H., & Covi, L. (1974). The Hopkins Symptom Checklist (HSCL): A self-report symptom inventory. *Behavioral Science, 19,* 1–15.

Derogatis, L. R., Lipman, R. S., Covi, L., Rickels, K., & Uhlenhuth, E. H. (1970). Dimensions of outpatient neurotic pathology: Comparison of a clinical versus an empirical assessment. *Journal of Consulting and Clinical Psychology, 34,* 164–171.

DiNardo, P. A., O'Brien, G. T., Barlow, D. H., Waddell, M. T., & Blanchard, E. B. (1983). Reliability of DSM-III anxiety disorders categories using a new structured interview. *Archives of General Psychiatry, 40,* 1070–1074.

Downing, R. W., & Rickels, K. (1974). Mixed anxiety-depression: Fact or myth? *Archives of General Psychiatry, 30,* 312–317.

Downing, R. W., Rickels, K., McNair, D. M., Lipman, R. S., Kahn, R. J., Fisher, S., Covi, L., & Smith, V. K. (1981). Description of sample, comparison of anxious and depressed groups, and attrition rates. *Psychopharmacology Bulletin, 17,* 94–97.

Endicott, J., Cohen, J., Nee, J., Fleiss, J. L., & Sarantakos, S. (1981). Hamilton Depression Rating Scale: Extracted from regular and change versions of the Schedule for Affective Disorders and Schizophrenia. *Archives of General Psychiatry, 38,* 98–103.

Endicott, J., & Spitzer, R. L. (1978). A diagnostic interview: The Schedule for Affective Disorders and Schizophrenia. *Archives of General Psychiatry, 35,* 837–844.

Eysenck, H., & Eysenck, S. B. G. (1968). *Manual for the Eysenck Personality Inventory.* San Diego: Educational and Industrial Testing Service.

Eysenck, H., & Eysenck, S. B. G. (1975). *Eysenck Personality Questionnaire.* San Diego: Educational and Industrial Testing Service.

Fawcett, J., & Kravitz, H. M. (1983). Anxiety syndromes and their relationship to depressive illness. *Journal of Clinical Psychiatry, 44,* 8–11.

Feighner, J. P., Robins, E., Guze, S. B., Woodruff, R. A., Winokur, G., & Munoz, R. (1972). Diagnostic criteria for use in psychiatric research. *Archives of General Psychiatry, 26,* 57–63.

Fleiss, J. L., Gurland, B. J., & Cooper, J. E. (1971). Some contributions to the measurement of psychopathology. *British Journal of Psychiatry, 119,* 647–656.

Foa, E. B., & Foa, U. G. (1982). Differentiating depression and anxiety: Is it possible? Is it useful? *Psychopharmacology Bulletin, 18,* 62–68.

Foster, S. L., & Cone, J. D. (1986). Design and use of direct observational procedures. In A.

Ciminero, K. Calhoun, & H. Adams (Eds.), *Handbook for behavioral assessment* (pp. 253–324). New York: Wiley.

Fowles, D. C., & Gersh, F. (1982). Neurotic depression: The endogenous-neurotic distinction. In R. A. Depue (Ed.), *The psychobiology of the depressive disorders* (pp. 55–80). New York: Academic Press.

Gardos, G. (1981). Is agoraphobia a psychosomatic form of depression. In D. F. Klein & J. Raskin (Eds.), *Anxiety: New research and changing concepts* (pp. 367–379). New York: Raven Press.

Gersh, F., & Fowles, D. C. (1982). Neurotic depression: The concept of anxious depression. In R. A. Depue (Ed.), *The psychobiology of the depressive disorders* (pp. 81–104). New York: Academic Press.

Gershon, E. S., Hamovit, J., Guroff, J. J., Dibble, E., Leckman, J. F., Sceery, W., Targum, S. D., Nurnberger, J. I., Goldin, L. R., & Bunney, W. E. (1982). A family study of schizoaffective, bipolar I, bipolar II, unipolar, and normal control probands. *Archives of General Psychiatry, 39,* 1157–1167.

Grinker, R. R., & Nunnally, J. C. (1965). The phenomena of depressions. In M. M. Katz, J. O. Cole, & W. E. Barton (Eds.), *The role of methodology and classification in psychiatry and psychopathology* (pp. 249–261). Chevy Chase, MD: US DHEW, NIMH.

Gurney, C., Roth, M., Garside, R. F., Kerr, T. A., Shapira, K. (1972). Studies in the classification of affective disorders: The relationship between anxiety states and depressive illness. *British Journal of Psychiatry, 121,* 162–166.

Hamilton, M. (1959). The assessment of anxiety states by rating. *British Journal of Medical Psychology, 32,* 50–55.

Hamilton, M. (1960). A rating scale for depression. *Journal of Neurology, Neurosurgery and Psychiatry, 23,* 56–62.

Hamilton, M. (1967). Development of a rating scale for primary depressive illness. *British Journal of Social and Clinical Psychology, 6,* 278–296.

Hamilton, M. (1982). Symptoms and assessment of depression. In E. S. Paykel (Ed.), *Handbook of affective disorders* (pp. 3–11). New York: Guilford Press.

Harris, E. L., Noyes, R., Crowe, R. R., & Chaudhry, D. R. (1983). Family study of agoraphobia: Report of a pilot study. *Archives of General Psychiatry, 40,* 1061–1064.

Hedlung, J. L., & Vieweg, B. W. (1979). The Hamilton Rating Scale for Depression: A comprehensive reivew. *Journal of Operational Psychiatry, 10,* 49–165.

Hesselbrock, V., Stabenau, J., Hesselbrock, M., Mirkin, P., & Meyer, R. (1982). A comparison of two interview schedules: The Schedule for Affective Disorders and Schizophrenia-Lifetime and the National Institute of Mental Health Diagnostic Interview Schedule. *Archives of General Psychiatry, 39,* 674–677.

Johnstone, E. C., Owens, D. G. C., Firth, C. D., McPherson, K., Dowie, C., Riley, G., & Gold, A. (1980). Neurotic illness and its response to anxiolytic and antidepressant treatment. *Psychological Medicine, 10,* 321–328.

Keller, M. B., & Shapiro, R. W. (1981). "Double Depression": Superimposition of acute depressive episodes on chronic depressive disorders. *American Journal of Psychiatry, 139,* 438–442.

Kendall, P. C., & Norton-Ford, J. D. (1982). *Clinical psychology: Scientific and professional dimensions.* New York: Wiley.

Kendell, R. E. (1977). The classification of depressions: A review of contemporary confusion. In G. D. Burrows (Ed.), *Handbook of studies on depression* (pp. 3–19). Amsterdam: Elsevier.

Kendler, K. S., Heath, A. C., Martin, N. G., & Eaves, L. J. (1987). Symptoms of anxiety and symptoms of depression. *Archives of General Psychiatry, 44,* 451–457.

Kerr, T. A., Roth, M., Schapira, K., & Gurney, C. (1972). The assessment and prediction of outcome in affective disorders. *British Journal of Psychiatry, 121,* 167–174.

Kerr, T. A., Schapira, K., Roth, M., & Garside, R. F. (1970). The relationship between the Maudsley Personality Inventory and the course of affective disorders. *British Journal of Psychiatry, 116,* 11–19.

Klein, D. (1981). Anxiety reconceptualized. In D. F. Klein & J. Raskin (Eds.), *Anxiety: New research and changing concepts* (pp. 235–266). New York: Raven Press.

Klerman, G. L. (1977). Anxiety and depression. In G. D. Burrows (Ed.), *Handbook of studies on depression* (pp. 49–68). Amsterdam: Elsevier.

Lauterbach, C. G. (1958). The Taylor A Scale and clinical measures of anxiety. *Journal of Consulting Psychology, 22,* 314.

Leckman, J. F., Merikangas, K. R., Pauls, D. L., Prusoff, B. A., & Weissman, M. M. (1983a). Anxiety disorders and depression: Contradictions between family study data and DSM-III conventions. *American Journal of Psychiatry, 140,* 880–882.

Leckman, J. F., Weissman, M. M., Merikangas, K. R., Pauls, D. L., & Prusoff, B. A. (1983b). Panic disorder increases risk of major depression, alcoholism, panic, and phobic disorders in affectively ill families. *Archives of General Psychiatry, 40,* 1055–1060.

Lipman, R. S. (1982). Differentiating anxiety and depression in anxiety disorders: Use of rating scales. *Psychopharmacology Bulletin, 18,* 69–77.

Lipman, R. S., Rickels, K., Covi, L., Derogatis, L. R., & Uhlenhuth, E. H. (1969). Factors of symptom distress. *Archives of General Psychiatry, 21,* 328–338.

Marks, I., & Lader, M. (1973). Anxiety states (anxiety neurosis): A review. *Journal of Nervous and Mental Disease, 156,* 3–18.

Matarazzo, J. D. (1983). The reliability of psychiatric and psychological diagnosis. *Clinical Psychology Review, 3,* 103–145.

Mendels, J., & Cochrane, C. (1968). The nosology of depression: The endogenous-reactive concept. *American Journal of Psychiatry Suppl., 124,* 1–11.

Mountjoy, C. Q., & Roth, M. (1982a). Studies in the relationship between depressive disorders and anxiety states: Part 2. Rating scales. *Journal of Affective Disorders, 4,* 127–147.

Mountjoy, C. Q., & Roth, M. (1982b). Studies in the relationship between depressive disorders and anxiety states: Part 2. Clinical items. *Journal of Affective Disorders, 4,* 149–161.

Mowbray, R. M. (1972). The Hamilton Rating Scale for depression: A factor analysis. *Psychological Medicine, 2,* 272–280.

Munjack, D. J., & Moss, H. B. (1981). Affective disorder and alcoholism in families of agoraphobics. *Archives of General Psychiatry, 38,* 869–871.

Murphy, J. M., Sobol, A. M., Neff, R. K., Olivier, D. C., & Leighton, A. H. (1984). Stability of prevalence: Depression and anxiety disorders. *Archives of General Psychiatry, 41,* 990–997.

Noyes, R., & Clancy, J. (1976). Anxiety neurosis: A 5-year followup. *Journal of Nervous and Mental Disease, 162,* 200–205.

Noyes, R., Clancy, J., Crowe, R. R., Hoenk, P. R., & Slymen, D. J. (1978). The familial prevalence of anxiety neurosis. *Archives of General Psychiatry, 35,* 1057–1059.

Pariser, S. F., Jones, B. A., Pinta, E. R., Young, E. A., & Fontana, M. E. (1979). Panic attacks: Diagnostic evaluation of 17 patients. *American Journal of Psychiatry, 136,* 105–106.

Parloff, M. B., Kelman, H. C., & Frank, J. D. (1954). Comfort, effectiveness and self-awareness as criteria of improvement in psychotherapy, *American Journal of Psychiatry, 3,* 343–351.

Price, R. A., Kidd, K. K., & Weissman, M. M. (1987). Early onset (under age 30 years) and panic disorder as markers for etiologic homogeneity in major depression. *Archives of General Psychiatry, 44,* 434–440.

Prusoff, B. A., & Klerman, G. L. (1974). Differentiating depressed from anxious neurotic outpatients. *Archives of General Psychiatry, 30,* 302–309.

Prusoff, B. A., & Weissman, M. M. (1981). Pharmacologic treatment of anxiety in depressed outpatients. In D. F. Klein & J. G. Rabkin (Eds.), *Anxiety: New research and changing concepts* (pp. 341–354). New York: Raven Press.

Radloff, L. S. (1977). The CES-D scale: A self-report depression scale for research in the general population. *Applied Psychological Measurement, 1,* 385–401.

Raskin, M., Peeke, H. V. S., Dickman, W., & Pinsker, H. (1982). Panic and generalized anxiety disorders: Developmental antecedents and precipitants. *Archives of General Psychiatry, 39,* 687–689.

Regier, D. A., Myers, J. K., Kramer, M., Robins, L. N., Blazer, D. G., Hough, R. L., Eatson, W. W., & Locke, B. Z. (1984). The NIMH Epidemiologic Catchment Area program. *Archives of General Psychiatry, 41,* 934–941.

Riskind, J. H., Beck, A. T., Brown, G., & Steer, R. A. (1987). Taking the measure of anxiety and depression: Validity of the reconstructed Hamilton scales. *Journal of Nervous and Mental Disease, 175,* 474–479.

Robins, L. N., Helzer, J. E., Croughan, J., & Ratcliff, K. S. (1981). National Institute of Mental Health Diagnostic Interview Schedule: Its history, characteristics, and validity. *Archives of General Psychiatry, 38,* 381–389.

Robins, L. N., Helzer, J. E., Weissman, M. M., Orvaschel, H., Gruenberg, E., Burke, J. D., & Regier, D. A. (1984). Lifetime prevalence of specific psychiatric disorders in three sites. *Archives of General Psychiatry, 41,* 949–958.

Roth, M., Gurney, C., Garside, R. F., & Kerr, T. A. (1972). Studies in the classification of affective disorders: Relationship between anxiety states and depressive illnesses—I. *British Journal of Psychiatry, 121,* 147–161.

Roth, M., & Mountjoy, C. Q. (1982). The distinction between anxiety states and depressive disorders. In E. S. Paykel (Ed.), *Handbook of affective disorders* (pp. 70–92). New York: Guilford Press.

Schapira, K., Kerr, T. A., & Roth, M. (1970). Phobias and affective illness. *British Journal of Psychiatry, 117,* 25–32.

Schapira, K., Roth, M., Kerr, T. A., & Gurney, C. (1972). The prognosis of affective disorders: The differentiation of anxiety states from depressive illnesses. *British Journal of Psychiatry, 121,* 175–181.

Seitz, F. C. (1970). Five psychological measures of neurotic depression: A correlation study. *Journal of Clinical Psychology, 26,* 504–505.

Sheehan, D. V., & Sheehan, K. H. (1982). The classification of anxiety and hysterical states, Part 1 (Historical review and empirical delineation). *Journal of Clinical Psychopharmacology, 2,* 235–244.

Spitzer, R. L., Endicott, J., Fleiss, J. L., & Cohen, J. (1970). Psychiatric status schedule: A technique for evaluating psychopathology and impairment in role functioning. *Archives of General Psychiatry, 23,* 41–55.

Spitzer, R. L., Endicott, J., & Robins, E. (1978). Research Diagnostic Criteria: Rationale and reliability. *Archives of General Psychiatry, 35,* 773–782.

Spitzer, R. L., & Fleiss, J. L. (1974). A re-analysis of the reliability of psychiatric diagnosis. *British Journal of Psychiatry, 125,* 341–347.

Spitzer, R. L., Forman, J. B. W., & Nee, J. (1979). DSM-III field trials: I. Initial interrater diagnostic reliability. *American Journal of Psychiatry, 136,* 815–817.

Spitzer, R. L., Skodol, A. E., Williams, J. B. W., Gibbon, M., & Kass, F. (1982). Supervising intake diagnosis: A psychiatric "Rashomon." *Archives of General Psychiatry, 39,* 1299–1305.

Spitzer, R. L., & Williams, J. B. W. (1983). *Instruction manual for the Structured Clinical Interview for DSM-III (SCID).* New York: NY State Psychiatric Institute, Biometrics Research Department.

Torgersen, S. (1985). Hereditary differentiation of anxiety and affective disorders. *British Journal of Psychiatry, 146,* 530–534.

Tuma, A. H., & Maser, J. D. (Eds.). (1985). *Anxiety and the anxiety disorders.* Hillsdale, NJ: Erlbaum.

Van Valkenburg, C., Akiskal, H. S., Puzantian, V., & Rosenthal, T. (1984). Anxious depression: Clinical, family history, and naturalistic outcome comparisons with panic and major depressive disorders. *Journal of Affective Disorders, 6,* 67–82.

Vye, C. (1986, November). *Positive and negative affect and the differentiation of depression and anxiety.* Paper presented at the Association for the Advancement of Behavior Therapy Convention, Chicago.

Watson, D., & Clark, L. A. (1984). Negative Affectivity: The disposition to experience aversive emotional states. *Psychological Bulletin, 96,* 465–490.

Watson, D., Clark, L. A., & Carey, G. (1988). Positive and negative affectivity and their relation to anxiety and depressive disorders. *Jouurnal of Abnormal Psychology, 97,* 346–353.

Watson, D., & Pennebaker, J. (in press). Health complaints, stress, and distress: Exploring the central role of Negative Affectivity. *Psychological Review.*

Weissman, M. M. (1985). The epidemiology of anxiety disorders: Rates, risks, and familial patterns. In A. H. Tuma & J. D. Maser (Eds.), *Anxiety and the anxiety disorders* (pp. 275–296). Hillsdale, NJ: Erlbaum.

Weissman, M. M., Leckman, J. F., Merikangas, K. R., Gammon, G. D., & Prusoff, B. A. (1984). Depression and anxiety disorders in parents and children. *Archives of General Psychiatry, 41,* 845–852.

Wing, J. K. (1970). A standard form of psychiatric present state examination and a method for standardizing the classification of symptoms. In E. H. Hare & J. K. Wing (Eds.), *Psychiatric epidemiology: An international symposium* (pp. 93–108). London: Oxford University Press.

Wing, J. K., Cooper, J. E., & Sartorius, N. (1974). *The measurement and classification of psychiatric syndromes: An introduction manual for the Present State Examination and CATEGO programme.* London: Cambridge University Press.

Woodruff, R. A., Guze, S. B., & Clayton, P. J. (1972). Anxiety neurosis among psychiatric outpatients. *Comprehensive Psychiatry, 13,* 165–170.

Zimmerman, M., Coryell, W., Wilson, S., & Corenthal, C. (1986). Evaluation of symptoms of major depressive disorder: Self-report *vs.* clinical ratings. *Journal of Nervous and Mental Disease, 174,* 150–153.

Zuckerman, M., Persky, H., Eckman, K. M., & Hopkins, T. R. (1967). A multitrait multimethod measurement approach to the traits (or states) of anxiety, depression and hostility. *Journal of Projective Techniques and Personality Assessment, 31,* 39–48.

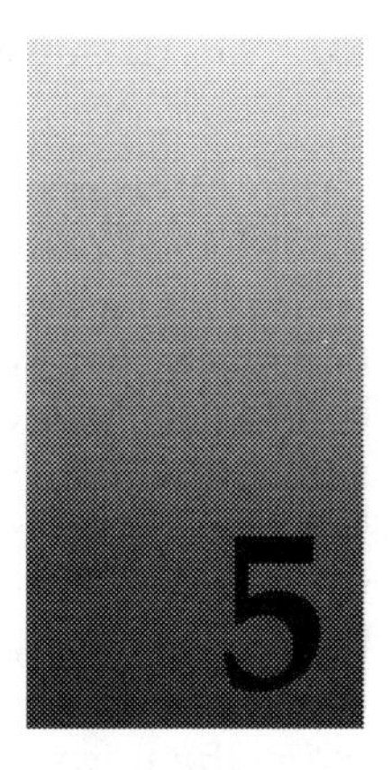

Self-Report Assessment of Depression and Anxiety

Ian H. Gotlib
Douglas B. Cane

I. Introduction

The last two decades have witnessed a renewed interest in the diagnosis and classification of mental disorders. In this context, particular attention has been given to depressive reactions and anxiety states. The purpose of this chapter is to examine a number of issues concerning the assessment, by self-report instruments, of depression and anxiety. We begin by describing the symptoms associated with the syndromes of depression and anxiety. The descriptions presented in this section are derived from the diagnostic criteria utilized in current systems of classification. As such, they reflect current clinical beliefs and standards re-

Note: Preparation of this chapter was facilitated by Grants MA 8574 from the Medical Research Council of Canada and #977-87-89 from the Ontario Mental Health Foundation to the first author.

Anxiety and Depression

garding the essential features and associated symptoms for these two disorders.

We next present a brief discussion of basic psychometric considerations, and then survey frequently used self-report measures of these two constructs. Included in this survey are measures designed to assess the severity of these syndromes and instruments that employ a checklist format to document the presence of various symptoms. Furthermore, we include not only self-report measures that assess a single construct, but also measures of depression and anxiety that are subscales of inventories assessing a broader range of symptomatology. We briefly describe the purpose, the method of construction, and the content of each scale. We also present the basic psychometric properties of each measure, such as internal consistency, test–retest reliability, and convergent validity, and, in a subsequent section, we assess the extent to which the content of each measure corresponds to the descriptions of depression and anxiety provided earlier. Because a key purpose of this chapter is to examine the nature of the relationship between depression and anxiety as assessed by self-report, a separate section is devoted to the issue of discriminant validity. Finally, we consider three explanations for the observed relationship among self-report measures of depression and anxiety, and conclude by outlining the implications of our review for the use of current self-report measures of these two constructs and for the development of new instruments.

II. Diagnostic Criteria

Depression. The most recent edition of the *Diagnostic and Statistical Manual of Mental Disorders* (DSM-III-R; American Psychiatric Association, 1987) describes two unipolar depressive disorders—major depression and dysthymia. For a diagnosis of major depression, the occurrence of one or more major depressive episodes must be established. DSM-III-R lists the following nine symptoms describing disturbances in affective, motivational, somatic, and cognitive functioning that may be present during a major depressive episode:

1. Depressed mood (or irritable mood in children and adolescents) most of the day, nearly every day. Feeling "depressed, sad, hopeless, discouraged."
2. Diminished interest or pleasure in all, or almost all, activities.
3. Significant weight loss or weight gain (not due to dieting) or decrease or increase in appetite.
4. Insomnia or hypersomnia.

5. Psychomotor agitation or retardation.
6. Fatigue or loss of energy.
7. Feelings of worthlessness or inappropriate guilt.
8. Diminished ability to concentrate or indecisiveness.
9. Recurrent thoughts of death or suicidal ideation.

These symptoms must represent a change from the previous functioning of the individual and must be present most of the day, nearly every day, for at least a 2-week period. During a major depressive episode, at least five of these nine symptoms must be present, and at least one of these symptoms must be either depressed mood or a loss of interest in, or failure to obtain pleasure from, most daily activities. Interestingly, DSM-III-R also lists anxiety, irritability, panic attacks, and phobias as commonly associated features of depression.

A current major depressive episode may further be classified as melancholic type if a specific pattern of symptoms and premorbid functioning is observed. The presence of five or more of the following symptoms is used to designate a depressive episode as melancholic: loss of interest or pleasure, lack of reactivity to usually pleasurable stimuli, depressed mood regularly worse in the morning, terminal insomnia, psychomotor retardation or agitation, weight loss, good premorbid personality functioning, one or more previous major depressive episodes followed by complete or near-complete recovery, and a previous good response to somatic antidepressant therapy.

Dysthymia is defined by the presence of depressed mood for a period of 2 or more years and by the presence of at least two of the following symptoms: poor appetite or overeating, insomnia or hypersomnia, poor concentration or difficulties making decisions, fatigue or low energy, low self-esteem, and feelings of hopelessness. For this diagnosis to be made, the individual cannot have been free of depressive symptoms for more than 2 months during the 2-year period, and there cannot have been a major depressive episode during this initial 2-year period. Following this initial period, major depressive episodes may be superimposed upon a diagnosis of dysthymia. A distinction is also made between secondary dysthymia, in which the mood disturbance is apparently related to a preexisting, nonmood disorder, and primary dysthymia, in which the mood disturbance does not appear to be related to a preexisting, nonmood, disorder.

Anxiety. DSM-III-R lists a number of anxiety disorders, including panic disorder, agoraphobia, social phobia, simple phobia, obsessive–compulsive disorder, posttraumatic stress disorder, and generalized anxiety disorder. However, because the vast majority of self-report measures of anxiety are attempting to assess generalized anxiety disorder, we will restrict our discussion to this form of anxiety. Where appropriate, we will direct the reader to self-report measures of other, more circumscribed types of anxiety.

The essential feature of a generalized anxiety disorder, according to DSM-III-R, is the presence for 6 months or longer of unrealistic or excessive anxiety and worry about two or more life circumstances. This diagnosis is not made if the anxiety or worry occurs only during the course of a mood disorder, such as major depressive episode, or if the focus of the worry or anxiety is another Axis I disorder. DSM-III-R criteria for a diagnosis of generalized anxiety disorder are presented in Table 5.1. Symptoms of anxiety may occur in the form of motor tension, autonomic hyperactivity, or vigilance and scanning. For a generalized anxiety disorder to be diagnosed, at least six of the symptoms listed in Table 5.1 must be present. Again, it is instructive to note that DSM-III-R lists "mild depressive symptoms" and "depressive disorder" as associated features of generalized anxiety disorder.

A comparison of the descriptions contained in DSM-III-R for uni-

Table 5.1
Summary of DSM-III-R Diagnostic Criteria for Generalized Anxiety Disorder

A. Unrealistic or excessive anxiety and worry about two or more life circumstances for a period of 6 months or longer.
B. The focus of the anxiety in A is unrelated to another Axis I disorder.
C. The disturbance does not occur only during the course of a mood disorder.
D. At least six of the following symptoms are often present:

Motor tension
1. Trembling, feeling shaky
2. Muscle tension or soreness
3. Restlessness
4. Fatigability

Autonomic hyperactivity
5. Shortness of breath
6. Heart palpitations or acceleration
7. Sweating or clammy hands
8. Dry mouth
9. Dizziness or lightheadedness
10. Nausea, diarrhea, or abdominal distress
11. Hot flashes or chills
12. Frequent urination
13. Trouble swallowing

Vigilance and scanning
14. Feeling on edge
15. Exaggerated startle response
16. Difficulty concentrating
17. Trouble falling or staying asleep
18. Irritability

polar depression and generalized anxiety, therefore, suggests that although differences exist with respect to the essential features of these disorders, there is considerable overlap with respect to their defining symptoms and associated features. To assess this possibility, we reviewed all of the symptoms enumerated at the beginning of Section II and in Table 5.1 and categorized each symptom as specific to depression, specific to anxiety, or common to both depression and anxiety (see Table 5.2). The essential features of a depressive episode, as defined in DSM-III-R, are depressed mood and a loss of interest in daily activities or a loss of pleasure from these activities. In contrast, the essential feature of anxiety is defined as an excessive or unrealistic anxiety and worry about life circumstances. However, in addition to these essential features, a number of other symptoms must be present to satisfy the criteria for both depression and anxiety. Of the nine symptoms included in the description of a major depressive episode, five (weight gain or loss, poor appetite, motor retardation, guilt or worthlessness, and thoughts of death) are specific to depression; the other four symptoms (restlessness, fatigue, diminished ability to concentrate, and insomnia, as well as irritability in some patients) also appear as criteria defining a generalized anxiety disorder. In addition, the poor appetite symptomatic of depression might also be consistent with the upset stomach characteristic of anxiety. Current definitions of depression and anxiety, then, do not appear to describe distinct, unrelated syndromes, but instead describe syndromes that overlap substantially with respect to their typical symptom patterns. Because this overlap has important implications for understanding the reasons underlying the relationships among self-report measures of depression and anxiety, we will return to a discussion of this issue later in the chapter.

Table 5.2
Distinctive and Overlapping Symptoms of Depression and Anxiety

Symptoms specific to depression	Symptoms common to depression and anxiety	Symptoms specific to anxiety
Dysphoric mood (depressed, hopeless)	Irritability	Excessive worry
Loss of interest	Agitation/restlessness	Autonomic hyperactivity
Weight loss/gain	Concentration difficulties	Exaggerated startle response
Poor appetite	Insomnia	Muscle tension
Motor retardation	Fatigue	
Guilt/worthlessness		
Thoughts of death		

III. Psychometric Issues

Before turning to a review of self-report measures of depression and anxiety, a brief presentation of certain psychometric concepts will be helpful. In order to evaluate the utility of any measurement procedure, information concerning its reliability and validity must be made available and assessed. Reliability refers to the proportion of variance in a set of scores that is due to true and stable differences among the individuals tested for the attribute that is being measured. While a number of procedures are available for deriving estimates of reliability, the reliability coefficients based on the split-half method, on measures of internal consistency, or on repeated administrations of the same test are most frequently encountered. In the split-half method, scores obtained from one-half of the test items are compared with those obtained from the other half. Measures of internal consistency make use of item- and total-score variance to calculate the average correlation among all of the test items. Finally, test–retest reliability can be estimated by correlating the scores obtained from administrations of the same test on different occasions. The interested reader is referred to Kendall and Norton-Ford (1982, pp. 227–228) for an extended discussion of reliability. We should note here, however, that test–retest reliability might not be particularly relevant in those instances in which temporal stability is not assumed to be a property of the attribute that is being assessed (e.g., state levels of depressed and anxious affect).

In contrast to reliability, evaluating the validity of a self-report measure is a more complex process that may involve a number of different procedures. While there are many different types of validity (Kendall & Norton-Ford, 1982, pp. 118–230), we think that content validity and construct validity are the most relevant to this chapter. Content validity refers to the extent to which the content of a test adequately samples the domain the test is intended to assess. With respect to the measurement of depression and anxiety, the content validity of a measure may be evaluated by comparing the items and descriptors included in the measure with the symptoms used to define the corresponding syndrome.

Construct validity refers to the extent to which performance on a measure is consistent with the theoretical concepts or constructs it is assumed to measure. Evidence for construct validity may be obtained either experimentally, by demonstrating that performance on a test is affected by certain manipulations in a manner predicted by theory, or correlationally, by examining the relationship of the test with other measures of the same and different constructs. Evidence of convergent validity is obtained when a test is found to correlate significantly with other established measures of the same construct. Thus, a self-report measure of depression is considered to have convergent validity to the extent to which it correlates with other valid measures or indicators of depression. In a similar manner, discriminant validity is established when a test or measure is found to have relatively low correlations with measures that are assumed to assess unrelated constructs. Thus, a measure of anxiety possesses discriminant validity to the extent to which it correlates with other measures of anxiety, but does not correlate with measures of variables that are essentially unrelated to anxiety (e.g., social class, intelligence). The establishment of construct validity is an ongoing process based upon an accumulation of evidence from a number of different sources. Because the concept of discriminant validity is of particular importance to a discussion of self-report measures of depression and anxiety, we will return to it later in the chapter.

IV. Self-Report Measures of Depression

There are numerous self-report instruments designed to measure depression or depressed affect. In fact, Moran and Lambert (1983) listed over 30 self-administered scales for the measurement of depression. However, only a handful have achieved widespread use, and it is these measures that we describe below.

Beck Depression Inventory. The Beck Depression Inventory (BDI) is probably the most frequently used self-report method of assessing depressive symptomatology. Originally developed by Beck, Ward, Mendelson, and Erlbaugh (1961) as an interviewer-assisted procedure, it consists of 84 self-evaluative statements grouped into 21 catagories that assess the affective, cognitive, motivational, and physiological symptoms of depression. Item categories include mood, pessimism, crying spells, guilt, irritability, sleep and appetite disturbance, and loss of libido. For each of these categories of symptoms, there is a graded series of four alternative statements, ranging from neutral (e.g., "I do not feel sad," "I don't feel disappointed in myself") to a maximum level of severity (e.g., "I am so sad or unhappy that I can't stand it," "I would kill myself if I had the chance"). The items are scored from 0 to 3, so that the total BDI score can range from 0 to 63. Generally, a total BDI score of 0–9 indicates a nondepressed state, 10–15 reflects a mild level of depression 16–23 reflects moderate depression, and 24–63 indicates a severe level of depression (Shaw, Vallis, & McCabe, 1985).

Kendall, Hollon, Beck, Hammen, and Ingram (1987) have recently outlined recommendations regarding the use of the BDI in research examining self-reported depression. Among other guidelines, Kendall et al. recommend the use of multiple assessments and suggest that the term *depression* be reserved for individuals with BDI scores of 20 or greater and concurrent, interviewer-based diagnoses; subjects selected only on the basis of BDI scores should be referred to as *dysphoric*. Finally, Kendall et al. caution that the practice of selecting subjects with extremely low BDI scores (0s and 1s) may produce a "nondepressed" group that is characterized by other forms of psychopathology (e.g., psychopathy, hypomania), and recommend the use of a control group that is statistically "average" in level of depression (i.e., BDI score between 4 and 6).

It is important to note that the BDI was not designed to yield a discrete diagnosis of depression; rather, it was constructed to measure depression as a single dimension of psychopathology that cuts across a wide variety of diagnostic categories. Its major focus, therefore, is on the depth or severity of depressive symptomatology as defined by the combination of the number, frequency, and intensity of symptoms. Consistent with its unidimensional intent, several investigators have reported high levels of internal consistency for the BDI (e.g., Beck & Beamesderfer, 1974; Strober, Green, & Carlson, 1981); split-half reliability coefficients average .86. Factor analyses with patients, however, have generally yielded three distinct factors: sad mood/negative sense of self, psychomotor retardation, and somatic depression (Beck & Beamesderfer, 1974; Vredenburg, Krames, & Flett, 1985; Weckowicz, Muir, & Cropley, 1967), although this pattern may not hold for nonclinical populations (cf. Golin & Hartz, 1979; Lips & Ng, 1985).

The BDI contains relatively few items related to feelings of anxiety, agitation, sleep disturbance, and specific somatic complaints. Furthermore, although the BDI was "not intended to reflect any theory regarding the etiology of depression" (Beck & Beamesderfer, 1974, p. 155), it does place a strong emphasis on cognitive symptomatology, an emphasis consistent with Beck's (1967) cognitive theory of depression. Both Depue and Monroe (1978) and Hughes, O'Hara, and Rehm (1982) have argued that, because of its strong emphasis on cognitive factors and its relative disregard of somatic concerns, the BDI is biased toward the milder forms of depression. Moreover, Vredenburg et al. (1985) recently presented data indicating that this problem is exacerbated by the use of the short form of the BDI (Beck & Beck, 1972).

Finally, with respect to convergent validity, the BDI correlates reasonably well with other self-report measures of depression and with clinician's ratings of severity of depression (e.g., Davies, Burrows, & Poynton, 1975; Schwab, Bialow, & Holzer, 1967), although the degree of concordance is attenuated with increasing severity (Carroll, Fielding, &

Blashki, 1973). The BDI is considered effective as a screening device; indeed, Hammen (1981) and Moran and Lambert (1983) have suggested that it is one of the most satisfactory self-rating instruments for assessing severity of depression.

Center for Epidemiological Studies Depression Scale. The Center for Epidemiological Studies Depression Scale (CES-D; Radloff, 1977) is a 20-item scale designed to measure the current level of depressive symptomatology in the general (i.e., nonpsychiatric) population. The items assess depressed mood, feelings of guilt, worthlessness, loneliness, hopelessness, psychomotor retardation, concentration problems, appetite loss, and sleep disturbance, although there is a particular emphasis on affective symptomatology. For each item, respondents indicate on a 4-point scale (0 to 3) how frequently they have experienced that symptom during the past week, ranging from "Rarely or none of the time" (less than 1 day) to "Most or all of the time" (5–7 days). Thus, total scores on the CES-D can range from 0 to 60. Radloff has suggested that a total score of 16, which demarcates the upper 20% of the score distribution in general population studies, may serve as a cutoff to differentiate "cases" of depression from noncases. More specifically, Barnes and Prosen (1985) have suggested that scores below 16 indicate that the respondent is "not depressed"; scores from 16 to 20 indicate "mild depression," scores from 21 to 30 indicate "moderate depression," and scores of 31 and greater indicate "severe depression."

Like the BDI, the CES-D was designed to measure depression as a single dimension of psychopathology that cuts across various diagnostic categories. Attesting to this unidimensional construction, Barnes and Prosen (1985) and Radloff (1977) have reported internal consistency coefficients of .84 and above. Despite this high reliability, however, the CES-D has consistently yielded three factors: depressed affect, positive affect, and somatic/retarded activities (Radloff, 1977; Roberts, 1980). The presence of a positive affect factor not found in factor analyses of the BDI may be due to the inclusion of positively worded items on the CES-D but not on the BDI. In fact, the separation of positive and negative affect on the CES-D is consistent with recent research suggesting that these are two independent dimensions, rather than opposite ends of a single bipolar factor (e.g., Gotlib & Meyer, 1986; Watson & Tellegen, 1985).

The CES-D has been found to correlate significantly with other measures of depression (cf. Radloff, 1977; Weissman, Sholomskas, Pottenger, Prusoff, & Locke, 1977), indicating acceptable convergent validity. Moreover, Weissman et al. reported the sensitivity of the CES-D (i.e., its capability to identify cases of depression) to be above .90 and its specificity (i.e., its ability to identify noncases) to be above .55. Despite these figures, however, the results of a number of studies suggest that the CES-D should not be used as a clinical diagnostic instrument. Boyd, Weissman, Thompson, and Myers (1982), for example, found that a significant proportion of the false positives on the CES-D received psychiatric or medical diagnoses other than depression. Lewinsohn and Teri (1982) also found that a score of 17 or greater on the CES-D predicted a diagnosis of depression with only 34% accuracy; scores of 16 and less, however, classified subjects as nondepressed with an 82% accuracy rate. On the basis of their results, Lewinsohn and Teri suggest that the CES-D could be used as an initial screening instrument. Those persons scoring low on the CES-D would be considered to be nondepressed, while those scoring high would be subjected to a subsequent clinical interview. Interestingly, the results of other investigations suggest that even this is too liberal a use of the CES-D. Myers and Weissman (1980) and Roberts and Vernon (1983) found a false negative rate of between 36 and 40% in their samples; that is, 40% of the individuals identified as depressed by the Schedule for Affective Disorders and Schizophrenia (SADS) criteria scored below 16 on the CES-D. Myers and Weissman suggest that the CES-D is an effective screening device for research, but not for clinical practice; in our view, this may not be a useful distinction.

MMPI-D and MMPI-D-30 Scales. The MMPI-D scale, one of the 10 clinical scales of the Minnesota Multiphasic Personality Inventory (Hathaway & McKinley, 1951), was originally developed to identify severely depressed patients. It consists of 60 statements to which patients respond true or false. The items reflect various aspects of depressive illness and were selected on the basis of their ability to identify a group of psychiatric patients exhibiting depressive symptomatology. Eleven items differentiated between depressed and nondepressed psychiatric patients, while the remaining 49 items discriminated between depressed patients and normals.

Certainly the MMPI is one of the most familiar psychological assessment instruments. Despite its empirical construction, however, the MMPI-D scale has been repeatedly criticized. For example, Snaith, Ahmed, Mehta, and Hamilton (1971) have questioned the construct validity of the scale because of the heterogeneity of its items and its complex and unreliable factor structure. In fact, Snaith et al. suggested that the MMPI-D scale may reflect personality factors rather than depressive illness. More recently, Nelson (1987) has suggested that using the MMPI-D scale for subject selection or group assignment may be misleading because one-third of the items on this scale, the "subtle" items, may play no role in defining depression. McNair (1974) has also expressed concerns about the lack of sensitivity of the MMPI to drug effects and the lack of a clear time reference period in the instructions. We should note, however, that Hollon and Mandell (1979) have taken exception to this conclusion and have suggested that the MMPI may compare favorably with other self-report measures as a potential measure of change in level of depression.

In an attempt to address these identified drawbacks of the scale, Dempsey (1964) constructed the MMPI-D-30, a 30-item version of the MMPI-D scale. Although the MMPI-D-30 is more nearly unidimensional than the MMPI-D scale, it nevertheless has limitations. For example, the item pool is still heterogeneous, but it does not sample from the entire range of depressive symptomatology, notably excluding items assessing somatic functioning. Finally, as Mayer (1977) notes, 25 items of the MMPI-D-30 also load on Comrey's (1957) neuroticism factor and, consequently, it is unclear exactly what is being measured by this scale.

Zung Self-Rating Depression Scale. The Zung Self-Rating Depression Scale (SDS; Zung, 1965) consists of 20 items identified in previous factor analytic studies of the syndrome of depression. Of the items, 10 are worded symptomatically positive and 10 are worded symptomatically negative. The 20 items assess *pervasive affect* (2 items), *physiological equivalents or concomitants* (10 items), and *psychological concomitants* (8 items). Respondents indicate whether each symptom is true of themselves "little or none of the time," "some of the time," "a good part of the time," or "most of the time." The SDS yields a numerical score that can be used to indicate both the presence and the severity of depressive symptomatology, regardless of specific diagnosis. It is important to note that no attempt was made to screen or evaluate potential items empirically before including them in the scale, and the final set of items was not tested for internal reliability. Blumenthal (1975), for example, reported that the positively worded items on the SDS load on a factor that is independent from the negatively worded, more "depressive" items, again indicating the independence of positive and negative affect. Moreover, scores on the SDS correlate −.28 with level of education, suggesting that better educated individuals are less likely to endorse depressive symptoms on the SDS (Glazer, Clarkin, & Hunt, 1981).

Carroll et al. (1973) have noted that the SDS lacks items assessing the depressive symptoms of guilt, retardation, hypochondriasis, and loss of insight and that it cannot be used for purposes of differential diagnosis. Furthermore, Glazer et al. (1981) have observed that normal adolescents and elderly persons both tend to score in the clinical range on this measure. Finally, although the SDS correlates moderately well with other self-report measures of depression, and particularly well with the BDI (cf. Schaefer et al., 1985; Zung, 1971), there is some evidence that it does not differentiate levels of severity within depressed populations and that it is not sensitive over a wide range of clinical depression (Carroll et al., 1973; Moran & Lambert, 1983). As Rehm (1976, p. 239) states, "The SDS is psychometrically unsophisticated [and its] use in behavioral practice and research is questionable pending stronger psychometric support."

V. Self-Report Measures of Anxiety

Although there are numerous self-report measures of various anxiety states, many of these are designed to assess specific fears or circumscribed, situation-specific anxiety (e.g., Fear Survey Schedule, Wolpe & Lang, 1964; Lang's Snake Questionnaire, Klorman, Weerts, Hastings, Melamed, & Lang, 1974; Social Avoidance and Distress Scale and the Fear of Negative Evaluation Scale, Watson & Friend, 1969; Acrophobic Questionnaire, Baker, Cohen, & Saunders, 1973; Test Anxiety Questionnaire, Mandler & Sarason, 1952). As we noted earlier, the most common type of self-report measure of anxiety assesses the type of anxiety that would best be characterized in DSM-III-R as generalized anxiety disorder, and it is these measures that are described below.

Taylor Manifest Anxiety Scale. The Taylor Manifest Anxiety Scale (TMAS; Taylor, 1953) consists of 50 true–false items. Two-hundred statements from the MMPI were judged by clinicians in terms of how representative they were of manifest anxiety, and 65 items for which there was at least 80% agreement were retained. These items were then administered to a college sample; the 50 items with the largest item-total correlations were retained for the final scale. Hilgard, Jones, and Kaplan (1951) reported a split-half reliability of .92 and Gocka (1965) obtained an internal consistency value of .92. The TMAS has also been found to possess high test–retest reliability, with Taylor (1953) reporting coefficients of .89, .82, and .81 for intervals of 3 weeks, 5 months, and 7–19 months, respectively. Norms for the TMAS are available for male and female psychiatric patients (Newton, 1968), medical patients (Swenson, Pearson, & Osborne, 1973), and college students (Graham, 1977).

The TMAS was originally developed to select subjects for studies of the effects of drive state on learning, and the evidence for the use of the TMAS in this context has been reviewed by Spence and Spence (1966). The TMAS has also been extensively used in other contexts and significant correlations have been reported between scores on the TMAS and other self-report measures of anxiety, such as the *Pt* scale of the MMPI (Brackbill & Little, 1954) and the IPAT Anxiety Scale (Bull & Strongman, 1971). Interpretation of TMAS scores is complicated, however, by the multidimensional nature of the scale and by its strong correlations with other types of personality measures. O'Conner, Lorr, and Stafford (1956), for example, reported five identifiable factors for the TMAS: chronic anxiety or worry, increased physiological activity, sleep disturbance associated with inner strain, personal inadequacy, and motor tension. The TMAS has also been found to correlate significantly with general measures of neuroticism (Bull & Strongman, 1971; Watson & Clark, 1984), negative self-concept (Donovan, Smythe, Paige, & O'Leary, 1975), and discomfort in social situations (Grossberg & Wilson, 1965). It appears, therefore, that the TMAS is a trait measure that assesses a number of different dimensions relating to general negative reactivity, dissatisfaction with the self, and discomfort in social or interpersonal situations.

Zung Self-Rating Anxiety Scale. Zung (1971) constructed the Self-Rating Anxiety Scale (SAS) based largely on DSM-II criteria for anxiety disorder, defined as a neurosis characterized by anxiety, overconcern, and panic and frequently accompanied by somatic symptoms. The SAS assesses 20 diagnostic criteria—5 affective symptoms and 15 somatic complaints. Responses for each of the 20 items are indicated on a 4-point scale, ranging from "none or a little of the time" to "most or all of the time," and are based on a 1-week time frame. To reduce the effect of response bias, the scoring of five items is reversed. Raw scores on the SAS are converted to an index score by dividing the total by the maximum possible score (80) and multiplying by 100. (The value of this index thus ranges from 25 to 100.) An index score below 44 is considered normal, while scores in the ranges of 45–55 and 56–100 are considered indicative of significant and severe anxiety, respectively.

Little information is available concerning the psychometric properties and structure of the SAS. Jegede (1977) obtained internal consistency (coefficient alpha) values of .69 in a normal sample and .81 in a group of psychiatric outpatients. With respect to validity, significant correlations have been obtained between the SAS and observer ratings of anxiety (Zung, 1974, 1979), although a correlation of only .30 was obtained between the SAS and another self-report measure of anxiety, the TMAS. Finally, scores on the SAS have been found to discriminate between normal subjects and psychiatric patients (Jegede, 1977; Zung, 1979) and between psychiatric patients with and without a diagnosed anxiety disorder (Zung, 1979). In summary, the SAS appears to have been constructed to measure commonly employed criteria for anxiety disorder, and initial investigations employing the SAS are encouraging. However, further investigation of the psychometric properties and structure of the SAS is still required.

State–Trait Anxiety Inventory. The State–Trait Anxiety Inventory (STAI; Spielberger, Gorsuch, & Lushene, 1970) is actually composed of two 20-item self-report measures developed to assess the separate concepts of trait and state anxiety in normal samples. The 20 state anxiety items are each scored on a 4-point scale of intensity, ranging from "not at all" to "very much so." The 20 trait anxiety items are scored on a 4-point frequency scale, ranging from "almost never" to "almost always." Individuals high on the dimension of trait anxiety are hypothesized to be sensitive to situations involving interpersonal relationships and threats to self-esteem, and to manifest state anxiety in these situations. On the trait form of this inventory, the A-Trait, subjects are instructed to respond on the basis of how they generally feel, while the state form, A-State, instructs subjects to respond according to their feelings at that particular moment. In contrast to the A-State, items on the A-Trait are expected to be relatively stable and unaffected by situational stress.

In constructing the STAI, Spielberger and his colleagues began with an initial pool of 177 items taken from the Taylor Manifest Anxiety Scale, the Welsh Anxiety Scale, and the IPAT Anxiety Scale, and eliminated items based on responses from large samples of college students. Form X of the STAI was published in 1970 and a revision, Form Y, was published in 1983. This latter form was intended to address problems of response bias, population specificity, and discriminant validity; the authors also attempted to eliminate items that appeared to be measuring symptoms of depression.

Both the state and trait measures have been found to possess high internal consistency (.86 to .95) and the trait form of the STAI has also demonstrated good test–retest reliability for intervals up to three months (.65 to .86; Spielberger et al., 1970). The trait form has been found to correlate significantly with other measures of anxiety and to discriminate normals from psychiatric patients. Similarly, scores on the state form have been found to change following relaxation training, viewing a disturbing film, or writing an exam (e.g., Kendall, Finch, Auerbach, Hooke, & Milulka, 1976), although given the face validity of the items on this scale, demand characteristics must remain a plausible explanation for these findings. Finally, Kendall et al. (1976) conducted a factor analysis on the STAI and obtained a three-factor solution accounting for 81% of the total variance. The first factor, labeled "A-Trait: Cognitive Anxiety," was composed of 14 of the 20 items from the trait form of the STAI; none of the state items loaded significantly on this factor. The remaining two factors were made up entirely of items from the state form, with 6 of the 10 negatively keyed items loading on the second factor ("A-State: Negative Descriptors") and 8 of the 10 positively keyed items loading on the final factor ("A-State: Positive Descriptors"). The evidence to date, therefore, suggests that the STAI is composed of independent measures of state and trait anxiety. The STAI has been widely employed in research involving clinical, medical, and student populations (see Smith & Lay, 1974, for additional information regarding the use of the STAI).

S-R Inventory of General Trait Anxiousness. The S-R Inventory of General Trait Anxiousness (S-R GTA; Endler & Okada, 1975) is a multidimensional measure of trait anxiety designed to assess an individual's predisposition to experience state anxiety in a number of different situations. The S-R GTA was developed to provide a more comprehensive assessment of trait anxiety than did other existing measures, such as the TMAS and the STAI, which primarily assess the traits of interpersonal or ego-threat anxiety (Endler & Shedletsky, 1973). The version of the S-R GTA described by Endler and Okada assesses trait anxiety on four different dimensions: interpersonal, physical danger, ambiguous or novel, and innocuous or routine. More recently, a fifth dimension, social evaluation, has been added (Flood & Endler, 1980). For each of the situations described on the S-R GTA, subjects indicate the extent to which each of nine different statements would generally describe their responses to the situation. Each statement is rated on a 5-point scale ranging from "not at all" to "very much." The statements assess three modes of responding: distress avoidance, autonomic physiological, and exhilaration approach. Estimates of internal consistency for these dimensions range from .62 for the innocuous dimension to .86 for the ambiguous dimension (Endler & Okada, 1975).

A number of studies have examined the extent to which responses to the S-R GTA predict state anxiety scores in different situations. The interactional model of anxiety, from which the S-R GTA is derived, predicts that individuals who differ on one dimension of trait anxiety will evidence different levels of state anxiety when confronted with a situation that is congruent with that dimension, but will not differ with respect to their responses to other, noncongruent dimensions. Consistent with this prediction, scores on the social evaluation dimension have been found to predict the level of state anxiety experienced in a test situation by high school students (Endler, King, Edwards, Kuczynski, & Diveky, 1983) and university students (Philips & Endler, 1982). S-R GTA scores on the social evaluation dimension have also been found to predict levels of state anxiety prior to an athletic competition (Flood & Endler, 1980). As expected, in each of these studies scores on the other dimensions of trait anxiety were not related to reported levels of state anxiety. Similar results have also been reported for the physical danger dimension of the S-R GTA. Kendall (1978), for example, found subjects with high scores on the physical danger dimension to respond with a greater increase in state anxiety in a physical danger context than did subjects with low scores on this dimension. High- and low-scoring subjects did not differ, however, in their responses to an evaluative dimension. Finally, similar differences were observed in this study between subjects with high and low scores on the evaluative dimension in an evaluative context, but not in a situation representing physical danger.

These findings regarding the social evaluation and physical danger dimensions of the S-R GTA, therefore, are consistent with the conceptualization underlying the construction of this measure. Empirical support for the other two dimensions of trait anxiety, however, has been equivocal. For example, although King and Endler (1982) reported a significant correlation between scores on the ambiguous dimension and changes in self-reported levels of anxiety before and after surgery, a stronger relationship was observed between these changed scores and the social evaluative dimension. The existence of separate dimensions for ambiguous and innocuous situations has also been questioned. A factor analysis of the S-R GTA by Endler, Magnusson, Ekehammer, and Okada (1976) revealed only two dimensions: interpersonal (ego threat) and physical danger. The situation representing innocuous or routine events was found to load primarily on the first dimension, whereas the ambiquous or novel situation was observed to load substantially on both dimensions. Finally, Mothersill, Dobson, and Neufeld (1986) found that subjects with high scores on the interpersonal (ego-threat) dimension reported higher levels of state anxiety for a situation perceived as ego threatening than did subjects with low scores on this dimension, but did not differ in their responses to a physical danger situation. However, support for independent dimensions representing ambiguous and innocuous situations was not obtained. Consistent with previous findings, the results of this study provided only partial support for the S-R GTA as a multidimensional measure of trait anxiety, with the interpersonal and physical danger dimensions appearing most promising. Results to date, however, are less encouraging regarding the assessment of additional dimensions of trait anxiety.

VI. Scales Measuring Both Depression and Anxiety

Costello–Comrey Anxiety and Depression Scales. The Costello–Comrey Depression (CC-D) and Anxiety Scales (CC-A; Costello & Comrey, 1967) were developed to provide measures of an individual's predisposition to experience depression and anxiety, respectively, and to discriminate between these affective states. Items selected from a number of existing scales were administered to a large university sample and, on the basis of repeated factor analyses, dimensions representing depression and anxiety were identified. The final scales were composed of items that were found to discriminate between these two affective states; nevertheless, correlations between the CC-D and CC-A have been found to range from .40 to .59. Items are rated on 9-point scales and are worded in both positive and negative directions. The CC-D is composed of 14 items. A split-half reliability of .90 was obtained for this scale when administered to a nonclinical sample. The CC-D has been found to correlate adequately with other self-report measures of depression in psychiatric populations (Mendels, Weinstein, & Cochrane, 1972). The CC-A is composed of nine items. A split-half reliability of .70 was reported for a university sample and a correlation of .72 was observed for the CC-A scores of psychiatric patients obtained at admission and again at discharge (Costello & Comrey, 1967).

Millon Clinical Multiaxial Inventory. The Millon Clinical Multiaxial Inventory (MCMI; Millon, 1983) was developed to provide a comprehensive assessment of both enduring personality characteristics and more acute clinical disorders in psychiatric populations. Each of the 20 scales on the MCMI was developed to measure a syndrome consistent with both current theories of personality and psychopathology and current diagnostic practice (i.e., DSM-III). Item selection for the MCMI was based on a three-stage process involving clinical populations. Scales were constructed using items that not only successfully discriminated the target diagnostic group from an undifferentiated psychiatric population, but also that covaried with other clinical scales in a manner consistent with current theories of personality and psychopathology. As a result, significant item overlap exists among the various scales.

The 175-item MCMI employs a true–false format, and actuarial base rate data are used in computing a patient's score on the various scales. Of particular relevance to the present chapter are the scales assessing depression and anxiety. The depression scale of the MCMI (MCMI-D) is a 36-item measure of the clinical syndrome of dysthymia, assessing cognitive, affective, and motivational symptoms of depression. This scale has been found to possess high internal consistency, acceptable test–retest reliabilities for intervals of 1 and 5 weeks (.78 and .66, respectively), and moderate correlations with other self-report measures of depression (Millon, 1983; J. O. Goldberg, Shaw, & Segal, 1987). J. O. Goldberg et al. have noted, however, that the MCMI-D scale does not assess vegetative depressive symptoms, such as appetite and weight loss, libido disturbance, and sleep difficulties. The 37-item anxiety scale of the MCMI (MCMI-A) assesses cognitive, behavioral, and physiological responses reflecting both generalized anxiety and specific phobias. This scale, too, has demonstrated high internal consistency, test–retest reliabilities of .80 and .68 for intervals of 1 and 5 weeks, respectively, and is moderately correlated with other measures of anxiety (Millon, 1983).

It is also important to note that substantial overlap exists between the items of the depression and anxiety scales of the MCMI, with a resulting intercorrelation of .93 for these two scales. In addition, response bias might affect scores on the MCMI-D and MCMI-A: only 4 of the 36 depression items and 1 of the 37 anxiety items are keyed "False."

Multiple Affect Adjective Checklist. The Multiple Affect Adjective Checklist (MAACL; Zuckerman & Lubin, 1965) is one of the most widely used instruments in research involving the assessment of emotional states. It was originally developed as a self-administered measure of the "negative affects" of depression, anxiety, and hostility. The depression and anxiety scales of the MAACL are derived from the earlier Depression Adjective Check Lists (DACL; Lubin, 1965, 1967/1981) and Affect Adjective Check List for Anxiety (AACL-A; Zuckerman, 1960), respectively.

The DACL are equivalent brief measures of depressed mood that were normed on depressed neuropsychiatric patients. The DACL consist of seven different lists of adjectives describing various feelings of depressed and elated mood. Each list contains 22 positive (depressed) and 10 or 12 negative (elated) adjectives, and respondents are required to check all of the words that describe their current feelings. The DACL are scored by adding all the positive words endorsed and the negative words not checked. Normative data are available for samples of students, senior citizens, adolescent delinquents, and psychiatric patients. Reliability estimates for the DACL with normal (i.e., nondepressed) samples are typically greater than .80. The DACL have been found to distinguish between depressed and nondepressed persons and to correlate modestly to strongly (.27 to .70) with other self-report measures and with clinical ratings of depression (e.g., Levitt & Lubin, 1975; Lubin, 1965; Tanaka-Matsumi & Kameoka, 1986). Furthermore, because of the large number of equivalent forms, the DACL are particularly suited for use in studies in which repeated measures of depressed mood are necessary. As Hammen (1981) notes, however, the greatest limitation of the use of this instrument is that it is a measure of depressed mood only; other aspects of the syndrome of depression, such as vegetative symptoms and cognitive dysfunction, are neglected.

The AACL-A was developed as a brief, objectively scored measure of anxiety that could be administered using different time sets. Items were selected empirically by comparing the responses of psychiatric patients diagnosed as anxious with those of nonanxious normals, and by comparing the responses of subjects in hypnotically induced states of high and low anxiety. The AACL-A consists of 21 positive and negative adjectives. Internal consistencies of .72 and .85 and test–retest reliabilities of .68 and .31 for a 1-week interval have been reported for the "general" and "today" forms of the AACL-A, respectively (Zuckerman, 1960). Moreover, the AACL-A has been found to correlate .52 to .65 with other self-report measures of anxiety. It has been widely used in outcome investigations with both student and psychiatric populations, and the "today" form of the AACL-A is frequently employed to assess transitory changes in anxiety. Nevertheless, as Borkovec, Weerts, and Bernstein (1977) note, little additional evidence regarding its reliability and interrelationships with other measures is available.

The depression scale of the MAACL consists of 20 positive and 20 negative adjectives, while the anxiety scale contains 10 positive and 11 negative adjectives. Scores for these scales are obtained by summing the number of negative adjectives endorsed by a subject and the number of positive adjectives not endorsed. Although Zuckerman and Lubin (1965) suggest that the MAACL be scored in this way to provide scores on the three subscales—depression, anxiety, and hostility—the results of a recent factor analysis conducted by Gotlib and Meyer (1986) on the MAACL adjectives yielded two large unipolar factors. Factor 1 was defined by negative adjectives and Factor 2 by positive adjectives from all three MAACL scales. Thus, it appears that the MAACL might be more appropriately used to yield independent scores on positive and negative affect, rather than as more discrete measures of depression and anxiety.

Symptom Checklist-90. The Symptom Checklist-90 (SCL-90; Derogatis, Lipman, & Covy, 1973) is a 90-item measure of symptomatic psychological distress designed for use with psychiatric and medical patients. Each item on the SCL-90 is rated on a 5-point scale ("not at all" to "extremely") to indicate the severity of the symptom over the past week. The inventory assesses nine clusters or primary symptom dimensions in addition to providing three global indices of distress. Five of these nine clusters were identified on the basis of factor analyses, while the remaining clusters were rationally created. Of relevance to the present chapter is the 13-item depression scale and the 10-item anxiety scale. Items on the depression scale assess such symptoms as dysphoric mood, decreased motivation and interest, feelings of hopelessness, and thoughts of suicide. The scale has been found to have high internal consistency (coefficient alpha of .90) and test–retest reliability for a 1-week period (Derogatis et al., 1973). With respect to concurrent validity, significant correlations have been reported between the SCL-90 depression scale and other depression measures.

The anxiety scale of the SCL-90 comprises 10 items assessing symptoms and signs of manifest anxiety, including nervousness, trembling, panic attacks, and somatic correlates of anxiety, such as a pounding heart. An internal consistency value of .85 and a test–retest reliability of .80 for a 1-week interval have been reported for this scale (Derogatis et al., 1973).

Profile of Mood States. The Profile of Mood States (POMS; McNair, Lorr, & Droppleman, 1971) was developed to assess short-term changes in six primary mood states. On the basis of repeated factor analyses conducted with samples of psychiatric patients and normals, dimensions labeled tension–anxiety, depression–dejection, anger–hostility, confusion–bewilderment, vigor–activity, and fatigue–inertia were identified. The 65 items on this checklist are each rated on a 5-point frequency scale, ranging from "not at all" to "extremely," for a 1-week time period. Reported internal-consistency coefficients for these dimensions range from .74 to .92, with test–retest reliabilities for a 20-day interval ranging from .65 to .74 (McNair et al., 1971). Separate male and female norms have been derived from a university health center sample. The POMS has been employed to assess change in clinical outcome studies (e.g., McNair, 1974).

There is one caveat that McNair et al. (1971) point out in their manual, but that seems to have been overlooked by investigators using this scale. For five of the six scales, the mood state measured by the scale is well described by the scale name. For the tension–anxiety scale, however, the authors are attempting to measure physical or muscular–skeletal tension rather than cognitive tension, anxiety, or the generalized feeling of nervousness and discomfort.

VII. Discriminant Validity

Having presented the major self-report measures of depression and anxiety and a brief discussion of the psychometric properties of each, we turn now to a more detailed discussion of the discriminant validity of these measures. Given the focus of this volume on distinctive and overlapping features of depression and anxiety, the concept of discriminant validity assumes major importance.

A large number of studies have yielded data relevant to the issue of the discriminant validity of measures of depression and anxiety. By and large, the results of these investigations suggest not only that measures of depression and anxiety both correlate highly with measures of other forms of psychopathology, but, further, that they also correlate highly with each other. Moreover, in studies in which various measures of emotional distress have been subjected to a factor analysis, measures of depression and anxiety invariably fall on the same factor.

Correlations with Other Measures. Several studies have found that self-report scales of depression and anxiety correlate similarly with other measures of psychopathology and psychological functioning. With respect to depression, for example, Dinning and Evans (1977) found that the BDI correlated significantly with all nine scales of the SCL-90 in a sample of psychiatric patients. Although the highest correlation of .70 was found with the SCL-90 depression scale, the BDI also correlated .67 with the SCL-90 anxiety scale. A number of other similar studies have yielded virtually identical results with both clinical and nonclinical samples. Both Weissman et al. (1977) and Amenson and Lewinsohn (1981), for example, found that scores on the CES-D correlated significantly (*rs* = .40 to .90) with scores on all nine SCL-90 subscales. Vernon and Roberts (1981) found that the correlation of the CES-D with the total score of the demoralization scale, a measure of general psychological distress, was as high as possible given the reliabilities of the two measures. Blatt, Quinlan, Chevron, McDonald, and Zuroff (1982) found the BDI to correlate significantly with 9 of the 10 clinical scales of the MMPI in a sample of psychiatric inpatients, and Lubin (1967/1981) reported significant correlations between the DACL and most of the clinical scales of the MMPI. Krantz and Hammen (1979) and Peterson, Calamari, Greenberg, Giffort, and Schiers (1983) found that all six factors of the Profile of Mood States were significantly intercorrelated. In fact, Peterson et al. reported that the depression scale correlated .74 to .90 with the other five scales. Finally, Gotlib (1984) administered measures of depression (BDI, MMPI-D-30, MAACL-D), anxiety (STAI, MAACL-A), and general distress (e.g., Dysfunctional Attitude Scale, Rathus Assertiveness Schedule, SCL-90, MAACL hostility) to 443 university students. As in the previous studies, all three measures of depression correlated significantly with all nine of the SCL-90 scales, as well as with the Dysfunctional Attitude Scale and the Rathus Assertiveness Schedule. In fact, a factor analysis of all the measures yielded a two-factor solution with the first factor, composed of all but the MAACL subscales, accounting for 50% of the total variance.

Similar results have been found for measures of anxiety. Donovan et al. (1975), for example, obtained significant correlations among the Taylor Manifest Anxiety Scale (TMAS), the Tennessee Self-Concept Scale, the Activity Preference Questionnaire, and Rotter's Internal–External Control Scale. On the basis of their results, Donovan et al. suggest that the TMAS is more accurately described as a measure of negative self-concept than of anxiety. In two studies described earlier, Dinning and Evans (1977) and Gotlib (1984) both found the STAI to correlate significantly with all nine subscales of the SCL-90, and Russell, Peplau, and Cutrona (1980) similarly found the STAI to correlate significantly with the UCLA Loneliness Scale. In fact, in a review of research conducted with the STAI, Chaplin (1984) notes that the STAI trait anxiety scale does not discriminate well between anxiety and general psychopathology. The STAI trait anxiety scale has been found to correlate with all of the MMPI clinical scales, with the Personality Research Form aggression and impulsivity scales, with the MAACL hostility scale, and with all the problem areas on the Mooney Problem Checklist. Reminiscent of the conclusions of Donovan et al., Chaplin suggests that the STAI appears to be related to general feelings of dissatisfaction with oneself, and not simply to anxiety. Finally, Friedman and Booth-Kewley (1987) recently conducted a meta-analysis of studies examining the relationship of emotional aspects of personality with asthma, arthritis, ulcers, headaches, and coronary heart disease. For our purposes, the important finding of this study is that for each of these disorders, the relationship with depression was virtually identical to the relationship with anxiety.

Correlations between Depression and Anxiety. It is apparent, therefore, that self-report measures of depression and anxiety both are significantly correlated with measures of other emotional states, personality characteristics, and other aspects of psychological and physical distress. Not surprisingly, a number of studies have also found that measures of depression and anxiety correlate strongly with each other. In one of the first studies to examine the relationship among self-report measures of depression and anxiety, Mendels et al. (1972) administered 11 self-report measures of depression and anxiety, including the BDI, Zung SDS, CC-D and CC-A, the three MAACL subscales, and the MMPI-D, to 76 female psychiatric inpatients. A principal components factor analysis with varimax rotation resulted in a two-factor solution which accounted for 68% of the total variance (53 and 15%, respectively). Mendels et al. found that all but two measures loaded greater than .70 on the first factor. Furthermore, all of the measures of depression and anxiety making up this first factor were significantly intercorrelated, with no correlation below .50.

Subsequent studies have obtained results consistent with those reported by Mendels et al. (1972). Indeed, significant correlations among various self-report measures of depression and anxiety have been found in samples of psychiatric patients (e.g., Davies et al., 1975; Evanson, Holland, Mehta, & Yasin, 1980; Hoffman & Overall, 1978), alcoholic inpatients (Pachman & Foy, 1978), medical outpatients (D. P. Goldberg,

Rickels, Downing, & Hesbacher, 1976), community residents (Orme, Reis, & Herz, 1986), and university students (Cane & Gotlib, 1985; Dobson, 1985a; Gotlib, 1984; Gotlib & Robinson, 1982; Hollon & Kendall, 1980; Krantz and Hammen, 1979; Meites, Lovallo, & Pishkin, 1980). In a prototypical study, Tanaka-Matsumi and Kameoka (1986) administered seven measures of depression and anxiety to a large sample of college undergraduates. They found that the correlations between the depression and anxiety scores were as high as the within-construct estimates of convergent validity. In fact, the BDI correlated more highly with measures of anxiety (STAI trait, TMAS) than it did with other measures of depression. The Zung SDS and Zung SAS correlated .71 with each other, higher than the SDS's correlations with two other depression measures and the SAS's correlations with two other anxiety measures.

It is also instructive to note that studies in which factor analyses have been conducted, such as the investigation by Mendels et al. (1972) described earlier, have been unable to separate empirically the constructs of depression and anxiety (cf. Dobson, 1985a; D. P. Goldberg et al., 1976; Gotlib, 1984; Gotlib & Meyer, 1986). For example, in conducting a factor analysis of responses to the General Health Questionnaire for a sample of medical outpatients, D. P. Goldberg et al. (1976) found that the first factor involved both depression and anxiety. D. P. Goldberg et al. stated that "it should perhaps be emphasized that both rotated and unrotated solutions have been examined up to the 7-factor solution and that there is no solution which produces anxiety items on one dimension and depressive items on another" (p. 65).

Similar conclusions can be drawn from studies examining the factor structure of the SCL-90 and the MCMI. With respect to the SCL-90, while a number of studies have provided evidence for a dimension assessing depression, no support has been obtained for the existence of a separate anxiety dimension. Items from the anxiety scale have been found, instead, either to be dispersed over the remaining factors (Clark & Friedman, 1983) or to combine with items from the depression scale to form a mixed anxiety–depression factor (Mazmanian, Mendonca, Holden, & Dufton, 1986). Factor analyses of the MCMI have also failed to obtain separate depression and anxiety dimensions. Flynn and McMahon (1984), for example, obtained a factor solution in which the first factor described a negativistic-avoidant personality type with associated depression, anxiety, and somatic complaints. Piersma (1986) also obtained a factor assessing depression, anxiety, and somatic concerns, but without the personality features described by Flynn and McMahon. From the perspective of this chapter, then, the most significant result of these studies is the absence of separate dimensions for depression and anxiety in any of the obtained factor solutions.

Finally, several investigators have examined the ability of self-report measures of depression and anxiety to discriminate individuals diagnosed as depressed from persons diagnosed as anxious. In one such study, Breslau (1985) assessed 310 women on the CES-D and on the Diagnostic Interview Schedule (DIS; Robins, Helzer, Croughan, & Ratcliff, 1981) criteria for major depressive disorder (MDD) and generalized anxiety disorder (GAD). With respect to predicting a diagnosis of MDD, the sensitivity of the CES-D (i.e., the accuracy with which it detected cases) was 87.5% and its specficity (i.e., the accuracy with which it identified noncases by the same criterion) was 73%. The predictive value of the CES-D, however, was only 15%: of the 292 women who did not receive a diagnosis of MDD, 79 (27%) scored 16 or greater on the CES-D. Interestingly, the figures for GAD are virtually identical to these: a sensitivity of 80%, a specificity of 73%, and a predictive value of 17%. In explaining the relatively low specificity of the CES-D for detecting current depression, Breslau cites the scale's inability to distinguish current major depression from past major depression or from current and past generalized anxiety. Moreover, an examination of the individual CES-D items also failed to identify any symptom as specific to either major depression or generalized anxiety. On the basis of these results, Breslau concluded that there is no support for the notion that the CES-D scale measures depression specifically.

More promising results were recently reported by Steer, Beck, Riskind, and Brown (1986), who used the BDI to differentiate a group of psychiatric outpatients diagnosed as depressed (MDD or dysthymic disorder) from a group diagnosed as anxious (GAD). A backward stepwise discriminant analysis indicated that two BDI items, sadness and loss of libido, each explained 18% of the discriminant space that differentiated the two groups. It is interesting to note that these are the two content items on the BDI that assess the two essential features described in DSM-III-R for a diagnosis of major depressive episode.

In concluding this section, we must concur with Mendels et al. (1972), who, 15 years ago, stated that "the literature, with only a few partial exceptions, is in agreement about the difficulty in discriminating between anxiety and depression" (p. 652). Mendels et al. go further, however, and suggest an explanation for this state of affairs:

> This is in keeping with the clinical observation that the content expressed by patients who are called either anxious or depressed is often very similar. Both groups of patients may mention dysphoria, rumination and worry, feelings of failure, worthlessness and guilt, tension, vague fears, sleep difficulties, somatic disturbances, feelings of loneliness and alienation, etc. The psychiatric interviewer probably makes his diagnostic judgment from other cues: whether the patient's behavior seems more mildly hyperactive and vigilant, or sad, despondent, and 'slowed down.'

> He may also make judgments as to the intensity of the complaints described: the sadness may seem more intense than the apprehension, for example. (p. 652)

Thus, Mendels et al. suggest that the self-reported symptomatology of depressed and anxious patients is very similar, although they may differ with respect to observed affect and overt behavior. Consequently, the lack of discriminating power of the measures examined in their study was due to the fact that they assessed only self-reported symptomatology. In the following section of this chapter, we consider this, as well as other possible explanations, for the low discriminant validity of self-report measures of anxiety and depression.

VIII. The Relationship among Self-Report Measures of Depression and Anxiety: Possible Explanations

It is clear from our review that self-report measures of depression and anxiety are highly intercorrelated. Moreover, although there have been a number of studies in which factor analyses were conducted on measures of depression and anxiety, none of these investigations identified two separate factors of depression and anxiety. In this section we offer possible reasons for the strength of the relationship among measures of anxiety and depression. More specifically, we briefly present what we believe are the three most probable explanations for the fact that these two constructs cannot be differentiated in self-report: First, and most likely, self-report measures of depression and anxiety might be, in large part, assessing symptoms that are common to both these constructs; second, responses to self-report measures of depression and anxiety might be tapping a single, underlying dimension of social desirability, or, more aptly, social *un*desirability; and third, symptoms of depression may often be present and secondary in anxiety disorders, and self-report measures are simply reflecting this co-occurrence.

Common Symptoms. Earlier in this chapter we reviewed DSM-III-R symptoms of depression and anxiety and we categorized each symptom as specific to depression, specific to anxiety, or common to both constructs (see Table 5.2). One likely explanation for the consistent finding of high intercorrelations among self-report measures of depression and anxiety is that items on these instruments assess not only symptoms specific to the construct in question, but might also assess symptoms that are common to the two disorders. Thus, measures of depression likely assess both symptoms specific to depression and symptoms common to depression and anxiety, while measures of anxiety assess both symptoms specific to anxiety and common symptoms. If this is in fact the case, the high correlations among these measures may be due to these common, overlapping symptoms. To examine this possibility we reviewed each of the measures described earlier in the chapter, with the exception of the MAACL, which is made up only of single adjectives. For each measure we calculated the number of items that assessed symptoms specific to depression, the number of items that assessed symptoms specific to anxiety, the number of items that assessed symptoms common to the two constructs, and the number of items that measured symptoms unrelated to DSM-III-R criteria for either depression or anxiety. We then calculated the proportion of items on each measure that assessed the intended construct (i.e., specific depression plus common items for depression measures, and specific anxiety plus common items for anxiety measures) and the proportion of items that assessed the unintended construct (i.e., specific anxiety plus common items for depression measures, and specific depression plus common items for anxiety measures). The results of this analysis are presented in Table 5.3.

As is evident from the data presented in Table 5.3, self-report measures of depression and anxiety vary considerably with respect to the proportion of items that actually assess only what the instrument intended. For example, whereas 76% of the items on the BDI assess symptoms of depression, less than half of the items on the MMPI-D and the MCMI-D measure depressive symptomatology, as defined by DSM-III-R criteria. Similarly, 90% of the SAS items measure symptoms of anxiety, whereas this is true of less than half of the STAI trait and the MCMI-A items.

Equally enlightening is the proportion of items for each measure that assesses the *unintended* construct. For the depression measures, 40% of the items on the SDS, the MMPI-D, and the MMPI-D-30 measure symptoms of anxiety; in contrast, none of the items on the CC-D assesses anxiety symptoms. Similarly, whereas almost half of the items on the STAI trait and 30% of the MCMI-A items measure symptoms of depression, none of the items on the S-R GTA and the CC-A assesses depressive symptomatology. The STAI trait, in fact, actually has more items that assess depression than assess anxiety. Finally, for each instrument we also calculated the ratio of the proportion of items assessing the intended construct to the proportion of items assessing the unintended construct. This ratio provides an alternative index of the relevance of the measures to their intended contruct. In this context, it is interesting to

Table 5.3
Content Analysis of Measures of Depression and Anxiety

Measure[a]	Items measuring depression (No.)	Common items (No.)	Items measuring anxiety (No.)	Unrelated items (No.)	Items measuring intended construct (%)	Items measuring unintended construct (%)	Ratio intended/ unintended
			Depression				
BDI (21)	12	4	1	4	76	24	3.17
SDS (20)	8	6	2	4	70	40	1.75
CES-D (20)	10	4	1	5	70	25	2.80
MMPI-D (60)	13	12	12	23	42	40	1.05
MMPI-D-30 (30)	10	7	5	8	57	40	1.43
SCL-90-D (13)	8	1	1	3	69	15	4.60
MCMI-D (36)	11	6	2	17	47	22	2.14
CC-D (14)	8	0	0	6	57	0	—
$\overline{X}$					61	26	
			Anxiety				
TMAS (50)	5	7	24	13	62	24	2.58
S-R GTA (9)	0	0	5	4	56	0	—
CC-A (9)	0	0	7	2	78	0	—
STAI-T (20)	5	4	4	7	40	45	0.89
STAI-S (20)	1	4	8	7	60	20	3.00
SAS (20)	0	3	15	2	90	15	6.00
SCL-90-A (10)	0	1	6	3	70	10	7.00
MCMI-A (37)	7	4	8	18	32	30	1.07
$\overline{X}$					61	18	

[a] Number of items for each measure is presented in parentheses.

note that the two SCL-90 scales and the two Costello–Comrey scales obtained the highest ratios among both the depression and the anxiety measures.

Table 5.3 clearly shows that measures of anxiety and depression overlap to a considerable extent. In fact, an average of 17% of the items on the measures of depression and 11% of the items on the anxiety questionnaires assess symptoms common to both constructs. Furthermore, an average of 31% of the items of all these questionnaires assess symptoms unrelated to both depression and anxiety. Overlap in both these areas, then, likely contributes to the high intercorrelations obtained among measures of these two constructs.

Social Desirability. It is unlikely, however, that overlap in the content of self-report measures of depression and anxiety accounts fully for the significant correlations observed among these measures. As we noted previously, the depression and anxiety scales constructed by Costello and Comrey (1967) contain no items relevant to the unintended construct. Indeed, these scales were constructed explicitly for the purpose of discriminating between these two affective states. Nevertheless, significant correlations have been reported between the CC-A and CC-D scales (e.g., Cane & Gotlib, 1985). In this context, it is likely that other factors, such as the operation of various response biases, also contribute to the observed relationship among measures of depression and anxiety. One such response bias is social desirability, defined as the tendency to endorse items that are socially desirable while not endorsing items that are socially undesirable (Edwards, 1957). Evidence of a significant association between social desirability and various self-report measures of depression and anxiety has been provided by a number of studies. Edwards (1957), for example, reported a correlation of .69 between the MMPI-D scale and the Edwards Social Desirability Scale (ESDS; Edwards, 1957), while Langevin and Stancer (1979) obtained a corresponding correlation of .81. Significant correlations have also been reported between the ESDS and other widely used measures of depression, such as the BDI (Langevin & Stancer, 1979; Tanaka-Matsumi & Kameoka, 1986) and the Zung SDS and the DACL (Tanaka-Matsumi & Kameoka, 1986). Tanka-Matsumi and Kameoka also found a significant relationship between the ESDS and several self-report measures of anxiety, with correlations ranging from .49 to .85. Finally, measures of depression and anxiety that are a part of inventories assessing a broader range of symptomatology have been found to correlate with measures of social desirability. For example, Mazmanian et al. (1986) found significant correlations between the SCL-90-D and SCL-90-A scales and a measure of social desirability.

There is evidence, therefore, that a significant correlation exists between measures of social desirability and measures of depression and anxiety. Two different interpretations of this relationship are possible. First, these correlations may indicate that self-report measures of depression and anxiety are influenced by a social desirability response set. That is, the responses of individuals to depression and anxiety questionnaires may be determined in part by the social desirability values of the items on these measures. Alternatively, this correlation may result from an overlap in the content of items on depression, anxiety, and social desirability questionnaires. Information relevant to this issue is provided by the Tanaka-Matsumi and Kameoka (1986) study described previously. In addition to the ESDS, which is not entirely satisfactory as a measure of social desirability given the large number of items on this scale that are also relevant to the measurement of psychopathology, subjects also completed the Marlow–Crowne Social Desirability Scale (MCSDS; Crowne & Marlow, 1960). Unlike the ESDS, items on the MCSDS are not particularly relevant to the measurement of psychopathology but, instead, describe behaviors that are socially desirable but unlikely to occur. As expected, a comparison of the correlations between various measures of depression and anxiety and the two measures of social desirability revealed smaller correlations with the MCSDS than with the ESDS (see also Radloff, 1977). Nevertheless, although attenuated, all correlations between the MCSDS and the depression and anxiety scales remained significant, indicating that subjects' self-reports of depression and anxiety were influenced by a social desirability response set.

Social (un)desirability, then, may be another factor contributing to the observed covariation between self-reports of depression and anxiety. Because symptoms of depression and anxiety are generally viewed as socially undesirable, some individuals may underreport their level of distress, resulting in biased but concordant scores on self-report measures of these states. Conversely, other individuals may exhibit a response set in which symptoms are endorsed more on the basis of their evaluative component than on their content. This negative response bias may be particularly relevant to the self-reports of depressed individuals, because a sense of worthlessness, ranging from feelings of inadequacy to negative self-evaluations, is one of the defining characteristics of the depressive syndrome. Consistent with their negative view of self, depressed individuals may be willing to acknowledge a broad range of symptomatology regardless of its specific content. As a result, significant correlations would be expected between self-report measures of depression and anxiety, or between depression and any other scale composed of undesirable symptoms.

Secondary Depression. The third explanation for the significant correlations among self-report measures of depression and anxiety involves the concept of secondary depression. The high frequency with which symptoms of depression and anxiety have been observed to co-occur may be due, in part, to the high prevalence of secondary depression found in individuals with an anxiety disorder. Individuals for whom the experience of anxiety is a persistent and pervasive feature of their lives are also likely to experience substantial disruption of, and impairment in, their vocational functioning and interpersonal relations. In fact, as we noted earlier in the chapter, DSM-III-R lists depressive symptoms as associated features of generalized anxiety disorder, and anxiety symptoms as associated features of depressive disorders. Not surprisingly, therefore, investigators examining the prevalence of secondary depression in samples of patients meeting diagnostic criteria for an anxiety disorder have reported rates ranging from 33 to 50% (e.g., Clancy, Noyes, Hoenk, & Slymen, 1978; Dealy, Ishiki, Avery, Wilson, & Dunner, 1981; Noyes, Clancy, Hoenk, & Slymen, 1980). In some instances, then, symptoms of depression and anxiety may be observed to covary because depression is one of the likely consequences of a chronic and persistent anxiety disorder.

Current self-report measures are not able to discriminate between depression and anxiety in cases in which symptoms of depression or anxiety occur as a consequence of the other disorder. In large part, this is because existing measures appear to assess only the dimensions of symptom frequency and severity. In order to discriminate between anxiety and depression in cases of a secondary disorder, additional information, such as the timing and context in which symptoms develop, the course of symptom development, and the duration of symptoms, is required. The assessment of these additional dimensions on self-report measures of depression and anxiety may be necessary in order to increase the discriminant validity of these measures.

IX. Conclusions

Consistent with previous reviews of the measurement of depression and anxiety (e.g., Dobson, 1985c; Mendels et al., 1972), our examination of the relationship between these two constructs leads us to conclude that, in general, existing self-report measures of depression and anxiety do not discriminate between these syndromes. In this final section we will examine the implications of this conclusion, both for the use of existing self-report measures and for the construction of new instruments.

Let us first consider existing measures. Table 5.2 indicated that there are clearly a number of symptoms, such as fatigue, insomnia, and concentration difficulties, that are common to both depression and anxiety. Given this overlap in symptomatology, we should also expect overlap in measures of these two constructs. Significant correlations between measures of depression and anxiety, or even actual overlap in the items themselves, do not necessarily indicate psychometric shortcomings or that the measures are not adequately or accurately assessing their intended construct; rather, they may simply reflect the overlap in the symptoms of these two constructs. Indeed, given the overlap in symptoms, we should be suspicious of measures of anxiety and depression that do *not* intercorrelate to some extent.

Nevertheless, it is evident from the analysis presented in Table 5.3 that self-report measures of depression and anxiety differ substantially in terms of the number of items they include that are specific to the unintended construct. This difference in content validity represents perhaps the most obvious criterion that might be used in determining the most appropriate measures of depression and anxiety. In this context, it seems reasonable to suggest that, in situations in which there is a need to discriminate between depression and anxiety, measures should not have a significant number of symptoms that are specific to the unintended construct. The MMPI-D, MCMI-D, TMAS, and MCMI-A would thus be eliminated on the basis of this concern.

A second criterion might then be that the ratio of "intended" to "unintended" items should be reasonably high. On the basis of this criterion, the SDS, MMPI-D-30, and STAI trait would be eliminated. Each of the remaining measures assesses no more than one symptom that is specific to the unintended construct. Indeed, the CC-D, CC-A, and S-R GTA do not assess any symptoms specific to the unintended construct. However, the CC-D contains only eight items assessing depressive symptomatology, and the CC-A and S-R GTA are composed of only seven and five anxiety items, respectively; moreover, none of these measures assesses any of the symptoms common to depression and anxiety. Therefore, although these three instruments meet the goal of minimizing the number of "unintended" items, they do so by restricting the range of symptoms they assess, such that the syndromes of depression and anxiety are not fully covered. These measures, too, should probably not be considered further.

This elimination process leaves three depression measures (BDI, CES-D, and SCL-90-D) and three measures of anxiety (STAI-S, SAS, and SCL-90-A). With respect to the depression measures, it is instructive to note that the SCL-90-D scale has only 9 items that measure depressive symptoms, compared with 16 for the BDI and 14 for the CES-D. Given that, in general, reliability increases with the number of items in a scale, the SCL-90-D scale could be eliminated simply because 9 relevant items may be insufficient for a reliable measure of depression. Similarly, the

SCL-90-A scale has only 7 items that measure symptoms of anxiety, compared with 18 for the SAS and 12 for the STAI state. Thus, the SCL-90-A scale could be eliminated on the same grounds.

On the basis of this analysis of content validity, then, we are left with the BDI and CES-D as the strongest measures of depression, and the STAI state and SAS as measures of anxiety. At this point, other psychometric properties of these measures, such as reliability and convergent and predictive validity, would need to be evaluated. Ultimately, the final choice of a self-report instrument must be made with reference to the particular context in which the measure is to be used. Although we have emphasized content validity in our discussion of these measures, we do not wish to imply that it should necessarily be given priority over other forms of validity. Nevertheless, in situations in which an important objective is to discriminate between the syndromes of depression and anxiety, this type of content analysis does provide valuable information.

With respect to the development of new instruments, several strategies are available for enhancing the discriminant validity of self-report measures of depression and anxiety. First, in situations in which high discriminant validity is a goal, measures could be developed that give greater emphasis to the distinctive features of these syndromes. Although current descriptions of depression and anxiety contain a number of common features, distinctive features—such as loss of interest and pleasure in depression and excessive worry in anxiety—are also evident. Indeed, Watson (1987; see also Watson & Kendall, this volume) has recently demonstrated that whereas negative affect is present in both depression and anxiety, only depression is also characterized by a lack of positive affect. Self-report measures that gave greater emphasis to these distinctive features may produce a more satisfactory separation of these two syndromes.

Discriminant validity may also be enchanced by ensuring that the content of self-report measures more faithfully reflects the criteria used to define depression and anxiety. Because of the need to assess symptoms common to both syndromes, this approach would certainly not eliminate overlapping content entirely. It would, however, eliminate the overlap introduced when measures include items that are not relevant to the intended construct, but that are related to the unintended construct. An example of this approach to the construction of a self-report measure is the Inventory to Diagnose Depression (IDD; Zimmerman & Coryell, 1987; Zimmerman, Coryell, Corenthal, & Wilson, 1986), which was developed to diagnose major depressive disorder using DSM-III criteria. Items on the IDD cover the entire range of symptoms used to diagnose major depressive disorder, and thresholds can be used to score a symptom as either present or absent. Although preliminary investigations of the IDD are encouraging, the relationship of this instrument to measures of anxiety has yet to be examined.

Discriminant validity of self-report measures of anxiety and depression may be further enhanced by a careful examination of the discriminant validity of individual items. Through the construction of a Differential Reliability Index (Jackson, 1970), the correlation of an item with both its intended scale and with scales assessing other constructs can be compared. Items with unacceptably low discriminant validity can then be identified and eliminated. Dobson (1985a), for example, employed this procedure as part of the development of a number of scales assessing situational predispositions for anxiety and depression. Evaluation of the psychometric properties of these scales revealed higher correlations between scales assessing the same construct than between scales assessing different constructs, and a factor analysis of these scales produced separate factors for anxiety and depression.

Finally, as we noted earlier, self-report measures of depression and anxiety may need to assess dimensions other than symptom patterns and severity in order to discriminate between these syndromes. Theories of depression and anxiety emphasize different etiological factors, with actual or perceived loss implicated in depression and evaluation of potential threat or danger regarded as central to the onset of anxiety. Self-report instruments do not assess etiology, but rather measure symptoms of depression and anxiety. It is possible that although different etiological processes are operative, they lead to similar outcomes, or symptoms. Thus, the fact that self-report measures ask respondents to indicate *how* they feel (and in what appears to be too general a manner), rather than *why* they feel this way, may contribute to their lack of differentiation between depression and anxiety. The development of self-report measures that are sensitive to these etiological differences, although a challenging and potentially difficult task, will represent an important step toward the goal of increasing the discriminant validity of self-report measures. As we continue to refine our efforts at measuring depression and anxiety through self-report questionnaires, we will move toward a better understanding of the true nature of the relationship between these two constructs.

References

Amenson, C. S., & Lewinsohn, P. M. (1981). An investigation into the observed sex difference in prevalence of unipolar depression. *Journal of Abnormal Psychology, 90,* 1–13.
American Psychiatric Association. (1987). *Diagnostic and statistical manual of mental disorders* (3rd ed., rev.). Washington, DC: Author.

Baker, B. L., Cohen, D. C., & Saunders, J. T. (1973). Self-directed desensitization for acrophobia. *Behaviour Research and Therapy, 11,* 79–89.

Barnes, G. E., & Prosen, H. (1985). Parental death and depression. *Journal of Abnormal Psychology, 94,* 64–69.

Beck, A. T. (1967). *Depression: Causes and treatment.* Philadelphia: University of Pennsylvania Press.

Beck, A. T., & Beamesderfer, A. (1974). Assessment of depression: The Depression Inventory. In P. Pichot (Ed.), *Psychological measurements in psychopharmacology* (pp. 151–169). Basel: Karger.

Beck, A. T., & Beck, R. W. (1972). Screening depressed patients in family practice: A rapid technique. *Postgraduate Medicine, 52,* 81–85.

Beck, A. T., Ward, C. H., Mendelson, M., Mock, J., & Erlbaugh, J. (1961). An inventory for measuring depression. *Archives of General Psychiatry, 4,* 53–61.

Blatt, S. J., Quinlan, D. M., Chevron, E. S., McDonald, C., & Zuroff, D. (1982). Dependency and self-criticism: Psychological dimensions of depression. *Journal of Consulting and Clinical Psychology, 50,* 113–124.

Blumenthal, M. D. (1975). Measuring depressive symptomatology in a general population. *Archives of General Psychiatry, 32,* 971–978.

Borkovec, T. D., Weerts, T. C., & Bernstein, D. A. (1977). Assessment of anxiety. In A. R. Ciminero, K. S. Calhoun, & H. E. Adams (Eds), *Handbook of behavioral assessment* (pp. 367–428). New York: Wiley.

Boyd, J. H., Weissman, M. M., Thompson, W. D., & Myers, J. K. (1982). Screening for depression in a community sample. *Archives of General Psychiatry, 39,* 1195–1200.

Brackbill, G., & Little, K. B. (1954). MMPI correlates of the Taylor scale of manifest anxiety. *Journal of Consulting Psychology, 18,* 433–436.

Breslau, N. (1985). Depressive symptoms, major depression, and generalized anxiety: A comparison of self-reports on CES-D and results from diagnostic interviews. *Psychiatry Research, 15,* 219–229.

Bull, R. H. C., & Strongman, K. T. (1971). Anxiety, neuroticism, and extroversion. *Psychological Reports, 29,* 1101–1102.

Cane, D. B., & Gotlib, I. H. (1985). Depression and the effects of positive and negative feedback on expectations, evaluations, and performance. *Cognitive Therapy and Research, 9,* 145–160.

Carroll, B., Fielding, J. M., & Blashki, T. G. (1973). Depression rating scales: A critical review. *Archives of General Psychiatry, 28,* 361–366.

Chaplin, W. F. (1984). The State Trait Anxiety Inventory. In D. J. Keyser & R. C. Sweetland (Eds.), *Test critiques* (Vol. 1, pp. 626–632). Kansas City, MO: Test Corporation of America.

Clancy, J., Noyes, R., Hoenk, P. R., & Slymen, D. J. (1978). Secondary depression in anxiety neurosis. *Journal of Nervous and Mental Disease, 166,* 846–850.

Clark, A., & Friedman, M. J. (1983). Factor structure and discriminant validity of the SCL-90 in a veteran population. *Journal of Personality Assessment, 47,* 396–404.

Comrey, A. L. (1957). A factor analysis of items on the MMPI Depression scale. *Educational and Psychological Measurement, 18,* 578–585.

Costello, C. G., & Comrey, A. L. (1967). Scales for measuring depression and anxiety. *Journal of Psychology, 66,* 303–313.

Crowne, D., & Marlow, D. (1960). A new scale of social desirability independent of psychopathology. *Journal of Consulting Psychology, 24,* 349–354.

Davies, B., Burrows, G., & Poynton, C. (1975). A comparative study of four depression rating scales. *Australian and New Zealand Journal of Psychiatry, 9,* 21–24.

Dealy, R. S., Ishiki, D. M., Avery, D. H., Wilson, L. G., & Dunner, D. L. (1981). Secondary depression in anxiety disorders. *Comprehensive Psychiatry, 22,* 612–618.

Deardorff, W. W., & Funabiki, D. (1985). A diagnostic caution in screening for depressed college students. *Cognitive Therapy and Research, 9,* 277–284.
Dempsey, P. A. (1964). Unidimensional depression scale for the MMPI. *Journal of Consulting Psychology, 28,* 364–370.
Depue, R. A., & Monroe, S. M. (1978). Learned helplessness in the perspective of the depressive disorders: Conceptual and definitional issues. *Journal of Abnormal Psychology, 87,* 3–20.
Derogatis, L. R. (1977). *SCL-90 administration, scoring, and procedures manual.* Baltimore: Johns Hopkins Press.
Derogatis, L. R., Lipman, R. S., & Covy, L. (1973). The SCL-90: An outpatient psychiatric rating scale. *Psychopharmacology Bulletin, 9,* 13–28.
Dinning, W. D., & Evans, R. G. (1977). Discriminant and convergent validity of the SCL-90 in psychiatric inpatients. *Journal of Personality Assessment, 41,* 304–310.
Dobson, K. S. (1985a). An analysis of anxiety and depression scales. *Journal of Personality Assessment, 49,* 522–527.
Dobson, K. S. (1985b). Defining an interactional approach to anxiety and depression. *Psychological Record, 35,* 471–489.
Dobson, K. S. (1985c). The relationship between anxiety and depression. *Clinical Psychology Review, 5,* 307–324.
Donovan, D., Smythe, L., Paige, A., & O'Leary, M. (1975). Relationships among locus of control, self-concept, and anxiety. *Journal of Clinical Psychology, 31,* 682–684.
Edwards, A. L. (1957). *The social desirability variable in personality assessment and research.* New York: Holt, Rinehart & Winston.
Endler, N. S., King, P. R., Edwards, J. M., Kuczynski, M., & Diveky, S. (1983). Generality of the interaction model of anxiety with respect to two social evaluation field studies. *Canadian Journal of Behavioral Science, 15,* 60–69.
Endler, N. S., Magnusson, D., Ekehammar, B., & Okada, M. (1976). The multidimensionality of state and trait anxiety. *Scandinavian Journal of Psychology, 17,* 81–96.
Endler, N. S., & Okada, M. (1975). A multidimensional measure of trait anxiety: The S-R Inventory of General Trait Anxiousness. *Journal of Consulting and Clinical Psychology, 43,* 319–329.
Endler, N. S., & Shedletsky, R. (1973). Trait vs. state anxiety, authoritarianism, and ego threat vs. physical threat. *Canadian Journal of Behavioral Science, 5,* 347–361.
Evanson, R. C., Holland, R. A., Mehta, S., & Yasin, F. (1980). Factor analysis of the Symptom Checklist-90. *Psychological Reports, 46,* 695–699.
Flood, M., & Endler, N. S. (1980). The interaction model of anxiety: An empirical test in an athletic competition situation. *Journal of Research in Personality, 14,* 329–339.
Flynn, P. M., & McMahon, R. C. (1984). An examination of the factor structure of the Millon Clinical Multiaxial Inventory. *Journal of Personality Assessment, 48,* 308–311.
Friedman, H. S., & Booth-Kewley, S. (1987). The "disease-prone personality": A meta-analytic view of the construct. *American Psychologist, 42,* 539–555.
Glazer, H. I., Clarkin, J. F., & Hunt, H. F. (1981). Assessment of depression. In J. F. Clarkin & H. I. Glazer (Eds.), *Depression: Behavioral and directive intervention strategies* (pp. 3–30). New York: Garland STPM Press.
Gocka, E. (1965). *American Lake norms for 200 MMPI scales.* Unpublished manuscript, Veterans Administration Hospital, American Lake, WA.
Goldberg, D. P., Rickels, K., Downing, R., & Hesbacher, P. (1976). A comparison of two psychiatric screening tests. *British Journal of Psychiatry, 129,* 61–67.
Goldberg, J. O., Shaw, B. F., & Segal, Z. V. (1907). Concurrent validity of the Millon Clinical Multiaxial Inventory Depression scales. *Journal of Consulting and Clinical Psychology, 55,* 785–787.

Golin, S., & Hartz, M. A. (1979). A factor analysis of the Beck Depression Inventory in a mildly depressed population. *Journal of Clinical Psychology, 35,* 322–325.

Gotlib, I. H. (1984). Depression and general psychopathology in university students. *Journal of Abnormal Psychology, 93,* 19–30.

Gotlib, I. H., & Meyer, J. P. (1986). Factor analysis of the Multiple Affect Adjective Check List: A separation of positive and negative affect. *Journal of Personality and Social Psychology, 50,* 1161–1165.

Gotlib, I. H., & Robinson, L. A. (1982). Responses to depressed individuals: Discrepancies between self-report and observer rated behavior. *Journal of Abnormal Psychology, 91,* 231–240.

Graham, J. R. (1977). *The MMPI: A practical guide.* New York: Oxford University Press.

Grossberg, J., & Wilson, H. K. (1965). A correlational comparison of the Wolpe–Lange Fear Survey Schedule and Taylor Manifest Anxiety Scale. *Behaviour Research and Therapy, 3,* 125–12O.

Gurtman, M. B. (1985). Self-Rating Depression Scale. In D. J. Keyser & R. C. Sweetland (Eds.), *Test critiques* (Vol. 3, pp. 593–603). Kansas City, MO: Test Corporation of America.

Hammen, C. L. (1981). Assessment: A clinical and cognitive emphasis. In L. P. Rehm (Ed.), *Behavior therapy for depression: Present status and future directions* (pp. 255–277). New York: Academic Press.

Hathaway, S. R., & McKinley, J. C. (1951). *The Minnesota Multiphasic Personality Inventory Manual* (rev. ed.). New York: Psychological Corporation.

Hilgard, E. R., Jones, L. V., & Kaplan, S. J. (1951). Conditioned discrimination as related to anxiety. *Journal of Experimental Psychology, 42,* 94–99.

Hoffman, N. G., & Overall, P. B. (1978). Factor structure of the SCL-90 in a psychiatric population. *Journal of Consulting and Clinical Psychology, 46,* 1187–1191.

Hollon, S. D., & Kendall, P. C. (1980). Cognitive self-statements in depression: Development of an Automatic Thoughts Questionnaire. *Cognitive Therapy and Research, 4,* 383–395.

Hollon, S. D., & Mandell, M. (1979). Use of the MMPI in the evaluation of treatment effects. In J. N. Butcher (Ed.), *New developments in the use of the MMPI* (pp. 241–302). Minneapolis: University of Minnesota Press.

Hughes, J. R., O'Hara, M. W., & Rehm, L. P. (1982). Measurement of depression in clinical trials: An overview. *Journal of Clinical Psychiatry, 43,* 85–88.

Jackson, D. N. (1970). A sequential system for personality scale development. In C. D. Spielberger (Ed.), *Current topics in clinical and community psychology* (Vol. 2, pp. 62–96). New York: Academic Press.

Jegede, R. O. (1977). Psychometric attributes of the Self-Rating Anxiety Scale. *Psychological Reports, 40,* 303–306.

Kendall, P. C. (1978). Anxiety: States, traits—situations? *Journal of Consulting and Clinical Psychology, 46,* 280–287.

Kendall, P. C., Finch, A. J., Auerbach, S. M., Hooke, J. F., & Mikulka, P. J. (1976). *Journal of Consulting and Clinical Psychology, 44,* 406–412.

Kendall, P. C., Hollon, S. D., Beck, A. T., Hammen, C. L., & Ingram, R. E. (1987). Issues and recommendations regarding use of the Beck Depression Inventory. *Cognitive Therapy and Research, 11,* 289–299.

Kendall, P. C., & Norton-Ford, J. D. (1982). *Clinical psychology: Scientific and professional dimensions.* New York: Wiley.

King, P. R., & Endler, N. W. (1982). Medical interventions and the interaction model of anxiety. *Canadian Journal of Behavioral Science, 14,* 82–91.

Klorman, R., Weerts, T. C., Hastings, J. E., Melamed, B. G., & Lang, P. J. (1974). Psychometric description of some specific-fear questionnaires. *Behavior Therapy, 5,* 401–409.

Krantz, S., & Hammen, C. (1979). Assessment of cognitive bias in depression. *Journal of Abnormal Psychology, 88,* 611–619.
Langevin, R., & Stancer, H. (1979). Evidence that depression rating scales primarily measure a social undesirability response set. *Acta Psychiatrica Scandinavia, 59,* 70–79.
Levitt, E. E., & Lubin, B. (1975). *Depression: Concepts, controversies, and some new facts.* New York: Springer.
Lewinsohn, P. M., & Teri, L. (1982). Selection of depressed and nondepressed subjects on the basis of self-report data. *Journal of Consulting and Clinical Psychology, 50,* 590–591.
Lips, H. M., & Ng, M. (1985). Use of the Beck Depression Inventory with three nonclinical populations. *Canadian Journal of Behavioural Science, 18,* 62–74.
Lubin, B. (1965). Adjective check lists for measurement of depression. *Archives of General Psychiatry, 12,* 57–62.
Lubin, B. (1967/1981). *Manual for depression adjective check lists.* San Diego: Educational and Industrial Testing Service.
Mandler, G., & Sarason, S. B. (1952). A study of anxiety and learning. *Journal of Abnormal and Social Psychology, 47,* 166–173.
Mayer, J. M. (1977). Assessment of depression. In P. McReynolds (Ed.), *Advances in psychological assessment* (Vol. 4, pp. 358–425). San Francisco: Jossey-Bass.
Mazmanian, D., Mendonca, J. D., Holden, R. R., & Dufton, B. (1986). *Psychopathology and response styles in the SCL-90 responses of acutely distressed persons* (Research Bulletin, Vol. 4, No. 4). St. Thomas, Canada: St. Thomas Psychiatric Hospital.
McNair, D. M. (1974). Self-evaluations of antidepressants. *Psychopharmacologia, 37,* 281–302.
McNair, D. M., Lorr, M., & Droppleman, L. F. (1971). *Profile of mood states.* San Diego: EdiTS/Educational and Industrial Testing Service.
Meites, K., Lovallo, W., & Pishkin, V. (1980). A comparison of four scales for anxiety, depression, and neuroticism. *Journal of Clinical Psychology, 36,* 427–432.
Mendels, J., Weinstein, N., & Cochrane, C. (1972). The relationship between depression and anxiety. *Archives of General Psychiatry, 27,* 649–653.
Millon, T. (1983). *Millon clinical multiaxial inventory manual* (3rd ed.). Minneapolis: Interpretive Scoring Systems.
Moran, P. W., & Lambert, M. J. (1983). A review of current assessment tools for monitoring changes in depression. In M. J. Lambert, E. R. Christensen, & S. S. DeJulio (Eds.), *The assessment of psychotherapy outcome* (pp. 304–355). New York: Wiley.
Mothersill, K. J., Dobson, K. S., & Neufeld, R. W. J. (1986). The interactional model of anxiety: An evaluation of the differential hypothesis. *Journal of Personality and Social Psychology, 51,* 640–648.
Myers, J. K., & Weissman, M. M. (1980). Use of a self-report symptom scale to detect depression in a community sample. *American Journal of Psychiatry, 137,* 1081–1084.
Nelson, L. D. (1987). Measuring depression in a clinical population using the MMPI. *Journal of Consulting and Clinical Psychology, 55,* 788–790.
Newton, J. R. (1968). Clinical normative data for MMPI special scales Critical Items, Manifest Anxiety, and Repression–Sensitization. *Journal of Clinical Psychology, 24,* 427–430.
Noyes, R., Clancy, J., Hoenk, P. R., & Slymen, D. J. (1980). The prognosis of anxiety neurosis. *Archives of General Psychiatry, 37,* 173–178.
O'Connor, J. P., Lorr, M., & Stafford, J. W. (1956). Some patterns of manifest anxiety. *Journal of Clinical Psychology, 12,* 160–163.
Orme, J. G., Reis, J., & Herz, E. J. (1986). Factorial and discriminant validity of the Center for Epidemiological Studies Depression (CES-D) Scale. *Journal of Clinical Psychology, 42,* 28–33.
Pachman, J. S., & Foy, D. W. (1978). A correlational investigation of anxiety, self-esteem

and depression: New findings with behavioral measures of assertiveness. *Journal of Behavior Therapy and Experimental Psychiatry, 9,* 97–101.

Peterson, R. A., Calamari, J., Greenberg, G., Giffort, D., & Schiers, B. (1983, August). *Evaluation of two strategies to reduce stress on supervisory staff in a residential facility for the DD.* Paper presented at the meeting of the Illinois American Association in Mental Deficiency, Homewood, IL.

Phillips, J. B., & Endler, N. S. (1982). Academic examinations and anxiety: The interaction model empirically tested. *Journal of Research in Personality, 16,* 303–318.

Piersma, H. L. (1986). The factor structure of the Millon Clinical Multiaxial Inventory (MCMI) for psychiatric inpatients. *Journal of Personality Assessment, 50,* 578–584.

Radloff, L. S. (1977). The CES-D Scale: A new self-report depression scale for research in the general population. *Applied Psychological Measurement, 1,* 385–401.

Rankin, R. J. (1963). Nonfunctioning Taylor manifest anxiety items. *Psychological Reports, 12,* 912.

Rehm, L. P. (1976). Assessment of depression. In M. Hersen & A. S. Bellack (Eds.), *Behavioral assessment: A practical handbook* (pp. 246–295). New York: Pergamon Press.

Roberts, R. E. (1980). Reliability of the CES-D in different ethnic contexts. *Psychiatry Research, 2,* 125–134.

Roberts, R. E., & Vernon, S. W. (1983). The Center for Epidemiologic Studies Depression Scale: Its use in a community sample. *American Journal of Psychiatry, 140,* 41–46.

Robins, L. N., Helzer, J. E., Croughan, J., & Ratcliff, K. S. (1981). The NIMH Diagnostic Interview Schedule: Its history, characteristics and validity. *Archives of General Psychiatry, 38,* 381–390.

Russell, D., Peplau, L. A., & Cutrona, C. E. (1980). The Revised UCLA Loneliness Scale: Concurrent and discriminant validity evidence. *Journal of Personality and Social Psychology, 39,* 472–480.

Schaefer, A., Brown, J., Watson, C. G., Plemel. D. DeMotts, J., Howard, M. T., Petrik, N., & Balleweg, B. J. (1985). Comparison of the validities of the Beck, Zung, and MMPI depression scales. *Journal of Consulting and Clinical Psychology, 53,* 415–418.

Schwab, J. J., Bialow, M. R., & Holzer, C. E. (1967). A comparison of rating scales for depression. *Journal of Clinical Psychology, 23,* 94–96.

Shaw, B. F., Vallis, T. M., & McCabe, S. B. (1985). The assessment of the severity and symptom patterns in depression. In E. E. Beckham & W. R. Leber (Eds.), *Handbook of depression: Treatment, assessment, and research* (pp. 372–407). Homewood, IL: Dorsey Press.

Smith, R. C., & Lay, C. D. (1974). State and trait anxiety: An annotated bibliography. *Psychological Reports, 34,* 519–594.

Snaith, R. P., Ahmed, S. N., Mehta, S., & Hamilton, M. (1971). Assessment of the severity of primary depressive illness: Wakefield Self-Assessment Depression Inventory. *Psychological Medicine, 1,* 143–149.

Spence, J. T., & Spence, K. W. (1966). The motivational components of manifest anxiety: Drive and drive stimuli. In C. D. Spielberger (Ed.), *Anxiety and behavior.* New York: Academic Press.

Spielberger, C. D., Gorsuch, R. L., & Lushene, R. E. (1970). *STAI manual for the State-Trait Anxiety Inventory.* Palo Alto, CA: Consulting Psychologists Press.

Steer, R. A., Beck, A. T., Riskind, J. H., & Brown, G. (1986). Differentiation of depressive disorders from generalized anxiety by the Beck Depression Inventory. *Journal of Clinical Psychology, 42,* 475–478.

Strober, M., Green, J., & Carlson, G. (1981). Utility of the Beck Depression Inventory with psychiatrically hospitalized adolescents. *Journal of Consulting and Clinical Psychology, 49,* 482–483.

Swenson, W. M., Pearson, J. S., & Osborne, D. (1973). *An MMPI sourcebook: Basic items, scale and pattern data on 50,000 medical patients.* Minneapolis: University of Minnesota Press.

Tanaka-Matsumi, J., & Kameoka, V. A. (1986). Reliabilities and concurrent validities of popular self-report measures of depression, anxiety, and social desirability. *Journal of Consulting and Clinical Psychology, 54,* 328–333.

Taylor, J. A. (1953). A personality scale of manifest anxiety. *Journal of Abnormal and Social Psychology, 48,* 285–290.

Vernon, S. W., & Roberts, R. E. (1981). Measuring nonspecific psychological distress and other dimensions of psychopathology. *Archives of General Psychiatry, 38,* 1239–1247.

Vredenburg, K., Krames, L., & Flett, G. L. (1985). Reexamining the Beck Depression Inventory: The long and short of it. *Psychological Reports, 56,* 767–778.

Watson, D. (1987, August). *A two-factor model of affect and its implications for psychopathology.* Paper presented at the annual convention of the American Psychological Association, New York.

Watson, D., & Clark, L. A. (1984). Negative Affectivity: The disposition to experience aversive emotional states. *Psychological Bulletin, 96,* 465–490.

Watson, D., & Friend, R. (1969). Measurement of social-evaluative anxiety. *Journal of Consulting and Clinical Psychology, 33,* 448–451.

Watson, D., & Tellegen, A. (1985). Toward a consensual structure of mood. *Psychological Bulletin, 98,* 219–235.

Weckowicz, T. E., Muir, W., & Cropley, A. J. (1967). A factor analysis of the Beck inventory of depression. *Journal of Consulting Psychology, 31,* 105–115.

Weissman, M. M., Sholomskas, D., Pottenger, M., Prusoff, B. A., & Locke, B. Z. (1977). Assessing depressive symptoms in five psychiatric populations: A validation study. *American Journal of Epidemiology, 106,* 203–214.

Wolpe, J., & Lang, P. J. (1964). *Fear Survey Schedule.* San Diego: Educational and Industrial Testing Service.

Zimmerman, M., & Coryell, W. (1987). The Inventory to Diagnose Depression (IDD): A self-report scale to diagnose major depressive disorder. *Journal of Consulting and Clinical Psychology, 55,* 55–59.

Zimmerman, M., Coryell, W., Corenthal, C., & Wilson, S. (1986). A self-report scale to diagnose major depressive disorder. *Archives of General Psychiatry, 43,* 1076–1081.

Zuckerman, M. (1960). The development of an Affect Adjective Check List for the measurement of anxiety. *Journal of Consulting Psychology, 24,* 457–462.

Zuckerman, M., & Lubin, B. (1965). *The Multiple Affect Adjective Check List.* San Diego, Educational and Industrial Testing Service.

Zung, W. W. K. (1965). A self-rating depression scale. *Archives of General Psychiatry, 13,* 508–516.

Zung, W. W. K. (1971). A rating instrument for anxiety disorders. *Psychosomatics, 12,* 371–379.

Zung, W. W. K. (1974). The measurement of affects: Depression and anxiety. In P. Pichot (Ed.), *Modern problems in pharmacopsychiatry* (Vol. 7, pp. 170–188). Basel: Karger.

Zung, W. W. K. (1979). Assessment of anxiety disorder: Qualitative and quantitative approaches. In W. E. Fann, I. Karacan, A. D. Porkorny, & R. L. Williams (Eds.), *Phenomenology and treatment of anxiety* (pp. 1–17). New York: Spectrum Press.

Anxiety and Depression in Children and Adolescents: Negative Affectivity or Separate Constructs?

A. J. Finch, Jr.
Julie A. Lipovsky
Charles D. Casat

I. Introduction

Clinical descriptions suggest that there is a high association between depression and anxiety in adults (e.g., Ayd, 1984) and children (e.g., Puig-Antich & Rabinovich, 1986). Eason, Finch, Brasted, and Saylor (1985) noted that theoretical distinctions between anxiety and depression are unclear and that clinically the two constructs may not be dis-

Anxiety and Depression

tinct. Rather, symptoms of both are seen concurrently, reflecting a broader category of generalized emotional distress termed *negative affectivity* (NA) by Watson and Clark (1984). These investigators examined assessment research on adults and found high correlations between self-report measures of anxiety, depression, and neuroticism. They noted that negative affectivity is a pervasive personality trait and that it generally is unrelated to measures of situation-specific anxiety. In this chapter we review the clinical and empirical evidence regarding the association between depression and anxiety in children and adolescents.

II. Diagnostic Definitions

Both anxiety and depression are ubiquitous emotional experiences that, in extreme forms, reflect a psychopathological process. A full review of the definitions of these constructs is beyond the scope of this chapter (but see Watson & Kendall, this volume), and we confine our discussion to those reports that describe both anxiety and depression in children and adolescents.

Classification systems of child psychopathology vary in the degree to which they distinguish between anxiety and depression. The *Diagnostic and Statistical Manual of Mental Disorders* (DSM-III-R; American Psychiatric Association, 1987) classifies anxiety disorders and affective disorders under separate categories for children and adults. In the *International Classification of Diseases-9* (ICD-9), anxiety and depressive disorders are classified separately under the broader category of "disturbance of emotions specific to childhood and adolescence." In contrast to these two systems, the World Health Organization (WHO) system (Rutter et al., 1969; Rutter, Shaffer, & Shepherd, 1975) includes eight categories. One of these categories is "neurotic disorder," which includes anxiety and depression. This system reflects the prevailing view in Great Britain, where both anxiety and depressive disorders are included within the general category of dysphoria (Werry, 1986).

Questioning the diagnostic reliability of the DSM-III and ICD-9 classification systems, Quay (1986a; 1986b; Quay & La Greca, 1986) suggests that they make an arbitrary distinction between anxiety and depression without demonstrating the independence of the disorders. He cites considerable empirical evidence to support his view that anxiety and depression reflect similar psychopathological processes. For example, in multivariate statistical analyses of child psychopathology, the second most frequently occurring dimension of pathology is labeled *anxiety–withdrawal–dysphoria* (Quay, 1986a). Several different labels have been employed to describe this broad-band grouping of behavior problems, including "internalizing" problems (Achenback, 1966, 1985; Achenbach & Edelbrock, 1978). Within this generalized grouping are sadness, depression, withdrawal, anxiety, somatic complaints, and fears (Achenbach, 1985).

There are no clear estimates of the prevalence of overlap between the symptoms of depression and anxiety in children. Furthermore, it is difficult to make a differential diagnosis when a child presents with both depression and anxiety. A number of suggestions have been given for making a diagnosis when a child presents with both anxiety and depression. Some authors have noted that many depressed individuals are also anxious but those who are anxious are less likely to be depressed (Foa & Foa, 1982; Hershberg, Carlson, Cantwell, & Strober, 1982; Bernstein & Garfinkel, 1986). Therefore, when one sees both anxiety and depression concurrently, the suggestion is to diagnose the individual as being depressed. A second suggestion is to designate the primary diagnosis on the basis of which disorder came first or which symptoms are most intense (Puig-Antich & Gittelman, 1979). Another proposal is that the diagnosis of separation anxiety should be limited to children who become distressed only when separated from a significant other (Puig-Antich & Gittelman, 1979). Finally, several symptoms do not overlap in anxiety and depression, including psychomotor retardation, suicidal ideation, anhedonia, decreased self-esteem, and inappropriate guilt seen in depressives but not associated with anxiety (Puig-Antich & Gittelman, 1979; Hershberg et al., 1982). The presence or absence of these distinguishing features is useful in making a differential diagnosis.

A. Anxiety in Depressed Children

There have been numerous attempts at classifying subtypes of depression in children (e.g., Malmquist, 1971; McConville, Boag, & Purohit, 1973). Although many reports of depression in childhood do not mention anxiety (Poznanski & Zrull, 1970; Kovacs & Beck, 1977; Carlson & Cantwell, 1980; Kashani, Venzke, & Millar, 1981; Poznanski, 1982), several classification systems have delineated anxiety symptoms as prominent in particular subtypes of childhood depression (e.g., Frommer, 1967; Cytryn & McKnew, 1972). School avoidance and other phobias have been labeled depressive equivalents that serve to mask underlying depression (e.g., Glaser, 1968). Frommer (1968) described three types of depression in childhood: enuretic, pure, and phobic. Somewhat different etiologies and clinical pictures were noted for these groups. Frommer suggested that depression should be suspected in a child if he or she complains of irrational fears; that is, anxiety.

Cytryn and McKnew (1972) studied 37 children aged 6 to 12 in an early attempt to clarify the classification of childhood depression. They described three distinct subtypes of depression: masked, acute, and chronic depressive reactions of childhood. The characteristic feature in masked depression was that depressive affect was not a major component of the illness and was generally overshadowed by the child's acting-out behavior. Anxiety was not generally a part of the clinical features of masked depression, but frequently was a prominent feature in the acute and chronic depressive reactions. The authors noted that the diagnostic category with which the acute or chronically depressed children might be confused was acute or chronic childhood anxiety. Although anxiety was part of the clinical picture, depression was considered to be the prominent problem of the children in their sample.

Cytryn, McKnew, and Bunney (1980) reformulated their views on the classification of depression in childhood by applying DSM-III criteria to their original sample. Children originally acutely or chronically depressed were found to fit the adult criteria for major depressive disorder, single episode or recurrent, respectively. Only one acutely depressed child was rediagnosed as having separation anxiety. Thus, many of these children did have affective disorder but some continued to have associated anxiety features. In most cases, the child's anxiety was not sufficient for a diagnosis of anxiety disorder.

Clinically, many depressed children present with anxiety symptoms. Kovacs (personal communication cited in Puig-Antich & Rabinovich, 1986) noted that 35% of a group of 54 children who presented with major depressive disorder or dysthymic disorder had a concomitant anxiety disorder diagnosis. Puig-Antich, Blau, Marx, Greenhill, and Chambers (1978) reported on a group of 13 children presenting with major depressive disorder. Separation anxiety as a symptom was present in all cases. In all of these cases the onset of the separation anxiety followed the onset of depression and therefore appeared as secondary.

Kovacs, Feinberg, Crouse-Novak, Paulauskas, and Finkelstein (1984) reported on the first stage of a longitudinal, prospective study of depressive disorders in childhood. They studied 65 children diagnosed as having a major depressive disorder, dysthymic disorder, or adjustment disorder with depressed mood. Using the Interview Schedule for Children, a 37-item structured interview designed to assess symptoms and symptom clusters associated with depression, they found that the most common nonaffective disorder existing concurrently with the depression was some type of anxiety disorder (separation anxiety, overanxious disorder, avoidant disorder, or phobic disorder). Of children with an adjustment disorder with depressed mood, 27% were found to have a concurrent anxiety disorder. Slightly higher percentages were found for children with major depressive disorder (33%) and dysthymic disorder

(36%). They found that the anxiety disorder generally postdated the onset of the dysthymic disorder, but was equally likely to predate, postdate, or be simultaneous with the onset of major depressive disorder or adjustment disorder. The presence or absence of anxiety did not appear to affect the remission of the depressive disorder.

B. Depression in Anxious Children

Anxiety disorders in childhood are generally classified into avoidant disorder, phobic disorder, obsessive–compulsive disorder, and separation anxiety. The latter is frequently equated with school avoidance or phobia (e.g., Gittelman-Klein & Klein, 1973; Bernstein & Garfinkel, 1986) and has been more widely studied in relation to depression than other types of anxiety disorders. Perhaps this is because school phobia differs from other childhood phobias in that the focus is on social relationships rather than the danger of physical harm (Achenbach, 1985).

An early report on children with school phobia (i.e., separation anxiety) noted that depressive symptoms were prominent in the disorder (Agras, 1959). In addition, depressive signs were found to occur in six of seven mothers of these children and the children's fathers were noted to have psychological difficulties. Agras described these children as being brought up within a family constellation of depression in which the child's parents were unable to resolve their depressive feelings and tended to minimize or deny painful affect in themselves or their children. Agras found that the parents' depression generally antedated the child's school phobia and appeared to be reactivated by the child's entrance into school.

More recent clinical reports of children with separation anxiety note that as many as 50% may have symptoms of depression (Waldron, Shrier, Stone, & Tobin, 1975) or clearly defined (e.g., DSM-III) affective disorders (Bernstein & Garfinkel, 1986). There have even been suggestions that school phobia is a symptom of depression (Glaser, 1968). Indirect support for this view comes from a study which found that the antidepressant imipramine was effective in relieving separation anxiety (Gittelman-Klein & Klein, 1973).

Several studies have examined the occurrence of depressive symptomatology in children with school phobia or separation anxiety. Bernstein and Garfinkel (1986) noted that in their sample of 26 children with school phobia, 50% had a concomitant DSM-III diagnosis of affective disorder. They subdivided their sample into four groups: affective disorder only, anxiety disorder only, both affective and anxiety disorder, and neither (largely conduct-disordered children). They found that children diagnosed with an affective disorder were most symptomatic regardless of whether they had a concomitant anxiety disorder or not. Children with both anxiety and affective disorder were more similar to children with an affective disorder than to children with an anxiety disorder. The authors noted that it was difficult to determine which disorder was primary in children with a dual diagnosis, but they suggested that depressed children are more likely to report anxiety than are anxious children likely to report depression. This finding is consistent with a number of previously cited works which suggested that many depressed individuals were anxious but that anxious individuals were less likely to be depressed (Foa & Foa, 1982; Hershberg et al., 1982; Bernstein & Garfinkel, 1986).

The co-occurrence of anxiety and depression has been implicated in school difficulties in general. Tisher (1983) compared a group of severe school refusers (possibly some were school phobic but there was likely a number of etiological factors significant to their school refusal) to a group of regular school attenders. Subjects were gathered from the general school population rather than from clinic referrals. School refusers were found to be more anxious and depressed (as measured by self-reports and parent reports) than were the regular attenders. In addition, school refusers scored higher on the anxiety and neuroticism scales, whereas regular attenders scored higher on the extraversion scale. These findings would seem to support the use of the negative affectivity construct in describing children with school refusal problems.

In addition to occurring with high frequency in children with school phobia, depressive symptoms have been found to be significant in obsessive–compulsive disorders of childhood (Puig-Antich & Rabinovich, 1986). Rapport et al. (1981) studied a group of nine adolescents who had a primary diagnosis of obsessive–compulsive disorder. Four of these adolescents also met diagnostic criteria for major depressive disorder at the time of admission to the psychiatric unit. In addition, the remaining five adolescents had symptoms of depression and all of the patients studied would have met criteria for major depressive disorder at some point in their lives. The authors noted that the depression was secondary to the onset of the obsessive–compulsive disorder in all cases and the depression was most severe with early onset of the anxiety disorder.

Additional support for the notion that anxiety and depression are closely related comes from a study of familial morbidity risks for psychiatric disorders in depressed and anxious children (Puig-Antich & Rabinovich, 1986). These authors found that children with separation anxiety symptoms who were not depressed had the same morbidity risk for major depressive disorder in first- and second-degree relatives as did children with major depressive disorder. No differences were found in morbidity risk for major depression in family members between children with major depression who did or did not have concomitant separation anxiety symptoms. Children with major depression and separation anxiety concomitantly were found to have a higher morbidity risk of alcoholism in their families than did children with major depression or separation anxiety alone. While these findings suggest a strong association between the two disorders, some differences may exist.

Overall, issues related to differentiating childhood anxiety and depression in the clinical setting are not resolved. Clinical observations of the high degree of association between depressive and anxiety symptoms and syndromes support the view that classification systems that attempt to differentiate affective and anxiety disorders may have limited diagnostic reliability and validity. Rather, the evidence from clinical reports is consistent with classifying anxiety and depression together within a broad-band category which reflects negative affectivity. Results of empirical studies to be reviewed below will provide additional support for this conclusion.

III. Methods of Assessment

Before we can examine the extensive assessment literature, we need to have a reasonable understanding of the various measurement instruments that have been employed. The present review of the methods of assessment in child and adolescent anxiety and depression is designed to provide information specifically focusing on the overlap and distinctiveness of the two constructs.

There are numerous methods for the assessment of psychopathology in children, including self-report measures, behavioral or observational methods, and interview schedules. Several of these have been designed specifically to assess either anxiety or depression. In addition, many personality inventories and symptom checklists include an internalizing (Achenbach, 1985) or anxiety–withdrawal–dysphoria (Quay, 1986a) factor composed of anxious, depressed, and withdrawing behaviors. Although a full review of assessment measures is beyond the scope of this chapter (see Kendall, Cantwell, & Kazdin, in press), those measures that have been employed most frequently in studies assessing the interrelationships between anxiety and depression are described below. As will be discussed later, these measures show little discriminant validity.

A. Self-Reports

Children's Depression Inventory (CDI). The CDI, developed by Kovacs (1980/1981), is a modification of the Beck Depression Inventory for adults. The inventory consists of 27 items designed to assess cognitive, behavioral, and neurovegetative signs of depression in children aged 7 to 17. Each item consists of three statements from which the child is instructed to choose the one that best describes him or her over the past 2 weeks. Each item is designed to assess a specific symptom of depression (i.e., crying, suicidal ideation, ability to concentrate on school work), and the three choices range from mild or limited symptomatology to severe or maladaptive symptomatology. Items are scored 0, 1, or 2 depending upon the statement chosen, with a score of 2 representing the most severe choice. Total scores on the CDI range from 0 to 54. Cutoff levels for varying degrees of depression have been established (Kovacs et al., 1977; Carlson & Cantwell, 1980).

Validity and reliability studies involving the CDI have provided varying results. The scale has been found to discriminate between children with an affective disorder and those with other psychiatric diagnoses in some studies (Carlson & Cantwell, 1980), but not in others (Saylor, Finch, Spirito, & Bennett, 1984). Internal consistency, split-half, and test–retest reliability data on the CDI from both clinical and normal populations have been reported in the literature and range from excellent (.94) to poor (.38) depending on the population and interval length (Saylor et al., 1984). Validity studies with the CDI have reported similarly inconsistent results (Finch & Rogers, 1984; Saylor et al., 1984).

Children's Depression Scale (CDS). This measure includes 48 items related to depression and 18 positive items that are presented to respondents on cards (Lang & Tisher, 1978). The respondent's agreement or disagreement with an item is indicated by sorting the item into one of five boxes (ranging from "very right" to "very wrong," with "don't know" as the midpoint). Items were gathered from the psychotherapy records and responses of depressed children, as well as from descriptions of depression found in the literature (Tisher & Lang, 1983). There are two major scales (depression and positive), each of which has subscales (affective response, social problems, self-esteem, preoccupation with own sickness and death, guilt, and pleasure). It is suitable for use with children aged 9 to 16 and there is a form to be completed by an adult that is intended to provide additional information about the child's functioning. The scale initially was administered to 96 children and successfully discriminated between three groups: severe school refusers, regular school attenders, and a clinical sample (with a variety of behavioral and emotional problems). The ability of the scale to differentiate between depressed children and children with other psychiatric diagnoses or normals has not been assessed systematically.

Little information is available regarding the validity and reliability of this assessment tool, and Tisher and Lang (1983) note that further research on the instrument is in progress. An internal consistency coefficient of .96 was reported; however, Kovacs (1980/1981) criticized the methodology of the consistency estimate because child and parent ratings were combined. The CDS and subscales have been found to correlate highly with the neuroticism scale of the Eysenck Personality Questionnaire (EPQ; Eysenck & Eysenck, 1968). The strongest correlations were found between the full depression and affective response subscale scores and EPQ neuroticism (Tisher & Lang, 1983), suggesting that the scale is a measure of NA rather than merely depression.

Revised Children's Manifest Anxiety Scale (RCMAS). This 37-item inventory of anxiety in children was devised by C. R. Reynolds and Richmond (1978) as a revision of the earlier, widely used Children's Manifest Anxiety Scale (Castenada, McCandless, & Palermo, 1956). Each item is a statement pertaining to a symptom of anxiety (i.e., "I worry a lot of the time") and the child is instructed to answer "yes" or "no." In addition to the total anxiety score, three factor scores can be assessed; these reflect physiological anxiety, worry and oversensitivity, and concentration anxiety. Finally, two Lie factors (combined for scoring purposes) are designed to detect a social desirability response bias (C. R. Reynolds & Paget, 1977).

Reliability and validity studies suggest that the RCMAS may be a good measure of chronic anxiety. Internal consistency and test–retest reliability coefficients >.80 have been reported in several studies (Finch & Rogers, 1984). Validity data have also been reported indicating that the RCMAS correlates well (>.80) with the A-trait scale of the State–Trait Anxiety Scale for Children (Spielberger, 1973), as well as correlating with teacher's rating of children's behavior in the classroom (Reynolds, 1982). As will be discussed in greater detail below, there is little discriminant validity between the RCMAS and measures of depression or internalization (e.g., Saylor et al., 1984; Shoemaker, 1987).

State–Trait Anxiety Inventory for Children (STAIC). The STAIC, developed by Spielberger (1973), is a self-report measure of anxiety in children. This inventory contains two scales, one assessing chronic anxiety (or trait) symptoms (i.e., "I worry about making mistakes," "I am shy"), and the other measuring temporary (or state) symptoms (i.e., "I feel upset," "I feel mixed-up"). Both scales consist of 20 items and the child is instructed to choose one of three answers that best describes how he/she is feeling at present (state) or how he/she typically feels (trait). A score of 1, 2, or 3 is obtained (with 3 being assigned to the most severe choice) on each item, and these are summed to yield total A-state and total A-trait scores.

Reliability and validity data on the STAIC generally support construct validity of this measure. Spielberger (1973) reported an internal consistency reliability of .82 and a test–retest coefficient of .65. Another reliability study, however, reported somewhat lower coefficients (r = .44; Finch, Montgomery, & Deardorff, 1974). Validity studies provide more consistent results supporting both the construct and concurrent validity of the measure. These studies found that the A-trait scale correlated well with the Children's Manifest Anxiety Scale and General Anxiety Scale for Children (Spielberger, 1973), that the scale could discriminate emotionally disturbed children from normal children (Montgomery & Finch, 1974), and that A-state scores in normal and emotionally disturbed children increased when the subjects were exposed to stressful situations (Newmark, Wheeler, Newmark, & Stabler, 1975; Finch, Kendall, Dannenburg, & Morgan, 1978). The evidence for discriminant validity of the STAIC is weak, with the A-trait portion of the scale correlating .42 with the depression factor of the POMS (Lira, White, & Finch, 1977) and high scores on this subscale being associated with high scores on the CDI (Saylor et al., 1984).

B. Behavioral/Observational

Child Behavior Checklist (CBCL). Achenbach and Edelbrock (1983, 1986, 1987) have developed three behaviorally based descriptive inventories designed to assess social competence, school performance, and behavior problems in children and adolescents. The three measures are similar in format and yield information about behavioral and emotional functioning from the child and his/her parents and teacher. Achenbach and Edelbrock have published three manuals, reporting on the construction and validation of the three forms of the checklist. They have investigated the psychometric properties of the measures extensively and the interested reader is referred to the manuals for such information.

The Youth Self-Report (CBCL-YSR) and Parent Report (CBCL-PRF) forms assess the child's social functioning, while the Teacher Report (CBCL-TRF) assesses school performance. The CBCL-YSR is appropriate for use with children aged 11 to 18 and requires a fifth-grade reading level. The CBCL-PRF and -TRF are appropriate for use with children aged 6 through 16 and there is an additional form of the CBCL-YSR suitable for children aged 2 to 4. Each form contains a wide variety of behavioral problems that were selected from a large pool of items acquired from the existing literature and from an anaylsis of the case histories of child psychiatric patients. The items have three response options: "not true," "somewhat true," and "very true." Each form of the checklist yields a behavior problem profile which is divided into internalizing, externalizing, and mixed scales. Each scale is further divided into a number of subscales that vary in content depending upon the child's age and sex. The CBCL-TRF yields *T* scores for each of the scales, which reflect norms for various age and sex groups.

Personality Inventory for Children (PIC). This inventory of 600 behavior problems is generally completed by someone familiar with the child. It is appropriate for use with children 3 to 16 years of age. Items are scored "true" or "false" and yield three validity scales, an adjustment scale, and 12 clinical scales which reflect different types of psychopathology. The depression subscale consists of 46 items. Test–retest reliabilities have been reported to be .93 (Wirt, Lachar, Klinedinst, & Seat, 1977). There is a 30-item anxiety scale which has been found to have a test–retest reliability of .76 to .91. There is a significant degree of item overlap between depression and anxiety subscales and these scales correlate .46 with each other.

Conners Parent Questionnaire (CPQ). The Conners Parent Questionnaire (Conners, 1973) is a 93-item checklist of symptoms commonly associated with behavior disorders in children. Eight factors have been demonstrated and are labeled as follows: conduct problems, anxiety, impulsive–hyperactive, learning problem, psychosomatic, perfectionism, antisocial, and muscular tension. In contrast to the Conners teacher rating scale, very little psychometric work has been done with this version of the scale.

Revised Behavior Problem Checklist (RBPC). The Revised Behavior Problem Checklist (RBPC) (Quay & Peterson, 1983) consists of 89 problem behaviors seen frequently in children and adolescents. Each behavior is rated on a 3-point scale by a teacher or parent. Factor analyses of ratings of normal children and psychiatric inpatients and outpatients have yielded four major factors: conduct disorder (CD), attention problems–immaturity (AP), anxiety–withdrawal (AW), and socialized aggression (SA). Two minor factors, psychotic behavior (PB) and motor tension excess (ME), are also assessed as subscales. Quay and Peterson (1983) found the RBPC to have adequate internal consistency with alpha reliability coefficients for the six factors ranging from .68 to .95. Test–retest reliabilities for a 2-month interval ranged from .49 to .83 for the six subscales. The RBPC has been found to discriminate between clinical and nonclinical samples. Of interest to the area of childhood depression and anxiety, the anxiety–withdrawal subscale encompasses a number of DSM-III categories, including separation anxiety, avoidant disorder, overanxious disorder, and dysthymic disorder. Quay and Peterson

(1983) suggest that this factor reflects internalizing symptoms of "neuroticism" and subjective distress.

C. Interview Schedules, Projectives, and Peer Measures

Schedule for Affective Disorders and Schizophrenia for School-Age Children (Kiddie-SADS). The Kiddie-SADS was developed by Puig-Antich and his colleagues (Chambers, Puig-Antich, & Tabrizi, 1978) for the purpose of assessing depression by a standardized clinical interview rather than through the usual unstructured assessment. The Kiddie-SADS is a downward extension of the adult SADS developed by Endicott and Spitzer (1978) and is for use with children 6 to 16 years of age. The interview assesses several diagnostic categories in addition to depression. There are 12 items which measure symptoms of depression, including depressive mood, guilt, anhedonia, and psychomotor retardation (Kazdin, 1981; Puig-Antich, Chambers, & Tabrizi, 1983). Kazdin (1981) reports that interrater reliability in scoring the Kiddie-SADS has ranged from .65 to .96. However, it is difficult to assess the psychometric properties of the instrument fully because many of the data relevant to the Kiddie-SADS have been presented in unpublished papers (Hodges & Siegel, 1985).

Rorschach Psychodiagnostic Method. Projective techniques are frequently used in the assessment of adolescents and children. Exner (1986) identified five Rorschach indicators of depression based on a series of studies with normal children, children who had effected or attempted suicide, and children who were identified as having depressive symptoms defined by DSM-III criteria. The Depression Index, composed of these indicators, is included in the structural summary. The five components of the Depression Index are Vistas > 0, Color-Shading Blend > 0, Egocentricity Index $< .30$ (or less than 1 standard deviation below the mean for the subject's age), sum of Achromatic Color > 2, and Morbid Responses > 3 (Exner, 1986).

The most frequently cited indicators of anxiety on the Rorschach have been shading (Y, T, V, and C) and inanimate movement (m; Exner, 1986; Auerbach & Spielberger, 1972; Burns, 1987). However, empirical research has yielded equivocal evidence regarding the validity of these indicators, possibly due to differences in administration and scoring between studies (Auerbach & Spielberger, 1972; Burns, 1987).

Peer Nomination Inventory of Depression (PNID). The PNID is a sociometric measure designed to assess symptoms of depression (Lefkowitz & Tesiny, 1980). The inventory consists of 20 items which are read to the children in group format. Each child responds to questions such as "Who worries a lot?" by marking peers' names who best fit the question. An item score (i.e., the number of times the child was nominated on a particular item) and a total score (i.e., number of nominations divided by the number of children in the class) are generated by the procedure. Estimates of internal consistency for the 13 depression items range from .34 to .85, and from .63 to .88 for the four happiness items. Test–retest reliability for a 2-month period was .79 for the 13 depression items and .74 for the four happiness items. Interrater reliability was .75. The PNID has been found to be modestly related (r = .41) to teacher ratings of depression (Kazdin, 1981), but it correlates poorly with children's self-report using the CDI (Kazdin, 1981; Saylor et al., 1984). Kazdin (1981) noted that the PNID has been shown to predict school performance, work skills, social behavior, locus of control, self-concept, and peer ratings of happiness and popularity.

IV. Assessment Research Evidence

A handful of researchers in the area of child assessment have shown interest in the interrelationship between anxiety and depression over the past decade, with the majority of these studies appearing in the past 3 to 4 years. These studies have examined children and adolescents from a variety of populations, including normals, outpatients, inpatients, and hospitalized pediatrics patients. As will be seen, evidence from the assessment literature consistently supports the notion of a construct of negative affectivity.

A. Monomethod Studies

Initial studies relied primarily upon self-reports as the method of assessment. An early study by Lira et al. (1977) examined the relationship between state–trait anxiety and various mood states in a sample of delinquent adolescents. Forty-one behavior-problem adolescents who were residents of a residential treatment facility were administered the STAIC and the Profile of Mood States (McNair, Lorr, & Droppleman, 1971). Of interest to our topic, the A-trait portion of the STAIC was significantly correlated (r = .42) with the depression factor of the POMS—a finding that is consistent with Watson and Clark's (1984) conceptualization of NA.

The relationship between anxiety and depression was more systematically assessed by Saylor et al. (1984), who administered the CDI, STAIC, RCMAS, and Test Anxiety Scale for Children to 63 psychiatric inpatients aged 7 to 15. Their sample was divided into "Hi" versus "Lo" depression based on a median split of CDI scores. Children who reported a high degree of depression on the CDI had higher RCMAS total and subscale scores and more test anxiety than those scoring low on the CDI. There were no differences between the groups on the state anxiety scale, but those reporting high depression scored higher on trait anxiety, suggesting that children who were depressed were also experiencing chronic anxiety. The results of this study suggested that there was little discriminant validity in self-report measures of anxiety and depression. It appeared that all of these measures reflect generalized emotional distress; that is, negative affectivity.

In an attempt to determine which aspects of anxiety and depression are most strongly related, Norvell, Brophy, and Finch (1985) administered the CDI, STAIC, and the RCMAS subscales (physiological anxiety, concentration anxiety, and worry/oversensitivity) to 30 inpatient children (mean age of 11 years, 6 months). They found a high correlation ($r = .70$) between the CDI and the RCMAS total score as well as moderate to high correlations between the CDI and RCMAS factor scores. The CDI was also correlated with A-state ($r = .46$) and A-trait ($r = .62$). The authors divided the CDI into two factors that were found to be differentially related to anxiety scores. The first factor reflected the child's level of self-criticism and self-deprecation and was not related to any of the anxiety measures. The second factor, termed *dysphoric mood,* was highly correlated with the RCMAS total score ($r = .71$) and its component subscales. Results of multiple regression equations using anxiety scores as predictors to the total CDI and two factor scores indicated that the physiological and concentration anxiety subscales of the RCMAS predicted both the CDI total score and dysphoric mood factor. The findings of this study suggest that depression as measured by the CDI is multidimensional, and that the overlap between depression and anxiety may reflect similarities in the affective experience rather than the cognitive component. The findings support Watson and Clark's (1984) concept of negative affectivity, which suggests that the affective experience of anxiety and depression are similar (see also Watson & Kendall, this volume). In addition, the findings are consistent with Puig-Antich and Gittelman's (1979) view that there are a number of nonoverlapping items between anxiety and depression, including psychomotor retardation and inappropriate guilt, which are seen in depression but not anxiety.

Shoemaker (1987) investigated the concurrent validity of the Achenbach CBCL-YSR in a sample of 98 child and adolescent psychiatric inpatients. He examined the CBCL-YSR in relation to the CDI, STAIC, and

RCMAS and found that these three measures were all significantly correlated with the internalizing factor of the YSR. These results support the notion of a broad-band dimension of psychopathology, whether it be labeled *internalizing* or *NA*.

The results of the single-method studies cast doubt on the distinctiveness of anxiety and depression in children and adolescents, and support the construct of negative affectivity. However, these conclusions are limited by the fact that all of these studies used only self-report measures with samples of inpatients. It may be that these measures are not sufficiently sensitive to detect differences between distinct forms of affective distress. Second, these studies employed severely emotionally disturbed children and adolescents who may have been experiencing such a high degree of affective distress that they endorsed items reflecting pathology in general. Finally, these respondents may have been unable to differentiate their own emotional responses. Thus multimethod studies using normals and pediatrics patients are needed to test the validity of the NA construct.

B. Multimethod Studies

In order to address the limitations of single-method studies, Leon, Kendall, and Garber (1980) assessed the behavior problems associated with depression in 42 elementary-school children. Groups of depressed and nondepressed children were identified using cutoff scores on the depression scale of the parent-completed PIC. Additional information from parents regarding the child's behavior was obtained using the Conners Parent Questionnaire and the hyperactivity scale of the PIC. Teachers completed the Conners Teacher Questionnaire. The child's self-report of depression was obtained using the CDI. Intellectual, psychomotor, and cognitive functioning were assessed by the Peabody Picture Vocabulary Test, Porteus Mazes, and Cognitive Processes Inventory for Children. Scores on the PIC depression scale were correlated with all of the Conners subscales, with the exception of the antisocial scale. The highest correlation was between two parent report measures, the PIC depression and the anxiety subscale of the CPQ (r = .56). Children rated as depressed by their parents were viewed by their teachers as passive and inattentive. There was a moderate correlation between the parent and child reports (r = .33), but, in general, the reports of the various respondents were not highly associated.

Kieffer and Siegel (1984) utilized parent (PIC), peer (PNID), teacher (global ratings and teacher nomination of depression), and self-reports (CDI and STAIC) to examine the relationship between anxiety and depression in a sample of 192 normal children in grades 4–6. The correlations between measures of depression across raters were significant but small in relation to correlations between different constructs as rated by the same individual. In other words, the correlational patterns reflected the method of assessment more than the trait/construct being measured. Children reporting a high degree of depression on the CDI also reported considerable anxiety and were rated as more depressed by teachers. There were no differences between high and low CDI scorers on parent or peer measures. Children rated depressed by their peers scored higher on the CDI, on both state and trait anxiety, and on the PIC-D than did children rated less depressed. Parents who rated their children as being depressed also rated their children as being anxious. Similarly, children described as depressed by their teachers were also rated as anxious by their teachers. Overall, the depression measures showed somewhat better convergent and divergent validity than did the anxiety scales.

Strauss, Forehand, Frame, and Smith (1984) administered the CDI to normal children in grades 2–5. They also obtained teacher-reported problems using the BPC, and teacher and peer nominations of social withdrawal. Subjects were assigned to "High" and "Low" depressed groups on the basis of their CDI scores (>19 and <5, respectively), generating two groups of 15 subjects each. Subjects in the "High" group scored significantly higher than those in the "Low" group on the RCMAS and its subscales, on the anxiety–withdrawal factor of the Teacher BPC; and on both the teacher- and peer-nominated withdrawal. Thus, children who reported themselves to be depressed also reported themselves to be anxious. In addition, those children who rated themselves as depressed were viewed by others in their school environment as displaying signs of both depression and anxiety. Clearly, most respondents in this study, both adults and children, had difficulty differentiating between anxiety and depression.

Eason et al. (1985) used self-report measures and clinicians' ratings based on a semistructured interview to assess anxiety and depression in a sample of 44 hospitalized pediatrics patients. Subjects were administered the CDI, RCMAS, and STAIC. In addition, each child was interviewed and rated on a measure of depression, the CDRS (Poznanski, Cook, & Carroll, 1979), and two measures of depression developed for this study, the Children's Anxiety Rating Scale (CARS) and the Anxiety Rating Scale for Children (ARSC). All measures were found to be highly correlated, and correlations between measures of anxiety and depression were lower than correlations between alternative measures of the same construct. Both self-reports and interviews appeared to be tapping the same construct, which the authors termed "emotional distress," thus revealing little discriminant validity between measures of anxiety and depression. The authors noted that the children they studied may have been experiencing vague symptoms of emotional distress that could not be easily differentiated or that the actual assessment measures employed were not refined sufficiently to discriminate between anxiety and depression.

Fifty children seen in an outpatient clinic with their mothers were studied by Treiber and Mabe (1987). The CDI and the RCMAS were administered to each child and the mothers completed these instruments to describe their child's behavior. There was a moderate degree of convergent validity between the reports of the children and their mothers (CDI: $r = .58$; RCMAS: $r = .43$). However, discriminant validity was poor, as the correlations between the anxiety and depression ratings within the same reporter were higher (mother: $r = .70$; child: $r = .65$). Similar to other investigators, these authors hypothesized that either (1) there was a significant degree of overlap between the constructs of anxiety and depression, or (2) the self-report instruments were poor measures of these constructs, because all seemed to be assessing nonspecific emotional distress.

Finch, Fryer, Saylor, Carek, and McIntosh (1987) examined the relationships between children's self-report, teacher report, and clinical interview material based on the Kiddie-SADS in their study of anxiety and depression in a sample of 53 child psychiatric inpatients. The results were supportive of the concept of negative affectivity and demonstrated poor discriminant validity for the constructs of anxiety and depression, whether measured by self-reports, teacher ratings, or clinical interviews. Based upon these findings, the authors concluded that anxiety and depression do not differ in children.

A similar study by Wolfe et al. (1987) examined the relationship between child and teacher reports in a sample of 102 child and adolescent psychiatric inpatients. Measures used in the study included the RCMAS, CDI, STAIC, and CBCL-TRF. The children's self-reports of anxiety and depression were significantly related (CDI–RCMAS: $r = .56$; CDI–A-state: $r = .52$; CDI–A-trait: $r = .36$) and the teacher report on the depression/social withdrawal scale correlated with the teacher's report on the anxiety scale ($r = .38$). There were no significant correlations between teacher and self-reports on either the measures of depression or of anxiety. However, both depression and anxiety measures were significantly related to the Internalizing scale score of the CBCL-TRF. Using a multiple regression analysis, these authors found that a combination of the anxiety self-reports (STAIC and RCMAS) and the CDI predicted the internalizing factor of the CBCL, suggesting that each of these instruments contributes to the broad-band dimension of negative affectivity.

Lipovsky, Finch, and Belter (in press) investigated the relationship between self-report and Rorschach measures of anxiety and depression in a sample of 60 adolescent psychiatric inpatients. The self-report measures employed were the CDI, MMPI (Depression and Psychasthenia scales), STAIC, and RCMAS. Results indicated that the CDI was more highly correlated with self-report measures of anxiety (including the MMPI Psychasthenia scale; *r*s ranged from .46 to .76) than it was with the MMPI Depression scale (r = .35). Moderate correlations (*r*s ranged from .27 to .35) were also found between the MMPI Depression scale and the anxiety self-report measures. The self-report measures and Rorschach indicators of anxiety were poorly related to one another. The only Rorschach indicator of depression which was associated with self-reported depression was the frequency of morbid content (CDI Morbid: r = .31; MMPI Depression–Morbid: r = .33). The number of shading responses on the Rorschach, reportedly related to anxiety (Exner, 1986; Burns, 1987), was significantly correlated with the MMPI Depression scale (r = .48), but was unrelated to the CDI or self-report measures of anxiety. As with the self-report measures, little discriminant validity was found between the Rorschach indicators of depression and anxiety, as both of the anxiety indicators (shading and inanimate movement) were significantly correlated with the overall Depression Index (Shading–Depression Index: r = .47; Inanimate Movement–Depression Index: r = .38).

To summarize the evidence from empirical assessment studies of anxiety and depression, there is no evidence to support notions that anxiety and depression are totally distinct clinical entities. Studies have examined the data from of a variety of sources (child, parent, teacher, and clinician) describing children and adolescents obtained from different populations (normals, outpatients, inpatients, and pediatrics patients). These studies have yielded consistent support for an overarching construct—that of negative affectivity. Alternatively, one might argue that the respondents or measures used were simply unable to differentiate the constructs of anxiety and depression.

V. Biological Correlates of Depression and Anxiety

The last few years have given rise to intensive research investigations of biologic correlates in the major psychiatric disorders. Fostered by the development of new laboratory technologies for the measurement of neurohormones and neurotransmitters, and by the adoption of criterion-based diagnostic systems such as the RDC and DSM-III, a massive amount of information has been generated. As is often the case, much of this information appears contradictory at this early stage. Yet there is an air of excitement over the possibility of identifying neurochemical and neurohormonal concomitants in the major disorders. Although a complete review of biologic correlates of depression and anxiety is beyond the scope of this chapter, some discussion is in order. Because work in the area of children's studies is currently sparse, adult investigations will be drawn upon freely in this section.

A. Neurotransmitters and Neurochemical Regulation in Depression

Norepinephrine (NE) is a catecholamine neurotransmitter produced by neurons of the sympathetic autonomic nervous system and centrally in the brain, where approximately 66% comes from neurons in the locus ceruleus (LC) (Copper, Bloom, & Roth, 1986). This neurotransmitter serves as a mediator of normal neurobiologic processes such as attention and arousal, learning and memory, sleep and activity cycles, temperature control and blood pressure. Complex interconnections exist between the LC and other neuronal pathways. These interconnections serve to regulate the organismic response to a variety of stimuli and conditions, thus maintaining a homeostatic balance.

Early work on biologic abnormalities in major affective disorders identified changes in the production of the principal metabolite of NE, 3-methoxy-4-hydroxyphenylglycol (MHPC), in patients with unipolar and bipolar depression. Such findings were reported by several research groups and led to the formation of the "catecholamine hypothesis" of depression (Schildkraut, 1965; Bunney, 1965). This hypothesis suggests that depression is caused by a functional decrease in NE, while in mania there is an increase.

A newer theory, the "dysregulation hypothesis," has been advanced to account for the multiplicity of findings in clinical and preclinical studies (Siever & Davis, 1985). This model recognizes the presence of many different subtypes of depressive disorders which are linked principally by common symptoms and behavior. This hypothesis implies that symptoms arise as a result of failure of one or more homeostatic mechanisms in the NE system, i.e., faulty neurotransmitter production or receptor sensitivity, together with a desynchronization of circadian and ultridian chronobiologic rhythms. Such disturbances lead to production of either agitated or retarded depressive pictures, with dysphoric, anxious, and vegetative symptoms. The nature of the underlying neurobiologic abnormalities may differ and exist in varying combinations in different individuals.

B. The Limbic–Hypothalamic–Pituitary Axis and Neurosecretory Factors

The limbic system of the brain is an interconnected series of neuronal structures thought to have a profound influence on the production of mood and affects (Carroll, Curtis, & Mendels, 1976). This system is a regulator of release of hypothalamic neurosecretory factors such as corticotropin-releasing factor (CRF) and thyrotropin-releasing hormone (TRH), which control anterior pituitary secretion (Roy-Byrne, Uhde, Gold, Rubinow, & Post, 1985). CRF is a principal stimulus to pituitary secretion of adrenocorticotropic hormone (ACTH), which regulates cortisol production by the adrenal cortex (Gold et al., 1984). TRH influences the release of thyroid-stimulating hormone (TSH) and ultimately the rate of thyroid secretions. TRH also has an influence on the pituitary production of prolactin (PRL) and human growth hormone (HGH) (Loosen & Prange, 1982). Inhibitory feedback loops normally maintain a homeostatic balance in the hypophyseal–pituitary–adrenal (HPA) and the hypophyseal–pituitary–thyroid (HPT) axes.

In normal functioning, NE exerts a tonic inhibitory influence on the limbic system. In depression, the NE system is dysfunctional, with effects found in abnormal functioning of the HPA and/or HPT systems, both in levels of various hormones secreted and in receptor sensitivity at the hypothalamic and pituitary levels (Gold et al., 1984; Loosen & Prange, 1982). While both may be dysregulated in depression (Targum, Sullivan, & Byrnes, 1982), there appears to be little correspondence between the HPA and HPT axes.

Disordered cortisol production as a result of HPA dysfunction has been repeatedly demonstrated in depression, especially of the endogenous subtype (Carroll et al., 1981). This is reflected by nonsuppression of cortisol in response to dexamethasone administration and in high levels of urinary free cortisol (Halbreich, Asnis, Shindledecker, Zumoff, & Nathan, 1985; Rosenbaum et al., 1983).

Antidepressants act to return the disregulated NE system to a more efficient equilibrium (Charney, Menkes, & Heninger, 1981). Tricyclic antidepressants (TCAs) increase functional NE in the synaptic cleft through reuptake inhibition and downregulation of NE receptors. Evidences of reregulation of the NE system are seen in decreased urinary MHPG, normalization of cortisol secretory patterns, restoration of normal sleep and activity patterns, and decrease in subjective symptomatology.

C. Neurochemical Regulation in Anxiety Disorders

A central role has also been postulated for the NE system in the production of anxiety symptoms (Uhde, Roy-Byrne, Vittone, Boulenger, & Post, 1985). The function of the NE system has been the focus of numerous investigations among normal adults in stressful circumstances, as well as among patients having panic disorder and agoraphobia. An inverse relationship between cerebrospinal fluid MHPG and state anxiety measured by the Multiple Affective Adjective Checklist (MAACL) has been noted in normal adult volunteers (Ballenger, Post, Jimerson, Lake, & Zuckerman, 1984). Yohimbine, an adrenergic receptor antagonist that increases NE system functioning, also increases subjective ratings of anxiety and nervousness in adults with agoraphobia and panic attacks, but fails to do so in normal controls (Breier, Charney, & Heninger, 1984). Patients having more frequent panic attacks (>2.5 per week) have a significantly greater response to yohimbine than do normals or those having fewer attacks. Conversely, clonidine, a NE agonist, decreases activity in the LC. Among panic patients given clonidine there is a decrease in MHPG and significant decreases in anxiety symptoms on the Spielberger State Anxiety Scale (Uhde et al., 1985), but no anxiolytic effects are seen among normal volunteers.

Decreased NE receptor density and affinity are noted in panic disorder patients when compared with normal controls. With a dysfunctional NE receptor system, homeostatic baance cannot be maintained, resulting in a prolongation of NE activity and production of panic symptoms. Postsynaptic NE alpha-1 and beta receptor dysfunction may occur also, creating a facilitation of NE excitation, with a resultant lowering of the threshold for weak stimuli and reinforcement of strong NE stimuli (Charney et al., 1981; Nesse, Cameron, Curtis, McCann, & Huber-Smith, 1984).

D. Neuroendocrine Function in Anxiety Disorders

Several neuroendocrine studies in panic disorder have been reported recently. Curtis, Cameron, and Nesse (1982) reported a 15% rate of cortisol nonsuppression by the dexamethasone suppression test (DST) among patients with a diagnosis of panic disorder or panic attacks with agoraphobia, while Lieberman et al. (1983) had no cases of DST nonsuppression among panic patients in a study where 10 of 22 controls with major depressive disorder (MDD) (45.4%) were nonsuppressors. Such a low figure for DST nonsuppression of cortisol among panic disorder patients contrasts with the 44.1% of MDD-diagnosed adults (Arana, Baldessarini, & Ornsteen, 1985).

E. Overlap of Neurochemical and Neurotransmitter Dysfunction in Depression and Anxiety Disorders

Much interest has been generated in the adult psychiatric literature regarding the relationship of MDD to panic disorder and agoraphobia with panic attacks (Dealy, Ishiki, Avery, Wilson, & Dunner, 1981; Breier et al., 1984; Charney, Heninger, Price, & Breier, 1986). A large overlap between the two disorders exists, with a 30% rate of occurrence of MDD in panic disorder (Breier et al., 1984). When such overlap occurs symptoms are more severe and disabling (Breier et al., 1984). Lesser (in press) has recently summarized competing positions regarding the conceptual relationship between panic and depressive disorders, identifying (1) a "unitary" model, in which the two are variants of the same disorder; (2) a "pluralistic" model, which holds that the two differ qualitatively; and (3) a "mixed" model, which takes an intermediate position but distinguishes between the two states. One interesting finding is that TCAs and monoamine oxidase inhibitors (MAOIs) appear equally useful in panic disorder and MDD (Klein & Fink, 1962; Pohl, Berchou, & Rainey, 1982). Other evidence is contradictory, however, with further studies required to help clarify this issue.

F. Neurochemical and Neuroendocrine Factors in Depression and Anxiety Disorders of Childhood

Empirical investigations have demonstrated that the diagnosis of MDD may be established in children using the unmodified RDC or DSM-III criteria (Puig-Antich et al., 1979; Poznanski, Mokros, Grossman, & Freeman, 1985). A strong familial loading for depression has been found in the relatives of child and adolescent probands with MDD (Puig-Antich, 1980). Weissman, Leckman, Merikangas, Gammon, and Prusoff (1984) found an excess of depressive and anxiety disorders in children of adult probands with depression, especially when the adults also had panic disorder.

Neuroendocrine abnormalities, principally cortisol response to dexamethasone, have been investigated extensively in children and adolescents (Casat, Arana, & Powell, in press). Pooled data for DST studies among children with MDD indicate a high rate on nonsuppression (69.7%). Measurement of 24-hour patterns of plasma cortisol secretion have failed to show consistent abnormalities in total secretion among prepubertal MDD subjects (Puig-Antich et al., 1984).

The relationship of separation anxiety disorder (SAD) in childhood to adult panic disorder and agoraphobia has been reviewed by several authors (Gittelman & Klein, 1984; Casat, 1988). Follow-back and follow-up studies of adults with panic disorder are only suggestive of a relationship between the two. Improvement of SAD children on phenelzine, imipramine, or alprazolam has been reported, but, again, this is only inferential of some sort of a relationship (Gittelman-Klein & Klein, 1971; Frommer, 1967; Bernstein & Garfinkel, 1986). Challenge studies with agents such as lactate, isoproterenol, yohimbine, or clonidine have not been undertaken in this age group because of ethical considerations. Flament et al. (1986) were unable to precipitate anxiety in children with SAD using 3 or 10 mg/kg of caffeine. Measures of plasma and urinary catecholamine metabolites have yet to be undertaken in children with SAD or in those with parents who have panic disorder.

A mixture of symptoms of anxiety and of major depression are noted frequently in children (Hershberg et al., 1982; Tisher, 1983; Puig-Antich & Rabinovich, 1986; Bernstein & Garfinkel, 1986), a finding similar to overlapping symptoms described in adults (Breier et al., 1984; Lesser, in press). Little information is currently available to clarify this issue. Puig-Antich and Rabinovich were able to conclude only that symptoms of separation anxiety did not affect psychobiologic correlates of MDD in prepubertal children, leaving the question completely open. Future investigations in this area may prove fruitful to the understanding of the relationships between childhood and adult forms of depressive and anxiety disorders.

VI. Conclusions and Implications

Clearly, the relationship between anxiety and depression in the young is complex. The evidence reviewed regarding the association between symptoms and syndromes of depression and anxiety is overwhelming. The existence of a generalized category of emotional distress such as negative affectivity is supported by data regarding the classification of psychopathology in childhood, by the clinical literature describing anxiety and depression, and by empirical studies investigating these constructs. Evidence from empirical studies suggests that respondents either are unable to differentiate between anxiety and depression, or that current assessment instruments and procedures are invalid—that is, that they lack the necessary discriminant validity. Furthermore, evidence from the biological literature seems to implicate many of the same biological mechanisms in both anxiety and depression. The consistency of findings raises the real question of whether distinguishing between these two constructs is useful, necessary, or possible. While it is obvious that clinicians, parents, teachers, and children themselves have considerable difficulty distinguishing between these two constructs, the two disorders do persist.

It has been suggested by Dobson (1985) that anxiety and depression exist along a continuum, with anxiety preceding depression. Although not specifically addressed in empirical studies, such a relationship is not inconsistent with the literature and would suggest that it is possible for individuals to be anxious without being depressed. A recent paper by Strauss, Last, Hersen, and Kazdin (in press) provides some support for this position. These authors investigated the relationship between anxiety and depression in a sample of 106 children and adolescents who were referred to an anxiety disorder clinic. Of their patients, 28% who were diagnosed as having an anxiety disorder also had a concurrent diagnosis of major depression. Interestingly, the group who had an anxiety disorder plus a major depression was older, exhibited more severe symptoms, and was more likely to be diagnosed as having an obsessive–compulsive disorder or agoraphobia. Equally as interesting was their finding that children and adolescents who were diagnosed only with an anxiety disorder did not differ from the psychopathological control group on either a global measure of anxiety or in symptoms of depression, while the group with both anxiety and depression diagnoses did. These results are consistent with the notion that anxiety and depression exist along the same continuum, with depression being toward the more disturbed end. Certainly, Dobson's continuum model would appear to be fruitful basis for additional research.

Future research should also focus on whether differentiating between anxiety and depression is related either to treatment response or the recurrence of disorder (Doerfler, Felner, Rowlison, Rayley, & Evans, 1987). Such research would help to demonstrate whether differentiating between them has any utility. In this regard, W. M. Reynolds and Coats (1986) recently found that depressed children who were treated with relaxation training showed marked improvement when compared to a waiting-list control group. Because relaxation training is generally regarded as a treatment for anxiety, this study provides further evidence of the lack of difference between anxiety and depression in children, and supports the position that the distinction is not useful.

Longitudinal studies, such as those under way by Kovacs et al. (1984), can help to broaden our knowledge of the etiology and natural course of psychopathological disorders in childhood and can help to delineate factors which may affect the presentation of anxiety and depression. Questions regarding the mechanisms by which children cope with their emotional difficulties should be another focus of further research.

Rutter et al. (1969) suggested that most neurotic disorders in children were less differentiated than neuroses in adults. Moreover, even when disorders could be specified as some particular subvariety of neurosis, it was uncertain whether this subdivision had much clinical meaning or predictive value. Certainly the findings reviewed in this chapter suggest that this statement is true for anxiety and depression in children. However, many investigators working in the area of child psychopathology continue to distinguish between anxiety and depression, despite the fact that there is little evidence to suggest that they actually differ or can be separated clinically. Whether this commitment to the distinction is based on a theoretical/ideological preference or simply on tradition is not clear.

Regardless of one's stance regarding the relationship between anxiety and depression in children, research in the area would clearly benefit from systematic attempts to eliminate overlapping items from measures. A quick examination of the items included in various tests, rating scales, and interviews of anxiety and depression will reveal many identical items. This overlapping content obviously contributes to the high correlations that are obtained between measures of depression and anxiety. This problem of overlapping items could be easily addressed and eliminated. However, we suspect that there is more at issue here than simple psychometric problems, and we wonder whether the overlapping items are not simply a symptom of overlapping constructs, rather than the cause.

It might be useful to look for patterns of behaviors in children who present with symptoms of depression and anxiety to determine if we can make meaningful distinctions or determine the natural history of the symptoms. There have been some suggestions that anxiety symptoms may precede depressive ones. However, these studies have been retrospective and have depended on the patients' recall of when certain symptoms appeared. The ability of individuals to recall accurately sequential information, even for clearly observable events, is very limited.

Prospective studies of disturbed children are badly needed before we can adequately address the question of the sequential relationship between anxiety and depression.

We propose that researchers begin to study more closely broad-band symptom clusters such as negative affectivity, internalization, and so on, and then carefully examine the behaviors and symptoms of children who clearly fall into one of these clusters to see if the symptoms can be divided into meaningful subclusters. By beginning with these broad-band clusters, it would be possible to then determine how they can best be subdivided. However, researchers should give serious consideration to the possibility that anxiety and depression are not separate in children and that it is futile to attempt to separate the disorders. We found little evidence from any area to support their separation. Perhaps we should put the distinction to rest.

Because of the strong affective component common to both anxious and depressive symptomatology, the term *negative affectivity* seems to provide a better description of the underlying pathology than does *internalization*. On the other hand, it may be that negative affectivity is a subcluster of internalization and that other groups of symptoms will emerge, such as somatization, day dreaming, and so on, that are not part of negative affectivity per se, but rather are part of a broader band cluster (such as internalization). It seems time to approach the area of child psychopathology from a slightly different direction and, as seems to be the case for anxiety and depression, some of our long-held beliefs may prove to be incorrect.

References

Achenbach, T. M. (1966). The classification of children's psychiatric symptoms: A factor analytic study. *Psychological Monographs, 80,* 1–37.

Achenbach, T. M. (1985). Assessment of Anxiety in children. In A. H. Tuma & J. D. Maser (Eds.), *Anxiety and the anxiety disorders.* Hillsdale, NJ: Erlbaum.

Achenbach, T. M., & Edelbrock, C. S. (1978). The classification of child psychopathology: A review and analysis of empirical efforts. *Psychological Bulletin, 85,* 1275–1301.

Achenbach, T. M., & Edelbrock, C. S. (1983). *Manual for the child behavior checklist and revised child behavior profile.* Burlington, VT: University of Vermont, Department of Child Psychiatry.

Achenbach, T. M., & Edelbrock, C. S. (1986). *Manual for the teacher's report form and teacher version of the child behavior profile.* Burlington, VT: University of Vermont, Department of Child Psychiatry.

Achenbach, T. M., & Edelbrock, C. S. (1987). *Manual for the youth self report form and self report version of the child behavior profile.* Burlington, VT: University of Vermont, Department of Child Psychiatry.

Agras, S. (1959). The relationship of school phobia to childhood depression. *American Journal of Psychiatry, 116,* 533–536.
American Psychiatric Association. (1987). *Diagnostic and statistical manual of mental disorders (3rd ed. rev.).* Washington, DC: Author.
Arana, G. W., Baldessarini, R. J., & Ornsteen, M. (1985). The dexamethasone suppression test for diagnosis and prognosis in psychiatry. *Archives of General Psychiatry, 42,* 1193–1204.
Auerbach, S. M., & Spielberger, C. D. (1972). The assessment of state and trait anxiety with the Rorschach test. *Journal of Personality Assessment, 36,* 314–335.
Ayd, F. J. (1984). Is it anxiety or depression? *Southern Medical Journal, 77,* 1269–1272.
Ballenger, J. C., Post, R. M., Jimerson, D. C., Lake, R., & Zuckerman, M. (1984). Neurobiological correlates of depression and anxiety in normal individuals. In R. M. Post & J. C. Ballenger (Eds.), *Neurobiology of mood disorder.* Baltimore, MD: Williams & Wilkins.
Bernstein, G., & Garfinkel, B. (1986). School phobia: The overlap of affective and anxiety disorders. *Journal of the American Academy of Child Psychiatry, 25,* 235–241.
Breier, A., Charney, D. S., & Heninger, G. R. (1984). Major depression in patients with agoraphobia and panic disorder. *Archives of General Psychiatry, 41,* 1129–1135.
Bunney, W. E., Jr. (1965). Norepinephrine in depressive reactions: A review. *Archives of General Psychiatry, 13,* 483–494.
Burns, N. G. (1987). *Rorschach Indices of Anxiety in Children: A correlational study with the State-Trait Anxiety Inventory for children.* Paper presented at the 1987 midwinter meeting of the Society for Personality Assessment, San Francisco.
Carlson, G. A., & Cantwell, D. P. (1980). A survey of depressive symptoms, syndrome, and disorder in a child psychiatric population. *Journal of Child Psychology and Psychiatry, 21,* 19–25.
Carroll, B. J., Curtis, G. C., & Meldels, J. (1976). Neuroendocrine regulation in depression: I. Limbic system-adrenal cortical dysfunction. *Archives of General Psychiatry, 33,* 1039–1044.
Carroll, B. J., Feinberg, M., Greden, J. F., Tarika, J., Albala, A. A., Haskett, R. F., James, N. M., Kronfol, L., Lohr, Steiner, M., de Vigne, J. P., & Young, E. (1981). A specific laboratory test for the diagnosis of melancholia. *Archives of General Psychiatry, 38,* 15–22.
Casat, C. D. (1988). Childhood anxiety disorders: A review of the possible relationship to adult panic disorder and agoraphobia. *Journal of Anxiety Disorders, 2,* 51–60.
Casat, C. D., Arana, G. A., and Powell, K. A. (in press). Use of the dexamethasone suppression test (DST) in children and adolescents with major depressive disorder (MDD). *American Journal of Psychiatry.*
Casat, C. D., & Powell, K. A. (1988). The dexamethasone suppression test in children and adolescents with major depressive disorders: A review. *Journal of Clinical Psychiatry, 49,* 390–393.
Castenada, A., McCandless, B. R., & Palermo, D. S. (1956). The Children's Form of the Manifest Anxiety Scale. *Child Development, 27,* 317–326.
Chambers, W. J., Puig-Antich, J., & Tabrizi, M. A. (1978). *The ongoing development of the Kiddie-SADS (Schedule of affective disorders and schizophrenia for school-age children).* Paper presented at the annual meeting of the American Academy of Child Psychiatry, San Diego.
Charney, D. S., Heninger, G. B., Price, & Breier, A. (1986). Receptor sensitivity and the mechanism of action of antidepressant treatment. *Archives of General Psychiatry, 38,* 1160–1180.
Charney, D. S., Menkes, D. B., & Heninger, G. B. (1981). Receptor sensitivity and the mechanism of action of antidepressant treatment. *Archives of General Psychiatry, 38,* 1160–1180.

Conners, C. K. (1973). Rating scales for use in drug studies with children. *Psychoparmacology Bulletin*, 23–31.

Cooper, J. R., Bloom, F. E., & Roth, R. H. (1986). *The biochemical basis of neuropharmacology (5th ed.)*. New York: Oxford University Press.

Curtis, G. C., Cameron, O. G., & Nesse, R. M. (1982). The dexamethasone suppression test in panic disorder and agoraphobia. *American Journal of Psychiatry, 139,* 1043–1046.

Cytryn, L., & McKnew, D. H. (1972). Proposed classification of childhood depression. *American Journal of Psychiatry, 129,* 63–69.

Cytryn, L., McKnew, D. H., & Bunney, W. E. (1980). Diagnosis of depression in children: A reassessment. *American Journal of Psychiatry, 137,* 22–25.

Dealy, R. S., Ishiki, D. M., Avery, D. H., Wilson, L. G., & Dunner, D. L. (1981). Secondary depression in anxiety disorders. *Comprehensive Psychiatry, 22,* 612–618.

Dobson, K. (1985). The relationship between anxiety and depression. *Clinical Psychology Review, 5,* 307–324.

Doerfler, L. A., Felner, R. D., Rowlison, R. T., Rayley, P. A., & Evans, E. (1987). *Depression in children and adolescents: A comparative analysis of the utility and construct validity of two assessment indices.* Manuscript submitted for publication.

Eason, L., Finch, A. J., Brasted, W., and Saylor, C. F. (1985). Inventories for the assessment of depression and anxiety in the pediatric setting. *Journal of Child Psychiatry and Human Development, 16,* 57–64.

Endicott, J., & Spitzer, R. L. (1978). A diagnostic interview: The schedule for affective disorders and schizophrenia. *Archives of General Psychiatry, 35,* 837–844.

Exner, J. E. (1986). *The Rorschach: A comprehensive system (2nd ed., Vol. 1).* New York: Wiley.

Eysenck, H., & Eysenck, S. (1968). *Manual for the Eysenck Personality Inventory.* San Diego: Educational and Industrial Testing Service.

Finch, A. J., Fryer, L. L., Saylor, C. F., Carek, D. J., & McIntosh, J. A. (1987). *Anxiety and depression in children: Negative affectivity or separate constructs?* Manuscript submitted for publication.

Finch, A. J., Kendall, P. C., Dannenburg, M. A., & Morgan, J. R. (1978). Effects of task difficulty on state-trait anxiety in emotionally disturbed children. *Journal of Genetic Psychology, 133,* 253–259.

Finch, A. J., Montgomery, L. E., & Deardorff, P. (1974). Reliability of State-Trait Anxiety with emotionally disturbed children. *Journal of Abnormal Child Psychology, 2,* 67–69.

Finch, A. J., & Rogers, T. (1984). Self-report instruments. In T. Ollendick & M. Hersen (Eds.), *Child behavioral assessment: Principles and procedures.* New York: Pergamon Press.

Flament, M., Rapoport, J. L., Zahn, T., Kahn, J. P., Berg, C. J., Scupi, B., & Ingersol, B. (1986, April). *Behavioral and physiological effects of caffeine in children with anxiety disorders and in normal controls.* Paper presented at the Panic Disorder Diologic Workshop, Washington, DC.

Foa, E. B., & Foa, U. G. (1982). Differentiating depression and anxiety: Is it possible? Is it useful? *Psychopharmacology Bulletin, 18,* 62–68.

Frommer, E. A. (1967). Treatment of childhood depression with antidepressant drugs. *British Medical Journal, i,* 729–732.

Frommer, E. A. (1968). Depressive illness in childhood. *British Journal of Psychiatry, 2,* 117–136.

Gittelman, R., & Klein, D. F. (1984). Relationship between separation anxiety and panic and agoraphobic disorders. *Psychopathology, 17*(Suppl. 1), 56–65.

Gittelman-Klein, R., & Klein, D. F. (1971). Controlled imipramine treatment of school phobia. *Archives of General Psychiatry, 25,* 204–207.

Gittelman-Klein, R., & Klein, D. F. (1973). School phobia: Diagnostic considerations in light of imipramine effects. *Journal of Nervous and Mental Disease, 156,* 199–215.

Glaser, K. (1968). Masked depression in children and adolescents. *American Journal of Psychotherapy, 21,* 565–574.

Gold, P. W., Chrousos, G., Kellner, C., Post, R. M., Roy, A., Augerinos, P., Schulte, H., Oldfield, E., & Loriaux, D. L. (1984). Psychiatric implications of basic and clinical studies with corticotropin-releasing factor. *American Journal of Psychiatry, 141,* 619–627.

Halbreich, U., Asnis, G. M., Shindledecker, R., Zumoff, B., & Nathan, S. (1985). Cortisol secretion in endogenous depression. *Archives of General Psychiatry, 42,* 904–908.

Hershberg, S. G., Carlson, G. A., Cantwell, D. P., & Strober, M. (1982). Anxiety and depressive disorders in psychiatrically disturbed children. *Journal of Clinical Psychiatry, 43,* 358–361.

Hodges, K. K., & Siegel, L. J. (1985). Depression in children and adolescents. In E. E. Beckham & W. R. Leber (Eds.), *Handbook of depression: Treatment, assessment, and research.* Homewood, IL: Dorsey Press.

Kashani, J. H., Venzke, R., & Millar, E. A. (1981). Depression in children admitted to hospital for orthopaedic procedures. *British Journal of Psychiatry, 138,* 21–25.

Kazdin, A. E. (1981). Assessment techniques for childhood depression: A critical appraisal. *Journal of the American Academy of Child Psychiatry, 20,* 358–375.

Kendall, P. C., Cantwell, D. P., & Kazdin, A. E. (1989). Depression in children and adolescents: Assessment issues and recommendations. *Cognitive Therapy and Research, 13,* 109–146.

Kieffer, M. L., & Siegel, L. J. (1984). Paper presented at the annual meeting of the American Psychological Association, Toronto.

Klein, D. F., & Fink, M. (1962). Psychiatric reaction patterns to imipramine. *American Journal of Psychiatry, 119,* 432–438.

Kovacs, M. (1980/1981). Rating scales to assess depression in school-aged children. *Acta Paedopsychiatrica, 46,* 305–331.

Kovacs, M., & Beck, A. T. (1977). An empirical–clinical approach toward a definition of childhood depression. In J. G. Schulterbrandt & A. Raskin (Eds.), *Depression in childhood: Diagnosis, treatment and conceptual models.* New York: Raven Press.

Kovacs, M., Betof, N. G., Celebre, J. E., Mansheim, P. A., Petty, L. K., & Reynak, J. J. (1977). *Childhood depression: Myth or clinical syndrome?* Unpublished manuscript, University of Pennsylvania, Philadelphia.

Kovacs, M., Feinberg, T. C., Crouse-Novak, M. A., Paulauskas, S. L., & Finkelstein, R. (1984). Depressive disorders in childhood. I. A longitudinal prospective study of characteristics and recovery. *Archives of General Psychiatry, 41,* 229–237.

Lang, M., & Tisher, M. (1978). *Children's Depression Scale.* Victoria, Australia: Australian Council for Educational Research.

Lefkowitz, M. M., & Tesiny, E. P. (1980). Assessment of childhood depression. *Journal of Consulting and Clinical Psychology, 48,* 43–50.

Leon, G. R., Kendall, P. C., & Garber, J. (1980). Depression in children: Parent, teacher, and child perspectives. *Journal of Abnormal Child Psychology, 8,* 221–235.

Lesser, I. M. (in press). The relationship between panic disorder and depression. *Journal of Anxiety Disorders.*

Lieberman, J. A., Brenner, R., Lesser, M., Coccaro, E., Borenstein, M., & Kane, J. M. (1983). Dexamethasone suppression tests in patients with panic disorder. *American Journal of Psychiatry, 140,* 917–919.

Lipovsky, J. A., Finch, A. J., Jr., & Belter, R. W. (in press). Assessment of anxiety and depression in hospitalized adolescents: Objective and projective measures. *Journal of Personality Assessment.*

Lira, F. T., White, M. J., & Finch, A. J. (1977). Anxiety and mood states in delinquent adolescents. *Journal of Personality Assessment, 41,* 532–536.

Loosen, P. T., & Prange, A. J. (1982). Serum thyrotropin response to thyrotropin-releasing hormone in psychiatric patients: A review. *American Journal of Psychiatry, 139,* 405–416.

Malmquist, C. P. (1971). Depression in childhood and adolescence. *New England Journal of Medicine, 284,* 887–893.

McConville, B. J., Boag, L. C., & Purohit, A. P. (1973). Three types of childhood depression. *Canadian Psychiatric Association Journal, 18,* 133–138.
McNair, D., Lorr, M., & Droppleman, L. (1971). *Manual for the Profile of Mood States.* San Diego: Educational and Industrial Testing Service.
Montgomery, L. E., & Finch, A. J. (1974). Validity of two measures of anxiety in children. *Journal of Abnormal Child Psychology, 2,* 293–298.
Nesse, R. M., Cameron, O. G., Curtis, G. C., McCann, D. S., & Huber-Smith, M. J. (1984). Adrenergic function in patients with panic anxiety. *Archives of General Psychiatry, 41,* 771–776.
Newmark, C. S., Wheeler, D., Newmark, L., & Stabler, B. (1975). Test induced anxiety with children. *Journal of Personality Assessment, 39,* 409–413.
Norvell, N., Brophy, C., & Finch, A. J. (1985). The relationship of anxiety to childhood depression. *Journal of Personality Assessment, 49,* 150–153.
Pearce, J., (1977). Depressive disorder in childhood. *Journal of Child Psychology and Psychiatry, 18,* 79–82.
Pohl, R., Berchou, R., & Rainey, J. M. (1982). Tricyclic antidepressants and monoamine oxidase inhibitors in the treatment of agoraphobia. *Journal of Psychopharmacology, 2,* 399–407.
Poznanski, E. O. (1982). The clinical phenomenology of childhood depression. *American Journal of Orthopsychiatry, 52,* 308–313.
Poznanski, E. O., Cook, S., & Carroll, B. (1979). A depression rating scale for children. *Pediatrics, 64,* 442–450.
Poznanski, E., Mokros, H. B., Grossman, J., & Freeman, L. N. (1985). Diagnostic criteria in childhood depression. *American Journal of Psychiatry, 142,* 1168–1173.
Poznanski, E. O., & Zrull, J. P. (1970). Childhood depression: Clinical characteristics of overtly depressed children. *Archives of General Psychiatry, 23,* 8–15.
Puig-Antich, J. (1980). Affective disorders in childhood. *Psychiatric Clinics of North America, 3,* 403–424.
Puig-Antich, J., Blau, S., Marx, N., Greenhill, L. L., & Chambers, W. (1978). Prepubertal major depressive disorder. *Journal of the American Academy of Child Psychiatry, 17,* 695–707.
Puig-Antich, J., Chambers, W., & Tabrizi, M. A. (1983). The clinical assessment of current depressive episodes in children and adolescents: Interviews with parents and children. In D. Cantwell & G. Carlson (Eds.), *Childhood depression* (pp. 157–179). New York: Spectrum.
Puig-Antich, J., & Gittelman, R. (1979). Depression in childhood and adolescence. In E. S. Paykel (Ed.), *Handbook of affective disorders.* London: Churchill.
Puig-Antich, J., Novacenko, H., Goetz, R., Corser, J., Davies, M., & Ryan, N. (1984). Cortisol and prolactin responses to insulin-induced hypoglycemia in prepubertal major depressives during and episode and after recovery. *Journal of the American Academy of Child Psychiatry, 23,* 49–57.
Puig-Antich, J., Perel, J. M., Lupatkin, W., Chambers, W. J., Shea, C., Tabrizi, M. A., & Stiller, R. L. (1979). Plasma levels of imipramine (IMI) and desmethylimipramine (DMI) and clinical response in prepubertal major depressive disorder. *Journal of the American Academy of Child Psychiatry, 18,* 661–677.
Puig-Antich, J., & Rabinovich, H. (1986). Relationship between affective and anxiety disorders in childhood. In R. Gittelman (Ed.), *Anxiety disorders of childhood.* New York: Guilford Press.
Quay, H. C. (1986a). Classification. In H. C. Quay & J. S. Werry (Eds.), *Psychopathological disorders of childhood.* New York: Wiley.
Quay, H. C. (1986b). A critical analysis of DSM-III as a taxonomy of psychopathology in childhood and adolescence. In T. Millon & G. L. Klerman (Eds.), *Contemporary directions in psychopathology: Toward the DSM-IV.* New York: Guilford Press.

Quay, H. C., & La Greca, A. M. (1986). Disorders of anxiety, withdrawal and dysphoria. In Quay, & J. S. Werry (Eds.), *Psychopathological disorders of childhood.* New York: Wiley.

Quay, H. C., & Peterson, D. R. (1983). *Interim manual for the Revised Behavior Problem Checklist (1st ed.).* Coral Gables, FL: University of Miami Press.

Rapport, J., Elkins, R., Langer, D., Sceery, W., Buchsbaum, M. S., Gillin, J. C., Murphy, D. L., Zahn, T. P., Lake, R., Ludlow, C., & Mendelson, W. (1981). Childhood obsessive–compulsive disorder. *American Journal of Psychiatry, 138,* 1545–1554.

Reynolds, C. R. (1982). *Convergent and divergent validity of What I Think and Feel: The Revised Children's Manifest Anxiety Scale.* Unpublished manuscript.

Reynolds, C. R., & Paget, K. D. (1981). Factor analysis of the Revised Children's Manifest Anxiety Scale for blacks, whites, males, and females. *Journal of Consulting and Clinical Psychology, 49,* 352–359.

Reynolds, C. R., & Richmond, B. O. (1978). What I think and feel: A revised measure of children's manifest anxiety. *Journal of Abnormal Child Psychiatry, 6,* 271–280.

Reynolds, W. M., & Coats, D. I. (1986). A comparison of cognitive-behavioral therapy and relaxation training for the treatment of depression in adolescents. *Journal of Consulting and Clinical Psychology, 54,* 653–660.

Rosenbaum, A. H., Maruta, T., Schatzberg, A. F., Orsulak, P. J., Jiang, N., Cole, J. O., & Schildkraut, J. J. (1983). Toward a biochemical classification of depressive disorders, VII: Urinary free cortisol and urinary MHPG in depressions. *American Journal of Psychiatry, 140,* 314–318.

Roy-Byrne, P. P., Uhde, T. W., Gold, P. W., Rubinow, D. R., & Post, R. M. (1985). Neuroendocrine abnormalities in panic disorder. *Psychopharmacolgy Bulletin, 21,* 546–550.

Rubin, R. T., Miller, R. G., Clark, B. R., Poland, R. E., & Arthur, R. J. (1970). The stress of aircraft carrier landings II. 3-methoxy-4-hydroxy-phenylglycol excretion in naval aviators. *Psychosomatic Medicine, 32,* 589–597.

Rutter, M., Lebovici, S., Eisenberg, L., Sneznevskij, A. V., Sadoun, R., Brooke, E., & Lin, T.-Y. (1969). A tri-axial classification of mental disorder in childhood. *Journal of Child Psychology and Psychiatry, 10,* 41–61.

Rutter, M., Shaffer, D., & Shepherd, M. (1975). *A multi-axial classification of child psychiatric disorders.* Geneva: World Health Organization.

Saylor, C. F., Finch, A. J., Jr., Spirito, A., & Bennett, B. (1984). The Children's Depression Inventory: A systematic evaluation of psychometric properties. *Journal of Consulting and Clinical Psychology, 52,* 955–967.

Schildkraut, J. J. (1965). The catecholamine hypothesis of affective disorders: A review of supporting evidence. *American Journal of Psychiatry, 122,* 509–522.

Shoemaker, O. S. (1987). *Concurrent validity of the Youth Self-report version of the Child Behavior Profile.* Unpublished manuscript.

Siever, L. J., & Davis, K. L. (1985). Overview: Toward a dysregulation hypothesis of depression. *American Journal of Psychiatry, 142,* 1017–1031.

Spielberger, C. D. (1973). *Preliminary manual for the State-Trait Anxiety Inventory for Children ("How I Feel Questionnaire").* Palo Alto, CA: Consulting Psychologists Press.

Strauss, C. C., Forehand, R., Frame, C., & Smith, K. (1984). Characteristics of children with extreme scores on the children's depression inventory. *Journal of Clinical Child Psychology, 13,* 227–231.

Strauss, C. C., Last, ., Hersen, ., & Kazdin, . (in press).

Targum, S. D., Sullivan, A. C., & Byrnes, S. M. (1982). Neuroendocrine relationships in major depressive disorders. *American Journal of Psychiatry, 139,* 282–286.

Tisher, M. (1983). School refusal: A depressive equivalent? In D. P. Cantwell & G. A. Carlson (Eds.), *Affective disorders in childhood and adolescence—An update.* Jamaica, NY: Spectrum.

Tisher, M., & Lang, M. (1983). The children's depression scale: Review and further developments. In D. P. Cantwell & G. A. Carlson (Eds.), *Affective disorders in childhood and adolescence: An update*. New York: Spectrum.

Treiber, F. A., & Mabe, P. A. (1987). Child and parent perceptions of children's psychopathology in psychiatric outpatient children. *Journal of Abnormal Child Psychology, 13,* 115–124.

Uhde, T. W., Roy-Byrne, P. P., Vittone, B. J., Boulenger, J.-P., & Post, R. M. (1985). Phenomenology and neurobiology of panic disorder. In A. H. Tuma & J. D. Maser (Eds). *Anxiety and the anxiety disorders*. Hillside, NJ: Erlbaum.

Waldron, S., Shrier, D. K., Stone, B., & Tobin, F. (1975). School phobia and other childhood neuroses: A systematic study of the children and their families. *American Journal of Psychiatry, 8,* 802–808.

Watson, D., & Clark, L. A. (1984). Negative affectivity: The disposition to experience aversive emotional states. *Psychological Bulletin, 96,* 465–490.

Weissman, M. M., Leckman, J. F., Merikangas, K. R., Gammon, G. D., & Prusoff, B. A. (1984). Depression and anxiety disorders in parents and children. *Archives of General Psychiatry, 41,* 845–852.

Werry, J. S. (1986). Diagnosis and assessment. In R. Gittelman (Ed.), *Anxiety disorders of childhood*. New York: Guilford Press.

Wirt, R. D., Lachar, D., Klinedinst, L. K., & Seat, P. D. (1977). *Multidimensional description of child personality: A manual for the Personality Inventory for Children*. Los Angeles: Western Psychological Services.

Wolfe, V. V., Finch, A. J., Saylor, C. F., Blount, R. L., Pallmeyer, T. P., & Carek, D. J. (1987). Negative affectivity in children: A multitrait-multimethod investigation. *Journal of Consulting and Clinical Psychology, 55,* 245–250.

Precursors and Concomitants

Major Life Events in Anxiety and Depression

Timothy W. Smith
Kenneth D. Allred

I. Introduction

A variety of scholars have agreed that anxiety and depression can be distinguished, at least in part, by the kinds of life events contributing to their development. Freud (1926/1959) argued that anxiety is a result of the danger or threat of losing a valued person or relationship, while sadness or depression results from the actual or perceived occurrence of such loss. Bowlby (1975) suggested that many types of threats in addition to threat of loss could produce anxiety, but agreed with the basic distinction. Implicit in such a distinction is a difference in the emotional tense of anxiety and depression (Katz, 1980). Anxiety results from the threat of a future loss or negative event, while depression is a response to a recent or previous event of this type. The diagnosis of a loved one as critically ill produces anxiety, while the death of a loved one produces sad and depressed mood. This distinction is widely made (e.g., Dobson, 1985; Katz, 1980; Malatesta & Wilson, 1988; Oatley & Boulton, 1985), and has an obvious intrinsic appeal.

Anxiety and Depression

This view of the role of life events in the negative affects would seem to generate relatively specific, testable hypotheses concerning the similarity and distinctness of anxiety and depression. The threat of a negative event and the occurrence of events which contain or produce such threats should elicit anxiety but not depression, as long as they do not represent losses themselves. Recent negative events or losses should produce depression but not anxiety, so long as they do not involve the threat of future negative events. Events that are losses *and* represent the danger of future negative events should produce a mixture of both affects. Much is known about the relationship between stressful events and depression, and the available data are consistent. Negative events increase the likelihood and severity of depressed mood and clinical depression. Less is known about the role of negative events in anxious mood and anxiety disorders, although the available evidence indicates that life events may operate in the predicted manner. However, in spite of the intuitive appeal of the argument that life events can distinguish between these two affective states, surprisingly little empirical evidence exists.

The purpose of this chapter is to review the empirical research on the role of life events in anxiety and depression, in an attempt to identify similar and distinguishable aspects of these emotions. Following a brief introduction to the conceptualization and measurement of life events, the most extensive literature, that concerning depression, will be reviewed. We will not attempt an exhaustive review; rather, we discuss the current status of this research, paying particular attention to its implications for understanding the similarities and differences between anxiety and depression. Next we review in more detail the smaller, more recently accumulated body of research on life stress and anxiety. The still smaller number of studies that simultaneously consider anxiety and depression is considered next.

As will be seen, the research raises many more questions than it answers. In an effort to facilitate the accumulation of helpful answers, we subsequently discuss methodological and conceptual issues to be considered in future research. Life stress research in general, and in particular research on life stress in depression, has generated important methodological and conceptual concerns that must be addressed in future work. Such methodological and conceptual concerns are made even more thorny when one is faced with the task of simultaneously considering anxiety and depression. Indeed, future research on this topic will benefit greatly from the ongoing efforts to distinguish between these affects at the level of theory and measurement, and many of these efforts are reviewed elsewhere in this volume.

II. Approaches to the Measurement of Life Stress

A. History and Current Techniques

Although particular instruments and methods vary in specific details, most approaches to the measurement of life stress share a common conceptual orientation. Potentially stressful, major life events are seen as "discrete, time-limited events requiring change or adaptation" (Perkins, 1982, p. 320). The notion that life events requiring adaptation contribute to the development of emotional disorders is not new. A rapid acceleration in the scientific study of the stress disorder hypothesis, however, followed the development of inventories for quantifying the occurrence and accumulation of recent life events.

The earliest of these inventories was the Schedule of Recent Experience (SRE), developed by Holmes and Rahe (1967). It consisted of a list of 43 life events (e.g., death of relative, change in job, moving, marriage, and divorce), and simply required subjects to indicate whether or not the event had been experienced in the past 6 to 12 months. Scores reflected the number of endorsed events. Realizing that not all events required the same degree of adaptation, Holmes and Rahe (1967) modified the scoring system in the Social Readjustment Rating Scale (SRRS). Again, subjects simply indicated which events they had experienced, but unlike the SRE the score reflected a sum of the preassigned weights corresponding to each endorsed event. Thus, the score is intended to represent the total amount of readjustment of Life Change Units (LCUs), combining positive and negative events (e.g., marriage vs. divorce).

The SRRS has historically been the workhorse of life events research. Further, most methodological developments have essentially been refinements in this approach. One recent line of development concerns the assignment of weights to events. Many conceptual approaches to stress suggest that a given event is not equally stressful for all individuals. Rather, the level of stress is determined by individual, subjective appraisals of events (e.g., Lazarus, 1966, Lazarus & Folkman, 1984). Further, many authors have argued, and data are relatively consistent with the assertion (for review, see Paykel, 1982), that negative events are much more strongly related to emotional distress than are positive events. One of the most widely used, "second-generation" life events measures, the Life Experience Survey (LES) reflects both of these concerns (Sarason, Johnson, & Siegel, 1978). A list of major life events is presented, and subjects are asked to (1) indicate which ones they have experienced and to (2) rate the valence or impact of each endorsed event from very negative to very positive. The three scores derived from the LES reflect the sum of the negative ratings, positive ratings, and the total, absolute value of impact ratings.

The Psychiatric Epidemiology Research Interview (PERI) is yet another approach to the issue of quantifying the adjustment demands of life events (Dohrenwend, Krasnoff, Askenasy, & Dohrenwend, 1982). Dohrenwend et al. (1982) argue that completely subjective ratings, as obtained by the LES, are problematic because they confound the event with the impact or outcome that they are hypothesized to predict. Differing impact ratings of similar events may, in part, reflect the influence of differing levels of emotional distress, thereby artificially inflating the correlation between stress and distress. They also argue that systems for selecting and weighting events, such as the one used with the SRRS, have been limited by the fact that they may not be representative of the general population. The PERI employs an expanded event list and an elaborate population-based weighting system. Although it is currently less widely used than other inventories, the approach reflects sophisticated and detailed attention to the thorny problem of developing a meaningful, unconfounded index of the level or degree of life change.

B. Recent Methodological and Conceptual Developments

The evolution of life event assessments reflects several methodological and conceptual issues. Beyond concerns about subjective versus general weighting, the valance of events, and representativeness of events and their weights, a variety of methodological and conceptual measurement issues have arisen in two decades of life event research (for reviews, see Monroe, 1982a; Perkins, 1982). Starting at a very basic level, for example, it is apparent that the long periods of retrospection required by most approaches (e.g., the previous 6–12 months) may produce inaccurate event totals (Monroe, 1982b). It is also true that many events may reflect the consequences rather than the cause of an emotional problem. The loss of a job or break up of a relationship could just as easily be the result rather than the cause of depression, for example. Further, *both* an increased level of stressful life events and emotional distress may actually reflect an underlying chronic disorder of some type (Depue & Munroe, 1986). These possibilities have led to increased effort to control or consider initial levels of psychopathology in prospective designs, and the separation of events that could not be the result of developing or established emotional dysfunction (e.g., death of a family member) from those that might be an effect of distress (e.g., loss of a job), as well as other methodological and conceptual refinements. Thus, recent critiques and empirical developments have moved this field well beyond simple studies of the correlation between retrospectively reported life events and concurrent levels of reported emotional distress (Monroe & Peterman, in press).

III. The Role of Life Events in Depression

The study of stressful life events as contributors to depression is an established aspect of psychopathology research. The resulting body of literature is far too large to review in detail in the present discussion, and such detail would quickly obscure our main purpose—identification of similarities and differences between anxiety and depression. As a result, we will discuss only the main features of this literature and its current foci, and refer the reader elsewhere for more detailed discussions (e.g., Paykel, 1982). Previous research in this area has produced two important concerns that we shall consider in our discussion. First, the simplest and most common studies in this area employ a concurrent or retrospective design. Current levels of depression are assessed, recent life events are reported, and the level or type of association is examined. Such studies are quite limited in comparison to prospective designs. As mentioned above, errors in recalling events may arise from typical forgetting, or from the effects of depression on memory, or from a retrospective justification or explanation of the affective disorder. Such errors can render the meaning of concurrent or retrospective results ambiguous. Prospective studies clearly provide the most compelling type of information.

A second important consideration involves the difference between mood and mood disorder. Depressed mood is clearly within the range of normal human emotional experience. It is quantitatively, but perhaps even qualitatively, distinct from the depressive disorders. As a result, we will distinguish between mood and mood disorder in the discussions of research on depression and the analogous research in anxiety. Finally, it should be noted that our review is restricted to major life events (e.g., moving, loss of job, divorce, and illness or death of a family member), rather than minor life events or daily irritants (e.g., Bowman & Luteijn, 1986; Zautra, Guarnaccia, & Reich, this volume).

A. Retrospective and Prospective Studies of Association

A now classic series of studies (e.g., Brown & Harris, 1978; Paykel et al., 1969) demonstrated that clinically depressed persons report an increased number of major life stressors in the year prior to the onset of the disorder. Relevant comparisons are made to a variety of controls, including nondepressed subjects for the same time period and depressed subjects during some other period. This association between the presence of clinical depression and the report of an increased number and severity of major life events is quite robust. Several large-scale studies have replicated the relationship in recent years (Billings, Cronkite, & Moos, 1983; Costello, 1982; Mitchell, Cronkite, & Moos, 1983).

Similar results have been widely demonstrated for depression in nonclinical populations. Current levels of self-reported depression in normal populations (e.g., college students) are associated with reports of increased numbers and/or rated severity of major life events (e.g., Hewitt & Dyck, 1986; Lakey & Heller, 1985; Nezu & Ronan, 1985; Rook, 1987; Smith, O'Keeffe, & Jenkins, 1988). This association between increased self-reports of depression and reported life events is statistically significant even when self-report biases (i.e., social desirability) are controlled (Lakey & Heller, 1985). Thus, both clinically and subclinically, there is a clear and consistent association between depression and the recent occurrence of major life events.

Well-controlled prospective studies are far less common, but also support the hypothesized relationship between major life events and the subsequent occurrence of depression. Studies defining depression in terms of clinical diagnosis (e.g., Surtees et al., 1986), as well as those defining depression in terms of continuous scores in a student (e.g., Linville, 1987) or community sample (Holahan & Moos, 1987; Fergusson & Horwood, 1984; Monroe, Bromet, Connell, & Steiner, 1986), have demonstrated that an increased level of major life events is associated with increased risk of the onset of depression. It is important to note that this prospective relationship is found even when the effects of prior mood are controlled. That is, depressed subjects at the follow-up are not simply subjects who were depressed initially and reported negative events while depressed. Consistent with the results of the retrospective studies then, an accumulation of major life events is associated with an increased risk of subsequent depression. Although the majority of the evidence comes from the less compelling retrospective studies (Lloyd, 1980), the more recent prospective studies provide clear support for the hypothesized role of life events in depression.

B. Recent Developments

Life events have also been examined in relation to specific problems in depressed groups. For example, within samples of clinically depressed patients, an elevated number of stressful life events is associated with increased risk of suicide attempts (Slater & Depue, 1981) and with more depression on follow-up after treatment (Billings & Moos, 1985).

Many of the recent efforts have been aimed toward improving the precision of life events as a predictor of depression. The life events–depression relationship, though consistently significant, is small. In an effort to improve the power of this predictive factor, researchers have examined several more specific relationships, suggesting for example, that the degree or nature of the association between life events and depression in prospective studies may depend in part on the initial levels of depressive symptoms (Monroe, 1982c; Monroe et al., 1986; Hammen, Mayol, de Mayo, & Marks, 1986).

Some research has suggested that life events may not be equivalently related to all depressive disorders. Roy, Breir, Doran, and Pickar (1985), for example, compared retrospective reports of life events in controls and patients suffering major depressive episodes with and without melancholia. Depressives without melancholia reported a greater accumulation of stressful events relative to controls, but patients with melancholia did not. Similarly, depressives with elevated levels of life stressors prior to initial onset respond better to treatment than do patients without any increased life events (Monroe, Bellack, Hersen, & Himmelhoch, 1983). Consistent with older notions of the endogenous–reactive distinction (Fowles & Gersh, 1979), such findings suggest that life events may be important in only some disorders within the depressive spectrum.

Other studies have examined specificity in terms of types of events. Earlier research suggested that negative life events were more strongly associated with depression than were positive events, and that social "exits" or losses of important relationships were most important (Paykel, 1982). Within the normal population, undesirable events for which the subjects felt responsible have been found to be more strongly related to depressed mood than are other types of events (Hammen & Mayol, 1982).

Perhaps the best developed models of specificity in life event–depression relationships are a group of approaches best described as diathesis–stress models. Such approaches argue that life events do not necessarily produce depression in all people. Rather, only people with some preexisting vulnerability (i.e., diathesis) are prone to the development of depression following major life events. For example, Blatt (1974) has suggested that highly dependent or self-critical persons are more prone to depression following an accumulation of stressful life events than are independent or self-accepting persons. This hypothesis has recently been supported in a study of depressed mood in a normal population (Smith et al., 1988). Cognitive vulnerability models suggest that individuals holding various irrational or dysfunctional attitudes are more likely to become depressed following negative life changes than are more realistic or rational persons. This hypothesis has also been supported by recent cross-sectional research (Hewitt & Dyck, 1986; Olinger, Kuiper, & Shaw, 1987). Finally, Oatley and Boulton (1985) have argued that depression occurs when stressful events disrupt the roles by which people define their worth, if they lack other sources of self-definition. These authors noted that people with few sources of self-definition are particularly vulnerable to such losses. Consistent with this notion, Linville (1987) recently demonstrated in a prospective study of normal subjects that stressful events are more strongly related to the development of depressed mood in individuals low in self-complexity than in persons with a more multifaceted self-concept, even when controlling for initial levels of depression. Such diathesis–stress or vulnerability approaches are not new (see Becker, 1979, for a review of older models), but recent empirical efforts have given this type of approach renewed importance.

Attention to specificity across types of depressive conditions, events, and vulnerability factors has shed new light on the role of life events in depression. It seems obvious that similar research in anxiety, and in comparisons of anxiety and depression, would profit from similar approaches.

IV. Life Events in Anxiety

When compared to the analogous literature on depression, research on the role of major life events in anxiety and anxiety disorders is sparse. In a sample of naval personnel and two samples of college students, Sarason et al. (1978) report significant concurrent correlations between negative life events and both state and trait measures of anxiety. Thus, similar to concurrent or retrospective studies of depression in normal populations, reported anxiety is consistently related to negative life events.

Several studies have examined the relationship of life events to the onset of clinical anxiety disorders in retrospective designs. Roy-Byrne, Geraci, and Linde (1986a) compared 44 outpatients with a Research Diagnostic Criteria (RDC; Spitzer, Endicott, & Robins, 1978) diagnosis of panic disorder with 44 healthy employees at the National Institutes of Health (NIH) clinical center matched for age, sex, and time of recall. Subjects were compared on the number, type, and effect of life events during the year prior to the onset of panic attacks. Life events were assessed using the PERI method of assessment (Dohrenwend et al., 1982), which was administered during a 60- to 90-minute personal interview. Results showed that while there were no differences between subjects in total number of events, panic patients experienced significantly more life events that happened to them personally (versus events occurring to spouses or children). Panic patients also reported a significantly greater number of events that were undesirable and uncontrollable and that caused lower self-esteem.

In a similar study, Faravelli (1985) compared 23 outpatients with a *Diagnostic and Statistical Manual of Mental Disorders* (DSM-III; American Psychiatric Association, 1980) diagnosis of a panic disorder with 23 healthy control subjects matched for age, sex, and social and educational level. Life events for the year prior to onset of illness were assessed through a semistructured interview. Results indicated that panic patients reported significantly more life events than did control subjects, especially in the month immediately prior to the onset of symptoms. Severe losses and severely threatening events demonstrated the largest differences across groups. In an attempt to control for possible general reporting biases, Pollard, Obermeier, and Lorn (1987) examined life events in a 12-month period prior to disorder onset in a group of agoraphobics, and in a smaller group of agoraphobics for whom the 12-month period did not coincide with onset. The onset group reported significantly more events than did the control group.

At least one study failed to find clear evidence of obvious life event precipitants in agoraphobics when compared to controls (Burglass, Clarke, & Kreitman, 1977). Several clinical descriptive studies report a large frequency of stressful events in anxiety disorder patients prior to onset, but they lack the kinds of controls required for clear support (e.g., Last, Barlow, & Obrieu, 1984). Nonetheless, the limited existing evidence appears to support the notion that stressful life events are associated with anxious mood and clinical anxiety disorders.

V. Studies of Anxiety and Depression

Few studies have directly compared the relationship of life events to anxiety and depression. Some studies have addressed indirectly related concerns. For example, Brown, Bifulco, Harris, and Bridge (1986) found that subclinical anxiety symptoms preceded the onset of depressive disorder, but only in depressives experiencing a precipitating stressful life event before onset. Similarly, Roy-Byrne, Geraci, and Linde (1986) found that panic disorder patients who reported a major loss or separation in the year before onset of the panic disorder were more likely to develop a subsequent depression than were patients without such an event. While these studies suggest that life events, anxiety, and depression may indeed be related in several interesting ways, they do not speak directly to the question of similarities and differences in the event–mood relationship in anxiety and depression.

In a more directly relevant study, Vinokur and Selzer (1975) examined the correlation of reported life events with measures of both anxiety and depression in a large community sample. Events reported for the previous 12 months were significantly correlated with current levels of both anxiety and depression, and with several other measures of emotional distress. These effects were primarily due to undesirable rather than desirable life events. Thus, general levels of recent negative life events were associated with diverse measures of adjustment, although no direct tests of specificity were reported. That is, the authors did not determine if the life events–depression and life events–anxiety relationships were independent, or instead reflected a more nonspecific relationship between life events and emotional distress.

In a more direct comparison, Monroe, Imhoff, Wise, and Harris (1983) examined the prospective relationship of life events to self-reports of both depression and anxiety in a sample of undergraduate students. Subjects completed the LES (Sarason et al., 1978), an interview about events endorsed on the survey, and a measure of general psychological distress (Goldberg, 1972) at the beginning of an academic semester. Near the end of the term, subjects completed the Beck Depression Inventory (Beck, 1967) and the state form of the State–Trait Anxiety Inventory (Spielberger, Gorsuch, & Lushene, 1970). Anxiety and depression demonstrated significant correlations both with total numbers of life events and with the degree of undesirability of events. When initial emotional distress was controlled in regression analyses, life events still predicted the subsequent development of depression. This result is consistent with the previously described prospective studies of life events and depression. Unlike the results for depression, however, when initial emotional distress was controlled, life events were no longer associated with subsequent levels of anxiety. Further, the correlation of depression with life events was significantly larger than the correlation of life events with anxiety. Monroe, Imhoff, Wise, and Harris (1983) argued that these results indicate that the effects of life events are specific to development of depression, given that this prospective relationship remained significant when controlling for previous distress. Within the confines of this population and these measures of affect and stress, then, it appears that life events are more strongly related to depression than to anxiety.

Clear evidence of overlapping and unique relationships of life events to anxiety and depression were observed in a study of clinical groups. Finlay-Jones and Brown (1981) selected a sample of women from those seeking outpatient health care. Using the Present State Examination (Wing, Nixon, Mann, & Leff, 1977) and multiple raters, the women were classified as psychiatric noncases (n = 119), depressed (n = 17), anxiety disorder (n = 13), or mixed anxiety and depression (n = 14). Cases were designated only if the condition had arisen in the previous year. Subjects were also interviewed about life events during the year before disorder onset, or the year before the interview in the case of the normal subjects. The Brown and Harris (1978) system was used to assess events, and events were further classified as instances of loss or danger. Losses included death of or separation from a loved one, loss of own health, loss of job or possessions, or the loss of a cherished idea. Danger events were those that raised the possibility of future crises or problems for the subject. The events were also rated in terms of severity.

Results indicated that severe life events were more frequent in each of the diagnostic groups than in the control group, indicating that stressful life events were equally important in anxiety and depression. The relative frequencies of severe loss and severe danger events, however, provided evidence of specificity. Significantly more depressed women, relative to women in both the anxiety and normal groups, reported severe losses in the 3 months prior to onset (65, 15, and 10%, respectively). Significantly more anxiety-disordered women, however, relative to depressed and normal control subjects, reported a severe danger event in the 3 months prior to onset (77, 47, and 12%, respectively). Mixed disorder patients, relative to controls, were more likely to have reported both a danger event (73 vs. 12%) and a loss event (80 vs. 10%). Thus, these findings are consistent with the assertion that major life events are associated with both anxiety and depressive disorders. However, they also show that different types of events are associated with the two types of clinically significant mood disturbances.

VI. Considerations for Future Research

The findings reviewed thus far suggest both similarities and differences in the role of life events in anxiety and depression. Direct comparisons are rare, however, and most studies are retrospective or contain other methodological limitations. Clearly, additional research is required before any definitive conclusions can be reached. In the following section, we discuss methodological and conceptual issues relevant to such future efforts.

A. Methodological Issues

Design and measurement problems plagued much of the earlier research on life events. As mentioned earlier, retrospective designs offer considerably less inferential power, with a variety potential artifacts (e.g., recall errors or distortion) and ambiguities concerning the direction of causality clouding results. Although the careful use of between-groups (e.g., normal *and* additional pathological groups) and within-groups controls (e.g., across onset-related and nonrelated periods) may facilitate the interpretation of retrospective studies, prospective designs are clearly superior. Given the paucity of direct comparisons of anxiety and depression, however, retrospective studies such as that of Finlay-Jones and Brown (1981) are currently valuable.

Also, as described above, a variety of techniques have evolved for the assessment of life events, and the ease of administration of self-report scales may come at the cost of somewhat less reliable data than can be obtained with the various interview measures in existence (cf. Brown & Harris, 1978; Dohrenwend et al., 1982; Perkins, 1982). Nevertheless, self-report methods of assessment are certainly useful for initial, exploratory studies in an area.

Regardless of the method, in any attempt to distinguish anxiety and depression, the dimensions or qualities of stressful events must be evaluated along with frequency and severity. Given that the relevant dimensions (e.g., danger, threat, loss) may be semantically similar to the items in anxiety and depression measures, researchers must be careful to ensure that item overlap does not artificially inflate the association between event dimensions ratings and measures of affect (Nicholls, Licht, & Pearl, 1982). Further, as described earlier, subjective ratings by subjects, as compared to independent ratings, represent a potential confounding of events and the disorders they are presumed to cause.

One of the most difficult methodological challenges to future research in this area concerns the empirical differentiation of anxiety and depression. That is, in order to study similarities and differences in anxiety and depression, assessment procedures must quantify these states as distinctly as possible. This is problematic at two levels. First, both as normal moods and as clinical disorders, anxiety and depression frequently co-occur (cf. Gersh & Fowles, 1979; Dobson, 1985). Second, existing measurement procedures have limited discriminant validity across the two constructs, exacerbating the problem of their actual co-occurrence. In other words, it is very difficult to identify empirically distinct features of two correlated constructs when the available assessment procedures share method variance as well. Little variance remains to be accounted for in studies of distinctive features or contributing factors. Overlapping measures and actual co-occurrence of the affects are problems at the level of clinical disorders (Dobson, 1985; Gersh & Fowles, 1979) and are severe problems in studies of normal mood. The results of several recent studies (Gotlib, 1984; Tanaka-Matsumi & Kameoka, 1986; Watson & Clark, 1984) indicate that in normal populations the cross-construct correlations for self-reports of anxiety and depression are virtually indistinguishable from the correlations among measures within each construct. This nearly total absence of discriminant or divergent validity makes it extremely difficult to study distinct features of normal anxiety and depression. Each of these measures may actually assess the broader trait of negative affectivity (Watson & Clark, 1984) or general dysphoria (Gotlib, 1984) in this population. This fact complicates the interpretation of studies attempting to discriminate general distress from anxiety or depression in this population (e.g., Monroe, Imhoff, Wise, & Harris, 1983). The development of better, more discriminating measures is an important task for future research.

A final methodological problem concerns the issue of chronic disorders, or chronic negative affect mentioned earlier (Depue & Monroe, 1986). As noted above, measures of anxious or depressed mood and anxiety or depressive disorders may reflect, in part, long-standing personality traits such as negative affectivity (Watson & Clark, 1984). This stable personality disposition is characterized by chronic anxious and depressed mood and negative emotional responsiveness. High-NA persons may also tend to rate life stressors as more upsetting. As a result, correlations between reports of life stress and dysphoric mood may reflect converging measurements of a single construct—negative affectivity (Depue & Monroe, 1986). Rather than simple reporting biases, the impact of chronic problems may also reflect the fact that these individuals actually *create* a more stressful and distressing environment in a reciprocally determined, self-perpetuating cycle (Wachtel, 1977). These possibilities make the interpretation of retrospective or concurrent designs even more ambiquous, and underscore the necessity of controlling for initial distress levels in prospective studies or separating chronically distressed from more normal subjects (Monroe et al., 1986).

B. Conceptual Issues

As noted above, recent research on the role of life events in depression has grown more specific in its focus. It seems likely that similar approaches might facilitate comparative studies of anxiety and depression.

Careful distinctions among subtypes of depressive and anxiety disorders, severity and chronicity of disorders, and types of events may hasten the accumulation of useful findings. Future life event typologies might focus on the distinction between loss and threat, as well as those distinctions in domain (e.g., achievement vs. interpersonal; Hammen, Marks, Mayol, & de Mayo, 1985) and in cognitive appraisal (Hammen & Mayol, 1982) that have been studied previously. The recent work of Higgins and his colleagues (Higgins, 1987; Higgins, Klein, & Strandman, 1985) may suggest additional event typologies useful in distinguishing anxiety and depression. Higgins has demonstrated that a discrepancy between one's personally defined ideal self and one's view of the actual self results in sad or depressed affect. In contrast, a discrepancy between one's view of the presumed ideal self endorsed by significant others (i.e., the "ought self"; "they think I ought to be") and the actual self produces more anxious, agitated moods. Events that differentially elicit these two types of self-discrepancy may, in turn, differentially elicit depression and anxiety.

Perhaps the most useful development in depression research has been the diathesis–stress approach. Vulnerabilities could include a variety of biological, cognitive, developmental, or social factors. In addition to specific event types, investigations of specific vulnerabilities for anxiety versus depression in one or more of these domains may provide evidence of distinct life stress effects. Recent evidence from a large twin study indicates that the patterns of correlations across different clusters of anxiety and depressive symptoms can be accounted for by a combination of environmental and genetic factors. Interestingly, while proneness to dysphoric emotion in general (i.e., common features of anxiety and depression) seemed to have a genetic basis, the unique features of anxiety and depression instead reflected environmental factors. That is, anxiety and depression may have the same genetic basis, but may be produced by different environmental factors (Kendler, Heath, Martin, & Eaves, 1987). Thus, distinct diatheses for anxiety and depression may not be genetic. Recent evidence of cognitive specificity in anxiety and depression (Beck, Brown, Steer, Eidelson, & Risking, 1987; Ingram, Kendall, Smith, Donnell, & Ronan, 1987) may contribute to the identification of distinct cognitive vulnerability factors. The identification of other areas of similarity and difference between anxiety and depression may facilitate theory-driven research on the differential effects of life stress.

VII. Summary and Conclusions

Existing research suggests that stressful life events play similar roles in anxiety and depression. Research on depression has clearly established stressful events as a contributing factor, and present research is attempting to refine this relationship by examining specific types of events, levels and types of depressive phenomena, and vulnerability factors. The analogous literature in anxiety is much smaller and less methodologically sophisticated. Although conclusions, as a result, must be tentative, stressful life events seem to contribute to anxious mood and anxiety disorders. The very limited information directly comparing anxiety and depression is consistent with prevailing but largely undocumented views on environmental contributions to these affects; events representing threat or future danger are more strongly associated with anxiety, while events representing a loss are more strongly associated with depression. The implicit appeal of this notion, together with the scant but enticing empirical support, should be enough incentive to spur additional research. Clearly, much additional research is needed before any firm conclusions can be drawn. Studies of life events may ultimately provide some indication as to how anxiety and depression are alike and how they are distinct. Fortunately, such future efforts can profit from two decades of methodological and conceptual refinements in life stress research.

References

American Psychiatric Association. (1980). *Diagnostic and statistical manual of mental disorders* (3rd ed.). Washington, DC: Author.

Beck, A. T. (1967). *Depression: Causes and treatment.* Philadelphia: University of Pennsylvania Press.

Beck, A. T., Brown, G., Steer, R. A., Eidelson, J. I., & Risking, J. H. (1987). Differentiating anxiety and depression: A test of the cognitive content-specificity hypothesis. *Journal of Abnormal Psychology, 96,* 179–183.

Becker, J. (1979). Vulnerable self-esteem as a predisposing factor in depressive disorders. In R. A. Depue (Ed.), *The psychobiology of the depressive disorders: Implications for the effects of stress* (pp. 317–334). New York: Academic Press.

Billings, A. G., Cronkite, R. C., & Moos, R. H. (1983). Social–environmental factors in unipolar depression: Comparisons of depressed patients and nondepressed controls. *Journal of Abnormal Psychology, 92,* 119–133.

Billings, A. G., & Moos, R. H. (1985). Psychosocial processes of remission in unipolar depression: Comparing depressed patients with matched community controls. *Journal of Consulting and Clinical Psychology, 53,* 314–325.

Blatt, S. (1974). Levels of object representation in analytic and introjective depression. *Psychoanalytic Study of the Child, 29,* 107–157.

Bowlby, J. (1975). *Attachment and loss: Vol. 2. Separation: Anxiety and anger.* London: Penguin.

Bowman, T. K., & Luteijn, F. (1986). Relations between the Pleasant Events Schedule, depression, and other aspects of psychopathology, *Journal of Abnormal Psychology, 95,* 373–377.

Brown, G. W., Bifulco, A., Harris, T., & Bridge, L. (1986). Life stress, chronic subclinical

symptoms, and vulnerability to clinical depression. *Journal of Affective Disorders, 11,* 1–19.
Brown, G. W., & Harris, T. O. (1978). *Social origins of depression.* London: Tavistock.
Buglass, D., Clarke, J., & Kreitman, N. (1977). A study of agoraphobic housewives. *Psychological Medicine, 7,* 73–86.
Costello, C. G. (1982). Social factors associated with depression: A retrospective community study. *Psychological Medicine, 12,* 329–339.
Depue, R. A., & Monroe, S. M. (1986). Conceptualization and measurement of human disorder in life stress research: The problem of chronic disturbance. *Psychological Bulletin, 99,* 36–51.
Dobson, K. S. (1985). The relationship between anxiety and depression. *Clinical Psychology Review, 5,* 307–324.
Dohrenwend, B. S., Krasnoff, L., Askenasy, A. R., & Dohrenwend, B. P. (1982). The Psychiatric Epidemiology Research Interview Life Events Scale. In L. Goldberger & S. Breznitz (Eds.), *Handbook of stress: Theoretical and clinical aspects* (pp. 332–363). New York: Free Press.
Ezquiaga, E., Gutierez, J. L. A., & Lopez, A. G. (1987). Psychosocial factors and episode number in depression. *Journal of Affective Disorders, 12,* 135–138.
Faravelli, C. (1985). Life events preceding the onset of panic disorder. *Journal of Affective Disorders, 9,* 103–105.
Fergusson, D. M., & Horwood, L. J. (1984). Life events and depression in women: A structural equation model. *Psychological Medicine, 14,* 881–889.
Finlay-Jones, R., & Brown, G. W. (1981). Types of stressful events and the onset of anxiety and depressive disorders. *Psychological Medicine, 11,* 803–815.
Fowles, D. C., & Gersh, F. (1979). Neurotic depression: The endogenous-neurotic distinction. In R. A. Depue (Ed.), *The psychobiology of the depressive disorder: Implications for the effects of stress* (pp. 55–80). New York: Academic Press.
Freud, S. (1926). *Hemmung, suymptom und angst.* [Reprinted as *Inhibitions, symptoms and anxiety* (standard ed., Vol. 20). London: Hogarth Press, 1959]
Gersh, F. S., & Fowles, D. C. (1979). Neurotic depression: The concept of anxious depression. In R. A. Depue (Ed.), *The psychobiology of the depressive disorders: Implications for the effects of stress* (pp. 81–104). New York: Academic Press.
Goldberg, D. P. (1972). *The detection of psychiatric illness by questionnaire.* New York: Oxford University Press.
Gotlib, I. H. (1984). Depression and general psychopathology in university students. *Journal of Abnormal Psychology, 93,* 19–30.
Hammen, C., Marks, T., Mayol, A., & de Mayo, R. (1985). Depressive self-schemas, life stress, and vulnerability to depression. *Journal of Abnormal Psychology, 94,* 308–319.
Hammen, C., & Mayol, A. (1982). Depression and cognitive characteristics of stressful life-event types. *Journal of Abnormal Psychology, 91,* 165–174.
Hammen, C., Mayol, A., de Mayo, R., & Marks, T. (1986). Initial symptom levels and the life-event-depression relationship. *Journal of Abnormal Psychology, 95,* 114–122.
Hewitt, P. L., & Dyck, D. G. (1986). Perfectionism, stress, and vulnerability to depression. *Cognitive Therapy and Research, 10,* 137–142.
Higgins, E. T. (1987). Self-discrepancy: A theory relating self and affect. *Psychological Review, 94,* 319–340.
Higgins, E. T., Klein, R., & Strandman, T. (1985). Self-concept discrepancy theory: A psychological model for distinguishing among different aspects of depression and anxiety. *Social Cognition, 3,* 51–76.
Holahan, C. J., & Moos, R. H. (1987). Risk, resistance, and psychological distress: A longitudinal analysis with adults and children. *Journal of Abnormal Psychology, 96,* 3–13.

Holmes, T. H., & Rahe, R. H. (1967). The Social Readjustment Rating Scale. *Journal of Psychosomatic Research, 11,* 213–218.

Ingram, R. E., Kendall, P. C., Smith, T. W., Donnell, C., & Ronan, K. (1987). Cognitive specificity in emotional distress. *Journal of Personality and Social Psychology, 53,* 734–742.

Katz, J. M. (1980). Discrepancy, arousal, and labelling: Towards a psychosocial theory of emotion. *Sociological Inquiry, 50,* 147–156.

Kendler, K. S., Heath, A. C., Martin, N. G., & Eaves, L. J. (1987). Symptoms of anxiety and symptoms of depression: Same genes, different environments? *Archives of General Psychiatry, 44,* 451–457.

Lakey, B., & Heller, K. (1985). Response bias and the relation between negative life events and psychological symptoms. *Journal of Personality and Social Psychology, 49,* 1662–1668.

Last, C., Barlow, D. H., & Obrieu, G. T. (1984). Precipitants of agoraphobia: Role of stressful life events. *Psychological Reports, 54,* 567–570.

Lazarus, R. S. (1966). *Psychological stress and the coping process.* New York: McGraw-Hill.

Lazarus, R. S., & Folkman, S. (1984). *Stress, appraisal and coping.* New York: Springer.

Linville, P. W. (1987). Self-complexity as a cognitive buffer against stress related illness and depression. *Journal of Personality and Social Psychology, 52,* 663–676.

Lloyd, C. (1980). Life events and depressive disorder reviewed: II. Life events as precipitating factors. *Archives of General Psychiatry, 37,* 541–548.

Malatesta, C. Z., & Wilson, A. (1988). Emotion/cognition interaction in personality development: A discrete emotions, functionalist analysis. *British Journal of Social Psychology, 27,* 91–112.

Mitchell, R. E., Cronkite, R. C., & Moos, R. H. (1983). Stress, coping, and depression among married couples. *Journal of Abnormal Psychology, 92,* 433–448.

Monroe, S. M. (1982a). Life events assessment: Current practices, emerging trends. *Clinical Psychology Review, 2,* 435–453.

Monroe, S. M. (1982b). Assessment of life events: Retrospective versus concurrent strategies. *Archives of General Psychiatry, 39,* 606–610.

Monroe, S. M. (1982c). Life events and disorder: Event-symptom associations and the course of the disorder. *Journal of Abnormal Psychology, 91,* 14–24.

Monroe, S. M., Bellack, A. S., Hersen, M., & Himmelhoch, J. M. (1983). Life events, symptom course, and treatment of outcome in unipolar depressed women. *Journal of Abnormal Psychology, 51,* 604–615.

Monroe, S. M., Bromet, E. J., Connell, M. M., & Steiner, S. C. (1986). Social support, life events, and depressive symptoms: A 1-year prospective study. *Journal of Consulting and Clinical Psychology, 54,* 424–431.

Monroe, S. M., Imhoff, D. F., Wise, B. D., & Harris, J. E. (1983). Prediction of psychological symptoms under high-risk psychosocial circumstances: Life events, social support, and symptom specificity. *Journal of Abnormal Psychology, 92,* 338–350.

Monroe, S. M., & Peterman, A. M. (in press). Life stress and psychopathology, In L. H. Cohen (Ed.), *Research on stressful life events: Theoretical and methodological issues.* New York: Sage.

Nezu, A. M., & Ronan, G. F. (1985). Life stress, current problems, problem solving, and depressive symptoms: An integrative model. *Journal of Consulting and Clinical Psychology, 53,* 693–697.

Nicholls, J. G., Licht, B. G., & Pearl, R. A. (1982). Some dangers of using personality questionnaires to study personality. *Psychological Bulletin, 92,* 572–580.

Oatley, K., & Bolton, W. (1985). A social-cognitive theory of depression in reaction to life events. *Psychological Review, 92,* 372–388.

O'Hara, M. W., Rehm, L. P., & Campbell, S. B. (1982). Predicting depressive symptomatology: Cognitive-behavioral model of post-partum depression. *Journal of Abnormal Psychology, 91*, 457–461.

Olinger, L. J., Kuiper, N. A., & Shaw, B. F. (1987). Dysfunctional attitudes and stressful life events: An interactive model of depression. *Cognitive Therapy and Research, 11*, 25–40.

Paykel, E. S. (1982). Life events and early environment. In E. S. Peykel (Ed.), *Handbook of affective disorders* (pp. 146–161). New York: Guilford Press.

Paykel, F. S., Myers, J. K., Dienelt, M. N., Klerman, G. L., Lindenthal, J. J., & Pepper, M. P. (1969). Life events and depression: A controlled study. *Archives of General Psychiatry, 21*, 753–760.

Perkins, D. V. (1982). The assessment of stress using life events scales. In L. Goldberger & S. Breznitz (Eds.), *Handbook of stress: Theoretical and clinical aspects* (pp. 320–331). New York: Free Press.

Phifer, J. F., & Murrell, S. A. (1986). Etiologic factors in the onset of depressive symptoms in older adults. *Journal of Abnormal Psychology, 95*, 282–291.

Pollard, C. A., Obermeier, H. J., & Lorn, K. J. (1987, November). *Life events and onset of agoraphobia: A comparative study*. Paper presented at the annual meeting of the Association for Advancement of Behavior Therapy, Boston.

Rabkin, J. G. (1982). Stress and psychiatric disorders. In L. Goldberger & S. Breznitz (Eds.), *Handbood of stress: Theoretical and clinical aspects* (pp. 566–584). New York: Free Press.

Rook, K. S. (1987). Social support versus companionship: Effects on life stress, loneliness, and evaluations by others. *Journal of Personality and Social Psychology, 52*, 1132–1147.

Roy, A., Breier, A., Doran, A. R., & Pickar, D. (1985). Life events in depression: Relationships to subtypes. *Journal of Affective Disorders, 9*, 143–148.

Roy-Byrne, P. P., Geraci, M., & Linde, T. W. (1986a). Life events and the onset of panic disorder. *American Journal of Psychiatry, 143*, 1424–1427.

Roy-Byrne, P. P., Geraci, M., & Linde, T. W. (1986b). Life events and course of illness in patients with panic disorder. *American Journal of Psychiatry, 143*, 1033–1035.

Sarason, I. G., Johnson, J. H., & Siegel, J. M. (1978). Assessing the impact of life changes: Development of the Life Experiences Survey. *Journal of Consulting and Clinical Psychology, 46*, 932–946.

Slater, J., & Depue, R. A. (1981). The contribution of environmental events and social support to serious suicide attempts in primary depressive disorder. *Journal of Abnormal Psychology, 90*, 275–285.

Smith, T. W., O'Keeffe, J. L., & Jenkins, M. (1988). Dependency and self-criticism: Correlates of depression or moderators of the effects of stressful events? *Journal of Personality Disorders, 2*, 160–169.

Spielberger, C. D., Gorsuch, R. L., & Lushene, R. E. (1970). *Manual for the State-Trait Anxiety Inventory*. Palo Alto, CA: Consulting Psychologists Press.

Spitzer, R. L., Endicott, J., & Robins, E. (1978). Research diagnostic criteria: Rationale and reliability. *Archives of General Psychiatry, 35*, 773–782.

Surtees, P. G., Miller, P., Ingham, J. G., Kreitman, N. D., Rennie, D., & Sashidharan, S. P. (1986). Life events and the onset of affective disorder: A longitudinal general population study. *Journal of Affective Disorders, 10*, 37–50.

Tanaka-Matsumi, J., & Kameoka, V. A. (1986). Reliabilities and concurrent validities of popular self-report measures of depression, anxiety, and social desirability. *Journal of Consulting and Clinical Psychology, 54*, 328–333.

Vinokur, A., & Selzer, M. L. (1975). Desirable versus undesirable life events: Their relationship to stress and mental distress. *Journal of Personality and Social Psychology, 32*, 329–337.

Wachtel, P. (1977). *Psychoanalysis and behavior therapy*. New York: Basic Books.
Watson, D., & Clark, L. A. (1984). Negative affectivity: The disposition to experience aversive emotional states. *Psychological Bulletin, 96*, 465–490.
Wing, J. K., Nixon, J. M., Mann, S. A., & Leff, J. P. (1977). Reliability of the PSE (ninth edition) used in a population study. *Psychological Medicine, 7*, 505–516.

The Effects of Daily Life Events on Negative Affective States

Alex J. Zautra
Charles A. Guarnaccia
John W. Reich

I. Introduction

There are many ways to conceptualize severe forms of negative affectivity, such as anxiety and depression, that arise from major personal upheavals. Psychological distress is not confined solely to major calamities, however. In the vernacular of everyday life, negative affects are common manifestations of inevitable conflicts between human desires and environmental constraints as they unfold throughout a day, week, or month. In this chapter we examine the force of these everyday events on symptoms of depression, anxiety, and negative affectivity in general,

Note: This work was supported by the National Institute on Aging (Grants R01-AG492401 and 2R01-AG04924-03). The authors wish to acknowledge the assistance of members of the Life Events and Aging Project team: John Finch and Barbara Maxwell and also Wendy Ramerth and David Pillow.

Anxiety and Depression

in hopes of coming closer to understanding the contribution of such events to emotional upset.

Our sense of proportion about the meaningfulness of human events argues against a central role of mundane events in the regulation of powerful emotions such as depression and anxiety. Only the most fragile and vulnerable would show adverse reactions to a single disagreeable small event. Nevertheless, a number of pioneering research studies have found that accumulations of small undesirable events within a given day, week, or month can "hassle" the adjustment process, even within normal populations, giving rise to strong negative affects (Eckenrode, 1984; Kanner, Coyne, Schaefer, & Lazarus, 1981; Reich & Zautra, 1983; Stone & Neale, 1983). Although measurement and design shortcomings in some of these studies limit the conclusions that can be reached, there is converging evidence to support a role for daily events in the regulation of negative affectivity.

There are a number of potential explanations for why small events may play an important role in the regulation of affective states. First, the events themselves, when occurring in high frequency, may represent a strain on the adjustment process, e.g., the day when nothing seems to go right. This would be in keeping with the formative hypothesis by Holmes and Rahe (1967) that life events can mount up to challenge the adjustment capacity of the organism. Even a game of tennis, according to Selye (1956), can put the person over the limit of the body's ability to tolerate change. Second, the events may imply an underlying disequilibrium in the person's ongoing relationship with the environment, and may serve as provocative reminders of long-standing problems which interfere with the person's ability to meet basic needs. Richard Lazarus (1978) provides a good example of this role for daily events:

> Although I believe it is true that people can be distressed over what seems at the moment to be trivialities, they are not really trivial at all in meaning, since they symbolize things that are very important to the person. The shoelace might break, but a major part of the psychological stress created thereby is the implication that one cannot control one's life, that one is helpless in the face of the most stupid of trivialities, or even worse, that one's own inadequacies have made the obstacle occur in the first place. This is what brings the powerful, stressful and pathogenic message that breaks one's morale. (p. 8)

This connection between daily events and negative affect suggests that the effects of such experiences should be studied within the context of wider difficulties with which the person is faced. Thus, in this paper, in addition to reviewing more generally the effects of daily events on negative affectivity, we look in depth at how the ramifications of two major stressful experiences, conjugal bereavement and physical disability, are manifested in daily life events of older adults. Small events are reviewed to see how such events may help explain changes in negative affective state that often accompany major life changes.

In this volume, anxiety and depression are compared for their similarities and their dissimilarities. There are two ways to proceed with this examination of affects. One way is to analyze the underlying structure and meaning of measures of the two conditions. The second is to examine correlates of anxiety and depression to identify factors differentially associated with their onset and duration. The latter approach is taken in this chapter as we examine whether the same or different patterns of association are found for the occurrence of daily events and depressive symptoms in comparison to anxiety. We used symptom scales to assess depressed affective states and anxiety. Because most studies of daily events have been conducted on normal samples, we have limited ourselves here to examining variations in subclinical levels of these negative affective states.

II. Why Small Events Are Important

Most life event research has been concerned with studying the effects of major life events (i.e., events on the order of marriage, divorce, or moving to a new part of the country) on mental and physical status (see Dohrenwend & Dohrenwend, 1974, 1981; Rabkin & Struening, 1976, for reviews of this research). The tradition of studying major life events started with the work of Holmes and Rahe (1967) using the Social Readjustment Rating Scale. This research conceptualized major events as the independent variable of interest. Often ignored in this research is the effect of small events and chronic stressors on mental and physical status. This less well-developed line of small-event research evaluates daily experiences as the predictors of interest (Epstein, 1979; Kanner et al., 1981; MacPhillamy & Lewinsohn, 1971; Stone & Neale, 1983; Zautra, Guarnaccia, & Dohrenwend, 1986).

The study of small daily events can make a contribution to the understanding of the stress/distress relationship. Research on small life events provides two advantages. By studying small events (1) some problems that are encountered when studying major events are avoided and (2) the measurement of small events provides information that is not provided by major life event scales. The research and conceptual problems that are avoided by studying small events are reviewed here.

Small events are much more discrete units of the person–environment interaction than are major events because they occur over relatively short periods of time. For example, major life events such as divorce from spouse may occur over a protracted length of time and involve a large number of components. A small event in the same category, such as an argument with a spouse, would occur over a much shorter length of time and is likely to be composed of a single or a small number of interactions. This specificity reduces the heterogeneity within event reports and permits greater reliability in scoring events on important stress dimensions such as desirability, size, and locus of causation. Being more easily discernible and discrete, the measurement of small events provides detailed information about the person–environment interactions that are missed in measures of major events.

In studying the connections between major events and distress, small events may prove to be a significant path in the causal chain. A number of plausible hypotheses that propose daily events as mediating or moderating the effects of major events on psychological distress can be constructed. Changes in daily life that result from major upheavals may constitute one of the most important means of transmission of effects over time. Further, individuals may be particularly sensitive to daily life events that carry specific thematic material such as loss of control, failure, or rejection. The assessment of these events provides important data to test such propositions.

From the standpoint of intervention, small events have another important advantage over major events. As in the above example of divorce from spouse versus argument with spouse, the small event is more mutable than the major event. An excess of small events, such as arguments with spouse, may be warning signs of ongoing problems; however, the ultimate result of such a series of small events is not wholly determined by these small events. Conversely, the major event in this example has little hope of reversal. Here daily events are indicators of ongoing processes involving "chronic burden(s)" (Dohrenwend & Dohrenwend, 1981) or ongoing difficulties (Brown & Harris, 1978). If small events are adequate indicators of ongoing problems in a person's relationship with the environment, then they may be used as timely indicators of a need for corrective actions.

Small events occur with greater frequency than major events. In order to have variance across subjects, major events are measured over periods from 6 to 24 months. In contrast, small-event reports will show sizable variance within a 1-month interval. This, along with the discrete nature of small events, makes them well suited to research that attempts to investigate the temporal and causal relationships between events and outcomes. Small events can be repeatedly measured within relatively short-duration contiguous time periods to test causal sequences of relations between measures. The shorter time intervals may also reduce problems in reliability of reporting of retrospective events (Jenkins, Hurst, & Rose, 1979; Monroe, 1982; Rabkin & Struening, 1976).

III. Development of the Inventory of Small Life Events (ISLE)

With few exceptions, the analyses reported in this chapter use the Inventory of Small Life Events (ISLE) as the daily event measure. The development of the ISLE is reported in detail in Zautra et al. (1986), and is described briefly here. The ISLE was developed as a small-event measure to complement the Psychiatric Epidemiology Research Interview (PERI) Major Life Events Scale (Dohrenwend, Krasnoff, Askenasy, & Dohrenwend, 1978). Zautra and Dohrenwend established explicit criteria for ISLE item inclusion. In order to be included the event had to (1) be an observable change in a person's life; (2) have a discrete beginning; (3) be objectively classifiable as either desirable or undesirable; and be (4) rated as requiring an average of 250 or less life change units using the parameters of Dohrenwend et al. (1978).

These criteria were chosen to improve the psychometric properties of this scale and remove potential confounds. By requiring that events on the ISLE be observable changes, there is less concern that the measure of small events is actually measuring distress (i.e., small event and distress measures may be confounded; see Dohrenwend & Shrout, 1985). This requirement removed subjective feeling states from the pool of potential small-event items. As items on the ISLE are at least in theory independently verifiable, there is less concern that the ISLE, as a small-event measure, is measuring other than what it is purported to measure. Establishing the independence of events *a priori* from distress measurement is especially important if methodologically sound advances are to be made in stress and coping research.

Requiring a discrete beginning eliminated routine day-in and day-out occurrences from the ISLE. In this way, it was ensured that the ISLE was not measuring ongoing situations, but rather event transactions with the environment that were distinct from daily routine. This is not to say that ongoing difficulties will not be reflected in the ISLE measure through their effect on daily events. The ISLE does not assess ongoing problematic situations directly, but rather detects their results when such situations erupt into undesirable events. With the inclusion of this criterion, the ISLE maintains the distinction of measuring event transactions apart from routine day-to-day occurrences and ongoing social strains. ISLE events, although small, should stand out from the normal course of peoples' daily lives.

The upper magnitude score of items chosen for inclusion in the ISLE is 250 Life Change Units (Holmes & Rahe, 1967) for events to still be considered as small. This cutoff point was also set to ensure that items on the ISLE did not overlap with the set of major events found on its companion instrument from the PERI.

Finally, ISLE items were written to be either clearly desirable or undesirable. This was done to facilitate research which investigates the differential effects of desirable and undesirable event occurrences on psychological outcome. In addition to the previous single linear dimension of "magnitude-of-required-readjustment," the desirability information on ISLE items allows research to address event desirability as a variable of interest.

Another central dimension of life events is the degree to which events are caused by and under the control of the person. A number of investigators have shown that events out of the person's control have different meaning in comparison to those for which the person is responsible (deCharms, 1972; Dohrenwend & Martin, 1979; Zautra & Reich, 1980). The ISLE event list was devised with these important distinctions in mind, so that independent raters could reach consensus on subgroups of items that were either internally or externally caused. In validation studies (Zautra et al., 1986), the ISLE was found to contain both internally caused and externally caused events (ratings of control were found to be highly correlated with ratings of causation). Along with ratings of magnitude and desirability, information about the cause/control of ISLE items allows researchers to investigate this dimension as a relevant factor that may determine how the event provokes negative affects.

As originally constructed the ISLE contains 178 items. Of these 80 are desirable and 98 are undesirable; 74 of the events have been identified as controllable, 41 as uncontrollable, and 56 as mixed on controllability. The events on the ISLE are divided into 13 categories by topical area. These categories include school, recreation, religion, money and finance, transportation, children, household, relations with family, love and marriage, crime and legal, social life, health and illness, and work. Exemplar items include: "Did poorly on an important test" (undesirable, internally caused); "Learned that child(ren) did particularly well in a school project" (desirable, mixed causation); "Neighborhood noise disrupted sleep" (undesirable, externally caused); and "Praised by spouse/mate" (desirable, mixed causation).

Assessment of Anxiety and Depressive Symptoms. Most researchers in this field have relied on symptom checklists and rating scales to identify levels of anxiety and depression. The work reported in this chapter is no exception. Here, anxiety refers to face-valid reports of anxious symptoms such as "nervousness" and "restlessness." Depression refers to feeling "sad," "downhearted," or "blue." In data analyzed for this chapter, we often take the additional step of assuring ourselves that the depression and anxiety items cluster into separate subscales (or factors) reliably, as the authors of those scales intended. We have employed both confirmatory and exploratory factor analyses to this end on the multiple scale inventories that we depend upon heavily herein: most notably the Veit and Ware (1983) Mental Health Inventory and the Dohrenwend, Shrout, Egri, and Mendelsohn (1980) PERI Demoralization Composite. The factor analyses confirm separate scales for anxiety and depressed affects. However, resulting scores are highly correlated, between .60 and .75 in most studies (including ours), prompting some investigators (e.g., Dohrenwend et al., 1980) to label them as part of a single underlying dimension such as demoralization. Because of this, we compare groups that show different patterns of depression and anxiety symptoms as a means of further examining the distinctiveness question with existing instruments. In passing, we note that we hope to see refinements in measures, perhaps as a result of the critical thinking on the underlying constructs of anxiety and depression found in other chapters in this volume.

IV. Daily Events and Negative Affects

Several recent studies have investigated the effects of undesirable and desirable ISLE events on anxiety and depressive symptoms in college students. Zautra et al. (1986) administered the ISLE, the Hopkins Symptom Checklist (Derogatis, Lipman, Rickels, Uhlenhuth, & Covi, 1974), and a checklist of the PERI major events measure (Dohrenwend et al., 1978) to 100 college students who participated in order to complete an experimental requirement for an introductory psychology course. The event administration took place in a large classroom where subjects were asked to report the frequency of occurrence of ISLE and PERI events during the past month, and each subject was given instructions to fill out the symptoms checklist on each of the next 4 days. The number of different undesirable ISLE events (not including health-related events) was associated with higher anxiety, $r(99) = .30$, and depressive symptoms, $r(99) = .33$, on the next day, with slightly lower but statistically significant correlations found for symptom reports 5 days later. The study also investigated whether internally caused and externally caused events had different effects on negative affective states. Internally caused undesirable events were more highly correlated with negative affects than were externally caused undesirable events, although both had significant relationships with reports of anxiety and depression. Desirable events were uncorrelated with negative affects but were associated with a separate measure of positive affect (Bradburn, 1969). In this study, several methodological controls were employed which strengthened confidence in the findings. The relationships obtained for small events were tested with and without the inclusion of health events, and the occurrence of major events was controlled statistically. The assessment of negative affective states was taken on four consecutive days following the assessment of events to avoid possible effects of transitory mood on event and symptom reporting (e.g., Teasdale & Fogarty, 1979).

Guarnaccia and Zautra (1988) studied the relationship of undesirable ISLE events on distress in a student health center clinic with a sample of 66 college students who requested psychological services and a comparison nonclinic sample of matched controls. The clinic sample had elevated scores ($p < .01$) on all subscales of the Hopkins Symptom Checklist, including both anxiety and depression subscales, and thus provided a test of whether the occurrence of ISLE events would be associated with symptoms for an identified patient population. For both patients and controls, higher numbers of undesirable events were associated with elevated scores on both anxiety and depression. Only small undesirable events that were rated as internally caused had significant effects for the clinic sample, however; $r(65) = .30$ for anxiety and $r(65) = .33$ for depression. For controls, both internally and externally caused events were associated with anxiety and depression. These findings were sustained in analyses controlling for the occurrence of major events. It is interesting that neither small nor major undesirable events predicted client status. Desirable events did appear to differentiate groups, even though such events were uncorrelated with negative affect. Those students who reported more positive transactions with their social networks were less likely to be in the student health center help-seeking sample.

In a study of high-risk families (Sandler, 1985), Pillow, Zautra, and Sandler (1988) administered an abridged version of undesirable events from the ISLE (80 items) to four groups of at-risk patients with children under age 18 who were coping with major family stressors, and a group of 73 control families through in-home interviews. One group of parents was recently conjugally bereaved ($n = 92$), one recently divorced ($n = 94$), another had an alcoholic spouse ($n = 26$), and a fourth an asthmatic child ($n = 99$). The interviews included an assessment of how frequently the events occurred in the past month. The PERI Demoralization Composite (Dohrenwend et al., 1980) was also administered to assess level of parent distress in the various groups. A confirmatory factor analysis identified a highly intercorrelated subfactor structure of the PERI Demoralization Composite, including factors of anxiety, sadness, self-esteem, confused thinking, and helplessness/hopelessness. The high-risk groups had significantly higher scores on all the above dimensions of demoralization in comparison to their controls. There were no distinctive patterns for anxiety in comparison to sadness or the other subscales of distress between groups.

In this study, ISLE events were scored as either recurrent stressors or nonrecurrent stressors: Those which happened 10 or more times in the past month were classified as recurrent, and were thought to detect more chronic strains than those which occurred less frequently. Interestingly, there was no correlation between the recurrent event scores and the counts of other events, supporting their classification as two distinct measures of daily stress. Both types of events occurred significantly more often in the high-risk groups in comparison to their controls.

The association between reports of undesirable events and symptoms was examined for each group. The relationships were uniform across conditions (including control families). All subscales of the PERI Demoralization Composite were elevated for those parents with more undesirable small events. Recurrent and nonrecurrent ISLE events were associated with higher anxiety [$rs(385) = .47$ and .42, respectively] and greater sadness [$rs(385) = .37$ and .35).

V. Attribution about Daily Events: Their Effects on Anxiety and Depression

A number of investigators have suggested that the effects of events on negative affective states depend more upon the cognitive response to those events than upon the events themselves (Abramson, Seligman, & Teasdale, 1978; Beck, 1967; Lazarus, & Launier, 1978). In order to explore such effects, Zautra, Guenther, and Chartier (1985) asked a group of 151 undergraduate students from an introductory psychology class to complete daily logs for 14 days and fill out postmeasures of depressive and anxiety symptoms using the Brief Symptom Inventory (Derogatis, 1977) and the Beck Depression Inventory (Beck, Ward, Mendelson, Mock, & Erbaugh, 1961). In the logs, the subjects were asked to list the most undesirable event they experienced each day and to rate the attributions they formed about the cause of each event, using the questions developed by Peterson et al. (1982), to tap attributional style. These questions asked the person to rate the cause of the event on dimensions of internality, stability, and globality. Undesirable daily events that were rated as internally caused, due to stable causes, and representative of more global difficulties were expected to be associated with increased negative affect. For simplicity, Zautra et al. (1985) averaged across the 14 days and used a composite index of harmful attributions that included the mean of internality, stability, and globality ratings for undesirable events weighted by the perceived importance of the event. These measures were then correlated with postscores on depression and anxiety.

The findings for anxiety and depression were nearly identical. The composite index of attributions made about daily undesirable events was correlated .28 and .31 with the two indices of depression used, and .33 with the anxiety subscale. Internal, stable, and global attributions showed the strongest relationships to both depression and anxiety. Unstable internal attributions for undesirable events were unrelated to either anxiety or depression. Effects specific to either anxiety or depression were not observed.

Some generalizations emerge from the studies just reviewed. Those persons who report a high number of undesirable events also tend to experience more negative affects. The increase in negative affectivity is nonspecific as a function of these events. Also, it is apparent that the careful measurement of daily events can reveal a number of important classes of events that contribute independently to the prediction of negative affective states. Locus of causation, desirability, and frequency of recurrence are all important characteristics of events and affect how they influence negative and positive affects. The person's attributions about the events also contribute to depression and anxiety.

VI. Small Events, Negative Mood, and Cognitions across Days

Interindividual studies which identify small events as potential sources of negative affective states suffer from one major methodological problem: the possibility that the association is a spurious one, due to the presence of other, unmeasured variables that account for subject differences in both events and negative affectivity. Investigators have attempted to resolve this problem in many ways, including matching subjects on important demographic variables and controlling statistically for the effects of other variables through the use of partial correlation and multiple regression techniques. Because all possible relevant variables in any one study can never be measured, one cannot be certain that all important sources of spuriousness have been accounted for in the analyses.

A better way around this problem is to study these processes intraindividually. Thus, we examined whether, for any given individual, variations in the daily occurrence of desirable and undesirable events would be associated with negative affects and anxious (i.e., stress-related) thoughts (Zautra and Ramerth, 1985). Eight undergraduate students were recruited and filled out daily self-report forms that included (1) the ISLE; (2) a list of items that assess the presence of negative and positive affects (Warr, Barter, & Brownbridge, 1983); (3) a list of 34 items which reflected "stressful" or anxious thoughts (Sandler, 1982); and (4) major life events using items from the PERI Major Life Events Scale (Dohrenwend et al., 1978). They did this self-monitoring for 61 consecutive days, turning in their reports each day to assure us of conscientious reporting. Desirable and undesirable ISLE event totals were taken, excluding health events in the analyses reported below. Major events revealed no significant effects across days due to their low frequency of occurrence.

The scores for each subject across the 61 days were analyzed separately, and the data from all eight subjects were combined into 488 (8×61) person-days for overall analysis. It is this person-day analysis we will report on here because it summarizes the findings well. The data were organized so that the data from the first day of all eight subjects were listed first, followed by the second day's scores of all subjects, etc., with the order of the subjects in the data file the same on each day.

This way of formatting the data allowed us to see the shape of the same-day relationship between events, moods, and thoughts, but also allowed us to detect and remove patterns of covariance between the person-day measures that were due either to stable differences between subjects across days, or correlations between scores on the same measures on adjacent days (what is known as autocorrelation).

Before attempting to compute the cross-correlations between event scores and affects, these variations due to person-days and adjacent days were removed so that the resulting set of person-day scores would show no statistically significant lagged relations. The approach taken was to prewhiten both event and negative affective outcome variables using ARIMA time-series methods (Catalano, Dooley, & Jackson, 1983; McCleary & Hays, 1980). In this approach a noise model is fit to the data and residualized scores are extracted to test against the predictor variables. The advantages of this approach are that each person-day score is independent, and systematic covariation due to scores adjacent in time or arising from the same person is eliminated.

After this prewhitening, the cross-correlation was computed to measure the level of association between the variables measured on the same person-day. The results of these analyses are shown in Table 8.1 for 488 person-days. Although not reported in detail here, we wish to add that the same pattern of findings also was found when analyzing individual subjects' time series.

Table 8.1 shows that daily variations in events are associated with systematic variations in mood and cognition. As can be seen, no apparent differences were observed in how events affected negative mood versus stressful (anxious) thoughts. Consistent with our prior findings (Zautra & Reich, 1983), desirable events appeared tangential to negative affects but were associated with positive mood. These findings provide more confirmation of the relationship between daily events and affective states. The contribution of individual differences and other stable sources of variability in event reports was controlled for by the ARIMA modeling procedures, and the conservative approach of prewhitening both series prior to analysis reduced the possibility of correlated errors contributing to the association found between variables. There is much more that is still unknown about the ebb and flow of everyday events,

Table 8.1
Same-Day Correlations of Desirable and Undesirable Events with Mood and Stress Thoughts[a]

	Desirable events	Undesirable events	Positive mood	Negative mood	Stress thoughts
Small desirable events	(.41)**	−.02	.36**	−.18*	−.05
Small undesirable events	—	(.52)**	−.27**	.40**	.41**
Positive mood	—	—	(.72)**	−.48**	−.38**
Negative mood	—	—	—	(.72)**	.61**
Stress thoughts	—	—	—	—	(.74)**

[a] Values in parentheses are lag 8 autocorrelations prior to prewhitening. $N = 472$ for cross-correlations of residualized series.
*$p < .01$; **$p < .001$.

and how such events jointly influence affects and cognitions both on the same day and on subsequent days (Zautra, Guarnaccia, Reich, & Dohrenwend, 1988). Nevertheless, this study of covariations in mood with daily events within subjects provides important further evidence of the substantial role played by these events in the regulation of negative affective states.

VII. Study of High-Risk Groups: Life Events and Aging Project (LEAP)

Thus far we have reviewed studies in which daily events were examined for their effects on general distress, and on anxiety and depression more specifically. However, to explore in greater detail whether different patterns of daily events might lead to distinctive patterns of negative affects, we selected for in-depth study two high-risk groups of elderly subjects, those who were recently (1) functionally disabled or (2) conjugally bereaved. These two high-risk groups were compared to each other and to matched controls on daily events, anxiety, and depression. We knew from previous work (Zautra, Guarnaccia, & Reich, 1987) that the disabled were both more anxious and more depressed than their controls, whereas the bereaved reported more depression but not more anxiety than their controls. Thus, we had groups exhibiting three patterns of negative affects: a group high on anxiety as well as depression, a group that was high on depression only, and a third group of controls matched to the others but without elevated scores on either depression or anxiety. Also, because the anxiety and depression elevations were reactive in that they arose in response to major life stresses, it was likely that if daily events played a role in the production of these distinctive patterns, they would do so here. Before reviewing the specific findings, we first provide a description of the design and methods of the overall project.

The sample consisted of 246 noninstitutionalized adults between the ages of 60 and 80. They were recruited from a wide variety of organizations, agencies, neighborhoods, mobile home parks, vital statistics records, and so on. Potential participants were interviewed by telephone using a detailed screening instrument assessing the recency and degree of their activity limitation (in the case of the disabled) or recency of bereavement (in the case of the bereaved).

A total of 710 residents were contacted; of these, 160 (23%) refused participation and 281 (40%) agreed to participate but did not meet screening criteria. The disabled sample consisted of 62 participants who suffered a recent disability due to accident or illness in the prior 3 months, or who experienced a significant worsening of an existing condition. The bereaved consisted of 61 participants conjugally bereaved within the past 6 months. A total of 123 control participants were matched on age, sex, and income to members in the two high-risk groups. These 123 controls were neither disabled within the past year nor conjugally bereaved within the past 2 years. Disability assessment was based on self-reported activity limitations taken from the CARE interview (Gurland et al., 1983).

The average age of the sample was 70 years; 80% were female and 2% were of minority status. In educational attainment, 75% had graduated from high school, 15% from college. There were no significant differences between the disabled, bereaved, and control groups on any of these variables. However, the bereaved group and their controls did report a slightly higher income than the disabled subjects and controls.

After being accepted into the study, participants were assigned to a trained female older adult interviewer. She arranged the first interview contact and continued interviewing them once a month for 10 months, and then for a 6-month follow-up period. Participants were paid $45 over the course of the project for their participation. Only data provided at the first interview are reported here.

The LEAP interviews included multiple measures of positive and negative affect. From the scales that were administered we selected two measures of anxiety and two for depression using subscales of two instruments, the Mental Health Inventory (MHI; Veit & Ware, 1983) and the PERI Demoralization Composite (Dohrenwend et al., 1980). For both inventories, our own confirmatory factor analyses supported the use of distinct scales of anxiety and depression symptoms from both interviews.

The MHI is a 38-item scale in which subjects are to respond with judgments of "How much of the time" they felt a variety of both positive and negative affective states. We will limit our discussion here to the MHI depression and MHI anxiety subscales. The items included on the MHI subscales were modified as a result of exploratory and confirmatory factor analyses performed on the LEAP date (Zautra et al., 1987). Internal consistency was high for both subscales with alpha = .91 for MHI depression (10 items) and .82 for MHI anxiety (10 items). Typical anxiety items concerned feelings of nervousness, anxiety, and restlessness (e.g., "Felt nervous or jumpy"). Depression items included "Felt downhearted and blue" and "Having nothing to look forward to."

The PERI Demoralization Composite assesses a range of correlated negative affective states including anxiety, dread, and helplessness/hopelessness. Based on exploratory and confirmatory factor analyses, PERI anxiety and PERI dread items were combined into one scale (seven items, alpha = .83). The PERI helplessness/hopelessness subscale was selected as a measure of depression (four items, alpha = .86). The PERI anxiety/dread subscales had items such as "Feared something terrible would happen" in addition to feelings of restlessness and anxiety. The PERI helplessness/hopelessness subscale contained items such as "How often have you felt completely hopeless about everything?"

Although both the PERI Major Events Scale and the ISLE were administered during the LEAP interviews to ensure a comprehensive assessment of life events, we discuss only the ISLE here (although similar procedures were followed for PERI events). The ISLE was revised to include negative and positive experiences that were more likely to occur to older adults. Some items were reworded to include, for example, events with grandchildren as well as children. The list of health events and complaints was expanded to assess health problems more intensively. In addition to the 199 small events on the ISLE, respondents were asked to identify additional events as the interviewer guided them through each of the 13 event categories. These 13 additional open-ended inquiries led respondents to report events that were not on the original lists. These events were read and scored by hand when they constituted 10% or more of the total number of small events reported in an interview. Approximately 20% of the interviews were hand scored in this manner. Through these procedures, we obtained a comprehensive picture of the small events occurring in the lives of these older adults.

A group of 17 expert raters, including members of the LEAP research team and the study interviewers, was used to obtain consensus judgments regarding whether the event could be properly classified as major or small, desirable or undesirable, controllable or uncontrollable, and internally or externally caused. In order for an event to be classified as desirable or undesirable, there had to be 90% agreement on its desirability among the raters. An event was classified as objectively controllable or uncontrollable if the average score for that item was more than 0.5 from the midpoint of the scale (range of 1 to 5) and the average rating was at least one-half a standard deviation from the same midpoint. Events which did not meet these criteria were considered mixed in causation. Magnitude estimation procedures were employed to classify events as major or small. The raters were asked to rate the degree of readjustment required for older adults as a function of each event. A set of items with fixed ratings was provided, one for each event category, and the other events were to be rated proportionately. Events were judged to be small if either the median rating was 200 units or less, or the median was below 226 and 7 of 10 ratings were between 225 and 275. For most categories of events the original magnitude estimates (Zautra et al., 1986) were sustained. However, many health events previously rated as small were rated too high to group them with other small events. Review of the content of those items suggested that these events were rated higher because they implied a more severe underlying disease state. We classified these events as health symptoms, distinct from major changes in health status, but also different in meaning from health discomforts such as a cold or flu, which do not carry added meaning regarding long-term health status.

Another important characteristic of the events was whether they represented recurrent stressors within a given month. Recurrent stressors identified respondents' chronic difficulties that were manifested in patterns of daily living. For events that occurred in the past month, respondents were asked whether the event happened once or twice or whether it happened more than twice. Events that happened more than twice in the past month were scored as recurrent small stressors; the remaining events were scored as nonrecurrent stressors.

A. Group Differences on Anxiety and Depression

As we discussed earlier, comparisons across the four groups revealed that the bereaved and the disabled both had elevated depression scores, but only the disabled reported consistently higher anxiety symptoms than their controls. Disability appeared to lead to pervasive deficits; on measures of positive affect and low self-esteem, the disabled group displayed more psychological disturbance than the other groups. In contrast, the bereaved were similar to their matched controls on self-esteem and positive affect measures as well as on anxiety indices.

Disability and bereavement differ on many dimensions, but perhaps among the most salient are the implications of the stressor for future capacity to adapt to change. Bereavement that is normative for the age group may not affect feelings of vulnerability toward future events because the event carries no implicit message of the person's lack of ability to cope with stress. The event causes an acute grief reaction akin to (but less intense than) clinical depression, but perceptions of self-efficacy remain intact. Neither self-esteem nor feelings of anxiety over future events were affected in comparison to selected controls. Disability, on the other hand, may threaten self-efficacy by signifying a major loss in the person's capacity to function independently, and the event may itself be life threatening and generate anxiety at a very basic level.

B. Frequency of ISLE Events across Groups

The lives of these elderly were eventful. The average subject reported 13.5 desirable small events and 4.0 undesirable small events, in addition to 5.3 health-related undesirable events for the past month. Comparisons between groups on event frequencies revealed that the disabled were different from their controls in a number of event categories, whereas the bereaved showed few differences. Most prominent were differences in daily health problems. The disabled reported an average of 0.9 new health problems in the past month compared with 0.2 such events for their controls (matched pair $t = 3.38$, $p < .001$), and they reported twice the number of daily health problems ($X = 7.6$) as their controls ($X = 3.7$); these differences were due to frequent reports of recurrent daily pain and activity limitation. The disabled also reported significantly fewer internally caused desirable events, particularly in the areas of family visits and recreation/social life, and slightly more undesirable social life events. The bereaved reported the occurrence of 0.3 major health problems (or the significant worsening of an existing problem) in comparison to 0.1 for their controls (paired $t = 2.87$, $p < .01$), but they did not report more daily health problems than did the controls. Of course there were no love and marriage events for the bereaved, either desirable or undesirable, but they did report more child and family desirable events than their controls ($t = 2.05$, $p < .05$) and fewer undesirable social events ($t = 2.67$, $p < .01$). Interestingly, both disabled and bereaved reported more health-promotion activities (such as changing to a healthy diet) than did their controls.

These event differences show patterns of daily living that are changed by the disruptions of disability and bereavement. The impact of disability was indeed more pervasive than the death of a spouse, although it is important to keep in mind that the bereaved respondents joined the study 4 to 6 months after the spouse died, so they had some time to recover from the initial disorganization that occurs following death of a spouse. For the bereaved there even appeared to be some changes for the better in the response of their social networks, as shown by increases in some desirable event categories and a decrease in undesirable events relative to controls. The increase in health-promotion activities of both disabled and bereaved groups perhaps indicates an increasing preoccupation with health concerns arising as a consequence of their recent traumatic experiencs. Whether these differences affect the psychological adjustment of these groups is examined next.

C. The Effects of Small Events: Their Role as Mediating Variables

If daily events are to play a role in the development and maintenance of depressed and/or anxious states, their role may be that of mediators, juxtaposed between major stresses and psychological distress—that is, they may be outcomes of the major stressor and a potential cause of elevations in the reports of anxiety and/or depression. The maintenance of depressive and/or anxious symptoms, therefore, would be attributable to how the person's everyday life is affected by major calamities such as disability and bereavement. Of course, we were also interested in how everyday events contributed to depressive symptoms and to anxiety independent of their role as mediators of the effects of major events. In this case we would anticipate essentially a replication of past findings that undesirable events were associated with elevations in both anxiety and depression, adding to the problems of disability and bereavement.

To test this proposition in each of the high-risk groups, we constructed a series of multiple regression tests predicting anxiety and depressive symptoms. We used hierarchical regression techniques to test whether daily events from the ISLE would account for differences between groups on depressive and anxiety symptoms. The groups were contrast coded to show the effects of disabled versus controls, bereaved versus controls, and bereaved versus disabled. These coded vectors were allowed to enter the regression equation only after forcing in event measures. If ISLE events were mediators of the relationship between group status and psychological disturbance, then the effects of group status should fall to nonsignificance after accounting for the effects of events.

The overall LEAP data set was comprehensive enough to allow a test of a competing approach to event/well-being relationships. Costa and McCrae (1980) have presented data to show that trait neuroticism predisposes people to negative affective reactions to events, and they have argued that personality factors and not life events predominate in influencing negative affectivity. Discussion of this issue is beyond the scope of this chapter, but we felt it was important to account for such effects because they could be the source of a spurious association between events and anxiety and depression. Therefore, in the tests of these relationships, neuroticism scores from the short form on the Eysenck scale (Eysenck & Eysenck, 1968) were added into the regression equation first to predict psychological disturbance, followed by events and the effect-coded group variables.

There were many subsets of event measures that could be justified on *a priori* grounds as important predictors of depression and anxiety. For simplicity, we narrowed the choices down to a small subset of variables that we thought would be most important; the total number of desirable events in the past month, the total number of undesirable events in the past month, and the number of health problems reported in the past month (separated into recurrent and nonrecurrent health problems). We followed up significant findings on these indicators with analyses of the subscales of events that contributed to the total score, so as to define with greater precision the type of event that was having an impact on the person's mental health.

Overall findings for two measures of anxiety are shown in Table 8.2, and for depression and helplessness/hopelessness, in Table 8.3. The findings from the two anxiety scales were comparable in most details as

Table 8.2
Multiple Regression Analysis of Two Anxiety Measures[a]

Step variable	Multiple R	Beta	R^2 change	t to enter
	MHI anxiety			
1. Neuroticism	.48	.37***	.23	8.04***
2. Small undesirable ISLE	.52	.14*	.04	3.46***
3. Small desirable ISLE	.54	−.09	.02	−2.34*
4. Health problems ISLE	.62	—	.09	—
Recurrent	—	.32***	—	−4.96***
Nonrecurrent	—	.13*	—	.96
5. Group variables	.62	—	.004	—
Disabled vs. controls	—	.08	—	.97
Bereaved vs. controls	—	−.03	—	−.00
Disabled vs. bereaved	—	−.06	—	−.12
	PERI anxiety/dread			
1. Neuroticism	.51	.39***	.26	8.73***
2. Small undesirable ISLE	.55	.06	.04	3.34***
3. Small desirable ISLE	.55	.04	.00	−.37
4. Health problems ISLE	.66	—	.14	—
Recurrent	—	.40***	—	6.24***
Nonrecurrent	—	.17**	—	1.45
5. Group variables	.66	—	.005	—
Disabled vs. controls	—	.07	—	.86
Bereaved vs. controls	—	.02	—	.87
Disabled vs. bereaved	—	−.05	—	−.60

[a] Betas provided are those with all variables in the equation.
$*p < .05$; $**p < .01$; $***p < .001$.

Table 8.3
Multiple Regression Analysis of Depressive Symptoms[a]

Step variable	Multiple R	Beta	R^2 change	t to enter
	MHI depression			
1. Neuroticism	.47	.36***	.22	7.78***
2. Small undesirable ISLE	.51	.25***	.04	3.33***
3. Small desirable ISLE	.53	−.18**	.03	−2.72**
4. Health problems ISLE	.56	—	.02	—
Recurrent	—	.18*	—	3.00**
Nonrecurrent	—	.07	—	−.05
5. Group variables	.60	—	.05	—
Disabled vs. controls	—	.14*	—	1.10
Bereaved vs. controls	—	.09	—	3.03**
Disabled vs. bereaved	—	−.18*	—	−2.65**
	PERI helplessness/hopelessness			
1. Neuroticism	.37	.25***	.14	5.88***
2. Small undesirable ISLE	.41	.15*	.03	2.73**
3. Small desirable ISLE	.45	−.15*	.03	−2.92**
4. Health problems ISLE	—	—	—	—
Recurrent	.53	.27***	.08	4.10***
Nonrecurrent	—	.13*	—	.26
5. Group variables	.54	—	.02	—
Disabled vs. controls	—	.14	—	1.76
Bereaved vs. controls	—	.04	—	1.26
Disabled vs. bereaved	—	−.07	—	−.51

[a] Betas provided are those with all variables in the equation.
$^{*}p < .05$; $^{**}p < .01$; $^{***}p < .001$.

well as in overall results. The neuroticism scale accounted for a substantial portion of variance in these subscales but did not diminish the effects of ISLE events. After accounting for neuroticism, the undesirable events, especially recurrent health events, were predictive of anxiety symptoms. The effects of daily events could account for all differences between groups on anxiety. Further inspection of the regression steps revealed that it was the recurrent health events that accounted for the differences between disabled and all other participants. The partial correlation of disabled status with anxiety scores dropped from .20 to .06 when daily health problems were added into the prediction equation for PERI anxiety/dread subscale, and the results were nearly identical for the MHI anxiety subscale.

The findings for depressive symptoms were similar to those found on anxiety, for the disabled. Differences between the disabled and their controls on depressive symptoms, including helplessness/hopelessness, could be wholly accounted for by differences between the two groups on recurrent health problems. One difference in these results in comparison to anxiety was that small desirable events lowered scores on depression consistently after accounting for all other predictors.

Unlike the findings for the disabled, differences between the bereaved and other groups on depressive symptoms remained when controlling for everyday events, including health problems. In comparison to the disabled, the bereaved had higher scores on MHI depression when controlling for ISLE health events. This result points to the fact that everyday health problems resulting from disability can explain the mental health effects of that disability, but there were no measurable daily event sequelae of bereavement that could fully account for the grief response.

D. Analysis of Daily Event Subtypes: Which Events Made the Difference to Mental Health Reports?

It was apparent from the above analyses that recurrent health problems were a major source of psychological upset measured by the ISLE for this population. The effects of desirable and undesirable events that were not health related were examined more closely to see if patterns of relationships could be discerned from the data to identify whether recurrent or nonrecurrent events were more potent, and whether internally or externally caused events were more likely to lead to depressed affect and/or symptoms of anxiety. In keeping with past research, undesirable events which showed mixed causation were included with those internally caused, and the desirable events which were rated as mixed on internal causation were included with the externally caused events. Among undesirable events, two classes of events showed consistently significant correlations with anxiety and depression: recurrent internally caused events and nonrecurrent externally caused events. The other two classes of events had little or no significant correlation with distress when the effects of the other event classes were controlled. Among desirable events, the internally caused events had the most consistent inverse relations with depression and anxiety, although no subscale of desirable events was associated with PERI anxiety.

These findings are consistent with a cognitive approach to understanding the effects of daily events. The events that carry the most implications for self-efficacy and esteem had the greatest impact on mental health measures: the internally caused desirable and undesirable events. In addition, the nonrecurrent externally caused undesirable events were associated with anxiety and depression, perhaps because of their unpredictability. Adaptation may also serve to reduce the aversiveness of recurrent undesirable events which are out of the person's control. Predictable but unavoidable hassles with the external environment, a traffic jam, for example, may be easier to accommodate than repeated failures to avoid potentially controllable events. The events that lead to vulnerability are those the person is responsible for; that the person is unable to prevent recurrence of the events may be the most salient dimension from the standpoint of negative affectivity. For desirable events, it would appear that effectance (White, 1959) may best describe these effects; the capacity to forge desirable outcomes appears central to mental health for these high-risk groups, a finding we have identified in past work (Zautra & Reich, 1983).

E. Interaction Effects of Undesirable Events and Group Status

The statistical procedures we followed permitted us to explore further whether daily events interacted with group status to affect mental health. In particular, we were interested in whether the occurrence of small undesirable events would exacerbate the difficulties for those groups "at risk" for anxiety and depression due to disability and bereavement. To test for these effects, we created interaction terms from the product of event measures (centered about the mean), and three group contrasts: disabled versus their controls, disabled versus bereaved, and bereaved versus their controls. For these tests, recurrent and nonrecurrent health problems were combined into one measure, as were non-health-related undesirable events. There were six possible interaction terms to enter into the regression equation at the last step, organized into two sets: those terms carrying the Group X Undesirable Events effects and those terms carrying the Group X Health Problems effects. These two sets were tested for their effects on four variables, yielding eight separate tests. In all these tests, the main effects of each of the variables were added into the equation first, using the variable sets shown in Tables 8.2 and 8.3. Then the one or the other set of interaction terms was added to the regression equation to test for those effects across each of the four variables. There were no significant interaction effects found for nonhealth undesirable events, so our discussion will concentrate on the Group X Health Problems interactions.

The two depression variables showed "bereaved by health problems" interaction effects. For PERI helplessness/hopelessness, the effect reached statistical significance, $t = 2.38$, $p < .02$; for MHI depression, the effect was marginally significant, $t = 1.75$, $p < .09$. Both effects were in the same direction; bereaved subjects who reported more health problems appeared to be more vulnerable to depressive symptoms than controls reporting the same number of health problems. There were no interaction effects predicting anxiety.

Given the number of analyses we performed, these findings should be viewed as only suggestive of the possible compounding effects of events with other events. Nevertheless, these results have important implications for the meaning of these everyday events in the production of anxiety and depression. Small daily events did not appear to carry specific affective consequences; they provoked either distressing or positive affects, but they did not specifically induce anxiety or depression. For the disabled, the force of the illness led to many everyday problems that apparently accounted for the adverse mental health effects of that stressor. Both the high anxiety and high depression scores of the disabled relative to their controls could be explained by group differences in everyday limitations and pain associated with the disability. Any lasting effect of the trauma of the major illness event itself could not be detected beyond that which was measurable in small events. The situation was different for bereavement, where the adverse effects of daily events could not account for the differences between the bereaved and their controls. The interaction effects suggest further that the bereaved had become more vulnerable to their own health problems, perhaps because of a thematic connection to the death of their spouse. If health problems themselves were tied specifically to increased anxiety, we would have expected interaction effects with anxiety, but not with depression for the bereaved. But none was observed. Instead, the vulnerability to a specific affective disturbance appeared to rest with more central threats to self-worth arising from major life stressors.

VIII. Summary

In this chapter we have examined whether the frequency of occurrence of daily events contributes to the presence of negative affects, particularly anxiety and depressive symptoms. We have confined ourselves to subclinical manifestations of these states and have limited the generalization of our results to those normal variations in feelings of anxiety and depression that are experienced as a part of everyday life.

Clearly there is no evidence to suggest differential patterns of negative affect in reaction to stressful daily events. These stressors appear to exert a nonspecific effect, raising both anxiety and depression. Further, we have shown that these influences cannot be accounted for by individual differences in the predisposition to experience negative events (i.e., neuroticism). Health problems had the strongest association with increases in negative affects. After that, undesirable events in which the person played a part had the strongest negative impacts; those that were recurrent as well as internally caused were the most influential.

These findings are consistent with the view that feelings of personal mastery play a central role in the maintenance of psychological well being, particularly among the elderly (Lawton, 1987; Pearlin & Schooler, 1978). Health problems and recurrent, internally caused undesirable events are likely to challenge personal beliefs of self-efficacy even among the hardiest individuals. When perceptions of competence are unaffected, life stress events may produce more localized effects. Such appeared to be the case among the bereaved subjects, who clearly evidenced more depressed affect in reaction to the death of their spouses but displayed no evidence of a significant disturbance in everyday life events or in general distress. The disabled, however, showed more severe deficits both in everyday events and in distress. Especially important were the health events, which, although they lie outside of the person's control, play a key role in perceptions of self-efficacy. Those events carry meaning both in themselves and in what they imply about future events, especially with regard to the person's capacity to cope effectively. That is, they imply vulnerability to life-threatening and/or chronic and painful illnesses.

From our data, desirable events appear to have two beneficial outcomes: they boost positive affects and they provide concrete evidence of self-efficacy that runs counter to feelings of helplessness/hopelessness arising from recurring encounters with undesirable outcomes. We have found that those desirable events that arise from the person's own efforts carry greater psychological benefit than those that depend upon the efforts of others. This should not be interpreted as a denial of the importance of social support networks. Support from others provides a coherent and responsive context within which the person attempts to defend against negative affects and promote positive feelings. However, the key to adaptation, in our view, remains with the self and the person's perceptions of future mastery. Those are strengthened most by desirable events that the person helped make happen. How the person's support network may amplify the effects of events is left unexamined in this chapter.

Much is left to future work on these topics. Our findings lead us to conclude that daily events have pervasive or more localized effects on negative affect, depending upon the underlying implications of the events on self-efficacy expectations. We have yet to examine closely how coping with these events affects adjustment. Surely simply the occurrence of events does not tell the whole story of adaptation to life stress. Also missing is an examination of individual differences in the illness and bereavement experiences. Bereavement is not a unitary phenomenon, nor is disability, and more needs to be learned of the characteristics of those stressors that are associated with negative affective reactions. We wish to emphasize here that everyday life remains a fertile ground for testing hypotheses on the maintenance of personal adjustment. The stresses contained therein are often reminders of what has been lost, or they provide new evidence to sustain apprehensions about future health and well-being. On the other hand, the daily desirable transactions can boost adjustment and expectations of recovery among those who are infirm, supporting a quality of life that is incompatible with chronic depression or lasting anxiety.

References

Abramson, L. Y., Seligman, M. E. P., & Teasdale, J. D. (1978). Learned helplessness in humans: Critique and reformulation. *Journal of Abnormal Psychology, 87,* 49–74.

Beck, A. T. (1967). *Depression: Clinical, experimental, and theoretical aspects.* New York: Harper & Row.

Beck, A. T., Ward, C. H., Mendelson, M., Mock, J., & Erbaugh, J. (1961). An inventory for measuring depression. *Archives of General Psychiatry, 4,* 561–571.

Bradburn, N. (1969). *The structure of psychological well-being.* Chicago: Aldine.

Brown, G. W., & Harris, T. (1978). *Social origins of depression.* New York: Free Press.

Catalano, R. A., Dooley, D., & Jackson, R. (1983). Selecting a time-series strategy. *Psychological Bulletin, 94,* 506–523.

Costa, P. T., & McCrae, R. R. (1980). Still stable after all these years: Personality as a key to some issues in adulthood and old age. In P. B. Baltes & O. G. Brim (Eds.), *Life span development and behavior* (Vol. 3, pp. 65–102). New York: Academic Press.

deCharms, R. (1972). Personal causation training in the schools. *Journal of Applied Social Psychology, 2,* 95–113.

Derogatis, L. R. (1977). *SCL-90 Administration, Scoring and Procedure Manual-I for the Revised Version and Other Instruments of the Psychopathology Rating Scale Series.* Baltimore, MD: Johns Hopkins University School of Medicine.

Derogatis, L. R., Lipman, R. S., Rickels, K., Uhlenhuth, E. H., & Covi, L. (1974). The Hopkins Symptom Checklist (HSCL): A self-report symptom inventory. *Behavioral Science, 19,* 1–15.

Dohrenwend, B. S., & Dohrenwend, B. P. (Eds.). (1974). *Stressful life events: Their nature and effects.* New York: Wiley.

Dohrenwend, B. S. , & Dohrenwend, B. P. (1981). *Stressful life events and their contexts.* New York: Prodist.

Dohrenwend, B. S., Krasnoff, L., Askenasy, A. R., & Dohrenwend, B. P. (1978). Exemplification of a method for scaling life events: The PERI life events scale. *Journal of Health and Social Behavior, 19,* 205–229.

Dohrenwend, B. S., & Martin, J. L. (1979). Personal versus situational determination of anticipation and control of the occurrence of stressful life events. *American Journal of Community Psychology, 7,* 453–468.

Dohrenwend, B. P., & Shrout, P. E. (1985). "Hassles" in the conceptualization and measurement of life stress variables. *American Psychologist, 40,* 780–785.

Dohrenwend, B. P., Shrout, P. E., Egri, G., & Mendelsohn, F. S. (1980). Non-specific psychological distress and other dimensions of psychopathology. *Archives of General Psychiatry, 37,* 1229–1236.

Eckenrode, J. (1984). Impact of chronic and acute stressors on daily reports of mood. *Journal of Personality and Social Psychology. 46,* 907–918.

Epstein,, S. (1979). The stability of behavior: On predicting most of the people much of the time. *Journal of Personality and Social Psychology, 37,* 1097–1126.

Eysenck, H. J., & Eysenck, S. B. G. (1968). *Manual for the Eysenck Personality Inventory.* San Diego: Educational and Industrial Testing Services.

Guarnaccia, C. A., & Zautra, A. J. (1988). *Life stress in a college health center clinic sample and a comparison sample.* Unpublished manuscript.

Gurland, B. J., Copeland, J. R., Kurlansky, J., Kelleher, M. J., Sharpe, L., & Dean, L. L. (1983). *The mind and mood of aging.* New York: Hawarth Press.

Holmes, T. H., & Rahe, R. H. (1967). The social readjustment rating scale. *Journal of Psychosomatic Research, 11,* 213–218.

Jenkins, C. D., Hurst, M. W., & Rose, R. M. (1979). Life changes. Do people really remember? *Archives of General Psychiatry, 36,* 379–384.

Kanner, A. D., Coyne, J. C., Schaefer, C., & Lazarus, R. S. (1981). Comparison of two modes of stress measurement: Daily hassles and uplifts versus major life events. *Journal of Behavioral Medicine, 4,* 1–39.

Lawton, M. P. (1987). *Aging, the environment and the decisions that create effective environments.* Invited address at the meeting of the American Psychological Association, New York.

Lazarus, R. S. (1978). *The stress and coping paradigm.* Paper presented at a conference organized by Carl Eisdorfer et al., *Critical evaluation of behavioral paradigm for psychiatric science,* Gleneden Beach, OR.

Lazarus, R., & Launier, R. (1978). Stress-related transactions between person and environment. In L. A. Pervin & M. Lewis (Eds.), *Perspectives in interactional psychology.* New York: Plenum.

MacPhillamy, D., & Lewinsohn, P. M. (1971). *The pleasant events schedule.* Mimeo, University of Oregon, Eugene.

McCleary, R., & Hays, R. A. (1980). *Applied time series analysis for the social sciences* (pp. 29–102). Beverly Hills, CA: Sage.

Monroe, S. M. (1982). Assessment of life events: Retrospective versus concurrent strategies. *Archives of General Psychiatry, 39,* 606–610.

Pearlin, L. I., & Schooler, C. (1978). The structure of coping. *Journal of Health and Social Behavior, 19,* 2–21.

Peterson, C., Semmel, A., Metalsky, G., Abramson, L., von Baeyer, C., & Seligman, M. E. P. (1982). The attributional style questionnaire. *Cognitive Therapy and Research, 6,* 287–300.

Pillow, D., Zautra, A. J., & Sandler, I. N. (1988). *Daily events and parental distress in high risk families.* Unpublished manuscript.

Rabkin, J. G., & Struening, E. L. (1976). Life events, stress, and illness. *Science, 194,* 1013–1020.

Reich, J. W., & Zautra, A. J. (1983). Demands and desires in daily life. *American Journal of Community Psychology. 11,* 41–58.

Sandler, I. N. (1982). Cognitive correlates of negative live events and social support as an approach to understanding the stress buffering effects. In R. D. Caplan (Chair), *Social support as a stress buffer.* Symposium conducted at the meeting of the American Psychological Association, Washington, DC.

Sandler, I. N. (1985). Arizona State University program for prevention research. In Kellam (Chair), *Prevention research: Five current research projects.* Symposium conducted at the meeting of the American Orthopsychiatric Association, New York.

Selye, H. (1956). *The stress of life*. New York: McGraw-Hill.

Stone, A. A., & Neale, J. M. (1983). Development of a methodology for assessing daily experiences. In A. Baum & J. E. Singer (Eds.), *Advances in environmental psychology: Environment and health* (Vol. 4, pp. 49–83). Hillsdale, NJ: Erlbaum.

Teasdale, J. D., & Fogarty, S. J. (1979). Differential effects of induced mood on retrieval of pleasant and unpleasant events from episodic memory. *Journal of Abnormal Psychology, 88,* 248–257.

Veit, C. T., & Ware, J. E. (1983). The structure of psychological distress and well-being in general populations. *Journal of Consulting and Clinical Psychology, 51,* 730–742.

Warr, P., Barter, J., & Brownbridge, G. (1983). On the independence of positive and negative affect. *Journal of Personality and Social Psychology, 44,* 644–651.

White, R. W. (1959). Motivation reconsidered: The concept of competence. *Psychological Review, 66,* 297–333.

Zautra, A. J., Guaraccia, C. A., & Dohrenwend, B. P. (1986). The measurement of small life events. *American Journal of Community Psychology, 14,* 629–655.

Zautra, A. J., Guaraccia, C. A., & Reich, J. W. (1987, August). *Stability of factor structure of mental health for older adults.* Paper presented at the 95th meeting of the American Psychological Association, New York.

Zautra, A. J., Guarnaccia, C. A., Reich, J. W., & Dohrenwend, B. P. (1988). The contribution of small events to stress and distress. In L. Cohen (Ed.), *Stressful life events: Theoretical and methodological issues*. Beverly Hills, CA: Sage.

Zautra, A. J., Guenther, R., & Chartier, G. (1985). Attributions for real and hypothetical events: Their relation to self-esteem and depression. *Journal of Abnormal Psychology, 94,* 530–540.

Zautra, A. J., & Ramerth, W. S. (1985). *College student small events study*. Unpublished raw data.

Zautra, A. J., & Reich, J. W. (1980). Positive life events and reports of well-being: Some useful distinctions. *American Journal of Community Psychology, 8,* 657–670.

Zautra, A. J., & Reich, J. W. (1983). Life events and perceptions of life quality: Developments in a two-factor approach. *Journal of Community Psychology, 11,* 121–132.

Affect and the Social Environment: The Role of Social Support in Depression and Anxiety

Joseph P. Stokes
David J. McKirnan

I. Introduction

The phenomenon of social support has generated a flood of publications in recent years. The basis for these works is the intuitively appealing assumption that support from other people has important effects on variables such as overall psychological well-being, rates of psychiatric disorder, and recovery from illness. The focus on social support is com-

Note: The order of author's names is arbitrary. The authors thank Peggy Peterson for her helpful contribution.

Anxiety and Depression

parable to the burst of attention paid to social stress as a source of health problems, for which the literature burgeoned in the late 1960s and 1970s. In each case researchers and clinicians have attempted to understand "person" variables—health status, psychopathology, or subjective stress—in terms of relatively objective environmental variables such as external events that require adaptive change or the availability of supportive others. Research on social support is distinctive, however, in its attempt to focus on health-promoting social resources, rather than to emphasize disorders, deficits, or problems, as is characteristic of much of psychological research.

A clear understanding of how specific events in the social environment affect health or well-being would obviously be helpful to the treatment and prevention of personal or social problems. However, despite a plethora of research, a clear, straightforward relationship between any given aspect of social support and any specific outcome variables has not been demonstrated. Rather, there has been a bewildering array of findings, many of them contradictory or frustratingly inconclusive.

Much of the difficulty in this field reflects the complexity and ambiguity of the phenomenon itself. The concept of social support has been defined in substantially different ways in different studies (or,in some studies, not defined at all), and as a consequence has been measured by a large number of instruments that vary considerably in quality and interpretability. Social support as a research field may eventually develop into what Kuhn (1970) describes as a mature science, in terms of a relatively unified paradigm that allows for systematic, theory-based research with comparability across studies. Or, it may simply go the way of the Tower of Babel. At present neither of these alternatives can be ruled out.

In this chapter we attempt to summarize what is known about the relationship between social support and the negative affective states of depression and anxiety. To evaluate the role of social support in these affective states, we will first have to discuss the nature of support.

II. The Nature of Social Support

A. Is Support in the Person or the Environment?

The study of social support began as an attempt to isolate features of the social environment that controlled internal physical or emotional states. As this field has evolved, conceptualizations of support have become more diverse, and presently range from a view of it as an environmental resource (e.g., Gottlieb, 1985) to a view of support as a cognitive-perceptual process within the individual (Cobb, 1976; Procidano & Heller, 1983; Wilcox, 1981). A central distinction is whether support should be viewed as an objective property of the social environment or as the perceptions of the focal person.

Many definitions of social support have emphasized behaviors relevant to specific coping needs. House (1981), for example, identified four such behaviors: (1) emotional support (expressions of caring and intimacy); (2) instrumental support (aid with a specific, concrete task); (3) informational support (cognitive guidance to help solve a problem or understand a situation); and (4) appraisal support (information used to evaluate one's personal performance). Both Kahn and Antonucci (1980) and Schaefer, Coyne, and Lazarus (1981) make similar distinctions among types of support. The assumption underlying these definitions is that failing to have one's needs met in these different areas is potentially stressful (e.g., lacking concrete assistance or information for a task that taxes one's personal resources) or directly decreases well-being (e.g., through the lack of the emotional support needed to maintain self-esteem while coping with adversity).

Other definitions of social support focus more explicitly on subjective perceptions. Heller, Swindle, and Dusenbury (1986), for example, described an activity as social support "if it is perceived . . . as esteem enhancing or if it involves the provision of stress-related interpersonal aid" (p. 67). Hobfoll and Stokes (1988) also defined social support in terms of "actual assistance or . . . a feeling of attachment to a person or group" (p. 499). These definitions emphasize that support may comprise not only task-related assistance, but a subjective sense of social connection, closeness, or esteem enhancement. They also indicate that support can result from specific interactions or behaviors, or from the simple existence of a relationship.

B. From Definition to Measurement

Objective Measures. Measures of support have been diverse, reflecting differences in the definition of the construct. One class of measures, which we are calling *objective* approaches, attempts to measure characteristics of the social environment independent of the respondent's subjective evaluation of that environment. The central assumption here is that certain objective or structural aspects of social networks are associated with increased support. One such measure, which was used in many early studies of social support, is marital status. This has the substantial advantage of being objective, simple, and reliably measured, although its validity as a measure of social support stems from the assumption that marriages are inherently supportive. *Structural* measures include the size of the person's social network, the number of interconnections among network members (i.e., network density), the number of close confidants in the person's network, and the frequency of contact with network members (see Turner, 1981).

Other objective social support measures assess specific interactions. One of the best known of these is the Inventory of Socially Supportive Behaviors (ISSB; Barrera, Sandler, & Ramsay, 1981), wherein respondents indicate how frequently they have received each of a set of fairly specific supportive behaviors, such as being given a loan. Related methods include having subjects keep logs or diaries of interactions (e.g., Hirsch, 1979, 1980; Wheeler & Nezlek, 1977) and having observers record and rate interactions (e.g., Glidewell, Tucker, Todt, & Cox, 1983).

Subjective Measures. In contrast to descriptions of a network or counts of the frequency of specific interactions, most measures of social support are inherently subjective. Respondents rate the availability of different forms of support, evaluate the overall quality of supportive relationships, or indicate their subjective satisfaction with their social support network as a whole. Some of these measures focus on specific interactions (e.g., Vaux, Riedel, & Stewart, 1987), although most assess highly generalized perceptions of support. The widespread use of such measures has influenced researchers' definitions of the construct, such that social support has increasingly come to mean some aspect of subjective appraisal. Hence, Coyne and DeLongis (1986) have noted that social support is now widely regarded as a personal experience, not an objective set of circumstances or a series of interactions.

There are two major reasons for this shift in the measurement (and conceptualization) of social support. First, objective and subjective measures of support are largely unrelated to one another (Hobfoll & Stokes, 1988; Sarason, Sarason, & Shearin, 1986; Schaefer et al., 1981). Studies that have explicitly attempted to predict subjective feelings about social support from more objective measures of networks have not been very successful (Hobfoll, Nadler, & Leiberman, 1986; Oritt, Behrman, & Paul, 1982; Stokes, 1983).

A second reason for the shift toward more subjective measures of support is the frequent finding that such measures bear a stronger relationship to adjustment and psychological distress than do more objective, quantifiable measures (Billings & Moos, 1982; Henderson, Byrne, & Duncan-Jones, 1981; Hirsch, 1980; Hobfoll & Stokes, 1988; Schaefer et al., 1981). For example, several studies using the ISSB as an objective support measure found it to be at best weakly related to psychological disorders, and to be substantially less predictive than were measures of subjective satisfaction with support (Barrera, 1981; L. H. Cohen, McGowan, Fooskas, & Rose, 1984; Sandler & Barrera, 1984). Thus, the greater predictive power of subjective support measures has led researchers to emphasize this conception of support rather than the original view of support as a feature of the social environment.

C. Individual Differences and Subjective Social Support

Although subjective measures of support produce higher correlations and thus appear to explain psychological outcomes better than do objective measures, using subjective measures raises difficult problems in interpretation. The relatively strong relationship between subjectively measured social support and psychological distress may be due largely to internal cognitive processes rather than support per se. That is, individual differences or personality factors may control perceptions of both social support and psychological distress (Levin & Stokes, 1986; Sarason et al., 1986; Watson & Clark, 1984). These states of mind may also influence more objective measures of support (e.g., number of confidants), insofar as they are based on self-report (Levin & Stokes, 1986). This raises the possibility that in many studies the predictor variable of support is seriously confounded with the criterion variable of distress or adjustment (see Dohrenwend, Dohrenwend, Dodson, & Shrout, 1984; Thoits, 1982).

The Role of Negative Affectivity. Negative affectivity (NA) is an individual difference variable that may underlie the relationship between perceived social support and psychological distress. NA is described by Watson and Clark (1984) as a broad personal disposition that subsumes trait anxiety, depression, and low self-esteem. People high in NA focus on negative aspects of themselves and others, and are generally dissatisfied with themselves and their lives. So, given adequate or even high levels of objective social support (e.g., numbers of friends, opportunities to receive attention or care from another), people high in NA might nonetheless have a negative view of the availability of support, or may feel dissatisfied with any support they received. Such people would also be more likely to report psychological distress or to exhibit actual psychopathology. According to this view, subjective dissatisfaction with social support, as well as the correlation of subjective support with psychological distress, reflects internal cognitive processes more than objective deficiencies in the person's social environment.

Several studies have addressed this possibility. Turner (1981) examined the relation of perceived support to measures of anxiety, depression, and anger (basically NA). Factor analysis showed the support items to form a factor separate from the items tapping well-being, leading Turner to conclude that subjective support and NA are not wholly the same construct. However, the support measure had moderate to high correlations with well-being (.33 to .48 over various samples), and interpretation of the factor analysis was substantially clouded by the fact that the support and well-being measures used very different response formats. The factor structure may have reflected only this difference in format. Other, longitudinal data from Turner's study indicated that subjective support and well-being at Time 1 predicted support at Time 2 as well as support at Time 1 predicted well-being at Time 2. Hence, it is unclear that these variables are empirically separable or that they have a straightforward causal relationship.

The Sarasons and their colleagues have found that people who perceived themselves as having high levels of social support and who were satisfied with their support were more happy, hopeful, and optimistic, and lower in anxiety, depression, and hostility (i.e., NA) than were those who perceived less support (Sarason, Levine, Basham, & Sarason, 1983; Sarason & Sarason, 1982). In a later paper Sarason et al. (1986) explicitly argued that perceptions of social support constitute an individual difference variable. They demonstrated that such perceptions were stable over a period of 3 years, more stable, in fact, than were measures of anxiety, depression, and hostility. S. Cohen, Mermelstein, Kamarch, and Hoberman (1985) and Gottlieb (1985) reported similar results and drew similar conclusions. These various results are consistent with the idea that perceived support is not simply a veridical report of social resources, but instead may be a product of ongoing psychological states within the individual.

Wherefore Objectivity? Both empirical and conceptual considerations have led researchers increasingly to consider social support to be a subjective state that varies more as a product of internal psychological processes than of external environmental events. Of course individual difference or personality variables are relevant to all social interactions, social support included. Still, the importance of social support to our understanding of social or personal problems is that it locates some of the cause of those problems in the social environment rather than in person. We thus share the concern expressed by several writers (Coyne & DeLongis, 1986; Gottlieb, 1985) that researchers have strayed too far from the original conception of social support as an environmental resource. If both perceived support and adjustment variables such as anxiety and depression are simply reflections of a higher order construct such as NA, then research relating perceived support to adjustment is trivial both from a conceptual and an applied perspective. These difficulties with a more subjective approach to social support will become clear as we turn now to consider literature relating social support to depression and anxiety.[1]

III. Social Support and Depression

Many writers have noted that the social environment must play an important role in causing depression. The concept of *reactive* depression, in fact, suggests that a person's response to some external (primarily social) event is the defining characteristic of an entire class of depressive episodes. It would seem obvious that if external social events can, in fact, precipitate depression, then the gain or loss of social support is a critical form of such events. However, a central issue here concerns the construct validity of social support and depression. Social withdrawal (or sense of isolation and social rejection) is characteristic of depression, making the relationship between depression and social support difficult to assess clearly: In many studies depression and support may simply be the same construct. These conceptual difficulties are often exacerbated by the use of subjective or perceptual measures of support that make it difficult to determine what actually constitutes support in a given study. We will return to this construct validity question repeatedly.

Assuming that social support and depression are separate constructs, there are several ways in which they may relate to each other. A lack of support may "cause" depression, either directly or indirectly. A direct effect would occur when a person suffers the loss of a confidant or companion and becomes depressed as a result of this lack of social support. More indirectly, the lack of adequate social support may leave a person vulnerable to becoming depressed in response to stress (Pearlin, Lieberman, Menaghan, & Mullan, 1981; Thoits, 1983).

The question of whether social resources affect mental health directly, or operate by buffering the impact of social stress, has been addressed frequently in the social support literature (S. Cohen & Wills, 1985). Proponents of direct or "main effects" argue that people who are integrated within a supportive network are less depressed and generally

[1]We considered reviewing also the literature relating loneliness to social support, anxiety, and depression, but have not done so because of the murky conceptual status of loneliness. Loneliness may be a reflection of lack of social support or, like anxiety and depression, it may be a manifestation of NA.

show better mental health than people without such support, regardless of how much stress they have experienced (S. Cohen & Wills, 1985; Schaefer et al., 1981; Thoits, 1982; Williams, Ware, & Donald, 1981). Proponents of the buffering hypothesis argue that social support primarily affects mental health among those experiencing high levels of stress (Brown & Harris, 1978; Cobb, 1976; Hirsch, 1980; Wilcox, 1981). Of course these two processes are not mutually exclusive.

As a third alternative, the causal relation between depression and social support may be reversed, such that depression erodes or alters the support available to the person. That is, people who are depressed for other reasons may act in a way that isolates them or decreases the probability of others offering support. Also, a person who is depressed may fail to perceive or to mobilize support that is objectively present or potentially available. Over time that perception may be self-fulfilling, insofar as others are alienated by the depressed person.

These three models of the relation between social support and depression are explored in more detail in separate sections below. These models obviously overlap, and each may accurately represent the particular circumstances of some people. Whatever the causal direction among these variables, the underlying theme in any investigation of these issues is demonstrating that depression is not simply the unfolding of an individual disposition based on biology or early learning, but is intimately related to the ongoing social environment.

A. Direct Effects of Social Support on Depression

1. Depression as a Loss of Reinforcement

More behaviorally oriented theories have attempted to understand depression as a consequence of a loss of reinforcement, a concept similar to loss of support. Lewinsohn's (1974) influential perspective holds that environmental changes, such as the loss of loved ones, could result in the loss of social rewards (i.e., recognition, concrete rewards, intimacy). According to Lewinsohn, the result of this process is that prosocial behavior gradually drops out of the person's repertoire, leading to the verbal and behavioral indicators of depression. Consistent with this perspective, Costello (1976) proposed that both anxiety and depression reflect changes in the response–reinforcement contingencies of the person's social environment. These affective states, while aversive, are adaptive in that they signal a need to shift toward new sources of reinforcement.

This perspective attempted to examine the cause of depression as a set of objective, clearly operationalizable events that are external to the person, with the putative advantage that it should lead to straightforward, behavioral forms of treatment. It was assumed that depression could be decreased by teaching people specific skills that would enable them to initiate social contacts with others and thereby build relationships that would provide social reinforcement for prosocial behaviors. Unfortunately, the simple behavioral perspective has not received consistent empirical support, nor has social skills training emerged as a consistent "cure" for depression.

Another issue concerns whether the loss involved in depression consisted of actual persons or sources of reinforcement, or of the reward value of activities that had previously served as reinforcers (Costello, 1972). Similarly, a debate has arisen around the role of self-reinforcement in people who are depressed. That is, people who are depressed may not have lost objective, external sources of reinforcement, but may simply lack the ability to give themselves the ongoing internal rewards necessary for persistent goal-directed or prosocial (i.e., nondepressed) behavior. The concepts of *reward value* and *self-reinforcement* both locate the cause of depression less in the social environment than in the cognitions of the depressed person. Consequently, this approach flounders on the question that plagues all research on the intersection of social support and depression, namely, that of separating cause from effect. Utimately, *losing reward value* may be just another way of saying that the person is depressed.

2. Social Exit Events and Depression

Researchers studying stressful life events have suggested that the loss of social support may lead to depression. Early research on stress and coping hypothesized that any substantial life change, even a positive change, would be stressful to the extent that it taxed the adaptive capacity of the person and would thus increase risk for psychopathology (Rabkin & Struening, 1976). Subsequent research made it clear that not all life events have equal effects, leading researchers to make distinctions between events that are controllable versus noncontrollable and undesirable versus desirable, and between social *exit* versus *entrance* events (Dohrenwend & Dohrenwend, 1974; Thoits, 1983). The latter distinction is directly relevant to this discussion, in that exit events are typically defined as the loss of an important other person (e.g., spouse or confidant), typically through events not wholly in the person's control (e.g., death or divorce).

Some of the most widely cited findings regarding exit events are from a study by Paykel and colleagues (1969) focusing on life events of depressed psychiatric patients and a matched community control sample. They distinguished entrance from exit events, and desirable from undesirable events. Entrance events were seen as stressful by virtue of requiring substantial adaptation to new circumstances, such as entry to a new marriage, while exit events were measured as the loss or disruption of a social resource. The frequency of entrance events was the same in the two groups, while exit events were five times more common in the depressed group and were reported by some 25% of the depressed sample. Similarly, desirable events were equally likely in both samples, but undesirable events (which subsumed exit events) were 2.6 times as likely among the depressed group and occurred in 45% of the depressed sample. These findings support the role of undesirable and, most relevant to this discussion, social exit events in precipitating depression.

Although the findings are interesting and suggestive, this study illustrates the general problem of confounded measures in this area. In contrasting the effect of entrance versus exit events there is a confounding between stress and lost social support: Leaving a marriage is presumably much more stressful than entering it. Paykel et al.'s results have been commonly interpreted as indicating the specific importance of loss of social support (i.e., exit events) as opposed to simple stress (entrance events) as a precursor to depression. Given the confound of stress and exit events in these data, such interpretations are questionable.

More serious is the confound between stressful life events and depression itself. The depressed and nondepressed groups differed most in the domain of marital conflict, and the most commonly reported single item was "arguments with one's spouse." These events are not concrete exits, but represent subjective judgments which may be biased by ongoing depression. Moreover, the depression may precede or cause the conflict, rather than the conflict leading to depression. Divorce or separation from a spouse is an exit event that is more objectively defined, but again the causal relationship is unclear: Separation may induce depression, but a preexisting depression may also be an important factor in leading to the separation.

More support for the role of exit events in depression was found in Slater and Depue's (1981) study of suicide attempters. They found that depressed patients who had attempted suicide had a higher proportion of independently verifiable life events after the onset of depression than did depressed patients who had not attempted suicide. Further, a much higher proportion of the life events experienced by suicide attempters were social exits resulting in the loss of a primary agent of social support (75 vs. 25% among controls). Although this study did not examine the onset of depression per se, it did demonstrate that an important sequela of depression—suicide attempt—is significantly more likely when a person has experienced a major, objectively defined loss of social support.

Contrary findings regarding the role of exit events come from a longitudinal study by Schaefer et al. (1981) that employed both structural and perceptual measures of social support. Their finding was that nonexit events were related to measures of positive and negative morale, whereas exit events were not. Depression was also not significantly related to exit events. Thus, stressful events that did not involve the loss of a significant other lowered morale; contrary to their hypothesis, loss events had no such effect. Perceived support related to positive morale and, more strongly, to depression, both cross-sectionally and over the 10-month study frame, whereas depression and morale at Time 1 did not predict support at Time 2. Hence, the effect of perceived support on depression seemed to be stronger than the effect of depression on perceived support.

The only consistent finding regarding the structural measure of network size was that it was correlated with more, not less, depression. The authors attempted to explain this paradoxical outcome by speculating that the demands placed on people with large networks may increase depression. This explanation is not very satisfactory, and is contrary to the idea that the presence of supportive others acts as a resource for mental health or psychological well-being. Other studies have also found that support worsened rather than bettered psychological well-being. Hobfoll and London (1986), for example, found several situations where social support was positively related to psychological distress. They proposed that the effects of support may depend upon other characteristics of the person or the situation; intimate relationships may occasionally be a source of stress by exposing people to the sorrows of others, or support may be aversive to people who enjoy mastering life challenges independently. Thus, different studies have generated dramatically different results regarding the effect of a gain or loss of support on depression.

These diverse findings illustrate the devilish complexity of assessing the role of social support in depression. Support can be assessed as subjective perceptions, as actual supportive interactions, or as the structure of a person's interpersonal environment. Exit events fall into the third category, in that they typically represent the loss of a supportive person. As measures of social support, however, exit events are problematic because of their inherent status as stressors. Further, as seems to be common in this general research area, the interpretation of results from various studies is hampered by an inconsistent use of technical terms and/or conceptual labels. Further, although an exit would seem to be a relatively objective event, inspection of these studies indicates that their measures often have a strong perceptual or subjective element, making interpretation even more difficult. Finally, the results of different studies vary dramatically, in part due to these differences in the conceptualization and measurement of support. For all these reasons we find it difficult to draw any conclusion regarding the degree to which loss of social support per se is a direct cause of depression.

B. Indirect, or Buffering, Effects of Support on Depression

1. Overview: Stress, Support, and Mental Health

In the last decade there has been a great deal of interest in the effect of stress on mental health. In addition to the direct relationship between stress and mental health, many studies in this area have examined the role of personal and social resources in mediating, or buffering, the effects of stress (S. Cohen & Wills, 1985). Much of the research relating social support to depression has tested this general buffering hypothesis. People who possess specific resources in the form of personal attributes or social support are hypothesized to be less vulnerable to becoming depressed (or psychologically distressed generally) in response to stress than are those without such resources.

Stress has typically been operationalized as the number of life events experienced over a particular period of time, using variations on the scales first developed by Holmes and Rahe (1967). More recent studies have focused on single events, either by having people nominate particularly stressful events (Moos, Cronkite, Billings, & Finney, 1986) or by selecting people who have recently experienced a specific stressful event (Hobfoll, 1985; Pearlin et al., 1981; McKirnan & Peterson, 1988). Many of the major events that have been studied in the area of depression have consisted of social exit events that involve the loss of an important person.

This research has typically assessed mental health via general symptom checklists (see Kessler, Price, & Wortman, 1985, for review), although depression has been examined as the outcome variable in several important studies (Brown & Harris, 1978; Lin & Dean, 1984; Pearlin et al., 1981). Many studies have measured depressive affect or ideation as a continuous variable using a standard scale such as the Beck Depression Inventory, although much of the research conducted among community samples has attempted to establish clinical categorizations of people as depressed or nondepressed.

2. Personal Resources as a Buffer of Stress

Several personal resources have been found to buffer the effects of life stress on depression and/or mental health. These have included perceived mastery or control (Kobasa, Maddi, & Courington, 1981; Menaghan, 1983; Pearlin et al., 1981), self-esteem (Kaplan, 1982; Hobfoll, 1985), cognitive appraisal (Folkman, Lazarus, Dunkel-Schetter, DeLongis, & Gruen, 1986), coping styles (Billings & Moos, 1981; Coyne & Lazarus, 1980; Folkman & Lazarus, 1986), and social competence (Menaghan, 1983). In general, people with these personal resources have been found to be more resilient to stress, in that a given level of stress induces lower levels of distress or depression among those who score high on these personal resource scales (see Hobfoll, 1985; Kessler et al., 1985; Thoits, 1983, for reviews).

Several personal resource variables may then reduce vulnerability to depression in response to stress. However, these variables overlap considerably with the construct of depression itself. For example, the general learned helplessness approach to depression maintains that a diminished perception of control or mastery over the environment causes or actually comprises depression (see Abramson, Seligman, & Teasdale, 1978). Similarly, self-esteem or perceived competence is integral to many theories of depression (Becker, 1977; Freden, 1982), and self-esteem and depression are components of negative affectivity (Watson & Clark, 1984; Levin & Stokes, 1986). Thus, research on personal resources well illustrates the general problem of confounded measures in studies of support and coping, in this case regarding a confound between hypothesized buffers and the outcome variable of depression. It may be most parsimonious to assume that people with such resources are simply less depressed to begin with or are characterologically less prone to respond to stress with depressive affect. Again, much of the problem lies in different classes of variables all being measured in the form of cognitions or psychological states.

3. Social Support as a Stress Buffer

Social support has been studied as the primary social—as opposed to personal—resource that should buffer the effect of stress on depression or mental health. Researchers generally hypothesize that people who lack an intimate relationship or social resources such as emotional or tangible support are more likely to respond to stress or environmental change by becoming depressed than are those with adequate support. Studies testing this hypothesis have used a variety of measures of support, again ranging from measures of objective social networks to subjective perceptions of support.

Studying perceived social support as a buffer for stress shares the difficulties encountered with personal resources: The subjective perception of support is inherently confounded with the state of depression. Despite this, perceived social support has been found to relate to some but not all measures of psychological distress within a given study, and some longitudinal studies have allowed for cross-lagged analyses, wherein perceived support at Time 1 predicts depression at Time 2 better than depression at Time 1 predicts subsequent support (Atkinson, Liem, & Liem, 1986; Schaefer et al., 1981). Thus, personality or individual difference variables may not account for all of the effects of perceived social support on depression. Nonetheless, it is difficult to interpret any study that relies solely on respondents' subjective sense of support.

Studies employing more objective measures of social support are easier to interpret, particularly if they are also longitudinal in design. Lin and Dean (1984), for example, using a longitudinal design in a community sample, found that the effect of stressful life events on depression was substantially reduced if support was sought and received subsequent to the event, both of which were assessed during the course of the study. This buffering effect was not found if the support person represented a "weak tie" to the respondent, indicating the importance of the source of support. Surtees (1980) also found differential effects for close versus more distant social ties in a longitudinal study of recovery from depression among adult psychiatric outpatients, although his data showed direct, not buffering effects of support.

The Brown and Harris Study and Replications. The best known study in this area is that of Brown and Harris (1978), who measured the onset of depression in an adult community sample of women. They used a relatively stringent criterion for depression (essentially a clinical diagnosis) and analyzed their results in terms of the number of women who became "cases" during a 1-year period. They differentiated *provoking agents* from *vulnerability factors.* Provoking agents (i.e., stress) primarily consisted of social exit events such as the death of a loved husband, or one's only confidant moving away. Vulnerability represented a circumstance that was not inherently stressful, but that decreased resources for dealing with stress. This could be thought of as a "negative" buffer, in that it enhanced rather than decreased the likelihood of becoming depressed in response to stress. The primary vulnerability factor was the lack of a confidant or an intimate relationship.

Brown and Harris' study has served as a prototype for a number of others. Oatley and Bolton (1985) reviewed these studies and isolated what they considered to be five close replications (i.e., that assessed the acute onset of clinical depression, employed female community samples, and used longitudinal designs.) Table 9.1 summarizes the results of the original and replicating studies in terms of the percentage of onset cases of depression among those who do or do not experience a major

Table 9.1
Average Percentage of Respondents Becoming Onset Cases of Depression in Six Community Studies, by Presence of Stressor and Intimate Relationship[a]

Stressor	Intimate relationship: Yes	Intimate relationship: No	(Marginal)
No	3.4	7.1	(5.3)
Yes	13.4	33.8	(23.6)
(Marginal)	(8.4)	(20.5)	

[a] Data taken from Oatley & Bolton (1985).

stressor (or *provoking event*), and who do or do not have a primary confidant or intimate relationship (*vulnerability*).[2]

The summary data in Table 9.1 clearly indicate the importance of both the general stress and the vulnerability factors. Across studies, those experiencing severely stressful events (primarily social exits) are about 4.5 times more likely to become depressed than are those who do not experience such a provoking agent. As well, those who are vulnerable by not having an intimate relationship are about 2.5 times more likely to become depressed than those who do have such social support. Thus, both of these factors appear to have a role in the onset of depression. Both Brown and Harris and Oatley and Bolton conclude that there is an interaction between these variables, such that stress has a significantly stronger effect among those who are vulnerable than among those who are not. However, these summary data do not support such an interaction. Respondents who were not vulnerable were about 4 times more likely to become depressed if they experienced a major stress than if they did not experience such stress, while those who were vulnerable were 4.8 times more likely to become depressed if they were stressed.[3]

A Return to the Confound Problem. Although these studies are among the best in this field, the status of both the buffering hypothesis

[2]The percentages in Table 9.1 were compiled by the present authors based on data presented by Oatley and Bolton (1985); see that source for relevant references. The percentage in each cell represents the total number of subjects in each cell over the six studies, divided into the sum of onset cases.

[3]Moreover, if the summary data are compiled by taking the average percentage in each cell across studies, thus weighting the results of each study equally, there is no evidence of an interaction effect whatsoever.

and the effect of support on depression generally is ambiguous in these data. Stress, vulnerability, and, to a great extent, the outcome measure of depression are inextricably confounded. Both stress and vulnerability represent some variation on social support, in the form of the presence or the acute loss of an important other person. The authors describe interaction effects among these variables as a way to make them less confounded or conceptually clearer. Vulnerability is said to not induce depression unless the person also experiences a major stressor, indicating that these variables have empirically different effects and thus represent different constructs. However, the data portrayed in Table 9.1 clearly show that this is not the case: Those made vulnerable by not having an intimate relationship are much more likely to become depressed than those who have a confidant, independent of stress level. As well, stress had similar effects on the likelihood of depression whether the respondent was vulnerable or not.

Despite the ambiguity in these data, Oatley and Bolton nonetheless argue that the distinction between provoking agents and vulnerability is valid because the two classes of variables are conceptually different. They propose that deciding whether a variable such as lack of social support is a provoking agent or a vulnerability factor can be accomplished only in the context of a particular person's situation. The most important distinction may be the duration of the circumstance: For a given person the death of a spouse may initially be a provoking factor (i.e., an acutely stressful role loss) that comes to represent more enduring vulnerability vis-à-vis the lack of a confidant.

We feel that stress and vulnerability are neither conceptually nor empirically distinct in this research. As a consequence the more general buffering hypothesis has not been adequately tested. Further, even the direct effect of (a loss of) support on depression is not supported by these findings insofar as the stress and vulnerability variables are themselves confounded with the criterion variable of depression. In many of these studies vulnerability is assessed as respondents' subjective judgment of the degree or quality of emotional support they receive, rather than, for example, the simple presence of a confidant. When vulnerability is assessed in this fashion it cannot be unequivocally distinguished from an early symptom of depression. Even the stress events suffer from this possible confound, in that marital or interpersonal difficulties are presumably most likely in those who already suffer some form of psychopathology. Thus, people who are already mildly depressed or who are predisposed toward depression may be more likely to suffer many of the stressors examined in this research. The confounds discussed in terms of direct effects (above) are also relevant here: One cannot assert unequivocally that either social support or stress as typically measured is objectively separable from depression; thus, it is problematic to say that either causes it.

Subjective versus Objective Support and Buffering. As we have seen, problems of interpretation are exacerbated in this literature by the use of perceptual or subjective measures of support. Hence, inconsistency in empirical support for the buffering hypothesis has been attributed to objective versus subjective measures of support in several studies. Both Aneshensel and Stone (1982) and Phifer and Murrell (1986), for example, found that support buffered the effects of stress on depression only when both stress and support were measured via respondents' subjective perceptions; more objective indices generally yielded only direct effects.

S. Cohen and Wills (1985) argued that this difference reflects a general phenomenon in stress and coping research. They concluded that subjective perceptions of support generally are associated with buffering effects, whereas structural support (e.g., the simple existence of a relationship) usually produces main effects but not interactions with stress in predicting mental health outcome variables. They further argued that this does not refute the buffering hypothesis, and that perceptions of support are important because buffering effects are to some extent cognitively mediated. For example, perceiving support might help one evaluate an event as relatively unstressful, or might increase one's perceived ability to cope. Similarly, Gottlieb (1985) proposed that subjective perceptions of available support are important because they affect appraisals of threat: Those who feel supported will feel less threatened by a given life event, and will thus experience less psychological distress, than will those who perceive that they lack social support.

Describing the buffering effect of support on depression as a *cognitive* as opposed to *objective* phenomenon has an intuitive appeal and appears to salvage the buffering hypothesis. However, simply describing these relationships as *cognitively mediated* does nothing to resolve the difficult problems that stem from confounded measures. If "perceiving support," "evaluating an event," "perceiving the ability to cope," and an outcome variable such as "psychological distress" are all subjective judgments that are under control of a common factor such as depression or NA, then correlations among these variables are trival.

Cohen and Wills reviewed studies that found buffering effects even when the stress and support measures were uncorrelated, as well as studies that found no buffering effects with explicitly confounded measures of stress and social exit. Based on these data, they concluded that "although a social exit confound may present a problem for interpretation of certain individual studies, it does not provide a tenable explanation for the literature as a whole" (p. 349). We disagree. At least in the area of depression, the nature of these variables as typically measured and the general trend of empirical findings make a confound the most plausible interpretation of many or most results.

More Integrative Approaches to the Buffering Hypothesis. If our review thus far has demonstrated anything with certainty, it is that research involving stress, coping, and psychopathology is difficult and complex. Although there has been an enormous amount of research on the stress and coping process, much of it involving the construct of social support, the amount of variance typically accounted for in this research has been disappointingly low (Dohrenwend & Dohrenwend, 1974; Rabkin & Struening, 1976). As yet, we really do not have a very good understanding of what accounts for differences in mental health outcomes among people experiencing stressful events. Hobfoll (1985) has argued that the field needs a conceptual framework which takes into account the larger social ecology of the stress process. Personal and environmental resources, as well as stress-inducing demands, need to be considered. He proposed that resources have a positive or negative effect (or none at all) for a given stressor depending on the appropriateness or "fit" of the resources for the type of situation and the needs of the person. Peterson and McKirnan (1987) also have argued that definitions of stress and support must consider the specific social context.

Pearlin and his colleagues (Pearlin & Schooler, 1978; Pearlin et al., 1981) developed a model of the stress process and its relationship to depression which is consistent with this conceptualization. The variables examined were chosen because of their particular relevance to the specific source of stress. In their model, life events create stress by intensifying role strains, which are defined as the "hardships, challenges, and conflicts or other problems that people come to experience over time in normal social roles" (Pearlin, 1983, p. 8). Role strains are seen as producing changes in self-esteem and perceived mastery, which themselves lead to depression.

Using a longitudinal design, Pearlin et al. (1981) examined the relationship between job disruption (i.e., being laid off) and depression. Cognitive coping strategies and social support—defined by the presence of a close confidant and/or a confiding relationship with the spouse—were assessed as buffer variables. Structural modeling analyses indicated that among people who experienced job disruption (high stress), those who used cognitive coping strategies experienced less economic strain and maintained a greater sense of mastery and self-esteem than those without cognitive coping strategies. Similarly, interactions involving social support showed it to buffer the effect of job disruption on self-esteem and sense of mastery.

Of course, this research does not solve all the problems we have discussed. For example, mastery and the presence of cognitive coping mechanisms are not obviously different variables. However, this study does more clearly demonstrate the importance of both personal and social resources for buffering the negative effects of social stress, because it measures stress in terms of an objectively verifiable, specific event that is less confounded with the outcome and buffering variables. Measuring a specific event chosen by the researcher has the danger of missing important stressors that people would have nominated themselves, but it does permit a clearer interpretation of results.

Peterson and McKirnan (1987) were also relatively successful in defining stress in a way that minimizes its overlap with support and depression, although their data demonstrated only main effects. They found that discrimination due to sexual orientation, as measured via relatively objective event checklists, was an important form of stress among homosexual males (see also McKirnan & Peterson, 1988). Both discrimination and low levels of social support (measured as respondents' number of confidants) induced more negative affect, with no evidence of interaction effects, using stress and vulnerability measures that were conceptually and empirically distinct.

C. The Effect of Depression on Social Support

The role of social support in causing depression is obviously of direct interest to clinicians or those interested in prevention. However, the alternate causal direction is also important: Ongoing depression may actually decrease the social support available to the person. To some extent the confounds we have been discussing thus far illustrate this process, in that it is likely that depression or NA leads the person to subjectively perceive less support. Depression may also decrease actual levels of support. Social withdrawal and/or a lack of social skills is a common symptom of depression and may keep the person from establishing or maintaining potentially supportive relationships. There is some evidence that individual differences in social competence affect people's abilities to develop relationships that can provide support or to use support that is available (Leavy, 1983; Sarason et al., 1986). As well, some aspects of depressive behavior may be aversive to other people and may therefore lead to social isolation or actual conflict. If this is the case, and if social support is important to affective stability generally, then depression may often represent a vicious cycle wherein social interactions that might help decrease the depression are precluded by the depressive symptoms.

Coyne (1976a) has made the most systematic statement of this theoretical position. He has proposed an interactional model of depression wherein the depressed person is active toward his/her social environment, but often in a destructive fashion: "The depressed person is able to engage others in his environment in such a way that support is lost and depressive information elicited" (p. 29). He asserted that depressed people initially elicit care and attention from those around them, particularly significant others. However, the irritating and often hostile/dependent interpersonal styles of depressed people, as well their sense of helplessness and lack of social skills, subsequently lead to spurious or inauthentic interactions wherein expressions of care from others become perfunctory or insincere. This disrupts the flow of accurate information to the depressed person, which exacerbates their often counterproductive help-seeking. Finally, the social behavior of the depressed person may elicit rejection or open hostility from people who had previously been important sources of support. Coyne argued that this vicious cycle maintains the depression beyond the time (or severity) that would be accounted for by "intrapersonal" or biological causes of depression.

Weissman and Paykel (1974) made a similar argument for the social origins of depression in discussing the role-related behaviors of adult female depression patients. They reviewed several studies indicating that depressed women are deficient in the social interactions that underlie a variety of basic social roles (worker, mother, housewife). This deficiency is said to disrupt their ongoing social interactions and, in our terms, decrease the social support available to them. This lack of support, together with any negative responses they elicit from others, constitutes a source of stress that perpetuates the depression.

Coyne has tested this general hypothesis, usually in laboratory experiments or simulated interactions. Several studies have shown that people who interact with a depressed person become more depressed, hostile, anxious, and rejecting of the depressed person. This effect appears to operate whether the depressed person is real or simulated, and whether the person is spoken to directly or over the telephone. Thus, there is some evidence that depressive behavior leads to rejection and to adverse emotional states in others (Coyne, 1976b; Hammen & Peters, 1978).

However, King and Heller (1984) failed to replicate this effect, and later argued (King & Heller, 1986) that any such effects are not specific to depression, but characterize any form of pathology. Doerfler and Chaplin (1985) have also argued that much of the laboratory-based research on this phenomenon is trivial, since it involves strangers who are interacting for brief periods of time rather than the significant others specified in Coyne's theory. Coyne (1985), however, argued that enough evidence has been gathered regarding spouses of depressed people (and others close to them) to suggest that the phenomenon is robust, and also to warrant therapeutic intervention in the depressed person's social network rather than just with the individual.

For example, Coyne et al. (1987) found that people who were living with a currently depressed outpatient reported substantially more social or personal burdens than did those who were living with outpatients not currently depressed. The most important of these burdens was the depressed person's lack of interest in social life. Further, a higher proportion of the partners of the depressed outpatients developed psychological disturbance scores that would recommend clinical intervention. Both these findings indicate that consistent, close contact with a currently depressed person is extremely trying. Although the authors did not actually measure social support for the depressed person, an erosion of support seems likely given the variables they did measure. Finally, this study indicates that the aversiveness of depressed people reported in other studies is not limited to brief interactions among strangers but can pervade even a close relationship.

Thus, several studies support the intuitively appealing hypothesis that depression can decrease actual social support. However, there is clearly a need for more research on this phenomenon. Longitudinal studies of depressed people would be particularly helpful. The ability to specify that an important social resource is adequate at the onset of a disorder, but is lost during the course of the depression, would powerfully support the hypothesis. Dependent measures should include the emotional stress felt by others that is emphasized in Coyne's theory, as well as the social withdrawal or loss of social skills that underlie more behavioral perspectives.

D. Summary—and Another Look at Individual Differences

Despite numerous studies, there is little convincing evidence that external events such as stress and/or social support underlie the onset or course of depression. The recurring confounds and interpretability problems of this area frustrate any clear conclusion. We feel that some social events must be relevant, and that a wholly biological or personal dispositional view of the etiology of depression is too limited. Still, the simple hypothesis that people become depressed because of stress or a loss of support, and that social support serves as a buffer to reduce the degree to which stress leads to depression, has not been convincingly supported in the available studies. Studies of the effect of depression on the emotional responses of others show mixed or controversial results, and such studies have typically not assessed actual social support.

A major difficulty in this area is that of confounds among measures of stress, support, and depression. Research that more explicitly recognized the very difficult construct validity problems in this area would go far in providing more interpretable results. Beyond this, however, is the inherent confound of the phenomena: It may simply be unreasonable to hypothesize that a wholly "external" environmental event causes depression, with the nature or frequency of such an event being completely independent of any characteristics of the person. Of course we can imagine a trauma or dramatic environmental event wholly outside of the person's control that may induce depression or distress, but as a general model of the onset of depression this may be unrealistic.

A more meaningful approach may be to abandon simple distinctions between social and personal causality, and to examine how personal dispositions both induce psychological states (such as depression) and affect interactions with the social environment. Both Freden (1982) and Becker (1977) have proposed psychosocial theories of depression that take this perspective. Freden (1982) suggested that social exit events tend to precipitate depression, and operate by decreasing self-esteem. He proposed that such events have particularly strong effects on people who are dispositionally more socially dependent: People who have unrealistic expectancies of relationships or who have high dependency needs are more likely to have relationships and/or life plans that do not work out, and will become more depressed in response to difficulties (i.e., stress) in this area. Becker (1977) also stressed the role of dependency, a construct that he based on earlier work of the symbolic interactionists or role theorists. Dependency stems from an overreliance on one source of self-definition; depression is likely if a dependent person loses the person, role, or activity that is integral to the source of self-definition. Two other dispositional factors that are central to his theory are (low) self-esteem and a rigid or limited repertoire of responses to stressful situations. Both of these are assumed to "set up" the person to experience social events that serve as the proximal causes of depression: People with these attributes are more likely to experience adverse life events and to respond to such events with more depression.

Brown and Harris (1978) made an argument similar to Becker's (1977). They explained some of their findings by proposing that women with low self-esteem tend to marry people in whom they cannot confide. In this view a personal disposition (chronic low self-esteem) leads people to establish an unstable or inadequate social support system, which fails to buffer them from the more proximal causes of depression (e.g., exit events, environmental change). Here "objective" social events are important, but their impact depends on preexisting characteristics of the person. Low self-esteem is not only associated with unpleasant affect, it is also a factor that creates social conditions that leave the person vulnerable to social or environmental stress.

Brugha (1984) also emphasized the importance of characterological traits in arguing for a "biosocial" view of social networks. He reviewed studies indicating that network size seems consistent across different cultures, as well as across demographic distinctions within a culture, such as rural versus urban status. Further, he argued that depressed patients' social networks, while smaller than those of people who are not depressed, are relatively stable over time and are unrelated to recent loss events. He thus proposed a traitlike quality to social support and/or network structures. Humans may have evolved with a general basal level of support necessary to adequate functioning, such that ongoing levels of support (at least in terms of numbers of "support people") may be determined more by biology than by culture. People who eventually become depressed may be those who are constitutionally deficient both in affective stability and in terms of their ability to garner or maintain a social support system. Again, external social events would still be relevant to the immediate onset of depression, insofar as a (biologically) vulnerable person would have neither the internal affective stability nor the external social resources to withstand stressful events.

These theories are similar in viewing external social events as influenced by stable characteristics of the person. Some people may be characterologically more likely to suffer stressful life events and/or to have inadequate social support systems to buffer the events they do experience. This view acknowledges that people actively create their social environment, yet differs from the perspective that the experience of stress or support is "nothing but" a manifestation of negative affectivity or incipient depression. Rather, both stress and support are seen as real events that serve as the proximal cause of depression, yet are themselves made more likely by a long-standing, highly generalized personal disposition (i.e., which serves as a more "distal" cause). Given the nature of these theories it would be extremely difficult to gather compelling empirical evidence regarding the origins and operation of any these personal dispositions. Problems of interpretability or confounded measures would be acute because many measures would have to be both subjective and retrospective. Nonetheless, the more integrative perspectives proposed by these authors may have heuristic value for taking this research area beyond its present impasse.

IV. Social Support and Anxiety

Very little has been written about the relation of social support and anxiety, yet intuitively the two constructs seem interconnected. Costello (1976) stated that "anxiety occurs when an anticipated event is expected to make demands for which the person is unprepared" (p. 23). Although many theorists would quarrel with the narrowness of this definition, it is a definition that implies a link between anxiety and social support. Definitions of social support usually mention behaviors or other resources that increase a person's ability to meet environmental demands. Thoits (1986), in fact, explicitly defined social support as coping assistance which would help reduce anxiety and/or depression. Social support that enhances esteem might also decrease anxiety by increasing one's perceived ability to cope. Social support that helps one feel socially connected might act directly to decrease anxiety associated with loneliness or more general existential concerns. In short, social support may assist coping and reduce anxiety either by providing direct coping assistance, by encouraging more effective problem-focused coping, or by influencing one's appraisal of the stressor.

A few studies have addressed the relation of social support to anxiety. Sarason (1981) demonstrated that social support can help the performance of students with high test anxiety. Social support was provided in two different ways in these studies. In one, groups of subjects met prior to an anagram-solving task and discussed the stresses and anxieties of university life, especially worries about evaluations. Another experiment used vicarious social support wherein subjects heard the experimenter provide esteem-building support and acceptance to a confederate who expressed concern about his ability. In both experiments social support had a positive influence on performance only among subjects who were high in test anxiety. Sarason suggested that social support had its effect by reducing the negative, self-depreciating cognitions that interfere with performance among test-anxious students. We should note that these experiments allow for a more confident interpretation than many studies in this area; support was actually manipulated, making it unconfounded with the outcome measures.

Fusilier, Ganster, and Mayes (1986) found that anxiety and depression both were related to perceived social support for a sample of men and women employed full time. Anxiety related most strongly to perceived support from co-workers but depression was correlated most strongly with support from family and friends. However, these results are clouded by a possible confounding via the use of subjective measures of both support and the outcome variables.

Factor analytic studies (see Schlenkler & Leary, 1982) reliably show that one class of anxiety-provoking stimuli concerns social or interpersonal factors. Schlenkler and Leary (1982) described social anxiety as occurring when "people are motivated to make a particular impression on others but doubt that they will do so" (p. 645). The subjective probability of creating a certain impression is largely a function of how one believes he or she is perceived by others. Our sense of such evaluations has at least two sources. The first is direct communications from others, which may be most effective via socially supportive behaviors. It follows, then, that social support can influence our perceptions of how others see us, which would directly influence our vulnerability to social anxiety. Second, people high in NA may have difficulty perceiving any behavior as supportive or caring and may assume relatively negative evaluations of themselves by others, thus eroding their confidence in their ability to make a desired impression. Thus, people who objectively lack social support, or who perceive themselves to be unsupported due to a personality variable such as NA, may respond with high social anxiety. Of course the alternate hypothesis is also tenable: Having high social anxiety may decrease one's social support, either because anxiety leads the person to feel unsupported or because other people actually withdraw from a chronically anxious person.

Unfortunately, few studies have directly tested these hypotheses. S. Cohen, Sherrod, and Clark (1986) provided some evidence related to the latter hypothesis that social anxiety may influence perceived support. Their subjects were entering college freshman who were assessed at two times. High social anxiety at Time 1 was associated with decreases in the perceived availability of having someone to talk to about one's problems between Times 1 and 2. Thus, high levels of social anxiety appeared to inhibit the development of supportive relationships or to disrupt existing supportive relationships.

Because few studies have explored the relation of social support and anxiety it is difficult to draw conclusions. The studies mentioned here suggest several avenues for future research. Social support may buffer the negative effects of anxiety on performance (Sarason, 1981), or anxiety may decrease support (Cohen et al., 1986). In short, the various possibilities linking depression and social support also apply to anxiety and support: Either might be viewed as a cause of the other. Of course, all the difficulties and confounds endemic to the depression–support literature apply here as well. Where support is measured via subjective perceptions it may relate to anxiety only because both anxiety and subjective support reflect a higher order construct such as NA. As well, a personal disposition such as social competence, which may be formed through early experiences with close relationships, might influence both anxiety and objective levels of social support.

V. Conclusions and Future Directions

As we have seen, any one of several causal relations between depression or anxiety and social support is possible. Low levels of support or sudden losses of supportive relationships may lead to depression or anxiety, or may fail to buffer one from the stressors that induce these states. Second, anxiety or depression may render one undesirable as a companion or confidant, or might be associated with a lack of the social skills needed to develop relationships and initiate supportive interactions. Finally, where social support is conceptualized as a subjective state it may relate to adjustment because both constructs reflect NA. Of course, all these processes may operate simultaneously, or may complement each other in a complex fashion.

As we discussed in Section III, other, more distal, variables may influence both depression and anxiety and people's ability to garner social support. Such variables may have their origin in early developmental experiences, in that successful relationships with early primary care-givers may serve as prototypes for later relationships through which one actively seeks support and intimacy (Kahn & Antonucci, 1980; Sarason & Sarason, 1982). Psychological dependence is central to several psychosocial theories of depression, and may have some heuristic value in explaining individual differences in social support and in psychopathology more generally. Self-esteem is a prime candidate here, since it is integral to theories of attachment, psychological development, and adult social functioning (e.g., Bowlby, 1969). Difficulties in early attachment relationships may preclude the development of the self-confidence or self-esteem necessary to solicit or maintain social resources, and may also create vulnerability to the characterological depression and anxiety that emerge as NA in adulthood. Both strong attention to construct validity and long-term, longitudinal research would be necessary to clarify these issues.

In summary, our reading of this literature is not very encouraging. Attempts to understand the relations of social support to depression and anxiety have not been very successful. Perhaps it does not make sense to try to create linear, causal models of stressful events or other provoking agents; social support, self-esteem, or other buffering or vulnerability factors; and depression, anxiety, or other indexes of psychopathology. The conceptual and empirical overlap among these variables may reflect their phenomenological overlap in the real world. Perhaps we need to recognize that the causality among these variables is mutual. Or maybe we need to abandon notions of causality altogether and to allow models that permit the co-occurrence of variables without implying causal relations.

One approach to these problems in this area would be to focus our research methods more toward direct observation, simple description, and in-depth analysis of the experiences of individuals (see Day, 1969; Stokes, 1987). The work of Giorgi (1985), Packer (1985), and others suggests that phenomenological approaches can be helpful in understanding psychological processes. Maybe we need to supplement our current methodologies, which emphasize the statistical testing of aggregate data, with methods that explore in depth the meaning of events and circumstances to individuals.

While innovative approaches to the study of social support and NA may be useful, more rigorous application of traditional, quantitative approaches is sorely needed. Social support has become a popular area of study in community psychology and in related fields such as social psychology and public health. The popularity and intuitive appeal of social support have, to some degree, obscured the lack of rigor and conceptual clarity that is characteristic of the area. Specifically, researchers must pay more attention to two aspects of this research: construct validity of the measures and testing falsifiable hypotheses. The constructs invoked and their measures must be conceptually and empirically separable. Learning that a subjective measure of social support correlates with a subjective measure of depression tells us little more than that people who are depressed are depressed. Also, future studies must be designed to test specific theory-based predictions. These suggestions, of course, are hardly novel; they reflect basic principles of the scientific method. Researchers studying the relation of social support to NA would do well to get back to these basics.

References

Abramson, L., Seligman, M. E. P., & Teasdale, J. P. (1978). Learned helplessness in humans: Critique and reformulation. *Journal of Abnormal Psychology, 87*, 49–74.

Aneshensel, C. S., & Stone, J. D. (1982). Stress and depression: A test of the buffering model of social support. *Archives of General Psychiatry, 39*, 1392–1396.

Atkinson, T., Liem, R., & Liem, J. (1986). The social costs of unemployment: Implications for social support. *Journal of Health and Social Behavior, 27*, 317–331.

Barrera, M. (1981). Social support in the adjustment of pregnant adolescents: Assessment issues. In B. H. Gottlieb (Ed.), *Social networks and social support* (pp. 69–96). Beverly Hills, CA: Sage.

Barrera, M., Sandler, I. N., & Ramsey, T. B. (1981). Preliminary development of a scale of social support: Studies in college students. *American Journal of Community Psychology, 9*, 435–447.

Becker, J. (1977). *Affective disorders*. Morristown, NJ: General Learning Press.

Billings, A. G., & Moos, R. H. (1981). The role of coping responses in attenuating the stress of life events. *Journal of Behavioral Medicine, 4*, 139–155.

Billings, A. G., & Moos, R. H. (1982). Social support and functioning among community and clinical groups: A panel model. *Journal of Behavioral Medicine, 5*, 295–311.

Bowlby, J. (1969). *Attachment and loss: Vol. 1. Attachment*. New York: Basic Books.

Brown, W., & Harris, T. (1978). *Social origins of depression*. London: Tavistock.

Brugha, T. S. (1984). Personal losses and deficiencies in social networks. *Social Psychiatry, 19*, 69–74.

Cobb, S. (1976). Social support as a moderator of life stress. *Psychosomatic Medicine, 38,* 300–314.
Cohen, L. H., McGowan, J., Fooskas, S., & Rose, S. (1984). Positive life events and social support and the relationship between life stress and psychological disorder. *American Journal of Community Psychology, 12,* 567–587.
Cohen, S., Mermelstein, R., Kamarch, T., & Hoberman, H. (1985). Measuring the functional components of social support. In I. G. Sarason & B. R. Sarason (Eds.), *Social support: Theory, research and application* (pp. 73–94). The Hague: Nijhoff.
Cohen, S., & Wills, T. A. (1985). Stress, social support, and the buffering hypothesis. *Psychological Bulletin, 98,* 310–357.
Cohen, S., Sherrod, D. R., & Clark, M. S. (1986). Social skills and the stress-protective role of social support. *Journal of Personality and Social Psychology, 50,* 963–973.
Costello, C. G. (1972). Depression: Loss of reinforcers or loss of reinforcer effectiveness? *Behavior Therapy, 3,* 240–247.
Costello, C. G. (1976). *Anxiety and depression.* Montreal: McGill-Queen's University Press.
Coyne, J. C. (1976a). Toward an interactional description of depression. *Psychiatry, 39,* 28–40.
Coyne, J. C. (1976b). Depression and the responses of others. *Journal of Abnormal Psychology, 85,* 186–193.
Coyne, J. C. (1985). Studying depressed persons' interactions with strangers and spouses. *Journal of Abnormal Psychology, 94,* 231–232.
Coyne, J. C., & DeLongis, A. (1986). Going beyond social support: The role of social relationships in adaptation. *Journal of Consulting and Clinical Psychology, 54,* 454–460.
Coyne, J. C., Kessler, R. C., Tal, M., Turnbull, J., Wortman, C. B., & Greden, J. F. (1987). Living with a depressed person. *Journal of Consulting Clinical Psychology, 55,* 347–352.
Coyne, J. C., & Lazarus, R. S. (1980). Cognitive style, stress perception, and coping. In I. L. Kutash & L. B. Schlesinger (Eds.), *Handbook on stress and anxiety: Contemporary knowledge, theory and treatment* (pp. 144–158). San Francisco: Jossey-Bass.
Day, W. F. (1969). Radical behaviorism in reconciliation with phenomenology. *Journal of the Experimental Analysis of Behavior, 12,* 315–328.
Doerfler, L. A., & Chaplin, W. F. (1985). Type III error in research on interpersonal models of depression. *Journal of Abnormal Psychology, 94,* 227–230.
Dohrenwend, B. S., & Dohrenwend, B. P. (Eds.). (1974). *Stressful life events: Their nature and effects.* New York: Wiley.
Dohrenwend, B. S., Dohrenwend, B. P., Dodson, M., & Shrout, P. E. (1984). Symptoms, hassles, social supports and life events: Problems of confounded measures. *Journal of Abnormal Psychology, 93,* 222–230.
Folkman, S., Lazarus, R. S., Dunkel-Schetter, C., DeLongis, A., & Gruen, R. J. (1986). Dynamics of a stressful encounter: Cognitive appraisal, coping and encounter outcomes. *Journal of Personality and Social Psychology, 50,* 992–1003.
Folkman, S., & Lazarus, R. S. (1986). Stress process and depressive symptomatology. *Journal of Abnormal Psychology, 95,* 107–113.
Freden, L. (1982). *Psychosocial aspects of depression.* New York: Wiley.
Fusilier, M. R., Ganster, D. C., & Mayes, T. M. (1986). The social support and help relationship: Is there a gender difference? *Journal of Occupational Psychology, 59,* 145–253.
Giorgi, A. (1985). Sketch of a psychological phenomenological method. In A. Giorgi (Ed.), *Phenomenology and psychological research.* Pittsburgh, PA: Duquesne University Press.
Glidewell, J. C., Tucker, S., Todt, M., & Cox, S. (1983). Professional support systems: The teaching profession. In A. Nadler, J. D. Fisher, & B. M. DePaulo (Eds.), *New directions in helping. Vol. 3: Applied perspectives in help-seeking and -receiving* (pp. 189–212). New York: Academic Press.

Gottlieb, B. H. (1985). Social support and the study of personal relationships. *Journal of Social and Personal Relationships, 2,* 351–375.
Hammen, C. L., & Peters, S. D. (1978). Interpersonal consequences of depression: Responses to men and women enacting a depressed role. *Journal of Abnormal Psychology, 91,* 231–240.
Heller, K., Swindle, R. W., Jr., & Dusenbury, L. (1986). Component social support processes: Comments and integration. *Journal of Consulting Clinical Psychology, 54,* 466–470.
Henderson, S., Bryne, D. G., & Duncan-Jones, P. (1981). *Neurosis and the social environment.* Sydney: Academic Press.
Hirsch, B. J. (1979). Psychological dimensions of social networks: A multimethod analysis. *American Journal of Community Psychology, 7,* 263–277.
Hirsch, B. J. (1980). Natural support systems and coping with major life changes. *American Journal of Community Psychology, 8,* 159–172.
Hobfoll, S. E. (1985). Personal and social resources and the ecology of stress resistance. In P. Shaver (Ed.), *Self, situations, and social behavior: Review of personality and social psychology* (pp. 265–290). Beverly Hills, CA: Sage.
Hobfoll, S. E., & London, P. (1986). The relationship of self concept and social support to emotional distress among women during war. *Journal of Social and Clinical Psychology, 4,* 189–203.
Hobfoll, S. E., Nadler, A., & Leiberman, Y. (1986). Satisfaction with social support during crisis: Intimacy and self-esteem as critical determinants. *Journal of Personality and Social Psychology, 52,* 296–304.
Hobfoll, S. E., & Stokes, J. P. (1988). The process and mechanics of social support. In S. Duck, D. F. Hay, S. E. Hobfoll, B. Ickes, & B. Montogomery (Eds.), *The handbook of personal relationships: Theory, research, and intervention.* Chicester, England: Wiley.
Holmes, T. H., & Rahe, R. H. (1967). The social readjustment rating scale. *Journal of Psychosomatic Research, 11,* 213–218.
House, J. S. (1981). *Work stress and social support.* Reading, MA: Addison-Wesley.
Kahn, R. L., & Antonucci, T. C. (1980). Convoys over the life cycle: Attachment, roles, and social support. In P. B. Baltes & O. G. Brim, Jr. (Eds.), *Lifespan development and behavior* (Vol. 3). New York: Academic Press.
Kaplan, H. B. (1982). Prevalence of the self-esteem motive. In M. Rosenberg & H. B. Kaplan (Eds.), *Social psychology of the self-concept* (pp. 139–151). Arlington Heights, IL: Harlan Davidson.
Kessler, R. C., Price, R. H., & Wortman, C. B. (1985). Social factors in psychopathology: Stress, social support and coping processes. *Annual Review of Psychology, 36,* 531–572.
King, D. A., & Heller, K. (1984). Depression and the response of others: A reevaluation. *Journal of Abnormal Psychology, 93,* 477–480.
King, D. A., & Heller, K. (1986). Depression and the response of others: Is the effect specific? *Journal of Abnormal Psychology, 95,* 410–411.
Kobasa, S. C., Maddi, S. R., & Courington, S. (1981). Personality and constitution as mediators in the stress-illness relationship. *Journal of Health and Social Behavior, 22,* 368–378.
Kuhn, T. S. (1970). *The structure of scientific revolutions* (2nd ed.). Chicago: University of Chicago Press.
Leavy, R. L. (1983). Social support and psychological disorder: A review. *Journal of Community Psychology, 11,* 3–21.
Levin, I., & Stokes, J. P. (1986). An examination of the relation of individual difference variables to loneliness. *Journal of Personality, 54,* 201–217.
Lewinsohn, P. M. (1974). A behavioral approach to depression. In J. R. Freiedman & M. M. Katz (Eds.), *The psychology of depression: Contemporary research and theory.* Washington, DC: V. H. Winston.

Lin, N., & Dean, A. (1984). Social support and depression: A panel study. *Social Psychiatry, 19,* 83–91.

McKirnan, D. J., & Peterson, P. (1988). Stress, expectancies, and vulnerability to substance abuse: A test of a model among homosexual men. *Journal of Abnormal Psychology, 97,* 461–466.

Menaghan, E. G. (1983). Individual coping efforts: Moderators of the relationship between life stress and mental health. In H. Kaplan (Ed.), *Psychosocial stress: Trends in theory and research* (pp. 157–194). New York: Academic Press.

Moos, R. H., Cronkite, R. C., & Billings, A. G., & Finney, J. W. (1986). *Health and Daily Living Form Manual.* Palo Alto, CA: Social Ecology Laboratory.

Oatley, K., & Bolton, W. (1985). A social-cognitive theory of depression in reaction to life events. *Psychological Review, 92,* 372–388.

Oritt, E. J., Behrman, J., & Paul, S. C. (1982, August). *Social support: Conditions related to satisfaction with received support.* Paper presented at a symposium at the annual convention of the American Psychological Association, Washington, DC.

Packer, M. J. (1985). Hermeneutic inquiry in the study of human conduct. *American Psychologist, 40,* 1081–1093.

Paykel, E. S., Meyers, J. K., Dienelt, M. N., Klerman, G. L., Lindenthal, J. J., & Pepper, M. P. (1969). Life events and depression: A controlled study. *Archives of General Psychiatry, 21,* 753–760.

Pearlin, L. I. (1983). Role strains and personal stress. In H. Kaplan, *Psychosocial stress: Trends in theory and research* (pp. 3–32). New York: Academic Press.

Pearlin, L. I., Lieberman, M. A., Menaghan, E. G., & Mullan, J. T. (1981). The stress process. *Journal of Health and Social Behavior, 22,* 337–356.

Pearlin, L. I., & Schooler, C. (1978). The structure of coping. *Journal of Health and Social Behavior, 22,* 337–356.

Peterson, P., & McKirnan, D. J. (1987). *Stress, social support and psychological distress among homosexual males: The effects of discrimination due to sexual orientation and social resources.* In review.

Phifer, J. F., & Murrell, S. A. (1986). Etiologic factors in the onset of depressive symptoms in older adults. *Journal of Abnormal Psychology, 95,* 282–291.

Procidano, M. E., & Heller, K. (1983). Measures of perceived social support from friends and family: Three validation studies. *American Journal of Community Psychology, 11,* 1–24.

Rabkin, J. G., & Struening, E. L. (1976). Life events, stress and illness. *Science, 194,* 1013–1020.

Sandler, I. N., & Barrera, M. (1984). Toward a multidimensional approach to assessing the affects of social support. *American Journal of Community Psychology, 12,* 37–52.

Sarason, I. G. (1981). Test anxiety, stress, and social support. *Journal of Personality, 49,* 101–114.

Sarason, I. G., Levine, H. M., Basham, R. B., & Sarason, B. R. (1983). Assessing social support: The social support questionnaire. *Journal of Personality and Social Psychology, 44,* 127–139.

Sarason, I. G., & Sarason, B. R. (1982). Concomitants of social support: Attitudes, personality characteristics, and life experiences. *Journal of Personality, 50,* 331–344.

Sarason, I. G., Sarason, B. R., & Shearin, E. W. (1986). Social support as an individual difference variable: Its stability, origins, and relational aspects. *Journal of Personality and Social Psychology, 50,* 845–855.

Schaefer, C., Coyne, J. C., & Lazarus, R. S. (1981). The health related functions of social support. *Journal of Behavioral Medicine, 4,* 381–406.

Schlenkler, B. R., & Leary, M. R. (1982). Social anxiety and self-presentation: A conceptualization and model. *Psychological Bulletin, 92,* 641–669.

Slater, J., & Depue, R. A. (1981). The contribution of environmental events and social support to serious suicide attempts in primary depressive disorder. *Journal of Abnormal Psychology, 90,* 275–285.

Stokes, J. P. (1983). Predicting satisfaction with social support from social network structure. *American Journal of Community Psychology, 11,* 141–152.

Stokes, J. P. (1987). On the usefulness of phenomenological methods. *Journal of Social Behavior and Personality, 2,* 57–62.

Surtees, P. G. (1980). Social support, residual adversity and depressive outcome. *Social Psychiatry, 15,* 71–80.

Thoits, P. A. (1982). Conceptual, methodological, and theoretical problems in studying social support as a buffer against life stress. *Journal of Health and Social Behavior, 23,* 145–159.

Thoits, P. A. (1983). Dimensions of life events that influence psychological distress: An evaluation and synthesis of the literature. In H. Kaplan, *Psychosocial stress: Trends in theory and research* (pp. 195–264). New York: Academic Press.

Thoits, P. A. (1986). Social support as coping assistance. *Journal of Consulting and Clinical Psychology, 54,* 416–423.

Turner, R. J. (1981). Social support as a contingency in psychological well-being. *Journal of Health and Social Behavior, 22,* 357–367.

Vaux, A., Riedel, S., & Stewart, D. (1987). Modes of social support: The Social Support Behaviors (SS-B) Scale. *American Journal of Community Psychology, 15,* 209–237.

Watson, D., & Clark, L. A. (1984). Negative affectivity: The predisposition to experience aversive emotional states. *Psychological Bulletin, 96,* 465–490.

Weissman, M. M., & Paykel, E. S. (1974). *The depressed woman.* Chicago: University of Chicago Press.

Wheeler, L., & Nezlek, J. (1977). Sex differences in social participation. *Journal of Personality and Social Psychology, 35,* 742–754.

Wilcox, B. L. (1981). Social support, life stress and psychological adjustment: A test of the buffering hypothesis. *American Journal of Community Psychology, 9,* 371–386.

Williams, A. W., Ware, J. E., Jr., & Donald, C. A. (1981). A model of mental health, life events and social supports applicable to general populations. *Journal of Health and Social Behaviors, 22,* 324–336.

Social Problem Solving and Negative Affective Conditions

Arthur M. Nezu
Thomas J. D'Zurilla

I. Introduction

Our focus is on the negative affective conditions that occur as the immediate and long-range effects of both major negative life events and current daily problems, as well as a person's maladaptive attempts to cope with these problems. We will argue that current daily problems are an important part of the phenomenon that we call *stress*, and that *social problem solving* (i.e., real-life problem solving) is an important coping strategy that mediates or moderates the affective experiences that are associated with stressful daily problems. A model of stress will be described that focuses on the reciprocal relations among negative life events, current daily problems, immediate and long-term emotional states, and coping activities, with an emphasis on problem solving. Experimental and correlational studies of the hypothesized relation between problem-solving coping and both immediate and long-range affective outcomes (depression and anxiety) will be reviewed. Finally, we provide speculations regarding the specificity/nonspecificity of problem-solving skills to both depression and anxiety.

Anxiety and Depression

II. The Concept of Stress

Despite the fact that stress research has been conducted for more than 50 years, there is still no universally accepted definition or conceptualization of stress. However, three general approaches can be identified: (1) the stimulus–response (S–R) model, (2) the stimulus–organism–response (S–O–R) model, and (3) the transactional approach. The latter approach is a relational, process-oriented model of stress that has evolved in recent years in an attempt to overcome the inadequacies of the first two more traditional approaches. All three will be briefly reviewed.

A. Stimulus–Response Model

The dominant stress paradigm over the years has been a simplistic S–R conceptualization that is based on the view that a person reacts passively to environmental stimuli. Within this general approach, some investigators have defined stress as an external stimulus, whereas others have defined it as a response. Stimulus definitions have focused on objective life events that place strong demands for readjustment on individuals (Dohrenwend & Dohrenwend, 1974; Holmes & Rahe, 1967). Most of the research based on this approach has focused on the effects of major stressful life events (e.g., divorce, death of a family member, career change, serious illness, earthquakes, floods, war). Although this research has demonstrated that a significant relation exists between major stressful events and both psychological and health outcomes, the results have not been consistently positive and the actual relation appears to be rather modest (Bloom, 1985; Billings & Moos, 1982; Nezu, 1986a). For example, according to one review (Christensen, 1981), the correlations between stressful events and psychological dysfunction cluster around only .30, which leaves over 90% of the variance in psychological symptomatology unexplained by stressful events. These findings have led other investigators to look elsewhere for significant sources of stress. One promising approach is to study the cumulative effects of specific daily stressful events (DeLongis, Coyne, Dakof, Folkman, & Lazarus, 1982; Kanner, Coyne, Schaefer, & Lazarus, 1981; Nezu, 1986a; Nezu & Ronan, 1985; Weinberger, Hiner, & Tierney, 1987).

Response definitions of stress within the S–R model have focused on the physiological and emotional effects of exposure to a stressor or strong demand for readjustment (Brady, 1980; Selye, 1983). A popular example of research based on this view of stress is Selye's (1983) work on the general adaptation syndrome, which describes a characteristic pattern of physiological responses and biochemical changes that results from continued exposure to a stressor. In addition to the work on physiological stress responses, other more psychologically oriented investigators have focused on negative emotional states (e.g., anxiety, depression, hostility) via self-report measures (Derogatis, 1982; Endler, 1980).

Although the S–R approach has contributed to our understanding of stress in general, it has been severely criticized in recent years because of its limited explanatory and predictive power, and also because of its simplistic, mechanistic view of human nature (Laux & Vossel, 1982; Lazarus & Folkman, 1984). For example, stimulus definitions have ignored or deemphasized important organismic variables that might mediate or moderate emotional stress responses, such as personal goals and commitments, perceptions, appraisals, and physiological changes. By the same token, the response definitions of stress have been criticized because they focus primarily on physiological and emotional responses, while giving little attention to antecedent stressors or to other stress-moderating properties of the person (e.g., cognitive appraisals, coping activities). Another problem with response definitions involves the difficulty in defining a stress response without reference to a stress stimulus (Lazarus & Folkman, 1984). Without first defining a stress stimulus, it is not possible to distinguish psychological stress from other forms of physiological or emotional arousal (e.g., arousal associated with exercise or sexual interactions). A definition of stress that includes *all* physiological–emotional arousal is not likely to further our understanding of stress-related dysfunctions or maladaptation.

B. Stimulus–Organism–Response Model

Early dissatisfaction with the S–R definitions of stress led to an expanded, somewhat more sophisticated S–O–R interactional model, which incorporates mediating organismic variables (Cofer & Apply, 1964; Levine, Weinberg, & Ursin, 1978; Spielberger, 1972). These moderating organismic variables include perceptions, appraisals, and various "personality mediators." The latter term refers to relatively stable social–behavioral characteristics (e.g., attitudes, commitments, behavioral patterns) that appear to increase or decrease the probability of negative stressful effects. One popular example of a stress-related personality mediator is the Type A behavior pattern, which is typified by impatience, aggressiveness, competitiveness, and compulsive achievement striving (Rosenhan & Chesney, 1982). The S–O–R model of stress can be called an *interactional* model in the sense that this term is used in an analysis of variance design. Experiments based on this model are designed to determine the separate and combined influences of different environmental and person variables on various types of emotional and physiological stress responses (cf. Hamberger & Lohr, 1984; Krohne & Laux, 1982). In addition, correlational studies have been conducted that assess the amount of variance in stress responses and adaptational outcomes that is accounted for by different environmental and person variables when analyzed separately and together (cf. Bloom, 1985; Nezu, 1987).

Whereas the S–O–R interactional model of stress represents a significant improvement over the old stimulus and response definitions, there remains a major limitation. The model still assumes a relatively passive human organism and a one-directional mode of determinism in nature, where influence begins with an environmental event or cause that activates certain organismic variables, which, in turn, affect certain response variables. This approach presents a static picture of stress-related phenomena that fails to recognize the important reciprocal relations among person and environmental variables that are involved in stressful life experiences, including the important role of active coping in moderating stress responses (Laux & Vossel, 1982; Lazarus & Folkman, 1984).

C. The Transactional Model

The transactional model of stress of Richard Lazarus and his associates represents an attempt to correct the limitations of the more traditional stress models by presenting a relational, process-oriented view of stress that incorporates and emphasizes both appraisal and coping processes (Lazarus, 1981; Lazarus & Lanier, 1978; Lazarus & Folkman, 1984). In this approach, stress is defined as a particular type of relation between the person and the environment in which demands (external and/or internal) are appraised by the person as taxing or exceeding his or her coping resources and influencing his or her well-being (Lazarus & Folkman, 1984). This relational view of stress assumes that people are active, thinking, problem-solving organisms that *interact* with their environment, instead of passive organisms that simply *react* to environmental stimuli. Within this model, the concept of a person–environmental interaction involves the process of reciprocal determinism (Bandura, 1977), where person and environmental variables are seen as constantly influencing and changing each other over time. Lazarus prefers to use the term *transaction* to describe this dynamic, interactional process in order to distinguish it from the interaction concept in the analysis of variance design, which usually implies unidirectional causality.

Another important characteristic of Lazarus' transactional approach concerns its focus on specific daily stressful events instead of on major stressful events (e.g., major life changes). These daily stressful events are the specific problems and "hassles" that occur in everyday living, such as having a dispute with one's spouse, being pressured by one's boss to work faster, having the car break down on a work day, or having one's teen-aged son or daughter demand to be allowed to stay out later. Although these daily stressful events are not as dramatic as major life events, recent research has suggested that they may have a greater influence on long-range health and psychological outcome (DeLongis et al., 1982; Kanner et al., 1981; Nezu, 1986a; Nezu & Ronan, 1985; Weinberger et al., 1987). Studies have not only found that daily stressful events are as good or better predictors of health and psychological dysfunction than major life events, but also that the primary influence of major life events may be indirect; that is, they increase the frequency of daily problems and hassles, which in turn have a negative effect on health and psychological outcomes (Nezu & Ronan, 1985; Weinberger et al., 1987).

III. A Transactional/Problem-Solving Model of Stress

Elsewhere, we have articulated both a transactional/problem-solving model of stress (D'Zurilla, 1986a, 1986b) and a related problem-solving formulation of depression (Nezu, 1986b, 1987; Nezu, Nezu, & Perri, 1989). These approaches focus on four major stress-related variables: (1) daily problems, (2) major stressful life events, (3) specific emotional states, and (4) problem-solving coping.

A. Daily Problems

Daily problems are the most common stressful life events. Ranging from trivial dilemmas (e.g., not being able to decide what tie to wear) to issues that are highly significant for well-being (e.g., ongoing difficulties with one's spouse), these stressful events occur frequently in everyone's life. A daily problem is defined as a specific life situation (either present or anticipated) that demands a response for effective or adaptive functioning, but for which no effective or adaptive coping response is immediately apparent or available to the person confronted with the situation, due to the presence of various obstacles (D'Zurilla & Goldfried, 1971). These obstacles may include novelty, ambiguity, uncertainty, conflicting stimulus demands, lack of resources, or some other personal or environmental constraint or deficiency. Daily problems are likely to be stressful if they are at all difficult and relevant to well-being (D'Zurilla, 1986a;

Nezu, 1986a; Lazarus & Folkman, 1984). A specific problem may be a single time-limited event (e.g., one's child gets caught stealing), a series of similar or related events (e.g., repeated unreasonable demands from one's boss), or a chronic, ongoing situation, such as the continuous presence of aversive stimulation (e.g., chronic arthritic pain) or the continuous absence of positive stimulation (e.g., loneliness).

The "demands" in the problematic situation may originate in the environment (e.g., objective task requirements) or within the person (e.g., a personal goal, need, or commitment). These demands are best described as perceived demands, rather than objective demands, since people are more likely to be influenced by their perceptions or appraisals of the demands in a particular problematic situation than by the actual demands themselves (Lazarus & Folkman, 1984). As such, a problem is *not* a characteristic of either the environment or person alone. Instead, a problem is best viewed as a particular type of person–environment relation, characterized by a perceived imbalance or discrepancy between demands and adaptive response availability, which can be expected to change over time, depending on changes in the environment, the person, or both.

B. Major Stressful Events

Major stressful events occur much less frequently than daily problems and, therefore, have less consistent impact on people. A major stressful event is considered to be a broad-scale life event that requires wide-ranging personal and social readjustment (Dohrenwend & Dohrenwend, 1974; Holmes & Rahe, 1967). The most common major stressful events involve major life changes, and include such events as divorce, change in careers, beginning college, the death of a family member, or a major material loss (e.g., losing all of one's savings in a stock market crash). Another type of major stressful event, which is less common and therefore affects less people, involves major physical danger or disaster, such as a flood or earthquake. These disasters, however, also can result in a major loss or life change. For example, an earthquake in California could result in the loss of one's home and a decision to relocate to another part of the country.

Although major stressful events by themselves appear to have a limited impact on long-term affective conditions (Christensen, 1981; Nezu & Ronan, 1985), when they do occur together with many difficult, unresolved daily problems, their long-term impact can be much greater (Nezu, 1986a; Nezu & Ronan, 1985).

C. Emotional States

In the transactional/problem-solving model, the concept of emotional states or emotional stress refers to a person's immediate emotional responses to a particular stressful life event (Mason, 1975). These emotional responses include perceived autonomic activity and other physical sensations, along with the subjective affective experiences that accompany them (Mandler, 1982). Emotional stress may vary in terms of the pattern and intensity of the autonomic activity and other physical responses, as well as the pattern, intensity, and subjective quality of the affective experiences (Ekman, Levenson, & Friesen, 1983). These variations may occur within the same person while in the same problematic situation, as well as across persons and situations (Schwartz & Weinberger, 1980).

The affective component of emotional stress is often described negatively as *distress,* meaning pain, suffering, or discomfort. Two common forms of negative emotional distress include depression and anxiety. The type of affective response that predominates in a particular stressful situation depends upon several interacting factors, including the type of stressor experienced, one's perception and appraisal of the stressor, the pattern of autonomic responses and biochemical changes that occur, and the nature and outcome of one's coping attempts (Leventhal & Nerenz, 1983).

D. Problem-Solving Coping

The fourth and most important variable in the transactional/problem-solving model of stress is problem-solving coping. According to Lazarus and Folkman (1984), the term *coping* refers to the cognitive and behavioral activities by which a person attempts to manage a stressful problematic situation. They have identified two general forms of coping: (1) problem-focused coping and (2) emotion-focused coping. Problem-focused coping is aimed at changing the objective problematic situation (i.e., the imbalance between demands and adaptive response availability) for the better. Emotion-focused coping, on the other hand, is aimed at managing the emotional stress that is associated with the problematic situation. In Lazarus and Folkman's transactional stress theory, problem solving is viewed as a form of problem-focused coping whose adaptive utility is limited to problematic situations that are appraised as changeable. When a stressful situation is appraised as unchangeable, the individual must rely on emotion-focused forms of coping in order to manage stress effectively.

In contrast with Lazarus and Folkman's view of problem solving as a form of problem-focused coping, we conceive of problem solving as a more versatile, flexible, and adaptive coping strategy. More specifically, within the present model, problem solving is defined as the *general coping process* by which a person attempts to identify, discover, or invent a solution, or adaptive coping response, for a particular problematic life situation (D'Zurilla, 1986a). As such, solutions might involve either active attempts to change the problematic nature of the situation, one's emotional reaction to it, or both (Nezu, 1987). Further, this process is distinguished from *coping performance,* which refers to solution implementation, or the performance of the specific coping responses that comprise the solution to the particular problem. Thus, coping performance is the outcome of the problem-solving process. The term *problem-solving coping* refers to the combination of problem solving *and* coping performance with regard to a particular problematic situation.

As it is conceived here, problem-solving coping has adaptive flexibility and versatility in that problem-solving goals may include problem-focused goals, emotion-focused goals, or both, depending on the nature of the problem and how it is appraised. Problem-focused goals would be emphasized in problematic situations that are appraised as potentially changeable, although emotion-focused goals may also be included when emotional stress is high. In problematic situations that are appraised as unchangeable, emotion-focused goals would be more desirable. In cases where the problematic situation is appraised *initially* as changeable, but later (due to unsuccessful problem-solving attempts) reappraised as unchangeable, then the problem can be reformulated to include emotion-focused goals, such as minimizing emotional distress, enhancing personal growth in some fashion, or maintaining a sense of self-worth. Thus, problem-solving coping is a general coping approach that can help people manage or adapt to any stressful situation, thereby enhancing perceived controllability and minimizing emotional distress, even in situations that cannot be changed for the better.

It is important to note that the distinction that is being made in this model between problem solving and coping performance is very important for research on the relation between the problem-solving *process* and problem-solving coping *outcomes* (D'Zurilla, 1986a; D'Zurilla & Nezu, 1987). To avoid confounding measures of process with measures of outcome, the process measure should focus on the skills and abilities that enable individuals to solve problems effectively, whereas the outcome measures should focus on either their reported solutions (specific coping responses or techniques) or their actual coping performance, as well as changes in various indices of psychopathology.

The positive effects of problem-solving coping have been demonstrated in two important process-oriented studies on real-life coping by Lazarus and his associates. In one study, Folkman, Lazarus, Dunkel-Schetter, DeLongis, and Gruen (1986) interviewed 170 community residents once each month for 6 months about how they coped with their most stressful situations during the previous week. A coping questionnaire was also administered during this time. Eight different types of coping activities were identified. Coping outcomes were assessed by asking subjects to rate the degree to which the problematic situations were resolved satisfactorily, as well as the quality of the emotional outcomes. The results showed that positive coping outcomes were significantly related to only two types of coping activities: (1) planful problem solving and (2) positive reappraisal (with an emphasis on emotional growth). Whereas Lazarus and his associates separate these two coping strategies, the present problem-solving coping model includes positive reappraisal as a part of the problem definition and formulation component of the overall problem-solving process (cf. D'Zurilla, 1986a; Nezu, 1987).

In a second study, Folkman and Lazarus (1987) used the same interview and questionnaire methods to investigate coping as a mediator of emotion. Emotion was assessed by asking subjects to indicate the extent to which they experienced each of a number of differing affective reactions (e.g., worry/fear, disgust/anger, pleasure/happiness) at the beginning, middle, and end of a stressful encounter. Two samples of subjects were included—a middle-aged population and an older sample over age 65. Regardless of age differences, the results showed that planful problem solving was significantly associated with less negative and more positive emotions in the stressful encounters. The authors' explanation for these results was that problem-solving coping can have both a direct and indirect effect on emotions. The direct effect is that people tend to feel better when they begin to do something constructively about a problem that is causing distress. The indirect effect is that problem solving can result in an improvement in the problematic situation, which should lead to a more favorable cognitive appraisal of the situation, and consequently, an improved emotional state.

E. The Social Problem-Solving Process

In the transactional/problem-solving model of stress, the problem-solving process is based on the social problem-solving model described extensively by us elsewhere (D'Zurilla, 1986a; D'Zurilla & Goldfried, 1971; D'Zurilla & Nezu, 1982; Nezu, 1987; Nezu, Nezu, & Perri, 1989). In this model, the problem-solving process has five interacting components: (1)

problem orientation, (2) problem definition and formulation, (3) generation of alternatives, (4) decision making, and (5) solution implementation and verification. The problem orientation component is different from the other four components in that it is a motivational process, whereas the other components consist of the specific skills and abilities that enable a person to solve a particular problem effectively. Problem orientation may be described as a set of orienting responses that consists of the immediate cognitive–affective–behavioral reactions of a person when first confronted with a problematic situation. These orienting responses include a particular type of attentional set (i.e., a sensitivity to problems) and a set of general and relatively stable beliefs, assumptions, appraisals, and expectations concerning life's problems and one's own general problem-solving ability. This cognitive set is based primarily on the person's past developmental and reinforcement history related to real-life problem solving. Depending on the specific nature of these cognitive variables, they may produce positive affect and approach motivation, which is likely to facilitate problem-solving performance, or they may produce negative affect and avoidance motivation, which may inhibit or disrupt problem-solving performance.

The remaining four components of the problem-solving process may be described as a set of specific skills or goal-directed tasks that enable a person to solve a particular problem successfully. Each task has its own distinct contribution toward the discovery of an adaptive solution or coping response in a particular problem-solving situation. The goal of problem definition and formulation is to clarify and understand the specific nature of the problem. This includes a reappraisal of the situation in terms of its significance for well-being and changeability. The initial problem appraisal involves the person's immediate response to an undefined problem based primarily on his or her past experiences with similar problems. After defining and formulating the nature of the problem more clearly and concretely, the person can then reappraise the problem more accurately.

The goal of the third component, generation of alternatives, is to make available as many solutions as possible in such a way as to maximize the likelihood that the "best" (most preferred) solution will be among them. The purpose of decision making is to evaluate (judge and compare) the available solution alternatives and to select the best one(s) for implementation in the actual problematic situation. Finally, the purpose of solution implementation and verification is to monitor the solution outcome and evaluate the "effectiveness" of the solution in managing the problematic situation.

Solution implementation, or coping performance, is included in the problem-solving process with verification (i.e., self-monitoring and evaluation) because it is the necessary prerequisite for verification. As noted above, however, solution implementation is separated from the problem-solving process when assessing problem-solving skills or abilities. A measure of solution implementation (e.g., rating of solution effectiveness) is, instead, a measure of problem-solving coping outcome, which should not be confused with the process of problem solving. Verification skills are a part of the problem-solving process, however, and should be included in a comprehensive assessment of problem-solving skills or abilities.

F. Interactions among Daily Problems, Major Stressful Events, Emotional States, and Problem Solving

In the transactional/problem-solving model, stress is viewed as a function of the reciprocal relations among daily problems, major stressful events, immediate emotional states, and problem-solving coping activities (D'Zurilla, 1986a; Nezu, 1987). These four stress-related variables are seen as constantly interacting (i.e., influencing and changing each other). Thus, in this approach, stress is a dynamic process that changes in intensity and quality over time.

According to our model, daily problems and major stressful events can influence each other. As suggested previously, a major stressful event, such as a major life change or loss, often precipitates the occurrence of a wide range of new daily problems with which a person must cope. For example, getting divorced can result in such problems as frequent disputes with one's ex-spouse, discipline problems with the children, attempts to locate a more affordable place to live, and difficulty meeting new people. It is important to note, however, that daily problems can also develop independently from major life changes as a normal part of daily living (Nezu, 1986a; Nezu & Ronan, 1985). An accumulation of these daily problems in a particular area of living may result eventually in a major life change, which in turn produces new additional daily problems. For example, a series of unresolved job-related problems (e.g., tardiness, conflicts with co-workers, missed deadlines) may result eventually in becoming fired (a major life change), which then could lead to other new daily problems, such as trying to find a new job, attempting to manage limited funds, and trying to maintain self-esteem.

Negative emotional conditions, such as depression and anxiety, may occur concurrently with or as a consequence of (1) particular conditions inherent in the objective problematic situation (e.g., harm or pain, ambiguity, conflict, novelty, complexity); (2) one's perception and appraisals of the problematic situation (e.g., perceived threat) and of one's own ability to cope with it (e.g., uncertainty, perceived uncontrollability); and (3) the outcomes of one's actual problem-solving coping attempts (e.g., ineffective attempts and/or the creation of new problems). Frequent successful coping attempts are likely to result in a reduction or minimization of immediate emotional distress and a reduced likelihood of long-term negative affective outcomes, such as depressive or anxiety disorders. However, if effective coping skills are lacking, or if extreme emotional distress impacts negatively on one's coping efforts, resulting in either reduced motivation, inhibition of problem-solving performance, or both (cf. J. E. Mitchell & Madigan, 1984), then the likelihood of long-term negative affective conditions will be increased. These negative outcomes may then increase the number and/or severity of daily problems (e.g., depression reduces motivation for job hunting), which in turn may lead to a major life change or loss (e.g., bankruptcy, divorce). In essence, each of the four major stress-related variables (daily problems, major stressful events, emotional states, problem-solving coping) influences each other to either escalate the stress process and eventually produce long-term negative affective outcomes, or to reduce the stress process and moderate these negative long-term effects. The type of outcome that results depends upon the nature of these four variables as they interact and change over time (see D'Zurilla, 1986a; Nezu, 1987; Nezu, Nezu, & Perri, 1989, for a more comprehensive discussion of these interaction effects).

G. Summary

A transactional/problem-solving model of stress has been presented which specifies the reciprocal relations among daily problems, major stressful life events, immediate emotional states, and problem-solving coping. Relevant to the present discussion, we argued that long-term negative affective states (i.e., anxiety and depression) can result from the interactions among two different sources of environmental stress (major life events and daily problems), immediate emotional reactions, and the nature of the problem-solving coping process. More specifically, if the outcome of the interactions within this model, primarily as a function of problem-solving coping, is negative (i.e., unsuccessful problem resolution), then long-term or *trait,* depression and/or anxiety is likely to occur. If one's attempts at problem solving, on the other hand, lead to effective problem resolution, then the probability of long-term negative affective conditions occurring becomes minimized. In the next section we will briefly describe the research that supports various aspects of this model, with specific reference to depression and anxiety.

IV. Problem Solving and Depression

The majority of the research addressing the relation between problem-solving deficits and negative affective conditions has focused on depression. This body of literature can be divided into studies that (1) have established the existence of a relation between problem solving and depression, (2) evaluated the moderating role that problem solving might serve concerning stress-related depression, and (3) assessed the effectiveness of treatment approaches for depression based on a problem-solving paradigm (Nezu, 1986b, 1987). These studies will be briefly described in this section.

A. Correlational Studies

The relation between problem-solving deficits and depressive symptomatology is supported initially by several correlational studies that have incorporated different measures of the problem-solving construct. The Means–End Problem Solving Procedure (MEPS; Platt & Spivack, 1975) is a measure that requests individuals to provide the means for achieving specific problem-solving goals for several problem situations. Each problem consists of a story stem that describes its beginning and actual outcome. Subjects are thus required to describe various actions that the story's protagonist would take in order to achieve the stated resolution. Using the MEPS, Gotlib and Asarnow (1979) assessed potential differences in interpersonal problem solving between depressed and nondepressed college students. Depressed subjects were designated as those who obtained a cutoff score of nine and above on the Beck Depression Inventory (BDI; Beck, Ward, Mendelson, Mock, & Erbaugh, 1961). In addition to these volunteers, who were solicited from introductory classes, students in treatment for depression at a campus counseling center also participated in this study. Thus, MEPS scores for the following four groups were compared: depressed and nondepressed college students, and depressed and nondepressed student counselees. Results indicated that both depressed groups performed less effectively on the MEPS than did both nondepressed groups. Additionally, these depression-associated differences in problem solving were not found to be a function of differences in intellectual functioning.

Consistent with the Gotlib and Asarnow (1979) study are several additional investigations that used the MEPS. Sacco and Graves (1984) found that depressed elementary school children, in comparison to nondepressed peers, showed poorer performance on the MEPS, as well as lower self-ratings on items assessing self-satisfaction with their interpersonal problem-solving performance. Additionally, Nezu and Kalmar (in press) found that within a group of nonreferred young adolescents (seventh graders), a strong relation did exist between MEPS scores and depressive symptoms. Further, Zemore and Dell (1983) found the MEPS to be significantly correlated with both the BDI and a measure of depression proneness. Specifically, university students with poor interpersonal problem-solving skills were found to be more depression prone than were students with good problem-solving skills.

In contrast to the above findings, Doerfler, Mullins, Griffin, Siegel, and Richards (1984) found no differences on the MEPS between depressed and nondepressed children, adolescents, and women college undergraduates. These authors speculate that their contradictory results were partially a function of the questionable external validity of the MEPS. Indeed, a number of investigators have questioned the psychometric adequacy of the MEPS, suggesting that caution is needed in drawing conclusions from studies that focus exclusively on this measure (see Butler & Meichenbaum, 1981; D'Zurilla, 1986a; D'Zurilla & Nezu, 1982; Kendall & Fischler, 1984). Mullins, Siegel, and Hodges (1985) also found no significant correlations between depression and interpersonal problem-solving ability as measured by a children's version of the MEPS among a population of nonreferred grade school children.

Using measures that assessed two specific problem-solving tasks (i.e., generating alternative solutions and decision making), Nezu and Ronan (1987) compared depressed and nondepressed college students regarding these particular problem-solving skills. Depressed subjects were designated as those who reported a score of 12 and above on the BDI. In the first of two studies reported, subjects were divided into four groups: depressed and nondepressed students who were asked to generate alternative solutions to an interpersonal problem, and depressed and nondepressed students who received specific training in this problem-solving skill. The assessment and training procedures were both developed in previous studies (D'Zurilla & Nezu, 1980; Nezu & D'Zurilla, 1981a). Results indicated that depressed subjects as a whole produced significantly less effective solutions than nondepressed subjects, but that training in this skill did increase the effectiveness of their performance. A third finding revealed that depressed individuals generated significantly fewer alternatives in general than nondepressed subjects. This finding is consistent with a study by D. J. G. Dobson and Dobson (1981) that found depressed individuals to be characterized by a conservative problem-solving style.

In the second study reported by Nezu and Ronan (1987), similar results with regard to decision-making performance were found. Specifically, depressed subjects were found to choose less effective alternatives to a series of interpersonal problems as compared to nondepressed persons. Again, training in this skill was found to be effective in facilitating better decision-making performance for both depressed and nondepressed subjects. The specific stimulus problems and alternative solutions used in this study were derived and validated in two previous studies (Nezu & D'Zurilla, 1979, 1981b).

Additional research has incorporated a third measure of social problem solving, the Problem Solving Inventory (PSI; Heppner & Petersen, 1982). The PSI is a self-report measure that assesses both self-appraised problem-solving behaviors and attitudes. In additional to an overall score, this inventory can be scored for three distinct dimensions that were previously identified through a factor analysis: (1) problem-solving confidence (belief that one can solve new problems); (2) approach–avoidance style (active attempts at generating a variety of alternative solutions to a problem as well as the use of a systematic method of reviewing the consequences of various problem-solving attempts); and (3) personal control (the ability to maintain self-control in problem situations). Whereas this measure essentially taps individuals' appraisal of their problem-solving ability, and thus is subject to validity problems inherent in any self-rating measure, PSI scores have been found to be significantly correlated with observational ratings of problem-solving behavioral competence (Heppner, Hibel, Neal, Weinstein, & Rabinowitz, 1982), as well as being unrelated to social desirability factors (Heppner & Petersen, 1982).

Using the PSI to distinguish between extreme groups among a college population, Nezu (1985) classified "ineffective problem solvers" and "effective problems solvers" as those subjects who scored 1 SD above and below the sample mean (the PSI is structured such that higher scores are indicative of less effective problem solving). In addition to differences on a variety of measures of psychological distress, results indicated that effective problem solvers reported significantly lower BDI scores than did ineffective problem solvers.

Three studies by Heppner and his associates incorporated a similar design to test various differences between effective and ineffective problem solvers among various populations of college students. With specific regard to depression, ineffective problem solvers were found to report significantly higher depression scores, as compared to effective problem solvers, as measured by (1) the depression scale of the Minnesota Multiphasic Personality Inventory (MMPI-D; Heppner & Anderson, 1985); (2) both the BDI and the Feelings and Concerns Survey, a measure of depressive mood experienced over the previous 4 years (Heppner, Baumgardner, & Jackson, 1985); and (3) both the Cornell Medical Index and the SCL-90 (Heppner, Kampa, & Brunning, 1987).

Because many of the above studies focused exclusively on depression-related deficits in problem solving among college students or subclinical populations, Nezu (1986c) conducted an investigation that involved clinically depressed individuals. The PSI served as the measure of problem solving in this study. Depressed individuals were identified as those subjects who had received a diagnosis of major depressive disorder according to criteria outlined by the *Diagnostic and Statistic Manual of Mental Disorders* (DSM III; American Psychiatric Association, 1980), as well as reported BDI scores of 16 and above and MMPI-D scores of $T > 70$. These individuals underwent a 90-minute semistructured interview based on guidelines suggested by the Schedule of Affective Disorders and Schizophrenia (Endicott & Spitzer, 1978). The mean BDI score for this group was 27.00, whereas the mean *T* score for the MMPI-D scale was 82.82. Their mean age was 42.88 years (range of 29 to 69). Diagnoses of unipolar, major depressive disorder were made independently by two clinicians, where the resulting kappa value of agreement reached .98.

Results from multivariate analyses indicated that these depressed subjects reported significantly higher scores across all three PSI dimensions (problem-solving confidence, approach–avoidance style, personal control) as compared to nondepressed individuals who were matched on various demographic variables. This finding suggests that the depression-related problem-solving deficits identified in previous studies with subclinical populations does extend to individuals experiencing depressive symptoms of clinical proportions.

In summary, although some contradictory evidence exists, a substantial number of studies, using different measures of interpersonal problem solving, have identified a strong correlation between depression and problem-solving deficits. A major limitation of this research, however, is the heavy reliance on subclinical populations as subjects. Only the Nezu (1986c) investigation involved subjects that had been reliably diagnosed as experiencing clinical depression. This criticism also applies to the general literatures regarding psychosocial aspects of depression (Gotlib, 1984; Nezu, Nezu, & Nezu, 1986), but future investigators in this area certainly should include more clinically depressed subjects. Further, with regard to the present discussion, it is also important to note that few of these studies assessed anxiety, and, therefore, it is not possible to know if this relation is specific between problem solving and depressive symptoms or if it is true for emotional problems in general.

B. Problem Solving as a Moderator of Stress-Related Depression

Although the above-mentioned research supports the existence of a strong relation between problem solving and depression, more relevant to the transactional model initially described in this chapter are a group of studies that specifically evaluated the role of problem solving as a buffer or attenuator of the negative effects of stressful events. Nezu, Nezu, Saraydarian, Kalmar, and Ronan (1986) found that problem solving, as measured by the PSI, served as a moderator between negative stressful life events and depressive symptoms among a university student population. Specifically, effective problem solvers under high levels of stress reported significantly lower BDI scores as compared to ineffective problem solvers under similar levels of high stress. These findings were further replicated by Nezu, Perri, Nezu, and Mahoney (1987) in a study that included a subject population of individuals diagnosed as experiencing major depressive disorder.

Because the above-mentioned studies were cross-sectional in nature, rival hypotheses regarding the effects of premorbid level of depression or biases related to depression-associated memory deficits about previous life events cannot be ruled out. Therefore, Nezu and Ronan (1988) conducted a prospective study with college students to determine whether problem-solving ability was an effective means of coping with stressful events concerning *consequent* depressive symptoms. Prior level of depression served as a covariate within the regression analyses to control for the influence of premorbid depressive level. Additionally, both the MEPS and PSI were used as measures of problem solving in order to increase the construct validity of the findings. Results for both measures indicated that all Stress × Problem Solving interactions were significant predictors of consequent depressive symptoms, even after the prior level of depression was statistically controlled. These findings suggest strongly that problem-solving effectiveness serves as an important moderator of stress-related depression. Put another way, ineffective problem-solving skills create a potential vulnerability for depression under stressful conditions.

In an attempt to expand upon a simple stress-dysfunction paradigm, Nezu and Ronan (1985) proposed a model that incorporates negative life stress, current problems, problem-solving coping, and depressive symptomatology. Results from an analog study involving 205 college students provided support for the following causal relations among these variables: (1) negative stressful events often result in an increase in problematic situations; (2) the degree to which individuals effectively cope with these problems is a function of their problem-solving ability; and (3) effective resolution of these problems serves to decrease the probability of depressive symptoms. These results were replicated in a subsequent study by Nezu, Perri, and Nezu (1987) that included clinically depressed individuals as subjects.

Previously in this chapter, social problem solving was defined as a broader concept than problem-focused coping. However, to the degree that problem-focused coping is subsumed under the process of problem solving, research attempting to evaluate the stress-buffering nature of problem-focused coping does impact on the general understanding of the relation among problem solving, stress, and depression. This research has been growing over the past few years. Billings, Moos, and their colleagues have conducted a series of studies that attempted to evaluate the efficacy of various classes of coping responses among both community groups and clinically depressed individuals. For example, R. E. Mitchell, Cronkite, and Moos (1983) compared 157 control couples with 157 couples wherein one of the partners was clinically depressed. Results indicated that a greater use of problem-focused coping was related to less severe depression for both depressed patients and their spouses.

This significant relation between problem-focused coping and depression (engaging in more problem-focused coping leads to less depression) was also evident in several additional studies that included (1) a general community sample (Billings & Moos, 1981), (2) depressed patients previously under treatment concerning differences regarding the presence or absence of symptom remission (Billings & Moos, 1985), (3) depressed patients seeking treatment at various out-patient facilities (Billings & Moos, 1984), and (4) depressed psychiatric patients as compared to demographically matched nondepressed controls (Billings, Cronkite, & Moos, 1983). Consistent with these findings is a study by Doerfler and Richards (1981) that examined differences among adult women who were successful or unsuccessful in self-initiated attempts to cope with depressive episodes. Successful women were found to engage in more problem-solving attempts.

In summary, in a variety of studies, problem-solving ability has been shown to be an important moderator of the likelihood that individuals will experience depression as a consequence of stress. In other words, problem-solving deficits may serve as a vulnerability factor that predisposes one to depression under stressful conditions. Further, it is important to note that several of the studies described in this section included subjects that had been reliably diagnosed as experiencing major depressive disorder according to DSM III criteria, thereby increasing the clinical relevance and validity of the findings. Yet, studies need to be conducted to also test for the specificity of these relations, since anxiety was not directly assessed.

C. Problem-Solving Therapy for Depression

If problem-solving deficits have been found to be related to depression, therapy based on overcoming such deficits should therefore lead to decreases in depressive symptomatology. Testing this hypothesis has been the specific goal of three outcome studies.

Hussian and Lawrence (1981) included 36 depressed nursing-home patients over 60 years of age in a study that tested the relative efficacy of social problem solving (PS) and social reinforcement (SR) approaches to treatment. A waiting-list control (WLC) condition was also included. Both treatment groups met for five 30-minute training sessions during a 1-week period. During a second treatment week, subjects in each condition were then assigned randomly either to continue in the same therapy or to participate in the other treatment approach. Thus, one PS subgroup continued to receive problem-solving training (PS–PS), whereas a second PS group received the SR condition (PS–SR). The initial SR group was also divided further to produce two groups: SR–SR and SR–PS. Finally, half of the WLC continued in this condition, whereas the other half participated in an informational control group.

Results of their study indicated a significant reduction in depression, as measured by the BDI, for only those groups that received problem-solving training (i.e., the differences between the SR–SR and control groups were nonsignificant). Additionally, the superiority of the PS condition was maintained at a 2-week follow-up assessment.

In another outcome study, Nezu (1986d) randomly assigned 26 depressed subjects to one of the following three groups: problem-solving therapy (PST), problem-focused therapy (PFT), and a waiting-list control (WLC). These subjects were community residents who were diagnosed as experiencing nonpsychotic, unipolar depression, according to Research Diagnostic Criteria (RDC; Spitzer, Endicott, & Robins, 1978).

In addition to meeting RDC criteria for a current episode of unipolar depression, subjects also had to report a score of 16 and above on the BDI and MMPI-D scores of $T > 70$. Exclusion criteria included the presence of mental retardation, psychotic symptomatology, active substance abuse, or current involvement in any form of psychological or pharmacological treatment for depression. Diagnoses of major depressive disorder were made independently by two clinicians where the resulting kappa value of agreement reached .96.

The PST condition in this study was based on a systematic model of problem solving as delineated by D'Zurilla and Nezu (1982), whereas the PFT group included discussions of current problems and depression-associated sources of stress, but did not provide for a systematic model for problem resolution. Treatment was conducted over eight 90-minute sessions.

Results of pre- and postanalyses indicated that PST subjects reported a significant decrease in their depressive symptoms, as measured by two scales, the BDI (mean change from 23.91 to 9.82) and the MMPI-D (mean change from 81.36 to 54.27), which was also found to covary with concurrent increases in problem-solving effectiveness, as measured by the PSI, and the adoption of an internal locus of control orientation. This improvement was found to be maintained at a 6-month follow-up assessment (mean BDI = 9.50; mean MMPI-D = 52.50). Moreover, PST subjects reported significantly lower posttreatment depression scores than did either the PFT (mean BDI = 18.00; mean MMPI-D = 67.32) or WLC groups (mean BDI = 21.00; mean MMPI-D = 76.33). Additional analyses indicated these changes to be clinically meaningful. For example, using BDI scores as the measure of depression, analyses indicated that 90.9% of the PST subjects showed improvement that was clinically meaningful, as compared to rates of 22.2% for PFT subjects and 16.7% for WLC subjects.

The purpose of a subsequent study by Nezu and Perri (1987) was twofold: (1) to provide a partial replication of the Nezu (1986d) study, and (2) to assess the relative contribution of the problem-orientation component of the overall problem-solving process in treating depressed individuals. A dismantling strategy was used to address these goals by assigning randomly 39 individuals who had been reliably diagnosed, according to RDC criteria, as experiencing major depressive disorder to one of three conditions: (1) problem-solving therapy; (2) abbreviated problem-solving therapy (APST); and (3) waiting-list control.

In addition to the BDI, the Hamilton Depression Rating Scale (HDRS; Hamilton, 1967), a measure of clinician ratings, was used to assess changes in depression. Estimates of interrater reliability (kappa values of agreement) between pairs of clinicians completing the HDRS were found to be .96 at pretreatment and .94 at the posttreatment assessment. Both treatment conditions included 10 2-hour therapy sessions conducted in groups by various pairs of advanced clinical psychology graduate students (counterbalanced by condition). Members of the PST condition were provided with training in all five components of the social problem-solving model (see p. 293). APST participants were provided with a similar package, with the exception of training in the problem orientation component.

Pretest analyses indicated initially that all three conditions were equivalent at pretreatment concerning both mean BDI (PST = 26.00; APST = 27.71; WLC = 27.27) and mean HDRS (PST = 24.07; APST = 25.29; WLC = 25.91) scores. Preanalyses and postanalyses indicated that subjects in the PST condition were found to display significantly lower levels of depressive symptoms at posttreatment (mean BDI = 6.57; mean HDRS = 7.71) as compared to both the APST (mean BDI = 13.00; mean HDRS = 13.07) and WLC (mean BDI = 24.73; mean HDRS = 21.00) subjects. Further, APST subjects reported significantly lower posttreatment depression scores than did WLC participants. Decreases in depressive symptoms were also found to be significantly correlated with increases in problem-solving ability, as measured by the PSI. These results were also found to be clinically significant.

A 6-month follow-up assessment revealed no significant differences between posttreatment and follow-up scores. In other words, the therapeutic benefits obtained by subjects in the PST condition were maintained. These results provide further support for problem-solving therapy as an effective treatment approach for unipolar depression. Moreover, this study suggests that whereas a version of problem-solving therapy without the problem-orientation component (APST) is significantly more effective than no treatment (WLC), the inclusion of the problem orientation component within the full problem-solving therapy package (PST) adds significantly to the overall effectiveness of such an approach.

Although only three studies thus far have been conducted to evaluate the efficacy of a problem-solving treatment approach for depression, they provide strong initial support for its effectiveness in reducing depressive symptomatology. More importantly, these studies suggest that decreases in depression were associated with increases in overall problem-solving ability (see Nezu, Nezu, & Perri, 1989, for a detailed clinical description of problem-solving therapy for depression).

D. Summary

The above-cited research provides support for (1) the existence of a strong relation between problem-solving deficits and depression; (2) the moderating role that problem solving plays in naturalistic settings concerning the likelihood that individuals will experience depressive symptoms under stressful conditions; and (3) the efficacy of a problem-solving therapy approach for unipolar depression. In the next section, we will briefly review the literature concerning problem-solving deficits and anxiety.

V. Problem Solving and Anxiety

In contrast to the literature concerning social problem solving and depression, only a handful of studies have specifically focused on the relation between social problem solving and anxiety. In the Nezu (1985) study previously described, "ineffective" problem solvers reported higher levels of both state and trait anxiety, as measured by the State–Trait Anxiety Inventory (STAI-Form X; Spielberger, Gorusch, & Luschene, 1970), as compared to "effective" problem solvers. Similarly,

Heppner et al. (1987) found corraborative results as measured by the anxiety scale of the SCL-90.

Nezu (1986e), using a university population, evaluated the mediating function that problem-solving ability (as measured by the PSI) serves regarding stressful life events and both state and trait anxiety. The anxiety constructs were measured by the STAI (Form X). Results from 310 subjects indicated that the probability that individuals would experience high levels of both state and trait anxiety, as a consequence of also experiencing high levels of stressful life events, was moderated by their problem-solving skills.

Focusing on a more clinically relevant population, Nezu and Carnevale (1987) evaluated the relation between posttraumatic stress disorder (PTSD) and interpersonal problem solving and coping. According to DSM-III, PTSD is considered primarily an anxiety disorder, with interpersonal difficulties being one of the core symptom clusters. Forty-three Vietnam veterans participated in this study and comprised the following four groups: (1) combat veterans with PTSD; (2) combat veterans with severe adjustment problems (AP) but not PTSD diagnosable, (3) combat veterans who were well adjusted (WA), and (4) veterans with little or no combat exposure who served during the Vietnam era (ERA). Results of multivariate analyses indicated that both the PTSD and AP groups reported less effective coping reactions (as measured by the Coping Reactions Inventory; Billings & Moos, 1981) and poorer problem solving (as measured by the PSI) concerning current life problems than did both the WA and the ERA groups. Further, PTSD subjects also reported less effective problem solving and less problem-focused coping reactions than did the AP subjects. These findings point to the specific relation between problem solving and one type of anxiety disorder. Further, we suggested that ineffective problem-solving coping with current stressors may serve to maintain the PTSD symptomatology.

Several investigators have proposed that deficits in social problem-solving skills may contribute to the development of another anxiety-based disorder—agoraphobia (Emmelkamp, 1982; Michelson, 1987). According to this view, the agoraphobic engages in avoidance behavior instead of problem solving to find effective ways to cope with stressful events. This hypothesis has been recently tested by Brodbeck and Michelson (1987). In this study, 23 female subjects with a primary diagnosis of agoraphobia with panic attacks were compared to a group of 20 normal controls on a variety of measures, one of which was the Interpersonal Problem-Solving Assessment Technique (Getter & Nowinski, 1981). This measure was used to assess the subjects' ability to generate alternative solutions and to select effective solutions to 24 problematic situations. The results indicated that the agoraphobic group was significantly deficient in contrast to the normal control subjects in both these problem-solving skills.

Several outcome studies focusing on stress or anxiety have included a problem-solving therapy condition or a problem-solving training component within a broader treatment program. Although a number of these studies have methodological problems that limit the conclusions that can be drawn (e.g., the unique contribution of problem-solving therapy was not evaluated), the overall results are quite promising. For a review of these studies, as well as clinical guidelines for a problem-solving approach to stress management, the reader is referred to D'Zurilla (1986a).

In summary, few studies have specifically addressed the relation between social problem-solving deficits and anxiety; those that have, with the exception of the Nezu and Carnevale (1987) and Brodbeck and Michelson (1987) studies, are limited in generalizability beyond a college population. However, the present review does suggest that increased research activity in the future, in this area, may provide not only for a better understanding of the relations among stress, coping, and anxiety, but may also point to potentially effective clinical interventions for anxiety reduction. We also recommend that future researchers deciding to include the STAI as a measure of anxiety use the revised form (Form Y; Spielberger, Gorusch, Luschene, Vagg, & Jacobs, 1983), as it is supposed to be a more pure assessment of the anxiety construct.

VI. Problem Solving, Depression, and Anxiety: The Specificity Question

Since problem-solving deficits appear to be related to both depression and anxiety, we would like to consider briefly the important question of specificity. That is, what variables determine when depression, anxiety, or both will be experienced as the immediate or long-term effect of social problem-solving deficits? Because empirical research on this issue is lacking, we can only speculate at this time about the relevant variables. We would like to emphasize, however, that in keeping with our transactional perspective, we believe that no single variable within the transactional/problem-solving model of stress is sufficient to account for the differentiation between depression and anxiety. As such, we are not suggesting that by sole virtue of inadequate problem-solving ability is one vulnerable to experience depression and/or anxiety. Rather, the quality of one's problem-solving skills interacts, in a reciprocal manner, with other important variables (e.g., major life events, daily problems, immediate emotional reactions, biological and genetic vulnerabilities) in combination to produce a *particular* negative affective state (depression, anxiety, or both). In this section, we will provide some brief speculations as to the influence of some of the variables that may contribute to the differentiation between depression and anxiety. It should be noted that such speculations should be viewed within the context of the controversy surrounding the question of whether depression and anxiety can be meaningfully differentiated (K. S. Dobson, 1985), and the existence of certain methodological problems concerning the use of subclinical populations and inappropriate assessment procedures to test these questions (cf. Gotlib, 1984; Nezu, Nezu, & Nezu, 1986).

1. *The Type of Stressor.* The specific type of stressful event may influence the nature of the immediate or long-term affective experience. Some studies have suggested, for example, that depression is most likely to occur as a function of events involving a significant loss (e.g., divorce, death of a family member, becoming unemployed; cf. Costello, 1980; Lewinsohn, 1974; Lin & Ensel, 1984; Lloyd, 1980). Anxiety, on the other hand, appears to be related more to events involving harm or conflict (Brady, 1980; Miller, 1980). Further, anxiety may also be the more probable affective state with problems or life events involving the threat or perceived threat of loss, harm, or conflict, and thus is more future oriented than depression with regard to the occurrence of stressful events (K. S. Dobson, 1985).

2. *The Amount of Stressors.* The number of precipitating stressful events in a person's life may also be related to this differentiation process. For example, Barrett (1979) found that depressed symptomatic individuals reported more stressful events in particular categories than did people with anxiety disorders. In general, the literature indicates that depressed individuals also report more stressful events than do both schizophrenics and normal controls (Rabkin, 1982).

3. *Influence of Biological Vulnerability.* Up to this point, little mention has been made of the influence of genetic or biological factors on negative affective states. Unfortunately, there has been little integration of biological and psychosocial research on depression (Thase, Frank, & Kupfer, 1985) or on other negative affective conditions. However, recent advances in the biology of affective disorders provide intriguing points of intersection that may be relevant to the present discussion. In particular, research has indicated that several common features exist between the types of neurochemical changes produced by stress and the biochemical factors associated with depression (Anisman & LaPierre, 1982). For example, clinical depression has been found to be related to both depletion of the brain amines norepinephrine and serotonin, with some evidence suggesting the involvement of acetylcholine as well (Schild-

kraut, 1974). Moreover, it is likely that neurotransmitter abnormalities act in combination (Anisman & LaPierre, 1982). In other words, it is the *balance* among neurotransmitter systems that provides the most appropriate framework from which to understand the influence of biochemical factors on depression.

Related to the present discussion, studies have also indicated that uncontrollable stress can result in the depletion of brain norepinephrine (Weiss, Glazer, & Pohorecky, 1976) and serotonin (Thierry, Blanc, & Glowinski, 1971) and an increase in acetylcholine (Anisman, Pizzino, & Sklar, 1980). As such, it can be argued that the experience of moderate to severe stress can induce the kinds of neurochemical and biological changes related to depressive symptomatology (Anisman & LaPierre, 1982; Sackheim & Weber, 1982). Theoretically, then, the presence (or absence) of a depression-related biochemical propensity may also act as one avenue by which individuals, under stressful conditions, become depressed, anxious, or both.

4. *Problem Orientation Variables.* Earlier we noted that the problem-orientation component of the social problem-solving process involves perceptions, appraisals, beliefs, and expectations concerning life's problems and one's problem-solving ability. The manner in which individuals perceive, appraise, and understand the negative events (major life changes and daily problems) in their lives (see Clark & Beck, Chapter 13, and Kendall & Ingram, Chapter 2, this volume), as well as their ability to cope with them, can influence whether they become depressed, anxious, or both (Nezu, Nezu, & Blisset, 1988). For example, if the death of a spouse is perceived as a major loss (due to a prior close relationship), feelings of grief and depression are more likely to occur than feelings of anxiety. On the other hand, if this death represents to another individual the *threat* of future harm, loss, or conflict (e.g., being alone and without future financial and social support), then anxiety may become the most predominant affective response. Further, if this person then appraises his or her problem-solving or coping ability negatively, and sees no hope of avoiding these future stressors, then he or she may become eventually depressed (Beck, Rush, Shaw, & Emery, 1979).

5. *Problem-Solving Performance.* The nature of the outcome of engaging in the other four problem-solving tasks (problem definition, generating alternatives, decision making, and solution implementation and verification) may also influence the differentiation process. For example, if ineffective problem solving leads to continual loss (or perceived loss) of reinforcement from one's social environment, it is likely that depression will occur (Lewinsohn, 1974; Nezu, 1986c, 1987; Nezu, Kalmar, Ronan, & Clavijo, 1986). Conversely, if such ineffective problem-solving coping leads to threats (actual or perceived) of future negative life events and problems, then anxiety might result.

It is obvious that the above hypotheses await much-needed future research. However, we believe a more complete understanding of the constructs of depression and anxiety involves an understanding of the relation between stressful events (both major life changes and daily problems) and problem-solving coping. Problem-solving deficits alone, then, should not be perceived as the etiological key by which to open the prize door which contains the answer to the question of who will become depressed or who will become anxious. Rather, it is the reciprocal interactions among all the variables within the transactional/problem-solving model that will best predict long-term affective outcome.

References

American Psychiatric Association. (1980). *Diagnostic and statistical manual of mental disorders* (3rd ed.). Washington, DC: Author.

Anisman, H., & LaPierre, Y. (1982). Neurochemical aspects of stress and depression: Formulations and caveats. In R. W. J. Neufeld (Ed.), *Psychosocial stress and psychopathology*. New York: McGraw-Hill.

Anisman, H., Pizzino, A., & Sklar, L. S. (1980). Coping with stress, norepinephrine depletion and escape performance. *Brain Research, 191,* 583–588.

Bandura, A. (1977). Self-efficacy: Toward a unifying theory of behavioral change. *Psychological Review, 84,* 191–215.

Barrett, J. E. (1979). The relationship of life events to the onset of neurotic disorders. In J. E. Barrett (Ed.), *Stress and mental disorder*. New York: Raven Press.

Beck, A. T., Rush, A. J., Shaw, B. F., & Emery, G. (1979). *Cognitive therapy of depression.* New York: Guilford Press.

Beck, A. T., Ward, C. H., Mendelson, M., Mock, J., & Erbaugh, J. (1961. An inventory for measuring depression. *Archives of General Psychiatry, 5,* 462–467.

Billings, A. G., Cronkite, R. C., & Moos, R. H. (1983). Social-environmental factors in unipolar depression: Comparisons of depressed patients and nondepressed controls. *Journal of Abnormal Psychology, 92,* 119–133.

Billings, A. G., & Moos, R. H. (1981). The role of coping responses and social resources in attenuating the impact of stressful life events. *Journal of Behavioral Medicine, 4,* 139–157.

Billings, A. G., & Moos, R. H. (1982). Psychosocial theory and research on depression: An integrative framework and review. *Clinical Psychology Review, 2,* 213–237.

Billings, A. G., & Moos, R. H. (1984). Coping, stress, and social resources among adults with unipolar depression. *Journal of Personality and Social Psychology, 46,* 877–891.

Billings, A. G., & Moos, R. H. (1985). Psychosocial processes of remission in unipolar depression: Comparing depressed patients with matched community controls. *Journal of Consulting and Clinical Psychology, 53,* 314–325.

Bloom, B. L. (1985). *Stressful life event theory and research: Implications for primary prevention* (DHHS Publication No. AMD 85-1385). Rockville, MD: National Institute of Mental Health.

Brady, J. V. (1980). Experimental studies of stress and anxiety. In I. L. Kutash, L. B. Scheslinger, & associates (Eds.), *Handbook on stress and anxiety*. San Francisco: Jossey-Bass.

Brodbeck, C., & Michelson, L. (1987). Problem-solving skills and attributional styles of agoraphobics. *Cognitive Therapy and Research, 11,* 593–610.

Butler, L., & Meichenbaum, D. (1981). The assessment of interpersonal problem-solving skills. In P. C. Kendall & S. D. Hollon (Eds.), *Assessment strategies for cognitive-behavioral interventions*. New York: Academic Press.

Christensen, J. F. (1981). Assessment of stress: Environmental, intrapersonal, and outcome issues. In P. McReynolds (Ed.), *Advances in psychological assessment* (Vol. 5). San Francisco: Jossey-Bass.

Cofer, C. N., & Apply, M. H. (1964). *Motivation: Theory and research*. New York: Wiley.

Costello, C. G. (1980). Loss as a source of stress in psychopathology. In R. W. J. Neufeld (Ed.), *Psychological stress and psychopathology*. New York: McGraw-Hill.

DeLongis, A., Coyne, J. C., Dakof, G., Folkman, S., & Lazarus, R. S. (1982). Relationship of daily hassles, uplifts, and major life events to health status. *Health Psychology, 1*, 119–136.

Derogatis, L. R. (1982). Self-report measures of stress. In L. Goldberger & S. Breznitz (Eds.), *Handbook of stress: Theoretical and clinical aspects*. New York: Free Press.

Dobson, D. J. G., & Dobson, K. S. (1981). Problem-solving strategies in depressed and nondepressed college students. *Cognitive Therapy and Research, 5*, 237–249.

Dobson, K. S. (1985). The relationship between anxiety and depression. *Clinical Psychology Review, 5*, 307–324.

Doerfler, L. A., Mullins, L. L., Griffin, N. J., Siegel, L. J., & Richards, S. C. (1984). Problem-solving deficits in depressed children, adolescents, and adults. *Cognitive Therapy and Research, 8*, 489–500.

Doerfler, L. A., & Richards, C. S. (1981). Self-initiated attempts to cope with depression. *Cognitive Therapy and Research, 5*, 367–371.

Dohrenwend, B. S., & Dohrenwend, B. P. (Eds.). (1974). *Stressful life events: Their nature and effects*. New York: Wiley.

D'Zurilla, T. J. (1986a). *Problem-solving therapy: A social competence approach to clinical intervention*. New York: Springer.

D'Zurilla, T. J. (1986b, November). A problem-solving approach to stress management and prevention. In A. M. Nezu (Chair), *Social problem solving: Recent advances in theory, research, and clinical applications*. Symposium conducted at the meeting of the Association for the Advancement of Behavior Therapy, Chicago.

D'Zurilla, T. J., & Goldfried, M. R. (1971). Problem solving and behavior modification. *Journal of Abnormal Psychology, 78*, 107–126.

D'Zurilla, T. J., & Nezu, A. (1980). A study of the generation of alternatives process in social problem solving. *Cognitive Therapy and Research, 4*, 67–72.

D'Zurilla, T. J., & Nezu, A. (1982). Social problem solving in adults. In P. C. Kendall (Ed.), *Advances in cognitive-behavioral research and therapy* (Vol. 1). New York: Academic Press.

D'Zurilla, T. J., & Nezu, A. M. (1987). The Heppner and Krauskopf approach: A model of personal problem solving or social skills? *Counseling Psychologist, 15*, 463–470.

Ekman, P., Levenson, R. W., & Friesen, W. V. (1983). Autonomic nervous system activity distinguishes among emotions. *Science, 221*, 1208–1210.

Emmelkamp, P. M. G. (1982). *Phobic and obsessive–compulsive disorders*. New York: Plenum.

Endicott, J., & Spitzer, R. L. (1978). A diagnostic interview: The Schedule for Affective Disorders and Schizophrenia. *Archives of General Psychiatry, 35*, 837–844.

Endler, N. S. (1980). Person–situation interaction and anxiety. In I. L. Kutash, L. B. Scheslinger, & associates (Eds.), *Handbook on stress and anxiety*. San Francisco: Jossey-Bass.

Folkman, S., & Lazarus, R. S. (1987). *Coping as a mediator of emotion*. Manuscript submitted for publication.

Folkman, S., Lazarus, R. S., Dunkel-Schetter, C., DeLongis, A., & Gruen, R. (1986). The dynamics of a stressful encounter: Cognitive appraisal, coping, and encounter outcomes. *Journal of Personality and Social Psychology, 50*, 992–1003.

Getter, H., & Nowinski, J. K. (1981). A free response test of interpersonal effectiveness. *Journal of Personality Assessment, 45,* 301–308.

Gotlib, I. H. (1984). Depression and general psychopathology in university students. *Journal of Abnormal Psychology, 93,* 19–30.

Gotlib, I. H., & Asarnow, R. F. (1979). Interpersonal and impersonal problem-solving skills in mildly and moderately depressed university students. *Journal of Consulting and Clinical Psychology, 47,* 86–95.

Hamberger, L. K., & Lohr, J. M. (1984). *Stress and stress management.* New York: Springer.

Hamilton, M. (1967). Development of a rating scale for primary depressive illness. *British Journal of Social and Clinical Psychology, 6,* 276–296.

Heppner, P. P., & Anderson, W. P. (1985). The relationship between problem-solving self-appraisal and psychological adjustment. *Cognitive Therapy and Research, 9,* 415–427.

Heppner, P. P., Baumgardner, A., & Jackson, J. (1985). Problem-solving self-appraisal, depression, and attributional style: Are they related? *Cognitive Therapy and Research, 9,* 105–113.

Heppner, P. P., Hibel, J. H., Neal, G. W., Weinstein, C. L., & Rabinowitz, F. E. (1982). Personal problem solving: A descriptive study of individual differences. *Journal of Counseling Psychology, 29,* 580–590.

Heppner, P. P., Kampa, M., & Brunning, L. (1987). The relationship between problem-solving self-appraisal and indices of physical and psychological health. *Cognitive Therapy and Research, 11,* 155–168.

Heppner, P. P., & Petersen, C. H. (1982). The development and implications of a personal problem solving inventory. *Journal of Counseling Psychology, 29,* 66–75.

Holmes, T. H., & Rahe, R. H. (1967). The social readjustment rating scale. *Journal of Psychosomatic Research, 11,* 213–218.

Hussian, R. A., & Lawrence, P. S. (1981). Social reinforcement of activity and problem-solving training in the treatment of depressed institutionalized elderly patients. *Cognitive Therapy and Research, 5,* 57–69.

Kanner, A. D., Coyne, J. C., Schaefer, C., & Lazarus, R. S. (1981). Comparison of two modes of stress measurement: Daily hassles and uplifts versus major life events. *Journal of Behavioral Medicine, 4,* 1–39.

Kendall, P.C., & Fischler, G. L. (1984). Behavioral and adjustment correlates of problem solving: Validation analyses of interpersonal cognitive problem-solving measures. *Child Development, 55,* 879–892.

Krohne, H. W., & Laux, L. (Eds.). (1982). *Achievement, stress, and anxiety.* New York: Hemisphere.

Laux, L., & Vossel, G. (1982). Theoretical and methodological issues in achievement-related stress and anxiety research. In H. W. Kronhne & L. Laux (Eds.), *Achievement, stress, and anxiety.* New York: Hemisphere.

Lazarus, R. S. (1981). The stress and coping paradigm. In C. Eisdorfer, D. Cohen, A. Kleinman, & P. Maxim (Eds.), *Theoretical bases for psychopathology.* New York: Springer.

Lazarus, R. S., & Folkman, S. (1984). *Stress, appraisal, and coping.* New York: Springer.

Lazarus, R. S., & Lanier, R. (1978). Stress-related transactions between person and environment. In L. A. Pervin & M. Lewis (Eds.), *Perspectives in interactional psychology.* New York: Plenum.

Leventhal, H., & Nerenz, D. R. (1983). A model for stress research with some implications for the control of stress disorders. In D. Meichenbaum & M. E. Jaremko (Eds.), *Stress reduction and prevention.* New York: Plenum.

Levine, S., Weinberg, J., & Ursin, H. (1978). Definition of the coping process and statement of the problem. In H. Ursin, E. Baade, & S. Levine (Eds.), *Psychobiology of stress: A study of coping men.* New York: Academic Press.

Lewinsohn, P. M. (1974). A behavioral approach to depression. In R. J. Friedman & M. M. Katz (Eds.), *The psychology of depression: Contemporary theory and research.* Washington, DC: Winston-Wiley.
Lin, N., & Ensel, W. M. (1984). Depression-mobility and its social etiology: The role of life events and social support. *Journal of Health and Social Behavior, 25,* 176–188.
Lloyd, C. (1980). Life events and depressive disorder revisited: II. Events as precipitating factors. *Archives of General Psychiatry, 37,* 541–548.
Mandler, G. (1982). Stress and thought processes. In L. Goldberger & S. Breznitz (Eds.), *Handbook of stress: Theoretical and clinical aspects.* New York: Free Press.
Mason, J. W. (1975). An historical view of the stress field. *Journal of Human Stress, 1,* 6–12.
Michelson, L. (1987). Cognitive-behavioral assessment and treatment of agoraphobia. In L. Michelson & L. M. Ascher (Eds.), *Anxiety and stress disorders: Cognitive-behavioral assessment and treatment.* New York: Guilford Press.
Miller, N.E. (1980).A perspective on the effects of stress and coping on disease and health. In S. Levine & H. Ursin (Eds.), *Coping and health* (NATO Conference Series III: Human factors). New York: Plenum.
Mitchell, J. E., & Madigan, R. J. (1984). The effects of induced elation and depression on interpersonal problem solving. *Cognitive Therapy and Research, 8,* 277–285.
Mitchell, R. E., Cronkite, R. C., & Moos, R. H. (1983). Stress, coping, and depression among married couples. *Journal of Abnormal Psychology, 92,* 433–448.
Mullins, L. L., Siegel, L. J., & Hodges, K. (1985). Cognitive problem-solving and life event correlates of depressive symptoms in children. *Journal of Abnormal Child Psychology, 13,* 305–314.
Nezu, A. M. (1985). Differences in psychological distress between effective and ineffective problem solvers. *Journal of Counseling Psychology, 32,* 135–138.
Nezu, A. M. (1986a). Effects of stress from current problems: Comparison to major life events. *Journal of Clinical Psychology, 42,* 847–852.
Nezu, A. M. (1986b), November). A problem-solving formulation of depression. In A. M. Nezu (Chair), *Social problem solving: Recent advances in theory, research, and clinical applications.* Symposium conducted at the meeting of the Association for the Advancement of Behavior Therapy, Chicago.
Nezu, A. M. (1986c). Cognitive appraisal of problem-solving effectiveness: Relation to depression and depressive symptoms. *Journal of Clinical Psychology, 42,* 42–48.
Nezu, A. M. (1986d). Efficacy of a social problem-solving therapy approach for unipolar depression. *Journal of Consulting and Clinical Psychology, 54,* 196–202.
Nezu, A. M. (1986e). Negative life stress and anxiety: Problem solving as a moderator variable. *Psychological Reports, 58,* 279–283.
Nezu, A. M. (1987). A problem-solving formulation of depression: A literature review and proposal of a pluralistic model. *Clinical Psychology Review, 7,* 121–144.
Nezu, A. M., & Carnevale, G. J. (1987). Interpersonal problem solving and coping reactions of Vietnam veterans with posttraumatic stress disorder. *Journal of Abnormal Psychology, 96,* 155–157.
Nezu, A., & D'Zurilla, T. J. (1979). An experimental evaluation of the decision-making process in social problem solving. *Cognitive Therapy and Research, 3,* 269–277.
Nezu, A., & D'Zurilla, T. J. (1981a). Effects of problem definition and formulation on the generation of alternatives in the social problem-solving process. *Cognitive Therapy and Research, 5,* 265–271.
Nezu, A., & D'Zurilla, T. J. (1981b). Effects of problem definition and formulation on decision making in the social problem-solving process. *Behavior Therapy, 12,* 100–106.
Nezu, A. M., & Kalmar, K. (in press). Stressful life events, problem solving, and psycho-

logical distress among young adolescents: An exploratory investigation. *Journal of Child and Adolescent Psychotherapy.*

Nezu, A. M., Kalmar, K., Ronan, G. F., & Clavijo, A. (1986). Attributional correlates of depression: An interactional model including problem solving. *Behavior Therapy, 17,* 50–56.

Nezu, A. M., Nezu, C. M., & Blisset, S. E. (1988). Sense of humor as a moderator of stress: A prospective analysis. *Journal of Personality and Social Psychology.*

Nezu, A. M., Nezu, C. M., & Nezu, V. A. (1986). Depression, general distress, and causal attributions among university students. *Journal of Abnormal Psychology, 95,* 184–186.

Nezu, A. M., Nezu, C. M., & Perri, M. G. (1989). *Problem-solving therapy for depression: Theory, research and clinical guidelines.* New York: Wiley.

Nezu, A. M., Nezu, C. M., Saraydarian, L., Kalmar, K., & Ronan, G. F. (1986). Social problem solving as a moderating variable between negative life stress and depressive symptoms. *Cognitive Research and Therapy, 10,* 489–498.

Nezu, A. M., & Perri, M. G. (1987, November). *Problem-solving therapy for unipolar depression: An initial dismantling investigation.* Paper presented at the meeting of the Association for the Advancement of Behavior Therapy, Boston.

Nezu, A. M., Perri, M. G., & Nezu, C. M. (1987, August). *Validation of a problem-solving/stress model of depression.* Paper presented at the meeting of the American Psychological Association, New York City.

Nezu, A. M., Perri, M. G., Nezu, C. M., & Mahoney, D. J. (1987, November). *Social problem solving as a moderator of stressful events among clinically depressed individuals.* Paper presented at the meeting of the Association for the Advancement of Behavior Therapy, Boston.

Nezu, A. M., & Ronan, G. F. (1985). Life stress, current problems, problem solving, and depressive symptoms: An integrative model. *Journal of Consulting and Clinical Psychology, 53,* 693–697.

Nezu, A. M., & Ronan, G. F. (1987). Social problem solving and depression: Deficits in generating alternatives and decision making. *Southern Psychologist, 3,* 29–34.

Nezu, A. M., & Ronan, G. F. (1988). Stressful life events, problem solving, and depressive symptoms among university students: A prospective analysis. *Journal of Counseling Psychology, 35,* 134–138.

Platt, J. J., & Spivack, G. (1975). *Manual for the Means-End Problem-Solving Procedure (MEPS): A measure of interpersonal cognitive problem-solving skills.* Philadelphia: Hahnemann Community Mental Health/Mental Retardation Center.

Rabkin, J. G. (1982). Stress and psychiatric disorders. In L. Goldberger & S. Breznitz (Eds.), *Handbook of stress: Theoretical and clinical aspects.* New York: Free Press.

Rosenhan, R. H., & Chesney, M. A. (1982). Stress, Type A Behavior, and coronary heart disease. In L. Goldberger & S. Breznitz (Eds.), *Handbook of stress: Theoretical and clinical aspects.* New York: Free Press.

Sacco, W. P., & Graves, D. J. (1984). Childhood depression, interpersonal problem solving, and self-ratings of performance. *Journal of Clinical Child Psychology, 13,* 10–15.

Sackheim, H. A., & Weber, S. L. (1982). Functional brain asymmetry in the regulation of emotion: Implications for bodily manifestations of stress. In L. Goldberger & S. Breznitz (Eds.), *Handbook of stress: Theoretical and clinical aspects.* New York: Free Press.

Schildkraut, J. J. (1974). Biogenic amines and affective disorders. *Annual Review of Medicine, 25,* 338–348.

Schwartz, G. E., & Weinberger, D. A. (1980). Patterns of emotional responses to affective situations: Relations among happiness, sadness, anger, fear, depression, and anxiety. *Motivation and Emotion, 4,* 175–191.

Seyle, H. (1983). The stress concept: Past, present, and future. In C. L. Cooper (Ed.), *Stress research: Issues for the eighties.* New York: Wiley.

Spielberger, C. D. (1972). Anxiety as an emotional state. In C. D. Spielberger (Ed.), *Anxiety: Current trends in theory and research* (Vol. 1). New York: Academic Press.

Spielberger, C. D., Gorusch, R. L., & Luschene, L. E. (1970). *Manual for the State-Trait Anxiety Inventory.* Palo Alto, CA: Consulting Psychologists.

Spielberger, C. D., Gorusch, R. L., Luschene, L. E., Vagg, P. R., & Jacobs, G. A. (1983). *Manual for the State-Trait Anxiety Inventory.* Palo Alto, CA: Consulting Psychologists.

Spitzer, R. L., Endicott, J., & Robins, E. (1978). Research Diagnostic Criteria: Rationale and reliability. *Archives of General Psychiatry, 36,* 773–782.

Thase, M. E., Frank, E., & Kupfer, D. J. (1985). Biological processes in major depression. In E. E. Beckham & W. R. Leber (Eds.), *Handbook of depression: Treatment, assessment, and research.* Homewood, IL: Dorsey Press.

Thierry, A. M., Blanc, G., & Glowinski, J. (1971). Effect of stress on the disposition of catecholamines localized in various intraneuronal storage forms in the brain stem of the rat. *Journal of Neurochemistry, 18,* 449–461.

Weinberger, M., Hiner, S. L., & Tierney, W. M. (1987). In support of hassles as a measure of stress in predicting health outcomes. *Journal of Behavioral Medicine, 10,* 19–31.

Weiss, J. M., Glazer, H. I., & Pohorecky, L. A. (1976). Coping behavior and neurochemical changes: An alternative explanation for the original "learned helplessness" experiments. In G. Serban & A. Kling (Eds.), *Animal models in human psychobiology.* New York: Plenum.

Zemore, R., & Dell, L. W. (1983). Interpersonal problem-solving skills and depression-proneness. *Personality and Social Psychology Bulletin, 9,* 231–235.

An Epidemiological Perspective on the Anxiety and Depressive Disorders

Carolyn L. Williams
James Poling

I. Introduction

Epidemiological research on mental disorders has undergone a major shift in recent years, away from prevalence studies of general psychological distress, to the study of both incidence and prevalence of specific mental disorders. Thus, epidemiology is becoming much more relevant to diagnosticians, researchers, and practicing clinicians alike, and current methods increase the likelihood of discovering risk factors associated with mental disorders (Weissman, 1987a). Epidemiology is the study of the distribution of diseases or physiological conditions in human populations and of the factors influencing that distribution (Lilienfeld & Lilienfeld, 1980). Epidemiologists are particularly in-

Note: The authors are grateful for the editorial comments of Mary Alice Schumacher of the Division of Epidemiology, University of Minnesota.

terested in the associations between diseases and time, place, and person; their eventual goal is to discover the causes of a disease in order to prevent it. The detection of potential causes is based on observational and descriptive procedures in clearly defined population groups, whereas prevention is demonstrated through preventive trials, or, in other words, randomized controlled experiments (Earls, 1987).

For anyone who doubts the relevance of epidemiology to important clinical issues in anxiety and depression, consider the changes made in the diagnostic system in the recently revised third edition of the *Diagnostic and Statistical Manual of Mental Disorders* (DSM-III-R; American Psychiatric Association, 1987). In the preceding DSM-III, many diagnoses, notably for the affective and anxiety disorders, were hierarchically organized with higher level disorders superseding lower ones (American Psychiatric Association, 1980). Thus, a patient diagnosed as having a major depression could not be diagnosed as having a panic disorder, even with all its symptoms. Because panic disorder was considered lower in the hierarchy than major depression, if its symptoms occurred with major depression, they were considered associated with the depression and not of diagnostic significance (American Psychiatric Association, 1980). However, findings from studies using epidemiological measures such as odds ratios (Boyd et al., 1984; see Table 11.1 for definition), as well as family studies (e.g., Leckman, Merikangas, Pauls, Prusoff, & Weissman, 1983; Weissman, 1985), failed to support this diagnostic practice and led to its elimination in the DSM-III-R (J. B. W. Williams, 1987).

Epidemiology provides data to help answer questions such as the distinctive and overlapping features of the anxiety and depressive disorders. Specifically, epidemiological research can tell us if anxiety and depression occur together (or are distributed similarly) in the population, have common risk factors, and respond to the same preventive efforts. However, determining this information is complicated by methodological issues that have not been completely resolved. Thus, before we attempt to summarize the relevant research on anxiety and depression, we will provide an overview of epidemiological concepts that apply to mental disorders and a discussion of methodological questions vital to interpreting the relevant results.

II. Overview of the Epidemiology of Mental Disorders

A. Concepts and Types of Studies

In order to interpret findings from epidemiological studies of anxiety and depression, a number of key concepts must be defined. Table 11.1

Table 11.1
Definitions of Epidemiological Terms[a]

Term	Definition
Case	An individual from a specific population who presents a specific disease, symptom, or abnormal test result. *Examples*—(1) An individual, selected randomly from the general population of a specified area during a specified time, with panic disorder as determined by a structured interview using DSM-III criteria; and (2) a woman, attending one of several primary care clinics during a 5-year period, who gives birth to a live infant and who receives a psychiatric diagnosis of major depressive episode according to DSM-III criteria within 6 months of the birth.
Population at risk	The reference group of individuals who could be affected by the condition being investigated. *Examples*—(1) Al individuals living in the same specified geographical area at the same time as the cases; and (2) all women of childbearing ages attending the same primary care clinics during the same time period as the cases.
Risk factor	A variable associated with an increased probability of the presence or future development of a particular disorder. *Examples*—(1) Autonomic nervous system dysfunction has been suggested as a risk factor for panic disorder; and (2) postpartum period is a risk factor for major depressive episode.
Incidence	The number of new cases of a disorder occurring in a general population during a specified period of time (e.g., 1 year) divided by the population at risk. Only incidence rates can be used to study etiological factors. Assessment at two points in time or a longitudinal study design is necessary to determine incidence data and, thus, etiological associations, for most mental disorders.
Prevalence	The ratio of both new and old cases in a population for a specified period of time (e.g., 6 months, known as the period prevalence and in contrast with point prevalence, which refers to the number of cases at a specified moment in time) divided by the population at risk. Most morbidity data for mental disorders are prevalence estimates (also known as rates), which limits the search for etiological factors.
Lifetime prevalence	The total number of individuals known to have had the disease or disorder for at least part of their

(*continued*)

Table 11.1
(*Continued*)

Term	Definition
	lives. It is used to estimate the lifetime risk of acquiring a disorder.
Morbid risk	The risk of ever experiencing a given disorder; in other words, a person's lifetime risk.
Relative risk	A basic epidemiologic measure of excess disease risk due to an exposure. The concepts of disease and exposure are general: disease may stand for any outcome, and exposure for any potential precursor of the outcome. Relative risk is computed as the probability of disease (incidence) among exposed people divided by the probability of disease among nonexposed people.
Odds ratio	A widely used measure in chronic disease epidemiology for estimating relative risk in circumstances when incidence data are unavailable, as in case–control studies (Table 11.2). The probabilities used to calculate relative risk can not be made in case–control studies because sampling is based on case–control status, rather than on exposed–nonexposed status. In case–control studies, the odds ratio can closely approximate relative risk if (1) the frequency of the disorder of interest in the population at risk is small (less than 10%) and (2) the study cases are representative of the cases in the population at risk and the controls are representative of the noncases in the population at risk. The odds of disease are the probability of disease divided by the probability of no disease, and the odds ratio is the odds among exposed people divided by the odds among nonexposed people.
Berksonian fallacy	The spurious association that can be observed in cases drawn from hospital settings between diseases or between a risk factor and a disease. These misleading associations occur because of the different probabilities of admission to a hospital for those with the disease, without the disease, and with the risk factor of interest. It has also been described as the clinician's illusion.
Genetic epidemiology	An emerging discipline concerned with the causes, distribution, and control of diseases in relatives of cases, including both biological and cultural factors.

[a] From Boyd & Weissman (1982); Boyd et al. (1984); Last (1983); Lilienfeld & Lilienfeld (1980); Morton & Chung (1978); Von Korff, Eaton, & Keyl (1985); Weissman (1985; 1987b).

Table 11.2
Epidemiological Study Designs[a]

Type and purpose of study	Design
Descriptive: Estimate frequency of a disorder and generate hypothesis	*Cross-sectional* (surveys and prevalence studies): estimate disease frequency and variations by person, place, and time in a sample from a reference population at one point in time
	Cohort (follow-up, incidence, or prospective studies): follow a sample over time and observe development of new disorders or recurrence of new episodes
Analytic: Identify risk factors and estimate their effect; test hypothesis	*Case–control* (retrospective): compare samples with particular disorders (cases) to samples who are similar to the cases with respect to the factors of interest, but without the disorders (controls)
Experimental: Manipulate a factor, by experiments of nature or by the investigators, and observe the effect	*Natural experiments*: study outome of experiments of nature (floods, nuclear accidents, fires, etc.) to determine their effects
	Laboratory experiments: estimate acute responses and their effect on components of the disorder
	Clinical trials: test the efficacy of treatment in the prevention of the disorder (prophylactic) or in the reduction of the disorder (therapeutic)
	Community interventions: test the efficacy of an intervention at the community level to modify a risk factor

[a] Reprinted with permission from Weissman (1987b, p. 579).

presents these terms, their definitions, and some examples relating to anxiety and depression.

Although many epidemiological study designs and procedures are familiar to behavioral scientists, some are known by different names and have methodological differences. Table 11.2, taken from Weissman (1987b), describes the types of epidemiological designs and their purposes.

B. Historical Background

Epidemiology is an eclectic discipline and its successes in preventing infectious diseases are noteworthy. It was established in the nineteenth century as a distinct discipline (Lilienfeld & Lilienfeld, 1980), and its initial emphasis on associating disease with place of origin is demonstrated by John Snow's tracing of the cause of cholera to a geographically defined water supply in London in the 1850s. Snow removed the handle from the Broad Street pump, thus ending a deadly outbreak of cholera.

Mental disorders drew the interest of several pioneer epidemiologists, including Edward Jarvis. Among his accomplishments were co-founding the American Public Health Association, acting as third president of the American Statistical Association, and reorganizing the eighth United States census (1860) so it could be used by epidemiologists and biometricians (Lilienfeld & Lilienfeld, 1980). Jarvis' (1855) study of "idiocy" and "insanity" in Massachusetts is a landmark in the epidemiology of mental disorders.

Another early epidemiological success in the study of mental disorders occurred when Goldberger demonstrated that pellagra was not an infectious disease, as was widely believed in the early twentieth century, but due to a deficiency of nicotinic acid or the absence of milk and eggs in the diet (Earls, 1987; Lilienfeld & Lilienfeld, 1980). Pellagra, which was eliminated with improved diet, accounted for a significant portion of persons institutionalized for mental disorders at that time, particularly in the southern United States.

Successes in studies of infectious diseases and nutritional disorders led to an application of epidemiological techniques to chronic diseases such as cancer and cardiovascular disease. However, epidemiological concepts and procedures developed for the infectious diseases are not always directly applicable to chronic disorders (Weissman, 1987b). Because chronic diseases are likely to have multiple etiologies, classic measures of infectious disease epidemiology (e.g., the length of time between exposure and disease onset, the study of the shape of epidemic curves) are not useful (Cassel, 1964). Chronic diseases develop slowly, causative factors may act over long periods of time, rates may change slowly over time, and precise onset is difficult to determine (Weissman, 1987b).

Fortunately, though, epidemiological methods have led to breakthroughs in some of the chronic diseases. For example, risk factors (Table 11.1) for cardiovascular disease (e.g., smoking, high cholesterol, high blood pressure) have been identified and demonstrated to be amenable to change or intervention. This has led to a reduction of mortality from cardiovascular disease, even without a comparable understanding of the underlying etiological mechanisms. These successes also may account for a renewed interest in the epidemiology of mental disorders, which best fits the chronic disease, rather than infectious disease, epidemiological model.

III. Concerns Relevant to Mental Disorders

Three issues are of particular relevance to the epidemiology of mental disorders: case definition, obtaining a representative sample of cases with rare disorders, and determining the onset of the disorder (Bromet, 1987). These must be considered when reviewing epidemiological research of anxiety and depression. How these issues are handled accounts for many of the differences in findings across studies.

A. Case Definition

In the first generation of studies (those conducted before World War II), researchers such as Jarvis, in nineteenth century Massachusetts, found prevalence rates (Table 11.1) around 3.6% for all mental disorders. However, the second generation of studies (those conducted after World War II through the 1970s) found prevalence rates around 20% for all disorders (Dohrenwend & Dohrenwend, 1982), a finding that is consistent with third-generation rates from the 1980s (e.g., Myers et al., 1984).

These three generations of research used different data collection methods, which obviously would account for some of the discrepancies in their findings. But, according to an analysis by Dohrenwend and Dohrenwend (1982), the main reason for the difference in prevalence was the substantial change in nomenclature, or case definition. What constituted a case (Table 11.1) of mental disorder was greatly broadened after World War II. Jarvis (1855) counted cases of "insanity and idiocy" for his prevalence estimates. Using today's nomenclature, Jarvis (1855) defined as cases only those individuals with psychotic disorders or moderate to profound mental retardation (he likely missed some highly functioning moderately retarded individuals). Because most individuals with anxiety and depressive disorders were not included as cases, first-generation studies tell us little about these two disorders.

The second-generation studies are more relevant to questions about anxiety and depression, since these conditions now were defined as mental disorders. However, problems in reliably classifying individuals, as well as the cost of this research, led many epidemiological researchers of this generation to rely on self-report instruments that purportedly measured such things as mental health, mental illness, psychiatric disorders, and emotional adjustment, rather than grouping individuals into distinct diagnostic categories. These instruments did not cover all symptoms of psychopathology, a fact that limits their ability to describe accurately the whole range of mental disorders. The scales consisted mostly of items assessing psychophysiological symptoms and some of the symptoms of depression and anxiety.

Although these scales contain items that are symptoms of anxiety and depression, it is important to distinguish between having some symptoms of a disorder and actually meeting the diagnostic criteria for the disorder. Dohrenwend and colleagues (Dohrenwend & Dohrenwend, 1982; Link & Dohrenwend, 1980) have examined the validity of these instruments, concluding that they actually measure a concept best labeled "demoralization," rather than mental disorders or mental illness. Demoralization frequently converges with diagnosable mental disorders, but it occurs at least as often in their absence. Demoralization is similar to a fever: when temperature is high, something is wrong, yet further assessment is necessary to determine the specific problem (Dohrenwend & Dohrenwend, 1982; Link & Dohrenwend, 1980).

Because many second-generation studies use instruments that include symptoms of anxiety and depression, some of their findings may provide hypotheses about the anxiety and depressive disorders. One fairly consistent finding across studies is a preponderance of women identified as cases. These data can lead to a false conclusion that mental illness is more common in women. A more reasonable hypothesis is that demoralization, and possibly the anxiety and depressive disorders, are more frequent in women, a supposition that is confirmed in third-generation work (e.g., Myers et al., 1984). One could generate other hypotheses about anxiety and depression from studies employing these self-report instruments, but it seems more reasonable to turn our attention to studies that identified as cases those who met specific diagnostic criteria for the anxiety and depressive disorders, rather than those who had some symptoms of the disorders and/or possibly other problems.

Some second-generation epidemiological investigators used other sources of information, rather than global assessment instruments. These researchers tended to work in England and other European countries, while Americans primarily relied on the previously described self-report inventories. European methods included clinical interviews by psychiatrists; obtaining information from relatives, physicians, and other key informants; and abstracting hospital and other public records. Consensus decisions about a subject's global psychiatric status were made by a panel of psychiatrists, using all the available information about an individual. Difficulties with this approach included the variability and quality of the available information across subjects in a study, as well as questions about whether diagnostic rules were applied uniformly within studies, and whether the procedures and diagnostic rules were comparable across studies (Robins et al., 1985). What is particularly troublesome for those interested in anxiety and depression is the lack of an internationally accepted definition of these disorders (Angst & Dobler-Mikola, 1985).

B. Obtaining a Representative Sample of Cases

A second methodological issue is how to obtain a representative sample of cases of anxiety and depression. On this question, there is some disagreement among epidemiological and clinical researchers. The epidemiologist recognizes the limitations of looking exclusively at cases already in treatment and attempting to generalize to all cases of the disorder. The Berksonian fallacy (Table 11.1) has long been recognized by epidemiologists as a major methodological problem when using hospital cases as samples.

Recent studies demonstrate that the Berksonian fallacy operates for psychiatric illness as well. Black, Winokur, and Nasrallah (1987) report that patients with affective disorders are probably referred for hospitalization more frequently if they also have a complicating physical disorder. Their findings indicate that complicating physical disorders, rather than psychiatric illness, account for the excessive natural deaths in these patients.

Cohen and Cohen (1984) provide a further description of the Berksonian fallacy, as applied to mental disorders, in what they call the "clinician's illusion" (i.e., falsely generalizing findings about the characteristics and course of a disorder, from a sample of patients who currently are in treatment, to the entire population contracting the illness). Samples of patients in psychiatric treatment more likely will contain cases of long duration compared to general population samples. Furthermore, most cases of mental disorders never receive treatment in the specialty mental health sector (Regier, Goldberg, & Taube, 1978; Shapiro et al., 1984; Weissman, 1987c). Shapiro and colleagues (1984) found that only 16–19% of individuals with affective disorders and 7–15% of individuals with anxiety/somatoform disorders visited a mental health specialist in a 6-month period. Those who visited a mental health specialist were more likely to have another DSM-III disorder than were those who went to a general medical provider (Shapiro et al., 1984). Diseases are more likely to covary in clinical samples because individuals with more than one disorder are more prone to seek treatment. Cases of anxiety and depression already receiving treatment in the mental health sector are a nonrepresentative subsample of all cases of the disorders, quite probably the most severe cases. Therefore, questions about the overlap between the anxiety and depressive disorders are best addressed using community-drawn samples, rather than clinical samples.

C. Determining Time of Onset

As is the case for other chronic diseases, time of onset is a crucial but difficult determination. At what point does an individual go from having one or several symptoms of a disorder to having (or meeting the diagnostic criteria for) the actual disorder? Is there a continuum of symptoms leading to disorder? Are self-reported symptoms preclinical or subclinical manifestations of disorder and thus risk factors for the disorder (Kaplan, Roberts, Camacho, & Coyne, 1987)? These are all questions that must be resolved by future work in this area. For the purposes of our discussion, we will concentrate on studies that meet DSM-III or DSM-III-R onset criteria.

Based on the issues described above, the greatest confidence should be given to findings coming from studies using specific diagnostic criteria for case definition, having a representative sample (community drawn) of all cases of anxiety and depression, and meeting specified onset criteria like those described in the DSM-III or DSM-III-R. These requirements are more likely to be met in studies from the third generation of research, primarily reported during the 1980s. A large number of these studies are from the National Institute of Mental Health's (NIMH) Epidemiological Catchment Area (ECA) program of research. The ECA is a university-based multisite (Baltimore, Johns Hopkins; Durham, Duke; Los Angeles, UCLA; New Haven, Yale; and St. Louis, Washington University) epidemiological project designed to determine incidence and prevalence for major DSM-III diagnoses, the use of health and mental health services by persons with these disorders, and risk factors for the disorders (Regier et al., 1984). All five sites used the same diagnostic instrument, a structured lay interview called the Diagnostic Interview Schedule (DIS), surveying over 18,000 adults selected from probability samples of noninstitutionalized persons. Longitudinal samples (collected over a 1-year period) and institutional samples also have been collected as part of the ECA (Weissman, 1987c).

IV. Distribution of Anxiety and Depressive Disorders

Incidence and prevalence should give us answers about any overlap in the anxiety and depressive disorders, by indicating if the two disorders are distributed similarly in the general population. Unfortunately, because of the issues described above, particularly those of case definition, unequivocal conclusions are elusive. Reviewers must describe broad categories when summarizing findings about these disorders, since there is so little agreement about more specific diagnoses. For example, Goodwin and Guze (1984) suggest that the important distinction is between primary and secondary affective disorders.

Primary affective disorder occurs in individuals with no psychiatric disorder other than mania or depression. Secondary affective disorder occurs in patients with a preexisting psychiatric illness other than mania or depression. The anxiety disorders occur commonly in those with secondary affective disorder, but other disorders, such as alcoholism, are also common. Distinguishing between a primary affective disorder and an anxiety neurosis is quite difficult because of the considerable symptom overlap in the two disorders (Goodwin & Guze, 1984). Chronology is usually the deciding factor: if anxiety symptoms predominate at first, then that is the diagnosis and vice versa. From their summary of epidemiological studies, Goodwin and Guze (1984) conclude that both the affective and anxiety disorders are among the most prevalent mental disorders in the population.

Boyd and Weissman (1981, 1982) classified studies of the affective disorders into those that provide rates for depressive symptoms, bipolar disorder, and nonbipolar disorders. They chose these categories because of international research supporting the existence of individuals with symptoms of depression not severe enough to warrant a clinical diagnosis, the fairly strong agreement on the classification of bipolar disorder (defined as one or more episodes of mania, whether or not the patient has had a depressive episode), and the relative lack of consensus on how to define or subdivide the nonbipolar disorders. Although Boyd and Weissman (1981, 1982) presented incidence, point prevalence, and lifetime prevalence (see Table 11.1 for definitions of these terms) for these classifications, unfortunately, for our purposes, comorbidity data for the anxiety disorders were not presented.

Studies from the ECA provide prevalence estimates for specific mental disorders using DSM-III criteria (with the exception of the exclusionary rules—no diagnoses are excluded) and using the DIS. Table 11.3 presents lifetime prevalence for the anxiety and affective disorders and any DIS disorder from four ECA sites reported by Karno and colleagues (1987). Data are not available currently for generalized anxiety disorder or posttraumatic stress disorder.

The ECA lifetime prevalence estimates indicate that both the anxiety and the depressive disorders occur frequently in the general population, with the anxiety disorders being the most prevalent of all conditions.

Table 11.3
ECA Lifetime Prevalence of Anxiety, Depression, and Any DIS Disorders[a,b]

Disorder	Los Angeles (n = 3125)	New Haven (n = 5034)	Baltimore (n = 3481)	St. Louis (n = 3004)
Affective disorders	8.9 (0.6)	10.0 (0.6)	6.5 (0.5)	8.1 (0.7)
Manic episode	0.5 (0.1)	1.3 (0.2)	0.7 (0.2)	1.1 (0.3)
Major depressive episode	6.4 (0.5)	7.2 (0.6)	4.0 (0.3)	5.6 (0.6)
Dysthymia	4.2 (0.4)	3.2 (0.3)	2.2 (0.3)	3.9 (0.5)
Anxiety disorders	13.5 (0.7)	10.5 (0.7)	25.1 (0.8)	11.2 (0.7)
Phobia	11.7 (0.6)	7.9 (0.6)	23.1 (0.8)	9.5 (0.6)
Panic disorder	1.5 (0.3)	1.5 (0.2)	1.5 (0.2)	1.6 (0.3)
Obsessive–compulsive disorder	2.1 (0.3)	2.7 (0.4)	3.1 (0.4)	1.9 (0.3)
Any DIS disorder	33.2 (1.0)	29.9 (1.0)	39.6 (0.9)	32.0 (1.2)

[a] Rates are based on the Diagnostic Interview Schedule (DIS), adjusted for gender and age, and expressed in percentages. Numbers in parentheses are standard errors.
[b] From Karno et al. (1987).

However, one must remember that ECA findings are contingent on the validity of the DIS. Parker (1987) recently questioned whether the lifetime prevalence rates generated by the DIS were accurate, suggesting reasons they may be suspect, including disagreement with the findings from previous studies. Parker (1987) described the difficulties in establishing the validity of the DIS and the poor agreement between lay interviewer-generated DIS diagnoses and psychiatric judgments, particularly for major depressive episode. He suggested that the validity of the DIS as a measure of lifetime psychiatric morbidity remains to be established. ECA researchers also recommend caution when interpreting their lifetime prevalence estimates until methodological issues are resolved (Regier, 1986).

Table 11.4 presents the 6-month prevalence of anxiety and depressive disorders currently available from the ECA (Burnam et al., 1987). Again, these rates indicate that the anxiety disorders are the most prevalent disorders in the general population, with the depressive disorders also being quite common. Rates vary across sites for some of the disorders, notably the phobias (i.e., ranging from 6.0 to 13.7). The rates also suggest that the disorders are heterogeneous and may contain some overlap. Information about comorbidity is of central concern to questions raised in this book, and needs to be addressed in future ECA studies.

A European study investigated the comorbidity of these disorders in

Table 11.4
ECA Six-Month Prevalence of Anxiety, Depression, and Any DIS Disorders[a,b]

Disorder	Los Angeles (n = 3125)	New Haven (n = 5034)	Baltimore (n = 3481)	St. Louis (n = 3004)	Piedmont, NC (n = 3921)
Affective disorder[c]	6.2 (0.5)	6.8 (0.5)	4.8 (0.4)	6.3 (0.6)	4.0 (0.3)
Manic episode	0.2 (0.1)	0.9 (0.2)	0.5 (0.1)	0.7 (0.2)	0.2 (0.1)
Major depressive episode	3.1 (0.3)	3.7 (0.4)	2.3 (0.3)	3.2 (0.5)	2.0 (0.3)
Anxiety/somatoform disorder	7.2 (0.5)	7.4 (0.6)	14.8 (0.8)	6.6 (0.6)	14.8 (0.9)
Phobia	6.3 (0.4)	6.0 (0.5)	13.2 (0.7)	5.5 (0.5)	13.7 (0.9)
Panic	0.9 (0.2)	0.6 (0.2)	1.0 (0.2)	0.9 (0.2)	0.7 (0.2)
Obsessive–compulsive disorder	0.7 (0.2)	1.5 (0.3)	2.1 (0.3)	1.3 (0.3)	2.2 (0.4)
Somatization	0.0 (0.0)	0.1 (0.1)	0.1 (0.1)	0.1 (0.1)	0.4 (0.1)
Any DIS disorder[c]	18.6 (0.8)	19.1 (0.8)	24.2 (1.0)	17.2 (1.0)	23.1 (1.0)

[a] Rates are based on the Diagnostic Interview Schedule (DIS) and are expressed per 100 persons, adjusted for gender and age. Numbers in parentheses are standard errors.
[b] From Burnam et al. (1987).
[c] Includes dysthymia.

a general population sample of 456 young adults (Angst & Dobler-Mikola, 1985). The investigators used diagnostic criteria from several systems, including the DSM-III, and classified cases of depression as major or minor. They found a 1-year prevalence of 7.0% for major depression, 4.4% for minor depression, and 8.9% for the anxiety disorders. Major depression overlapped with 36% of the cases of anxiety disorder, and minor depression overlapped with 60% of the cases of anxiety disorders. The anxiety disorders overlapped with 28% of the cases of major depression and 21% of the cases of minor depression. Symptom overlap was great, even in the nonoverlapping cases. The overlapping cases were more severely disturbed than those with single disorders. These results are suggestive of a continuum of anxiety and depressive disorders, with cases having both disorders being the most severely affected. However, the youth of this sample (i.e., 22 to 23 years) must be considered, as the disorders may progress and become more distinct as the subjects age.

V. Risk Factors for Anxiety and Depressive Disorders

Epidemiologists are concerned not only with incidence and prevalence derived from descriptive studies, but also with risk factors, typically identified through analytic studies using a case control design (Table 11.2). A number of potential risk factors have been studied for the mental disorders, including anxiety and depression. This section will summarize findings from risk factor studies for these two disorders, with the goal of determining if they share similar risk factors. In doing so, we will indicate whether we are describing risk factors for symptoms or diagnosed disorders.

A. Gender

Being female carries with it a greater risk for both depressive symptoms and disorders, across a number of studies with differing methodologies (Boyd & Weissman, 1982; Hirschfeld & Cross, 1982; Kovess, Murphy, & Tousignant, 1987; Weissman, 1987c). Roughly twice as many women as men have nonbipolar depressive disorders in industrialized countries, and this female-to-male ratio decreases slightly with bipolar disorder (Boyd & Weissman, 1982). Because it is found in population studies, this gender difference is real and not simply due to help-seeking behavior or reporting bias.

Less information is available for the anxiety disorders, yet there appears to be a preponderance of females with these disorders as well. Weissman (1985) and Von Korff, Eaton, and Keyl (1985) report ECA data indicating that panic disorder and simple panic attacks are more common in women than men. Obsessive–compulsive disorder and agoraphobia also occur more frequently in women (Weissman, 1985). In fact, the rates for agoraphobia are 2 to 4 times higher in females (Weissman, 1985); these rates are consistent with Dobson's report (1985) that the anxiety neuroses averaged 2.17 times higher for women than men. ECA data concerning generalized anxiety disorder and posttraumatic stress disorder are not yet available. As in all ECA studies, Von Korff and colleagues' study (1985) did not use the DSM-III exclusionary criteria for the anxiety disorders (e.g., they did not exclude a diagnosis of panic disorder if a subject had major depression, schizophrenia, somatization disorder, or agoraphobia).

B. Age

Findings of age differences for both depressive symptoms and bipolar disorder are inconsistent. Boyd and Weissman's (1982) earlier review indicated that both incidence and prevalence of nonbipolar depression reach a peak in women from 35 to 45, with another possible increase after age 55. They suggest that the evidence for men is less clear, but their rates apparently increase with age. However, Hirschfeld and Cross (1982) conclude that both depressive symptoms and syndromes are more prevalent at younger ages and Weissman (1987c) reports ECA findings that major depression is most prevalent in young persons (18 to 44 years), particularly ages 25 to 34. ECA data for panic disorder, obsessive–compulsive disorder, and agoraphobia showed no strong relationship with age (Weissman, 1985), except in Von Korff and colleagues' (1985) report of a decrease in panic attacks across three levels of severity (from symptoms to disorder) for persons 65 years and older.

C. Social Class

No consistent pattern of social class differences has been demonstrated for the nonbipolar disorders, although studies suggest an inverse relationship between social class and depressive symptoms and an increase in bipolar disorder in upper socioeconomic classes (Boyd & Weissman, 1982; Hirschfeld & Cross, 1982). Again, less information is available for the anxiety disorders, although educational level (one component of social class) was reported unrelated to panic disorder or obsessive–compulsive disorder (Weissman, 1985). On the other hand, agoraphobia occurred twice as often in less educated persons (Weissman, 1985).

Findings are inconsistent, however, with Von Korff et al. (1985) reporting highly variable prevalence rates by educational level for panic attacks and disorder, with a tendency for persons with less than a high school education to have higher rates.

D. Marital Status

Research on this risk factor demonstrates the need to study males and females separately, as there appears to be an interaction effect. One must also consider that divorce or marital separation may be an outcome of the disorder, rather than a risk factor. With those caveats in mind, it appears that depressive symptoms and disorders are more common in the divorced and separated (Hirschfeld & Cross, 1982; Kovess et al., 1987; Weissman, 1987c). Absence of a satisfying intimate heterosexual relationship has been shown to be a risk factor for depressive disorders (Boyd & Weissman, 1982), as is being in an unhappy marriage (Weissman, 1987c). Von Korff and colleagues (1985) also found a strong association between marital status and prevalence of panic attacks across three levels of severity. Separated and divorced individuals had substantially higher rates than the married.

E. Race/Ethnicity

A number of variables have to be controlled when studying race or ethnicity as a risk factor. Social class, gender, and accessibility of treatment for nonwhites, for example, must all be considered. Generally, when these variables are controlled, few racial or ethnic differences are found for either the anxiety or depressive disorders (Boyd & Weissman, 1982; Hirschfeld & Cross, 1982; Von Korff et al., 1985; Weissman, 1985, 1987c). ECA data from Los Angeles comparing Mexican-Americans and non-Hispanic whites showed relatively few ethnic differences for the anxiety and depressive disorders. However, older (>40 years) Mexican-American women had the highest 6-month prevalence rate of current phobia. These older Mexican-American women also had a slightly, but not significantly, higher rate of major depression (Burnam et al., 1987). Non-Hispanic whites reported more lifetime prevalence of major depression than did Mexican-Americans in Los Angeles (Karno et al., 1987).

F. Urban–Rural Residence

Urban environments have been suggested as risk factors for neurotic disorders such as anxiety and depression (Hirschfeld & Cross, 1982).

However, studies of this risk factor are quite limited and, if only treatment-facility cases are used, the confounding effects of limited accessibility and lower acceptability of treatment in rural areas are a major problem. Other variables (e.g., gender, age, race, education, and migration) also must be controlled. ECA data indicate that the prevalence of major depression is lower in rural areas, whereas the prevalence of dysthymia (a depressive disorder), obsessive–compulsive disorder, or agoraphobia (anxiety disorders) does not differ in urban and rural settings. However, these findings are from only one ECA site, North Carolina, and it is uncertain if they will generalize to other areas (Blazer et al., 1985). Although Kovess and colleagues (1987) confirmed the finding that rural residents have lower rates of depression than do urban residents, their study suggested that the broad classification into rural and urban environments should be refined, and that subgroups within those environments (e.g., the nonemployed or divorced) should be studied separately.

G. Family History

There is a growing evidence of a familial pattern for both the anxiety and depressive disorders (Weissman, 1985, 1987c). In fact, family studies using an epidemiological approach (sometimes referred to as "genetic epidemiology"; Table 11.1) provide some of the strongest support for overlap in anxiety and depressive disorders. The Yale family–genetic study investigated 215 probands (82 normals and 133 with major depression), 1331 of their adult first-degree relatives, and 194 of their children (ages 6–17). Diagnostic information was obtained from numerous sources: direct interview (40% of the total sample), medical records, and family history from multiple informants. Diagnostic estimates were then made by a panel of raters. The modified Research Diagnostic Criteria (Spitzer, Endicott, & Robins, 1977) was used for all probands and adult first-degree relatives. Diagnosis for the child sample was based on the DSM-III.

The results of the Yale study demonstrated that the first-degree relatives of probands with major depression plus an anxiety disorder were at a greater risk for major depression, as well as anxiety disorders, than were the relatives of depressed persons without an anxiety disorder (Leckman, Merikangas, Pauls, Prusoff, & Weissman, 1983). This risk remained higher even if the anxiety disorder and the major depressive episode occurred at different times.

The highest rates of psychiatric difficulties were found in the first-degree relatives of probands with major depression and panic disorder. These persons showed increased rates of major depression, anxiety disorders, and alcoholism in comparison with the relatives of both the normal and depressed-only probands. The relatives of probands with major depression and generalized anxiety disorder evidenced an increase in major depression when compared to relatives of normal and major depression-only probands (Leckman, Weissman, Merikangas, Pauls, & Prusoff, 1983).

The children of probands with depression, as compared to those of normal probands, were at increased risk of depression. The highest overall rate of impairment occurred in the children of probands having both depression and panic disorders. They were particularly susceptible to separation anxiety and major depression (Weissman, 1985). In her review of the Yale family–genetic study, Weissman (1985) concluded that (1) major depression and anxiety disorders probably are heterogeneous diagnostic categories and (2) panic disorder and major depression may have a common underlying diathesis.

H. Disasters and Other Catastrophic Events

Disasters, combat and war experiences, and refugee movements all have been associated with increased psychiatric symptoms and disorders, particularly anxiety and depression (e.g., Bromet & Schulberg, 1987; Dent, Tennant, & Goulston, 1987; Mangelsdorff, 1985; C. L. Williams & Westermeyer, 1986). The most common psychiatric diagnoses found in the aftermath of disasters are major depression, generalized anxiety disorder, and posttraumatic stress disorder (Bromet & Schulberg, 1987). Psychiatric casualties or combat stress reactions have been common throughout military history (Mangelsdorff, 1985). Similar findings were reported for refugee movements, which frequently involved catastrophic events, including death and torture. Across many different refugee groups, in different periods of time and with different researchers and methodologies, refugees were reported to have higher prevalence of depression and anxiety disorders than general population samples (C. L. Williams & Westermeyer, 1986).

I. Recent Stressful Life Events

Less catastrophic, more ordinary stressful life events (e.g., divorce, death of a family member, loss of a job) also have been suggested as risk factors for both the anxiety and the depressive disorders. These studies are reviewed elsewhere in this book and so will not be described in detail here. What is significant for this discussion is that life events characterized by loss experiences and an inability to control one's environment have been hypothesized as risk factors for both the anxiety (Raskin, Peeke, Dickman, & Pinsker, 1982; Von Korff et al., 1985) and the depressive disorders (Boyd & Weissman, 1982; Hirschfeld & Cross, 1982).

J. Negative Childhood Experiences

Although research is inconclusive about whether negative childhood experiences, such as early parental death or a disruptive, hostile home environment, are relevant factors, they have been hypothesized as risk factors for both anxiety and depression (Boyd & Weissman, 1982; Raskin et al., 1982; Von Korff et al., 1985).

VI. Preventive Efforts for Anxiety and Depressive Disorders

Results from clinical trials and community intervention could provide definitive answers to the questions about the overlap between anxiety and depression. If these experimental epidemiological studies indicated that the incidence of both disorders can be lowered by the same preventive interventions, then we would have further evidence of their similarity. The converse would suggest that the disorders are different. Unfortunately, such clinical trials and community interventions have not been conducted. In fact, Earls (1987) suggests that the research base for developing a preventive trial for the affective disorders is not strong. However, rates from the ECA and other epidemiological studies indicate a relatively high frequency of anxiety and depression in the general population, with a significant amount of suffering, making them, in our view, prime candidates for preventive efforts.

Because loss has been suggested as a risk factor for both disorders, recently bereaved individuals could be targeted for future clinical trials (Osterweis, Solomon, & Green, 1984). Programs for the recently bereaved should be evaluated not only for their potential to decrease symptoms of anxiety and depression, but also for their ability to reduce the incidence of these disorders in this at-risk population. Disaster victims, including combat veterans and refugees, are another at-risk population for these disorders, and crisis intervention is supported by the research data (Bromet & Schulberg, 1987; Mangelsdorff, 1985; C. L. Williams, in press).

VII. Summary and Conclusions

Epidemiological research indicates that the anxiety and depressive disorders are among the most frequent mental disorders in the community, and, that they share some common risk factors. Firm conclusions from epidemiology about the distinctive and overlapping features of these disorders are obstructed by methodological issues, primarily case definition. However, third-generation research, exemplified by the ECA program of NIMH, has made considerable progress toward more definitive answers.

There is epidemiological evidence of overlap in these disorders, particularly from information about their prevalence and comorbidity in community samples. The overlap is not 100%, as the variability in prevalence estimates in Tables 11.3 and 11.4 indicates. Both disorders share common risk factors, including the importance of family history; the preponderance of females; the association with marital separation, divorce, or lack of a satisfying relationship; the role of catastrophic life events; and the association with loss experiences and an inability to control one's environment. Because these findings indicate that similar populations are at risk for anxiety and depression (e.g., the recently bereaved or divorced, disaster victims, combat veterans, and refugees), they suggest possibilities for similar preventive trials for the two disorders.

However, given the current state of knowledge, epidemiology's greatest potential contribution toward answering the questions raised in this volume is in the area of methodology. Epidemiology outlines procedures that must be considered when addressing these questions. We have highlighted the importance of case definitions and of having representative samples of all cases, not just those drawn from clinical populations. Findings will vary depending upon whether one's definition includes actual disorders or merely symptoms of disorders.

The Berksonian fallacy, or clinician's illusion, describes the problems inherent in trying to generalize from a sample of patients to all persons with the disorder. Clinical samples can provide very important information about clinical populations, but should not be used to generalize about all persons with the disorder of interest or the natural course of the disorder. These methodological guidelines can be used to evaluate the findings from studies of anxiety and depression, as well as in designing future studies of these disorders.

References

American Psychiatric Association. (1980). *Diagnostic and statistical manual of mental disorders* (3rd ed.). Washington, DC: Author.

American Psychiatric Association. (1987). *Diagnostic and statistical manual of mental disorders* (3rd ed., rev.). Washington, DC: Author.

Angst, J., & Dobler-Mikola, A. (1985). The Zurich Study: VI. A continuum from depression to anxiety disorders? *European Archives of Psychiatry and Neurological Sciences, 235,* 179–186.

Black, D. W., Winokur, G., & Nasrallah, A. (1987). Is death from natural causes still excessive in psychiatric patients? A follow-up of 1593 patients with major affective disorder. *Journal of Nervous and Mental Disease, 175,* 674–680.

Blazer, D., George, L. K., Landerman, R., Pennybacker, M., Melville, M. L., Woodbury, M., Manton, K. G., Jordon, K., & Locke, B. (1985). Psychiatric disorders: A rural/urban comparison. *Archives of General Psychiatry, 42,* 651–656.

Boyd, J. H., Burke, J. D., Gruenberg, E., Holzer, C. E., Rae, D. S., George, L. K., Karno, M., Stoltzman, R., McEvoy, L., & Nestadt, G. (1984). Exclusion criteria of DSM-III: A study of co-occurrence of hierarchy-free syndromes. *Archives of General Psychiatry, 41,* 983–989.

Boyd, J. H., & Weissman, M. M. (1981). Epidemiology of affective disorders: A reexamination and future directions. *Archives of General Psychiatry, 38,* 1039–1046.

Boyd, J. H., & Weissman, M. M. (1982). Epidemiology. In E. Paykel (Ed.), *Handbook of affective disorders* (pp. 109–125). New York: Guilford Press.

Bromet, E. J. (1987, June). *Epidemiology of mental disorders.* Course presented at the 22nd Graduate Summer Session in Epidemiology, Minneapolis, MN.

Bromet, E. J., Schulberg, H.C. (1987). Epidemiologic findings from disaster research. In R. E. Hales & A. J. Frances (Eds.), *American Psychiatric Association Annual Review* (Vol. 6, pp. 676–689). Washington, DC: American Psychiatric Press.

Burnam, M. A., Hough, R. L., Escobar, J. I., Karno, M., Timbers, D. M., Telles, C. A., & Locke, B. Z. (1987). Six-month prevalence of specific psychiatric disorders among Mexican-Americans and non-Hispanic whites in Los Angeles. *Archives of General Psychiatry, 44,* 687–694.

Cassel, J. (1964). Social science theory as a source of hypotheses in epidemiological research. *American Journal of Public Health, 54,* 1482–1488.

Cohen, P., & Cohen, J. (1984). The clinician's illusion. *Archives of General Psychiatry, 41,* 1178–1182.

Dent, O. F., Tennant, C. C., & Goulston, K. J. (1987). Precursors of depression in World War II veterans 40 years after the war. *Journal of Nervous and Mental Disease, 175,* 486–490.

Dobson, K. S. (1985). The relationship between anxiety and depression. *Clinical Psychology Review, 5,* 307–324.

Dohrenwend, B. P., & Dohrenwend, B. S. (1982). Perspectives on the past and future of psychiatric epidemiology. *American Journal of Public Health, 72,* 1271–1279.

Earls, F. (1987). Toward the prevention of psychiatric disorders. In R. E. Hales & A. J. Frances (Eds.), *American Psychiatric Association Annual Review* (Vol. 6, pp. 664–675). Washington, DC: American Psychiatric Press.

Goodwin, D. W., & Guze, S. B. (1984). *Psychiatric disorders* (3rd ed.). New York: Oxford University Press.

Hirschfeld, R. M. A., & Cross, C. K. (1982). Epidemiology of affective disorders. *Archives of General Psychiatry, 39,* 35–46.

Jarvis, E. (1855). *Report on insanity and idiocy in Massachusetts by the Commission on Lunacy under resolve of the Legislature of 1854.* Boston: William White, Printer to the State.

Kaplan, G. A., Roberts, R. E., Camacho, T. C., & Coyne, J. C. (1987). Psychosocial predictors of depression: Prospective evidence from the Human Population Laboratory Studies. *American Journal of Epidemiology, 125,* 206–220.

Karno, M., Hough, R. L., Burnam, A., Excobar, J. I., Timbers, D. M., Santana, F., & Boyd, J. H. (1987). Lifetime prevalence of specific psychiatric disorders among Mexican-Americans and non-Hispanic whites in Los Angeles. *Archives of General Psychiatry, 44,* 695–701.

Kovess, V., Murphy, H. B. M., & Tousignant, M. (1987). Urban–rural comparisons of depressive disorders in French Canada. *Journal of Nervous and Mental Disease, 175,* 457–465.

Last, J. M. (Ed.). (1983). *A dictionary of epidemiology.* New York: Oxford University Press.

Leckman, J. F., Merikangas, K. R., Pauls, D. L., Prusoff, B. A., & Weissman, M. M. (1983). Anxiety disorders and depression: Contradictions between family study data and DSM-III conventions. *American Journal of Psychiatry, 140,* 880–882.

Leckman, J. F., Weissman, M. M., Merikangas, K. R., Pauls, D. L., & Prusoff, B. A. (1983). Panic disorder and major depression. *Archives of General Psychiatry, 40,* 1055–1060.

Lilienfeld, A. M., & Lilienfeld, D. E. (1980). *Foundations of epidemiology* (2nd ed.). New York: Oxford University Press.

Link, R., & Dohrenwend, B. P. (1980). Formulation of hypotheses about the ratio of untreated to treated cases in the true prevalence studies of functional psychiatric disorders in adults in the United States. In B. P. Dohrenwend, B. S. Dohrenwend, M. S. Gould, B. Link, R. Neugebauer, & R. Wunsch-Hitzig, (Eds.), *Mental illness in the United States: Epidemiological estimates.* New York: Praeger.

Mangelsdorff, A. D. (1985). Lessons learned and forgotten: The need for prevention and mental health interventions in disaster preparedness. *Journal of Community Psychology, 13,* 239–257.

Morton, N.E., & Chung, C. S. (Eds.). (1978). *Genetic epidemiology.* New York: Academic Press.

Myers, J. K., Weissman, M. M., Tischler, G. L., Holzer, C. E., Leaf, P. J., Orvaschel, H., Anthony, J. C., Boyd, J. H., Burke, J. D., Kramer, M., & Stoltzman, R. (1984). Six-month prevalence of psychiatric disorders in three communities. *Archives of General Psychiatry, 41,* 959–967.

Osterweis, M., Solomon, F., & Green, M. (Eds.). (1984). *Bereavement: Reactions, consequences, and care.* Washington, DC: National Academy Press.

Parker, G. (1987). Editorial: Are the lifetime prevalence estimates in the ECA study accurate? *Psychological Medicine, 17,* 275–282.

Raskin, M., Peeke, H. V. S., Dickman, W., & Pinsker, H. (1982). Panic and generalized anxiety disorders: Developmental antecedents and precipitants. *Archives of General Psychiatry, 39,* 687–689.

Regier, D. A. (1986). General discussion of chapter 4. In J. Barrett & R. M. Rose (Eds.), *Mental disorders in the community: Findings from psychiatric epidemiology* (p. 69). New York: Guilford Press.

Regier, D. A., Goldberg, I. D., & Taube, C. A. (1978). The de facto U.S. mental health services system: A public health perspective. *Archives of General Psychiatry, 35,* 685–693.

Regier, D. A., Myers, M., Kramer, L. N., Robins, L. N., Blazer, D. G., Hough, R. L., Eaton, W. W., & Locke, B. Z. (1984). The NIMH Epidemiologic Catchment Area Program. *Archives of General Psychiatry, 41,* 934–941.

Robins, L. N., Helzer, J. E., Orvaschel, H., Anthony, J. C., Blazer, D. G., Burnam, A., & Burke, J. D. (1985). The Diagnostic Interview Schedule. In W. W. Eaton & L. G. Kessler (Eds.), *Epidemiologic field methods in psychiatry* (pp. 143–170). Orlando, FL: Academic Press.

Shapiro, S., Skinner, E. A., Kessler, L. G., Von Korff, M., German, P. S., Tischler, G. L., Leaf, P. J., Benham, L., Cottler, L., & Regier, D. A. (1984). Utilization of health and mental health services. *Archives of General Psychiatry, 41,* 971–978.

Spitzer, R. L., Endicott, J., & Robins, E. (1977). *Research diagnostic criteria for a selected group of functional disorders* (3rd ed.). New York: New York State Psychiatric Institute, Biometrics Research Division.

Von Korff, M., Eaton, W., & Keyl, P. (1985). The epidemiology of panic attacks and disorder: Results from three community surveys. *American Journal of Epidemiology, 122,* 970–981.

Weissman, M. M. (1985). The epidemiology of anxiety disorders: Rates, risks, and familial patterns. In A. H. Tuma & J. D. Maser (Eds.), *Anxiety and the anxiety disorders* (pp. 275–296). Hillsdale, NJ: Erlbaum.

Weissman, M. M. (1987a). Psychiatric epidemiology: Foreward. In R. E. Hales & A. J. Frances (Eds.), *American Psychiatric Association Annual Review* (Vol. 6, pp. 572–573). American Psychiatric Press.

Weissman, M. M. (1987b). Epidemiology overview. In R. E. Hales & A. J. Frances (Eds.), *American Psychiatric Association Annual Review* (Vol. 6, pp. 574–588). Washington, DC: American Psychiatric Press.

Weissman, M. M. (1987c). Advances in psychiatric epidemiology: Rates and risks for major depression. *American Journal of Public Health, 77,* 445–451.

Williams, C. L. (1989). Prevention programs for refugees: An interface for mental health and public health. *Journal of Prevention, 9.*

Williams, C. L., & Westermeyer, J. (Eds.). (1986). *Refugee mental health in resettlement countries.* Washington, DC: Hemisphere.

Williams, J. B. W. (1987). DSM-III-R preview: Revised classification for anxiety disorders. *Hospital and Community Psychiatry, 38,* 245–246.

Anxiety and Depression in Seasonal Affective Disorders

Siegfried Kasper
Norman E. Rosenthal

I. Introduction

Seasonal changes in behavior and physiology have been recognized in humans since ancient times, and cases in whom those seasonal changes occurred on a regular and predictable basis have been documented since the middle of the last century (Esquirol, 1845; Griesinger, 1845; Pilcz, 1901; Hellpach, 1911; Kraepelin, 1921; Kraines, 1957). As early as the second century A.D. Areteus noted that "the seasons of summer and of autumn engender mania and melancholy, and spring brings it to a crisis" (1856).

However, only in the past 6 years has a substantial effort been made to gather together a large number of patients with regularly occurring seasonal mood changes, resulting in the description of a syndrome called seasonal affective disorder (SAD) by Rosenthal et al. (1984). It emerged that SAD is a condition characterized by regular fall and winter

Note: Kasper's research was supported by the German Research Foundation (DFG).

Anxiety and Depression

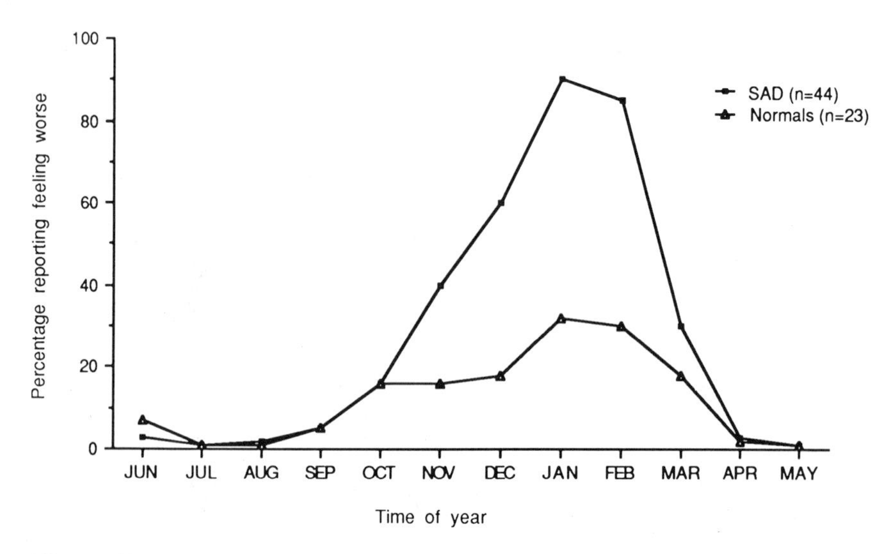

Figure 12.1
Relative frequency distribution of seasonal changes in general well-being, as reported retrospectively on the Seasonal Pattern Assessment Questionnaire (SPAQ; Rosenthal et al., 1987b) by diagnosed SAD patients and normal controls in Washington, D.C. (39° of latitude north of the equator).

depressions alternating with nondepressed periods in the spring and summer. Furthermore, it can be demonstrated that even normals feel worse during the winter months (see Figure 12.1), but this change is exaggerated in SAD subjects. During winter SAD patients experience a variety of symptoms, including changes in mood and energy and the occurrence of anxiety and irritability. In addition, most patients with SAD crave carbohydrates and overeat during their winter depressions.

Psychopathological changes in SAD are recurrent and predictable, and it is therefore possible to study patients prospectively and follow them through the different seasons. It has by now been firmly established that the symptoms of SAD, including depressed mood and anxiety, can be reversed by exposing the patient to bright artificial light. As anxiety and depression are among the "core symptoms" of SAD, we will review and discuss them together with the clinical picture of SAD, where they show the most pronounced seasonal occurrence. Furthermore, we will describe the relevance of seasonal rhythms in animals to SAD and also to the effects of phototherapy in humans, which, together with the reported animal studies, may provide insight into the underlying pathophysiology of this disorder.

II. Seasonal Affective Disorder (SAD)

A. Recruitment of SAD Patients

In order to obtain a large sample, the NIMH research group (Rosenthal et al., 1984) recruited patients by means of newspaper articles. There are certain problems involved in recruiting via the media; for example, the attraction of inappropriate subjects, who may distort their histories in order to be included in a research study. Nevertheless, this technique was initially necessary, as the syndrome had not been generally recognized by local psychiatrists and physicians, who might otherwise have been in a position to refer patients to the program. This approach has been surprisingly successful. Large numbers of responses have generally followed all recruitment efforts, and inappropriate applicants have, in general, been screened out without too much difficulty. Since these initial studies, the syndrome has been more widely recognized by the psychiatric community, resulting in referrals from psychiatrists and general practitioners.

All people who responded to the recruitment or were referred to the NIMH outpatient clinic filled out a Seasonal Pattern Assessment Questionnaire (SPAQ; Rosenthal, Genhardt, Sack, Skwerer, & Wehr, 1987b), and those whose histories sounded suitable were screened by a trained clinician. If suitable, they were included in a study. Inclusion criteria for studies of SAD were (1) a lifetime history of major affective disorder as diagnosed by the Research Diagnostic Criteria (Spitzer, Endicott, & Robins, 1978); (2) regularly occurring fall/winter depressive episodes remitting in the spring or summer, at least two of which occurred during consecutive winters; (3) no other major psychiatric disorder [Axis I, *Diagnostic and Statistical Manual of Mental Disorders* (DSM-III; American Psychiatric Association, 1980)], and (4) no regularly changing psychosocial variables which might account for the recurrent seasonal mood changes. This characterization has led to the description of the diagnostic criteria for "seasonal pattern" in DSM-III-R (American Psychiatric Association, 1987):

1. There has been a regular temporal relationship between the onset of an episode of bipolar disorder (including bipolar disorder NOS) or recurrent major depression (including depressive disorder NOS) and a particular 60-day period of the year (e.g., regular appearance of depression between the beginning of October and the end of November). (Note: Do not include cases in which there is an obvious effect of seasonally

related psychosocial stressors, e.g., regularly being unemployed every winter.)

2. Full remissions (or a change from depression to mania or hypomania) also occurred within a particular 60-day period of the year (e.g., depression disappears from mid-February to mid-April).
3. There have been at least three episodes of mood disturbances in three separate years that demonstrated the temporal seasonal relationship defined in (1) and (2); at least two of the years were consecutive.
4. Seasonal episodes of mood disturbance, as described above, outnumbered any nonseasonal episodes of such disturbance that may have occurred by more than three to one.

Thus far we have studied a total number of 246 patients who fit the criteria for SAD, and whose demographic and clinical features are presented in Tables 12.1 and 12.2.

Table 12.1
Clinical and Demographic Features of 246 SAD Patients[a]

Feature	Value
Age (years)	37.6 ± 9.4
Age of onset (years)	22.2 ± 10.9
Sex ratio (F/M)	202 : 44 (9 : 2)
Length of depressions (months)	5.2 ± 1.3
Psychiatric diagnosis	
Bipolar II	81%
Bipolar I	7%
Unipolar	12%
Family history (at least one affected first-degree relative)	
Major affective disorder	55%
Alcohol abuse	36%
Previous treatment history	
No treatment	26%
Antidepressants	42%
Lithium	10%
Thyroid	10%
Hospitalization	
For depression	3%
For mania	8%
ECT	2%

[a] Data derived from studies at NIMH, 1981–1987.

Table 12.2
Symptoms Reported by 246 SAD Patients during Winter[a]

Variable	Symptoms reported	Patients (%)
Activity	Decreased	95
Affect	Sadness	96
	Irritability	86
	Anxiety	87
Appetite	Increased	71
	Decreased	18
	Mixed	1
	No change	11
	Carbohydrate craving	72
Weight	Increased	76
	Decreased	10
	Mixed	13
	No change	13
Libido	Decreased	59
Sleep	Increased duration	83
	Earlier onset	69
	Change in quality	64
	Daytime drowsiness	73
Other	Symptoms milder near equator (n = 100)	89
	Menstrual difficulties (n = 185)	58
	Work difficulties	86
	Interpersonal difficulties	93

[a] Data derived from studies at NIMH, 1981–1987.

B. Demographic Features

The majority of patients (83%) have been women. Many patients recall disliking winter as far back as they can remember, but in most cases the winter problems become severe in the third decade of life. However, there is considerable variation in age of onset and we have observed individuals whose problems began before age 10 (Rosenthal, Carpenter, James, Parry, & Rogers, 1986a). Most patients (81%) met lifetime Research Diagnostic Criteria for bipolar II affective disorder (recurrent depressions with a history of hypomania; Spitzer et al., 1978); a minority of patients (12%) were diagnosed as unipolar depressives. A high proportion of patients report a history of major affective disorder (55%) or alcohol-related problems (36%) in at least one affected first-degree relative.

As is shown in Table 12.1, 26% of our patients had never received any psychiatric treatment before entering our program. The rest had been treated with psychotherapy, either alone or in conjunction with lithium carbonate (10%), tricyclic antidepressants (42%), thyroid supplements (10%), or a combination of these. Few patients had been previously hospitalized and only two patients had received electroconvulsive treatment.

C. Clinical Characteristics

The average length of winter depression in our sample is 5.2 ± 1.3 months. Some patients complain of transient anxiety as early as August or September. It is unclear whether this late summer anxiety, which some describe as a feeling of panic, is due to anticipation of the approaching winter or whether it has a biological basis of its own. Depressive symptoms usually begin in October or November, and increasing sleep length and a change in food preference are frequently the earliest signs. Patients find it difficult to wake up in the morning and set about their daily tasks, and they report a distinct craving for carbohydrates. Both of these symptoms generally become worse as winter advances.

Table 12.2 points out the frequency of complaints in the 246 SAD patients so far investigated by our group. Among the most frequently reported symptoms are decreased activity (95%), sadness (96%), irritability (86%), anxiety (87%), weight gain (71%), carbohydrate craving (72%), decreased libido (59%), hypersomnia (83%), and interpersonal (93%) and work difficulties (86%). Less common are the more classic depressive complaints such as decreased appetite (18%) and weight loss (10%).

While SAD patients fulfill standard diagnostic criteria for major depression, they frequently manifest typical depressive features (Beeber & Pies, 1983; Liebowitz et al., 1984), such as overeating, oversleeping, and weight gain. These symptoms and others that characterize SAD are either not represented in the Hamilton Depression Rating Scale (HDRS; Hamilton, 1967) (e.g, social withdrawal) or are scored inversely (e.g, hypersomnia, hyperphagia). In order to represent these symptoms in studies of SAD we designed an atypical depression scale modeled on the HDRS (Rosenthal et al., 1987b). Items on this scale include fatigue, social withdrawal, increased appetite, increased eating, carbohydrate craving, weight gain, and hypersomnia. Some of the patients show atypical vegetative symptoms when their depressions are less severe, but as the severity increases, the vegetative symptoms shift to a typical, "endogenous" picture. The overall degree of severity of depression in SAD may vary considerably. Most patients suffer depressions of mild to moderate severity but some become markedly depressed and even suicidal.

D. Reverse SAD (Summer Depression)

Wehr, Skwerer, Jacobsen, Sack, and Rosenthal (1987) and Boyce et al. (1987, personal communication) recently identified a type of seasonal affective disorder in which the seasonal pattern is opposite to what is known for SAD patients. In this reverse form patients regularly become depressed in the spring and summer and are euthymic, hypomanic, or manic in fall and winter. The symptomatology is quite similar to that in SAD patients. Patients' observations and self-experiments, and our own preliminary studies (Wehr et al., 1987), have suggested that seasonal changes in environmental temperature may help to trigger mood swings in this group of patients. Some patients reported that they did not have symptoms when they lived further north; others reported that when they traveled south in the spring, their summer depressions began earlier than usual. Thus, it seems that environmental factors may play a significant role in this form of seasonal affective disorder, and manipulation of the environment could perhaps be beneficial in these cases. Two findings suggest the possibility that the two forms of seasonal affective disorder are related: (1) both forms have been reported to occur in the same patients either over the course of a year or at different times in the course of their illness; and (2) different forms of SAD may occur in different members of a family. Controlled studies of environmental factors in patients with SAD are obviously necessary, and then will establish which environmental factors are important in triggering, maintaining and resolving episodes.

E. Differential Diagnosis of SAD

The frequently mild-to-moderate levels of depression in SAD, coupled with the atypical vegetative symptoms, have created diagnostic difficulties. Specifically, several physical illnesses must be considered in the differential diagnosis of SAD. These include hypothyroidism, hypoglycemia, and chronic viral conditions such as mononucleosis. Our patients have frequently been evaluated for these conditions, generally with negative results.

III. Seasonality as a Dimension in Normals and SAD Patients

Following the consistently reported success of phototherapy in SAD patients (for a review, see Rosenthal, Sack, Skwerer, Jacobsen, & Wehr, in press-c), researchers have questioned whether other segments of the population might also benefit from this treatment. To our knowledge, Kraepelin (1921) was the first who compared the winter depressions and spring hypomanias in manic depressive patients with the emotional changes that even healthy individuals experience at the change of the seasons (see Fig. 12.1). This observation is compatible with the idea that the seasonal changes found in SAD patients might be the extreme end of a behavioral spectrum, which can be also observed in normals to a lesser extent. In an epidemiological survey, Terman (in press) noted that about 25% of the population of New York City complain of symptoms that resemble the psychopathology observed in SAD patients, albeit to a milder degree. In order to evaluate whether normal individuals who do not present as SAD patients might also benefit from light treatment, we studied the effects of bright light in 62 normal individuals (Rosenthal, Rotter, Jacobsen, & Skwerer, in press-b; Kasper et al., in press). Only those normal individuals with a history of mild SAD-like symptoms (S-SAD) benefited from phototherapy. The beneficial effects of phototherapy are thus not universal and may be seen only in individuals susceptible to changes in environmental light. This finding of reported seasonal changes and the beneficial effect of phototherapy in some normals may have practical implications for establishing optimal environ-

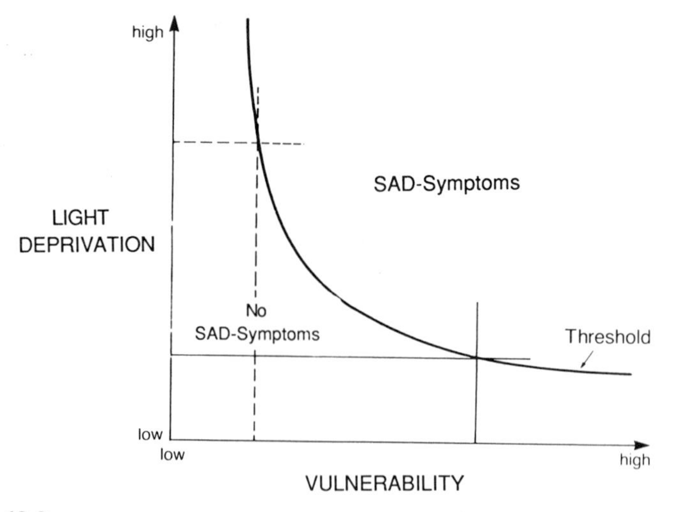

Figure 12.2
Relationships between the degree of vulnerability to develop SAD symptoms and the amount of light deprivation. The dashed lines and solid lines represent the possible relationship in subsyndromal individuals (S-SAD; Kasper et al., in press) and in SAD patients, respectively. Vertical lines indicate the development and involution of SAD symptoms with the amount of light and might therefore reflect the effect of phototherapy.

mental lighting conditions even for nonpsychiatric populations. It would be of interest to determine what physiological and biochemical processes underlie such a susceptibility to develop symptoms related to the seasons. It appears that there are certain seasonally changing environmental variables that cause an alteration in mood, activity, anxiety and energy levels, and sleep in many normal people. In vulnerable individuals these changes may reach symptomatic levels, whereas in normals they may be regarded as acceptable fluctuations.

Figure 12.2 summarizes the hypothetical relationship between an individual's vulnerability to develop SAD symptoms and the degree of light deprivation. Thus, individuals with a low degree of vulnerability might reach the threshold for SAD symptoms only after severe light deprivation. On the other hand, individuals with a high degree of vulnerability might develop symptoms after even small decreases in available light. The former description might represent subsyndromal SAD individuals and the latter the more severely affected SAD patients.

IV. Relevance to SAD of Seasonal Rhythms in Animals

Seasonal rhythms in many different behavioral and physiological processes are common among animals. For instance, many species have evolved rhythms of reproduction so that offspring are born during the spring, when weather conditions and food availability are optimal for their survival. In addition, animals have developed mechanisms for conserving energy and thereby enhancing their chances of surviving the winter. Somehow, the information that the climate is changing must be conveyed to the organism to induce these behavioral changes. Daylength, or photoperiod, has been shown to be the most widely important seasonal time cue among a variety of animal species (Immelman, 1973). However, other factors, such as a decrease in the environmental temperature, interact with the shortened photoperiod (Hoffmann, Davidson, & Steinberg, 1982) to induce seasonal changes such as weight gain.

Two physiological processes in animals have been studied in an attempt to understand the mechanisms by which environmental changes may influence human behavior: (1) seasonal rhythms of reproduction, which are linked to the secretion of melatonin by the pineal gland; and (2) rhythms of energy conservation. We will describe these two aspects and discuss why they may be heuristic for SAD and perhaps for other types of affective disorders as well.

A. Seasonal Rhythms of Reproduction

The secretion of melatonin by the pineal gland has been shown to be a major mechanism responsible for mediating the effects of the changing seasons on behavior in various animal species (Lincoln, 1983; Tamarkin, Baird, & Almeida, 1985). Pineal melatonin is secreted nocturnally on a circadian basis, a rhythm generated by the suprachiasmatic nuclei of the hypothalamus. Environmental light impinges on the retina from which the photic information is conveyed to the suprachiasmatic nuclei via the retinohypothalamic tracts, and from there, by a series of neurons, to the pineal gland (Hoffman, 1981). Light exposure affects melatonin secretion in at least two ways: it influences the timing of (entrains) melatonin secretion, and also has a direct suppressant effect on its secretion (Lewy, Sack, & Singer, 1985a). The pattern of melatonin secretion has been shown to be critical for mediating the effects of photoperiod on seasonally varying behaviors in several species (Tamarkin et al., 1985). The specific feature of the melatonin secretory pattern responsible for conveying photoperiodic information has not been determined in all cases. Variables of potential importance include the duration, amplitude, and timing of the secretion. In two species that have been particularly well studied, the sheep and the Djungarian hamster, duration of melatonin secretion appears to be the critical parameter (Carter & Goldman, 1983; Bittman, Dempsey, & Karsch, 1983). In these two species, melatonin acts on reproductive functioning in opposite ways. A long duration of melatonin secretion, such as occurs in winter, inhibits reproductive functioning in hamsters but stimulates it in sheep. This latter observation has been used by farmers, who have added melatonin to the feed of sheep to stimulate them to give birth more than once a year (Lincoln, 1983). Besides melatonin, the secretion of other behaviorally active hormones, such as prolactin, is also photoperiodically controlled in some lower mammals (Pelletier, 1973).

Jacobsen, Wehr, and Rosenthal (in press) discussed the reproductive pattern of a relatively small sample of 91 SAD patients (69 female and 22 male) with 219 offspring. In this preliminary report there is some evidence that patients with SAD give birth to children in a seasonal pattern that is greater in amplitude and different in distribution from that of the general United States population. Their pattern of childbirth is in keeping with their symptomatology. In other words, in the summer months, when patients are feeling energetic and their sex drive is high, conceptions are more likely to occur. Conversely, in the winter, when they withdraw socially and have a reduced libido, they are less likely to conceive. Thus their peak season for childbirth is May and June and fewest births occur in August through November, a pattern different from that of the general United States population, in which the peak is in July to October. One may speculate as to whether SAD is purely a pathological development or whether it was once an adaptive mechanism, conferring an advantage on those individuals who bred seasonally. According to this latter view, a number of behaviors that covary with low libido, such as social withdrawal and decreased energy, might have been a part of this adaptive mechanism. In modern times, however, we have good control over our indoor environment and food is available throughout the year. Therefore, it could be argued, this once adaptive mechanism is now a handicap, as it limits the capacity to function efficiently throughout the year.

B. Seasonal Rhythms of Energy Conservation

Just as it is necessary for the survival of the species that the offspring are born during the gentle weather of spring, so it is also important that the adult animal develops a strategy for surviving the extreme cold and shortage of food that occur in the winter. Different species have adopted different behaviors for storing energy sources and decreasing energy utilization to cope with these extreme conditions (Dark & Zucker, 1985). Thus hamsters, for example, store energy in the form of body fat and become obese in the winter (Bartness & Wade, 1984; Elliot et al., 1984; Hoffmann et al., 1982; Wade, 1983). Voles, on the other hand, actually conserve energy by losing weight, thus decreasing their energy requirements, and continue to forage during the winter months. They compensate for the lost thermal insulation by developing a long winter pelage, which insulates their bodies as efficiently as would the fat they have lost (Dark & Zucker, 1985).

Lange (1928) first compared the cyclical mood and energy changes seen in manic depression to the seasonal rhythms of hibernating animals. Patients with SAD also frequently refer to their state of "hibernation." There is extensive evidence, dating back to the end of the last century, that humans tend to increase weight in the fall and winter and to lose it most easily in the spring and summer (Attarzadeh, 1983). Humans also reveal seasonal changes in food choice, which appear to be independent of the availability of different types of food. For example, a study at the NIMH cafeteria has shown that purchases of starchy foods declined significantly during spring and summer months (Zifferblatt, Curtis, & Pinsky, 1980). Patients with SAD generally show an exaggeration of these population trends. Most of them gain weight, overeat, and crave carbohydrates; many of their other symptoms, such as increased sleeping, social withdrawal, and decreased sex drive, can also be viewed as having an energy-conserving function. Conversely, the hypomanic symptoms of spring can be regarded as energy-dissipating behaviors. The changing seasons, which are associated with changing energy requirements and food availability, are naturally occurring stimuli for these different sets of behaviors and suggest comparison with seasonal energy-conserving behaviors in other animals.

Just as photoperiod has been shown to be an important time cue for synchronizing seasonal rhythms of reproduction in animals, it is similarly important in regulating seasonal rhythms of weight gain and loss. Shortening of the photoperiod has been shown to induce weight gain in hamsters (Hoffmann et al., 1982; Wade, 1983), an effect observed even when the animals were blinded or pinealectomized (Hoffmann et al., 1982). However, when animals were both pinealectomized and blinded, the effects of photoperiod were lost, suggesting that multiple mechanisms are responsible for the photoperiodically mediated changes in weight and metabolism. Besides photoperiod, changes in environmental temperature have also been shown to influence seasonal fluctuations in weight (Hoffmann et al., 1982). It is therefore conceivable that changes in temperature interact with changes in environmental light to produce the symptoms of SAD. Just as bright light exposure has been beneficial to SAD patients, therapeutic changes in ambient temperature may also prove to be a promising line of treatment for affective disorder patients, most notably, perhaps, for those with reverse SAD.

V. Phototherapy for SAD

Although the sun has been worshipped for its life-giving properties since ancient times, it was not until the industrial revolution that humans deprived themselves of exposure to sunlight and subsequently realized how important exposure to sunlight was for health. Books were written on the concept of exposing patients to artificial light sources for therapeutic purposes (Humphris, 1924; Kellogg, 1910; Kovacs, 1924). However, there are important distinctions between the treatments outlined in these earlier texts and the phototherapy currently in use. These earlier clinicians regarded phototherapy as a broad-spectrum treatment for a wide variety of illnesses; to our knowledge, only Kellogg (1910) comments on the usefulness of light treatment for mood disorders. In contrast, phototherapy is currently regarded as being helpful only in certain types of patients, and the emphasis is now placed on light exposure to the eyes rather than the skin.

Since the first anecdotal observations and the single case report of

Lewy, Kern, Rosenthal, and Wehr (1982), our knowledge about phototherapy for treatment of SAD has increased rapidly and phototherapy is now regarded as an established and accepted treatment (Rosenthal et al., in press-c). Numerous groups have documented robust antidepressant responses to bright artificial light in depressed patients with SAD (Checkley, Winton, & Franey, 1986; Hellekson, Kline, & Rosenthal, 1986; James, Wehr, Sack, Parry, & Rosenthal, 1985; Jacobsen, Wehr, Skwerer, Sack & Rosenthal, in press; Köhler & Pflug, in press; Lewy, Sack, Miller, & Hoban, 1987; Rosenthal et al., 1984, 1985, 1987a; Terman, Quitkin, & Terman, 1986; Thompson, Isaacs, Stainer, & Miles, 1986; Wehr et al., 1986, 1987; Wirz-Justice et al., 1986, 1987; Yerevanian, Anderson, Grota, & Bray, 1986). So far, the efficacy of phototherapy has been studied predominantly in patients with SAD, and its use with other disorders has not been thoroughly explored. Relatively weak antidepressant responses to phototherapy have been reported in patients with nonseasonal major depression (Kripke, 1985; Kripke, Gillin, & Mullaney, in press; Kripke, Risch, & Janowsky, 1983), though more recent studies, using a longer duration of light treatment, have yielded more encouraging preliminary results (Dietzel, Saletu, Lesch, Sieghardt, & Schjerve, 1986; Kripke, Mullaney, Savides, & Gillin, in press; Peter, Räbiger, & Kowalik, 1986). Other investigators have reported some success in using phototherapy for jet lag (Czeisler & Allan, 1987a; Daan & Lewy, 1984), for shift-work difficulties (Eastman, 1987), for delayed sleep-phase syndrome (Lewy and Sack, 1986b), and for the treatment of alcohol withdrawal symptoms (Dietzel et al., in press).

Among SAD patients, symptom predictors of good phototherapeutic response are hypersomnia, severity of diurnal variation, reverse diurnal variation (mood and energy worse later in the day), and anxiety (Jacobsen, Wehr, Sack, & Rosenthal, 1986). Anecdotally we have found that those relatively rare SAD patients afflicted with severe endogenous depression respond worst to phototherapy. The antidepressant effect usually appears after 3 days, and when the lights are withdrawn, relapse into depression frequently takes at least a few days.

Figure 12.3 demonstrates the treatment effects of 1 week of phototherapy in 47 SAD patients. After phototherapy, a reduction of the scores of the used assessment scales of over 50% compared to baseline ratings can be achieved in most of the characteristic symptoms for SAD. Since the HDRS is used in all studies evaluating the antidepressant effects of phototherapy, the percentage improvements in Figures 12.4 and 12.5 as well as in Tables 12.3 and 12.4 refer to the percentage change in HDRS ratings (total score) when the scores after treatment are compared with the values before treatment. In addition to the HDRS we developed and used a 7-item supplementary scale which is particularly

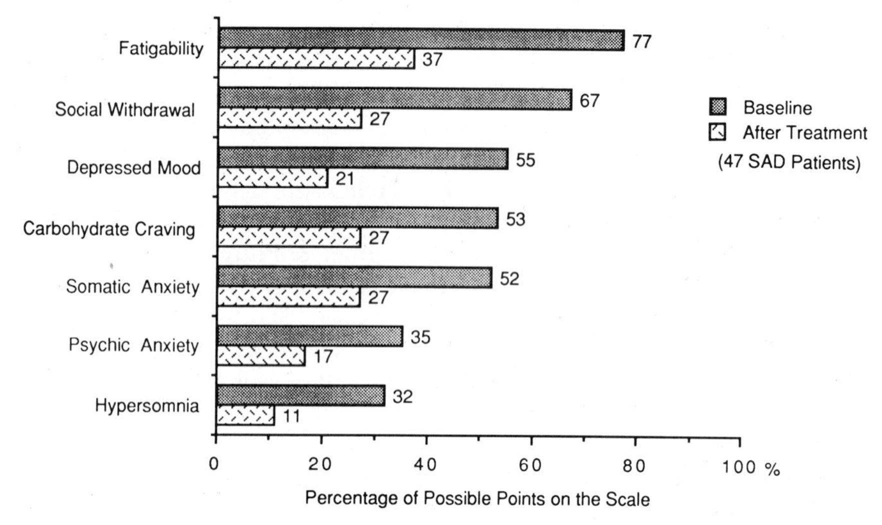

Figure 12.3
Effect of bright light on several characteristic symptoms in SAD as measured by objective ratings (Hamilton Depression Rating Scale, Hamilton, 1967; supplementary items, Rosenthal et al., 1987b). Since the individual items of these scales differ in their scaling, the results are expressed as percentages of the maximum of possible points which can be achieved on the item.

relevant to the symptoms of SAD and their improvement with phototherapy (Rosenthal et al., in press-a).

One problem in interpreting these studies on phototherapy is that, because the nature of the intervention is apparent to the subject, double-blind studies cannot be performed and therefore it is especially difficult to rule out placebo effects. Most of the studies have used raters who were blind to the nature or condition of the treatment interventions, which reduces the problem of researcher bias. Attempts have also been made to reduce patient bias and to develop plausible control treatments; for example, dim light controls have shown a considerably weaker response than bright light treatment (Figure 12.4, Table 12.3). While all effective antidepressant treatments probably capitalize on placebo effects to some extent, the existence of some specific therapeutic factor in phototherapy is suggested by the diversity of researchers who have noted its efficacy in controlled studies (Figure 12.4, Table 12.3), the repeated and consistent responses within individual patients, a characteristic time course of response to treatment and relapse following withdrawal of treatment (usually a latency of about 2 to 4 days for both phenomena), the existence of a dose-response curve (both for duration and intensity), and the lack of a significant correlation between pretreatment expectations and the effects of phototherapy.

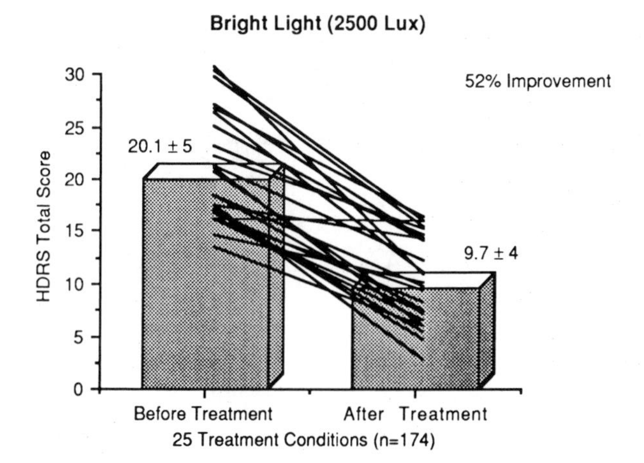

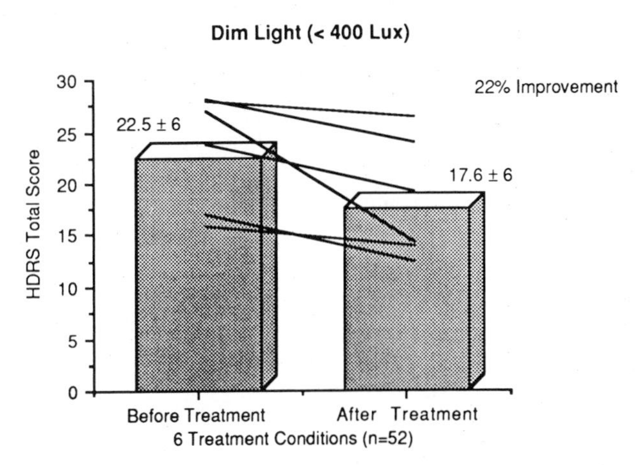

Figure 12.4
Comparison of 15 studies in which bright light was used with 6 studies in which dim light was used for treatment of SAD patients. The individual values of the different treatment conditions are listed in Table 12.3 (see also text). Improvement reflects the percentage change in HDRS ratings (total score) when the scores after treatment are compared with the values before treatment. HDRS, Hamilton Depression Rating Scale (Hamilton, 1967).

Table 12.3
Phototherapy in SAD Patients with Bright and Dim Light[a]

Treatment and author	Number of patients	HDRS[b] Baseline	HDRS[b] Posttreatment	Improvement (%)
Bright light				
Rosenthal et al. (1984)	9	17.7	6.7	62
James et al. (1985)	9	24.3	13.4	45
Rosenthal et al. (1985)	13	26.5	13.6	49
Checkley et al. (1986)	11	29.6	15.2	49
Hellekson et al. (1986)	6	12.8	5.3	59
		20	6.4	68
		20.4	5.2	75
Terman et al. (1986)	28	16.2	4.7	71
		15.4	5.9	68
		16.8	13.5	20
Thompson et al. (1986)	11	13.9	9.5	32
		16.1	7.6	53
Wehr et al. (1986)	7	26	15.7	40
		29.1	14.7	49
Wirz-Justice et al. (1986)	12	30	10.1	66
Yerevanian et al. (1986)	4	16.7	2	88
	4	16.4	4	76
Jacobsen et al. (in press)	16	22.4	13.9	38
		21.6	14.6	32
Lewy et al. (1987)	8	15.4	6.6	57
		15.4	15.2	1
		15.4	8.6	44
Rosenthal et al. (1987a)	12	17.8	9	49
Wehr et al. (1987)	10	25.6	10.3	60
Wirz-Justice et al. (1987)	14	20.5	11.6	43
25 treatment conditions	174	20.08 ± 5	9.7 ± 4	52
Dim light				
Rosenthal et al. (1984)	9	15.1	13.2	13
Rosenthal et al. (1985)	6	27.1	25.7	5
James et al. (1985)	9	23	18.4	20
Checkley et al. (1986)	11	27.4	23.2	22
Thompson et al. (1986)	11	16.3	11.7	28
Wirz-Justice et al. (1986)	6	26.3	13.5	49
6 treatment conditions	52	22.5 ± 6	17.6 ± 6	22

[a] Data are based on different computations of individual data shown in published graphs or tables. For more distinct presentation the different treatment conditions of these studies are listed in this table under the heading of bright or dim light, regardless of the design, cross-over or parallel, in which they have been originally studied. Within a cross-over design, withdrawal scores immediately preceding a phototherapy condition are used as baseline; given successive treatments without withdrawals (Lewy et al., 1987), the pretreatment score is used. In most studies the duration of phototherapy was 1 week.
[b] Mean scores of Hamilton Depression Rating Scale (HDRS, total score; Hamilton, 1967).

Table 12.4
Phototherapy in SAD Patients at Different Times of the Day[a]

Treatment and author	Number of patients	HDRS[b] Baseline	HDRS[b] Posttreatment	Improvement (%)
Morning + evening light therapy				
Rosenthal et al. (1984)	9	17.7	6.7	62
Rosenthal et al. (1985)	13	26.5	13.6	49
Checkley et al. (1986)	11	29.6	15.2	49
Hellekson et al. (1986)	6	20	6.4	68
Terman et al. (1986)	28	16.2	4.7	71
Thompson et al. (1986)	12	13.9	9.5	32
Wehr et al. (1986)	7	29.1	14.7	49
Wirz-Justice et al. (1986)	12	30	10.1	66
Lewy et al. (1987)	8	15.4	8.6	44
Rosenthal et al. (1987a)	12	17.8	9	49
10 treatment conditions	107	21.6 ± 6	9.8 ± 4	55
Morning light therapy				
Hellekson et al. (1986)	6	12.8	5.3	59
Terman et al. (1986)	17	15.4	5.9	68
Yerevanian et al. (1986)	4	16.7	2	88
Jacobsen et al. (in press)	16	22.4	13.9	39
Lewy et al. (1987)	8	15.4	6.6	57
Wirz-Justice et al. (1987)	14	20.5	11.6	43
6 treatment conditions	65	17.2 ± 4	7.5 ± 4	56
Evening light therapy				
James et al. (1985)	9	24.3	13.4	45
Buckwald et al. (in press)	11	15.4	7.4	52
Hellekson et al. (1986)	6	20.4	5.2	75
Terman et al. (1986)	12	16.8	13.5	20
Yerevanian et al. (1986)	4	16.4	4	76
Lewy et al. (1987)	8	15.4	15.2	1
Wehr et al. (1987)	7	25.6	10.3	60
7 treatment conditions	57	19.2 ± 4	9.9 ± 4	48

[a] Data are based on different computations of individual data shown in published graphs or tables. For more distinct presentation the different treatment conditions of these studies are listed in this table under the aspect of timing, regardless of the design, cross-over or parallel, in which they have been originally studied. Within a cross-over design, withdrawal scores immediately preceding a phototherapy condition are used as baseline; given successive treatments without withdrawals (Lewy et al., 1987), the pretreatment score is used. In most studies the duration of phototherapy was 1 week.
[b] Mean scores of Hamilton Depression Rating Scale (HDRS, total score; Hamilton, 1967).

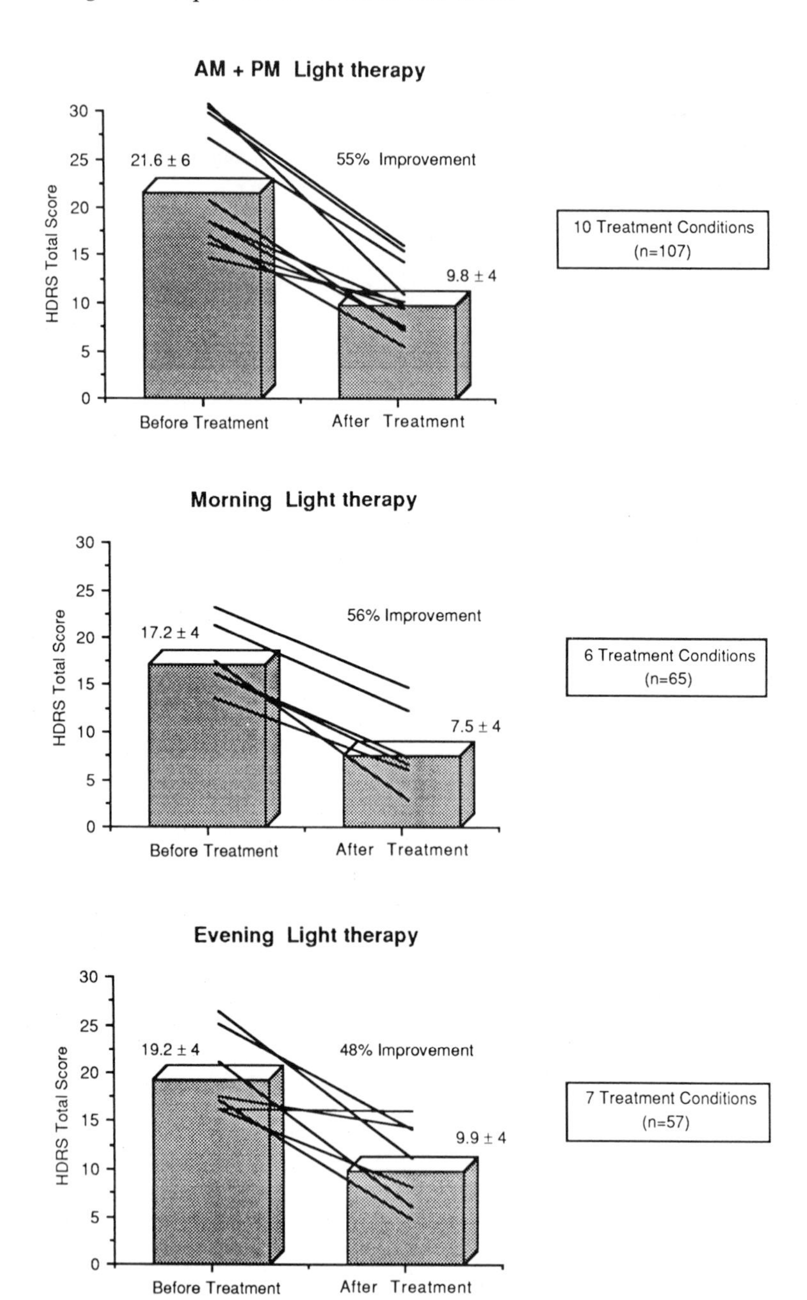

Figure 12.5
Phototherapy at different times of the day. Individual values of the different treatment conditions are listed in Table 12.4 (see also text). Improvement reflects the percentage change in HDRS ratings (total score) when the scores after treatment are compared with the values before treatment. HDRS, Hamilton Depression Rating Scale (Hamilton, 1967).

VI. Practical Aspects of Phototherapy

The light source most frequently used for phototherapy has been full-spectrum fluorescent light (Vitalite). Six or eight 40-watt tubes have been inserted into a rectangular metal fixture, 2 by 4 feet, with a reflecting surface behind them and a plastic diffusing screen in front. Patients have been asked to place the box at eye level, either horizontally on a desk or table, or vertically on the ground. They have been asked to sit approximately 3 feet away from the lights and to stare at them for a few seconds each minute. The intensity of light measured at 3 feet from this light source is 2500 lux, the amount of light to which one would be exposed by looking out of a window on a spring day. This is five to ten times brighter than ordinary room lighting. This technique is not the only possible way to administer phototherapy. However, it is well tested, safe, and effective. It has been shown to alleviate symptoms in approximately 80% of the over 120 patients treated at the NIMH, and a high percentage of cases treated at other centers as well. Researchers who have used the above technique agree that it is an effective antidepressant in SAD (for a review see Rosenthal et al., in press-c). However, there is disagreement concerning the specific parameters of light treatment that are necessary or optimal for producing this response. A further discussion of these areas is of importance both in establishing optimal guidelines for phototherapy administration and in attempting to understand the physiological mechanisms involved in phototherapy.

A. Intensity

In phototherapy studies, intensity has been measured as illuminance, i.e., the amount of light incident on the patient, as opposed to the amount of light leaving the light source or the perceived brightness of the source. Illuminance has generally been reported in lux. Intensity of the light source was the first parameter to be studied systematically; its importance was suggested by the finding that suppression of nocturnal melatonin secretion required high-intensity light (2500 lux), which is far brighter than ordinary room light (Lewy, Wehr, Goodwin, Newsome, & Markey, 1980).

To determine the importance of intensity in phototherapy, researchers have used a variety of control light treatments of lower intensity (400 lux or less). Figure 12.4 and Table 12.3 summarize the findings of 15 investigations using bright light, and 6 studies in which dim light conditions were administered to patients with SAD. In most studies the duration of phototherapy was 1 week. The results of these studies are based on computations of individual data shown in published graphs or tables of the quoted publications. Irrespective of the design of these studies, whether cross-over or parallel, different treatment conditions can be extracted. Within a cross-over design, withdrawal scores immediately preceding a phototherapy condition are used as baseline; given successive treatments without withdrawals (Lewy et al., 1987), the pretreatment score is used. These comparisons clearly demonstrate the superiority of bright over dim light.

Except for the research of Czeisler and Allan (1987b) and Terman (in press), no study used intensities of light greater than 2500 lux. The latter group found that phototherapy can be shortened with higher intensities. It seems reasonable to conclude, on the basis of most studies, that intensity of the light source is an important parameter in achieving an antidepressant effect. The exact threshold probably varies from patient to patient, and in our experience some subjects appear to benefit even from light intensities somewhat lower than 2500 lux. However, dose-response curves for light intensity have not been systematically studied.

B. Timing

There has been considerable interest as to whether timing of light treatment is important in achieving an antidepressant response to phototherapy. Researchers have investigated this question along two separate theoretical lines. The first was derived from studies of photoperiodic control of seasonal rhythms in animals, where the modulatory effects of light on behavior have depended on exposure to light at certain critical times of the day outside of the usual winter photoperiod (Hoffman, 1981). The second approach was suggested by Lewy et al. (1987), and was patterned along the lines of the phase-advance hypothesis of nonseasonal depression (Papousek, 1975; Wehr, Goodwin, Duncan, & Gillin, 1979). The latter group hypothesized that patients with SAD become depressed during the winter because the timing of their circadian rhythms is abnormal. According to this theory, light exposure at certain critical times of the day might correct this abnormality, thereby exerting an antidepressant effect.

The existing controversy with regard to the phase-advance theory remains unresolved. Findings supporting the theory have been reported by Terman et al. (1986) and Lewy et al. (1987); in contrast, contradictory data have been reported by Hellekson et al. (1986), Terman et al. (1986), and Wirz-Justice et al. (1987). Figure 12.5 and Table 12.4 show a comparison of studies in which phototherapy was applied at different times of the day. These are grouped according to whether the light was administered during the morning only (6 studies), during the evening only

(7 studies), or during both times (10 studies). The overall response rates for these three groups were 56, 48, and 55% respectively. The mean HDRS scores at baseline and after treatment are also comparable across the different timing conditions; thus, it does not seem that time of day significantly affects the effectiveness of phototherapy in SAD.

C. Duration

In general, the relationship between dosage of an effective drug and the obtained response can be represented graphically as a dose-response curve. It is reasonable to wonder whether such a relationship exists for the phototherapy of SAD. We have already encountered a type of dose-response relationship in studying the intensity of light required for a therapeutically relevant response. However, the dose-response relationship can also be studied as a function of duration.

Most study outcomes are based on 1 week of phototherapy, and within this time frame SAD patients have been exposed to artificial light for 1–5 hours daily. Several groups have studied the importance of duration of light treatment in influencing the outcome of phototherapy (Lewy and Sack, 1986a; Terman et al., 1986; Wirz-Justice et al., 1987). Based on this limited number of studies and on unpublished observations, it appears as though a duration-response curve probably exists for the phototherapy of SAD and that patients who do not respond to phototherapy at first may subsequently respond when the duration of therapy is increased. Conversely, patients who are doing well on treatment may lose part or all of the effect if the duration of light exposure is reduced.

D. Spectrum

Most investigators have used full-spectrum fluorescent light in their phototherapy studies. The initial rationale for using this light source was its strong resemblance to the spectrum of natural sunlight. However, the question arises as to which wavelength is optimal for the efficacy of phototherapy. This is of interest for both practical and theoretical reasons. Practical reasons involve the potentially toxic effects of ultraviolet light to eyes and skin. Theoretically, it is important to know what photopigments and photoreceptors are involved in the original transduction of light into the nerve impulses in the retina, the presumptive neuroanatomical portal of the antidepressant response (Wehr et al., 1987). Knowledge of the spectral characteristics of the photopigments involved in the antidepressant response to phototherapy will increase our understanding of the neuroanatomy and neurophysiology of this response.

The data of A. J. Lewy and colleagues (personal communication) suggest that ultraviolet (UV) rays do not influence the efficacy of light treatment. Yerevanian et al. (1986) treated nine SAD patients with an incandescent light source and found it to be an effective antidepressant. Thus, the available data suggest that neither UV nor full-spectrum light is essential for the antidepressant effects of phototherapy in SAD. In a recent study, Rosenthal et al. (1987a) compared 2500 lux of full-spectrum light with two different colored fluorescent lights, red and blue, controlling for intensity as measured by the number of photons per unit area. They found that the full-spectrum light had a superior antidepressant effect to the colored lights, but this did not reach statistical significance. Both colored lights appeared to have some antidepressant effects, but it is possible that these might have been due to a placebo alone. Further research along these lines may help us to learn more about the retinal receptors involved in this response. However, large numbers of subjects and the use of several wavelengths would be necessary to resolve this question definitely.

E. Presentation of Light

Different ways of presenting light therapy to the individual have been considered. For example, the lighting may be direct or indirect, at eye level or above eye level, in front of the individual or to the side. The relative efficacy of those different methods has theoretical and practical implications, as they provide information regarding both the underlying pathophysiology of SAD and the neuroanatomical pathways involved in the antidepressant response.

Only one controlled study has specifically addressed this issue. Wehr et al. (1987) compared the effects of skin versus eye exposure in eleven SAD patients and found the eye exposure to be significantly superior. In our controlled studies of phototherapy we have asked our subjects not to stare at the lights but to glance at them for a few seconds every minute. We do not know whether it is even necessary for subjects to glance directly at the light periodically, or whether it would be just as effective for them to be exposed constantly to indirect light. If the latter is true, it would imply that the effects of light are mediated via the periphery of the retina and therefore, presumably, via the rods. Yerevanian et al. (1986) reported that indirect light was an effective antidepressant in nine SAD patients, which would appear to corroborate the importance of a peripheral retinal mechanism.

F. Side Effects

Most patients tolerate phototherapy well and it is rather unusual for someone to need to discontinue treatment because of side effects. Perhaps because of this, there have not yet been any systematic surveys of side effects. Side effects about which patients most commonly complain are eye strain, headaches, and irritability. Eyestrain and headaches often decrease after a few days of treatment, and may be minimized by decreasing duration or distance from the source and then gradually building up exposure again. When irritability occurs, it resembles the hypomanic symptoms seen in spring and summer and generally responds well to decreasing the duration of treatment. To date, we have not encountered any manic episodes among typical SAD patients, although we did observe one such episode in a patient with several atypical features, and a few other cases have been observed by other researchers. We have not yet encountered problems with the eyes or skin even after chronic use of light for several years. However, it is possible that the use of light sources emitting ultraviolet radiation could pose a hazard to the skin or the eyes with long-term use, as has been shown for the skin in humans exposed to an extensive amount of sunlight (Granstein & Sober, 1982).

VII. Psychobiology of SAD and the Physiological Effects of Phototherapy

In addition to the research strategies that are used in major affective disorders, SAD offers the unique opportunity that the psychopathological state can be reliably reversed by light exposure or again induced by light deprivation; this allows one to conduct cross-over studies. A further advantage in studying phototherapy, as compared with other antidepressant treatments, is that the results are not confounded by the presence of psychopharmacological medication.

In order to determine the extent to which SAD patients share neuroendocrine, neurotransmitter, or sleep-related abnormalities found in other patients with affective or anxiety disorders, extensive biological investigations have been performed, especially by the NIMH group. Although some promising new observations have been made in the area of immune function and evoked potentials, which will be discussed below, most of the findings have been negative. The mechanism of action of phototherapy is closely linked to the psychobiology of SAD but has not yet been satisfactorily explained. Among the several theories which have been proposed, the melatonin and phase-shift hypotheses have been the basis for several earlier studies. However, newer theories should take into account the observed effects of bright light on neurotransmitter, immune and electrophysiological systems.

A. Melatonin

The melatonin hypothesis was based on the importance of this substance in regulating seasonal rhythms in animals (Tamarkin et al., 1985; Lincoln, 1983), and on the observation that light that was bright enough to suppress melatonin secretion (2500 lux) had significant antidepressant effects, whereas light that was too dim to suppress melatonin secretion was ineffective. Our group has investigated the melatonin hypothesis in several ways: (1) by measuring plasma melatonin levels in SAD patients and normals in summer and winter, and in SAD patients before and after effective phototherapy. (Rosenthal et al., 1986b); (2) by administering melatonin orally to SAD patients successfully treated with phototherapy to see whether the symptoms of SAD would reemerge (Rosenthal et al., 1986b); (3) by administering the beta-adrenergic blocking agent, atenolol, which is known to suppress nocturnal melatonin secretion, in an attempt to mimic the effects of light pharmacologically (Rosenthal et al., in press-a); and (4) by administering pulses of light early in the morning and late at night, thereby extending the length of the day and suppressing melatonin secretion, and then comparing this treatment to the administration of pulses of light during the day, administered in such a way as not to suppress melatonin secretion (Wehr et al., 1986).

In summary, the findings of these studies were as follows: (1) Nocturnal melatonin levels were significantly lower in patients than in normals in winter, but treatment with bright artificial light did not alter the amplitude or duration of melatonin secretion; it is noteworthy that lower nocturnal melatonin levels have been reported in the literature for patients with major depression (Brown et al., 1985). (2) The administration of melatonin did not reinduce symptoms of SAD, as measured by the 21-item Hamilton Depression Rating Scale (Hamilton, 1967), but a significant exacerbation of the supplementary symptoms (overeating, oversleeping, weight gain, carbohydrate craving, fatigue, and social withdrawal) could be noted. (3) The administration of atenolol was not statistically superior to placebo in 19 SAD patients. However, 3 of the 19 patients reported repeated and sustained responses to atenolol, and relapsed when atenolol was withdrawn. (4) Pulses of light administered early and late in the day suppressed melatonin, whereas those administered toward the middle of the day did not. However, both treatment conditions were equally and significantly effective as antidepressants (Wehr et al., 1986). Thus, while there was some suggestion that melatonin secretion may play a role in the development of depressive symptoms in SAD, and that the modification of melatonin secretion may be involved in the effects of phototherapy, at least in certain cases, it does not appear that melatonin secretion has the same pivotal role in these processes as it does in mediating seasonal rhythms of behavior in animals.

B. Phase-Shift Hypothesis

The phase-shift hypothesis was inspired by the observation of Lewy et al. (1985a,b) that the onset of melatonin secretion during dim light is shifted later in the winter than in the summer. Based on the animal literature on the phase-shifting capacity of light (de Coursey, 1960; Hoban & Sulzman, 1985) and the observation that bright light was necessary to suppress human melatonin (Lewy et al., 1980), this latter group postulated that exposing humans to bright light at different times of the day would shift rhythms in different directions and to different degrees. The observed seasonal phase changes in the timing of the onset of melatonin secretion suggested to these authors that rhythms needed to be advanced in order to be returned to their summer phase position and that light, by inducing such phase advances, was capable of reversing the winter depressive symptoms. This hypothesis was supported by their observation in eight patients with SAD that 2 hours of light treatment in the morning was significantly more effective than 2 hours in the evening (Lewy et al., 1987). Further support for this hypothesis came from Terman et al. (1986), who replicated this finding.

However, there are several studies that would tend to refute this hypothesis. Figure 12.5 and Table 12.4 demonstrate that light administered both in the morning and evening, or in the evening alone, is as effective as morning light; and only one study (Lewy et al., 1987) shows that evening light has no beneficial effect. Based on animal studies, one would not expect that light treatments during the day would have any significant effect on the timing of circadian rhythms (Pittendringh, in press). In addition, our studies of sleep architecture, circadian temperature, and plasma cortisol, melatonin, and prolactin did not confirm that these rhythms were phase delayed in patients with SAD, nor did we find that a combination of morning and evening phototherapy (which was effective in reversing the winter symptoms of SAD) was associated with any change in circadian phase (Rosenthal et al., in press-d). Thus we do not believe at this time that phase shift per se is responsible for the symptomatic improvement seen after phototherapy.

C. Photochemical Hypothesis

The effect of light on brain metabolism has been studied and summarized already by Hollwich (1955). In accordance with these findings, light therapy has been shown to work by stimulating receptors in the eye as opposed to working via the skin (Wehr et al., 1986). Thus, light impinges on the retina where it is converted into neural impulses, which are transmitted to the brain, probably along the retino-hypothalamic tract (Kappers, 1960; Kappers, Smith, & De Vries, 1979). This presumably causes certain chemical changes to occur in the brain, reversing the neurochemical abnormalities found in SAD, and thereby reversing the symptoms of the condition. This theory should be further investigated by studies that actually show neurochemical changes in neurotransmitter or neuromodulator systems.

The complexity of the neurotransmitter and neuromodulatory systems complicates our investigation into the pathogenesis of the disease and makes it unlikely that only one neurostransmitter system is involved. However, the most extensively studied neurotransmitter systems in depression, serotonin, dopamine, and norepinephrine, seem a logical starting point in these investigations. We measured the concentrations of 5-hydroxyindoleacetic acid (5-HIAA), homovanillic acid (HVA), and 3-methoxy-4-hydroxyphenylglycol (MHPG) in cerebrospinal fluid of six patients being treated with bright and dim light phototherapy. No statistically significant differences in mean CSF monoamine metabolite concentrations could be attributed to phototherapy with bright and dim light.

Deficient serotonergic transmission in the central nervous system has been postulated as a potential cause of depression (Murphy, Campbell, & Costa, 1978). Carlsson, Svennerholm, and Winblad (1980), in a postmortem study of people who died from nonneurological nonpsychiatric conditions, found that hypothalamic serotonin concentration decreased from fall into winter, when it reached its nadir. Furthermore, Wurtman and colleagues (Fernstrom & Wurtman, 1972; Wurtman & Wurtman, 1984) have data from both animal and human studies suggesting that dietary carbohydrate increases serotonin synthesis and serotonergic transmission. Thus the carbohydrate craving seen in patients with SAD may represent a complex behavioral–biochemical feedback loop that serves to replenish depleted brain serotonin levels. Another hypothesis regarding the biological basis of depression is that this psychopathological state is associated with a noradrenergic deficiency (Schildkraut, 1965). Consistent with this theory we found that lower norepinephrine plasma levels were associated with a greater degree of depression in untreated patients, and that phototherapy appeared to "normalize" the orthostatic rise of norepinephrine in patients (Skwerer et al., in press).

D. Neuroendocrine Investigations

Apart from melatonin, interest in hormonal abnormalities in SAD has focused on the hypothalamic–pituitary–adrenal axis, the hypothalamic–pituitary–thyroid axis, and prolactin. TSH, T_3 and T_4, and prolactin are of special interest for SAD, because they have been shown to be temperature sensitive. For instance, in a warm ambient temperature the thyroid hormones decrease (Bartels & Jensen, 1985; Beck, Reinhardt, Kendel, & Schmidt-Kessen, 1976; Mc Lellan, Riley, & Davies, 1979; O'Malley et al., 1984) whereas prolactin rises (Christensen, Jørgensen, Møller, Møller, & Ørskov, 1985).

No consistent picture has emerged with respect to hypothalamic–pituitary–thyroid (HPT) function in SAD, but there are some trends which suggest possibilities for future research. SAD patients had higher plasma T_4 levels in the winter compared to healthy controls. Other thyroid hormones (free T_4, T_3, and TSH) did not differ significantly among patients and controls. As mentioned before, increased thyroid levels have been found in lower ambient temperatures. If these higher values in the HPT function are upheld in SAD, this might indicate a greater sensitivity to cold in this population. Additional longitudinal studies of thyroid function are needed to clarify whether the HPT axis is disturbed in SAD.

Plasma prolactin levels have been reported to be mildly elevated in the morning (Jacobsen, Sack, Wehr, Rogers, & Rosenthal, in press) and low in the afternoon (Depue, Arbisi, Spoont, Leon, & Ainsworth, in press) in SAD patients compared to normal subjects. Furthermore, low 24-hour plasma prolactin values have been reported in 15 SAD patients compared with 9 normal controls (Skwerer et al. in press). In a separate study the NIMH group also found reduced 24-hour prolactin profiles in 6 SAD patients compared with 6 normal controls in the winter but not in the summer (N. E. Rosenthal et al., unpublished observations). Thus the majority of the data suggests decreased prolactin secretion in SAD in the winter. We failed to detect any difference in the timing of the prolactin rhythm in patients and controls studied during the winter under dim light conditions, and like Depue et al. (in press) we also did not find any effect of light treatment (2500 lux; 2.0 hours, morning and evening) on prolactin levels in patients and normal controls.

Finally, we have found no significant differences among patients and controls in mean cortisol levels or in the timing or amplitude of the cortisol rhythm. Furthermore, no alleviation from suppression by dexamethasone has been noted (James et al., 1986).

E. Further Areas of Research

Further effects of bright light in SAD have been explored, and these are summarized below. Although they are discussed at the end of the chapter, they are nevertheless exciting and are likely to be areas of ongoing future research.

In the winter, depressed SAD patients often complain of decreased ability to concentrate and process information; this improves as they gradually reach a euthymic state as they progress through the spring and summer. Active processing of information by the brain can be measured by studying the P300 component of the event-related brain potential (ERP). In the visual modality, Duncan and Rosenthal (1986) have demonstrated that the visual P300 component of the ERP is enhanced by bright light in patients who respond to this treatment. Moreover, the degree of P300 amplitude enhancement correlated with the amount of antidepressant response. It is noteworthy, however, that this relationship between mood improvement and increased P300 amplitude is not apparent following auditory stimuli. The specificity of this response to different stimuli is important because SAD patients are considerably more fatigued before than after light treatment, and fatiguability is one of the intervening variables in event-related brain potential recording. The differential response in auditory versus visual information processing suggests that a positive response to phototherapy is associated with a significant increase in the attentional resources that are needed to process visual information.

In a recently completed study, Skwerer et al. (1987) found abnormally elevated lymphocyte transformation in response to mitogen stimulation *in vitro.* Furthermore, they showed that phototherapy modifies the ability of peripheral blood lymphocytes of SAD patients to respond to mitogen stimulation. After exposure to bright light, the lymphocyte transformation was reduced in SAD patients to levels similar to those of normal controls. Depressed states have previously been associated with altered immune function (Schleifer et al., 1984; Stein, Keller, & Schleifer, 1985). It is conceivable that the observed effect of light on both lymphocytes and mood in depressed patients undergoing phototherapy may provide a clue to understanding the biology of SAD and the mechanism of phototherapy.

VIII. Conclusions

Changes in affect (including depressed mood, anxiety, and irritability), increases in appetite, weight, and duration of sleep, decreases in libido, and difficulties in accomplishing tasks characterize the psychopathology of patients with seasonal affective disorders. These symptoms can be treated by phototherapy, and the efficacy of this treatment has been widely demonstrated and generally acknowledged. Whereas seasonal variations in depression as a clinical syndrome have been studied thoroughly, there are no studies addressing seasonal variations in anxiety disorders. To date, the value of phototherapy in the treatment of nonseasonal syndromes has not as yet been thoroughly explored. For example, no study has focused on the effects of light in different anxiety disorders. Because anxiety is one of the "core symptoms" of SAD and depressed mood is present in most anxiety states, this line of research seems worth pursuing.

Seasonality of mood and behavior appears to be a dimension affecting many different people, including normal individuals and those with conditions other than SAD. Such a history can be elicited by a simple standardized self-administered questionnaire, the Seasonal Pattern Assessment Questionnaire (SPAQ; Rosenthal et al., 1987). It is noteworthy, that exposure to bright environmental light seems to alter mood and behavior only in those individuals with a history of seasonal changes in these variables.

The biological mechanisms underlying the seasonal changes in SAD are as yet unknown. Studies of seasonal change in animal reproductive function and energy balance may enhance our understanding of the underlying pathophysiology. Moreover, the effect of phototherapy can be used as a probe to investigate state-dependent changes in SAD and can thereby further elucidate the biological mechanisms involved in these changes. Research into this question in SAD is facilitated because the symptomatic response to phototherapy occurs predictably within a few days and is not confounded by drug effects, a variable that complicates other biological studies.

References

American Psychiatric Association. (1980). *DSM-III. Diagnostic and statistical manual of mental disorders* (3rd ed.). Washington, DC: Author.

American Psychiatric Association. (1987). *DSM-III-R. Diagnostic and statistical manual of mental disorders* (3rd ed. rev.). Washington, DC: Author.

Areteus. (1856). *The extant works,* F. Adams (Ed. and Trans.). London: Sydenham Society.

Attarzadeh, F. (1983). Seasonal variation in stature and body weight. *International Journal of Orthodontics, 21,* 3–12.

Bartels, P. D., & Jensen, P. (1985). Ambient temperature and thyrotropin concentration in serum. *Clinical Chemistry, 31,* 1407–1408.

Bartness, T. J., & Wade, G. N. (1984). Photoperiodic control of body weight and energy metabolism in Syrian hamsters (*Mesocricetus auratus*): Role of pineal gland, melatonin, gonads, and diet. *Endocrinology, 114*, 492–498.

Beck, U., Reinhardt, H., Kendel, K., & Schmidt-Kessen, W. (1976). Temperature and endocrine activity during sleep in man. *Archiv für Psychiatrie und Nervenkrankheiten, 222*, 245–256.

Beeber, A. R., & Pies, R. W. (1983). The nonmelancholic depressive syndromes. An alternative approach to classification. *Journal of Nervous and Mental Disease, 171*, 3–9.

Bittman, E. L., Dempsey, J., & Karsch, F. J. (1983). Pineal melatonin secretion drives the reproductive response to daylength in the ewe. *Endocrinology, 113*, 2276–2283.

Brown, R., Kocsis, J. H., Caroff, S., Amsterdam, J., Winokur, A., Stokes, P. E., & Frazer, A. (1985). Differences in nocturnal melatonin secretion between melancholic depressed patients and control subjects. *American Journal of Psychiatry, 142*, 811–816.

Buckwald, B., McGrath, R. E., & Resnick, E. V. (in press). Preliminary evidence on the effectiveness of L-tryptophan as a treatment for seasonal affective disorder. *American Journal of Psychiatry*.

Carlsson, A., Svennerholm, L., & Winblad, B. (1980). Seasonal and circadian monoamine variations in human brains examined postmortem. *Acta Psychiatrica Scandinavica, 61*, 75–83.

Carter, D. S., & Goldman, B. D. (1983). Antigonal effects of timed melatonin infusion in pinealectomized male Djungarian hamsters (*Phodopus sungorus*): Duration is the critical parameter. *Endocrinology, 112*, 1257–1261.

Checkley, S., Winton, F., & Franey, C. (1986, June). *Antidepressant effects of light in seasonal affective disorder*. Paper presented at the Royal College of Psychiatry, Southhampton, England.

Christensen, S. E., Jørgensen, O., Møller, N., & Ørskov, H. (1985). Body temperature elevation, exercise and serum prolactin concentrations. *Acta Endocrinologica, 109*, 458–462.

Czeisler, C. A., & Allan, J. S. (1987a). Acute circadian phase reversal in man via bright light exposure: Application to jet-lag. *Sleep Research, 16*, 605.

Czeisler, C. A., & Allan, J. S. (1987b). Rapid phase shifting in humans requires bright light. *Chronobiologia, 14*, 167.

Daan, S., & Lewy, A. J. (1984). Scheduled exposure to daylight: A potential strategy to reduce "jet lag" following transmeridian flight. *Psychopharmacology Bulletin, 20*, 566–568.

Dark, J., & Zucker, I. (1985). Seasonal cycles in energy balance: Regulation by light. In R. J. Wurtmann, M. J. Baum, & J. T. Potts (Eds.), *The medical and biological effects of light. Annals of the New York Academy of Sciences, 453*, 170–181.

de Coursey, P. (1960). Daily light sensitivity in a rodent. *Science, 131*, 159–184.

Depue, A. R., Arbisi, P., Spoont, M. R., Leon, A., & Ainsworth, B. (in press). Dopamine functioning in the behavioral facilitation system and seasonal variation in behavior: Normal population and clinical studies. In N. E. Rosenthal & M. Blehar (Eds.), *Seasonal affective disorders and phototherapy*. New York: Guilford Press.

Dietzel, M., Saletu, B., Birsak, L., Veit, I., Marx, B., & Lesch, O. (in press). Biologisch aktives Licht: eine wirksame Therapie im schweren Alkoholentzug. In B. Pflug (Ed.), *Chronophamakologie, Chronobiologie*. Stuttgart & New York: Fischer Verlag.

Dietzel, M., Saletu, B., Lesch, O. M., Sieghardt, W., & Schjerve, M. (1986). Light treatment in depressive illness. *European Neurology, 25*, (Suppl. 2), 93–103.

Duncan, C. C., & Rosenthal, N. E. (1986). *Effects of phototherapy on brain potentials in patients with seasonal affective disorder: A pilot study*. Paper presented at the annual meeting of the Society for Psychophysiological Research, Montreal. (Abstract No. 26).

Eastman, C. I. (1987). Bright light in work–sleep schedules for shift workers: Application of circadian rhythms principles. In L. Rensing, V. van der Heiden, & M. C. Mackey

(Eds.), *Temporal disorder in human oscillatory systems* (pp. 176–185). Berlin: Springer-Verlag.

Elliot, J. A. (1976). Circadian rhythms and photoperiodic time measurements in mammals. *Federation Proceedings, 35,* 2339–2346.

Esquirol, E. (1845). *Mental maladies: A treatise on insanity,* E. K. Hunt (Trans.), (pp. 275–315). Philadelphia: Lea & Blanchard.

Fernstrom, J. D., & Wurtman, R. J. (1972). Brain serotonin content: Physiological regulation by plasma neutral amino acids. *Science, 178,* 414–416.

Granstein, R. D., & Sober, A. J. (1982). Current concepts in ultraviolet carcinogenesis. *Proceedings of the Society for Experimental Biology and Medicine, 170,* 115–125.

Griesinger, W. (1845). *Die Pathologie und Therapie der psychischen Krankheiten* (p. 175). Stuttgart: A. Krabbe.

Hamilton, M. (1967). Development of a rating scale for primary depressive illness. *British Journal of Social and Clinical Psychology, 6,* 278–296.

Hellekson, C. J., Kline, J. A., & Rosenthal, N. E. (1986). Phototherapy for seasonal affective disorder in alaska. *American Journal of Psychiatry, 143,* 1035–1037.

Hellpach, W. (1911). *Die geopsychischen Erscheinungen.* Leipzig.

Hoban, T. M., & Sulzman, F. M. (1985). Light effects on circadian timing system of a diurnal primate, the squirrel monkey. *American Journal of Physiology, 249,* 274–280.

Hoffman, K. (1981). Photoperiodism in vertebrates. In J. Aschoff (Ed.), *Handbook of behavioral neurobiology* (pp. 449–473). New York: Plenum.

Hoffman, R. A., Davidson, K., & Steinberg, K. (1982). Influence of photoperiod and temperature on weight gain, food consumption, fat pads and thyroxine in male golden hamsters. *Growth, 46,* 150–162.

Hollwich, F. (1955). Der Einfluss des Augenlichtes auf die Regulation des Stoffwechsels. *Klinische Monatsblätter für Augenheilkunde, 23,*(Beih.), 95–136.

Humphris, F. H. (1924). *Artifical sunlight and its therapeutic uses* (pp. 221–223). London: Oxford University Press.

Immelmann, K. (1973). Role of the environment in reproduction as source of predictive information. In D. S. Farner (Ed.), *Breeding biology of birds* (pp. 121–147). Washington, DC: National Academy of Sciences.

Jacobsen, F. M., Sack, D. A., Wehr, T. A., Rogers, L. B. S., & Rosenthal, N. E. (in press). Neuroendocrine responses to 5-hydroxytryptophane in seasonal affective disorder (SAD). *Archives of General Psychiatry.*

Jacobsen, F. M., Wehr, T. A., & Rosenthal, N. E. (in press). The pineal and seasonal reproduction in seasonal affective disorder. In P. Pancheri L. Zichella (Eds.), *Biorhythms and stress in the physiopathology of reproduction.* Washington, DC: Hemisphere.

Jacobsen, F. M., Wehr, T. A., Sack, D. A., & Rosenthal, N. E. (1986). *Predictors of response to phototherapy in seasonal affective disorder.* Paper presented at the 139th annual meeting of the American Psychiatric Association. Abstract No. 150.

Jacobsen, F. M., Wehr, T. A., Skwerer, R. A., Sack, D. A., & Rosenthal, N. E. (in press). Morning- versus midday-phototherapy opf seasonal affective disorder. *American Journal of Psychiatry.*

James, S. P., Wehr, T. A., Sack, D. A., Parry, B. L., Rogers, L. B. S., & Rosenthal, N. E. (1986). The dexamethasone suppression test in seasonal affective disorder. *Comprehensive Psychiatry, 27,* 224–226.

James, S. P., Wehr, T. A., Sack, D. A., Parry, B. L., & Rosenthal, N. E. (1985). Treatment of seasonal affective disorder with light in the evening. *British Journal of Psychiatry, 147,* 424–428.

Kappers, A. J. (1960). The development, topographical relations and innervations of the epiphysis cerebri in the albino rat. *Zeitschrift für Zellforschung und Mikroskopische Anatomie, 52,* 163–215.

Kappers, A. J., Smith, A. R., & De Vries, R. A. C. (1979). The mammalian pineal gland and its control of hypothalamic activity. In J. Ariens Kappers & P. Pevet (Eds.), *The pineal gland in vertebrates including man. Progress in Brain Research, 52,* 149–174.

Kasper, S., Rogers, L. B. S., Yancey, A., Skwerer, R. G., Schulz, P. M., & Rosenthal, N. E. (in press). Phototherapy in individuals with and without subsyndromal seasonal affective disorder. *Archives of General Psychiatry.*

Kellogg, J. H. (1910). *Light therapeutics: A practical manual of phototherapy for the student and practitioner.* Battle Creek, MI: Good Health Publishing Co.

Köhler, W. K., & Pflug, B. (in press). Lichttherapie depressiver Erkrankungen. In H. Häfer, H. Heimann, & B. Pflug (Eds.), *Aktuelle Psychiatrie.* Stuttgart: Fischer Verlag.

Kovacs, R. (1924). *Electrotherapy and the elements of light therapy* (pp. 367–167). Philadelphia: Lea & Febiger.

Kraepelin, E. (1921). *Manic-depressive insanity and paranoia,* G. M. Robertson (Ed.); R. M. Barclay (Trans.). Edinburgh: Livingstone.

Kraines,S. (1957). *Mental depressions and their treatment.* New York: Macmillan.

Kripke, D. F. (1985). Therapeutic effects of bright light in depressed patients. In R. J. Wurtmann, M. J. Baum, & J. T. Potts (Eds.), *The medical and biological effects of light. Annals of the New York Academy of Sciences, 28,* 270–281.

Kripke, D. F., Gillin, J. C., & Mullaney, D. J. (in press). Treatment of major depressive disorders by bright white light for five days. In A. Halaris (Ed.), *Chronobiology and neuropsychiatric disorders.* New York: Pergamon Press.

Kripke, D. F., Mullaney, D. J., Savides, T. J., & Gillin, J. C. (in press). Phototherapy for nonseasonal major depressive disorders. *Journal of Biological Rhythms.*

Kripke, D. F., Risch, S. C., & Janowsky, D. (1983). Bright white light alleviates depression. *Psychiatry Research, 10,* 105–112.

Lange, J. (1928). Die endogenen und reaktiven Gemütserkrankungen und die manisch–depressive Konstitution. In O. Bumke (Ed.), *Handbuch der Geisteskrankheiten* (Vol. 6). Berlin: Springer-Verlag.

Lewy, A. J., Kern, H. A., Rosenthal, N. E., & Wehr, T. A. (1982). Bright artificial light treatment of a manic-depressive patient with a seasonal mood cycle. *American Journal of Psychiatry, 139,* 1496–1498.

Lewy, A. J., & Sack, R. L. (1986a). Minireview: Light therapy and psychiatry. *Proceedings of the Society for Experimental Biology and Medicine, 183,* 11–18.

Lewy, A. J., & Sack, R. L. (1986b). Melatonin physiology and light therapy. *Clinical Neuropharmacology, 9,* 196–198.

Lewy, A. J., Sack, R. L., Frederickson, R. H., Reaves, M., Denney, D., & Zielske, D. R. (1983). The use of bright light in the treatment of chronobiologic sleep and mood disorders: The phase-response curve. *Psychopharmacology Bulletin, 19,* 523–525.

Lewy, A. L., Sack, R. L., Miller, S., & Hoban, T. M. (1987). Antidepressant and circadian phase-shifting effects of light. *Science, 235,* 352–354.

Lewy, A. J., Sack, R. L., & Singer, C. M. (1985a). Melatonin, light and chronobiological disorders. In D. Evered & S. Clark (Eds.), *Photoperiodism, melatonin and the pineal* (pp. 231–252). London: Pitman.

Lewy, A. J., Sack, R. L., & Singer, C. M. (1985b). Immediate and delayed effects of bright light on human melatonin production: Shifting "dawn" and "dusk" shifts the dim light melatonin onset (DLMO). *Annals of the New York Academy of Sciences, 28,* 253–259.

Lewy, A. J., Wehr, T. A., Goodwin, F. K., Newsome, D. A., & Markey, S. P. (1980). Light suppresses melatonin secretion in humans. *Science, 210,* 1267–1269.

Lewy, A. J., Wehr, T. A., Goodwin, F. K., Newsome, D. A., & Rosenthal, N. E. (1981). Manic-depressive patients may be supersensitive to light. *Lancet, I,* 383–384.

Liebowitz, M. R., Quitkin, F. M., Steward, J. W., McGrath, P. J., Harrison, W., Rabkin, J., Tricamo, E., Markowitz, J. S., & Klein, D. F. (1984). Phenelzine vs. imipramine in atypical depression. *Archives of General Psychiatry, 41,* 669–667.

Lincoln, G. A. (1983). Photoperiodism: Melatonin as a seasonal time cue: A commercial story. *Nature, 302,* 755.

McLellan, G. H., Riley, W. J., & Davies, C. P. (1979). Season variation in serum-thyroxine. *Lancet, I,* 883–884.

Murphy, D. L., Campbell, L., & Costa, J. L. (1978). Current status of the indoleamine hypothesis of affective disorders. In M. A. Di Mascio & A. Killam (Eds.), *Psychopharmacology: a generation of progress* (pp. 1223–1234). New York: Raven Press.

O'Malley, B. P., Richardson, A., Cook, N., et al. (1984). Circadian rhythms of serum thyrotropin and body temperature in euthyroid individuals and their responses to warming. *Clinical Science, 67,* 433–437.

Papousek, M. (1975). Chronobiologische Aspekte der Zyklothymie. *Fortschritte der Neurologie, Psychiatrie und ihrer Grenzgebiete, 43,* 381–440.

Pelletier, J. (1973). Evidence for photoperiodic control of prolactin release in rams. *Journal of Reproduction and Fertility, 35,* 143–147.

Peter, K., Räbiger, U., & Kowalik, A. (1986). Erste Ergebnisse mit Bright-Light (Phototherapie) bei affektiven Psychosen. *Psychiatrie, Neurologie und Medizinische Psychologie, 38,* 384–390.

Pilcz, A. (1901). *Die periodischen Geistesstörungen.* Fischer Verlag: Jena.

Pittendringh, C. S. (in press). The photoperiodic phenomena: Seasonal modulation of the "day" within. *Journal of Biological Rhythms.*

Rosenthal, N. E. (in press). Light therapy in the treatment of affective disorders. *Manual of Psychiatric Treatment.*

Rosenthal, N. E., Brainard, G. C., Sherry, D., Skwerer, R. G., Waxler, M., Kelly, K., Sack, D. A., Wehr, T. A., & Schulz, P. M. (1987a). *Effects of different light wavelength in SAD.* Paper presented at the 140th annual meeting of the American Psychiatric Association. (Abstr. No. 13).

Rosenthal, N. E., Carpenter, C. J., James, S. P., Parry, B. L., & Rogers, S. L. B. (1986a). Seasonal affective disorder in children and adolescents. *American Journal of Psychiatry, 143,* 356–358.

Rosenthal, N. E., Genhardt, M., Sack, D. A., Skwerer, R. G., & Wehr, T. A. (1987b). Seasonal affective disorder: Relevance for treatment and research of bulimia. In J. I. Hudson & H. G. Pope (Eds.), *Psychbiology of bulimia.* Washington, DC: American Psychiatric Press.

Rosenthal, N. E., Jacobsen, F. M., Sack, D. A., Arendt, J., James, S. P., Parry, B. L., & Wehr, T. A. (in press-a). Atenolol in seasonal affective disorder: A test of the melatonin hypothesis. *American Journal of Psychiatry.*

Rosenthal, N. E., Rotter, A., Jacobsen, F. M., & Skwerer, R. G. (in press-b). No mood-altering effects found following treatment of normal subjects with bright light in the morning. *Psychiatry Research.*

Rosenthal, N. E., Sack, D. A., Carpenter, C. J., Parry, B. L., Mendelsohn, W. B., & Wehr, T. A. (1985). Antidepressant effects of light in seasonal affective disorder. *American Journal of Psychiatry, 142,* 163–170.

Rosenthal, N. E., Sack, D. A., Gillin, J. C., Lewy, A. J., Goodwin, F. K., Davenport, Y., & Mueller, P. S. (1984). Seasonal affective disorder; a description of the syndrome and preliminary findings with light therapy. *Archives of General Psychiatry, 41,* 72–80.

Rosenthal, N. E., Sack, D. A., Jacobsen, F. M., James, S. P., Parry, B. L. P., Arendt, J., Tamarkin, L., & Wehr, T. A. (1986b). Melatonin in seasonal affective disorder. *Journal of Neural Transmission, 21*(Suppl. 2). 257–267.

Rosenthal, N. E., Sack, D. A., Skwerer, R. G., Jacobsen, F. M., & Wehr, T. A. (in press-c). Phototherapy of seasonal affective disorder. *Journal of Biological Rhythms.*
Rosenthal, N. E., Skwerer, R. G., Sack, D. A., Duncan, C. C., Jacobsen, F. M., Tamarkin, L., & Wehr, T. A. (in press-d). *Psychopharmacology Bulletin.*
Schildkraut, J. (1965). Catecholamine hypothesis of affective disorders. *American Journal of Psychiatry, 122,* 509–522.
Schleifer, S. J., Keller, S. E., Meyerson, A. T., Raskin, M. J., Davis, L., & Stein, M. (1984). Lymphocyte function in major depressive disorder. *Archives of General Psychiatry, 41,* 484.
Skwerer, R. G., Duncan, C. C., Sack, D. A., Jacobsen, F. M., Tamarkin, L., Kasper, S., Wehr, T. A., & Rosenthal, N. E. (in press). The biology of seasonal affective disorder and phototherapy. *Journal of Biological Rhythms.*
Skwerer, R. G., Rosenthal, N. E., Wehr, T. A., Jacobsen, F. M., Sack, D. A., Paciotti, G. F., Kelly, K. A., & Tamarkin, L. (1987). *Photoimmunology and seasonal affective disorder.* Paper presented at the 42nd annual meeting of the Society of Biological Psychiatry. (Abstr. No. 265).
Spitzer, R. L., Endicott, J., & Robins, E. (1978). Research diagnostic criteria: Rationale and reliability. *Archives of General Psychiatry, 35,* 773–782.
Stein, M., Keller, S., & Schleifer, S. (1985). The hypothalamus and the immune response. In H. Weiner, M. A. Hofer, & A. H. Stunker (Eds.), *Brain behavior and bodily disease.* New York: Raven Press.
Tamarkin, L., Baird, C. J., & Almeida, O. F. (1985). Melatonin: A coordinating signal for mammalian reproduction. *Science, 227,* 714–720.
Terman, M. (in press). On the question of mechanism in phototherapy: Considerations of clinical efficacy and epidemiology. *Journal of Biological Rhythms.*
Terman, M., Quitkin, F. M., & Terman, J. S. (1986). Light therapy for SAD: Dose regimens. Paper presented at the 139th annual meeting of the American Psychiatric Association. (Abstr. No. 121).
Thompson, C., Isaacs, G., Stainer, S., & Miles, A. (1986). Seasonal affective disorder—Phototherapy and salivary melatonin. Paper presented at the 15th C.I.N.P. Congress, Puerto Rico. (Abstract No. 263).
Wade, G. N. (1983). Dietary obesity in golden hamsters: Reversibility and effects of sex and photoperiod. *Physiology and Behavior, 114,* 131–137.
Wehr, T. A., et al. (1988). *Seasonal affective disorder with summer depression and winter hypomania.* Manuscript submitted for publication.
Wehr, T. A., Goodwin, F. K., Duncan, W. C., & Gillin, J. C. (1979). Phase advance of the circadian sleep–wake cycle as an antidepressant. *Science, 206,* 710–713.
Wehr, T. A., Jacobsen, F. M., Sack, D. A., Arendt, J., Tamarkin, L., & Rosenthal, N. E. (1986). Phototherapy of seasonal affective disorder. Time of day and suppression of melatonin are not critical for antidepressant effects. *Archives of General Psychiatry, 43,* 870–875.
Wehr, T. A., Skwerer, R. M., Jacobsen, F. M., Sack, D. A., & Rosenthal, N. E. (1987). Eye-versus skin-phototherapy of seasonal disorder. *American Journal of Psychiatry, 144,* 753–757.
Wirz-Justice, A., Bucheli, B., Graw, P., Kielholz, P., Fisch, H. U., & Woggon, B. (1986). Light treatment of seasonal affective disorder in Switzerland. *Acta Psychiatrica Scandinavica, 74,* 193–204.
Wirz-Justice, A., Schmid, A. C., Graw, P., Kräuchi, K., Pöldinger, W., Fisch, H. U., & Buddeberg, C. (1987). Dose relationships of morning bright white light in seasonal affective disorders (SAD). *Experientia, 43,* 574–576.
Wurtman, R. J., & Wurtman, J. J. (1984). Nutritional control of central neurotransmitters.

In K. M. Pirke & D. Ploog (Eds.), *The psychobiology of anorexia nervosa.* (pp. 4–11). Berlin: Springer-Verlag.

Yerevanian, B. I., Anderson, J. L., Grota, L. J., & Bray, M. (1986). Effects of bright incandescant light on seasonal and nonseasonal major depressive disorder. *Psychiatry Research, 18,* 355–364.

Zifferblatt, S. M., Curtis, C. S., & Pinsky, J. L. (1980). Understanding food habits. *Journal of the American Dietetic Association, 76,* 9–14.

IV Treatment

Cognitive Theory and Therapy of Anxiety and Depression

David A. Clark
Aaron T. Beck

I. Introduction

The last two decades have witnessed a resurgence in theory, research, and practice focused on the cognitive concomitants of psychopathology (Mahoney, 1987). Consequently, a growing number of investigators are examining cognitive dysfunction in psychological disorders. In addition, a variety of cognitive and cognitive–behavioral (CB) interventions have been developed for treating psychopathological states.

Hollon and Beck (1986) have defined cognitive and CB therapies as "approaches that attempt to modify existing or anticipated disorders by virtue of altering cognitions or cognitive processes" (p. 443). A number of these therapeutic approaches have been accepted as plausible treatments for anxiety and/or depression. These include Beck's (Beck, Rush, Shaw, & Emery, 1979; Beck & Emery, 1985) cognitive therapy (CT), Ellis' (1962) rational emotive therapy (RET), Meichenbaum's (1977) self-instructional training (SIT) and stress inoculation therapy, and Goldfried, DeCantecco, and Weinberg's (1974) systematic rational restructuring (SRR).

Anxiety and Depression

Despite their common cognitive orientation, these therapeutic approaches differ in many respects. Differences are evident in the primary cognitive constructs targeted for change, the methods used to achieve this change, their range of application and the quantity of empirical research supporting their efficacy, and the extent to which therapeutic practice is derived from a distinct cognitive model of psychopathology.

Beck's CT has emerged as one of the most widely accepted of these treatment approaches. It is derived from his schema-based information-processing model of psychological disturbance and focuses on surfacelike thoughts and images as well as processing distortions and underlying maladaptive beliefs. CT emphasizes an empirical hypothesis-testing approach to modify cognitive dysfunction. It has been employed successfully with a variety of disorders (Beck & Rush, 1988), although its strongest empirical support is in the treatment of depression. However, preliminary evidence suggests that CT may prove effective with certain anxiety disorders as well as with panic attacks. The primary focus of this chapter is on Beck's CT of depression and anxiety, although other cognitive and CB treatment approaches will be discussed where applicable. The chapter is divided into three sections: (1) presentation of an integrated information-processing model of anxiety and depression in which the similarities and differences in cognitive functioning between these disorders are emphasized, (2) an outline of the CT treatment of anxiety, panic disorder, and depression, and (3) a brief review of the empirical status of cognitive and CB treatments of anxiety and depression.

II. Anxiety and Depression: Toward an Integrated Theory of Information Processing

A. Basic Tenets of the Cognitive Model

In order to survive, humans must process information from their environment. Consequently, we actively construct our reality by selecting, transforming, encoding, storing, and retrieving information about ourselves and the world around us. This information-processing activity in turn affects our emotional and behavioral responses.

In psychopathological conditions systematic biases are introduced into the processing of information. These cognitive distortions reflect the excessive functioning or malfunctioning of normal cognitive processes (Beck, 1987; Beck & Emery, 1985). As noted by Kendall (1985), cognitive deficiencies (acting without thinking or failing to engage in the processing of relevant information) are also prominent in certain types of psychopathology, such as impulsive acting-out and aggressive behaviors. Nevertheless, the cognitive dysfunction in anxiety and depression primarily reflects the distortion of information, although cognitive deficiencies may also be evident to a lesser degree. Thus the various anxiety disorders are associated with an exaggeration of the normal survival mechanism. Anxious patients incorrectly perceive threat or danger to their survival and judge themselves incapable of effectively coping with this threat, whereas normal persons are able to make a reasonably accurate assessment of the possibility of harm to their personal domains (Beck & Rush, 1988). In depression, one sees a maladaptive appraisal of events involving loss or deprivation. With nondepressed individuals, a loss may trigger a temporary withdrawal from both activities and emotional involvements. Depressed individuals, on the other hand, show persistent withdrawal as a result of appraising their current negative circumstances as pervasive, global, and irreversible (Beck & Emery, 1985). In addition, cognitive deficiencies may contribute to the depressive state in the form of problem-solving deficits.

According to the cognitive model, this faulty information-processing system leads to the affective, behavioral, motivational, and physiological symptoms of anxiety and depression. However, the cognitive model does not assert that biased information processing is the sole cause of psychopathology: genetic, developmental, hormonal, physical, and psychological factors may also be involved in the etiology of disorders such as anxiety and depression. As a result, the model contends that cognitive factors are an intrinsic part of a syndrome and so function to maintain psychopathologic states (Beck, 1967, 1976, 1987).

Recently Ingram and Kendall (1986) proposed a taxonomic system for categorizing the various constructs used in information-processing theories of psychopathology. They suggested that most cognitive variables can be classified as referring to cognitive structure, propositions, operations, or products, though some variables may fall into more than one category. Cognitive structure is defined as the manner in which data are internally organized or represented, while cognitive propositions refer to the actual information stored in the structures. Cognitive operations are the numerous procedures or processes by which the components of the system interact, while cognitive products are viewed as output resulting from the functioning of the information-processing system.

Ingram and Kendall's (1986) classificatory scheme is a useful framework for discussing information-processing models of psychopathology. Under this scheme four concepts can be identified which are basic to

Beck's cognitive theory. These constructs operate in a reciprocal, interactional manner but vary in terms of function, accessibility, temporality, and specificity/generality. First, information exists in structures called schemata. Second, these structures give rise to cognitive operations and processes that distort incoming information. Third, as a by-product of maladaptive schemata and biased cognitive processing, negative thoughts and images dominate the stream of consciousness. Finally, relatively stable, broadly based schemata may cluster to form personality dimensions. These dimensions are thought to contribute to an individual's vulnerability to psychopathology.

B. Schemata

Schemata are functional structures of relatively enduring representations of prior knowledge and experience (Beck, 1987; Greenberg & Beck, in press-a). These cognitive structures direct the screening, encoding, differentiating, organizing, and retrieving of environmental stimuli (Beck, 1967; Beck et al., 1979). Because of the vast array of stimuli impinging upon the organism, schemata provide an economical method for processing information. Stimuli consistent with existing schemata are elaborated and encoded, while inconsistent information is ignored or forgotten (Greenberg, Vazquez, & Alloy, 1988). However, this "top-down processing" may sacrifice accuracy to economy. As a result, systematic errors may be introduced into the information-processing system by the activation of prepotent, idiosyncratic, maladaptive schemata (Beck et al., 1979). A by-product of this activation and faulty information processing is a distorted interpretation of reality.

Both structural and propositional (i.e., content) characteristics are important in understanding schematic influences in psychopathology. The idiosyncratic, maladaptive schemata in psychological disorders tend to be more rigid, impermeable, and concrete than the adaptive, flexible schemata of normal individuals (Beck, 1967). Furthermore, these dysfunctional schemata may organize into clusters dealing with diverse situations. If these schematic constellations or sets become too overinclusive, encompassing a variety of situations, then a broadly based, superordinate, organizing principle, labeled a *mode,* is operating (Beck & Emery, 1985). Modes are particularly prominent in psychopathological states, such that individuals may exhibit modes for depression, fear or danger, narcissism, paranoia, and the like.

In cognitive theory, various psychopathological syndromes are differentiated by the content or propositional nature of their schemata. Thus, the schematic organization of the clinically depressed individual is dominated by an overwhelming negativity. That is, depressives see themselves, the world around them, and their future in a negative fashion (Beck et al., 1979). This negative cognitive triad means that depressives become preoccupied with possible adverse consequences and ignore any positive interpretations or events (Beck, 1987). They see themselves as inadequate, deprived, and worthless, they perceive the world as hostile, rejecting, and as presenting insurmountable obstacles, and view the future as predetermined failure and hopelessness. In essence, then, a constrictive mode operates in depression whereby the individual withdraws from events and conserves energy in response to a pervasive negativity.

In anxiety states, the characteristic cognitive mode is one of threat or danger to one's personal domain (Beck & Emery, 1985). This cognitive mode results in the anxious person being hypervigilant for stimuli signaling possible danger or threat. The individual focuses on the dangerous aspects of a situation, while the safety features may be completely ignored. Furthermore, this cognitive mode influences a person's self-appraisal such that an exaggerated sense of vulnerability is experienced. In anxiety states, estimates of the degree of danger or threat to one's personal domain are maximized, while self-appraisals of one's ability to cope with the situation are minimized (Beck & Weishaar, in press).

The various subsyndromes of anxiety are further differentiated by their dominant cognitive constellation. In generalized anxiety disorder (GAD), a variety of life situations are interpreted as threatening to one's self-concept. When in threatening situations, the anxious person experiences lower self-confidence and perceptions of inadequacy. Patients with panic disorder are likely to interpret any unexplained symptom or sensation as a sign of some forbidding physical or mental catastrophe. This catastrophic misinterpretation, in turn, intensifies the patient's hypervigilance to bodily sensations (D. M. Clark, 1986a). In agoraphobia, the patient associates panic attacks with particular situations and so develops an avoidance of the fear stimuli. However, the agoraphobic may enter the fear situation if she or he perceives quick access to a place of safety (e.g., home, hospital, physician) when any frightening bodily sensation is perceived (Beck & Emergy, 1985). Finally, in simple phobias, the anticipated physical or psychological harm is represented in well-defined, specific situations. The exaggerated sense of danger and underestimation of one's coping abilities lead to the conclusion that avoidance is the best remedy. One also sees this cognitive set in the evaluation phobias (i.e., social, speech, test anxiety) wherein one fears being disparaged by others.

C. Cognitive Operations

Maladaptive schemata give rise to systematic bias in the way information from the environment is perceived and interpreted. A number of cognitive operations that result in the maintenance of anxiety and depression have been identified (Beck, 1967; Beck et al., 1979). These include *arbitrary inference* (drawing a conclusion in the absence of evidence or in favor of contradictory evidence); *selective abstraction* (taking a detail out of its context while ignoring the more prominent features of the situation); *overgeneralization* (formulating a conclusion based on one or more isolated events and then applying this concept across diverse situations); *magnification and minimization* (distorting the importance of an event); *personalization* (relating external events to oneself in the absence of data); and *absolutistic, dichotomous thinking* (tendency to evaluate all experiences in terms of one of two mutually exclusive categories).

Although each of these cognitive distortions is evident to some degree in all psychopathological states, their importance will vary across disorders. Depressives selectively attend to the negative features of a situation and ignore the positive. Errors or mishaps are personalized and their negative effects are exaggerated and overgeneralized.

In anxiety states, distorted information processing is evident in situations perceived as threatening. This faulty processing confirms the person's view of impending danger and increased vulnerability. Danger cues are perceived and accentuated while safety signals are either ignored or minimized. Stimulus generalization may occur with a range of stimuli being interpreted as threatening. Anxious individuals selectively recall any past or present experience consistent with their perception of danger. Finally, they appear unable to distinguish between stimuli signaling safety and those indicating threat. Thus, the net result is a hypervigilance for threat-related cues and heightened sense of vulnerability.

D. Cognitive Products

As a product of the information-processing system, patient self-verbalizations reflect the content of their cognitive structures as well as their biased interpretation of events. Two types of cognitive product particularly relevant to psychopathological states are (1) voluntary thoughts or images and (2) automatic thoughts. Both types comprise the internal dialogue and so are relatively accessible to awareness. Moreover, they tend to be transient, statelike phenomena, easily influenced by the prevailing mood state and current situational demands.

Automatic thoughts are verbal or visual ideation that are involuntary and repetitive in nature, and seem plausible to the individual at the time of their occurrence. They differ from voluntary cognitions in the degree of control associated with their occurrence. Automatic thoughts are involuntary intrusions of which the patient may not always be aware. Consequently, individuals may need training to accurately identify their automatic thoughts and images.

Despite these characteristic differences, voluntary and automatic cognitions are both products of the underlying activated schemata. In depression, both types of mental events will contain themes of loss, failure, rejection, incompetence, and hopelessness. In anxiety states, themes of possible physical or mental harm as well as a negative self-view in coping with the fear situation will dominate.

E. Cognitive Vulnerability

Strong individual differences clearly exist in the development of anxiety and depression. Some individuals are more susceptible to these disorders than others when confronted with stressful life circumstances. High rates of relapse are common, with some individuals showing a persistence of the disorder across many years. To explain this, cognitive theory asserts that, among other things, certain individuals do show a cognitive vulnerability which predisposes them toward development of anxiety or depression.

Cognitive theory assumes that depressive and anxious schemata remain dormant until activated by particular environmental events. Thus prepotent depressive schemata will dominate when triggered by events perceived as loss or deprivation. Anxious schemata involving a fight or flight reaction will be triggered by events perceived as physically or psychologically threatening.

An individual's vulnerability will depend, to a great extent, on his or her personality structure (Beck, 1987). In cognitive theory, personality attributes or traits are viewed as superordinate schemata. Two major personality dimensions have been identified as possible vulnerability factors: *autonomy* and *sociotropy*. The autonomous personality values independence, freedom of action, privacy, and self-determination, while the sociotropic person places a high premium on interpersonal relations, acceptance, and affection (Beck, 1987; Beck, Epstein, & Harrison, 1983).

The prepotent depressive or anxious schemata comprising these personality dimensions remain relatively inactive until triggered by specific psychosocial stressors. For autonomous individuals, any event involving defeat or deprivation which is perceived as infringing on their independence, self-determination, or competence will trigger depression-related schemata and lead to a depressive disorder. Events involving possible harm or danger may also be perceived as encroaching on one's independence and so lead to an increased sense of vulnerability. Conversely, sociotropic individuals will develop depression or anxiety when events involving loss or danger, respectively, are perceived as limiting their social acceptance and personal attractiveness. Vulnerability to depression or anxiety, then, is viewed as resulting from a congruence between specific types of psychosocial stressors and certain personality structures.

F. Empirical Status of Cognitive Theory

In recent years empirical research has investigated the various hypotheses of cognitive theory. Early studies focused primarily at the level of cognitive product. However, subsequent research has attempted to assess cognitive structure more directly by investigating biases in the encoding and retrieval of information.

Cognitive Products. In a study of 50 clinically depressed patients, Beck (1967) noted that the dominant ideation of these patients involved themes of negative self-evaluation, hopelessness, and negative view of the world. Since then, a number of self-report questionnaires, such as the Automatic Thoughts Questionnaire (Hollon & Kendall, 1980), Cognitions Checklist (Beck, Brown, Steer, Eidelson, & Riskind, 1987), and Crandell Cognition Inventory (Crandell & Chambless, 1986), have been developed to assess depressive ideation in a more objective, systematic manner. A number of studies using these instruments have documented that depressed patients do, in fact, report a more negative view of self, world, and future than do nondepressed psychiatric controls (Beck *et al.*, 1987; Blackburn, Jones, & Lewin, 1986; Crandell & Chambless, 1986; Dobson & Shaw, 1986; Eaves & Rush, 1984; Harrell & Ryon, 1983; Hollon, Kendall, & Lumry, 1986).

Fewer studies have investigated the content of self-referent thinking in anxious individuals. Beck, Laude, and Bohnert (1974) and, in a later study, Hibbert (1984), found that GAD patients reported ideation involving themes of physical or psychological threat to one's personal domain. More recently, anxious cognitions have been assessed using a more structured objective format. Self-report measures such as the Anxious Self-Statement Questionnaire (Kendall & Hollon, 1987), Agoraphobia Cognitions Questionnaire (Chambless, Caputo, Bright, & Gallager, 1984), and Cognitions Checklist have demonstrated that anxious individuals (i.e., GAD, panic and social phobic disorders) report more ideation involving threat and inability to cope than do nonanxious controls.

Thus, moderately strong empirical evidence supports the view that in anxiety states, thoughts and images involving danger, vulnerability, and absence of safety dominate the internal dialogue.

Cognitive Operations. A number of laboratory studies have found that depressives do process information in a biased manner, but only if the material is self-referent in nature. Compared to nondepressed psychiatric controls, depressed patients (1) underestimate the success of their performance (Buchwald, 1977; Loeb, Beck, & Diggory, 1971), (2) monitor significantly more negative and fewer positive interpersonal behaviors when viewing a videotape of their role-play interactions (Roth & Rehm, 1980), (3) overestimate the negative and/or underestimate the positive feedback received subsequent to task performance (DeMonbreun & Craighead, 1977; Finkel, Glass, & Merluzzi, 1982; Nelson & Craighead, 1977), and (4) exhibit a negative perceptual bias when presented with brief tachistoscopic displays of pleasant, unpleasant, and neutral words (Powell & Hemsley, 1984). However, a few studies have failed to confirm these findings. For example, MacLeod, Tata, and Mathews (1987) did not find quicker perception of negative words by depressed patients in a lexical decision experiment while Craighead, Hickey, and DeMonbreun (1979) failed to find differences in perception of feedback between mildly depressed and nondepressed students.

Taken together, there is strong empirical evidence that a depressive mood state does bias one's perception against positive self-referent information. The data, however, have been less consistent in demonstrating an enhanced processing for negative self-referent material. It may be that in milder depressive-like states one may only find a blocking of positive information. As one progresses to a more severe clinical depression, an enhanced processing of negative material may also become apparent (Beck & D. A. Clark, 1988). Thus studies using analog subjects may fail to find a cognitive bias for negative self-referent stimuli.

Empirical support for the view that anxious patients show a heightened sensitivity to threat-related cues comes from a variety of experimental paradigms. For example, two studies have shown that GAD patients tend to interpret ambiguous stimuli in a threatening manner (Bulter & Mathews, 1983; Eysenck, Mathews, & Richards, 1987).

With the dichotic listening task, agoraphobic, social phobic, and obsessive–compulsive patients show a heightened sensitivity to fear-related words presented in the unattended channel (Burgess, Jones, Robertson, Radcliffe, & Emerson, 1981; Foa & McNally, 1986). Mathews and MacLeod (1986), however, failed to find enhanced recognition for unattended threat words, though these stimuli did cause more task interference for anxious than for control subjects. Overall, then, there is evidence that anxious patients selectively perceive threat and danger stimuli.

A number of studies have shown that threat stimuli demand more processing resources in anxious than in nonanxious individuals (Mathews & MacLeod, 1987). Mathews and MacLeod (1985) found that anxious patients evidenced greater interference from threat-related words in a Stroop color-naming task. Watts, McKenna, Sharrock, and Trezise (1986) reported that spider phobics were selectively disrupted in the color-naming task by spider-related words.

In a final experiment, MacLeod, Mathews, and Tata (1986) employed a visual probe detection task to show that anxious patients do show an attentional shift toward threat stimuli. The results from this study show that anxious individuals will automatically and selectively attend to threatening stimuli in their environment.

Cognitive Structure. Dysfunctional schemata have been directly investigated by employing either structured self-report instruments or measures of process variables such as encoding and retrieval. Among the former, the Dysfunctional Attitudes Scale (DAS) is currently the most widely adopted measure of underlying dysfunctional attitudes and beliefs. Although the DAS was originally intended to measure beliefs associated with depression, recent evidence suggests it may assess more general maladaptive attitudes (Hollon et al., 1986). Nonetheless, the DAS has been related to measures of depression severity (Dobson & Breiter, 1983; Dobson & Shaw, 1986) and can differentiate depressed from nondepressed psychiatric and normal control groups (Hamilton & Abramson, 1983; Hollon et al., 1986). Furthermore, there is some indication that high pretreatment DAS scores may be predictive of poorer treatment response (Keller, 1983) or subsequent relapse (Rush, Weissenburger, & Eaves, 1986; Simons, Murphy, Levine, & Wetzel, 1986). These results, then, suggest that the DAS may be tapping a stable cognitive component of depression (Dobson & Shaw, 1986).

Schemata have been directly investigated by assessing their effects on the encoding and retrieval of personally relevant information. A number of studies have employed a self-referent encoding task (SRET) to assess self-schemata. Subjects are presented with a list of positive, negative, and neutral trait adjectives and are asked to rate whether each adjective is self-descriptive. An incidental recall and/or recognition task follows presentation of the list. It is assumed that the type of trait adjective judged self-descriptive, response latencies when making these self-rating decisions, and the types of words recalled, will all reflect the nature of an individual's self-schemata.

Mixed results have been obtained with this paradigm. Most studies report that depressives endorse more negative self-descriptives than do controls (e.g., Bradley & Mathews, 1983; Clifford & Hemsley, 1987; Derry & Kuiper, 1981; Dobson & Shaw, 1987; Greenberg & Alloy, 1987; Roth & Rehm, 1980). In a clinical study, Greenberg and Beck (in press-b) also found that depressed patients endorsed more negative world- and future-relevant trait adjectives than did nondepressed psychiatric controls. However, no significant differential effects have been found in the amount of time taken to make the self-referential decision (e.g., Bradley & Mathews, 1983; Derry & Kuiper, 1981; Dobson & Shaw, 1987). The incidental recall and recognition tasks have yielded inconsistent results. Some studies have found that depressed patients recall/recognize more negative than positive trait words (Bradley & Mathews, 1983; Derry & Kuiper, 1981; Dunbar & Lishman, 1984), while others have not found such biased recall/recognition (Clifford & Hemsley, 1987; Davis, 1979; Dobson & Shaw, 1987; Roth & Rehm, 1980). However, Teasdale and his colleagues have reported that nondepressed subjects exposed to a sad mood induction do show enhanced recall of negative self-referent adjectives (D. M. Clark & Teasdale, 1985; Teasdale & Russell, 1983). Moreover, a number of researchers have found that depressives have equivalent recall rates for positive and negative material as compared to the significant positive recall bias of nondepressed controls (e.g., Breslow, Kocsis, & Belkin, 1981; Greenberg & Alloy, 1987; Kuiper & Derry, 1982).

A number of studies have investigated factors affecting the retrieval of preexperimentally stored information. Depressed mood, whether naturally occurring or experimentally induced, is more likely to elicit the recall of unpleasant than pleasant memories, while the opposite retrieval pattern is associated with an elated mood state (e.g., D. M. Clark & Teasdale, 1982; Teasdale & Taylor, 1981; Teasdale, Taylor, & Fogarty, 1980). Furthermore, depression is associated with a quicker recall of unpleasant than pleasant past memories (Lloyd & Lishman, 1975; Teasdale & Fogarty, 1979).

Fewer studies have directly investigated cognitive structure in anxiety disorders. In two experiments, Nunn, Stevenson, and Whalan (1984) found that agoraphobics had biased recall for fear-relevant information on both prose and trait adjective tasks. O'Banion and Arkowitz (1977) found that high socially anxious subjects had better recognition memory for evaluative adjectives than did low socially anxious individuals. Greenberg and Beck (in press-b) found that clinically anxious subjects did recall more negative than positive anxiety-relevant trait adjectives. However, Mogg, Mathews, and Weinman (1987) failed to find an enhanced recall for threatening or negative material in their group of anxious patients.

In summary, self-report measures have consistently demonstrated the prominence of negative self-schemata in depressive states. The results from laboratory research are less consistent, although many studies have shown an enhanced encoding and retrieval of negative material as well as a concomitant decrement in the processing and recall of positive information. It may be that in mild depressive states one only finds a failure to show the biased positive self-schemata of the nondepressed. The actual predominance of negative self-schemata may be found only in the more severe clinical states of depression (Greenberg & Alloy, 1987; Kuiper & Derry, 1982). With anxiety states, the few studies that have investigated schema effects have generally supported the view that anxious patients have a schematic organization that emphasizes danger, threat, and vulnerability.

Cognitive Vulnerability. Research on cognitive vulnerability typically involves comparisons between currently depressed subjects, remitted depressives, and nondepressed controls using various cognitive measures. Cognitive theory predicts that remitted depressives do have negative schemata, although in an attenuated form, since they are now relatively inactive. However, at the cognitive product level, there should be no difference between remitted depressives and nondepressed controls, since the depressive schemata are not activated during remission.

According to the cognitive vulnerability hypothesis, the DAS scores (as a measure of schemata) of remitted depressives should remain elevated, if this measure is indeed tapping a vulnerability marker. In fact, the empirical results have been rather mixed. Consistent with the theory, some studies reported that the DAS scores of remitted patients remain significantly elevated (Dobson & Shaw, 1986; Eaves & Rush, 1984; Reda, Carpiniello, Secchiaroli, & Blanco, 1985), while others found that with remission DAS scores return to the normal range (Hamilton & Abramson, 1983, Silverman, Silverman, & Eardley, 1984; Simons, Garfield, & Murphy, 1984). Adopting a more rigorous experimental approach, Teasdale and Dent (1987) employed the SRET to assess self-schema in remitted and never-depressed women. Consistent with the vulnerability hypothesis, they found that the remitted depressives rated more of the negative global depressive trait adjectives self-descriptive, showed poorer recall of positive trait words in the neutral and induced depressed mood conditions, and evidenced better recall of the global negative trait adjectives when in the induced mood state. However, Hammen (1985) reported on two studies from her own laboratory in which a negative self-schema, as indicated by recall bias on the SRET, was found to be state-dependent and not predictive of subsequent depression. She concluded that instead of being a vulnerability factor in depression, the negative self-schema may play a concomitant or maintaining role in the disorder.

We would argue that Hammen's (1985) conclusion regarding the negative self-schema may be premature. First, the studies reviewed in this article were based on depressed college student samples. While we recognize that college students can become depressed, nevertheless it is likely that the depressive experience of these subjects differs in important ways from that of self-referred clinic-based depressed patients. For instance, a review of the SRET research indicates that a pervasive dominant negative self-schema may be evident only in the more severe forms of depression. Second, most studies rely on the incidental recall of trait adjectives as the sole measure of schemata. Recently this task has been critized as an inappropriate measure of schema strength (Dobson & Shaw, 1987; Ferguson, Rule, & Carlson, 1983). Finally, cognitive theory postulates that it is the co-occurrence of certain types of psychosocial stressors with specific superordinate schemata (i.e., personality traits) that places an individual at high risk for depression. In fact, in her review, Hammen (1985) also proposed a cognitive–environmental model to predict the occurrence of depression.

A few studies have investigated the interaction between life events and dysfunctional attitudes in predicting depression. Persons and Rao (1985) found no evidence of increased depression as a function of an interaction between irrational beliefs and life events. Wise and Barnes (1986) reported that depression did reflect an interaction between negative life events and dysfunctional attitudes, but this was applicable only to their normal and not their clinical sample. Olinger, Kupier, and Shaw (1987) also found that more stressful life events and high DAS scores predicted increased depression scores in a student sample. Employing a memory retrieval task to assess self-schemata, Hammen, Marks, Mayol, and deMayo (1985) reported an interaction between dependent schemata and negative interpersonal events in predicting levels of depression in a student sample. The combination of self-critical schemata and negative achievement events produced a much weaker effect.

As mentioned previously, Beck (1987) has identified two personality dimensions which may represent cognitive vulnerability markers for depression: sociotropy and autonomy. To assess these dimensions, the Sociotropy/Autonomy Scale (SAS) was developed and has shown acceptable levels of reliability and validity (Beck et al., 1983; Robins, 1985). At present, only preliminary research has been conducted with the SAS. Robins and Block (1985), for example, found that depression in students correlated with sociotropy but not autonomy. Furthermore, this relation was strengthened by the occurrence of recent negative life events (both social and autonomous). In a mood induction study, Robins (1986) found that listening to social rejection tapes had a more depressive effect on high sociotropic students. Once again, autonomy was not related to mood.

To date, the full interactional model has not been sufficiently researched to allow any firm conclusions regarding cognitive vulnerability to depression. The preliminary data are encouraging for sociotropy as a possible vulnerability marker. Although the initial findings are less encouraging for autonomy, it may be that this factor is relevant for a much smaller number of depressives (e.g., D. J. Pilon, personal communication, December 15, 1986). Furthermore, there is some evidence that recovered depressives continue to show negative self-schemata, though in an attenuated form. These results, then, provide some support for the concept of cognitive vulnerability as a predisposing factor in depression.

G. The Content-Specificity Hypothesis

A main tenet of cognitive theory is that differentiation between various types of psychopathology is evident in the content of the schemata, automatic thoughts, and biased interpretations apparent in these disorders. Thus, each disorder has a specific cognitive profile. In depression, the cognitive profile involves the negative view of self, world, and future, while in anxiety disorders it consists of fear of physical or psychological harm.

Cognitive theory postulates that it is this difference in cognitive content that determines the type of psychological disturbance experienced (Beck, 1976). This cognitive specificity is at variance with Ellis' RET, in which a few core irrational beliefs are thought to underlie all emotional disorders (Ellis, 1977).

A number of studies have investigated the specificity issue at the cognitive product level. Utilizing student samples, measures of depressive cognitions show a higher correlation with depressive mood than with other noncorresponding mood states (D. A. Clark, 1986; Harrell, Chambless, & Calhoun, 1981; Thorpe, Barnes, Hunter, & Hines, 1983). Furthermore, Wickless and Kirsch (1988) found that anxious and anger cognitions evidenced higher correlations with their corresponding mood states. In a study comparing psychometrically defined groups of depressed, test-anxious, and nondepressed–nonanxious students, Ingram Kendall, Smith, Donnell, and Ronan (1987) found that depressed students reported significantly more negative self-referent automatic thoughts, while the test-anxious subjects reported significantly more automatic anxious cognitions. In a clinical study, Beck et al. (1987) found that depressive and anxious cognitions, as assessed by the CCL, were differentially correlated with the Hamilton Rating Scales for depression and anxiety, respectively. In addition, depressed patients scored significantly higher on the CCL Depression scale while GAD patients scored significantly higher on the CCL Anxiety scale. Together these results demonstrate content specificity at the cognitive product level.

Turning to cognitive processes, Beck and Emery (1985, p. 103) noted differences in the way depressed and anxious individuals interpret their environment. The negative appraisals of the depressed are global, pervasive, and exclusive. Depressives are absolute about their negative self-evaluation; they mourn the loss of all sources of gratification, and they expect failure to continue well into the future. In contrast, anxious individuals are more specific and selective in their appraisals. Their negative self-evaluation is more tentative—they anticipate possible damage to their goals and relations with others, and are afraid of possible failure and its consequences.

Currently only a few studies have directly compared the cognitive processing of anxious and depressed individuals. Butler and Mathews (1983) compared the interpretations of anxious and depressed patients regarding ambiguous scenarios. However, the depressed subjects evidenced as much anxiety as the anxious sample, thus making interpretation of the results equivocal. Based on the Attributional Style Questionnaire, Ingram et al. (1987) found that compared to the anxious group, the depressed students minimized positive and maximized negative experiences. Brown, Beck, Steer, and Riskind (1986) found that depressed patients (diagnosis of major depressive disorder) had significantly higher likelihood estimates for negative events than did patients with a generalized anxiety disorder. MacLeod et al. (1986) found that the attentional bias for threat stimuli was evident only with anxious but not depressed subjects. Together these preliminary investigations suggest considerable specificity at the cognitive processing level.

At the schema level, Greenberg and Alloy (1987) investigated content specificity in 60 students classified into depressed, anxious–nondepressed, and nondepressed–nonanxious groups. Using an SRET paradigm, they found that the anxious-nondepressed group recalled more anxiety-relevant adjectives, while the mixed depressed–anxious subjects rated as self-descriptive more negative depression-relevant trait words. Ingram et al. (1987) found that the depressed subjects had enhanced recall of depression-relevant trait adjectives while the test-anxious group evidenced biased recall for anxiety-relevant stimuli. Greenberg and Beck (in press-b) found that, compared to the anxious patients, the clinically depressed group showed enhanced recall for depression-relevant words. The anxious patients, on the other hand, were the only group to recall more negative than positive anxiety-relevant adjectives.

Finally, Beck, Riskind, Brown, and Steer (1988) reported that depressed patients endorsed significantly more hopelessness about the future than did anxious patients.

In summary, the content-specificity hypothesis of cognitive theory is evident at all three levels of cognitive functioning. At the product level, thoughts involving harm and danger, and cognitions dealing with loss and failure, are associated with their corresponding mood state. Differences are also evident between anxiety and depression in how information is processed and the types of maladaptive schemata underlying the faulty information-processing system. Clearly, more empirical studies are needed directly comparing the cognitive functioning of anxious and depressed patients.

H. Treatment Implications of the Content-Specificity Hypothesis

Given differences in the faulty information processing associated with anxiety and depression, one would expect differences in the cognitive treatment of these disorders. One difference noted by P. C. Kendall (personal communication, October, 1987) concerns the differential responsiveness of anxious and depressed patients to evidence contrary to their dysfunctional beliefs. The negative maladaptive beliefs of the depressed seem to crumble when confronted with contradictory evidence. On the other hand, anxious individuals will continue to express conviction in their belief of possible danger despite repeated exposure to contrary evidence.

This apparent differential responsiveness to evidence derives from the fact that in depression faulty thinking takes the form of *knowing* while in anxiety one finds a *questioning* mode of thought. That is, depressed patients have absolute beliefs as manifested by statements such as "always" or "never" (knowing mode). Since the belief is absolute, any contradictory evidence can disconfirm the absoluteness of the belief. For example, if a patient believes that "Nobody likes me" or "I can never get what I want," and then has a successful social experience (which the therapist has already prepared the patient to observe and integrate), then this absolute belief is weakened. It does not take many disconfirmations of this type to shift the patient from the absolutistic mode, to a more moderate mode which includes both knowing and questioning. In this moderate mode, facts are not taken as absolute and are now permeable to questioning and new evidence. Thus, individuals can now engage in "metacognition," i.e., questioning their beliefs.

With anxiety, the patient is already in a questioning mode but one devoid of any security or certainity. Thus, the anxious patient believes that nothing can be assumed. Granted there is no absolute certainty in this world, but there is a pragmatic or relative certainty. In order to function normally we must operate under certain reasonable assumptions (e.g., we will continue to breathe, we will not get struck by lightning, all of our friends will not desert us). However, once an individual begins operating within a questioning mode, it is possible to move from accepting reasonable assumptions to operating under no assumptions at all. Thus, in the therapy of anxiety we facilitate a progression from living under no assumptions to living under pragmatic assumptions. This is done by structuring experiences so that patients learn that they are exaggerating the probability of harm as well as the consequences of aversive events.

In CT of anxiety we first tackle the problem of exaggerated probabilities by having the patient confront "dangerous" situations (exposure therapy) and learn through this experience that the probabilities of harm are not as great as expected. For example, in the elevator phobia, exposure therapy would involve riding on the elevator with the patient. The therapeutic situation seems to give the patient a type of "super" monitor (metacognition) which can override the automatic monitor or calculator that is generating high-probability aversive predictions. The presence of the therapist thus induces a cognitive set which enables the patient to process the negative information coming from the automatic monitor and to thus reset or recalibrate the calculator.

Having readjusted the patient's formula of risk, the therapist then focuses on the possible consequences assigned to aversive events. This was first described by Ellis as "catastrophizing and awfullizing." We do this by demonstrating logically to the patient that the aversive consequences are actually on a continuum of which only the very end (death) represents the patient's fantastic expectations. For example, a failure at public speaking could, at the far end of the continuum, result in the patient's career collapsing and in ending up friendless and on Skid Row. But there are many points on the continuum that are considerably more probable. For instance, the patient may feel bad and the audience may be sympathetic. The individual might take public-speaking lessons and do better the next time.

Finally, we also can reduce the perceived threat of situations by helping with the patient's coping resources. The patient can be trained, for example, to deal with the immediate behavioral and physiological consequences of the threat (inhibition, rapid heart rate, subjective anxiety) through training in relaxation, focusing, distraction, and the like. Furthermore, skills training and role playing can be introduced not only as a form of exposure but as a means of changing the equation of threat/resources.

In summary, the cognitive therapist must take into account differences in the faulty thinking evident in anxiety and depression. While the basic tenets of the therapy will be similar, the specific strategies necessary to achieve change will differ across disorders. With this in mind, we now consider the various ingredients found in CT of anxiety and depression.

III. Cognitive Therapy of Anxiety and Depression

A. General Considerations

Cognitive therapy is a structured, time-limited, problem-solving psychotherapy aimed at modifying the faulty information processing evident in psychological disturbances. To achieve its aims, CT utilizes both verbal procedures and behavioral techniques. The treatment focuses on modifying cognitive functioning at the cognitive product, processing, and schema levels.

Three core assumptions form the basis of CT. First, it is assumed that in order to effect real change in psychological functioning, one must modify the manner in which an individual processes information. Second, since faulty or maladaptive information-processing structures and operations are an integral part of the symptomatology of psychopathological disturbances, CT is applicable to a variety of psychological disorders. And finally, because each disorder has a unique cognitive profile, CT must be specifically tailored to the various types of psychopathology.

During the initial sessions, CT focuses on symptomatic relief by training the patient to identify and evaluate negative cognitions and automatic thoughts. Concurrently, the therapist helps patients identify the errors in their thinking and to test the erroneous inferences derived from this biased cognitive processing. This aspect of CT facilitates the shift from a maladaptive automatic mode of information processing to a more adaptive controlled type of processing (Ingram & Hollon, 1986). Toward the latter phase of treatment, the cognitive therapist focuses on the identification and evaluation of the underlying dysfunctional beliefs and assumptions that perpetuate psychological disturbance. This is a crucial aspect of treatment because it enhances relapse prevention and the erosion of treatment gains.

The therapeutic relationship is an important aspect of CT. During the initial session, the cognitive therapist must establish rapport with the patient and model the kind of collaborative approach which is the essence of CT. The therapist must assess the sources of distress and dysfunction and work with the patient to specify treatment goals. The patient provides the "data" for each treatment session (e.g., thoughts, images, beliefs) and shares the responsibility for setting an agenda and deciding on homework tasks.

Three concepts are fundamental to the CT treatment process. First, a spirit of *collaborative empiricism* is encouraged. Patient and therapist act as "coinvestigators" who examine support for or against the patient's dysfunctional cognitions and beliefs. Second, the therapist utilizes a form of questioning known as the *socratic dialogue*. Through careful questioning the therapist guides patients toward accepting logical conclusions concerning the unrealistic nature of their erroneous assumptions and beliefs (Beck & Weishaar, in press). Finally, the maladaptive beliefs and attitudes are modified through a process of *guided discovery*. The therapist directs the treatment process in a manner that facilitates patients' discovery of their maladaptive thinking and errors of logic. New experiences (i.e., behavioral experiments) are designed which promote the acquisition and consolidation of new skills and modes of thinking. Cognitive therapists do not tell patients what they are thinking, nor do they cajole patients into accepting new beliefs or assumptions. Rather, therapists help patients evaluate their current maladaptive style of thinking and adopt a more realistic perspective.

During the initial session, it is imperative that the therapist educate the patient in the cognitive model. By providing an explanation for the patient's psychological distress as well as a treatment rationale, this engenders a sense of trust in the treatment process. It also increases the patient's motivation to enter into the collaborative relationship, and so promotes initial symptomatic relief. In fact, it is not possible to help a patient who does not accept the cognitive model or treatment rationale. Recently Winfrey and Goldfried (1986) also emphasized the importance of the treatment rationale in setting the stage for therapeutic change. Teasdale (1985) argued that an essential ingredient of psychological treatment for depression is the provision of an explanation for the patient's current psychological distress and a rationale for its amelioration. He noted that a credible treatment rationale acts to counter the patient's "depression about depression." Whatever the exact mechanism, it is clear that setting the context for treatment is a necessary aspect of the therapeutic change process.

CT utilizes two general approaches to change cognitive functioning. First, the cognitive therapist engages in a process of verbal examination and logical analysis of the patient's thoughts and beliefs in order to highlight logical inconsistencies, contradictory evidence, and other errors in thinking. Moreover, the therapist focuses on "hot cognitions" that are affectively charged (Safran & Greenberg, 1986). By focusing on emotionally arousing thoughts and beliefs, the cognitive therapist promotes learning in the patient.

CT does not rely solely on verbal procedures to achieve change in cognitive functioning. Hollon and Beck (1986) noted that a major difference between CT and other cognitive therapies such as RET is its emphasis on empirical hypothesis testing as a means to achieve change in maladaptive beliefs. The cognitive therapist sets up behavioral experiments, usually in the form of homework assignments, through which patients test the veracity of their belief system. For example, the first author recently had a patient presenting with social anxiety. One of the beliefs expressed by this patient was the conviction that he was the only one among his work colleagues to show any evidence of nervousness. In addition, he believed that nervousness always undermines one's performance. As a homework assignment, it was agreed that over the next week, the patient would observe and record any signs of nervousness exhibited by his work colleagues. Also, he was to rate their level of nervousness and the adequacy of their performance. The following week the patient reported, much to his surprise, that nervousness was more common than he had originally thought and that most people were able to perform quite adequately despite their manifest anxiety. For this patient, the behavioral experiment disconfirmed a long-standing belief that anxiety was a sign of abnormality and weakness and a significant detriment to performance.

B. Specific Intervention Strategies in Cognitive Therapy

Because published treatment manuals for CT with depression (Beck et al., 1979) and anxiety (Beck & Emery, 1985) are now available, only a brief review of CT intervention strategies is presented below. These strategies can be grouped into two broad categories, cognitive and behavioral techniques.

Cognitive Interventions. Cognitive interventions include provision of a treatment rationale (discussed above), self-monitoring of negative automatic thoughts and images, evaluation of dysfunctional cognitions and images, testing/evaluation of cognitive distortions, and identifying and modifying maladaptive beliefs and assumptions. Within the first session, the therapist assists the patient in identifying pertinent automatic thoughts and images. In depression, negative automatic thoughts are usually so persistent and pervasive that they are easily elicited within the session. In anxiety disorders, the threat-related cognitions and images may be less accessible due to their situational specificity (D. M. Clark, 1986b). Consequently, the therapist may have to prime these cognitions through an anxiety induction procedure (see discussion below).

Once the automatic thoughts are identified, each is evaluated through a process of inductive questioning. Evidence regarding the realistic (i.e., adaptive) nature of these cognitions is gathered from past and present experiences.

An important component of CT involves training the patients to identify distortions in their thinking. For example, in depression, dichotomous thinking can be modified by building up a continuum between extreme categories, while personalization and overgeneralization are corrected by redefining the problem. In anxiety states, "decatastrophizing" is accomplished by encouraging the patient to consider the actual consequences of the dreaded catastrophe. Also, images associated with this "catastrophic thinking" can be modified through a number of imaging techniques outlined by Beck and Emery (1985, pp. 214–227).

Toward the latter part of the treatment program, the cognitive therapist identifies underlying beliefs and assumptions by noting recurrent themes in the patient's dysfunctional thinking (Safran, Vallis, Segal, & Shaw, 1986). Use of the vertical column technique with the Daily Record of Dysfunctional Thoughts can facilitate discovery of maladaptive underlying assumptions. Modification of these beliefs is achieved through logical persuasion and empirical hypothesis-testing assignments.

Behavioral Procedures. CT recognizes that experience is the most effective way to change existing thoughts and beliefs. By emphasizing an empirical hypothesis-testing approach, maladaptive beliefs are disconfirmed and more adaptive thinking is verified. Behavioral experiments are presented in a collaborative, hypothesis-testing manner, usually as part of a homework assignment.

The behavioral techniques utilized in CT can be grouped into six broad categories. First, behavioral activation strategies are particularly suited for testing the pervasive negativity and hopelessness of the depressed patient. Tasks such as weekly activity scheduling, graded task assignment, and pleasure/mastery rating assignments are useful in dislodging depressotypic beliefs.

Second, behavioral coping strategies are especially useful in countering beliefs of ineffectiveness and failure in dealing with one's environment. The depressed patient may be taught problem-solving skills, interpersonal behaviors, assertiveness, or antiprocrastination strategies. In anxiety states, techniques such as progressive muscle relaxation, controlled breathing, and distraction challenge the patients' belief in their vulnerability by providing them with tools for dealing with anxiety.

Third, in panic disorder it is useful to induce a panic attack within the session by having the patient overbreathe, overexercise, or imagine the fear situation. This task helps decatastrophize the consequences of experiencing the bodily sensations associated with panic attacks, enables the patient to reattribute the bodily sensations to the effects of overbreathing or physical exertion, and engenders within the patient a greater sense of control over the panic state.

Fourth, graded *in vivo* exposure tasks are a crucial aspect of CT for agoraphobia and simple phobias. The patient is encouraged to enter the fear situation to gather information on negative thinking and distorted cognitive processing (e.g., catastrophizing), to practice anxiety coping skills, and to test out anxiotypic beliefs concerning danger and vulnerability.

Fifth, behavioral rehearsal and role playing are used to consolidate changes in maladaptive thinking. Role playing can be especially useful in helping patients develop a more adaptive style of thinking. In later sessions, the therapist can play the "devil's advocate" by trying to persuade patients to readopt their former maladaptive beliefs and faulty information processing. The patient counters the therapist's "temptations" by insisting on the inherent fallacies of the maladaptive beliefs and the more realistic nature of the new style of thinking.

Finally, the cognitive therapist must devise direct behavioral tests of maladaptive beliefs. For example, pleasure-predicting exercises are often very useful in challenging the negativity of the depressed patient. Toward the end of treatment, the therapist may instruct the anxious patient to actually induce the anxiety symptoms while in the fear situation. This constitutes the ultimate in exposure to fear sensations. It demonstrates to patients that they can control their anxiety and that the catastrophic consequences they so actively seek to avoid will not materialize.

IV. Empirical Status of Cognitive Therapy of Anxiety and Depression

We will now review the literature on the efficacy of CT. Although the primary focus is on Beck's CT, other CB treatment approaches will be mentioned when relevant.

A. Cognitive Therapy Outcome Studies of Depression

Beck's CT is the only cognitive or cognitive–behavioral approach that has been extensively researched as a treatment for depression. In a meta-analysis of CT for depression, Dobson (in press) identified 21 outcome studies reported between 1976 and mid-1986. A number of reviews have already evaluated the efficacy of CT (e.g., Blackburn, 1985; Hollon & Beck, 1986; Hollon & Najavits, in press), so we will merely summarize the findings.

Acute Treatment Response. Most outcome studies concern the efficacy of CT as a treatment for the acute symptomatic phase of depression. Dobson (in press) identified five studies that found CT more effective than either a no-treatment group or a waiting-list control group. However, these studies did not include an attention-placebo condition to control for possible nonspecific treatment effects.

CT has already been compared to other forms of psychotherapy for depression. Although some studies found CT superior to behavior therapy or insight-oriented psychotherapy (McLean & Hakstein, 1979; Shaw, 1977; Taylor & Marshall, 1977), others have found CT equivalent to behavior therapy (Maldonado, 1982; Wilson, Goldin, & Charbonneau-Powis, 1983).

CT has shown its efficacy in comparison with antidepressant drug treatment. Four studies found CT superior to drug treatment (Blackburn, Bishop, Glen, Whalley, & Christie, 1981—general practice sample; Dunn, 1979; Maldonado, 1982; Rush, Beck, Kovacs, & Hollon, 1977), while three studies found CT equivalent to drug therapy (Blackburn et al., 1981—inpatient sample; Hollon et al., 1985; Murphy, Simons, Wetzel, & Lustman, 1984). Four studies found the combination of CT plus antidepressants more effective than drugs alone (Blackburn et al., 1981—both samples; Maldonado, 1982; Teasdale, Fennell, Hibbert, & Amies, 1984), whereas two found equivalence (Hollon et al., 1985; Murphy et al., 1984). Finally, three studies found CT alone as effective as the combination treatment (Beck, Hollon, Young, Bedrosian, & Budenz, 1985; Maldonado, 1982; Murphy et al., 1984), while one found superiority of the CT plus drug treatment modality (Hollon et al., 1985).

Prevention of Relapse. Several studies have shown that, compared to antidepressant drug treatment, CT may reduce relapse rates over a 1- to 2-year period (Blackburn, Eunson, & Bishop, 1986; Evans et al., 1985; Simons et al., 1986). However, Kovacs, Rush, Beck, and Hollon (1981) found comparable relapse rates for the CT and imipramine groups at a 1-year follow-up. Overall, then, there is strong evidence that CT may have a prophylactic effect. Relapse rates of 60% are commonly reported for antidepressant drug treatment without maintenance, while rates of about 30% are evident in groups treated with CT (Hollon & Najavits, in press).

B. Cognitive and Cognitive–Behavioral Outcome Studies of Clinical Anxiety Disorders

Although a number of outcome studies have investigated CB treatments of simple phobias and the evaluative anxieties, most used analog rather than fully clinical samples. The interested reader is directed to recent reviews of this literature (Haaga & Davison, 1986; Hollon & Beck, 1986; Hollon & Najavits, in press).

Generalized Anxiety Disorders (GAD). Only a few studies have investigated the efficacy of CT or CB treatment of GAD. Woodward and Jones (1980) reported that a combined treatment of self-statement modification and systematic desensitization was superior to either condition alone. Barlow et al. (1984) found that a combination of CT and Meichenbaum's stress inoculation training was more effective than a waiting-list control condition. Durham and Turvey (1987) compared CT alone with a behavior therapy plus self-statement replacement group. The two groups did not differ at posttreatment, but by the 6-month follow-up the GAD outpatients treated with CT maintained or improved while the behavior therapy group reverted toward their pretreatment anxiety level. Lindsay, Gamsu, McLaughlin, Hood, and Espie (1987) recently compared CT, anxiety management therapy (AMT), benzodiazepine treatment, and a waiting-list control condition in 40 general practice patients with chronic anxiety. At posttreatment, the CT and AMT groups showed the most consistent and significant improvements on various measures of anxiety. At the 3-month follow-up, the CT group had the greatest number of subjects reporting clinically meaningful improvement. These results, then, suggest that CT may be an effective intervention for GAD.

Agoraphobia. A few studies have investigated the efficacy of cognitive strategies in treating agoraphobics. Emmelkamp, Kuipers, and Eggeraat (1978) compared cognitive treatment (i.e., cognitive treatment rationale, discussion of Ellis' irrational beliefs, and self-instructional training) with *in vivo* exposure. The behavioral treatment was significantly more effective than the cognitive modality. In a second study, Emmelkamp and Mersch (1982) found that combined cognitive treatment plus exposure was no more effective then each treatment alone. However, at a 1-month follow-up the cognitive-only treatment proved to be as effective as the exposure treatment.

More recently, Emmelkamp, Brilman, Kuiper, and Mersch (1985) found that prolonged *in vivo* exposure was more effective in treating agoraphobia than self-instructional training or RET. Mavissakalian, Michelson, Greenwald, Kornblith, and Greenwald (1983) found that the addition of self-instructional training to exposure treatment was less effective than adding paradoxical intention, although, at a 6-month follow-up the self-instructional group had improved markedly. However, it is likely that self-instructional training is less appropriate with agoraphobics. Kendall (1984, p. 155) has noted that self-instructions are theoretically tied to "inhibitory" behavior (e.g., impulsivity). Consequently self-instructional training may be more effectively used to inhibit excessive behavior than to overcome behavioral deficiencies (e.g., the extensive avoidance behavior of agoraphobics). Finally, Williams and Rappoport (1983) found that the addition of a cognitive component to a behavioral treatment of driving fear did not enhance gains in an agoraphobic sample.

Overall, these results are not supportive of the efficacy of cognitive treatment for agoraphobia, whether alone or in combination with behavioral treatments (Hollon & Beck, 1986). There is some suggestive evidence, however, that cognitive strategies help maintain and even promote posttreatment gains. However, it should be noted that the studies of Emmelkamp and colleagues may not have adequately tested the cognitive approach. Their treatment conditions often involved unusually short durations, they placed too much emphasis on self-instructional training, and the more effective hypothesis-testing approach was never included in any of their outcome studies.

Panic Disorder. D. M. Clark (1986a) has proposed a cognitive approach to the treatment of panic. Panic attacks are viewed as resulting from catastrophic misinterpretations of certain bodily sensations. Sensations such as heart palpitations, breathlessness, dizziness, and lightheadedness are interpreted as signs of heart attack, seizure, fainting, going crazy, or loss of control. These somatic sensations may be caused by a prior state of heightened anxiety (as in the case of an agoraphobic entering a crowded shop), by a fluctuation in emotional state (excitement, anger), or by overbreathing in response to a stressor. Whatever the initial factor precipitating the sensations, it is the catastrophic misinterpretation that triggers the panic attack.

It is known that CO_2 inhalation, hyperventilation, and sodium lactate infusion are more likely to trigger panic attacks in patients with panic disorder than in nonpanic individuals (e.g., Rapee, 1986). Additional data have indicated that these stimuli will trigger attacks only if the patient makes a catastrophic misinterpretation of the bodily sensations produced by these agents (Rapee, Mattick, & Murrell, 1986). These findings are consistent with cognitive models of panic.

Based on cognitive theory, a treatment strategy for panic has been proposed which emphasizes the identification of somatic misinterpretations, an evaluation of the accuracy of these perceptions through logical analysis and empirical verification, and the causal reattribution of the sensations to the effects of overbreathing. To facilitate this reattribution process, a panic induction exercise is carried out in which patients are requested to hyperventilate for 2 minutes. To date, two uncontrolled treatment trials have found this cognitive–behavioral approach to be effective in reducing the frequency and severity of panic attacks and general anxiety (D. M. Clark, Salkovskis, & Chalkey, 1985; Salkovskis, Jones, & D. M. Clark, 1986). Currently comparative outcome treatment trials of cognitive therapy for panic disorder are in progress in Oxford, England, and Philadelphia.

V. Conclusions

We have presented an integrated information-processing model that highlights the similarities and differences of cognitive dysfunction in depressive and anxious states. It was proposed that anxiety and depression exhibit similar cognitive structural and operational dysfunctions but differ in the content and output of the faulty information-processing system. The model postulates that latent, prepotent maladaptive schemata, when triggered by appropriate environmental stressors, will give rise to cognitive distortions and negative, dysfunctional thoughts and images. Thus, cognitive factors are involved in both the maintenance of, and vulnerability to, anxiety and depression. Empirical evidence was strongest for the existence of negativistic thinking and distorted cognitive processing in both psychological disorders.

Results are less consistent for the structural concepts of the model, due, in part to methodological difficulties inherent in measuring underlying schemata. Consequently, research on cognitive vulnerability, though encouraging, is currently inconclusive.

The content-specificity hypothesis has received some empirical support, at least at the cognitive product level. Thoughts of loss and failure are associated with depression, while cognitions of harm and danger are involved in anxiety states. However, more research investigating content specificity at the cognitive processing and schematic levels is clearly needed. Comparative studies involving anxious and depressive samples are still rare in research on cognitive functioning.

Based on the cognitive model, we described a treatment approach that focused on change at the cognitive product, processing, and schematic levels. To achieve this, verbal persuasion and empirical hypothesis-testing strategies are used. The efficacy of CT for depression has been established, while evidence for its effectiveness with anxiety states and panic disorder is only preliminary at this time.

Many questions remain unresolved. At the theoretical level, questions needing further investigation concern the most appropriate experimental methodology for assessing schemata, the adequacy of the interactional model of cognitive vulnerability, and evidence of content specificity at the processing and schematic levels. Issues involving who will benefit from CT, for how long, and by what treatment processes are important for disentangling the active therapeutic ingredients of cognitive interventions. In our opinion, knowledge on these issues will be better advanced by adopting a more comparative research strategy involving samples of both anxious and depressed patients.

References

Barlow, D. H., Cohen, A. S., Waddell, M. T., Vermilyea, B. B., Klosko, J. S., Blanchard, E. B., & DiNardo, P. A. (1984). Panic and generalized anxiety disorders: Nature and treatment. *Behavior Therapy, 15,* 431–449.

Beck, A. T. (1967). *Depression: Causes and treatment.* Philadelphia: University of Pennsylvania Press.

Beck, A. T. (1976). *Cognitive therapy of the emotional disorders.* New York: New American Library.

Beck, A. T. (1987). Cognitive model of depression. *Journal of Cognitive Psychotherapy, 1,* 2–27.

Beck, A. T., Brown, G., Steer, R. A., Eidelson, J. Z., & Riskind, J. H. (1987). Differentiating anxiety and depression utilizing the Cognition Checklist. *Journal of Abnormal Psychology, 96,* 179–183.

Beck, A. T., & Clark, D. A. (1988). Anxiety and depression: An information processing perspective. *Anxiety Research, 1,* 23–36.

Beck, A. T., & Emery, G. (1985). *Anxiety disorders and phobias: A cognitive perspective.* New York: Basic Books.

Beck, A. T., Epstein, N., & Harrison, R. (1983). Cognitions, attitudes, and personality dimensions in depression. *British Journal of Cognitive Psychotherapy, 1,* 1–16.

Beck, A. T., Hollon, S. D., Young, J., Bedrosian, R. C., & Budenz, D. (1985). Treatment of depression with cognitive therapy and amitriptyline. *Archives of General Psychiatry, 42,* 142–148.

Beck, A. T., Laude, R., & Bohnert, M. (1974). Ideational components of anxiety neurosis. *Archives of General Psychiatry, 31,* 319–325.

Beck, A. T., Riskind, J. H., Brown, G., & Steer, R. A. (1988). Levels of hopelessness in DSM-III disorders: A test of the cognitive model of depression. *Cognitive Therapy and Research, 12,* 459–469.

Beck, A. T., & Rush, A. J. (1988). Cognitive Therapy. In H. J. Kaplan & B. J. Sadock (Eds.), *Comprehensive textbook of psychiatry IV.* Baltimore, MD: Williams & Wilkins.

Beck, A. T., Rush, A. J., Shaw, B. F., & Emery, G. (1979). *Cognitive therapy of depression.* New York: Guilford Press.

Beck, A. T., & Weishaar, M. E. (in press). Cognitive therapy. In D. Wedding & R. Corsin (Eds.), *Current psychotherapies* (4th ed.). Itasca, IL: Peacock.

Blackburn, I. M. (1985). Depression. In B. P. Bradley & C. Thompson (Eds.), *Psychological applications in psychiatry*. Chichester, England: Wiley.

Blackburn, I. M., Bishop, S., Glen, I. M., Whalley, L. J., & Christie, J. E. (1981). The efficacy of cognitive therapy in depression: A treatment trial using cognitive therapy and pharmacotherapy, each alone and in combination. *British Journal of Psychiatry, 139*, 181–189.

Blackburn, I. M., Eunson, K. M., & Bishop, S. (1986). A two-year naturalistic follow-up of depressed patients treated with cognitive therapy, pharmacotherapy and a combination of both. *Journal of Affective Disorders, 10*, 67–75.

Blackburn, I. M., Jones, S., & Lewin, R. J. P. (1986). Cognitive style in depression. *British Journal of Clinical Psychology, 25*, 241–251.

Bradley, B., & Mathews, A. (1983). Negative self-schemata in clinical depression. *British Journal of Clinical Psychology, 32*, 173–181.

Breslow, R., Kocsis, J., & Belkin, B. (1981). Contribution of the depressive perspective to memory function in depression. *American Journal of Psychiatry, 138*, 227–229.

Brown, G., Beck, A. T., Steer, R. A., & Riskind, J. H. (1986). *Differentiating anxiety from depression: The Cognition Checklist, Fantasied Outcome Test, Hopelessness Scale, and Self Concept Test.* Paper presented at the annual meeting of the Society for Psychotherapy Research, Wellesley, MA.

Buchwald, A. M. (1977). Depressive mood and estimates of reinforcement frequency. *Journal of Abnormal Psychology, 86*, 443–446.

Bulter, G., & Mathews, A. (1983). Cognitive processes in anxiety. *Advances in Behavior Research and Therapy, 5*, 51–62.

Burgess, I. S., Jones, L. M., Robertson, S. A., Radcliffe, W. N., & Emerson, E. (1981). The degree of control exerted by phobic and non-phobic verbal stimuli over the recognition behaviour of phobic and nonphobic subjects. *Behaviour Research and Therapy, 19*, 233–243.

Chambless, D. L., Caputo, G. C., Bright, P., & Gallagher, R. (1984). Assessment of fear in agoraphobics: The Body Sensations Questionnaire and the Agoraphobic Cognitions Questionnaire. *Journal of Consulting and Clinical Psychology, 52*, 1090–1097.

Clark, D. A. (1986). Cognitive-affective interaction: A test of the "specificity" and "generality" hypotheses. *Cognitive Therapy and Research, 10*, 607–623.

Clark, D. M. (1986a). A cognitive approach to panic. *Behaviour Research and Therapy, 24*, 461–470.

Clark, D. M. (1986b). Cognitive therapy for anxiety. *Behavioural Psychotherapy, 14*, 283–294.

Clark, D. M., Salkovskis, P. M., & Chalkley, A. J. (1985). Respiratory control as a treatment for panic attacks. *Journal of Behavior Therapy and Experimental Psychiatry, 16*, 23–30.

Clark, D. M., & Teasdale, J. D. (1982). Diurnal variation in clinical depression and accessibility of memories of positive and negative experiences. *Journal of Abnormal Psychology, 91*, 87–95.

Clark, D. M., & Teasdale, J. D. (1985). Constraints on the effects of mood on memory. *Journal of Personality and Social Psychology, 48*, 1595–1608.

Clifford, P. I., & Hemsley, D. R., (1987). The influence of depression on the processing of personal attributes. *British Journal of Psychiatry, 150*, 98–103.

Craighead, W. E., Hickey, K. S., & DeMonbreun, B. G. (1979). Distortion of perception and recall of neutral feedback in depression. *Cognitive Therapy and Research, 3*, 291–298.

Crandell, C. J., & Chambless, D. L. (1986). The validation of an inventory for measuring depressive thoughts: The Crandell Cognitions Inventory. *Behaviour Research and Therapy, 24*, 403–411.

Davis, H. (1979). Self-reference and the encoding of personal information in depression. *Cognitive Therapy and Research, 3,* 97–110.
DeMonbreun, B. G., & Craighead, W. E. (1977). Distortion of perception and recall of positive and neutral feedback in depression. *Cognitive Therapy and Research, 1,* 311–329.
Derry, P. A., & Kuiper, N. A. (1981). Schematic processing and self-reference in clinical depression. *Journal of Abnormal Psychology, 90,* 286–297.
Dobson, K. S. (in press). A meta-analysis of the efficacy of cognitive therapy for depression. *Journal of Consulting and Clinical Psychology.*
Dobson, K. S., & Breiter, H. J. (1983). Cognitive assessment of depression: Reliability and validity of three measures. *Journal of Abnormal Psychology, 92,* 107–109.
Dobson, K. S., & Shaw, B. F. (1986). Cognitive assessment with major depressive disorders. *Cognitive Therapy and Research, 10,* 13–29.
Dobson, K. S., & Shaw, B. F. (1987). Specificity and stability of self-referent encoding in clinical depression. *Journal of Abnormal Psychology, 96,* 34–40.
Dunbar, G. C., & Lishman, W. A. (1984). Depression recognition-memory and hedonic tone: A signal detection analysis. *British Journal of Psychiatry, 144,* 376–382.
Dunn, R. J. (1979). Cognitive modification with depression-prone psychiatric patients. *Cognitive Therapy and Research, 3,* 307–317.
Durham, R. C., & Turvey, A. A. (1987). *Cognitive therapy versus behavior therapy in the treatment of chronic general anxiety: Outcome at discharge and at six months follow-up.* Unpublished manuscript, Royal Dundee Hospital, Tayside Area Clinical Psychology Department, Dundee, Scotland.
Eaves, G., & Rush, J. A. (1984). Cognitive patterns in symptomatic and remitted unipolar major depression. *Journal of Abnormal Psychology, 93,* 313–340.
Ellis, A. (1962). *Reason and emotion in psychotherapy.* New York: Lyle Stuart.
Ellis, A. (1977). The basic clinical theory of rational-emotive therapy. In A. Ellis & R. Grieger (Eds.), *Handbook of rational-emotive therapy.* New York: Springer.
Emmelkamp, P. M. G., Brilman, E., Kuiper, H., & Mersch, P. P. (1985). The relative contribution of self-instructional training, rational emotive therapy, and exposure *in vivo* in the treatment of agoraphobia. *Behavior Modification, 2,* 53–59.
Emmelkamp, P. M. G., Kuipers, A. C. M., & Eggeraat, J. B. (1978). Cognitive modification versus prolonged exposure *in vivo:* A comparison with agoraphobics as subjects. *Behaviour Research and Therapy, 16,* 33–42.
Emmelkamp, P. M. G., & Mersch, P. P. (1982). Cognition and exposure *in vivo* in the treatment of agoraphobia: Short-term and delayed effects. *Cognitive Therapy and Research, 6,* 77–90.
Evans, M. D., Hollon, S. D., DeRubeis, R. J., Piasecki, J., Tuason, V. B., & Garvey, M. J. (1985). *Relapse/recurrence following cognitive therapy and pharmacotherapy for depression: IV. Two-year follow-up in the CPT project.* Unpublished manuscript, University of Minnesota and the St. Paul-Ramsey Medical Center, Minneapolis, St. Paul, MN.
Eysenck, M. W., Mathews, A., & Richards, A. (1987). *Anxiety and the interpretation of ambiguity.* Unpublished manuscript, Birkbeck College and St. George's Hospital Medical School, London.
Ferguson, T. J., Rule, B. G., & Carlson, D. (1983). Memory for personally relevant information. *Journal of Personality and Social Psychology, 44,* 251–261.
Finkel, C. B., Glass, C. R., & Merluzzi, T. V. (1982). Differential discrimination of self-referent statements by depressives and nondepressives. *Cognitive Therapy and Research, 6,* 173–183.
Foa, E. B., & McNally, R. J. (1986). Sensitivity to feared stimuli in obsessive-compulsives: A dichotic listening analysis. *Cognitive Therapy and Research, 10,* 477–485.
Goldfried, M. R., DeCantecco, E. T., & Weinberg, L. (1974). Systematic rational restructuring as a self control technique. *Behavior Therapy, 5,* 247–254.

Greenberg, M. S., & Alloy, L. B. (1987). *Depression versus anxiety: Schematic processing of self- and other-referent information.* Manuscript in preparation, Center for Cognitive Therapy and Northwestern University, Evanston, IL.

Greenberg, M. S., & Beck, A. T. (in press-a). Cognitive approaches to psychotherapy: Theory and therapy. In R. Plutchik & H. Kellerman (Eds.), *Emotion and psychotherapy.* (Vol. 5).

Greenberg, M. S., & Beck, A. T. (in press-b). Depression versus anxiety: A test of the content specificity hypothesis. *Journal of Abnormal Psychology.*

Greenberg, M. S., Vazquez, C. V., & Alloy, L. B. (1988). Depression versus anxiety: Difference in self and other schemata. In L. B. Alloy (Ed.), *Cognitive processes in depression.* New York: Guilford Press.

Haaga, D. A., & Davison, G. C. (1986). Cognitive change methods. In F. H. Kanfer & A. P. Goldstein (Eds.), *Helping people change: A textbook of methods* (3rd ed.). Elmsford, NY: Pergamon Press.

Hamilton, E. W., & Abramson, L. Y. (1983). Cognitive patterns and major depressive disorder: A longitudinal study in a hospital setting. *Journal of Abnormal Psychology, 92,* 173–184.

Hammen, C. L. (1985). Predicting depression: a cognitive-behavioral perspective. In P. C. Kendall (Ed.), *Advances in cognitive-behavioral research and therapy* (Vol. 4). Orlando, FL: Academic Press.

Hammen, C., Marks, T., Mayol, A., & deMayo, R. (1985). Depressive self-schemas, life stress, and vulnerability to depression. *Journal of Abnormal Psychology, 94,* 308–319.

Harrell, T. H., Chambless, D. L., & Calhoun, J. F. (1981). Correlational relationships between self-statements and affective states. *Cognitive Therapy and Research, 5,* 159–173.

Harrell, T. H., & Ryon, N. B. (1983). Cognitive-behavioral assessment of depression: Clinical validation of the Automatic Thoughts Questionnaire. *Journal of Consulting and Clinical Psychology, 51,* 721–725.

Hibbert, G. A. (1984). Ideational components of anxiety: Their origin and content. *British Journal of Psychiatry, 144,* 618–624.

Hollon, S. D., & Beck, A. T. (1986). Cognitive and cognitive-behavioral therapies. In S. L. Garfield & A. E. Bergin (Eds.), *Handbook of psychotherapy and behavior change* (3rd ed.). New York: Wiley.

Hollon, S. D., DeRubeis, R. J., Evans, M. D., Tuason, V. B., Weimer, M. J., & Garvey, M. J. (1985). *Combined cognitive-pharmacotherapy versus cognitive therapy alone and pharmacotherapy alone in the treatment of depressed outpatients: Differential treatment outcome in the CTP project.* Unpublished manuscript, University of Minnesota and the St. Paul-Ramsey Medical Center, Minneapolis, St. Paul, MN.

Hollon, S. D., & Kendall, P. C. (1980). Cognitive self-statements in depression: Development of an Automatic Thoughts Questionnaire. *Cognitive Therapy and Research, 4,* 383–395.

Hollon, S. D., Kendall, P. C., & Lumry, A. (1986). Specificity of depressotypic cognitions in clinical depression. *Journal of Abnormal Psychology, 95,* 52–59.

Hollon, S. D., & Najavits, L. (in press). Review of empirical studies on cognitive therapy. In A. J. Rush & A. T. Beck (Eds.), *American Psychiatric Association review of psychiatry: Vol. 7. Cognitive therapy.* Washington, DC: American Psychiatric Association.

Ingram, R. E., & Hollon, S. D. (1986). Cognitive therapy of depression from an information processing perspective. In R. E. Ingram (Ed.), *Information processing approaches to clinical psychology.* Orlando, FL: Academic Press.

Ingram, R. E., & Kendall, P. C. (1986). Cognitive clinical psychology: Implications of an information processing perspective. In R. E. Ingram (Ed.), *Information processing approaches to clinical psychology.* Orlando, FL: Academic Press.

Ingram, R. E., Kendall, P. C., Smith, T. W., Donnell, C., & Ronan, K. (1987). Cognitive specificity in emotional disorders. *Journal of Personality and Social Psychology, 53,* 734–742.

Keller, K. E. (1983). Dysfunctional attitudes and the cognitive therapy for depression. *Cognitive Therapy and Research, 7,* 437–444.

Kendall, P. C. (1984). Cognitive processes and procedures in behavior therapy. In C. M. Franks, G. T. Wilson, P. C. Kendall, & K. D. Brownell (Eds.), *Annual Review of Behavior Therapy* (Vol. 10). New York: Guilford Press.

Kendall, P. C. (1985). Toward a cognitive-behavioral model of child psychopathology and a critique of related interventions. *Journal of Abnormal Child Psychology, 13,* 357–372.

Kendall, P. C., & Hollon, S. D. (1987). *Development of an Anxious Self-Statement Inventory.* Unpublished manuscript, Temple University, Philadelphia.

Kovacs, M., Rush, A. J., Beck, A. T., & Hollon, S. D. (1981). Depressed outpatients treated with cognitive therapy or pharmacotherapy. *Archives of General Psychiatry, 38,* 33–39.

Kuiper, N. A., & Derry, P. A. (1982). Depressed and nondepressed content self reference in mild depressives. *Journal of Personality, 50,* 67–80.

Lindsay, W. R., Gamsu, C. V., McLaughlin, E., Hood, E. M., & Espie, C. A. (1987). A controlled trial of treatments for generalized anxiety. *British Journal of Clinical Psychology, 26,* 3–15.

Lloyd, G. G., & Lishman, W. A. (1975). Effect of depression on the speed of recall of pleasant and unpleasant experiences. *Psychological Medicine, 5,* 173–180.

Loeb, A., Beck, A. T., & Diggory, J. (1971). Differential effects of success and failure on depressed and nondepressed patients. *Journal of Nervous and Mental Disease, 152,* 106–114.

MacLeod, C., Mathews, A., & Tata, P. (1986). Attentional bias in emotional disorders. *Journal of Abnormal Psychology, 95,* 15–20.

MacLeod, C., Tata, P., & Mathews, A. (1987). Perception of emotionally valenced information in depression. *British Journal of Clinical Psychology, 26,* 67–68.

Mahoney, M. J. (1987). The cognitive science and psychotherapy: Patterns in a developing relationship. In K. S. Dobson (Ed.), *Handbook of cognitive psychotherapies.* New York: Guilford Press.

Maldonado, A. (1982). Terapia de conducta y depression: Un analisis experimental de los modelos conductal y cognitivo [Cognitive and behavior therapy for depression: Its efficacy and interaction with pharmacological treatment]. *Revista de Psicologia General y Applicada, 37,* 31–56.

Mathews, A., & MacLeod, C. (1985). Selective processing of threat cues in anxiety states. *Behaviour Research and Therapy, 23,* 563–569.

Mathews, A., & MacLeod, C. (1986). Discrimination of threat cues without awareness in anxiety states. *Journal of Abnormal Psychology, 95,* 131–138.

Mathews, A., & MacLeod, C. (1987). An information-processing approach to anxiety. *Journal of Cognitive Psychotherapy: An International Quarterly, 1,* 105–115.

Mavissakalian, M., Michelson, L., Greenwald, D., Kornblith, S., & Greenwald, M. (1983). Cognitive-behavioral treatment of agoraphobia: Paradoxical intention vs. self-statement training. *Behaviour Research and Therapy, 21,* 75–86.

McLean, P. D., & Hakstein, A. R. (1979). Clinical depression: Comparative efficacy of outpatient treatments. *Journal of Consulting and Clinical Psychology, 47,* 818–836.

Meichenbaum, D. (1977). *Cognitive-behavior modification: An integrative approach.* New York: Plenum.

Mogg, K., Mathews, A., & Weinman, J. (1987). Memory bias in clinical anxiety. *Journal of Abnormal Psychology, 96,* 94–98.

Murphy, G. E., Simons, A. D., Wetzel, R. D., & Lustman, P. J. (1984). Cognitive therapy and pharmacotherapy. *Archives of General Psychiatry, 41,* 33–41.

Nelson, R. E., & Craighead, W. E. (1977). Selective recall of positive and negative feedback, self-control behaviors, and depression. *Journal of Abnormal Psychology, 86,* 195–201.

Nunn, J. D., Stevenson, R. J., & Whalan, G. (1984). Selective memory effects in agoraphobic patients. *British Journal of Clinical Psychology, 23,* 195–201.

O'Banion, K., & Arkowitz, H. (1977). Social anxiety and selective memory for affective information about the self. *Social Behavior and Personality, 5,* 321–328.

Olinger, L. J., Kuiper, N. A., & Shaw, B. F. (1987). Dysfunctional attitudes and stressful life events: An interactive model of depression. *Cognitive Therapy and Research, 11,* 25–40.

Persons, J. B., & Rao, P. A. (1985). Longitudinal study of cognitions, life events, and depression in psychiatric inpatients. *Journal of Abnormal Psychology, 94,* 51–63.

Powell, N., & Hemsley, D. R. (1984). Depression: a breakdown of perceptual defence? *British Journal of Psychiatry, 145,* 358–362.

Rapee, R. (1986). Differential response to hyperventilation in panic disorder and generalized anxiety disorders. *Journal of Abnormal Psychology, 95,* 24–28.

Rapee, R., Mattick, R., & Murrell, E. (1986). Cognitive mediation in the affective components of spontaneous panic attacks. *Journal of Behavior Therapy and Experimental Psychiatry, 17,* 245–253.

Reda, M. A., Carpiniello, B., Secchiaroli, L., & Blanco, S. (1985). Thinking, depression, and antidepressants: Modified and unmodified depressive beliefs during treatment with amitriptyline. *Cognitive Therapy and Research, 9,* 135–143.

Robins, C. J. (1985). *Construct validation of the sociotropy–autonomy scale: A measure of vulnerability to depression.* Paper presented at the annual meeting of the Eastern Psychological Association, Boston.

Robins, C. J. (1986). *Effects of simulated social rejection and achievement failure on mood as a function of sociotropic and autonomous personality characteristics.* Manuscript submitted for publication.

Robins, C. J., & Block, P. (1985). *Depression: Specific interactions of personality variables and life events.* Poster presented at the annual meeting of the American Psychological Association, Los Angeles.

Roth, D., & Rehm, L. (1980). Relationships among self-monitoring processes, memory, and depression. *Cognitive Therapy and Research, 4,* 149–157.

Rush, A. J., Beck, A. T., Kovacs, M., & Hollon, S. (1977). Comparative efficacy of cognitive therapy and pharmacotherapy in the treatment of depressed outpatients. *Cognitive Therapy and Research, 1,* 17–37.

Rush, A. J., Weissenburger, J., & Eaves, G. (1986). Do thinking patterns predict depressive symptoms? *Cognitive Therapy and Research, 10,* 225–236.

Safran, J. D., & Greenberg, L. S. (1986). Hot cognition and psychotherapy process: An information processing/ecological approach. In P. C. Kendall (Ed.), *Advances in cognitive-behavioral research and therapy* (Vol. 5). Orlando, FL: Academic Press.

Safran, J. D., Vallis, T. M., Segal, Z. V., & Shaw, B. F. (1986). Assessment of core cognitive processes in cognitive therapy. *Cognitive Therapy and Research, 10,* 509–526.

Salkovskis, P. M., Jones, D. R. O., & Clark, D. M. (1986). Respiratory control in the treatment of panic attacks: Replication and extension with concurrent measurement of behavior and pCO_2. *British Journal of Psychiatry, 148,* 526–532.

Shaw, B. F. (1977). Comparison of cognitive therapy and behavior therapy in the treatment of depression. *Journal of Consulting and Clinical Psychology, 45,* 543–551.

Silverman, J. S., Silverman, J. A., & Eardley, D. A. (1984). Do maladaptive attitudes cause depression? *Archives of General Psychiatry, 41,* 28–30.

Simons, A. D., Garfield, S. L., & Murphy, G. E. (1984). The process of change in cognitive therapy and pharmacotherapy for depression. *Archives of General Psychiatry, 41,* 45–51.

Simons, A. D., Murphy, G. E., Levine, J. L., & Wetzel, R. D. (1986). Cognitive therapy and pharmacotherapy for depression: Sustained improvement over one year. *Archives of General Psychiatry, 43,* 43–48.

Taylor, F. G., & Marshall, W. L. (1977). Experimental analysis of a cognitive-behavioral therapy for depression. *Cognitive Therapy and Research, 1,* 59–72.

Teasdale, J. D. (1985). Psychological treatments for depression: How do they work? *Behaviour Research and Therapy, 23,* 157–165.

Teasdale, J. D., & Dent, J. (1987). Cognitive vulnerability to depression: An investigation of two hypotheses. *British Journal of Clinical Psychology, 26,* 126–133.

Teasdale, J. D., Fennell, M. J. V., Hibbert, G. A., & Amies, P. L. (1984). Cognitive therapy for major depressive disorder in primary care. *British Journal of Psychiatry, 144,* 400–406.

Teasdale, J. D., & Fogarty, S. J. (1979). Differential effects of induced mood in retrieval of pleasant and unpleasant events from episodic memory. *Journal of Abnormal Psychology, 88,* 248–257.

Teasdale, J. D., & Russell, L. M. (1983). Differential effects of induced mood on the recall of positive, negative and neutral words. *British Journal of Clinical Psychology, 22,* 163–171.

Teasdale, J. D., & Taylor, R. (1981). Induced mood and accessibility of memories: An effect of mood state or of induction procedure? *British Journal of Clinical Psychology, 20,* 39–48.

Teasdale, J. D., Taylor, R., & Fogarty, S. J. (1980). Effects of induced elation–depression on the accessibility of memories of happy and unhappy experiences. *Behaviour Research and Therapy, 18,* 339–346.

Thorpe, G. L., Barnes, G. S., Hunter, J. E., & Hines, D. (1983). Thoughts and feelings: Correlations in two clinical and two nonclinical samples. *Cognitive Therapy and Research, 7,* 565–574.

Watts, F. N., McKenna, F. P., Sharrock, R., & Trezise, L. (1986). Colour naming of phobic-related words. *British Journal of Psychology, 77,* 97–108.

Wickless, C., & Kirsch, I. (1988). *Cognitive correlates of anger, anxiety, and sadness. Cognitive Therapy and Research, 12,* 367–377.

Williams, S. L., & Rappoport, A. (1983). Cognitive treatment in the natural environment for agoraphobics. *Behavior Therapy, 14,* 299–313.

Wilson, P. H., Goldin, J. C., & Charbonneau-Powis, M. (1983). Comparative efficacy of behavioral and cognitive treatments of depression. *Cognitive Therapy and Research, 7,* 111–124.

Winfrey, L. L., & Goldfried, M. R. (1986). Information processing and the human change process. In R. E. Ingram (Ed.), *Information processing approaches to clinical psychology.* Orlando, FL: Academic Press.

Wise, E. H., & Barnes, D. R. (1986). The relationship among life events, dysfunctional attitudes, and depression. *Cognitive Therapy and Research, 10,* 257–266.

Woodward, R., & Jones, R. B. (1980). Cognitive restructuring treatment: A controlled trial with anxious patients. *Behaviour Research and Therapy, 18,* 401–407.

Behavioral Treatments for Anxiety and Depression

Edna B. Foa
Barbara Olasov Rothbaum
Michael J. Kozak

I. Introduction

With the development of behavioral techniques, the last two decades have brought encouraging developments in the treatment of anxiety and depression. Syndromes such as agoraphobia and obsessive–compulsive disorder that once had bleak prognoses are now amenable to change. Moreover, substantial knowledge has accumulated about the effects of different treatment procedures for anxiety and depression, as well as about specific variables associated with treatment efficacy. In discussing the treatment of anxiety and depression, we will consider the classification of these disorders, discuss theoretical formulations, and finally review the treatment literature. We first discuss anxiety, then depression.

Note: Support for the preparation of this chapter was provided in part by NIMH Grants MH 42178 and MH 31634 awarded to the first author.

Anxiety and Depression

II. Anxiety Disorders

A. Definition and Description

Historically, behavior therapists focused on reducing neurotic fear and anxiety without making a distinction between types of fears (Leitenberg, Agras, Barlow, & Oliveau, 1969; Watson, Gaind, & Marks, 1972; Wolpe, 1958). More recently, the *Diagnostic and Statistical Manual of Mental Disorders* (DSM-III and DSM-III-R; American Psychiatric Association, 1980, 1987) classifications of anxiety disorders have been used in selecting subjects for outcome studies. It is therefore pertinent to review the eight anxiety disorders listed in the DSM-III-R: panic disorder, with and without agoraphobia, agoraphobia without a history of panic disorder, social phobia, simple phobia, obsessive–compulsive disorder, posttraumatic stress disorder, and generalized anxiety disorder.

Whereas this classification system provides clear descriptions for the identification of anxiety disorders, no theoretical dimensions are offered. Several such dimensions were proposed by Foa, Steketee, and Young (1984). These include the presence or absence of avoidance behaviors, external fear cues, and absence of anticipated harm. Given the nonexternal cues for fear (e.g., thoughts, physiological responses, impulses) occur in every anxiety problem, eight categories emerge from all possible combinations of these three dimensions. In Figure 14.1, these categories are mapped against the DSM-III-R classifications of anxiety.

It is apparent that some disorders are more homogeneous with respect to this classification. Panic-disordered individuals with agoraphobia, for example, are quite homogeneous: most fear their own physiological responses because they signal potential harm. To protect themselves from such harm, agoraphobics avoid arousing situations. Thus, all three types of fear cues comprise the agoraphobic fear structure. In contrast, obsessive–compulsive disorder is highly heterogeneous. Some obsessive–compulsives are similar to agoraphobics in that their fear contains all three types of fear cues (e.g., fear that contamination by germs that will lead to illness), whereas other obsessive–compulsive fear structures may not include external cues or any anticipated harm.

The value of any classification of psychopathology depends partly on its usefulness for selecting therapy. A relationship between treatment procedures and types of fears has already been proposed for phobias (Chambless, Foa, Groves, & Goldstein, 1980), for obsessive–compulsives (Foa, Steketee, & Ozarow, 1985), and for anxiety disorders in general (Foa & Kozak, 1986). Here, we will try to relate different fear structures to treatment outcomes and to hypothesized deficits specific to anxiety disorders.

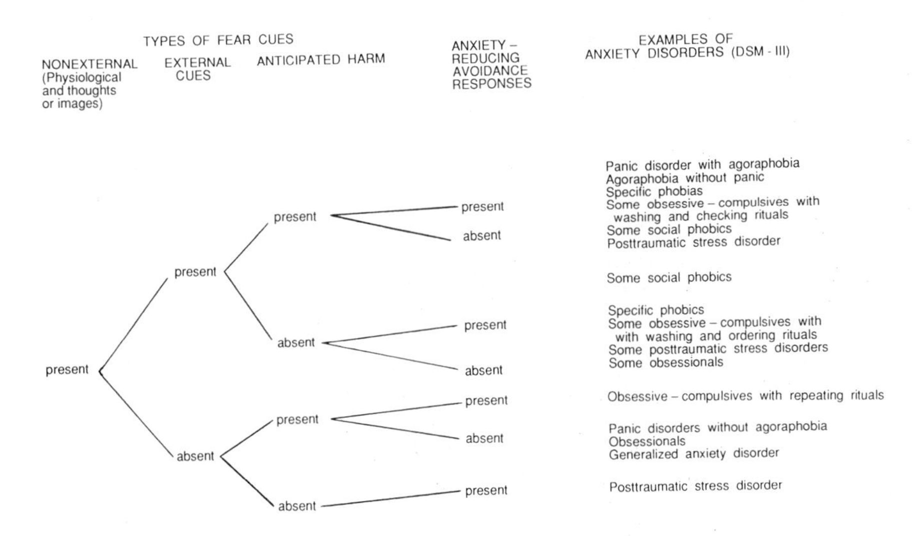

Figure 14.1
Functional analysis of anxiety disorder. (Adapted from Foa, Steketee, & Young, 1984.)

B. Theoretical Perspectives

Traditionally, behaviorists have focused on the conceptualization and treatment of phobias. Characterized by intense anxiety to circumscribed stimuli and a strong tendency to their avoidance, phobias have been formulated by learning theorists as involving both classical and operant conditioning. The most popular behavioral formulation is Mowrer's (1960) two-factor learning theory, which proposes that two types of learning, classical and instrumental, occur in the acquisition of fear and avoidance. In the first stage, via temporal contiguity, a previously neutral stimulus becomes associated with an unconditioned stimulus (UCS) that innately evokes discomfort or fear. The neutral stimulus then acquires aversive properties such that its presence elicits anxiety; it now becomes a conditioned stimulus (CS) for fear responses. When this conditioned stimulus is paired with a neutral stimulus, the latter also becomes aversive and will evoke fear responses. Through this process of higher order conditioning, many stimuli, including words, images, and thoughts, acquire the capacity to engender anxiety. The number of conditioned stimuli is further increased via a process of stimulus generalization: Stimuli that are similar to the original CS also become anxiety eliciting. The second stage consists of the development of learned responses, i.e., avoidance or escape responses, which decrease or terminate the discomfort arising from the presence of the conditioned stimuli.

Notwithstanding criticisms of the two-stage theory (e.g., Bolles, 1970; Herrnstein, 1969; Rachman, 1976), it does offer a useful account of the maintenance of avoidance behavior as stemming from its anxiety-reducing properties (Hodgson & Rachman, 1972; Carr, 1971).

If phobias are thought to involve conditioned responses, then therapeutic procedures should resemble extinction paradigms, i.e., weakening the association between the CS (fear stimulus) and the conditioned response (CR; anxiety response). To this end, Wolpe (1958) developed treatment by systematic desensitization, based on the hypothesis of reciprocal inhibition. Accordingly, pairing a response incompatible with anxiety (i.e., relaxation) with feared stimuli forms a new association and replaces the undesired association between the feared stimuli and fear response. Whereas this treatment technique is effective with some anxiety disorders, the hypothesis of reciprocal inhibition has not received empirical support (Kazdin & Wilkerson, 1976).

Recently, with the recognition of the inability of behavioral stimulus–response (S–R) theories to account for the "meaning" of fear situations (i.e., danger, threat), there has been a shift to information-processing theories (Reiss, 1980). One such theory has been proposed by Foa and Kozak (1986). Their starting point was Lang's (1977, 1979) analysis of fear as a network in memory that includes three kinds of information: (1) information about the feared stimulus situation; (2) information about verbal, physiological, and overt behavioral responses; and (3) interpretive, semantic information. This information structure is conceived of as a program for escape or avoidance behavior.

Foa and Kozak argued that if a fear structure is indeed a program to escape danger, it must involve information that stimuli and/or responses are *dangerous*, as well as information about physiological activity preparatory for escape. Thus, a fear structure is distinguished from other information structures not only by the stimulus and response elements, but also by certain meaning information it contains, i.e., information about danger. As will be discussed in the section on classification, anxiety disorders can be conceptualized as reflecting specific fear structures.

How can an established fear structure be dismantled to alleviate anxiety symptoms? Foa and Kozak (1986) suggested that two conditions are required for the reduction of fear. First, the fear memory must be activated. That is, as suggested by Lang (1977), if the fear structure remains in storage unaccessed, it will not be available for modification. Second, they proposed that information must be provided which includes elements "incompatible with some of those that exist in the fear structure, so that a new memory can be formed. This new information, which is at once cognitive and affective, has to be integrated into the evoked information structure for an emotional change to occur" (p. 22). Exposure to information consistent with a fear memory would be expected to strengthen the fear.

Information incompatible with associations between stimuli and anxiety responses must be provided during therapy. Indeed, systematic desensitization is a deliberate attempt to provide such information via associating relaxation with the feared stimuli. In flooding, confrontation is prolonged in order to allow response decrements (habituation), which dissociates the fear responses and the feared stimuli.

Corrective information also addresses the meaning associated with stimuli and responses (i.e., threat associations). Foa and Kozak (1985) suggested that several types of meaning elements characterize the fear structures of those who manifest anxiety disorders. First, there is the concept that anxiety will persist forever in the situation. Second, there are overestimated probabilities that the fear stimuli and/or the fear responses will cause either psychological (e.g., going crazy, losing control) or physical (e.g., dying, being ill) harm. Third, the anticipated consequences have an excessive negative valence, i.e., are extremely aversive for the individual. The erroneous concept of persistent anxiety is corrected via habituation during confrontation with the feared situation. Correction of patients' overestimates of eventual harm often requires repeated exposures; such changes are reflected in long-term habituation. Valence seems to change through observations of others' mild reactions to the same event as well as through habituation.

C. Fear Structures in the Anxiety Disorders

The different anxiety disorders have been conceptualized as reflecting different fear structures (Foa & Kozak, 1985). We will consider the hypothesized structural characteristics of each disorder.

Panic Disorder with Agoraphobia. The prevailing conceptualization of panic disorder with agoraphobia focuses on the fear of fear hypothesis (Goldstein & Chambless, 1978; Weekes, 1976). Accordingly, agoraphobics are afraid of interoceptive cues associated with fear or anxiety; they perceive anxiety as dangerous, leading to either physical harm (e.g., heart attacks) or psychological harm (e.g., going crazy, being embarrassed). Stimulus elements (e.g., supermarkets) are not evaluated as intrinsically threatening: the danger associated with them lies in the anxiety they evoke. Accordingly, treatment for this disorder should aim at correcting the threat value associated with the fear responses.

Panic Disorder without Agoraphobia. This disorder is distinguished by the absence of specific stimulus elements in its fear structure and the absence of avoidance behavior. Like agoraphobics, these patients construe anxiety responses as dangerous but do not develop spurious stimulus–response associations.

Social Phobias. Social fears are characterized by unusually high negative valence for social scrutiny and criticism as well as by overestimation of their likelihood. In addition, anxiety responses are associated with social criticism. Thus, the social fear structure includes associations about social situations and anxiety responses, perception of social encounters as threatening (e.g., criticism), and interpretation of anxiety responses as eliciting criticism and therefore as being harmful.

Simple Phobias. The fear structure of simple phobias consists of pathological stimulus–response associations and of the overestimation of the probabilities of harm associated with the stimulus situation. For example, the dog phobic experiences anxiety about dogs and supposes them to be ferocious. This mistaken evaluation inspires avoidance which precludes structural change via corrective information.

Obsessive–Compulsive Disorder. Several types of fear structures occur in obsessive–compulsives. The patient who fears contracting venereal disease from public bathrooms and exhibits washing rituals has a fear structure that includes disordered associations among stimulus and response elements and mistaken evaluations about the harm from the stimulus situation. For other obsessive–compulsives, fear responses are associated with evaluative elements rather than with a particular stimulus set. For example, patients who are disturbed by perceived asymmetry and reduce anxiety by rearranging objects do not fear the objects themselves, nor do they anticipate disaster from the asymmetry. It appears from the examples cited that no one form of fear structure is common to obsessive–compulsives. Foa and Kozak (1985) suggested that one unifying variable is an impairment in the interpretive rules for making inferences about harm. Typically, obsessive–compulsives base their beliefs about danger on the *absence* of disconfirming evidence and often fail to make inductive leaps about general safety from specific disconfirmations regarding danger.

Posttraumatic Stress Disorder. Among the various anxiety disorders, posttraumatic stress is the only one which is defined in part by a precipitating event. Stimulus and response associations regarding that event form the basic fear structure for this disorder. Since the precipitating events are of the sort which would be stressful for almost anyone, it is the *persistence* of the fear structure, rather than simply its formation, that is pathological (see Foa, Steketee, & Rothbaum, in press, for further discussion).

Generalized Anxiety Disorder. This disorder, like panic disorder without agoraphobia, is not distinguished by stimulus content. Rather, the primary pathological features of this fear structure are intense response elements associated with negative valence (i.e., anxiety is bad), which become temporarily linked to various negatively valent stimulus structures.

III. Treatment of Anxiety Disorders

Early learning theorists and behavior therapists did not distinguish among types of pathological fears, assuming mechanisms of acquisition and of maintenance to be the same for all fears. Consonant with this lumping approach, early behavior therapy studies examined outcome of a given therapeutic procedure using a mixed sample of anxiety disorders (e.g., Gelder, Marks, & Wolff, 1967). At the same time, researchers' attempts to define differences among the anxiety disorders were manifested in efforts at classification (Marks, 1969). Accordingly, later studies utilized homogeneous populations in examining treatment efficacy. In this chapter, we will present the treatment literature using the DSM-III-R anxiety disorder classification.

Two sets of behavioral procedures have been commonly employed in the treatment of anxiety disorders: exposure-based procedures and anxiety management techniques.

Exposure Techniques. Exposure treatment is a set of techniques whose common denominator is patients' confrontation with their feared situations. These techniques can be divided according to the medium of exposure (imaginal vs. *in vivo*), the length of exposure (short vs. long), and level of arousal during exposure (low vs. high). When the various exposure procedures are ordered along these dimensions, systematic desensitization (SD) (Wolpe, 1958), where exposure is imaginal, brief, and minimally arousing, occupies one extreme position. In direct contrast is *in vivo* flooding (Marks, 1972), where exposure is to actual life events, is prolonged, and is designed to elicit high levels of anxiety.

SD was the first exposure technique. As described originally, it consists of imagining confrontation with feared situations or objects. The therapist describes short scenarios which focus on the feared stimulus (e.g., "you are five feet away from the *snake*"). Patients are instructed to imagine the scenarios as vividly as possible for a short period of time. Although some fear is said to be necessary, attempts are made to minimize fear during imagery, usually via relaxation. The scenes are arranged hierarchically, with the least fearful one presented first. Each scene is repeated until it ceases to elicit anxiety. Variants of SD include *in vivo* and imaginal graded exposure without relaxation. When exposure begins with highly feared stimuli, is prolonged, and elicits high levels of anxiety, the treatment technique is called flooding, which can be implemented either imaginally or *in vivo* until some reduction in anxiety occurs.

Anxiety Management Techniques (AMT). Whereas exposure techniques are designed to activate fear and promote habituation, AMT aims toward anxiety reduction by providing patients with skills to control fear. Among such techniques are relaxation training (e.g., Bernstein & Borkovec, 1973; Jacobson, 1938), stress inoculation training (Meichenbaum, 1974), cognitive restructuring (Beck, 1972; Ellis, 1977), breathing retraining (Clark, Salkovskis, & Chalkley, 1985), social skills training (Becker, Heimberg, & Bellack, 1987), and distraction techniques (e.g., thought stopping; Wolpe, 1973). The most widely used of these techniques is deep muscle relaxation training defined by Wolpe (1985) as the "activity of the undoing of the tonic contraction of muscle fibers" (p. 101). It affects the autonomic nervous system such that sympathetic responses are attenuated, i.e., heart rate and breathing slows and blood pressure falls.

Exposure techniques are used when the disorder involves excessive avoidance and treatment aims for both activation and modification of the fear structure. AMT, on the other hand, is used when anxiety pervades daily functioning. In this case there is no need to activate the fear as much as manage it. In the following sections we discuss the efficacy of behavioral treatments with the various anxiety disorders. The order of presentation follows the historical development of these techniques.

A. Simple Phobias

The efficacy of SD with simple phobics was validated in numerous studies of subclinical fears (cf. Marks, 1972), as well as with specific phobics (Cooper, Gelder, & Marks, 1965; Marks & Gelder, 1965). When compared with other therapeutic procedures, including hospitalization, insight, groups, and individual psychotherapy, SD was superior (Gelder et al., 1967). Moreover, phobics who failed to benefit from traditional psychotherapy later improved when treated with SD (Gelder & Marks, 1968). However, treatment by desensitization usually includes homework assignments for *in vivo* confrontations to augment imaginal exposure conducted in the therapist's office. Because Barlow, Leitenberg, Agras, and Wincze (1969) obtained only a 50% transfer from imaginal SD to real-life situations without homework assignments, the effect of SD may not be as impressive as initially claimed.

Imaginal flooding was also found effective with simple phobics. Studies with clinical populations showed equivalent effectiveness for SD and imaginal flooding (Marks, Boulougouris, & Marset, 1971; Gelder et al., 1973; Crowe, Marks, Agras, & Leitenberg, 1972). Evidence as to the superiority of *in vivo* versus imaginal exposure has been found (Barlow et al., 1969). Crowe et al. (1972) found *in vivo* graded exposure superior to SD. In a similar vein, Watson et al. (1972) found that fear, as measured by heart rate, was higher during *in vivo* exposure to feared situations, although patients had previously habituated to them during imaginal exposure. In all the above studies, subjects were simple phobics. As noted by Mathews (1978) "the available evidence suggests that direct exposure is always superior with simple phobics" (p. 399). The efficacy of *in vivo* exposure was again evidenced recently with height phobics and driving phobics (S. L. Williams, Dooseman, & Kleinfield, 1984; S. S. Williams, Turner, & Peer, 1985).

One hypothesized mechanism of change through exposure therapy is physiological habituation. With prolonged exposure, decreases in heart rate, reported fear, and (sometimes) electrodermal activity have been found both within and between sessions (cf. Foa & Kozak, 1986). However, the general rule that heart rate decreases with fear reduction is apparently contradicted in blood/injury phobics. These individuals show a diphasic pattern culminating in decreased heart rate and blood pressure, and sometimes fainting, when exposed to their feared situations. This parasympathetic pattern has been evidenced during bloodletting (e.g., Graham, 1961), and the viewing of films of violence (Carruthers & Taggart, 1973) and of surgical procedures (Curtis & Thyer, 1983; Ost, Sterner, & Lindahl, 1984).

Fainting in blood/injury phobics has been treated successfully by graded exposure (Nimmer & Kapp, 1974; Curtis & Thyer, 1983). However, because of the vasodepressor component of blood injury fear, Kozak and Montgomery (1981) introduced a muscle tensing, in combination with exposure, to treat fainting successfully. The tensing procedure probably inhibits fainting during exposure by activating the venous pump and increasing heart rate and cardiac output by the mechanism of cardiac–somatic coupling (Kozak & Miller, 1985). The tensing technique has also been found effective in group studies of exposure therapy for fear of blood/injury (Ost, Sterner, & Lindahl, 1984; Ost & Sterner, 1987).

B. Agoraphobia

The effects of SD with agoraphobia are less impressive than with simple phobias (Gelder et al., 1967; Gelder & Marks, 1966; Yorkston, Sergeant, & Rachman, 1968). In reviewing the behavioral treatment of agoraphobia, Jansson and Ost (1982) concluded that SD was ineffective with this population.

In comparing the responsiveness of simple phobics and agoraphobics to SD and imaginal flooding, Marks et al. (1971) found the former to profit equally from the two techniques, whereas the latter improved with flooding but not with desensitization. In a replication and extension of this study, Gelder et al. (1973) concluded that both desensitization and flooding were superior to placebo control treatment, and were equally effective for both disorders. Inspection of the results, however, suggests that for the behavior-test measure, flooding was superior to desensitization for agoraphobics.

There are several possible explanations for the differential effect of SD on the two disorders. If, as suggested before, the core pathology of agoraphobia is response-threat associations, i.e., "fear of fear," then flooding may provide a better match to its fear structure. First, SD usually emphasizes description of the stimulus situation, which is more relevant to simple phobics, rather than description of the responses, which is more relevant to agoraphobics. Second, flooding probably generates more interoceptive physical responses, which are at the core of the agoraphobic fear. Third, therapy that encourages confrontation with intense anxiety may relate implicitly that anxiety is not dangerous, thereby contradicting the agoraphobic's notion that fear is dangerous. SD, on the other hand, attempts to minimize anxiety, perhaps reinforcing the patient's beliefs that anxiety may be dangerous.

Chambless et al. (1980) found flooding in conjunction with intravenously administered barbiturates less effective than flooding alone. Since the drug led to lower anxiety during flooding, and to inferior outcome, it appears that anxiety during exposure may be important for fear reduction with agoraphobics. Some support for this notion comes from Watson and Marks' (1971) finding that agoraphobics profited from anxiety-evoking images even when irrelevant to their problems. Similarly, I. Hand (personal communication) found that agoraphobics who experienced panic in the first few exposure sessions improved more than those who did not. Perhaps for agoraphobics, the experience of certain physical responses increased the matching with their fear structure, thereby enhancing its activation and facilitating change.

With the increased interest in cognitive therapy for anxiety disorders (Beck, Emery, & Greenberg, 1985), several studies have investigated the relative efficacy of *in vivo* exposure and various cognitive techniques. Emmelkamp, Bulman, Kuiper, and Mersch (1986) noted the equivocal results found across these studies. In general, exposure *in vivo* was superior to rational-emotive training (RET) and self-instructional training, although the latter two produced some improvement (Emmelkamp et al., 1986; Marchione, Michelson, Greenwald, & Dancu, 1987).

Whereas *in vivo* exposure was always superior to imaginal exposure with simple phobics, the results are equivocal with agoraphobics. With the latter, variants of *in vivo* confrontations were found equivalent to one another (Emmelkamp, 1974; Emmelkamp & Ultree, 1974; Everard, Rijken, & Emmelkamp, 1973) and imaginal flooding was inferior to *in vivo* exposure on some measures (Emmelkamp & Wessels, 1975; Stern & Marks, 1973). Also, with agoraphobics, Mathews et al. (1974) found these two forms of exposure equivalent, except for one measure on which *in vivo* exposure was superior.

The efficacy of *in vivo* exposure with agoraphobics was evidenced in many studies (cf. Emmelkamp, 1982; Mathews, Gelder, & Johnston, 1981), some with long-term follow-up (Emmelkamp & Kuipers, 1979; Mavissakalian & Michelson, 1983; McPherson, Brougham, & McLaren, 1980; Munby & Johnston, 1980). However, McPherson et al. (1980) reported that only 10% of their participants were completely symptom free, with 66% being stabilized at a functional level. More pessimistic results, 4.6% symptom free, were reported by Marks (1971).

Most of the clinical studies on the efficacy of *in vivo* exposure involved agoraphobics and obsessive–compulsives. From parametric studies we have learned that prolonged exposure is better than short exposure (Rabavilas, Boulougouris, & Stephanis, 1976; Stern & Marks, 1973), that massed practice is better than spaced practice sessions (Foa, Jameson, Turner, & Payne, 1980), and that self-exposure is better than modeled exposure (Roper, Rachman, & Marks, 1975). Graded exposure is equivalent to abrupt exposure (Boersma, Den Hengst, Dekker, & Emmelkamp, 1976; Hodgson, Rachman, & Marks, 1972), and group exposure is equivalent to individual exposure (Emmelkamp & Emmelkamp-Benner, 1975; Hafner & Marks, 1976). Although the contribution of a therapist in designing the exposure regimen and encouraging the patient to follow the program may be significant, the presence of a therapist during exposure seems unnecessary (Emmelkamp, 1974; Emmelkamp & Kraanen, 1977; Mathews et al. 1981; Michelson, 1986). Neither did spouse-assisted exposure enhance treatment efficacy (Emmelkamp, 1982; Mathews, Jannoun, & Gelder, 1979).

Earlier studies employed exposure directed by a therapist, either in groups or individually (e.g., Hand, Lamontagne, & Marks, 1974); more recently, programs utilizing the patient's natural support systems have been devised. Mathews, Teasdale, Munby, Johnston, and Shaw (1977) developed a home-based treatment program actively involving the patient's spouse in planning and encouraging practice. In comparison with clinic-based treatments used earlier by the authors, the home-based program produced equivalent immediate change compared to the clinic-based treatment and superior gains during follow-up. Moreover, Barlow, O'Brien, and Last (1984) asserted that drop-out rates were lower in this type of program. This advantage of incorporating spouses in treatment was reported by Cerney, Barlow, Craske, and Himaldi (1987) and by Cobb, Mathews, Childs-Clarke, and Blowers (1984). Arnow, Taylor, Agras, and Telch's (1985) results indicated that it was not the spouse's participation in treatment per se, but the consequent improvement in the relationship that mediated the advantage. Instructions may not have to be given at home nor by a therapist. Self-help books and computer programs were found equivalent to psychiatrist-aided instructions (Ghosh & Marks, 1987). Results were comparable to therapist-aided exposure in previous studies (e.g., Hafner and Marks, 1976).

Several studies compared the relative efficacy of pharmacological and behavioral treatments of agoraphobia. Four studies to date have compared the separate and combined effects of imipramine and behavior therapy (Marks et al., 1983; Telch, Agras, Taylor, Roth, & Gallen, 1985; Mavissakalian & Michelson, 1983; Zitrin, Klein, & Warner, 1980). All found behavior therapy to be effective, either with or without a therapist. The results regarding imipramine's effects were more equivocal, ranging from mild effects (Marks et al., 1983; Telch et al., 1985) to strong effects (Mavissakalian & Michelson, 1986; Zitrin et al., 1980). Three of the four studies found that the combination of behavior therapy and imipramine was superior (except for Marks et al., 1983).

In summary, exposure *in vivo* appears to be the most effective therapy for avoidance in agoraphobia, although imaginal exposure may also be helpful. Panic attacks, however, seem to be best controlled via a combination of pharmacological and behavioral treatments, notably imipramine and exposure (Telch et al., 1985). Home-based programs appear to be more efficient and effective, produce less attrition, and promote continuous progress in contrast to the ceiling effect found in therapist-aided exposure. The advantage of including the spouse in the treatment program seems to be mediated by enhanced marital communication.

C. Panic Disorder

Until recently, exposure treatments were not applied to patients with panic disorder without agoraphobia due to the absence of an identifiable external stimulus to which the patient could be exposed. It is only with the reconceptualization of agoraphobia and panic disorder (PD) as "fear of fear" (suggesting that interoceptive responses act as the feared stimuli) that behaviorists have developed effective treatment strategies. In addition to the fear-of-fear influence, the recognition of the role of hyperventilation in the production of panic attacks has spawned new treatments. It has been shown that increased ventilation reduces the amount of carbon dioxide in the lungs. This reduces the CO_2 blood concentration, increasing blood pH (more alkaline). These changes produce sensations such as numbness, dizziness, palpitations, lump in the throat, blurred vision, nausea, and breathlessness, which may not be unpleasant in themselves but when interpreted as dangerous become alarming.

The similarity of these responses to those experienced during panic attacks has led many researchers to suggest that hyperventilation may play an important role in the production of panic attacks (e.g., Clark et al., 1985). This model became the basis for a program which demonstrated the link between hyperventilation and panic and provided breathing retraining to control hyperventilation. This treatment consists of two 30- to 60-minute sessions delivered once per week. It proved highly effective in reducing frequency of panic attacks and self-reported anxiety for patients who suffered from panic attacks as well as from fear of experiencing panic (Clark et al., 1985).

In a successful replication of this treatment, Salkovskis, Jones, and Clark (1986) found that patients' initial resting CO_2 levels were significantly lower than found in a matched nonpatient control group and increased to normal levels during the course of treatment. These results support the mechanisms hypothesized by the model.

A treatment program nearly identical to that of Clark and Salkovskis has been tested by Sokol-Kessler, Beck, Greenberg, Berchick, and Wright (1987). However, the number of sessions was much greater (mean of 28 sessions). Compared with supportive therapy, this program was found more effective in reducing panic attacks and fear of fear (Sokol-Kessler & Beck, 1987).

There are three possible explanations for the success of this program: First, repeated hyperventilation can be viewed as an exposure to the feared interoceptive cues, which leads to habituation. Second, the breathing exercises can be conceived as a specific anxiety management technique. The proponents of this program (e.g., Beck et al., 1985; Clark et al., 1985) favor a third explanation: Recognition of the similarity between hyperventilation-related responses and panic-related responses promotes reinterpretation of the latter as benign, thereby disassociating their danger meaning.

A direct test of the hypothesis that exposure to interoceptive cues is effective for PD was conducted by Griez and Van Den Hout (1986). PD individuals and agoraphobics participated in the study of a cross-over design wherein half of the subjects received CO_2 inhalation therapy before administration of beta blockers (propanolol); the remaining received the two procedures in the reversed order. The results indicated the general effectiveness of the CO_2–propanolol package. CO_2 was more effective than propanolol in reducing fear of fear and avoidance.

D. Obsessive–Compulsive Disorder

No controlled prospective studies have been conducted to evaluate the effects of systematic desensitization on obsessive–compulsive disorder (OCD). The available case reports, however, suggest its ineffectiveness with these patients (Beech & Vaughn, 1978, Cooper, Gelder, & Marks, 1965).

The application of *in vivo* exposure to OCD is complicated by the nature of the fear: the physical removal of a feared object or situation does not necessarily constitute escape. Contamination is perceived to continue long after the object is removed. In contrast, for simple phobics and agoraphobics, removal from the feared situation constitutes escape and therefore terminates the fear response. In 1966, Victor Meyer described a treatment program for obsessive–compulsives addressing this problem, which included (1) exposure, i.e., contact with discomfort-evoking stimuli and (2) response prevention, i.e., the blocking of ritualistic behavior. Through the use of these two procedures, exposure was prolonged and avoidance or escape was blocked. At follow-up, 80% of the patients thus treated were improved (Meyer, Levy, & Schnurer, 1974).

A series of studies conducted at the Maudsley Hospital in London found variants of exposure more effective than relaxation and modeling, with about 75% of the patients showing significant improvement (Hodgson et al., 1972; Marks, Hodgson, & Rachman, 1975, Rachman, Hodgson, & Marks, 1971; Rachman, Marks, & Hodgson, 1973; Roper et al., 1975). Hundreds of patients around the world have been treated successfully with exposure and response prevention, attesting to the robust effect of this procedure (Boersma et al., 1977; Boulougouris, 1977; Boulougouris, Rabavilas, & Stefanis, 1977; Emmelkamp, Van Der Helm, van Zanten, & Plochy, 1980; Foa & Goldstein, 1978).

In a series of experiments, Foa and her colleagues investigated the relative contributions of the various treatment components. With few exceptions, in previous studies, exposure was conducted *in vivo* only. Yet, the fears seen in OCD, especially checkers, are characterized by feared consequences that cannot be realized *in vivo*. In comparing checkers who received *in vivo* exposure in addition to response prevention to those who received imaginal exposure in addition to the other two components, Foa, Steketee, Turner, and Fischer (1980) found no differences immediately posttreatment. However, at a 9-month follow-up, four of the eight who had received exposure *in vivo* relapsed to various degrees, whereas those who had been given both imaginal and *in vivo* exposure maintained their gains.

Several studies evaluated the contributions of exposure and of response prevention to treatment outcome (Foa, Steketee, & Milby, 1980; Steketee, Foa, & Grayson, 1982). *In vivo* exposure mainly affected reported anxiety and avoidance of contaminants, whereas response prevention influenced ritualistic behavior. A combination of the two procedures was superior both at posttreatment and at follow-up.

Exposure and response prevention is effective with OCs who manifest overt rituals, the majority of individuals suffering from this disorder. Only 10% of obsessive–compulsives do not evidence such rituals. The success rate with these individuals is considerably lower. Two procedures have been used: thought stopping and imaginal exposure. In a cross-over design, Emmelkamp and Kwee (1977) found that only one of the three patients who received exposure evidenced improvement, and none who received thought stopping improved. In the second investigation, Stern (1978) compared the efficacy of *satiation* (a variant of exposure) with thought stopping. The results of this study were again disappointing; less than 30% improved with satiation, and thought stopping was ineffective. In sum, we have developed good treatments for ritualizers, but not for ruminators.

E. Social Phobias

Investigations of exposure-based treatments with socially anxious patients have been limited until recently. The majority of the studies from the 1970s and early 1980s used volunteer subjects, for whom systematic desensitization has been consistently effective. In contrast, the few studies of clinical populations have found SD relatively ineffective. Marzillier, Lambert, and Kellett (1976) compared SD with social skills training (SST) and a waiting-list control. Social functioning improved immediately following both treatments, but at follow-up the SD group lost its gains. Neither treatment produced reduction in self-reported anxiety. Conversely, Trower, Yardley, Bryant, and Shaw (1978) found self-reported anxiety decreased following both SD and SST but social functioning improved only after SST. Shaw (1979) described a flooding group that improved as much as did the SD and SST groups in the Trower et al. (1978) study. Emmelkamp (1982) concluded that "desensitization is of limited value with socially anxious patients [and that] social skills training seems to be of more value in the treatment of social anxiety" (p. 135).

Ost, Jerremalm, and Johansson (1981) examined the effectiveness of SST versus relaxation in socially anxious outpatients who were either "physiologically reactive" or "behaviorally reactive". Although both treatments were generally effective, skills training worked better for behaviorally reactive patients and relaxation worked better for physiologically reactive patients. In a later study, Jerremalm, Jansson, and Ost (1986) compared relaxation to stress inoculation training (SIT). "Cognitively" reactive patients faired better with SIT on one thought measure and three self-report measures, and physiologically reactive patients did equally well with both treatments on all measures. The authors noted that the classification of cognitive versus noncognitive reactors may not have been reliable, whereas the classification used in the previous study was more stable over time.

The effectiveness of SST was also evidenced in a study of socially dysfunctional patients who received this training either alone or in combination with cognitive modification (Stravinsky, Marks, & Yule, 1982). Both treatments increased frequency of social behavior and reduced subjective anxiety, but there were no significant differences between the treatments. Without a control group, alternative explanations for the effects (such as passage of time, contact with therapist) cannot be ruled out.

Whereas exposure *in vivo* has been recognized to be preferable for agoraphobics and obsessive–compulsives, not until the mid-1980s was this technique systematically investigated with social phobics. A controlled study comparing exposure *in vivo* with exposure plus anxiety management training was conducted by Butler, Cullington, Munby, Amies, and Gelder (1984). Socially anxious outpatients were divided into three groups: waiting-list, exposure plus AMT, or exposure plus associative therapy (placebo). On measures of phobia and avoidance, both treatment groups improved more than the waiting-list group, evidencing the efficacy of exposure treatment for social phobia. The combination of exposure plus AMT was found more effective than exposure alone. In another study, exposure *in vivo* in groups was compared to self-instructional training and rational emotive therapy (Emmelkamp, Mersch, Vissia, & Van Der Helm, 1985). All three treatments were equally effective in reducing anxiety; only on one measure, pulse rate, was exposure superior.

Heimberg, Becker, and their colleagues developed a group treatment program for social phobics which consisted of imaginal exposure, exposure *in vivo,* and cognitive restructuring (P. G. Heimberg, Becker, Goldfinger, & Vermilyea, 1985; R. G. Heimberg et al., 1986). They compared this to a credible placebo (group discussion of topics relevant to social phobia). Exposure consisted of confronting simulated phobic events conducted during the therapy session. Improvement was evidenced for both treatments, with superiority of the cognitive–behavioral package on only two measures, clinician measures of phobic severity and self-reported discomfort.

Mattick and Peters (in press) compared weekly group treatment of social phobics who received therapist-aided exposure with exposure plus cognitive restructuring. Treatment included exposure to actual life situations in which patients were instructed to remain until anxiety subsided. The cognitive restructuring resembled Ellis' RET. Results indicated improvements in both treatment groups, which were maintained at follow-up. The combination treatment yielded improvement on social behavioral and self-rated avoidance as well as on other measures. These results and those of Butler et al. converge to indicate that, for social phobics, the combination of exposure and cognitive therapy is preferable. Compared to other anxiety disorders, perhaps social phobia is mediated more by evaluative processes rather than by mistaken stimulus–response associations. This may also account for the superiority of SST over SD. The latter focuses on correcting stimulus–response associations whereas the former focuses on changing self-evaluation of one's social competence.

F. Generalized Anxiety Disorder

Until recently, there were no behavioral treatments for generalized anxiety disorder (GAD), previously labeled "free-floating anxiety" or "perasive anxiety." The few existing interventions for pervasive anxiety focused on anxiety responses themselves. Goldfried (1971), for example, extended the use of systematic desensitization to encompass all stressful situations. Rather than conceptualizing SD as a technique to dissociate conditioned stimuli from anxiety responses, Goldfried viewed it as a method of teaching patients how to cope with anxiety. Along the same lines, Suinn and Richardson (1971) developed a technique called anxiety management training (AMT), which consisted of exposure to stressful situations and rehearsal of anxiety management techniques.

Common to these approaches, as well as to Meichenbaum and Turk's (1976) stress inoculation training, is the assumption that GAD reflects deficits in the management of anxiety rather than conditioned fear to nondangerous situations. Patients are exposed to an anxiety-evoking situation not for anxiety to habituate, but in order to learn ways to manage anxiety.

In the last 5 years, several authors have studied treatment programs for GAD based on the hypothesis that these patients are deficient in anxiety management skills and therefore should receive AMT (Suinn & Richardson, 1971). Despite this recognition, no controlled studies applying AMT to GAD patients were conducted until the present decade. In many of the studies, people with panic attacks were included and thus "pure" GAD studies are difficult to find.

Jannoun, Oppenheimer, and Gelder (1982) compared AMT to a no-treatment period in a multiple-baseline design utilizing a modification of Suinn and Richardson's treatment (Suinn, 1974). This self-help program included self-monitoring of anxiety and reading instruction booklets containing information on anxiety, muscle relaxation, and positive self-statements. AMT was more effective than no treatment in reducing anxiety. Moreover, patients continued to use these skills even after the termination of treatment.

This pilot study was the basis for a larger investigation by the Oxford group (Butler, Covington, Hibbert, Klimes, & Gelder, 1987). Patients were allocated randomly to AMT or to a waiting-list condition. Results on all anxiety measures indicated improvements in the treatment group which were maintained at 3- and 6-month follow-ups. The waiting-list group did not change at all during the waiting period, but after receiving AMT, reached the same level of improvement as the treatment group.

Another treatment for GAD was devised by the Albany group (Barlow et al., 1984) and was compared to a waiting-list condition. Treated subjects received progressive relaxation and frontalis electromyogram (EMG) biofeedback combined with cognitive–behavioral therapy. The behavioral components were based on Meichenbaum and Turk's (1973) SIT and on Beck et al.'s (1985) cognitive therapy for anxiety. A clear treatment effect emerged. Interestingly, GAD and panic disorders (PDs) responded equally well to treatment. However, PDs responded primarily to relaxation whereas GAD benefited somewhat more from the cognitive intervention. Gains were maintained at 3- and 12-month follow-ups.

Borkovec, Mathews, and their colleagues began programmatic research to identify the active ingredients of cognitive–behavioral approaches to GAD. They compared cognitive therapy plus relaxation, nondirective therapy plus relaxation, and relaxation alone (Borkovec et al., in press). Subjects were students recruited through classes and advertisements who met diagnostic criteria for GAD. All treatments produced therapeutic gains but the cognitive therapy resulted in greater gains than did the other treatment conditions on most measures.

In a second study, Borkovec and Mathews (1987) repeated the comparison of cognitive therapy to nonspecific treatment, adding a coping desensitization condition closely related to AMT, using a nonstudent clinical sample. All groups improved significantly from pretreatment, but no differences between groups were found at posttreatment or at follow-up. The magnitude of improvement was comparable to that found in other treatment studies using equivalent measures (e.g., State–Trait Anxiety Inventory; STAI), which found significant differences between treatment and no-treatment groups (e.g., Barlow et al., 1984; Butler et al., 1987). Because relaxation was included in all conditions, it may have been the active ingredient in the treatment. Indeed, there were significant correlations, which did not differ across groups, between relaxation practice and therapist's ratings of improvement. In addition, patients who became anxious during relaxation ("relaxation-induced anxiety" did not improve as much as the others.

Blowers, Cobb, and Mathews (1987) compared nondirective counseling to AMT (relaxation plus brief cognitive therapy) and to a waiting-list group. The two therapy groups received self-help booklets: *Understanding Anxiety* was given to the counseling group and *Coping with Anxiety* was given to the AMT group. Results indicated very few group differences between the two active treatments. However, the AMT group fared better than the waiting-list group whereas the counseling group did not. These results support Borkovec and Mathews' findings, although the improvement with AMT found by Blowers et al. was less than in other studies using AMT, possibly due to the exclusion of exposure instructions. Perhaps, as suggested by Mathews (1984) and by Foa and Kozak (1986), fear activation may be a crucial feature of more successful treatments. In the absence of exposure, relaxation and cognitive methods may be only slightly more potent than a nonspecific treatment such as counseling.

G. Posttraumatic Stress Disorder

SD was employed effectively by Wolff (1977) to treat the fears of a 20-year-old female raped 7 years earlier. In a series of nine cases, S. M. Turner (1979) found that SD effected improvement in measures of fear, anxiety, depression, and social adjustment. Similar results were reported by Frank and Stewart (1984) and by Becker and Abel (1981). Recent comparisons between SD and cognitive therapy with rape victims indicated no group differences (Frank et al., 1988).

Flooding has been markedly successful for Vietnam veterans with posttraumatic stress disorder (Fairbank & Keane, 1982; Keane & Kaloupek, 1982; Minisek, 1984). There are few reports of its application to rape victims. Imaginal flooding proved effective for several physical and sexual assault victims (Haynes & Mooney, 1975) and for a case of incest (Rychtarik, Silverman, Van Landingham, & Prue, 1984). The use of flooding in sexual assault victims has drawn pointed criticism (Kilpatrick, Veronen, & Resick, 1982; Kilpatrick & Best, 1984). However, its efficacy with Vietnam veterans and the successes cited above suggest that flooding holds promise for rape victims.

Holmes and St. Lawrence (1983) concluded from their review of treatments for rape victims that "the most promising treatment strategies appear to be those which provide victims with specific coping mechanisms and alternative responses to anxiety" (p. 430). A treatment package utilizing stress inoculation training that aims at providing such coping strategies for rape victims was adopted by Kilpatrick and Veronen (Kilpatrick & Veronen, 1983; Veronen & Kilpatrick, 1983).

In a study of SIT, Veronen and Kilpatrick (1982) selected only victims who showed elevated fear and avoidance to specific phobic stimuli 3 months postrape. Clear improvements were found, but conclusions from the data are limited by the absence of control conditions. A comparison between SIT, assertion training, supportive psychotherapy plus information, and a waiting-list control was conducted by Resick, Jordan, Girelli, Hutter, and Marhoefer-Dvorak (in press). Results indicated that all three treatments were effective in reducing fear, with no group differences evident. Improvement was maintained at a 6-month follow-up on rape-related fear measures, but not on depression, self-esteem, and social fears. No improvements were found in the waiting-list group.

A study comparing SIT, imaginal exposure to the assault, supportive counseling, and a waiting-list group is presently being conducted by Foa and Olasov Rothbaum with assault victims meeting diagnostic criteria for posttraumatic stress disorder (PTSD). Preliminary analysis indicates the superiority of SIT over exposure, counseling, and the waiting-list condition, although all groups are showing some improvement (Olasov & Foa, 1988). It is interesting to note that this is the first study to find exposure inferior to other treatments for anxiety disorders.

Although the behavioral treatment for PTSD was employed first with war veterans, no data from controlled group outcome studies are available to date. Several single case studies have been published (Fairbank, Gross, & Keane, 1983; Fairbank & Keane, 1982; Johnson, Gilmore, & Shenoy, 1982; Keane & Kaloupek, 1982; Schindler, 1980) demonstrating the efficacy of a variety of techniques in which the patient was exposed imaginally to the original traumatic event. SD (Schindler, 1980), flooding in imagination (e.g., Fairbank & Keane, 1982; Keane, Fairbank, Caddell, Zimering, & Bender, 1985), and flooding *in vivo* with material associated with the traumatic event (Johnson et al., 1982) appeared to be equally therapeutic. Most of these case reports, however, included other techniques as well, such as anger control or relaxation training, and thus the contribution of exposure to the overall efficacy is unclear.

PTSD resulting from other traumas (e.g., accidents) has also been successfully treated with behavioral techniques. McCaffey and Fairbank (1985) reported on two PTSD cases: one resulted from a helicopter crash and the other resulted from a series of automobile accidents. Treatment included relaxation training, imaginal exposure, and self-directed *in vivo* exposure. Improvement in PTSD symptoms was substantial; only modest changes in reported anxiety were noted.

In summary, reliving traumatic events seems helpful in reducing PTSD symptoms following war and accidents, and it may be helpful with rape victims. At present, however, SIT is the most well-evidenced procedure for survivors of sexual assault with PTSD.

IV. The Behavioral Treatment of Depression

As is apparent from the above review, behavior therapy has made substantial theoretical and practical contributions to the understanding and treatment of anxiety. In the 1970s, following the pioneering work of Ferster (1965), attention was drawn to depression. Unlike the DSM-III criteria for defining the samples, which were adopted in treatment studies of anxiety, no one common practice has been adopted for defining the samples in treatment studies of depression. Severity of depression is assessed via standardized scales such as the Beck Depression Inventory (BDI), the Minnesota Multiphasic Personality Inventory (MMPI), and the Hamilton Depression Rating Scale (HDRS). Some researchers have also used the Research Diagnostic Criteria (RDC; Spitzer, Endicott, & Robins, 1978), and the Schedule for Affective Disorders and Schizophrenia (SADS; Endicott & Spitzer, 1978). For example, Lewinsohn classifies a person as depressed according to criteria derived from the MMPI and the clinical interviews, thus viewing depression as a psychopathological entity. Ferster, on the other hand, defines depression solely on the basis of behavioral observations.

A. Behavioral Theories of Depression

Pleasant Events Deficiency. Following Skinner's (1953) view of depression as an interruption of behaviors previously reinforced by the social environment, behaviorists have conceptualized depression as an extinction phenomenon. Accordingly, Ferster (1965, 1966) viewed depression as a reduced rate of behaviors brought about by a decrease in positive reinforcement in the person's life. This decrease may have resulted from a number of life events such as death of partner, loss of job, divorce, or dislocation. This decrease takes the form of psychomotor and cognitive retardation. Consequently, Ferster (1973) expanded his model to account for the passivity of depressed individuals, noting their limited, negative, and fixed view of the world. Thus, his later formulation addressed cognitive and perceptual aspects as well as behavioral manifestations of depression.

Following Ferster's view and Lazarus' (1968) position that depression is a "function of inadequate and/or insufficient reinforcers" (p. 84), Lewinsohn (1974, 1975) hypothesized that low rate of positive reinforcement can explain parts of the depressive syndrome. By defining depression as a "psychopathological condition whose existence can be defined in terms of the occurrence (frequency and intensity) of certain kinds of behaviors and symptoms" (p. 24), he took the position that a common antecedent (e.g., low rate of positive reinforcement) underlies all depressions.

Unlike Ferster, Lewinsohn has stressed the importance of response-contingent reinforcement rather than frequency of reinforcement. Accordingly, the degree of response-contingent reinforcement depends on the number of activities a person may find rewarding, the availability of these activities in a person's environment, and the skillfulness of a person in maximizing positive reinforcement and minimizing punishment.

Support for the hypothesis that depressed individuals lack response-contingent reinforcers comes from several studies (Lewinsohn & Amenson, 1978; Lewinsohn & Graf, 1973; Lewinsohn & Libet, 1972). In these studies depressed psychiatric patients were compared with normal controls on the Pleasant Events Schedule (PES; MacPhillamy & Lewinsohn, 1971) and on daily ratings on the Depression Adjective Checklist (DAC; Lubin, 1965). Significant correlations between mood and pleasant activity level were found, especially with respect to interpersonal activities.

Social Skills Deficits. According to Lewinsohn (1975), depressed individuals lack social skills and therefore may be less able than others to find alternative sources of personal pleasure after losing previous sources. The hypothesis regarding deficits in social skills is consistent with the results of Libet and Lewinsohn (1973), who found that depressed subjects showed slower response time, fewer conversations with others, and fewer positive responses when approached by others. Similarly, clinically depressed psychiatric patients were found to engage less frequently in social interactions than were nondepressed patients (Youngren & Lewinsohn, 1980).

The relationship between depression and assertive behavior was further explored by Sanchez and Lewinsohn (1980), who found that assertiveness was negatively correlated with depression. Moreover, it served as a good predictor of the next day's mood. Lewinsohn, Mischel, Chaplin, and Barton (1980) compared perceived social competence of depressed and nondepressed patients as well as of normal controls. Observers rated depressed patients as slightly less socially competent than nondepressed patients and normals. Interestingly, normal individuals rated themselves as more socially competent than did those who observed them. It appears, then, that the depressed patients were more realistic than normals in assessing their level of social competence. Perhaps, as suggested by Miller and Seligman (1975), "realistic pessimism" may breed depression.

A problem with the work of Lewinsohn and Ferster is the assumption of a one-to-one correspondence between one's perception of the reinforcer and its reinforcement value (valence). This problem has been recognized by Costello (1972), who found evidence that depression involves a "general loss of reinforcer *effectiveness.*" Unlike Ferster, who proposed that the cause of depression was the absence of positive reinforcement, or Lewinsohn, who focused on the contingency of reinforcers on responses, Costello stressed the inability of the depressed individual to derive pleasure from existing reinforcers. Supportive of this formulation are the findings of Lewinsohn and MacPhillamy (1974) and MacPhillamy and Lewinsohn (1973) that the subjective enjoyability of pleasant events is lower in depressed than in nondepressed individuals regardless of age or activity level.

Additional evidence for the impact of one's perception of events on depression is the finding that depressed individuals are hypersensitive to aversive stimuli (Lewinsohn, Lobitz, & Wilson, 1983). It stands to reason that such sensitivity would lead to a greater tendency to avoid and withdraw from unpleasant situations. This, in turn, would result in greater isolation, and, consequently, in decreased opportunity to acquire social skills. On the basis of several studies exploring the relationship between social skills and depression, Lewinsohn (1975) concluded that: "individuals who: (a) are active; (b) are quick to respond; (c) are relatively insensitive to an aversive person; (d) do not miss chances to react; (e) distribute their behaviors fairly evenly across members in group situations; and (f) emit the functional positive reinforcing events, maximize the rate of positive reinforcement elicited, i.e., are socially skillful." (p. 44).

Other investigators have also stressed the lack of social skills in maintaining, and perhaps causing, depression. Indeed, depressed persons repeatedly have been found to be deficient in social skills (Ekman & Friesen, 1974; Lewinsohn et al., 1980; Weissman & Paykel, 1974). In a summary of social skills training approaches to the treatment of depression, Becker and Heimberg (1984) delineate the following assumptions:

1. Depression is a result of an inadequate schedule of positive reinforcement contingent on the person's nondepressed behavior.
2. A meaningful portion of the most salient positive reinforcers in the adult world are interpersonal in nature.
3. A meaningful portion of the noninterpersonal rewards in adult life may be received or denied, contingent on the person's interpersonal behavior.
4. Therefore, any set of treatment techniques that helps the depressed patient increase the quality of his or her interpersonal behavior should act to increase the amount of response-contingent positive reinforcement and thereby decrease depressive affect and increase the rate of nondepressed behavior.

Self-Monitoring Deficits. Similar to Costello, Rehm (1977) proposed that depression is caused by the individual's *perception* of external events and their own behavior as opposed to the event or behavior itself. This approach is based on Kanfer's (1970, 1971) view of self-control as altering the probability of a response in the absence of external influences. Three processes were postulated to operate in a closed-loop feedback model: self-monitoring, self-evaluation, and self-reinforcement (Kanfer, 1971). Rehm applied these concepts to identify specific deficits associated with depression. The self-monitoring of depressed individuals differs from normals in two ways: First, they are more attentive to negative events, and second, they attend more to the immediate rather than the delayed outcome of behavior. Deficits in the self-evaluation process include frequent failure to make accurate internal attributions of causality and the tendency to set stringent criteria for evaluating themselves. Deficits in the self-reinforcement mechanism, according to Rehm, are particularly important in accounting for depression, which is characterized by a low rate of self-reward and high rate of self-punishment.

Some support for this theory has been provided by Gottlieb (1981). Depressed and nondepressed psychiatric inpatients and nondepressed normals were presented with 30 nonsense syllables followed by slides of three-syllable words. After a resting period they were shown additional slides, each containing three syllables, one of which was presented previously. Subjects were instructed to press either a button indicating self-reward for making a good choice or a button indicating self-punishment for making a bad choice. As predicted by the theory, depressed patients self-administered fewer rewards and more punishments than normals.

However, the depressed patients did not differ from nondepressed psychiatric patients. In addition, depressed patients overestimated the number of self-punishments and underestimated the number of self-reinforcements, whereas the other groups reported their behavior accurately. Gottlieb suggested that low rate of self-reinforcement may be characteristic of global psychopathology, but the deficit in recall of self-reinforcement and self-punishment is specific to depression.

Self-reinforcement processes in depressed and nondepressed psychiatric inpatients were also examined by Lobitz and Post (1979). Subjects were administered several tasks and were asked to rate their expectations for success, to evaluate their actual success, and to reward themselves with as many tokens as they thought they deserved for their success. They were also asked to rate other patients on the same variables. The results indicated that depressed patients showed lower self-expectation and lower self-evaluation than did nondepressed patients, despite the absence of actual performance differences between the groups. The authors concluded that the low self-reinforcement was mediated by the low initial expectations for success rather than by deficits in the self-reinforcement process; however, the data do not allow causal interpretation.

B. Behavioral Treatments of Depression

It is apparent from the above discussion that the guiding principle of the behavioral treatment of depression is to increase perceived rewards. A number of treatments derived from behavioral theories of depression have been developed.

These techniques can be divided into four major categories: changing the environment, changing the individual's skillfulness in interacting with the environment, increasing the pleasantness and decreasing the aversiveness of these interactions, and increasing self-reinforcement. Whereas some investigators stress one approach over another, typically a combination of techniques is used.

Increasing Pleasant Events. Lewinsohn and his colleagues have developed a treatment aimed at increasing pleasant events for depressed individuals (Lewinsohn, Antonuccio, Steinmetz, & Teri, 1984). The program begins by requesting patients to monitor their daily activities to increase awareness of the interaction between environmental events and mood state. Next, patients are trained to relax to facilitate enjoyment of activities and decision making. Patients are encouraged to identify pleasant events which elevate mood and to increase the frequency of these events. Particular emphasis is placed on social interactions and the patient's current level of social functioning. Evidence for a consistent relationship between mood and the rate of pleasant events has been presented by Lewinsohn and Graf (1973) and MacPhillamy and Lewinsohn (1974).

The relationship between depression and reinforcement was explored in a treatment study by Lewinsohn, Youngren, and Grosscup (1979). They found a positive relationship between improvement in depression and an increase in pleasant events, which evidenced the efficacy of their treatment program and the validity of their theory. Additional support for the relationship of activity and mood comes from a study by R. W. Turner, Ward, and Turner (1979), who compared four conditions: increased activity, expectancy control, self-monitoring, and attention control. All subjects improved; the increased-activity group showed significantly greater gains than the others. Evidence for nonspecific factors emerged in a study by Zeiss, Lewinsohn, and Munoz (1979). Depressed outpatients received treatment focusing either on interpersonal skills, cognitions, or pleasurable events. All treatments significantly relieved depression, but no treatment had specific impact on its target variables. All patients improved on most dependent variables, regardless of whether the variables were addressed directly in the treatment.

Lewinsohn and his colleagues have formalized the above procedures into a highly structured group treatment program called The Coping With Depression Course (CWD), which consists of 12 2-hour sessions over the course of 8 weeks. This program includes a theoretical explanation of depression, relaxation training, scheduling training, rethinking, and social skills practice. The program, described in detail in Lewinsohn et al. (1984), adopts an educational stance, incorporating a text (Lewinsohn, Munoz, Youngren, & Zeiss, 1978), a workbook (Brown & Lewinsohn, 1979), and an instructor's manual (Steinmetz et al., 1979). Three outcome studies on the CWD course were conducted (Brown & Lewinsohn, 1984; Steinmetz, Lewinsohn, & Antonuccio, 1983; Teri & Lewinsohn, 1981, 1985). The results indicated that the CWD course alleviated depression and was not significantly different from the individual therapy.

Social Interaction Therapy. This treatment program is based on McLean's (1976) social learning theory which views depression as a loss of ability to control the interpersonal environment. McLean suggested the use of six therapeutic techniques aimed at training patients in communication, social interaction, behavioral productivity, cognitive self-control, assertiveness, decision making, and problem solving. Some components of this therapy are shared with other programs. What may be unique to McLean's program is the emphasis on communication training with the inclusion of the spouse or significant other.

In an outcome study by McLean, Ogston, and Graver (1973), depressed individuals and their spouses received either social interaction therapy or drug therapy, and/or more general psychosocial therapy. Social interaction therapy was superior on Depression Adjective Checklist scores posttreatment and 3 months thereafter. In addition, significant treatment effects were found for original presenting problems such as social withdrawal, sleep disturbance, impaired concentration, inability to make decisions, suicidal preoccupation, poor communication with spouse, sexual dissatisfaction, and minimal interest in hobbies and activities. In a more recent study, moderately depressed patients were randomly assigned to one to four treatment conditions: social interaction therapy, short-term traditional psychotherapy, relaxation training, and medication (McLean & Hakstian, 1979). The results demonstrated the superiority of the social interaction group at posttreatment but not at a 3-month follow-up. Additionally, the social interaction group showed only a 5% attrition rate as opposed to 26–36% in the other conditions. The least effective treatment was traditional psychotherapy.

Social Skills Training for Treatment of Depression. Bellack, Hersen, and Himmelhoch (1980) developed treatment aimed at enhancing the social skills of depressed individuals. The rationale was that depressed individuals lack assertiveness (Sanchez & Lewinsohn, 1980; Wolpe, 1979), and Lewinsohn's (1975) idea was that depressed individuals lack the behaviors to elicit positive responses. The program had four components: (1) social skills training, (2) social perception training, (3) practice (including homework), and (4) self-evaluation and self-reinforcement.

Evidence for the efficacy of social skills training for the treatment of depression has been provided by several sources. Wells, Hersen, Bellack, and Himmelhoch (1979) reported promising results with four depressed patients. Later applications of this treatment also evidenced its efficacy (Bellack, Hersen, & Himmelhoch, 1983; Hersen, Bellack, & Himmelhoch, 1980). Bellack et al. (1981) compared four treatments with depressed females: amitriptyline, social skills training plus amitriptyline, social skills training plus placebo, and psychotherapy plus placebo. No differences were detected in group means: each treatment produced clinically meaningful changes in depression and social functioning. However, the social skills plus placebo group had the least number of dropouts and the greatest number of improved patients. These effects, however, were not found in a later study (Hersen, Bellack, Himmelhoch, & Thase, 1984) with a larger sample. It appears that psychosocial treatment is competitive with pharmacotherapy in ameliorating depression. Given the side effects of drugs and the rate of relapse upon drug withdrawal, perhaps social skills training appears preferable to a drug intervention for many depressed individuals, although drug interventions are often more economical.

Further evidence for the impact of interpersonal skills on depression was provided by Sanchez, Lewinsohn, and Larson (1980), who compared assertion training and traditional group psychotherapy. The former was more effective than the latter in enhancing self-reported assertiveness and relieving depression. LaPointe and Rimm (1980) compared assertiveness training, cognitive therapy, and insight-oriented psychotherapy and found that all groups improved equally in depression, rationality, and assertiveness. At follow-up, however, none of the assertiveness group had sought further treatment in contrast with 18% of the cognitive therapy group and 45% of the insight therapy group.

Self-Control Therapy. Rehm's (1977) self-control model of depression posits deficits in self-monitoring, self-evaluation, and self-reinforcement. Fuchs and Rehm (1977) developed a group treatment program which consisted of three phases: self-monitoring of activities and daily mood, self-evaluation training stressing realistic goal setting and evaluation of oneself, and self-reinforcement practice. When compared to nonspecific group therapy and to a waiting-list control (Fuchs & Rehm, 1977), this therapy group showed greater reduction in self-reported and behavioral depression as well as in reduction of overall pathology (as measured by MMPI). Improvement was maintained at a 6-week follow-up.

A comparison between self-control therapy and assertion training revealed some specificity of treatment effects: self-control subjects improved more on measures of self-control whereas assertion skills subjects improved more on assertion skill measures. On measures of depression, self-control therapy was better at posttreatment and at follow-up (Rehm, Fuchs, Rosh, Kornblith, & Romano, 1979). Additional studies supporting the efficacy of self-control therapy for depression are summarized in Rehm (1977).

More recently, Rehm and his colleagues have examined the different components of self-control therapy. Rehm et al. (1981) compared five groups of self-control therapy: self-monitoring only, self-monitoring plus self-evaluation, self-monitoring and self-reinforcement, all three components, and a waiting-list period. All active treatment groups fared better than waiting-list controls on measures of depression and no differences were found among the active treatments. The finding of no differences among treatment components was replicated by Kornblith, Rehm, O'Hara, and Lamparski (1983). The authors were particularly surprised at the failure of the self-reinforcement component to show superiority and suggested that the high complexity of the procedure hindered its effectiveness. In support of this explanation, they cited the poor compliance with the self-reinforcement procedure. Alternatively, the authors proposed that possible ceiling effects may have obscured the efficacy of self-reinforcement. This phase was always presented last and patients may have already improved before its implementation. But, if such ceiling effects are present after self-monitoring alone, then self-reinforcement appears to be nonessential. A better design for evaluating the individual effects of the three components of self-control would involve between subjects' comparisons of self-monitoring, self-evaluation, and self-reinforcement.

Roth, Bielski, Jones, Parker, and Osborn (1982) compared modification of self-control therapy with self-control therapy plus antidepressant medication (desipramine). Both groups showed improvement in depressive symptoms; the combined treatment showed more rapid improvement, but no differences were detected at posttreatment and a 3-month follow-up.

Summary. The common denominator of the various approaches to depression is the hypothesis that underlying depression is a deficiency in the availability of positive reinforcement. Where do they diverge? What distinguishes each is the supposed *source* of this deficiency. For Lewinsohn, it is the environment; for social skills training advocates, it is the interpersonal behavior of the depressed individual; for self-control theorists, it is the perception of the relationship of environmental events and behavior. The hypothesized source of the deficit entails the type of procedures developed to modify that deficit. Lewinsohn and his colleagues, for example, initially focused on enriching the environment to increase positive reinforcement. With the development of the theory, the importance of social behavior was recognized and social skills training was implemented. Social skills programs focus on modifying behavior for more interpersonal reinforcement, and, secondarily, on shaping interpretations of others' behavior. Self-control therapy aims at equipping the depressed individual with the ability for self-reinforcement. All three approaches have been found effective in reducing depression.

V. Similarities and Differences in Treatments of Anxiety and Depression

The behavioral treatments of depression and anxiety reflect specific behavioral theories of their psychopathology. Both depression and anxiety are thought to involve two types of impairments: skills deficits and mistaken interpretations of events.

Treatments for anxiety decrease autonomic responding and discomfort as well as correct misconceptions about danger. Treatments for depression increase reward-seeking behavior as well as enhance the perception that rewards have been received. Because both anxiety and depression are negative affective states, their treatment involves procedures which directly reduce discomfort. In addition, treatments for both anxiety and depression aim at altering perceptions of contingencies among actions and outcomes. Specifically, treatments of anxiety teach individuals that harm is noncontingent on protective actions. Conversely, treatment of depression trains depressed patients to recognize the existing contingencies among their actions and attained rewards.

Behavioral treatments of anxiety can be grouped into anxiety management techniques and exposure procedures. The former promote autonomic self-control and enhance task performance. For example, to reduce test anxiety, treatment typically includes training in test taking and in relaxation for use in testing situations. Exposure procedures, on the other hand, are designed to confront the patient with the absence of contingency among escape, avoidance, and danger. To teach agoraphobics that keeping heart rate low does not protect them from cardiac arrest, they are exposed to situations that produce increased heart rate. Patients thereby learn that increased heart rate is not dangerous and does not require careful avoidance.

For depression, behavioral treatments can be divided into techniques aimed at increasing the availability of rewards, the skills to obtain them, and the capacity to recognize them as such. Lewinsohn's early program exemplifies the first procedure in which patients are instructed to schedule pleasant events. Social skills training (e.g., Bellack, Hersen, & Himmelhoch, 1980) exemplifies the second type. Improved social skills are thought to increase the likelihood of gaining satisfying social interactions. Rehm's self-control therapy emphasizes the interpretation of external and internal events to facilitate recognition of positive events when they occur.

Behaviorists perceive depression as characterized by poverty of positive experiences. Therefore, all the behavioral treatments attempt to facilitate such experiences. The treatments are distinguished, however, in their emphasis on the contingency between patient's actions and rewarding events. It is unclear whether increased access to positive events is sufficient to relieve depression, or whether *earning* the rewards (i.e., experience of contingencies) is necessary. Simply increasing pleasant events constitutes a basic ingredient of Lewinsohn's approach. On the other hand, social skills programs emphasize response-contingent rewards. If what must be learned is a contingency between actions and rewards, then programs which institute this contingency should be more successful than programs which simply provide rewards. This issue awaits further study.

Whereas treatments for anxiety and depression share some features, they differ in important aspects which reflect differences in the nature of anxiety and depression. Treatments for both disorders attempt to reduce discomfort directly and to correct misperceptions of response-contingent events. They differ, however, in two ways. First, treatment for anxiety reduces autonomic responding whereas treatment for depression increases overt activity. Second, anxiety treatment weakens perceived associations between actions and harmful outcomes, whereas many antidepressive procedures strengthen perceived response-reward contingencies.

Accordingly, one would not treat a depressed individual who underestimates the contingency between actions and outcomes via exposure procedures used for anxiety disorders. For example, a socially anxious patient might receive imaginal exposure to social criticism and rejection. This would be exactly the opposite of what the depressed individual requires, and might be expected to strengthen perceptions that the world is noxious. What the depressed person needs to learn is that actions can lead to rewards in the world. On the other hand, training an obsessive–compulsive patient to seek pleasant events is irrelevant to the erroneous perceptions that need to be corrected. What the obsessive–compulsive patient needs is to reduce overestimates of the contingency between self-protective behavior and harm.

Implicit in the organization of this chapter is a conceptual distinction between anxiety and depression. However, the co-occurrence of anxiety and depression is frequently observed and their theoretical interrelationship is as yet insufficiently understood. Nevertheless, patients can often be characterized as predominantly depressed or anxious and can be treated accordingly. Thus, our presentation reflects the state of behavior therapy at present. Although there are behavioral treatments for anxiety and for depression, there are no such techniques specific to anxious depression.

References

American Psychiatric Association. (1980). *Diagnostic and statistical manual of mental disorders* (3rd ed.). Washington, DC: Author.

American Psychiatric Association. (1987). *Diagnostic and statistical manual of mental disorders-Revised.* Washington, DC: Author.

Arnow, B., Taylor, C. B., Agras, W. S., & Telch, M. J. (1985). Enhancing agoraphobia treatment outcome by changing couple communication patterns. *Behavior Therapy, 16,* 452–467.

Barlow, D. H., Cohen, A. S., Waddell, M. J., Vermilyea, B. B., Klosko, J. S., Blanchard, E. B., & DiNardo, P. A. (1984). Panic and generalized anxiety disorders: Nature and treatment. *Behavior Therapy, 15,* 431–449.

Barlow, D. H., Leitenberg, H., Agras, W. S., & Wincze, J. P. (1969). The transfer gap in systematic desensitization: An analogue study. *Behaviour Research and Therapy, 7,* 191–196.

Barlow, D. H., O'Brien, G. T., & Last, C. G. (1984). Couples treatment of agoraphobia. *Behavior Therapy, 15,* 41–58.

Beck, A. T. (1972). *Depression: Causes and treatment.* Philadelphia: University of Pennsylvania Press.

Beck, A. T., Emery, G., & Greenberg, R. L. (1985). *Anxiety disorders and phobias: A cognitive perspective.* New York: Basic Books.

Becker, R. E., & Abel, G. C. (1981). Behavioral treatment of victims of sexual assault. In S. M. Turner, K. S. Calhoun, & H. E. Adams (Eds.), *Handbook of clinical behavior therapy* (pp. 347–379). New York: Wiley.

Becker, R. E., & Heimberg, R. G. (1984). Cognitive-behavioral treatments for depression: A review of controlled clinical research. In A. Dean (Ed.), *Depression in multidisciplinary perspectives* (pp. 209–234). New York: Brunner/Mazel.

Becker, R. E., Heimberg, R. G., & Bellack, A. S. (1987). *Social skills training treatment for depression.* New York: Pergamon Press.

Beech, H. R., & Vaughn, M. (1978). *Behavioral treatment of obsessive-states.* New York: Wiley.

Bellack, A. S., Hersen, M., & Himmelhoch, J. (1980). Social skills training for depression: A treatment manual. *JSAS Catalog of Selected Documents in Psychology, 10,* 92.

Bellack, A. S., Hersen, M., & Himmelhoch, J. (1981). Social skills training compared with pharmacotherapy and psychotherapy in the treatment of unipolar depression. *American Journal of Psychiatry, 138,* 1562–1567.

Bellack, A. S., Hersen, M., & Himmelhoch, J. M. (1983). A comparison of social skills training, pharmacotherapy, and psychotherapy for depression. *Behaviour Research and Therapy, 21,* 101–107.

Bernstein, D. A., & Borkovec, T. D. (1973). *Progressive relaxation training.* Champaign, IL: Research Press.

Blowers, C. M., Cobb, J. P., & Mathews, A. M. (1987). Treatment of generalized anxiety disorders. A comparative study. *Behaviour Research and Therapy, 25,* 493–502.

Boersma, K., Den Hengst, A., Dekker, J., & Emmelkamp, P. M. G. (1976). Exposure and response prevention: A comparison with obsessive–compulsive patients. *Behaviour Research and Therapy, 14,* 19–24.

Bolles, R. C. (1970). Species-specific defense reactions and avoidance learning. *Psychological Review, 77,* 32–48.

Borkovec, T. D., & Mathews, A. M. (1987). Treatment of non-phobic anxiety disorders. *Journal of Consulting & Clinical Psychology, 55,* 883–888.

Borkovec, T. D., Mathews, A. M., Chambers, A., Ebrahimi, S., Lytle, R., & Nelson, R. (in press). The effects of relaxation training with cognitive therapy or non-directive therapy and the role of relaxation induced anxiety in the treatment of generalized anxiety. *Journal of Consulting and Clinical Psychology.*

Boulougouris, J. C. (1977). Variables affecting the behavior modification of obsessive–compulsive patients treated by flooding. In J. L. Boulougouris & A. D. Rabavilas (Eds.), *The treatment of phobic and obsessive–compulsive disorders.* New York: Pergamon Press.

Boulougouris, J. C., Rabavilas, A. D., & Stefanis, C. (1977). Psychophysiological responses in obsessive–compulsive patients. *Behaviour Research and Therapy, 15,* 221–230.
Brown, R., & Lewinsohn, P. M. (1979). *A psychoeducational approach to the treatment of depression: Comparison of group, individual, and minimal contact procedures.* Unpublished mimeo, University of Oregon, Eugene.
Brown, R., & Lewinsohn, P. M. (1984). A psychoeducational approach to the treatment of depression: Comparison of group, individual, and minimal contact procedures. *Journal of Consulting and Clinical Psychology, 52,* 774–783.
Butler, G., Covington, A., Hibbert, G., Klimes, I., & Gelder, M. (1987). Anxiety management for persistent generalized anxiety. *British Journal of Psychiatry, 151,* 535–542.
Butler, G., Cullington, A., Munby, M., Amies, P., & Gelder, M. (1984). Exposure and anxiety management in the treatment of social phobia. *Journal of Consulting and Clinical Psychology, 52,* 642–650.
Carr, A. T. (1971). Compulsive neurosis: Two psychophysiological studies. *Bulletin of the British Psychological Society, 24,* 256–257.
Carruthers, M., & Taggart, P. (1973). Vagotonicity of violence: Biomedical and cardiac responses to violent films and television programmes. *British Medical Journal, 3,* 384–389.
Cerney, J., Barlow, D. H., Craske, M. G., & Himaldi, W. G. (1987). Couples treatment of agoraphobia: A two-year follow-up. *Behavior Therapy, 18,* 401–415.
Chambless, D. L., Foa, E. B., Groves, G. A., & Goldstein, A. J. (1980). Flooding with Brevital in the treatment of agoraphobia: Counter-effective? *Behaviour Research and Therapy, 17,* 243–251.
Clark, D. M., Salkovskis, P. M., & Chalkley, A. J. (1985). Respiratory control as a treatment for panic attacks. *Journal of Behavior Therapy and Experimental Psychiatry, 16,* 23–30.
Cobb, J. P., Mathews, A. M., Childs-Clarke, A., & Blowers, C. M. (1984). The spouse as co-therapist in the treatment of agoraphobia. *British Journal of Psychiatry, 144,* 282–287.
Cooper, J. E., Gelder, M. G., & Marks, I. M. (1965). Results of behaviour therapy in 77 psychiatric patients. *British Medical Journal, 1,* 1222–1225.
Costello, C. G. (1972). Depression: Loss of reinforcers or loss of reinforcer effectiveness? *Behavior Therapy, 3,* 240–247.
Crowe, M. J., Marks, I. M., Agras, W. S., & Leitenberg, H. (1972). Time-limited desensitization implosion and shaping for phobic patients: A cross-over study. *Behaviour Research and Therapy, 10,* 319–328.
Curtis, G., & Thyer, B. (1983). Fainting on exposure to phobic stimuli. *American Journal of Psychiatry, 140,* 771–774.
Ekman, P., & Friesen, W. V. (1974). Non-verbal behavior in psychopathology. In R. J. Friedman & M. M. Katz (Eds.), *The psychology of depression: Contemporary theory and research.* New York: Wiley.
Ellis, A. (1977). The basic clinical theory and rational-emotive therapy. In A. Ellis & R. Grieger (Eds.), *Handbook of rational-emotive therapy.* New York: Springer.
Emmelkamp, P. M. G. (1974). Self-observation versus flooding in the treatment of agoraphobia. *Behaviour Research and Therapy, 12,* 229–237.
Emmelkamp, P. M. G. (1982). *In vivo* treatment of agoraphobia. In D. L. Chambless & A. J. Goldstein (Eds.), *Agoraphobia.* New York: Wiley.
Emmelkamp, P. M. G., Bulman, E., Kuiper, H., & Mersch, P. P. (1986). The treatment of agoraphobia: A comparison of self-instructional training, rational emotive therapy, and exposure *in vivo. Behavior Modification, 10,* 37–53.
Emmelkamp, P. M. G., & Emmelkamp-Benner, A. (1975). Effects of historically portrayed modeling and group treatment on self-observation. A comparison with agoraphobics. *Behaviour Research and Therapy, 13,* 135–139.

Emmelkamp, P. M. G., & Kraanen, J. (1977). Therapist-controlled exposure *in vivo:* A comparison with obsessive–compulsive patients. *Behaviour Research and Therapy, 15,* 491–495.
Emmelkamp, P. M. G., & Kuipers, A. C. M. (1979). Agoraphobia: A follow-up study four years after treatment. *British Journal of Psychiatry, 134,* 352–355.
Emmelkamp, P. M. G., & Kwee, K. G. (1977). Obsessional ruminations: A comparison between thought-stopping and prolonged exposure in imagination. *Behaviour Research and Therapy, 15,* 441–444.
Emmelkamp, P. M. G., Mersch, P. P., Vissia, E., & Van Der Helm, M. (1985). Social phobia: A comparative evaluation of cognitive and behavioral interventions. *Behaviour Research and Therapy, 23,* 365–369.
Emmelkamp, P. M. G., & Ultree, K. A. (1974). A comparison of successive approximation and self-observation in the treatment of agoraphobia. *Behavior Therapy, 5,* 605–613.
Emmelkamp, P. M. G., Van Der Helm, M., van Zanten, B. L., & Plochy, I. (1980). Contributions of self-instructional training to the effectiveness of exposure *in vivo:* A comparison with obsessive–compulsive patients. *Behaviour Research and Therapy, 18,* 61–66.
Emmelkamp, P. M. G., & Wessels, H. (1975). Flooding in imagination versus flooding *in vivo.* A comparison with agoraphobics. *Behaviour Research and Therapy, 13,* 7–15.
Endicott, J., & Spitzer, R. L. (1978). A diagnostic interview: The schedule for affective disorders and schizophrenia. *Archives of General Psychiatry, 35,* 837–844.
Everaerd, W. T. A. M., Rijken, H. M., & Emmelkamp, P. M. G. (1973). A comparison of "flooding successive approximation" in the treatment of agoraphobia. *Behaviour Research and Therapy, 11,* 105–117.
Fairbank, J. A., Gross, R. T., & Keane, T. M. (1983). Treatment of posttraumatic stress disorder: Evaluation of outcome with a behavioral code. *Behavior Modification, 7,* 557–568.
Fairbank, J. A., & Keane, T. M. (1982). Flooding for combat-related stress disorders: Assessment of anxiety reduction across traumatic memories. *Behavior Therapy, 13,* 499–510.
Ferster, C. B. (1965). Classification of behavior pathology. In L. Krasner & L. P. Ullmann (Eds.), *Research in behavior modification.* New York: Holt, Rinehart, & Winston.
Ferster, C. B. (1966). Animal behavior and mental illness. *Psychological Record, 16,* 345–356.
Ferster, C. B. (1973). A functional analysis of depression. *American Psychologist, 28,* 857–870.
Foa, E. B., & Goldstein, A. (1978). Continuous exposure and complete response prevention of obsessive–compulsive neurosis. *Behavior Therapy, 8,* 821–829.
Foa, E. B., Jameson, J. S., Turner, R. M., & Payne, L. L. (1980). Massed versus spaced exposure sessions in the treatment of agoraphobia. *Behaviour Research and Therapy, 18,* 333–338.
Foa, E. B., & Kozak, M. J. (1985). Treatment of anxiety disorders: Implications for psychopathology. In A. H. Tuma & J. D. Maser (Eds.), *Anxiety and the anxiety disorders.* Hillsdale, NJ: Erlbaum.
Foa, E. B., & Kozak, M. J. (1986). Emotional processing of fear: Exposure to corrective information. *Psychological Bulletin, 99,* 20–35.
Foa, E. B., Steketee, G. S., & Milby, J. B. (1980). Differential effects of exposure and response prevention in obsessive–compulsive washers. *Journal of Consulting and Clinical Psychology, 48,* 71–79.
Foa, E. B., Steketee, G. S., & Ozarow, B. J. (1985). Behavior therapy with obsessive–compulsives: From theory to treatment. In M. Mavissakalian (Ed.), *Obsessive–compulsive disorders: Psychological and pharmacological treatments.* New York: Plenum Press.

Foa, E. B., Steketee, G., & Rothbaum, B. (in press). Behavioral/cognitive conceptualizations of post-traumatic stress disorder. *Behavior Therapy.*

Foa, E. B., Steketee, G. S., Turner, R. M., & Fischer, S. C. (1980). Effects of imaginal exposure to feared disasters in obsessive–compulsive checkers. *Behaviour Research and Therapy, 18,* 449–455.

Foa, E. B., Steketee, G. S., & Young, M. (1984). Agoraphobia: Phenomenological aspects, associated characteristics, and theoretical considerations. *Clinical Psychology Review, 4,* 431–457.

Frank, E., Anderson, B., Stewart, B. D., Dancu, C., Hughes, C., & West, D. (1988). Efficacy of cognitive behavior therapy and systematic desensitization in the treatment of rape trauma. *Behavior Therapy, 19,* 403–420.

Frank, E., & Stewart, B. D. (1984). Depressive symptoms in rape victims. *Journal of Affective Disorders, 1,* 269–277.

Fuchs, C. Z., & Rehm, L. R. (1977). A self-control behavior therapy program for depression. *Journal of Consulting and Clinical Psychology, 45,* 206–215.

Gelder, M. G., Bancroft, J. H., Gath, D., Johnston, B. W., Mathews, A. W., & Shaw, P. M. (1973). Specific and non-specific factors in behaviour therapy. *British Journal of Psychiatry, 123,* 445–462.

Gelder, M. G., & Marks, I. M. (1966). Severe agoraphobia: A controlled prospective trial of behaviour therapy. *British Journal of Psychiatry, 112,* 309–319.

Gelder, M. G., & Marks, I. M. (1968). Desensitization and phobias: A crossover study. *British Journal of Psychiatry, 114,* 323–328.

Gelder, M. G., Marks, I. M., & Wolff, H. H. (1967). Desensitization and psychotherapy in the treatment of phobic states: A controlled enquiry. *British Journal of Psychiatry, 113,* 53–73.

Ghosh, A., & Marks, I. M. (1987). Self-treatment of agoraphobia by exposure. *Behavior Therapy, 18,* 3–16.

Goldfried, M. R. (1971). Systematic desensitization as training in self-control. *Journal of Consulting and Clinical Psychology, 37,* 228–235.

Goldstein, A. J., & Chambless, D. L. (1978). A reanalysis of agoraphobia. *Behavior Therapy, 9,* 49–57.

Gottlieb, I. H. (1981). Self-reinforcement and recall: Differential deficits in depressed and nondepressed psychiatric inpatients. *Journal of Abnormal Psychology, 90,* 521–530.

Graham, D. T. (1961). Prediction of fainting in blood donors. *Circulation, 23,* 901–906.

Griez, E., & Van Den Hout, M. A. (1986). CO_2 inhalation in the treatment of panic attacks. *Behaviour Research and Therapy, 24,* 145–150.

Hafner, R. J., & Marks, I. M. (1976). Exposure *in vivo* of agoraphobics: Contributions of diazepam, group exposure, and anxiety evocation. *Psychological Medicine, 6,* 71–88.

Hand, I., Lamontagne, Y., & Marks, I. M. (1974). Group exposure *in vivo* for agoraphobics. *British Journal of Psychiatry, 124,* 588–602.

Haynes, S. N., & Mooney, D. K. (1975). Nightmares: Etiological, theoretical, and behavioral treatment considerations. *Psychological Record, 25,* 225–236.

Heimberg, P. G., Becker, R. E., Goldfinger, K., & Vermilyea, J. A. (1985). Treatment of social phobia by exposure, cognitive restructuring, and homework assignments. *Journal of Nervous and Mental Disease, 173,* 236–245.

Heimberg, R. G., Becker, R. E., Kennedy, C. R., Dodge, C. S., Zollo, L., & Hope, D. (1986). *Treatment of social phobia with cognitive-behavioral therapy versus education and support: Posttest and follow-up.* Paper presented at the annual meeting of the Association of Behavior Therapy, Chicago.

Hersen, M., Bellack, A. S., & Himmelhoch, J. M. (1980). Treatment of unipolar depression with social skills training. *Behavior Modification, 4,* 547–556.

Herrnstein, R. J. (1969). Method and theory in the study of avoidance. *Psychological Review, 76,* 71–88.

Hersen, M., Bellack, A. S., Himmelhoch, J. M., & Thase, M. E. (1984). Effects of social skills training, amitriptyline, and psychotherapy in unipolar depressed women. *Behavior Therapy, 15,* 21–40.

Hodgson, R. J., & Rachman, S. (1972). The effects of contamination and washing in obsessional patients. *Behaviour Research and Therapy, 10,* 111–117.

Hodgson, R. J., Rachman, S., & Marks, I. M. (1972). The treatment of chronic obsessive–compulsive neurosis: Follow-up and further findings. *Behaviour Research and Therapy, 10,* 181–189.

Holmes, M. R., & St. Lawrence, J. S. (1983). Treatment of rape-induced trauma: Proposed behavioral conceptualization and review of the literature. *Clinical Psychology Review, 3,* 417–433.

Jacobson, E. (1938). *Progressive relaxation.* Chicago, IL: University of Chicago Press.

Jannoun, L., Oppenheimer, C., & Gelder, M. (1982). A self-help treatment program for anxiety state patients. *Behavior Therapy, 13,* 103–111.

Jansson, L., & Ost, L. (1982). Behavioral treatment for agoraphobia: An evaluative review. *Clinical Psychology Review, 2,* 311–336.

Jerremalm, A., Jansson, L., & Ost, L. G. (1986). Cognitive and physiological reactivity and the effects of different behavioral methods in the treatment of social phobia. *Behaviour Research and Therapy, 24,* 171–180.

Johnson, C. H., Gilmore, J. D., & Shenoy, R. Z. (1982). Use of a feeding procedure in the treatment of a stress-related anxiety disorder. *Journal of Behavior Therapy and Experimental Psychiatry, 13,* 235–237.

Kanfer, F. H. (1970). Self-regulation: Research issues and speculations. In C. Neuringer & J. L. Michael (Eds.), *Behavior modification in clinical psychology.* New York: Appleton-Century-Crofts.

Kanfer, F. H. (1971). The maintenance of behavior by self-generated stimuli and reinforcement. In A. Jacobs & L. B. Sachs (Eds.), *The psychology of private events: Perspectives on covert response systems.* New York: Academic Press.

Kazdin, A. E., & Wilkerson, L. A. (1976). Systematic desensitization and nonspecific treatment effects: A methodological evaluation. *Psychological Bulletin, 83,* 229–258.

Keane, T. M., Fairbank, J. A., Caddell, J. M., Zimering, R. T., & Bender, M. E. (1985). A behavioral approach to assessing and treating post-traumatic stress disorder in Vietnam veterans. In C. R. Figley (Ed.), *Trauma and its wake* (pp. 258–294). New York: Brunner/Mazel.

Keane, T. M., & Kaloupek, D. G. (1982). Imaginal flooding in the treatment of a post-traumatic stress disorder. *Journal of Consulting and Clinical Psychology, 50,* 138–140.

Kilpatrick, D. G., & Best, C. L. (1984). Some cautionary remarks on treating sexual assault victims with implosion. *Behavior Therapy, 15,* 421–423.

Kilpatrick D. G., & Veronen, L. J. (1983). Treatment for rape-related problems: Crisis intervention is not enough. In L. H. Cohen, W. L. Claiborn, & G. A. Specter (Eds.), *Crisis intervention.* New York: Human Sciences Press.

Kilpatrick, D. G., Veronen, L. J., & Resick, P. A. (1982). Psychological sequelae to rape: Assessment and treatment strategies. In D. M. Doleys, R. L. Meredith, & A. R. Ciminero (Eds.), *Behavioral medicine: Assessment and treatment strategies.* New York: Plenum Press.

Kornblith, S. J., Rehm, L. A., O'Hara, M. W., & Lamparski, D. M. (1983). The contribution of self-reinforcement training and behavioral assignments to the efficacy of self-control therapy for depression. *Cognitive Therapy and Research, 7,* 499–528.

Kozak, M. J., & Miller, G. A. (1985). The psychological and physiological process of therapy in a case injury scene elicited fainting. *Journal of Behavior Therapy and Experimental Psychiatry, 16,* 139–145.

Kozak, M. J., & Montgomery, G. K. (1981). Multimodal behavioral-treatment of recurrent injury-scene-elicited fainting (vasodepressor syncope). *Behavioral Psychotherapy, 9,* 316–332.

Lang, P. J. (1977). Imagery in therapy: An information processing analysis of fear. *Behavior Therapy, 8,* 862–886.

Lang, P. J. (1979). A bio-informational theory of emotional imagery. *Psychophysiology, 16,* 495–512.

LaPointe, K. M., & Rimm, D. C. (1980). Cognitive, assertive, and insight oriented group therapies in the treatment of reactive depression in women. *Psychotherapy: Theory, Research and Practice, 17,* 312–321.

Lazarus, A. A. (1968). Learning theory and the treatment of depression. *Behaviour Research and Therapy, 6,* 83–89.

Leitenberg, H., Agras, W. S., Barlow, D. H., & Oliveau, D. C. (1969). Contribution of selective positive reinforcement and therapeutic instructions to systematic desensitization therapy. *Journal of Abnormal Psychology, 74,* 113–118.

Lewinsohn, P. M. (1974). Clinical and theoretical aspects of depression. In K. S. Calhoun, H. E. Adams, & K. M. Mitchell (Eds.), *Innovative treatment methods in psychopathology,* New York: Wiley.

Lewinsohn, P. M. (1975). The behavioral study and treatment of depression. In M. Hersen, R. M. Eisler, & P. M. Miller (Eds.), *Progress in behavioral modification* (Vol. 1). New York: Academic Press.

Lewinsohn, P. M., & Amenson, C. S. (1978). Some relations between pleasant and unpleasant mood-related events. *Journal of Abnormal Psychology, 87,* 644–654.

Lewinsohn, P. M., Antonuccio, D. O., Steinmetz, J. L., & Teri, L. (1984). *The coping with depression course: A psychoeducational intervention for unipolar depression.* Eugene, OR: Castalia.

Lewinsohn, P. M., & Graf, M. (1973). Pleasant activities and depression. *Journal of Consulting and Clinical Psychology, 41,* 261–268.

Lewinsohn, P. M., & Libet, J. (1972). Pleasant activities, activity schedules, and depression. *Journal of Abnormal Psychology, 79,* 291–295.

Lewinsohn, P. M., Lobitz, W. C., & Wilson, S. (1983). "Sensitivity" of depressed individuals to aversive stimuli. *Journal of Abnormal Psychology, 81,* 259–263.

Lewinsohn, P. M., & MacPhillamy, D. J. (1974). The relationship between age and engagement in pleasant activities. *Journal of Gerontology, 29,* 290–294.

Lewinsohn, P. M., Mischel, W., Chaplin, C., & Barton, R. (1980). Social competence and depression: The role of illusory self-perceptions. *Journal of Abnormal Psychology, 89,* 203–217.

Lewinsohn, P. M., Munoz, R. F., Youngren, M. A., & Zeiss, A. M. (1978). *Control your depression.* Englewood Cliffs, NJ: Prentice-Hall.

Lewinsohn, P. M., Youngren, M. A., & Grosscup, S. J. (1979). Reinforcement and depression. In R. A. DePue (Ed.), *The psychobiology of depressive disorders: Implications for the effects of stress.* New York: Academic Press.

Libet, J., & Lewinsohn, P. M. (1973). The concept of social skill with special reference to the behavior of depressed persons. *Journal of Consulting and Clinical Psychology, 40,* 304–312.

Lobitz, W. C., & Post, R. D. (1979). Parameters of self-reinforcement and depression. *Journal of Abnormal Psychology, 88,* 33–41.

Lubin, B. (1965). Adjective checklists for the measurement of depression. *Archives of General Psychiatry, 12,* 57–62.

MacPhillamy, D. J., & Lewinsohn, P. M. (1971). *Pleasant events schedule.* Unpublished mimeo, University of Oregon, Eugene.
MacPhillamy, D. J., & Lewinsohn, P. M. (1973). *Studies on the measurements of human reinforcement and on the relationship between positive reinforcement and depression.* Unpublished mimeo, University of Oregon, Eugene.
MacPhillamy, D. J., & Lewinsohn, P. M. (1974). Depression as function of levels of desired and obtained pleasure. *Journal of Abnormal Psychology, 83,* 651–657.
Marchione, K. E., Michelson, L., Greenwald, M., & Dancu, D. (1987). Cognitive behavioral treatment of agoraphobia. *Behaviour Research and Therapy, 25,* 319–328.
Marks, I. M. (1969). *Fears and phobias.* London: Heineman.
Marks, I. M. (1971). Phobic disorders four years after treatment: A prospective follow-up. *British Journal of Psychiatry, 118,* 683–688.
Marks, I. M. (1972). Flooding and allied treatments. In W. Agras (Ed.), *Behavior modification: Principles and clinical applications.* Boston: Little, Brown.
Marks, I. M., Boulougouris, J., & Marset, P. (1971). Flooding versus desensitization in the treatment of phobic disorders. *British Journal of Psychiatry, 119,* 353–375.
Marks, I. M., & Gelder, M. G. (1965). A controlled retrospective study of behaviour therapy in phobic patients. *British Journal of Psychiatry, 111,* 571–573.
Marks, I. M., Gray, S., Cohen, D., Hill, R., Mawson, D., Ramm, E., & Stern, R. S. (1983). Imipramine and brief therapist-aided exposure in agoraphobics having self-exposure homework. *Archives of General Psychiatry, 40,* 153–162.
Marks, I. M., Hodgson, R., & Rachman, S. (1975). Treatment of chronic obsessive–compulsive neurosis by *in vivo* exposure. *British Journal of Psychiatry, 127,* 349–364.
Marzillier, J. S., Lambert, C., & Kellett, J. (1976). A controlled evaluation of systematic desensitization and social skills training for social inadequate psychiatric patients. *Behaviour Research and Therapy, 14,* 225–228.
Mathews, A. M. (1978). Fear-reduction research and clinical phobias. *Psychological Bulletin, 85,* 390–404.
Mathews, A. (1984, September). *Cognitive processes in generalized anxiety.* Paper presented at the meeting of the European Association for Behaviour Therapy, Brussels.
Mathews, A. M., Gelder, M. G., & Johnston, D. W. (1981). *Agoraphobia: Nature and treatment.* New York: Guilford Press.
Mathews, A. M., Jannoun, L., & Gelder, M. (1979, September). *Self-help methods in agoraphobia.* Paper presented at the Conference of the European Association of Behavior Therapy, Paris.
Mathews, A. M., Johnston, D. W., Lancashire, M., Munby, D., Shaw, P. M., & Gelder, M. D. (1974). Imaginal flooding and exposure to real phobic situations: Treatment outcome with agoraphobic patients. *British Journal of Psychiatry, 129,* 362–371.
Mathews, A., Teasdale, J., Munby, M., Johnston, D., & Shaw, P. (1977). A home-based treatment program for agoraphobia. *Behavior Therapy, 8,* 915–924.
Mattick, R. P., & Peters, L. (1988). Treatment of severe social phobia. *Journal of Consulting and Clinical Psychology, 56,* 251–260.
Mavissakalian, M., & Michelson, L. (1983). Tricyclic antidepressants in obsessive–compulsive disorder: Antiobsessional or antidepressant agents? *Journal of Nervous and Mental Disease, 171,* 301–306.
Mavissakalian, M., & Michelson, L. (1986). Agoraphobia: Relative and combined effectiveness of therapist-assisted *in vivo* exposure and imipramine. *Journal of Clinical Psychiatry, 47,* 117–122.
McCaffrey, R. J., & Fairbank, J. A. (1985). Post-traumatic stress disorder associated with transportation accidents: Two case studies. *Behaviour Therapy, 16,* 406–416.
McLean, P. D. (1976). Therapeutic decision making in the behavioral treatment of depres-

sion. In P. O. Davidson (Ed.), *The behavioral management of anxiety, depression, and pain.* New York: Bruner/Mazel.

McLean, P. D., & Hakstian, A. R. (1979). Clinical depression: Comparative efficacy of outpatient treatments. *Journal of Consulting and Clinical Psychology, 47,* 818–836.

McLean, P. D., Ogston, K., & Graver, L. (1973). A behavioral approach to the treatment of depression. *Journal of Behavior Therapy and Experimental Psychology, 4,* 323–330.

McPherson, E. J., Brougham, L., & McLaren, S. (1980). Maintenance of improvement in agoraphobic patients treated by behavioral methods—A four year follow-up. *Behaviour Research and Therapy, 18,* 150–152.

Meichenbaum, D. (1974). Self-instructional methods. In F. H. Kanfer & A. P. Goldstein (Eds.), *Helping people change.* New York: Pergamon Press.

Meichenbaum, D. H., & Turk, D. (1973). *Stress inoculation: A skills training approach to anxiety management.* Unpublished manuscript, University of Waterloo, Waterloo, Ontario, Canada.

Meichenbaum, D., & Turk, D. (1976). The cognitive-behavioral management of anxiety, anger, and pain. In P. O. Davidson (Ed.), *The behavioral management of anxiety, depression, and pain.* New York: Brunner/Mazel.

Meyer, V., Levy, R., & Schnurer, A. (1974). A behavioral treatment of obsessive–compulsive disorders. In H. R. Beech (Ed.), *Obsessional states.* London: Methuen.

Michelson, L. (1986). Treatment consonance and response profiles in agoraphobia: The role of individual differences in cognitive, behavioral and physiological treatments. *Behaviour Research and Therapy, 24,* 263–275.

Miller, W. R., & Seligman, M. E. P. (1975). Depression and the perception of reinforcement. *Journal of Abnormal Psychology, 82,* 62–73.

Minisek, N. A. (1984). *Flooding as a supplemental treatment for Vietnam veterans.* Paper presented at the Third National Conference on Post-Traumatic Stress Disorders, Baltimore, MD.

Mowrer, O. A. (1960). *Learning theory and behavior.* New York: Wiley.

Munby, M., & Johnston, D. W. (1980). Agoraphobia: The long-term follow-up of behavioral treatment. *British Journal of Psychiatry, 136,* 418–427.

Nimmer, W. H., & Kapp, R. A. (1974). A multiple impact program for the treatment of an injection phobia. *Journal of Behavior Therapy and Experimental Psychiatry, 5,* 257–258.

Olasov, B., & Foa, E. (1988, May). Behavioral treatment of post-traumatic stress disorder. In *PTSD: Its psychopathology and treatment.* Symposium conducted at the 14th annual convention of the Association for Behavior Analysis, Philadelphia.

Ost, L. G., Jerremalm, A., & Johansson, J. (1981). Individual response patterns and the effects of different behavioral methods in the treatment of social phobia. *Behaviour Research and Therapy, 19,* 1–16.

Ost, L. G., Sterner, U., & Lindahl, I. L. (1984). Physiological responses in blood phobics. *Behaviour Research and Therapy, 22,* 109–117.

Ost, L. G., & Sterner, U. (1987). *Applied tension: A specific behavioral method for treatment of blood phobia.* Unpublished manuscript, University of Uppsala, Psychiatric Research Center, Uppsala.

Rabavilas, A. D., Boulougouris, J. C., & Stefanis, C. (1976). Duration of flooding sessions in the treatment of obsessive–compulsive patients. *Behaviour Research and Therapy, 14,* 349–355.

Rachman, S. (1976). The passing of the two stage theory of fear and avoidance: Fresh possibilities. *Behaviour Research and Therapy, 14,* 125–138.

Rachman, S., Hodgson, R., & Marks, I. M. (1971). The treatment of chronic obsessive–compulsive neurosis. *Behaviour Research and Therapy, 9,* 237–247.

Rachman, S., Marks, I. M., & Hodgson, R. (1973). The treatment of obsessive-compulsive neurotics by modelling and flooding *in vivo*. *Behaviour Research and Therapy, 11*, 463–471.

Rehm, L. P. (1977). A self-control model of depression. *Behavior Therapy, 8*, 787–804.

Rehm, L. P., Fuchs, C. Z., Rosh, D. M., Kornblith, S. J., & Romano, J. M. (1979). A comparison of self-control and assertion skills treatments of depression. *Behavior Therapy, 10*, 429–442.

Rehm, L. P., Kornblith, S. J., O'Hara, M. W., Laniparski, D. M., Romano, J. M., & Volkin, J. I. (1981). An evaluation of major components in a self-control therapy program for depression. *Behavior Modification, 5*, 459–489.

Reiss, S. (1980). Pavlovian conditioning and human fear: An expectancy model. *Behavior Therapy, 11*, 380–396.

Resick, P. A., Jordan, C. G., Girelli, S. A., Hutter, C. K., & Marhoefer-Dvorak, S. (in press). A comparative outcome study of behavioral group therapy for sexual assault victims. *Behavior Therapy*.

Roper, G., Rachman, S., & Marks, I. (1975). Passive and participant modeling in exposure treatment of obsessive–compulsive neurotics. *Behaviour Research and Therapy, 13*, 271–279.

Roth, D., Bielski, R., Jones, M., Parker, W., & Osborn, G. (1982). A comparison of self-control therapy and combined self control therapy and antidepressant medication in the treatment of depression. *Behavior Therapy, 13*, 133–144.

Rychtarik, R. G., Silverman, W. K., Van Landingham, W. P., & Prue, D. M. (1984). Treatment of an incest victim with impolsive therapy: A case study. *Behavior Therapy, 15*, 410–420.

Salkovskis, P. M., Jones, P. R. O., & Clark, D. M. (1986). Respiratory control in the treatment of panic attacks: Replication and extension with concurrent measurement of behavior and pCO_2. *British Journal of Psychiatry, 148*, 526–532.

Sanchez, V., & Lewinsohn, P. M. (1980). Assertive behavior and depression. *Journal of Consulting and Clinical Psychology, 48*, 119–120.

Sanchez, V. C., Lewinsohn, P. M., & Larson, D. W. (1980). Assertion training: Effectiveness in the treatment of depression. *Journal of Clinical Psychology, 36*, 526–529.

Schindler, E. E. (1980). Treatment by systematic desensitization of a recurring nightmare of a real life trauma. *Journal of Behavior Therapy and Experimental Psychiatry, 11*, 53–54.

Shaw, P. (1979). A comparison of three behaviour therapies in the treatment of social phobia. *British Journal of Psychiatry, 134*, 620–623.

Skinner, B. F. (1953). *Science and human behavior*. New York: Free Press.

Sokol-Kessler, L., & Beck, A. T. (1987, May). *Cognitive treatment of panic disorder*. Paper presented at the annual meeting of the American Psychiatric Association, Chicago.

Sokol-Kessler, L., Beck, A. T., Greenberg, R. L., Berchick, R. J., & Wright, F. D. (1987, May). *Cognitive therapy of panic disorder: a non-pharmacological alternative*. Paper presented at the annual meeting of the American Psychiatric Association, Chicago.

Spitzer, R. L., Endicott, J., & Robins, E. (1978). Research diagnostic criteria: Rationale and reliability. *Archives of General Psychiatry, 35*, 773–782.

Steinmetz, J., Antonuccio, D., Bond, M., McKay, G., Brown, R., & Lewinsohn, P. M. (1979). *Instructors manual, coping with depression*. Unpublished mimeo, University of Oregon, Eugene.

Steinmetz, J., Lewinsohn, P. M., & Antonuccio, D. (1983). Prediction of individual outcome in a group intervention for depression. *Journal of Consulting and Clinical Psychology, 51*, 331–337.

Steketee, G., Foa, E. B., & Grayson, J. B. (1982). Recent advances in the behavioral treatment of obsessive-compulsives. *Archives of General Psychiatry, 39*, 1365–1371.

Stern, R. S. (1978). Obsessive thoughts: The problem of therapy. *British Journal of Psychiatry, 132,* 200–205.

Stern, R., & Marks, I. M. (1973). Brief and prolonged flooding: A comparison in agoraphobic patients. *Archives of General Psychiatry, 28,* 270–276.

Stravinsky, A., Marks, I. M., & Yule, W. (1982). Social skills problems in neurotic outpatients: Social skills training with and without cognitive modification. *Archives of General Psychiatry, 39,* 1378–1385.

Suinn, R. (1974). Anxiety management training for general anxiety. In R. Suinn & R. Weigel (Eds.), *The innovative therapy: Critical and creative contributions.* New York: Harper & Row.

Suinn, R. M., & Richardson, D. (1971). Anxiety management training: A nonspecific behaviour therapy program for anxiety control. *Behavior Therapy, 2,* 498–510.

Telch, M. J., Agras, W. S., Taylor, C., Roth, W. T., & Gallen, C. G. (1985). Combined pharmacological and behavioral treatment for agoraphobia. *Behaviour Research and Therapy, 23,* 325–335.

Teri, L., & Lewinsohn, P. M. (1981). *A comparison of individual and group treatments for depression.* Unpublished manuscript, University of Oregon, Eugene.

Teri, T., & Lewinsohn, P. M. (1985). Individual and group treatment of unipolar depression: Comparison of treatment outcome and identification of predictors of successful treatment outcome. *Behavior Therapy, 17,* 215–228.

Trower, P., Yardley, K., Bryant, B. M., & Shaw, P. (1978). The treatment of social failure: A comparison of anxiety-reduction and skills acquisition procedures on two social problems. *Behavior Modification, 2,* 41–60.

Turner, R. W., Ward, M. F., & Turner, D. W. (1979). Behavioral treatment for depression: An evaluation of therapeutic components. *Journal of Clinical Psychology, 35,* 166–175.

Turner, S. M. (1979). *Systematic desensitization of fears and anxiety in rape victims.* Paper presented at the Association for the Advancement of Behavior Therapy, San Francisco.

Veronen, L. J., & Kilpatrick, D. G. (1982, November). Stress inoculation training for victims of rape: Efficacy and differential findings. In *Sexual violence and harassment.* Symposium conducted at the 16th annual convention of the Association for Advancement of Behavior Therapy, Los Angeles.

Veronen, L. J., & Kilpatrick, D. G. (1983). Stress management for rape victims. In D. Meichenbaum & M. E. Jaremko (Eds.), *Stress reduction and prevention.* New York: Plenum.

Watson, J. P., Gaind, R., & Marks, I. M. (1972). Physiological habituation to continue phobic stimulation. *Behaviour Research and Therapy, 10,* 269–278.

Watson, J. P., & Marks, I. M. (1971). Relevant and irrelevant fear in flooding—A crossover study of phobic patients. *Behavior Therapy, 2,* 275–293.

Weekes, C. (1976). *Simple effective treatment of agoraphobia.* New York: Hawthorn Books.

Weissman, M. M., & Paykel, E. S. (1974). *The depressed woman: A study of social relationships.* Chicago, IL: University of Chicago Press.

Wells, K. C., Hersen, M., Bellack, A. S., & Himmelhoch, J. (1979). Social skills training in unipolar nonpsychotic depression. *American Journal of Psychiatry, 136,* 1331–1332.

Williams, S. L., Dooseman, G., & Kleinfield, E. (1984). Comparative effectiveness of guided mastery and exposure treatments for intractable phobias. *Journal of Consulting and Clinical Psychology, 52,* 505–518.

Williams, S. S., Turner, S. M., & Peer, D. E. (1985). Guided mastery and performance desensitization treatments for severe agoraphobia. *Journal of Consulting and Clinical Psychology, 53,* 237–247.

Wolff, R. (1977). Systematic desensitization and negative practice to alter the aftereffects of a rape attempt. *Journal of Behavior Therapy and Experimental Psychiatry, 8,* 423–425.
Wolpe, J. (1958). *Psychotherapy by reciprocal inhibition.* Stanford, CA: Stanford University Press.
Wolpe, J. (1973). *The practice of behavior therapy.* New York: Pergamon Press.
Wolpe, J. (1979). The experimental model and treatment of neurotic depression. *Behaviour Research and Therapy, 17,* 555–565.
Wolpe, J. (1985). Deep muscle relaxation. In A. S. Bellack & M. Hersen (Eds.), *Dictionary of behavior therapy techniques* (pp. 101–104). New York: Pergamon Press.
Yorkston, N. J., Sergeant, H. G. S., & Rachman, S. (1968). Methodexitone relaxation for desensitizing agoraphobic patients. *Lancet, ii,* 651–653.
Youngren, M. A., & Lewinsohn, P. M. (1980). The functional relation between depression and problematic interpersonal behavior. *Journal of Abnormal Psychology, 89,* 333–341.
Zeiss, A. M., Lewinsohn, P. M., & Munoz, R. F. (1979). Nonspecific improvement effects in depression using interpersonal skills training, pleasant activity schedules, or cognitive training. *Journal of Consulting and Clinical Psychology, 47,* 427–439.
Zitrin, C. M., Klein, D. E., & Warner, M. G. (1980). Treatment of agoraphobia with group exposure *in vivo* and imipramine. *Archives of General Psychiatry, 37,* 63–72.

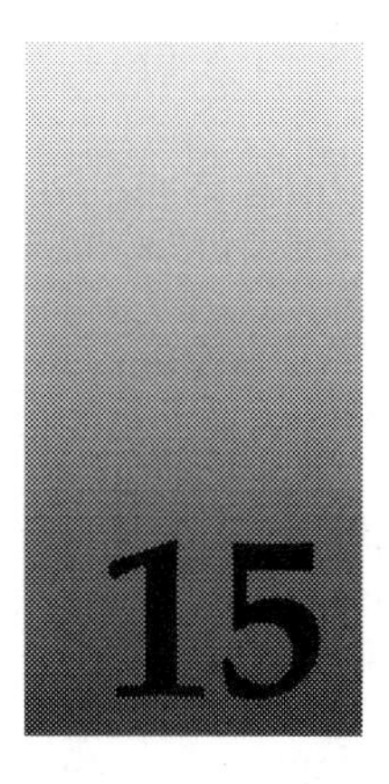

The Treatment of Anxiety and Depression: The Process of Affective Change

Jeremy D. Safran
Leslie S. Greenberg

I. Introduction

In this chapter we will describe the conceptualization and treatment of depression and anxiety from the perspective of the affective processes involved. The treatment approach we will be describing should not be considered a new form of psychotherapy. Many of the interventions that we will be describing are employed in different forms of psychotherapy, ranging from psychodynamic therapy, to gestalt therapy, to client-centered therapy, to cognitive therapy. The common theme, however, is that they focus on underlying emotional processes.

The focus on this topic from an affective perspective is part of a systematic attempt on our part to clarify the role that emotion plays in psychotherapeutic change (Greenberg & Safran, 1980, 1981, 1984a, 1984b, 1987; Safran & Greenberg, 1982a, 1982b, 1986, 1987, 1988). Emotion is a fundamental aspect of what it is to be human. Emotion is

Anxiety and Depression

central to the enterprise of psychotherapy. This is taken for granted in the common culture. Nonpsychologists are always puzzled by our assertions on the role of emotion in therapy, because they assume that anything written on psychotherapy will automatically take into account the central role that emotion plays.

In the last 30 years, however, the preoccupation of experimental psychology with behavioral and cognitive perspectives has pushed emotion into the background and accorded it a secondary role in the understanding of human functioning and the psychotherapy change process. A by-product of this emphasis has been the tendency to focus on maladaptive emotional experiences, to view emotion as disruptive to the problem-solving process, and to look for ways to dampen or curtail emotional experience (Greenberg & Safran, 1984a; Mahoney, 1980).

Our contention is that by focusing attention on the role that emotion plays in human functioning and on the role that various affective processes can play in psychotherapy, we can provide a perspective on the process of psychotherapy in the treatment of both depression and anxiety that can help to further clarify our understanding of the way in which change takes place.

Central to our position is the assumption that emotion plays an adaptive role in human functioning, and that psychological problems such as anxiety and depression often arise when clients avoid, block, or interrupt potentially adaptive emotional experience. Thus, many of the interventions we will be describing help clients to become aware of how they interrupt their emotional experience, and to learn to access their affective experience more fully.

A second assumption is that emotional experiences—if fully allowed or processed—are inherently transient in nature and that the complete processing of emotional experience leads to a shift to other emotional experiences. In contrast, chronic, unchanging maladaptive emotional states result from interruption or incomplete processing of emotional experiences. An important principle of affectively oriented therapy thus involves working with clients to help them overcome their avoidance of complete emotional processing in order to allow normal, organismically healthy shifts in emotional experience to take place.

An important factor underlying the interruption of emotional experiences is that clients do not accept their emotions and fear the consequences of feeling and expressing them more completely. An important task for the affectively oriented therapist is to help clients come to accept their emotional experience and to challenge their fears about experiencing their feelings more fully. This attitude of acceptance of emotional experience must be conveyed by the therapist both explicitly and implicitly. For this reason it is vital for the affectively oriented therapist to believe that emotional experience is fundamentally adaptive in nature, and to have faith that the full experiencing of primary emotional experience will lead to a shift in that experience. The conceptual framework we articulate in this chapter will hopefully provide therapists with a theoretical rationale that is useful in this respect. Nevertheless, there is no substitute for therapists directly experiencing these processes and learning to trust their own emotional experience.

Although we will organize our comments around the treatment of anxiety and depression as distinct disorders, we believe that ultimately these diagnostic categories are too heterogeneous to provide therapists with the kinds of context-sensitive, differentiated guidelines that are most useful for linking specific interventions to specific in-session states (Greenberg & Safran, 1987; Rice & Greenberg, 1984). Our approach to affectively oriented treatment involves systematically mapping out a variety of different affective information-processing dysfunctions and a variety of different affective processes that lead to change (Greenberg & Safran, 1987). These affective information-processing deficits and relevant interventions do not correspond in any one-to-one fashion to traditional diagnostic categories. Two different clients meeting criteria for different diagnostic classifications may at various times exhibit similar affective processing deficits, and may benefit from similar affective interventions. Moreover, the same client may demonstrate different affective processing deficits at different points in time (or even at different points in the same session), and may benefit from different affective interventions at those points in time. The optimal interventions are thus responsive to the particular client state and processing difficulty at the time.

These concerns notwithstanding, we believe that it can be of some use to consider anxiety and depression as distinct diagnostic entities, for purposes of illustrating certain general affective information-processing themes relevant to our understanding of psychological problems and their treatment. We regard anxiety and depression as general response constellations that have become wired into the human organism through a process of evolutionary adaptation. As Engel (1962) observed, depression corresponds to an organismic reaction pattern of conservation/withdrawal, while anxiety corresponds to a reaction pattern of flight/fright. In theory, both of these response systems had survival value in the environment of ecological adaptedness, although they may currently be maladaptive. This general perspective on anxiety and depression has also been advocated by Bowlby (1969, 1973, 1980) and Beck & Emery (1985).

Although this broad conceptualization provides a starting point for our analysis of anxiety and depression, a more detailed and refined analysis will have to await the establishment of a conceptual framework provided by our discussion of the relationship between emotion, information processing, and behavior.

II. Information Processing and Biological Adaptation

A. Concepts

There are two key concepts that are essential to our analysis of the nature of depression and anxiety and of the role that affectively oriented interventions play in the treatment of these problems. The first concept is information processing and the second is biological adaptation. We will consider each of these in turn.

The perspective we present on the role of emotion in psychotherapy is articulated within the basic framework of cognitive psychology. Fundamental assumptions of this framework are that human beings actively construct representations of their world and that it is theoretically useful to clarify the fashion in which information is registered, processed, stored in memory, and retrieved.

Cognitive theory typically focuses on the fashion in which information about the external world is processed. There is, however, another type of information-processing activity that is equally significant—internally generated information. We regard emotion as a form of internally generated information; i.e., information about the self in interaction with the world (Greenberg & Safran, 1984a, 1987; Safran & Greenberg, 1986, 1987).

In order to understand the nature and function of this internally generated form of information processing, a second concept is useful—biological adaptation. The principle of biological adaptation asserts that different species characteristics have evolved to fit the demands of a specific environmental niche through a process of natural selection. Given this perspective, it is important to analyze the role that the characteristic of interest may have played in the evolutionary adaptation of the species. This conceptual strategy has developed out of Darwin's (1872/1955) pioneering work on biological structure and evolution, and is a fundamental feature of contemporary ethology (Hinde, 1966/1970; Lorenz, 1973/1977).

B. Behavioral Systems

A behavioral system is a concept originating in ethology that was developed to account for patterns of behavior that are presumed to be wired into a species through an evolutionary process (Hinde, 1966/1970; Tinbergen, 1951). Behavioral systems vary with respect to complexity and with respect to how fixed or flexible they are.

Human beings and other phylogenetically advanced species commonly exhibit a type of behavioral system that is more complex and flexible than the type of fixed action patterns found in less advanced species. This more complex type of action pattern is referred to as a set-goal system (Bowlby, 1969).

A set-goal system operates by activating different behaviors or behavioral sequences that increase the probability of attaining a specific outcome. The particular sequence of enacted behaviors, however, is not rigid or stereotyped as in the case of the fixed action pattern. Once a general goal is selected a variety of specific behaviors may be enacted, and the specific behaviors being enacted are modified in response to ongoing feedback about their effectiveness in obtaining the desired goal. The most well-studied set-goal pattern in human beings is attachment behavior.

We regard attachment theory (Bowlby, 1969) as central in our understanding of emotional development, anxiety, and depression. Attachment behavior is a biologically wired-in behavioral system that functions to maintain proximity to the attachment figure. Attachment behavior has evolved in many species because of its role in contributing to survival. In human beings, maintaining proximity to attachment figures has a readily apparent survival function for the young, who are helpless without the support and protection of attachment figures. Even in the mature adult, the probability of survival is increased when individuals can maintain cooperative relationships with their peers. This was particularly true in the primitive conditions in which the human species evolved, wherein survival on a daily basis was dependent on the availability of others who could assist in providing protection from predators and in obtaining food and shelter.

Careful and systematic observation of infants has demonstrated that when the attachment figure is available and accessible, attachment behaviors may consist of activities such as checking for availability with the eyes or the ears or exchanging occasional glances or greetings. If the attachment figure appears less accessible, however, or if the infant is startled or threatened by something in the environment, attachment behaviors may include clinging, following, calling, or crying (Bowlby, 1969).

Attachment relationships play a crucial role in emotional development. Many of the most intense emotions are elicited in the course of negotiating relationships to attachment figures. For example, love is associated with the experience of establishing a bond with an attachment figure. Anxiety is experienced at the threat of loss—and sadness with the actual loss—of an attachment figure. Joy is experienced upon being reunited with an attachment figure.

Experiences with attachment figures play a crucial role in emotional development; moreover, memories for these events are coded in emotional form and play a central role in the establishment of subsequent relationships.

III. Emotion

A. Basic Perspective

Our perspective on emotion (Greenberg & Safran, 1987) has been substantially influenced by a variety of theorists who advocate an evolutionary and biosocial perspective on emotion (e.g., Izard, 1977; Plutchik, 1980; Tomkins, 1980) and by those who combine this approach with a cognitive perspective (Arnold, 1960; Leventhal, 1982, 1984).

This perspective starts with the hypothesis that the basic structure for emotional experience is neurologically hard-wired into the human organism. This structure is provided by a central neural mechanism that is analogous to the language acquisition device in Chomsky's (1980) linguistic theory, and it functions as a template for emotional experience. This innate emotion mechanism contains the neural code for specific expressive motor configurations corresponding to specific primary emotions.

As Piaget (1952) recognized, there is something fundamental about the sensory motor system. A child's first responses to the world are sensory motor in nature, and he or she comes to know the world through his or her actions upon it. Consistent with theorists who advocate a motor theory of mind (e.g., Turvey, 1977; Weimer, 1977), we argue that, even after the more mature human develops sophisticated cognitive representations of the world, cognition remains tied to this more basic and fundamental expressive motor level. Motor metatheories of mind view consciousness as intrinsically linked to motor action. In the motor metatheory of consciousness, the mind is seen as a specialized organ of action in the world rather than as a type of computer or "thought machine." Thus, thought is seen as a type of skilled action (Mahoney & Gabriel, 1987; Weimer, 1977). Computer metaphors conceptualize the process of knowledge representation in terms of the coding of abstract logical propositions. As Zajonc and Markus (1984) argue, however, information can also be represented at the expressive motor level.

We hypothesize that in the young, specific patterns of expressive motor responses are automatically elicited by environmental stimuli. The newborn infant engages in immediate, perceptual motor appraisals of the environment. These appraisals evoke biologically programmed motor responses prior to any learning. These primitive hard-wired expressive motor responses form the core for the development of subsequent emotional experience. Some are directly instrumental. For example, the tensing of muscles associated with the fear response prepares the organism to escape from danger. Other responses serve a communicative function. Thus, for example, facial patterning associated with fear might signal to another individual to come to the threatened individual's assistance. Facial patterning associated with affection promotes bonding.

Although the newborn infant comes equipped with hard-wired, adaptive expressive motor responses prior to any learning, these responses subsequently become elaborated through a process of learning. From the moment of birth, the infant develops memory stores consisting of specific expressive motor responses, relevant eliciting stimuli, associated images, and autonomic arousal. These memories are developed and elaborated over time and play a central role in emotional experience. Thus, while the neurological substrate and expressive motor configurations for basic emotions (Izard, 1977; Tompkins, 1980) are hard-wired into the organism, these hard-wired configurations form only the basic templates for human emotions. Within the constraints established by these templates, there is room for a tremendous amount of subtlety and idiosyncratic variation in an individual's emotional life.

There affective memory structures, or schemata, are discussed in somewhat different terms by different theorists (e.g., Bower, 1981; Lang, 1983; Leventhal, 1984). However, the themes common to these different theories of emotional memory are that (1) emotions are coded in memory as a number of different subsidiary components, and (2) the activation of one or more of these components can automatically activate or lower the threshold for the activation of other components. When an emotion schema or prototype is activated, a synthetic process takes place at a preattentive level, which integrates the information generated through this process with the perception of new eliciting stimuli that are both external and internal to the organism (Leventhal, 1982, 1984; Greenberg & Safran, 1987; Safran & Greenberg, 1986). In this fashion, emotion, cognition, and action are fused through a type of preattentive information processing that combines information both internal and external to the organism.

In our view, the physiological and expressive motor behaviors associated with emotion are best understood as action tendencies or action dispositions (Lang, 1983). Emotions provide internally generated feedback that activates the biologically wired-in behavioral systems described earlier. For example, a feeling of affection may activate the attachment system in an infant. Whether or not a specific behavioral system becomes fully activated is contingent both upon how fully the relevant emotional information is processed and upon decisions executed by higher level processing.

Emotions provide us with organismic feedback that allows us to adapt to our environment. This feedback results from an automatic perceptual appraisal process in which input is processed through the schematic structures that have developed within the organism over its lifetime. New information generated through interaction with the environment is evaluated with reference to these internal structures and evokes an emotional response that falls within the basic parameters established by the hard-wiring of the organism.

Emotions can thus be viewed as a form of tacit meaning (Guidano, 1987; Mahoney & Gabriel, 1987). Emotional experience tells what events mean to us as biological organisms. They inform us of action dispositions that are evoked in us. These action dispositions are grounded in the biological imperatives dictated by the hard-wiring of the human organism as it has adapted to its ecological niche.

B. The Interruption of Emotional Experience

A central underlying premise in our perspective is that it is often the avoidance of, or interruption of, current emotional experiencing (Perls, Hefferline, & Goodman, 1951) that plays a part in both anxiety- and depression-related problems. It is the clients' sense that they *should feel* a certain way that prevents them from experiencing what they *are* feeling.

Helping clients thus involves teaching them to acknowledge and accept their current emotional experience. This, in turn, helps them to accept who they are and what is happening, rather than focusing on who they *should* be and what they feel *should* be happening. By becoming aware of how he or she is interrupting or avoiding internal experience, as well as the nature of the fears underlying this avoidance, the client can gradually choose to reduce this avoidance or interruption when ready. At the same time, it is absolutely essential to respect the client's fear of the internal experience, and to convey the message that he or she need attend to that experience only when ready. Any attempt to push the client too quickly is completely antithetical to the general principle of acceptance of the self that the therapist wishes to convey.

Because the interruption of emotional experience often takes place at an automatic, reflexive level, it is often important to help clients become aware of the precise ways in which they are interrupting their emotional experience. People develop varied and idiosyncratic ways of interrupting emotional experience. Although the general notion of interruption of emotional experience obviously bears some similarity to the psychoanalytic concept of defense mechanisms, there is an important difference. In an affectively oriented approach to treatment, rather than working on the basis of a preestablished classification of defensive styles, it is important to explore and discover the precise and unique fashion in which each individual client interrupts their emotional experience. In addition, what is being defended against in our view is not a primitive antisocial drive, but a painful and potentially adaptive emotional experience.

Once clients become more aware of *how* they are interrupting their emotional experience, they will become more aware of *when* they are interrupting their emotional experience. They can then make a choice as to whether or not they wish to continue this process of interruption, or whether they wish to attend to the emotional experience that is being blocked. Clients use a variety of interruptive styles.

Some clients minimize or invalidate their emotional experience. For example, it is not uncommon for clients to tell themselves that they do not have any right to feel whatever they are feeling (e.g., sad, hurt, angry), or that their feelings are unwarranted or foolish. Others automatically divert their attention so as not to attend to inner experience. In other situations, clients interrupt their emotional experiences by catastrophizing about the potential consequences of feeling and/or expressing their emotions. For example, clients may believe that they will never stop crying if they allow themselves to experience sadness. Other clients may believe that they will be rejected if they fully experience and express certain emotions.

It is often important for clients to distinguish between experiencing and expressing their feelings. Allowing oneself to fully experience one's anger or sadness does not necessarily mean that one must express it in the situation. People can experience their emotions, and then make a decision as to whether or not they wish to express them at that particular point in time. When, however, clients believe that expression and experience of emotions are inextricably linked, fear of the consequences of expressing an emotion may interrupt the initial experience of that emotion.

Whether or not clients choose to express their feelings at a given point in time, fully experiencing their emotions can be beneficial in and of itself. The failure to fully experience one's emotions results in a general sense of confusion, vagueness, and uncertainty. When, however, clients begin to allow themselves to experience their emotions fully, they become more clear about who they are, what they need, and what they want in a given situation.

Often clients interrupt their emotional experiences by distracting themselves or deflecting their attentional focus (Polster & Polster, 1973). It is not uncommon, for example, for clients to become preoccupied with trivial or unimportant issues when they begin to experience a threatening feeling.

Emotional experiences are also commonly interrupted through muscular contractions (Perls et al., 1951). Clients who are beginning to experience a threatening or anxiety-provoking experience will often adopt a rigid posture and contract muscles associated with expressive motor behaviors linked to the relevant emotion. The use of muscular contraction to suppress and control emotional experience was noted and described in detail by Darwin (1872) in the nineteenth century and more recently by Laird (1984). In clinical practice this type of muscular contraction is often accompanied by an inhibition of the respiratory system, because inhibition of the diaphragm muscles associated with respiration can be an effective way of controlling a variety of other muscles. Regardless of the specific fashion in which the client interrupts his or her emotional experience, the general therapeutic strategy consists of working with the client to attend to the current process of interruption in order to convert an automated process to a controlled process (Schiffrin & Schneider, 1977).

Having examined the relationship between emotion, information processing, and behavior, and having described how emotional experience is interrupted, we will now discuss the processes underlying anxiety and depression.

IV. Anxiety

Anxiety can be viewed as a biologically wired-in form of feedback about potential danger situations (Bowlby, 1973). There are various forms of behavior that are associated with fear and anxiety, including: hypervigilance, inhibition of action, trembling or crying, cowering, hiding, running away, and seeking contact with others. Human beings are genetically predisposed to respond to specific types of situations with anxiety.

Bowlby (1973), reviewing the empirical literature on situations that commonly elicit anxiety in infants, lists four general categories: (1) sudden noises, and sudden changes in physical situations such as sudden changes in illumination, unexpected movements, and so on, (2) strangers, (3) animals, and (4) darkness, especially darkness when alone. These situations elicit anxiety without learning.

There is one stimulus situation readily evoking anxiety that stands out as having special status: the fear of being alone. Being alone functions as a moderating variable in all of the above fear-eliciting stimulus situations. As we have seen, the fundamental premise of attachment theory is that attachment behavior promotes proximity to other people, thus reducing the possibility of vulnerability to predators and increasing the possibility of survival.

Anxiety is not a unitary phenomenon. In the clinical situation the experience of anxiety can reflect a number of different underlying processes. Depending upon the specific psychological process involved, different therapeutic interventions may be appropriate. In this section we will describe a number of different processes that can underlie anxiety and describe interventions that can be effective for dealing with each of them. The list of anxiety processes that we will articulate is in no sense intended to be exhaustive. Nor should these various processes be considered pure diagnostic types. In a given individual any combination of different processes may be in evidence at a given point in time. We will discuss five different anxiety processes: insecure attachment, fear of negative evaluation, anxiety secondary to primary emotion, anxiety secondary to avoidance, and catastrophizing. We will also discuss relevant interventions from an affective perspective.

A. Insecure Attachment

The first general anxiety process takes place in an individual who has never developed the type of secure attachment relationship that is necessary to engage in the type of exploratory behavior required to master naturally occurring childhood fears.

Some extremely important information regarding the development of various anxiety disorders comes from the empirical observation of different patterns of infant/mother attachment relationships. Ainsworth (1982) and others (e.g., Main, 1983; Pastor, 1981) have consistently observed that infants vary considerably in the extent to which they use the attachment figure as a secure base from which to explore and master unfamiliar and potentially anxiety provoking situations. A dimension that is extremely useful for classifying these observations concerns the *security* of the child's attachment. The secure child is one who is able to explore novel situations relatively freely using the mother or attachment figure as a base. Securely attached children will thus roam around and explore their environment, returning from time to time to the attachment figure, or simply visually checking to ensure that the attachment figure is available and responsive.

In contrast, the *insecurely* attached child engages in minimal exploratory behavior, even in the attachment figure's presence. The insecure child is not able to use the attachment figure as a base for exploration, becomes extremely distressed in the mother's absence, and may not greet the mother upon her return.

The balance between withdrawal and exploration thus appears to be mediated by the child's belief that the attachment figure will be available and responsive when necessary. As Bowlby (1973) suggests, individuals with multiple anxiety problems may never have developed the type of secure attachment relationships necessary to engage in exploratory behaviors that are essential for purposes of developing a sense of familiarity with, and mastery of, the environment.

As the behavioral and cognitive behavioral traditions have long recognized, getting the client to engage in active exploratory behaviors is an extremely important step in the treatment of a variety of fear avoidance and anxiety-related problems. This is only possible, however, when the therapist is seen as emotionally available to provide the type of secure base for exploration that the client's attachment figures may not have provided.

Although empirical research indicates that *in vivo* exposure is effective in treating various anxiety problems, it should be noted that a client will benefit from exposure treatment only if he or she will engage in the behavioral program in the first place (Emmelkamp & Foa, 1983). In our experience, a number of clients with various types of fear avoidance problems (circumscribed phobias, social anxiety, agoraphobia) simply will not engage in behavioral programs at the beginning of therapy. In these cases a trusting therapeutic relationship must gradually develop before the client is able to engage in the type of exploratory behavior necessary for dealing with their anxiety problems. If the client is extremely untrusting and experiences social anxiety and intimacy problems, this can require a slow and painstaking therapeutic process through which the therapist gradually uses the therapeutic interaction to disconfirm the client's dysfunctional beliefs about interpersonal relationships (Safran, 1984a, 1984b; Safran & Segal, in press).

In the case of anxious individuals with a history of extremely poor attachment relationships—and subsequent interpersonal problems and social anxiety—it may be important that they fully access dysfunctional cognitive-affective structures relating to important interpersonal relationships. This can create an opportunity for new information to be entered into their dysfunctional cognitive-affective structures at an experiential level. These cognitive-affective structures relating to interpersonal relationships can be thought of as internal working models (Bowlby, 1969; Safran & Segal, in press) about interpersonal relationships which are encoded in terms of specific episodic memories, images, and somatic and neuromuscular memories. As Lang (1983) points out, the relevant principles of operation of these networks may be similar ways to those underlying a subroutine in a computer program. In order to restructure or modify the subroutine, it is necessary to access it.

The relevant anxiety-laden memory structures, however, may not be accessible unless the individual experiences the anxiety that is associatively linked to them. In individuals with a history of insecure attachment relationships, relevant interpersonal memories are often associated with painful feelings surrounding the frustration of interpersonal needs. These painful feelings, such as feelings of rejection or resentment, are often avoided or interrupted, thus making it difficult to access the relevant cognitive-affective schemas. However, as clients develop a trusting relationship with their therapists over time, they may be more willing to tolerate the pain and anxiety associated with these memory structures.

Research conducted by the Mount Zion group (Weiss, Sampson, & The Mount Zion Psychotherapy Research Group, 1987) suggests that if these cognitive-affective schemas are to be accessed, the therapist must behave in a fashion which disconfirms the client's pathogenic beliefs about interpersonal relationships. For example, if the client believes that significant others will not tolerate any displays of independence, the therapist who truly accepts his client's independence can provide a powerful disconfirming impact.

At this point, associated memories, feelings of longing for support and nurturing, and feelings of pain and anger about previous interpersonal relationships may emerge. Once the client is able to experience and express his or her feelings of longing for interpersonal contact, a truly empathic response by the therapist can help to restructure his or her belief that attachment figures will be unavailable. As this cognitive-affective schema begins to change, the client may then find it easier to engage in the type of exploratory behavior necessary to master his or her fears of the environment.

B. Fear of Negative Evaluation

Another important factor producing anxiety is the fear of rejection and negative evaluation by others. Given the centrality of attachment behavior in human beings, it is no surprise that social anxiety and related issues are important clinical problems.

There are both similarities and differences in the way that affectively oriented therapy and cognitive behavioral therapy treat these problems. Both approaches stress the importance of accessing the client's negative predictions, expectations, and self-statements. However, cognitive and affective approaches fundamentally differ in the manner in which change then takes place.

Cognitive behavioral treatment involves challenging the client's negative predictions and negative self-statements using both logic and empirical evidence (Beck & Emery, 1985). The information that is employed to challenge the client's negative self-statements is thus external to the client. In contrast, the affectively oriented approach maintains that logic is often inadequate for modifying anxiety, since the information can be coded in expressive motor, rather than propositional or conceptual form. As previously indicated, the first major principle in any affectively oriented intervention is that the targeted emotional structure must first be accessed before change can take place. Thus, for example, one would never intervene by examining automatic thoughts that the client has written down over the week and subjecting them to some type of logical scrutiny. Instead, it is always important, for the client to access the relevant dysfunctional cognitive processes in an emotionally alive fashion during the session.

Moreover, once the negative self-statements or automatic thoughts are accessed, the therapist does not encourage the client to refute them on rational grounds. The affective perspective theorizes that anxiety results from a perceptual motor appraisal of events that reflects the individual's entire history of learning about himself or herself in relationship to other people. Any attempt to modify this expressive motor or perceptual motor appraisal through logical means would be a perpetuation of the clients' own maladaptive strategy of trying to talk themselves out of their feelings or to control themselves through reason. In fact, the therapist's attempt to impose logic on the client may obscure the fundamental perceptual motor appraisal that is essential to access before any change can take place (Greenberg & Safran, 1981, 1987; Safran & Greenberg, 1982a).

Once this emotional appraisal has been accessed, there are a number of mechanisms through which change can take place. The first mechanism involves gaining a tangible emotional sense of the impact of one's subjective construal upon one's experience. In this process, clients, by articulating their expectations or negative self-criticisms in an emotionally alive fashion, move from seeing the cause of the anxiety as external to viewing it as internal. Rather than continuing to locate the source of criticism externally, they begin to gain an experientially alive sense of the way in which they are evaluating themselves.

It is important to emphasize here that this process involves more than recognizing at an intellectual level that one is self-critical or that one causes one's own anxiety. Instead, it is a powerful emotional experience in which one literally steps outside of the process and *sees* what one is doing to oneself.

We emphasize this distinction, because clinicians who we are supervising will often say to us that their clients already know that they are being self-critical. There is, however, a difference between intellectual knowledge and experiential recognition of the role that one plays in the process (Strachey, 1934). Once clients have had this type of experiential recognition of the role that they play in generating their own anxiety, this can serve as a reference point to which they can return to in future anxiety experiences.

The fact that a client has had this type of experiential recognition on one occasion, however, does not mean that he or she will never experience anxiety again. Instead, it is necessary for clients to cultivate an ongoing experiential awareness of how they create their own anxiety. This involves the cultivation of what is referred to in psychoanalysis as *the observing ego* or what Deikman (1982) has referred to as *the observing self* that plays such a central role in the Eastern mystical traditions.

A second important affective mechanism for challenging anxiety-related cognitions is through the arousal of adaptive emotional responses (Greenberg & Safran, 1987). A useful intervention for activating this mechanism is the "two chairs" procedure in gestalt therapy (Greenberg, 1979, 1984). In this intervention the client sits in one chair and articulates anxiety-provoking cognitions by assuming the role of the internal critic. He or she is asked to articulate self-evaluations and catastrophic cognitions in a concrete, vivid, and immediate fashion by directing them at an empty chair. The client is then instructed to shift to the empty chair and to respond to the pressure coming from the other chair. It is important to note that the client is not instructed to stand up to the pressure, or challenge the message being directed at him or her from the other chair. Instead, he or she is instructed to respond in a fashion congruent with the way in which he or she is actually feeling at the moment. The objective of this intervention is to heighten the clients' awareness of what they are truly feeling rather than to encourage the client to challenge catastrophic cognitions in a rational fashion.

The therapist then shifts the client back to the critical or catastrophizing chair and encourages him or her to direct more pressure at the empty chair. The therapist encourages the client to be as specific as possible and to intensify the pressure. For example, a client who was experiencing extreme evaluation anxiety around authority figures was encouraged to pressure himself by telling the other chair exactly how he should be when he is with his boss. In the first chair the client said: "You should be extremely sharp, intelligent, bright, and perceptive. There is no room for any dullness, or slowness. You have to make a good impression!"

He was then instructed to move to the empty chair and to respond to this pressure by describing what he was experiencing in that moment. The client responded: "I feel like I'll never be able to be the way you're telling me to be. I feel really anxious, small, and helpless." He was then instructed to move back to the first chair and to respond to this. The client continued to pressure himself, and the therapist instructed him to be as specific as possible and to intensify his pressure.

In this fashion the therapist instructs the client to shuttle back and forth between the two chairs, always speaking in a fashion which reflects his or her immediate emotional response to verbalizations of the other chair. This process helps to partial out and separate the two parts of the internal conflict: the part that creates the pressure, or what Horney (1950) referred to as the idealized self, and the part that experiences that pressure.

A number of processes are facilitated by maintaining the separation between the two parts in this internal dialogue. First, both sides become clearer and more intense, and the experience of the internal struggle deepens. The client begins to identify with the part that creates the pressure. As this takes place he or she shifts from experiencing himself or herself exclusively as an anxious victim, to a position of agency, as he or she identifies more fully with the part that is doing the pressuring.

Second, clients are able to experience both parts more fully. Often, this deeper level of experiencing is prevented by premature resolutions in which clients attempt to cope with the conflict by talking themselves out of their feelings, by being rational, by avoiding painful emotions.

However, as the two sides of the conflict intensify and deepen, the client experiences the full force of his or her self-pressuring in an emotionally immediate fashion. A spontaneous emotional shift often begins to occur in the chair at which the pressure is directed. In response to the continued and intensified pressure, an emotional response begins to emerge which reflects a biologically adaptive reaction to the pressure, which has now become externalized through the "two chairs" intervention (Greenberg, 1984). Sometimes the client responds to the pressure with anger; sometimes the client responds to the pressure with sadness and tears, or with intense fear.

Any deep and authentically experienced emotion of this type seems to reflect a primary, adaptive organismic response that stems from a genuine part of the self that has been submerged, inhibited, or obscured by constant self-imposed injunctions and admonitions as to how one should feel or behave. As this primary emotional response emerges, the self-pressuring begins to soften and the individual begins to experience some of his or her true feelings. In this fashion, a more compassionate stance toward the self begins to emerge (Greenberg, 1980, 1984).

Thus, by separating out the two sides of the conflict, intensifying the self-pressure, and encouraging clients to stay with their true feelings in response to the self-pressure, the therapist nurtures the emergence of a true self that is grounded in clients' ongoing emotional experience. As this emotional experience emerges more clearly, clients begin to develop compassion for themselves and reduce their attempts to control their emotional experience. In this technique, the internally generated pressure responsible for the anxiety is challenged by an internally generated affective experience, rather than from any form of logical clarification or from the evaluation of one's experience against the criterion of external reality.

C. Anxiety as a Secondary Response to a Primary Emotion

When an individual has learned, as a result of specific developmental experiences, that the activation of a specific behavioral system disrupts or threatens his or her relationship with attachment figures, experiencing information linked to that behavioral system can provoke anxiety. As previously indicated, human beings are genetically predisposed to experience anxiety in response to the threat of disruption in interpersonal relatedness.

For example, an individual may learn that the experience of emotions such as anger or sadness will disrupt his or her relationships with attachment figures. Because of this, expressive motor behaviors associated with those emotions are experienced as threatening. The experience of expressive motor behaviors associated with these emotions can thus result in the subjective experience of anxiety, and a subsequent failure to fully attend to and process this internally generated information.

Thus, a wide range of action dispositions can trigger anxiety as a result of learning experiences with significant others. When this occurs, anxiety blocks the processing of potentially adaptive emotional information. For example, a client whose presenting problem was free-floating, generalized anxiety reported that she had been extremely anxious the evening prior to the therapy session and that her anxiety was not connected to anything in particular. The therapist worked with her to reconstruct the details of the situation as vividly as possible. Through a careful reconstruction of images and feelings immediately preceding her intense increase in anxiety, she was able to reexperience a vague feeling of tension and irritability that was different in quality from her typical, generalized experience of anxiety. Further exploration of the situation revealed that the strange and uncomfortable feelings occurred when her boyfriend was 2 hours late for a date.

Through a process of vividly imaging this situation and attending to the expressive motor behaviors associated with the emotional experience (e.g., tension in the jaw, clenched fists), the client was able to become aware of her anger toward her boyfriend. As she became clearly aware of this anger, the anxiety disappeared. Through fully experiencing this anger, the client was eventually able to clarify in her mind the action she wished to take should this situation arise again, and she resolved that she was not willing to tolerate this kind of discourtesy. In situations of this type, free-floating anxiety can be a clue to the clinician that a potentially adaptive primary emotion that threatens the client's sense of interpersonal relatedness is not being fully synthesized.

Certain types of clients have difficulty synthesizing a number of important emotional experiences and tend to experience a variety of different emotions as anxiety. Chambliss and Goldstein (1982), for example, point out that agoraphobics often have difficulty labeling and differentiating different emotional states and tend to experience a variety of different emotions as diffuse anxiety. According to Chambliss and Goldstein, agoraphobics have difficulty linking their anxiety to relevant interpersonal antecedents. Consistent with this observation, our experience has been that agoraphobics tend to focus on the expressive motor component of their emotions and to interpret this information somatically. This is extremely frightening to the agoraphobic who does not understand what is happening to him or her, and imagines that either something is physically wrong or that he or she is dying or going crazy. The agoraphobic thus experiences secondary anxiety in response to this misinterpreted somatic information (Beck & Emery, 1985; Chambliss & Goldstein, 1982).

A number of authors have pointed out that a core theme for agoraphobics often has to do with the dysfunctional need to maintain absolute control in all situations (Chambliss & Goldstein, 1982; Guidano & Liotti, 1983; Liotti, 1986). Our own experience suggests that this need for control is often part of a basic lack of acceptance of one's internal experience—a belief that one's private thoughts and associated feelings, whether they be sadness, anger, or fear, are simply unacceptable.

It is not surprising then, that as Liotti (1984) has pointed out, treatment procedures such as progressive relaxation can sometimes lead to an increase in anxiety, rather than the desired decrease. Although this effect may at first glance appear paradoxical, the relinquishing of control that is part and parcel of relaxation training may prove quite threatening to the individual who feels a need to maintain control at all costs. We are not, however, suggesting that the therapist should help the agoraphobic to increase his or her sense of control. Rather, we are suggesting that the therapist should gradually and sensitively work toward helping agoraphobics relinquish control at their own pace, as they gradually become more accepting of their own internal experience.

Another common feature in agoraphobia is what has been described as a fear of fear (e.g., Beck & Emery, 1985; Chambliss & Goldstein, 1982). The agoraphobic is often extremely intolerant of his or her own anxiety, and begins to catastrophize and panic at the least sign of anxiety. We consider this tendency to be part of a larger and more general tendency to be intolerant of one's own emotional experience. We try to teach our agoraphobic clients that while their internal experience may be threatening to them, it is ultimately a valuable source of information (Liotti, 1986). We thus encourage them—at their own pace—to attend to and make sense of their emotional experience.

This invariably involves developing some capacity to tolerate anxiety, rather than avoiding it and any experience associated with it. For this reason, we rarely use formal relaxation training, since it is vital to teach agoraphobics that it is important to gradually accept internal experience rather than to dampen it. We encourage agoraphobic clients to move beyond their anxiety about anxiety and to begin to become aware of what they are avoiding and how they are avoiding it. In some cases, the client is avoiding external situations that are threatening (e.g., social gatherings, confrontations with authority figures, contacts with people of the opposite sex). In addition, however, they are often avoiding their own internal experience. Again, when this occurs it is important to work with clients to explore what they fear about that experience, as well as the specific maneuvers they use in order to avoid it.

D. Catastrophic Anxiety

Anxiety also results from anticipating the future rather than living in and fully experiencing the present. To the extent that an individual is fully experiencing the present, anxiety about anticipated catastrophes in the future will be decreased. A classic Zen parable illustrates this point:

> A man travelling across a field encountered a tiger after him. Coming to a precipice, he caught hold of the root of a wild vine and swung himself down over the edge. The tiger sniffed at him from above. Trembling, the man looked down to where, far below, another tiger was waiting to eat him. Only the vine sustained him. Two mice, one white and one black, little by little started to gnaw away at the vine. The man saw a luscious strawberry near him. Grasping the vine with one hand, he plucked the strawberry with the other. How sweet it tasted! (Reps, 1971, p. 32)

This process of being able to live in the present and experience one's feelings as they really are, rather than anticipating the future, is often important in reducing anxiety. Cognitive behavioral treatment for catastrophic anxiety involves calculating the logical probabilities that an undesired event will actually take place. In contrast, the affective approach involves helping the client to realize that there are limits on the extent to which the future can be controlled. Anxiety results from the tendency to control that which cannot be controlled. The person is therefore trained to focus attention on the present, not the future.

E. Multiple Anxiety Concerns Secondary to Avoidance

Many clients shift from one anxiety-provoking preoccupation to another without ever fully exploring their true feelings about any specific event. These clients thus skim over the surface of multiple anxiety-related concerns without ever fully examining any one of them. It is thus like a stone skipping over the water instead of sinking into it. No one issue is ever resolved; instead, the anxiety generated by one concern appears to activate thoughts about other concerns that are associatively linked by the anxiety. In these situations we find that it is necessary to work with the client to explore one specific concern in detail. Often the client is avoiding exploring his or her feelings about a specific concern in any depth, because the feelings themselves generate anxiety. The feelings thus generate a type of secondary anxiety which further maintains an anxiety cycle.

V. Depression

As previously stated, we agree with a number of theorists (e.g., Beck, 1987; Bowlby, 1980; Engel, 1962) who propose that depression corresponds to an organismic response pattern of conservation/withdrawal. It is important to distinguish between the organismic response pattern of depression and the emotion of sadness (Beck, Rush, Shaw, & Emery, 1979; Bowlby, 1980; Greenberg & Safran, 1987). Sadness is an adaptive primary emotion that occurs in response to loss. The experience of sadness motivates the individual to attempt to recover that which is lost either directly or through replacement. The expression of sadness also promotes bonding and social cohesiveness by eliciting nurturing responses in others (e.g., Huebner & Izard, 1983). We hypothesize that the subjective experience of sadness is the result of an information-processing activity that informs the individual of his or her response to loss as a biological organism. This type of internal feedback motivates the individual to act in a fashion which will recover the lost object or compensate for it. In contrast, the depressed individual no longer attempts to recover the lost object. The key feature of depression is hopelessness (Beck, 1976).

In this section we will examine a variety of different depressive processes and discuss intervention from an affective perspective. The specific processes to be examined are (1) deactivation of behavioral systems, (2) cognitive disconnection of response from situation, (3) depressive cognitive-affective sequences, (4) apathy associated with harsh internal standards, and (5) incomplete emotional processing.

A. Deactivation of Behavioral Systems

A central hypothesis about depression is that this organismic response constellation in one way or another involves what Bowlby (1980) refers to as a deactivation of behavioral systems. When the individual feels that the exertion of further effort is futile or dangerous, the normal link between emotional information processing and action can become broken in a number of ways.

In situations of this type, the synthesis of emotional information associated with specific behavioral systems may be blocked or incomplete. One example is the depressed individual who experiences a general sense of numbness and emptiness, but does not experience a full and complete sense of sadness. Another example is a depressive who has difficulty experiencing and/or expressing anger. A third example would be the depressed individual who has difficulty experiencing feelings of warmth toward others.

In all of these situations the depressed individual may fail to synthesize relevant emotional information to varying degrees. When this occurs, interventions can consist of challenging dysfunctional beliefs that block the synthesis of the emotional experience, or of directing the individual's attention to expressive motor behavior that is not being fully synthesized.

This inability to synthesize the emotion leaves the person feeling powerless and helpless because they are robbed of their response. For example, a severely depressed male inpatient described a situation in which the resident responsible for coordinating his treatment on the ward had behaved in a manner which he interpreted as condescending. When the therapist asked him how he felt about this situation, he maintained that he felt numb, and that there was nothing he could do. The client's response in this situation was consistent with a general sense of powerlessness and helplessness that had been observed in him over the course of therapy.

The therapist then asked the client to describe the last interaction of this kind in concrete, vivid detail. As the client described the incident the therapist observed tension in the client's jaw. He directed the client's attention to his jaw and asked him to describe his experience. The client reported that he was feeling tense and irritated. As he continued to describe the incident the therapist noticed that his right hand was clenching in what appeared to be a partial fist. When the therapist drew his attention to the hand, the client suddenly became extremely quiet.

Exploration of his experience at this point revealed that the client feared the possible consequences of becoming angry. He reported a concern that the resident would retaliate and throw him off the ward. Articulating his tacit belief in this fashion helped the client to recognize how he was blocking his own emotional experience. Making his fear explicit also helped to reduce this inhibition as he spontaneously began to question the validity of the assumption that the resident would retaliate.

Now, as he continued to describe the incident, his subjective experience of his own emotional response continued to deepen. As the therapist continued to draw his attention to his nonverbal behaviors and somatic sensations the client was actually able to speak in an emotionally alive fashion about his anger at the resident. At this point the therapist asked him what he wanted from the resident. In this process it is always important for the therapist to help clarify the desire and potentially adaptive action disposition that is implicit in the experienced emotion (Greenberg & Safran, 1987).

The client reported that he wanted the resident to know his feelings and to treat him with respect. The next session the client reported that, over the course of the week, he had become aware of feeling angry with the resident during their meeting and that he had spontaneously confronted him. Whereas previously he had felt numb and dead inside, he now reported feeling alive and having more of a sense of control in his life. This was the beginning of an important emotional shift.

Another example involves a 29-year-old woman who had been severely depressed for 2 years, and who presented with severely blunted affect. In response to probes by the therapist she reported that she felt nothing inside—that she felt completely dead. As she spoke about a number of devastating events she had experienced (e.g., being physically abused by her boyfriend), the therapist noticed a faint, half-smile on her lips. He drew her attention to the smile and asked her what her experience was at that point. The client indicated that she had not been aware of her smile, but that she was now aware of a vague feeling of discomfort.

Further exploration revealed a desire to control whatever feelings she might be having because of a general sense that they might be unacceptable to the therapist. The therapist then instructed her to focus on and report any somatic sensations she experienced as she described the relationship with her boyfriend. The client reported a heavy feeling in her eyelids and a painful, heavy feeling in her solar plexus. As she focused on these sensations she began to experience and report a sense of overwhelming sadness. At this point the therapist noticed her smiling again and asked her to report her experience. The client indicated that she was feeling self-conscious and self-critical about her sadness.

Further exploration revealed some important tacit attitudes and beliefs linked to her inability to process internally generated information related to sadness. The client expressed a belief that expressing sadness would be an acknowledgement of weakness and vulnerability, and that it would drive people away or allow them to take advantage of her. She also feared that her sadness would never end if she allowed herself to experience it.

Over the course of therapy she became better able to experience and express her sadness as a result of attending more fully to associated somatic expression. This process was further facilitated as she became more aware of the way in which her beliefs and fears inhibited the experience, and as she saw that the therapist did not reject her when she expressed sadness. As she allowed herself to experience her sadness she began to feel more self-compassionate and less self-critical.

Her increased experience of sadness was painful, but she also began to experience an increasing sense of internal aliveness. It was the inability to experience the sadness that had left her feeling empty and depressed. She reported that although the pain was in a sense more intense than it had been before, it was preferable to the sense of deadness and emptiness she had felt for the last 2 years. Moreover, as she began to experience her sadness more fully she became motivated to reach out to other people, and to be more open to the nurturance and support that they might provide.

B. Cognitive Disconnection of Response from Situation

Another common form of dysfunctional affective information processing in depression is what Bowlby (1980) refers to as the cognitive disconnection of response from situation. In many cases, when an individual has learned through important developmental experiences that the activation of behavioral systems associated with certain types of emotion predictably leads to the disintegration of interpersonal relationships, he or she may synthesize the expressive motor components but fail to connect the feeling with the relevant interpersonal event.

When clients experience a lack of focus and immediacy in their general emotional state, a useful intervention consists of helping them to reestablish the connection between the emotional experience and the relevant eliciting event. The client is thus encouraged to deal with *specific* examples and to link the emotional experience to *specific* interpersonal events. For example, a general sense of hopelessness may disappear when the client is able to identify an underlying sense of powerlessness and hopelessness related to a specific interpersonal event (e.g., the interaction with the therapist, or a recent interaction with his or her spouse).

When a set of affective responses becomes disconnected from the eliciting interpersonal situation, depression results from the individual focusing attention on himself or herself, rather than toward the relevant interpersonal event. This results in a morbid preoccupation with the self, or a generalized, aimless anger, bitterness, or hopelessness rather than a focused emotion, directed at a specific and immediate interpersonal event.

For example, a male client who felt belittled and slighted by something the therapist had said experienced a sense of irritation, but was not able to connect this feeling to the immediate interaction. He was thus left with a global, vague sense of irritation and bitterness. This contributed to a general sense of aimlessness and helplessness. Instead of focusing outside on the immediate interaction, the client became preoccupied with his own ill-defined feelings. Instead of anger and irritability, the client experienced a *general* sense of bitterness and helplessness, which is what he communicated to his therapist. The focus of his attention thus became the *self* rather than the *self-in-interaction* with others. He was thus out of contact with his immediate environment and continued to be preoccupied with negative, self-critical ruminations.

In situations of this type, the intervention consists of helping clients to sharpen their emotional experience and to reconnect it to the relevant environmental event. It is important to move beyond a general sense of bitterness toward an immediate and clearly felt experience of anger that is directed at someone in particular. Similarly, the client must move beyond a general, global sense of being hurt and victimized toward an immediate sense of feeling hurt about something specific.

The experience of bitterness arises when primary and potentially adaptive anger becomes blocked, either because of a fear of the consequences or from a feeling of hopelessness. When the anger becomes associated with a feeling of helplessness and powerlessness it can become transformed into a kind of self-righteous bitterness in which the individual feels victimized and derives perverse satisfaction out of seeing others as wrongdoers, and the self as noble and as unjustly violated.

Because of the importance of helping clients connect their feelings to particular ongoing experiences, it can be useful to work either in groups or with events that take place in the therapeutic relationship. In a group situation, the therapist has the opportunity to help the client learn to attend to his or her immediate emotional experience, and to share it through interactions with other group members. Groups provide an ideal opportunity to help clients explore and clarify their fears of interactions linking their emotional experience to specific interactions in the immediate present.

In the same fashion, any feelings that clients have about their interactions with the therapist can help them to learn about the ways in which they disconnect their emotional response from relevant interpersonal events, and to explore the fears associated with this type of avoidance. They can then go through the corrective emotional experience of reestablishing a response–event connection while discovering that the consequences are not necessarily disastrous.

A useful marker for this type of intervention occurs when something takes place in the therapeutic relationship that the therapist hypothesizes might constitute grounds for certain affects (e.g., hurt, sadness, and anger), whereas the client responds with a very generalized, unfocused, feeling that does not appear to be linked to anything particular. For example, the therapist is unavoidably late for a session and the client expresses a general feeling of being unhappy or disgruntled, but not at the therapist. Another example would be the situation in which the client is dissatisifed with his or her progress in therapy and feels angry at himself or herself, but is not able to experience or express any sense of anger or disappointment with the therapist.

We are not advocating that the therapist make assumptions about what the client is feeling or that the therapist should interpret the client's feeling for him or her. We are, however, suggesting that on the basis of all available information (e.g., a general understanding of human nature, specific knowledge about the client, and his or her own feelings toward the client), the therapist establish hypotheses about missing emotional response–interpersonal event links that can guide intervention, and then be alert for any signs of these that can be brought to the client's awareness. For example, if the client complains about a general sense of irritability and anger, the therapist can ask "Who are you angry at?" If the client speaks about a general sense of powerlessness and hopelessness, the therapist can ask "How are you feeling about what's happening right now?"

Another useful marker for interventions of this type is what is called in psychodynamic theory an *allusion to transference* (Gill, 1982). If the client describes an emotionally charged event that is taking place in another context and that bears a plausible thematic relationship to the current therapeutic interaction, the therapist may choose to explore a possible link between the two events. For example, in one session the client appeared irritated when the therapist attempted to empathically reflect his statement. The client began to speak about how angry and fed up he was with mental health professionals in general, because of their inability to understand his experience, and their unwillingness to take the time to understand. At this point, the therapist intervened by saying to the client "I was aware that when I made my last comment you looked kind of irritated, and wondered if you are experiencing any of the feelings you are talking about towards me?"

There are two additional points worth making about the process of response–event disconnection and the relevant therapeutic intervention. First, therapists should not make the assumption that all narratives that are thematically related to therapeutic relationship are allusions to that relationship, or that it is necessarily useful to make the link even when they are. Rather, the therapist may wish to explore the potential link in a specific situation in which the client appears to have difficulty connecting emotional responses to interpersonal events, and the narrative presented by the client bears a plausible structural relationship to current events in the therapeutic relationship.

Second, we are not assuming that the client who presents a narrative that might possibly allude to the therapeutic relationship is consciously trying to tell the therapist something in symbolic form. We hypothesize that the client may be unclear about the link between the emotional response and the current interpersonal event. The client may, however, wish to convey his current experience to the therapist, and it may be that episodic memories that are linked to the current emotion in a cognitive-affective schema may be activated and thus primed or easily accessible.

Finally, in connecting an emotional response to the therapeutic relationship, the objective is not so much one of helping the client gain insight into current interpersonal dynamics as it is to promote a type of experiential learning in which he or she actually practices connecting emotional responses to interpersonal events in the present, and discovers that the consequences are not catastrophic.

C. Faulty or Depressive Cognitive–Affective Sequences

When clients experience the general sense of hopelessness typically associated with depression, it is often useful to explore the specific cognitive-affective sequence that leads to feelings of hopelessness in particular situations. As Glass and Arnkoff (1982) have argued in the field of cognitive assessment, it is important that we move beyond a rudimentary quantification of the frequency of positive versus negative self-statements to a more detailed sequential analysis of relevant cognitions. Similarly, we believe that it is important for the clinician to capture as accurately as possible the complex cognitive-affective sequences that are characteristics of the client in distress (Greenberg & Safran, 1987).

The guiding principle in this type of assessment is to expand or stretch out the emotional monologue that normally occurs automatically and instantaneously, in order to allow both the client and therapist to gain a better understanding of the sequence of affective reasoning that leads to the hopelessness. For example, the client may begin to feel hurt by something that the therapist had said, but then immediately disqualifies those feelings and collapses into a numb, confused sense of hopelessness. Or, the client may begin to stand up to his or her own internal self-criticism, but then at some point turns on himself/herself, crushes any biologically adaptive self-assertion, and thus feels hopeless.

The "two chairs" procedure from gestalt therapy can be a very useful way of bringing to life, slowing down, expanding, and dramatizing these problematic cognitive-affective performance sequences. For example, a client began a session upset that she was not progressing quickly enough. Using the "two chairs" procedure, the therapist instructed her to pressure the empty chair in the same way she was currently pressuring herself. She was then instructed to move to the empty chair and to respond in a fashion consistent with her current experience. In this fashion the client move back and forth between the two chairs, alternately pressuring herself and experiencing and reporting her feelings in response to that pressure. After five minutes of this, as the pressure intensified, the client began to experience some anger in the second chair.

"I'm sick and tired of you pressuring me!" she said to the other chair. At this point she moved into the other chair and said: "You have no right to get angry, you useless lump of clay!" She then moved back to the other chair and was overcome with an incredible feeling of hopelessness. At this point, the therapist drew her attention to the way in which she had ruthlessly undercut herself and extinguished the one spark of self-assertion and acceptance she had experienced. This seemed to result in a realization experience for the client and this insight translated into an experiential shift the following week. In the next session, the client began by criticizing herself in a similar fashion for not progressing quickly enough. The therapist began to use the "two chairs" intervention again and a cognitive-affective sequence similar to the one in the previous session emerged. At a certain point in the sequence the client began to become angry at the chair for being critical of her.

As in the previous session she changed chairs and responded to this anger by intensifying her self-criticism. The client then moved back to the other chair and said: "Oh no . . . you're not going to do that to me this time! I've had it with this pressure. I'm moving as quickly as I can!"

It is important to point out that in such cases clients are not explicitly trained to challenge their self-criticism. Rather, by drawing their attention to the precise way in which they undercut themselves emotionally, they become more aware of what they are doing to themselves, and more able to recognize it when it is happening.

Often, a self-criticism which is especially undercutting will emerge when a cognitive-affective sequence is explored in this fashion. These self-criticisms are typically phrases or combinations of words that have a special, idiosyncratic meaning for the client. Sometimes they are linked to important developmental experiences. For example, one client, who had a serious orthopedic problem when younger, undercut his adaptive emotional experience by calling himself a helpless cripple. The potency of specific self-inflicted psychological insults or this type often does not become clear to either the client or therapist until specific cognitive-affective sequences are stretched out and assessed in an emotionally alive fashion.

Evocative responding (Rice & Saperia, 1984) can also be used to reevoke in a lively fashion the experience from a past problematic situation. By visually recreating the original scene it becomes possible to track the moment-by-moment internal processes that led to a negative problematic reaction such as a depressed or resigned feeling. Once these sequences are available in a lively form they become amenable to change.

D. Apathy Associated with Harsh Internal Standards

A common pattern underlying chronic states of depression involves a constant, ongoing struggle to satisfy or appease harsh dysfunctional beliefs about the way one *should* be in order to be acceptable as a person. Clients engaged in this type of internal struggle often derive very little satisfaction or enjoyment out of life and experience a constant state of lifelessness and apathetic dysphoria.

Because of their lack of enthusiasm and full-hearted engagement in the tasks they are performing, they often function in a suboptional fashion. This creates a vicious cycle. They are constantly feeling disappointed in themselves because they cannot satisfy the unreasonable demands of their harsh internal standards. Moreover, objectively their performance may suffer because they engage in these tasks half-heartedly and resentfully. Finally, they are not able to enjoy their leisure time because of a constant sense of guilt over not accomplishing what they believe they should be accomplishing. This difficulty in fully engaging in the task at hand may manifest itself in the therapeutic situation as well. Thus, the client may participate in the process of therapy with the same kind of grudging, half-hearted involvement that they apply to the other tasks in their life.

The intervention here focuses on helping the client to act in a way that is connected to their own affective experience, rather than from an externalized sense of what they should be doing. To begin this process it is vital that they obtain a clearer sense of what they feel and want, and that they start treating that experience as valid. A client may, for example, feel resentful about doing a certain task. In a situation such as this, the process of fully experiencing that resentment, and then consciously and intentionally deciding not to complete the task, may be an important part of the change process.

For example, one client was constantly procrastinating at work and then carrying his work home with him on weekends in order to complete it. When the weekend arrived he would feel more and more depressed and often find himself retiring to bed, rather then doing the work he had planned to do. An important part of the change process for him involved fully experiencing resentment at the harsh demands of his own internal standards, and then *intentionally* and *actively* deciding not to work on the weekend, rather then passively avoiding work. Once he had done this he was able to enjoy himself on the weekend. In turn, he experienced renewed energy on Monday and found it easier to do his work. This initiated a process of shifting the source of his motivation from an externalized sense of what he should be doing to an internal sense of what he wanted to do.

It may be clarifying to contrast the current perspective with a cognitive behavioral perspective on depression. In Beck's (Beck et al., 1979) cognitive therapy, for example, scheduling of activities that will afford an increased sense of mastery and pleasure plays an important role in the treatment of depression. In contrast, the current perspective would not involve *scheduling* mastery or pleasure activities *in this specific context*. An affective perspective suggests that until a client is able to gain a tangible sense of what he or she really wants in an emotionally alive fashion, there is a danger that any scheduled activity will be experienced as an external imposition. Activities that are scheduled to provide a sense of mastery may seem like a good idea, but may ultimately be sabotaged in the same way that previous plans have been. Activities that are scheduled to provide a sense of pleasure may not be carried through because the client feels too guilty.

There is often a concern that unless the depressed clients continue some minimal level of activity, they will become even more depressed. The current intuition, however, is that an important part of the change process involves a kind of surrendering or "letting go." In this process it is important for clients to stop pushing themselves to do things. Instead a type of "letting go" takes place, in which clients surrender to their inner feelings and begin to gain a sense of what they really want to do, rather than what they should do. Therapists using this approach must have faith that that this process of "letting go" will not ultimately result in even greater passivity and depression.

In cases where clients are only half-heartedly engaged in the tasks of therapy, it is important that they become aware of their resentment of the belief that they *should* be working in therapy. If clients are able to experience and express this sense of grudging resentment, they can begin the process of becoming more internally motivated.

E. Incomplete Emotional Processing

The failure to experience a complete emotional sequence leads to the maintenance of a number of incomplete emotional sequences or behavioral systems that are incompatible with one another and thus block each other. This perspective is consistent with data demonstrating that depressed individuals are more likely than nondepressed individuals to experience persevering motivational states that intrude into working memory, thereby claiming processing capacity that may be needed for the enactment of new goals and intentions (Kuhl & Helle, 1986).

As Izard (1977) argues, emotional states usually are transient in nature. Interrupted emotion sequences, because they have been stored in schematic emotional memory in this incompletely processed state, have a tendency to persevere. Because of this, they inhibit the establishment of new goals and the enactment of behaviors to obtain those goals.

Clinically, one often observes that depressed clients experience unresolved grief and/or anger toward significant others. These feelings can be either left over from the past or can stem from more recent interpersonal conflicts or losses. The therapeutic work of expressing these feelings to completion—thereby finishing unfinished business—can be most helpful in restructuring the schematic representation of self and other (Greenberg & Safran, 1987). The presence of unfinished business in depression is indicated by the patient's lingering feeling of resignation and helplessness in response to losses in significant interpersonal relationships.

In these situations the person has had strong emotional responses which were interrupted at the time and not expressed to any satisfactory degree. This interruption of the response disempowered the person, which in turn led to feelings of resignation and hopelessness. Reactivation and completion of the emotional expression in the safety of the therapeutic situation produces feelings of recovery and relief and a sense of empowerment. Once this process has occurred, individuals are able to restructure their view of themselves and the significant other by incorporating other facets of their experience into their internal representation of the relationship.

Thus, clients who grew up with scornful, rejecting parents may have learned to suppress their anger and tendency to fight back, and have therefore developed a strong sense of helpless defeat. A remobilization in therapy of the interrupted anger and self-assertion can lead to a revitalization and the motivation to try again. The completion of unfinished business allows the person to respond to the current situation fully, without the intrusion of the painful experience which previously demanded processing capacity and interfered with the person's ability to respond optimally.

Working with unfinished business is best facilitated by the creation of a dialogue with the imaginary significant other in an empty chair (Perls et al., 1951; Greenberg & Safran, 1987). In this process the person clearly expresses feelings of anger and sadness which were previously undifferentiated. Completion of this expression leads to a more balanced and understanding view of the other, who was previously viewed in entirely negative terms. The effectiveness of this intervention for resolving anger is currently being evaluated (Daldrup, Beutler, Engle, & Greenberg, in press).

VI. Conclusion

In this chapter, we have outlined a general perspective on the affective conceptualization and treatment of anxiety and depression. We have distinguished between anxiety and depression as two different organismic response constellations, one corresponding to fight/flight, and the other corresponding to conservation/withdrawal.

Although it is possible to make this distinction in general terms, we have emphasized that the various cognitive-affective processes underlying both anxiety and depression are heterogeneous in nature. Moreover, the dysfunctional processes underlying anxiety and depression are not entirely distinct. In keeping with this perspective, we have described a number of dysfunctional cognitive-affective processes underlying anxiety and depression, as well as affectively oriented interventions that deal with specific dysfunctional cognitive-affective processes.

In clinical practice, it is our assessment of the relevant underlying process on a moment-by-moment basis that guides intervention (Greenberg & Safran, 1987; Rice & Greenberg, 1984) rather than a static diagnosis of anxiety or depression. This helps the clinician to respond flexibly to ongoing changes in clinical process rather than to be locked in by a static diagnosis. A particular client may, for example, display both anxiety secondary to a primary emotion and apathy associated with harsh internal standards, at different points in the same session. The clinical observation regarding the overlapping nature of dysfunctional affective processes underlying anxiety and depression is consistent with empirical evidence regarding the difficulty in distinguishing the two disorders empirically (Dobson, 1985; Strian & Klicpera, 1984; Swinson & Kirby, 1987).

The interventions we have described derive from a number of different psychotherapeutic traditions. What distinguishes the therapeutic approach articulated in this chapter is not the surface features of the interventions employed, but rather the use of a specific conceptual perspective to understand the *process* through which the interventions operate. This perspective begins with the fundamental assumption that emotional experience plays a potentially adaptive role in human functions, and that psychological problems often result from the interruption or avoidance of emotional experience.

References

Ainsworth, M. D. S. (1982). Attachment: Retrospect and prospect. In C. M. Parkers & J. Stevenson-Hinde (Eds.), *The place of attachment in human behavior*. New York: Basic Books.

Arnold, M. B. (1960). *Emotion and personality*. New York: Columbia University Press.

Beck, A. T. (1976). *Cognitive therapy and the emotional disorders*. New York: International Universities Press.

Beck, A. T., & Emery, G. (1985). *Anxiety disorders and phobias: A cognitive perspective*, New York: Basic Books.

Beck, A. T., Rush, A. J., Shaw, B. F., & Emery, G. (1979). *Cognitive therapy of depression*. New York: Guilford Press.

Bower, G. H. (1981). Mood and memory. *American Psychologist, 36*, 129–148.

Bowlby, J. (1969). *Attachment and loss: Vol. I. Attachment*. New York: Basic Books.

Bowlby, J. (1973). *Attachment and loss: Vol. II. Separation, anxiety, and anger*. New York: Basic Books.

Bowlby, J. (1980). *Attachment and loss: Vol. III: Loss: Sadness and depression*. London: Hogarth Press.

Chambliss, D. L., & Goldstein, A. J. (1982). *Agoraphobia: Multiple perspectives on therapy*. New York: Wiley.

Chomsky, N. (1980). *Rules and representations*. New York: Columbia University Press.

Daldrup, R. J., Beutler, L. E., Engle, D., & Greenberg, L. S. (in press). *Focused expressive psychotherapy: A Gestalt psychotherapy intervention for individuals with constricted affect*. New York: Guilford Press.

Darwin, C. (1872). *The expression of emotions in man and animal*. New York: Philosophical Library, 1955.

Deikman, A. J. (1982). *The observing self: Mysticism and psychotherapy*. Boston: Beacon Press.

Dobson, K. S. (1985). The relationship between anxiety and depression. *Clinical Psychology Review, 49*, 305–324.

Emmelkamp, P. M. G., & Foa, E. B. (1983). Failures are a challenge. In E. B. Foa & P. M. G. Emmelkamp (Eds.), *Failures in behavior therapy*. New York: Wiley.

Engel, G. L. (1962). Anxiety and depression-withdrawal: The primary affects of unpleasure. *International Journal of Psychoanalysis, 43*, 89–97.

Foa, E. B., Steketee, G., Grayson, J. B., & Doppelt, H. (1983). Treatment of obsessive–compulsives: When do we fail? In E. B. Foa & P. M. G. Emmelkamp (Eds.), *Failures in behavior therapy*. New York: Wiley.

Gill, M. M. (1982). *Analysis of transference I: Theory and technique*. New York: International Universities Press.

Glass, C., & Arnkoff, D. (1982). Thinking cognitively: Selected issues in cognitive assessment and therapy. In P. C. Kendall (Ed.), *Advances in cognitive-behavioral research and therapy*. New York: Academic Press.

Greenberg, L. S. (1979). Resolving splits the two-chair technique. *Psychotherapy: Theory, Research and Practice, 16*, 310–318.

Greenberg, L. S. (1980). The intensive analysis of recurring events from the practice of Gestalt therapy. *Psychotherapy: Theory, Research and Practice, 17*, 143–152.

Greenberg, L. S. (1984). A task analysis of intrapersonal conflict resolution. In L. N. Rice & L. S. Greenberg (Eds.), *Patterns of change: Intensive analysis of psychotherapy process*. New York: Guilford Press.

Greenberg, L. S., & Safran, J. D. (1980). Encoding information processing and cognitive behavior therapy. *Canadian Psychologist, 21*, 59–66.

Greenberg, L. S., & Safran, J. D. (1981). Encoding and cognitive therapy: Changing what clients attend to. *Psychotherapy: Theory, Research and Practice, 18*, 163–169.

Greenberg, L. S., & Safran, J. D. (1984a). Hot cognition: Emotion coming in from the cold. A reply to Rachman & Mahoney. *Cognitive Therapy and Research, 8*, 591–598.

Greenberg, L. S., & Safran, J. D. (1984b). Integrating affect and cognition: A perspective on therapeutic change. *Cognitive Therapy and Research, 8*, 559–578.

Greenberg, L. S., & Safran, J. D. (1987). *Emotion in psychotherapy*. New York: Guilford Press.

Guidano, V. F. (1987). *Complexity of the self*. New York: Guilford Press.

Guidano, V. F., & Liotti, F. (1983). *Cognitive processes and the emotional disorders*. New York: Guilford Press.

Hinde, R. A. (1966). *Animal behavior: A synthesis of ethology and comparative psychology*. New York: McGraw-Hill. (2nd ed., 1970).

Horney, K. (1950). *Neurosis and human growth*. New York: Norton.

Huebner, R. R., & Izard, C. E. (1983). *Mother's responses to infants' facial expressions of sadness, anger, and physical pain*. Unpublished manuscript.

Izard, C. E. (1977). *Human emotions*. New York: Plenum.

Kuhl, J., & Helle, P. (1986). Motivational and volitional determinants of depression: The degenerated intentions hypothesis. *Journal of Abnormal Psychology, 95*, 247–251.

Laird, J. D. (1984). The real role of facial response in the experience of emotion: A reply to Tourangeau and Ellsworth, and others. *Journal of Personality and Social Psychology, 47*, 909–917.

Lang, P. J. (1977). Imagery and therapy. *Behavior Therapy, 8,* 862–886.
Lang, P. J. (1983). Cognition in emotion: Concept and action. In C. Izard, J. Kagan, & R. Zajonc (Eds.), *Emotion, cognition and behavior,* New York: Cambridge University Press.
Lang, P. J. (1984). In C. Izard, J. Kagan, & R. Zajonc (Eds.), *Emotion, cognition and behavior.* London & New York: Cambridge University Press.
Leventhal, H. (1982). The integration of emotion and cognition: A vew from the perceptual-motor theory of emotion. In M. S. Clarke & S. T. Fiske (Eds.), *Affect and cognition.* Hillsdale, NJ: Erlbaum.
Leventhal, H. (1984). A perceptual-motor theory of emotion. In L. Berkowitz (Ed.), *Advances in experimental social psychology* (Vol. 17, pp. 117–182). New York: Academic Press.
Liotti, G. (1984). Cognitive therapy, attachment theory and psychiatric nosology: A clinical and theoretical inquiry into their interdependence. In M. A. Reda & M. J. Mahoney (Eds.), *Cognitive psychotherapies.* Cambridge, MA: Ballinger.
Liotti, G. (1986). Structural cognitive therapy. In W. Dryden & W. Golden (Eds.), *Cognitive behavioral approaches to psychotherapy.* London: Harper & Row.
Lorenz, K. (1973). *Behind the mirror.* New York: Harcourt Brace Jovanovich. (English translation 1977)
Mahoney, M. J. (1980). Psychotherapy and the structure of personal revolutions. In M. J. Mahoney (Ed.), *Psychotherapy process: Current issues and future directions.* New York: Plenum.
Mahoney, M. J., & Gabriel, T. J. (1987). Psychotherapy and cognitive sciences: An evolving alliance. *Journal of Cognitive Psychotherapy, 1,* 39–59.
Main, M. (1983). Exploration, play, and cognitive functioning related to infant–mother attachment. *Infant Behavior and Development, 6,* 167–174.
Pastor, D. L. (1981). The quality of mother–infant attachment and its relationship to toddlers' initial sociability with peers. *Developmental Psychology, 17,* 326–335.
Perls, F. S., Hefferline, R., & Goodman, P. (1951). *Gestalt therapy.* New York: Dell.
Piaget, J. (1952). *The origins of intelligence in children.* New York: International Universities Press.
Piaget, J. (1954). *Construction of reality in the child.* New York: Basic Books.
Plutchik, R. (1980). *Emotion: A psychoevolutionary synthesis.* New York: Harper & Row.
Polanyi, M. (1966). *The tacit dimension.* New York: Doubleday.
Polster, E., & Polster, M. (1973). *Gestalt therapy integrated.* New York: Brunner/Mazel.
Reps, P. (1971). *Zen flesh, Zen bones: A collection of Zen and pre-Zen writings.* Garden City, NY: Doubleday.
Rice, L., & Greenberg, L. S. (1984). *Patterns of change intensive analysis of psychotherapeutic process.* New York: Guilford Press.
Rice, L., & Saperia, E. P. (1984). Task analysis of the resolution of problematic reactions. In L. R. Rice & L. S. Greenberg (Eds.), *Patterns of change: Intensive analysis of psychotherapy process.* (pp. 29–66). New York: Guilford Press.
Safran, J. D. (1984a). Assessing the cognitive-interpersonal cycle. *Cognitive Therapy and Research, 8,* 333–348.
Safran, J. D. (1984b). Some implications of Sullivan's interpersonal theory for cognitive therapy. In M. A. Reda & M. J. Mahoney (Eds.), *Cognitive psychotherapies: Recent developments in theory, research, and practice.* Cambridge, MA: Ballinger.
Safran, J. D., & Greenberg, L. S. (1982a). Cognitive appraisal and reappraisal implications for clinical practice. *Cognitive Therapy and Research, 6,* 251–258.
Safran, J. D., & Greenberg, L. S. (1982b). Eliciting hot cognitions in cognitive behavior therapy: Rationale and procedural guidelines. Canadian Psychology, 23, 83–87.
Safran, J. D., & Greenberg, L. S. (1986). Hot cognition and psychotherapy process: An information processing/ecological approach. In P. C. Kendall (Ed.), *Advances in cognitive-behavioral research and therapy* (Vol. 5). New York: Academic Press.

Safran, J. D., & Greenberg, L. S. (1987). Affect and the unconscious: A cognitive perspective. In R. Stern (Ed.), *Theories of the unconscious.* Hillsdale, NJ: Analytic Press.
Safran, J. D., & Greenberg, L. S. (1988). Feeling, thinking and acting: A cognitive framework for psychotherapy integration. *Journal of Cognitive Psychotherapy: An international quarterly,* 103–131.
Safran, J. D., & Segal, Z. (in press). Cognitive therapy: *An interpersonal process perspective.* New York: Basic Books.
Shiffrin, R. M., & Schneider, W. (1977). Controlled and automatic human information processing. II: Perceptual learning, automatic attending, and a general theory. *Psychological Review, 84,* 127–190.
Strachey, J. (1934). The nature of the therapeutic action of psychoanalysis. *International Journal of Psychoanalysis, 15,* 127–159.
Strian, F., & Klicpera, C. (1984). Anxiety and depression in affective disorders. *Psychopathology, 17,* 37–48.
Swinson, R. P., & Kirby, M. (1987). The differentiation of anxiety and depressive symptoms. In B. F. Shaw, Z. V. Segal, T. M. Vallis, & F. E. Cashman (Eds.), *Anxiety disorders: Psychological and biological perspectives.*
Tinbergen, N. (1951). *The study of instinct.* London: Oxford University Press.
Tomkins, S. S. (1980). Affect as amplifications: Some modifications in theory. In R. Plutchik & H. Kelerman (Eds.). *Emotion: Theory, research and experience* (Vol. I), New York: Academic Press.
Turvey, M. T. (1977). Preliminaries to a theory of action with reference to vision. In R. Shaw & J. Bransford (Eds.), *Perceiving acting and knowing: Toward an ecological psychology.* Hillsdale, NJ: Erlbaum.
Weimer, W. B. (1977). A conceptual framework for cognitive psychology motor theories of the mind. In R. Shaw & J. Bransford (Eds.). *Perceiving acting and knowing: Toward an ecological psychology.* Hillsdale, NJ: Erlbaum.
Weiss, J., Sampson, H., & The Mount Zion Psychotherapy Research Group. (1987). *The psychoanalytic process: Theory, clinical observation, and empirical research.* New York: Guilford.
Zajonc, R. B., & Markus, H. (1984). Affect and cognition: The hard interface. In C. E. Izard, J. Kagan & R. B. Zajonc (Eds.), *Emotions, cognition and behavior.* Cambridge: Cambridge University Press.

Summary and Conclusions

Common and Differentiating Features of Anxiety and Depression: Current Findings and Future Directions

David Watson
Philip C. Kendall

I. Introduction

The primary purpose of this volume has been to examine the anxiety and depressive disorders, not only in isolation (as is too commonly done), but in relation to one another. The authors have been especially concerned with identifying features unique to each disorder, as well as those common to both. An enormous literature has been reviewed in the preceding chapters, and the underlying trends are complex and not always easily discerned. Therefore, in this final section we will summarize and integrate the key findings and briefly note their implications for future theorizing and research.

II. Common (Nonspecific) Features

A. The Strong Correlation between Anxiety and Depression

The central finding in this area—to which we must necessarily return again and again—is that anxious and depressive states are strongly correlated with one another. Simply put, individuals who report significant levels of one state are also likely to experience comparable amounts of the other. Furthermore, this empirical co-occurrence is quite robust and general. It has been demonstrated in diverse subject samples (e.g., children, college students, normal adults, psychiatric patients), and with various types of assessment. That is, self-report measure of anxiety and depression are highly correlated (see Finch, Lipovsky, & Casat, Chapter 6; Gotlib & Cane, Chapter 5; Watson & Kendall, Chapter 1), but so are teachers' and clinicians' ratings of the two syndromes (Clark, Chapter 4; Finch, Lipovsky, & Casat, Chapter 6). Finally, because anxious and depressive symptoms also frequently co-occur, many patients receive both types of diagnoses (Clark, Chapter 4; Williams & Poling, Chapter 11).

B. Explanations for the Correlation: Current Methods of Assessment

Why are anxiety and depression so strongly related? To some extent, their co-occurrence reflects the way in which they are currently measured. Two points seem especially important. First, Clark (Chapter 4) and Gotlib and Cane (Chapter 5) note that that current conceptualizations of anxiety and depression share several symptom criteria. For example, in the *Diagnostic and Statistical Manual of Mental Disorders* (DSM-III-R; American Psychiatric Association, 1987), symptoms such as restlessness, fatigability, loss of energy, difficulty concentrating, and insomnia are criteria for both anxiety and depressive disorders. We emphasize that this is not necessarily inappropriate—if these symptoms are, in fact, meaningful criteria of both types of disorder, then it is certainly valid to include them in both. However, this content overlap inevitably produces some correlation between the disorders and the measures designed to assess them.

Second, Gotlib and Cane (Chapter 5) demonstrate that many commonly used assessment scales are simply poor measures of the intended constructs. Gotlib and Cane show that, regardless of their label, self-report scales in this area tap symptomatology relevant to anxiety, depression, and several other disorders. Thus, these measures generally lack discriminant validity—that is, although they are significantly correlated with other measures of the target disorder, they are similarly related to measures of other disorders as well. It is noteworthy that most of these scales were developed before the co-occurrence problem was widely appreciated, when discriminant validity was not viewed as an important concern. Clearly, new measures need to be developed with a greater regard for discriminant validity, a point we will return to later.

C. Explanations for the Correlation: Co-occurrence of Affects and Symptoms

Clearly, however, these methodological problems are insufficient to explain the strong observed correlation between anxiety and depression. The two disorders remain highly related even when valid, nonoverlapping measures are used. Perhaps the most basic explanation for their co-occurrence is that anxiety and depression are both negative affective conditions involving substantial levels of subjective distress. Furthermore, as we discussed in Chapter 1, subjective distress is characterized by a very strong general factor, so that the various negative emotions (fear, anger, guilt, sadness, etc.) tend to co-occur. Thus, although anxious mood is centered on the emotion of fear, whereas depression is best characterized by sadness or grief, these negative affects are themselves strongly correlated empirically. Consequently, anxious and depressed mood are highly related to one another.

More generally, Clark (Chapter 4) demonstrates that other nonoverlapping manifestations of anxiety and depression are also empirically correlated, so that many individuals will report clinically significant symptoms of both disorders. For example, patients with anxiety disorders are also likely to report various depressive symptoms, such as loss of appetite and suicidal ideation; conversely, depressed patients frequently experience significant levels of anxious symptomatology (e.g., autonomic symptoms associated with panic). Given these symptom data, it is not surprising that the full-blown clinical disorders also strongly co-occur. In fact, Clark (Chapter 4) summarizes data suggesting that approximately half of the patients diagnosed as having one type of disorder also receive some diagnosis of the other (see also Williams & Poling, Chapter 11).

D. Common Precursors and Concomitants

The book's contributors have also noted several general classes of precipitating and/or concomitant factors that are common to the two disorders. Some of these factors may further explain the strong association between them; others may simply reflect it.

Nezu and D'Zurilla (Chapter 10) conclude that deficits in problem-solving abilities lead to various negative affects, including both anxiety and depression. Regarding more specific deficits, Foa, Olasov Rothbaum, and Kozak (Chapter 14) discuss Lewinsohn's (1975) argument that depressed individuals lack the social skills necessary to obtain reinforcement from the environment. Similarly, Stokes and McKirnan (Chapter 9) review the literature indicating that the loss of social support (which may reflect deficient social skills) is associated with depression and other negative consequences. However, neither poor social skills nor the loss of social support have been widely studied in relation to anxiety, so it is currently unclear whether they represent common or differentiating features.

Stressful life events also show nonspecific effects with regard to anxiety and depression. Smith and Allred (Chapter 7) considered the impact of major life changes, while Zautra, Guarnaccia, and Reich (Chapter 8) examined the literature regarding more mundane daily life events. Both reviews showed that negative life events (whether major or minor) are generally associated with substantial levels of subjective distress, including both anxiety and depression. At the level of mundane events, Zautra et al. conclude that the effects are largely nonspecific—that is, negative daily events are associated with comparable increases in anxiety, depression, and other negative affects as well. However, although Smith and Allred also find that major life changes are associated with heightened levels of both anxiety and depression, they also find some evidence for specificity (to be discussed later).

Several contributors (see especially Clark & Beck, Chapter 13; Foa, Olasov Rothbaum, & Kozak, Chapter 14; Kendall & Ingram, Chapter 2) have emphasized that anxiety and depression are both strongly characterized by maladaptive cognitive processes. That is, anxiety and depression both involve a negative self-view, heightened self-focused attention, negative automatic thoughts, and dysfunctional beliefs. Anxious and depressed patients also tend to have rigid and concrete cognitive structures (Clark & Beck, Chapter 13), to misinterpret events in the environment (Foa et al., Chapter 14), and to exhibit biased, negativistic information processing, both in the encoding of incoming material, and in the retrieval of stored information (Clark & Beck, Chapter 13; Kendall & Ingram, Chapter 2). However, although anxiety and depression share several dysfunctional cognitive *processes,* they show some specificity in their cognitive *content,* as we will discuss later.

Safran and Greenberg (Chapter 15), also working from an information-processing perspective, view emotions as adaptive responses that are biologically "hard-wired" at birth, but that are also subject to various learning influences. Most importantly, when the communication of an affect results in negative consequences, an individual will likely stop expressing it, and may stop consciously experiencing it as well. This dysfunctional blocking of emotional experience leads to various responses, including anxiety or depression, where anxiety is viewed as a flight/fight response, and depression is seen in terms of conservation/withdrawal. Thus, Safran and Greenberg's model contains both nonspecific and discriminating features with regard to the two disorders.

Finally, several authors (Clark, Chapter 4; Finch, Lipovsky, & Casat, Chapter 6; Watson & Kendall, Chapter 1; Williams & Poling, Chapter 11) review evidence indicating that at least some forms of anxiety and depression may share a common biological/genetic diathesis. Specifically, the data strongly suggest some commonality between panic disorder and major depression: Family and twin studies indicate that these disorders are genetically related, while psychopharmocological studies have demonstrated that both can be effectively treated with tricyclic antidepressants (see Clark, Chapter 4; Watson & Kendall, Chapter 1).

III. Critical, Differentiating Features

Despite their strong correlation, and the many common features we have noted, anxiety and depression are clearly not identical or interchangeable constructs. The contributors to this volume discussed several important distinctive aspects of the two disorders that we will briefly summarize in the following section. We emphasize that although each of these aspects has received some support as a critical feature, more research is needed to determine the ultimate value of each as a differentiator. Moreover, as we will see, these differences between anxiety and depression are best viewed as *relative,* rather than *absolute*—that is, most of these features can be found in both disorders, but they more strongly or centrally characterize one or the other.

A. Cognitive Content

Several contributors have noted that the content of the maladaptive cognitions seen in both anxiety and depression differs systematically between the two disorders (Clark & Beck, Chapter 13; Foa, Olasov Rothbaum, & Kozak, Chapter 14; Kendall & Ingram, Chapter 2; Rehm, Chapter 3). Specifically, anxiety is associated with an uncertain, future-oriented cognitive state in which the individual anticipates the possibility of threat or harm. In contrast, depression is more a past-centered state in which the individual focuses on some actual or perceived loss, failure, or degradation: Depressives tend to view the future pessimistically as an inevitable, hopeless extension of the past and present (Clark & Beck, Chapter 13; Kendall & Ingram, Chapter 2; see also Beck, Brown, Steer, Eidelson, & Riskind, 1987; Tellegen, 1985). Again, however, we emphasize that these divergent cognitive modes represent relative, rather than absolute, differences between the disorders (e.g., Beck et al., 1987).

These content differences are paralleled in the biased processing and retrieval of information seen in the two disorders. Compared to depressives, anxious patients are more hypervigilant to signs of threat or harm in the environment, and characteristically overestimate the possibility of danger (Clark & Beck, Chapter 13; Foa et al., Chapter 14); they also differentially recall stimuli related to anxiety and threat (Clark & Beck, Chapter 13; Kendall & Ingram, Chapter 2; see also Ingram, Kendall, Smith, Donnell, & Ronan, 1987). Conversely, depressives differentially process and recall information related to loss and failure; they also tend to discount positive self-referent information (Clark & Beck, Chapter 13; Foa, Olasov Rothbaum, & Kozak, Chapter 14; Kendall & Ingram, Chapter 2).

A related difference concerns the self-views of anxious and depressive individuals. As noted earlier, both disorders involve a negative self-schema, but this negative self-view appears to be a stronger and more central aspect of depression (Clark & Beck, Chapter 13; Foa, Olasov Rothbaum, & Kozak, Chapter 14; Kendall & Ingram, Chapter 2). More than the anxious, depressives view themselves as worthless, unlovable, and rejected by others. They also have a stronger sense of perceived failure and incompetence. Foa et al. (Chapter 14) review evidence indicating that depressives have low expectations for success, and that they characteristically see themselves as incapable of performing the behaviors necessary for success or reward. Thus, the picture in depression is one of generally lower self-esteem, with a greater perceived sense of worthlessness and ineffectuality.

B. Life Stress

As noted earlier, Smith and Allred (Chapter 7) found that negative life changes are associated with increased levels of both anxiety and depression. However, they also reported some interesting evidence for specificity. First, negative events were more highly correlated with depression than anxiety when initial distress levels were controlled, indicating a stronger association with the former. Second, specific types of events were differentially associated with the two disorders. That is, events involving a loss (e.g., death of a spouse) were more strongly related to depression, whereas those involving threat or danger were differentially associated with anxiety. This pattern obviously parallels the cognitive content differences noted previously, and suggests that they may have a realistic basis in the life experiences of anxious and depressed individuals. However, Smith and Allred emphasize the tentative nature of these findings, especially given the dearth of studies relating life stress to anxiety.

C. Pleasurable Affects and Events

As we have discussed, anxiety and depression are both states of high negative affect. The positive emotions, however, are differentially related to the two disorders. Specifically, depression—but not anxiety—involves the loss of pleasurable life events and a corresponding deficit in positive emotional experiences (e.g., joy, excitement, enthusiasm; see Foa, Olasov Rothbaum, & Kozak, Chapter 14; Gotlib & Cane, Chapter 5; Rehm, Chapter 3; Watson & Kendall, Chapter 1). That is, both disorders are states of strong subjective distress (i.e., high levels of negative affect), but only depression involves an additional affective *deficit*—the absence of enjoyable, pleasurable activities (i.e., low levels of positive affect). Behavioristic models of depression describe this phenomenon in terms of reinforcement; they emphasize that depressed individuals obtain insufficient reinforcers from the environment (see Foa, Olasov Rothbaum, & Kozak, Chapter 14; Rehm, Chapter 3). Watson and Kendall (Chapter 1), on the other hand, focus on the affective deficit itself (i.e., the absence of positive emotional experiences).

Foa et al. (Chapter 14) discuss various explanations for this pleasure deficit. Ferster's (1973) early behavioristic model emphasized the lack of available reinforcers in the environment, whereas Lewinsohn (1974, 1975) stressed the importance of response-contingent reward. In both of these views, depressives lack a sufficient number of rewarding, pleasurable activities in their lives. However, other models deemphasize the role of the environment, and focus instead on the inability of the depressed individual to derive pleasure from normally hedonic activities, either for psychological (e.g., Costello, 1972) or biological reasons (Klein, 1974; Meehl, 1975).

It must be emphasized that these environmental and person-centered explanations are not necessarily incompatible. Each may apply to different subtypes of depression—some depressives may lack sufficient reinforcement in their environment, whereas others are incapable of deriving satisfaction from normally rewarding events. It is also possible that both processes can be observed in the same individual. For example, because of their decreased ability to experience pleasure, depressives may reduce their rate of reward-seeking behavior, thus leading to an objective lack of reinforcement in their lives as well.

D. Behavioral Differences

Consistent with this view, various contributors have commented on the reduced level of adaptive, reward-seeking behavior in depression (Foa, Olasov Rothbaum, & Kozak, Chapter 14; Safran & Greenberg, Chapter 15). Generally speaking, depression can be viewed as a withdrawal from normal patterns of behavior (Safran & Greenberg, Chapter 15). Thus, it is associated with a lower level of behavior and a lower level of autonomic arousal than anxiety (Foa, Olasov Rothbaum, & Kozak, Chapter 14; Rehm, Chapter 3; Safran & Greenberg, Chapter 15; see also Akiskal, 1985). Kasper and Rosenthal (Chapter 12), in fact, speculate that depression may have originally been an evolutionarily adaptive response of energy conservation. In any event, because of this reduced level of activity, behavioral treatments for depression frequently involve *increasing* the patient's level of adaptive behavior.

Anxiety, in contrast, is viewed more as a flight/fight response, with concomitant autonomic symptoms and heightened arousal (Foa, Olasov Rothbaum, & Kozak, Chapter 14; Rehm, Chapter 3; Safran & Greenberg, Chapter 15; see also Akiskal, 1985). Rehm (Chapter 3) and Safran and Greenberg (Chapter 15) both discuss the possible evolutionary significance of this flight/fight pattern. Anxiety is also associated with increased levels of maladaptive responding (e.g., phobic avoidance behaviors, compulsive rituals, and the autonomic symptoms of panic). Thus, behavioral treatment of anxiety typically focuses on *eliminating or reducing* these maladaptive responses.

E. Temporal Patterning Differences

Several contributors have noted that some forms of depression show interesting temporal patterning effects that apparently reflect systematic, endogenous oscillations. Some depressive disorders vary in frequency over the course of the year (winter onset is more common; Kasper & Rosenthal, Chapter 12) and in intensity over the course of the day (e.g., worse in the morning in melancholia; Clark, Chapter 4; Watson & Kendall, Chapter 1). The reasons for these systematic fluctuations in depression are not yet clear, but several investigators have suggested that they reflect a basic disruption of the normal circadian rhythm that may be etiologically implicated in some forms of the disorder (see Healy & Williams, 1988, for review). Less attention has been given to anxiety in this area, but the available research suggests that it does not exhibit comparably strong or consistent patterns (e.g., Clark, Watson, & Leeka, 1988). Thus, these patterning differences would seem to be a promising area for future exploration.

IV. Implications of the Findings and Directions for Future Research

The data discussed in this volume clearly have significant implications for future research and theorizing on anxiety and depression. We will begin by noting some important directions for future research.

A. Research Implications

Above all, the discussions in the preceding chapters underscore the necessity for more (and more systematic) research in this area. For example, several contributors noted the relative paucity of research on anxiety in the literatures they examined (Clark & Beck, Chapter 3; Kasper & Rosenthal, Chapter 12; Nezu & D'Zurilla, Chapter 10; Stokes & McKirnan, Chapter 9), making it difficult if not impossible to identify common versus differentiating factors in these areas.

Moreover, the findings have important implications for how future research should be conducted. Most importantly, the data demonstrate that anxiety and depression are so highly correlated that they cannot be meaningfully studied in isolation from one another. Thus, future research should—whenever possible—examine both types of disorder concurrently. Without the concomitant assessment of both affects, it is virtually impossible to interpret any significant effects that emerge.

For example, if an investigator finds that a measure of dysfunctional attitudes is significantly correlated with a self-report depression scale, it is inappropriate to conclude that dysfunctional attitudes are specifically related to depression. That is, given the strong observed correlations between self-report measures of anxiety and depression, it is highly likely that a similar correlation would be obtained between dysfunctional attitudes and anxiety. Furthermore, because of the general distress factor noted previously, almost any subjective distress measure will likely yield comparable results. Indeed, recent studies (Gotlib, 1984; Nezu, Nezu, & Nezu, 1986; Zurawski & Smith, 1987) indicate that many measures of dysfunctional attitudes, irrational beliefs, and attributional style are nonspecifically related to diverse indicators of subjective distress, including depression, anxiety, hostility, unassertiveness, and psychosomatic complaints.

Because of this general distress factor, the specificity of relationships can never be assumed. If a single affect is studied in isolation, the safest conclusion is that any observed effects reflect general, nonspecific distress, rather than any single affect or disorder (for an extended discussion, see Kendall, Hollon, Beck, Hammen, & Ingram, 1987). Thus, a better approach is to examine anxiety, depression, and other types of distress (e.g., anger, unassertiveness, loneliness) concurrently. If several affects show comparable effects, then one can conclude that the findings simply reflect the general distress factor. On the other hand, if only one affect shows a significant relation—or if it has a stronger association that remains significant even when the influence of the other affects is partialled out—then one has evidence for specificity.

Several recent articles exemplify this more comprehensive approach, investigating the specificity of factors such as automatic thoughts, attributional style, cognitive interference, and biased information processing (Ingram et al., 1987); thought content (Beck et al., 1987); attributional style and attitudes toward the self (Ganellen, 1988); and positive and negative affective states (Watson, Clark, & Carey, 1988). Future studies along these lines will surely enhance our understanding of depression and anxiety.

Also needed are studies that directly examine the relation between anxiety and depression at various levels, including further investigations of the content of—and correlations among—self-report and clinical rating scales; analyses of symptom and diagnostic co-occurrence; and family, twin, and pharmacological studies of common biological/genetic diatheses (see Clark, Chapter 4; Finch, Lipovsky, & Casat, Chapter 6; Gotlib & Cane, Chapter 5; Williams & Poling, Chapter 11). Ideally, such studies should use only measures that have been shown to have acceptable convergent and discriminant validity.

In this regard, the construct validation of anxiety and depression measures is another important topic for future research. The most informative approach involves a multitrait–multimethod design in which anxiety and depression (and perhaps other constructs as well) are assessed in various ways (e.g., through self-report, teachers' or clinicians' ratings, symptom or diagnostic data). Wolfe et al. (1987) provide an excellent demonstration of the value of this design in testing the convergent/discriminant validity of measures of related constructs (see also

Clark, Chapter 4; Finch, Lipovsky, & Casat, Chapter 6; Gotlib & Cane, Chapter 5).

In exploring the commonality between depression and anxiety, it is also important to examine relations among more specific syndromes. Clark (Chapter 4), for example, concluded that—at least at the symptom level—certain of the anxious and depressive disorders are more differentiable than others. Specifically, symptoms of panic disorder/agoraphobia can be clearly differentiated from those of endogenous depression, whereas manifestations of generalized anxiety disorder are not easily separable from those of dysthymia. These data caution us against adopting a simplistic model in which anxiety and depression are viewed as monolithic entities, and indicate that the relations among specific disorders deserve further examination.

Finally, several contributors have noted that the course, duration, and temporal relation of the disorders need to be examined more thoroughly (Clark, Chapter 4; Gotlib & Cane, Chapter 5; Kendall & Ingram, Chapter 2). For example, Clark (Chapter 4) found that although the mere presence of depressed affect was not a useful discriminating factor, persistently depressed mood significantly differentiated depressed from anxious patients. Thus, future research should not simply assess anxiety and depression on a single occasion, but should study their course and duration over time (see also Breier, Charney, & Heninger, 1985).

B. Assessment Implications

Several contributors have demonstrated that many existing anxiety and depression instruments are inadequate measures of the target disorders (see especially Clark, Chapter 4; Gotlib and Cane, Chapter 5). As discussed previously, the primary problem is that these measures are highly correlated with one another and with other types of subjective distress as well. These correlations are not confined simply to self-reports, but are also found with many clinical measures (e.g., clinicians' ratings, symptom, and diagnostic instruments). Further, these measures generally show poor discriminant validity, so that their validity as specific measures of anxiety or depression is highly suspect. However, this is not to say that these measures are therefore worthless or uninteresting. In fact, most are good, reliable measures of general distress or dysphoria, which is a dimension of considerable psychological significance (see Gotlib, 1984; Kendall et al., 1987; Watson & Clark, 1984; Wolfe et al., 1987; Zurawski & Smith, 1987).

Given the poor discriminant validity of most existing measures, the development of more specific and differentiated measures of anxiety and depression should clearly be a major focus of future research. Improved differentiation can be achieved in various ways. An obvious and easy first step is to remove any symptomatology that is not clearly relevant to the target construct (for examples and a discussion, see Gotlib & Cane, Chapter 5). Another possibility is to remove item content that is common to the two disorders (Clark, Chapter 4; Gotlib & Cane, Chapter 5). Riskind, Beck, Brown, and Steer (1987) used this latter approach with the Hamilton Psychiatric Rating Scales for Anxiety (Hamilton, 1959) and Depression (Hamilton, 1960). Because of their substantial content overlap, the standard Hamilton scales are strongly correlated with one another. However, by reducing this overlap, Riskind et al. were able to lower this correlation somewhat, and to improve the discriminant validity of the resulting scales.

The critical, differentiating features we reviewed previously also offer a useful guide for future assessment. As noted by various contributors (e.g., Clark, Chapter 4; Gotlib & Cane, Chapter 5; Watson & Kendall, Chapter 1), many existing measures overemphasize phenomena that—although they are certainly relevant to the anxiety and depressive disorders—are nevertheless common to both. Depression and anxiety scales that strongly weight these nonspecific features will inevitably be strongly correlated with one another.

Thus, to improve discrimination, more weight should be given to those aspects of the disorders that successfully differentiate between them. For example, rather than emphasizing the experience of negative affect or subjective distress (a feature common to both anxiety and depression; see Finch, Lipovsky, & Casat, Chapter 6; Watson & Kendall, Chapter 1), depression measures should more strongly assess the lack of positive emotional experiences (a critical, differentiating feature). Similarly, rather than simply assessing the presence of negative thoughts and beliefs, anxiety and depression scales should measure cognitive content that is specific to each (see Clark & Beck, Chapter 13; Kendall & Ingram, Chapter 2). Beck et al. (1987) recently used this approach to develop content-specific measures of depression and anxiety that showed good convergent/discriminant validity when correlated with clinical ratings of the disorders.

Greater attention to these differentiating features should improve the discrimination between anxiety and depression measures. Nevertheless, it is unrealistic to believe that perfect differentiation is possible (or even desirable, a point we will return to shortly). That is, anxiety and depression scales are likely to remain significantly related, even when these critical aspects are strongly weighted. Clark (Chapter 4) noted that even the symptoms that best differentiate the disorders reflect relative, rather than absolute, differences between them. That is, they are not invariably present in one disorder and absent in the other; rather, they are simply more frequently reported in one than the other.

Moreover, many of these critical features are themselves strongly correlated with one another. For example, we have mentioned that anxious thought content is dominated by anticipated threat or harm, whereas depressive cognitions focus more on loss and failure. And, as noted previously, Beck et al. (1987) developed content-specific scales of anxiety and depression that showed good convergent/discriminant validity in relation to clinical ratings. However, in two patient samples, these scales correlated .58 and .57 with one another. Thus, a large number of patients reported cognitions characteristic of both disorders—that is, they reported thoughts related to both loss/failure and danger/threat. It seems inevitable that a great many patients will report symptoms and manifestations of both disorders, regardless of how they are conceptualized and assessed.

This leads us to consider the related issue of how strongly measures of anxiety and depression *should be related*. We believe that better discrimination (i.e., a lower intercorrelation) is desirable, but we do not thereby assume that increasing differentiation invariably yields better validity. On the contrary, it seems likely that beyond a certain point greater discriminant validity will be achieved at the expense of good convergent validity. For example, suppose one were to eliminate entirely the nonspecific negative affect/subjective distress component from depression scales, making them instead measures of (the lack of) positive emotionality. This would certainly produce better differentiation of depression from anxiety, but at what cost? It seems unlikely that one can assess depression validly without tapping subjective distress; hence, this approach would probably lead to significantly poorer convergent validity.

The danger is that an overemphasis on discrimination may lead to the development of measures that do not optimally assess the underlying disorders. Thus, any attempt at improved differentiation should be carefully examined, and its implications for both convergent and discriminant validity should be fully investigated. For example, Clark (Chapter 4) noted that that clinicians' ratings of anxiety and depression are more independent when they are generated as part of a diagnostic process. Is this greater independence associated with increased or lowered diagnostic validity? Only further research can answer this question.

C. Clinical/Diagnostic Implications

Many of the considerations noted in the last section apply here as well. First, as was discussed earlier, clinical manifestations of anxiety and depression also strongly co-occur. Thus, many individuals report clinically significant symptoms of both disorders; in fact, approximately half of those with one type of disorder diagnosis also receive some diagnosis of the other (Clark, Chapter 4; Williams & Poling, Chapter 11).

Given this strong co-occurrence, greater attention should be focused on the differential diagnosis of the anxious and depressive disorders. Consistent with our earlier discussion, differentiation could be improved in various ways—by reducing the importance of overlapping symptom criteria (e.g., restlessness, loss of energy, inability to concentrate, insomnia), by deemphasizing common, nonspecific symptomatology (e.g., loss of appetite, suicidal ideation, dysphoric mood), and by giving greater weight to distinctive aspects of the disorders (e.g., cognitive content differences, lack of pleasurable experiences in depression). Again, however, efforts at improved differentiation may lead to unforseen and undesirable sequelae; thus, the consequences of any criterion changes should be carefully investigated.

Another possible approach to this problem is to recognize that anxiety and depression cannot be meaningfully differentiated in many patients; that is, to recognize formally the existence of a large, nondifferentiable subgroup of patients with mixed anxiety/depression (see Clark, Chapter 4; Gersh & Fowles, 1979). Adopting this approach would involve restructuring Axis I of the DSM-III-R (APA, 1987) so that the anxiety and depressive disorders are no longer classified separately, but are instead combined into a superordinate *mood disorders* category. Within this broadened grouping, individuals who exhibit predominantly anxious symptomatology would be placed within the *anxiety disorders* subcategory, whereas those reporting mostly depressive complaints would be put into the depressive spectrum. Finally, those reporting comparable levels of both would be given the diagnosis of anxious depression; or, recognizing the nonspecific nature of subjective distress, it might be preferable to use a more inclusive term, such as *generalized mood disorder*.

Regardless of the specific classification scheme that is adopted, the accumulated data suggest that a substantial number of patients could be put into a mixed anxiety/depression group (see Clark, Chapter 4; see also Breier, Charney, & Heninger, 1985: Gersh & Fowles, 1979). Given its size and potential importance, this mixed patient group surely warrants more research attention.

Clark (Chapter 4) suggests a parallel development for Axis II. Specifically, she proposes the creation of a new personality disorder—which might be termed *dysphoric personality disorder*—for patients who report chronic, intense, and nonspecific distress [these would be extreme cases of what Watson and Clark (1984) call "high Negative Affectivity" individuals]. This category would likely draw patients who are currently included in the anxiety disorders (especially those with generalized anxiety disorder), the depressive spectrum (notably those diagnosed with dysthymia), and the personality disorders (e.g., avoidant personality disorder). Again, this is likely to be a large and important patient group that deserves further study.

V. Concluding Remarks

A recurrent theme in this volume is that anxiety and depression are closely related constructs, both theoretically and empirically. Indeed, given the strong correlation between them, it has become increasingly clear that they cannot be meaningfully studied in isolation, but must necessarily be examined together. The contributing authors have reviewed various topics relevant to their interrelation, have noted some problems and gaps in the existing research, and have suggested several promising avenues for future study. Obviously, work in this area has only just begun. If this volume serves to stimulate further inquiry into the relation between depression and anxiety, then it has served its purpose.

References

Akiskal, H. S. (1985). Anxiety: Definition, relationship to depression, and proposal for an integrative model. In A. H. Tuma & J. D. Maser (Eds.), *Anxiety and the anxiety disorders* (pp. 787–797). Hillsdale, NJ: Erlbaum.

American Psychiatric Association. (1987). *Diagnostic and statistical manual of mental disorders* (3rd ed., rev.). Washington, DC: Author.

Beck, A. T., Brown, G., Steer, R. A., Eidelson, J. I., & Riskind, J. H. (1987). Differentiating anxiety and depression: A test of the cognitive content specificity hypothesis. *Journal of Abnormal Psychology, 96,* 179–183.

Breier, A., Charney, D. S., & Heninger, G. R. (1985). The diagnostic validity of anxiety disorders and their relationship to depressive illness. *American Journal of Psychiatry, 142,* 787–797.

Clark, L. A., Watson, D., & Leeka, J. (1988). *Diurnal variation in positive affect: A robust psychobiological phenomenon.* Manuscript submitted for publication.

Costello, C. G. (1972). Depression: Loss of reinforcers or loss of reinforcer effectiveness? *Behavior Therapy, 3,* 240–247.

Ferster, C. B. (1973). A functional analysis of depression. *American Psychologist, 28,* 857–870.

Ganellen, R. J. (1988). Specificity of attributions and overgeneralization in depression and anxiety. *Journal of Abnormal Psychology, 97,* 83–86.

Gersh, F. S., & Fowles, D. C. (1979). Neurotic depression: The concept of anxious depression. In R. A. Depue (Ed.), *The psychobiology of the depressive disorders: Implications for the effects of stress* (pp. 81–104). New York: Academic Press.

Gotlib, I. H. (1984). Depression and general psychopathology in university students. *Journal of Abnormal Psychology, 93,* 19–30.

Hamilton, M. (1959). The assessment of anxiety states by rating. *British Journal of Medical Psychology, 32,* 50–55.

Hamilton, M. (1960). A rating scale for depression. *Journal of Neurology, Neurosurgery, and Psychiatry, 23,* 56–61.

Healy, D., & Williams, J. M. G. (1988). Dysrhythmia, dysphoria, and depression: The interaction of learned helplessness and circadian dysrhythmia in the pathogenesis of depression. *Psychological Bulletin, 103,* 163–178.

Ingram, R. E., Kendall, P. C., Smith, T. W., Donnell, C., & Ronan, K. (1987). Cognitive specificity in emotional distress. *Journal of Personality and Social Psychology, 53,* 734–742.

Kendall, P. C., Hollon, S. D., Beck, A. T., Hammen, C. L., & Ingram, R. E. (1987). Issues and recommendations regarding use of the Beck Depression Inventory. *Cognitive Therapy and Research, 11,* 289–299.

Klein, D. F. (1974). Endogenomorphic depression: A conceptual and terminological revision. *Archives of General Psychiatry, 31,* 447–454.

Lewinsohn, P. M. (1974). Clinical and theoretical aspects of depression. In K. S. Calhoun, H. E. Adams, & K. M. Mitchell (Eds.), *Innovative treatment methods in psychopathology* (pp. 63–120). New York: Wiley.

Lewinsohn, P. M. (1975). The behavioral study and treatment of depression. In M. Hersen, R. M. Eisler, & P. M. Miller (Eds.), *Progress in behavioral modification* (Vol. 1, pp. 19–64). New York: Academic Press.

Meehl, P. E. (1975). Hedonic capacity: Some conjectures. *Bulletin of the Menninger Clinic, 39,* 295–307.

Nezu, A. M., Nezu, C. M., & Nezu, V. A. (1986). Depression, general distress, and causal attributions among university students. *Journal of Abnormal Psychology, 95,* 184–186.

Riskind, J. H., Beck, A. T., Brown, G., & Steer, R. A. (1987). Taking the measure of anxiety and depression: Validity of reconstructed Hamilton Scales. *Journal of Nervous and Mental Disease, 175,* 474–479.

Tellegen, A. (1985). Structures of mood and personality and their relevance to assessing anxiety, with an emphasis on self-report. In A. H. Tuma & J. D. Maser (Eds.), *Anxiety and the anxiety disorders* (pp. 681–706). Hillsdale, NJ: Erlbaum.

Watson, D., & Clark, L. A. (1984). Negative Affectivity: The disposition to experience aversive emotional states. *Psychological Bulletin, 96,* 465–490.

Watson, D., Clark, L. A., & Carey, G. (1988). Positive and Negative Affectivity and their relation to anxiety and depressive disorders. *Journal of Abnormal Psychology, 97,* 346–353.

Wolfe, V. V., Finch, A. J., Jr., Saylor, C. F., Blount, R. L., Pallmeyer, T. P., & Carek, D. J. (1987). Negative Affectivity in children: A multitrait-multimethod investigation. *Journal of Consulting and Clinical Psychology, 55,* 245–250.

Zurawski, R. M., & Smith, T. W. (1987). Assessing irrational beliefs and emotional distress: Evidence and implications of limited discriminant validity. *Journal of Counseling Psychology, 34,* 224–227.

Index

A

Adjective Check List for Anxiety, 148–149
Affective change, 455–485
Affective disorders, *see also* Depression
  diagnostic categories, 86
  and disasters, 334
  prevalence, 328–329
Affectivity, *see also* Emotion; Negative Affectivity (NA); Positive Affectivity (PA)
  analyses of mood, 9–12
  assessment, 20–22
  correlation with symptoms, 14–16
  negative emotions, 7–9, 117
  positive emotions, 9–12, 19–22, 499–500
  relation to anxiety and depression, 3–22, 117
  relation to endogenous depression, 19–20
Agoraphobia, 5, 36, 84, 87, 103–104, 110–115, 213, 402–403, 417, 422–424, 428, 472
  heritability, 117
  prevalence, 328–329
  relation to depression, 103–104, 110–115
Agoraphobia Cognitions Questionnaire (ACQ), 386
Anxiety
  adolescents, 171–196
  affective change processes, 455–485
  behavioral theory, 55–74, 415–419
  behavioral treatments, 419–433
  biological correlates, 188–192
  catastrophic, 473–474
  children, 171–196
  cognitive features, 32–38, 44–48, 60
  cognitive theory, 379–396
  cognitive therapy, 396–405
  cognitive-behavioral treatment, 467–468
  common features with depression, 494–497
  comorbidity with depression, 97–99, 109–116, 328–330, 336
  as conditioned emotional response, 64–66
  correlation with depression, 4–5, 29–31, 92–94, 155–160, 494
  daily life events, 225–229
  diagnostic categories, 87–88, 505–507
  diagnostic criteria, 87–88, 133–135
  differentiating from depression, 122, 497–501
  emotional basis, 6–9
  and emotional processing, 464–474
  epidemiology, 317–336
  factor analyses, 94–95
  future directions, 501–506
  information processing model, 380–394
  life events, 205–219
  and performance, 60
  pharmacological treatments, 118
  plus depression, 118–121
  rating scales, 89–94
  related to affect, 3–21
  as secondary response, 471–473
  self-reports, 142–150, *see also* individual scales by name
  social problem solving, 285–310
  social supports, 275–279
  stress and coping, 67–68
  symptom overlap with depression, 102–109, 135
  thought content, 32–38

Anxiety Diagnostic Interview Schedule (ADIS), 89
Anxiety Management Training (AMT), 420, 429–431
Anxious Self-Statement Questionnaire (ASSQ), 35, 386
Assessment, *see also* individual scales by name
  behavioral/observational, 180–182
  with children and adolescents, 177–183
  diagnostic, 88–92, 97–99
  discriminant validity, 84, 95–97, 150–155, 503–505
  future directions, 503–505
  interviews with children, 182–183
  issues, 83–196, 503–505
  of life events, 207–209
  of positive affect, 21–22
  self-report, 131–163, 494–495
  of social support, 255–257
At risk, 319–320, *see also* Epidemiology
Attachment, 459, 465–467
Attributional Style Questionnaire (ASQ), 393
Attributions, 36, 48, 70, 436, 504
  about daily life events, 233–234
Automatic questioning, 35–36, 394
Automatic thoughts, 31, 73, 384–385, 468, 502
Automatic Thoughts Questionnaire (ATQ), 21, 32–33, 35, 47, 386

B

Beck Depression Inventory (BDI), 4, 12, 137–139, 151–154, 161, 215, 234, 297–298, 301–304, 433
  recommendations for, 40, 137
Behavioral models, 55–76, 415–419
Behavioral treatments, 419–433
Bereavement, 240–242, 248–249
Biofeedback, 430
Bioinformational theory, 66–67
Biological adaptation, 458
Biological correlates of affectivity
  in children, 188–192

C

Center for Epidemiological Studies Depression Scale (CES-D), 139–140
Child Behavior Checklist (CBCL), 180–181, 184–188
Children
  anxiety in depressed children, 173–175
  biological correlates of depression and anxiety, 188–192
  depression in anxious children, 175–177
  school phobia, 175
Children's Depression Inventory (CDI), 13, 177–178, 183–188
Children's Depression Scale (CDS), 178–179
Clinician's illusion, 325, 337
Cognitions Checklist, 386
Cognitive content of anxiety and depression, 497–498
Cognitive Interference Questionnaire (CIQ), 33
Cognitive operations, 43–48, 384, 387–388
Cognitive products, 44–48, 384–387
Cognitive propositions, 43–48
Cognitive structures, 43–48, *see also* Schemata
  fear-related, 417–419
Cognitive taxonomy, 43–45, 381–384
Cognitive theory, 379–396, 458
Cognitive therapy
  anxiety, 396–400
  behavioral procedures, 399-400
  cognitive strategies, 398–399
  depression, 396–400
  empirical status, 400–404
Cognitive-behavioral perspectives, 27–54
  in anxiety, 32–38, 44–48, 60, 415–419
  in depression, 44–48, 72–75, 379–396, 433–437
Collaborative empiricism, 397
Comorbidity of anxiety and depression, 97–99, 109–116, 328–330, 336
Conditioning theory, 415–417
Conners Parent Questionnaire (CPQ), 181, 185
Costello-Comrey Anxiety and Depression Scales, 146–147, 161
Covi Anxiety Scale, 93, 95
Crandell Cognition Inventory, 386

D

Depression
  adolescents, 171–196
  affective change processes, 455–485

antidepressant medications, 6, 118, 190
behavioral theory, 55–74, 68–72, 433–437
behavioral treatments, 437–443
biological correlates, 188–192
children, 171–196
cognitive disconnection, 477–480
cognitive features, 44–48
cognitive theory, 44–48, 72–75, 379–396
cognitive therapy, 396–405, 431–432, 483
common features with anxiety, 494–497
comorbidity with anxiety, 97–99, 109–116, 328–330, 336
correlation with anxiety, 4–5, 29–31, 92–94, 155–160, 494
daily life events, 225–229
deactivation, 475–477
diagnostic criteria, 86, 132–133
differentiating from anxiety, 122, 497–501
dysfunctional beliefs, 482–484
emotional basis, 6–9
endogenous subtype, 19–20, 107, 121
epidemiology, 317–336
factor analyses, 94–95
faulty cognitions, 480–482
future directions, 501–506
information processing, 37–38, 380–394
interactional model, 272
and loss of reinforcement, 69–70, 260–261, 499–500
major life events, 205–219
plus anxiety, 118–121
rating scales, 89–94
related to basic emotions, 6–9
related to positive and negative affect, 3–31, 499–500
seasonal affective disorder, 341–369
self-control theory, 71–72, 440–441
self-reports, 131–142, 146–150
social interaction therapy, 438–439
social problem solving, 285–310
social skills training, 439–440
social supports, 253–279
symptom overlap with anxiety, 102–109, 135
thought content, 32–38
Depression Adjective Check Lists (DACL), 148–149
Dexamethasone suppression test (DST), 191–192
Diagnosis, *see also* DSM-III-R
differential, 5, 83–123, 505–507
mood and syndrome overlap, 97–99
overlap, 109–121
primary categories, anxiety, 87–88
primary categories, depression, 85–87
proposed new categories, 123, 506
reliability of clinical ratings, 88–92
specific symptoms, 99–108
Diagnostic and Statistical Manual: Third Edition—Revised, *see* DSM-III-R
Diagnostic Interview Schedule (DIS), 18, 89–90, 326
Diathesis-stress, 211–212, 218, 497, *see also* Vulnerability
Differential emotions theory, 7
Disability, 240–242, 248–249
DSM-III-R, 17–19, 28, 57–58, 62–63, 85–89, 97, 105, 113, 116, 123, 132–137, 154–156, 172, 181–182, 213, 300, 318, 325–327, 343, 414, 494, 506
dysphoric personality disorder, 506
generalized mood disorder, 123, 506
Dysfunctional Attitudes Scale (DAS), 47, 151, 388, 390
Dysphoric personality disorder, 506
Dysregulation hypothesis, 189
Dysthymia, 17–18, 133

E

Edwards Social Desirability Scale (ESDS), 158–159
Emotion, *see also* Affectivity
appraisal process, 468–469
basic perspectives, 460–464
and faulty cognitions, 480–482
incomplete processing, 484–485
interrupted experience, 462–464
mood descriptions, 9–12
negative, 7–8
positive, 9–12, 19–22, 499–500
primary, 6–9
Endogenous depression, 19–20, 86, 107, 121
Epidemiology, 110, 317–336
definition of terms, 319–321
Exposure, 400, 402, 419–424, 426–429, 432

F

Factor analysis, 11–12, 94–95, 138, 153, 184, 258, 276

Fear, 7
  of fear, 422, 425, *see also* Agoraphobia
  of negative evaluation, 467–471

G

Generalized Anxiety Disorder (GAD), 84, 87–88, 107, 110, 113, 134, 334, 383, 386–387, 402, 419, 429–431
  diagnostic criteria, 87–88, 134
  pharmacological treatment, 118
Genetic data, 5–6, 117–118, 122–123, 176–177, 333–334, 497

H

Hamilton Rating Scale of Anxiety (HRSA), 89, 92–93, 97
Hamilton Rating Scale of Depression (HRSD), 89, 90, 92–93, 97, 346, 353–358, 364, 433
Heritability, *see* Genetic data
High-risk groups
  elderly, 237–241
  families, 232
Hopkins Symptom Check List (HSCL), 13–16
Hyperventilation, 425

I

Incidence, 319, 326–330, *see also* Epidemiology
Information processing, 37–38
  and affect, 457–458
  and behavioral systems, 458–460
  and biological adaptation, 458–460
Inventory of Small Life Events (ISLE), 229–237, 239, 241
Inventory of Socially Supportive Behaviors (ISSB), 2566

L

Life Change Units (LCU), 207, 230
Life events, 391, 496, 498–499
  cognitive approach, 245
  desirable, 236
  major, 205–219, 290–291
  measurement, 207–209
  methodological issues, 216–217
  minor, 225–248, 295–296
  undesirable, 236
Life Experiences Survey (LES), 207–208
Longitudinal follow-ups, 116

M

Marlowe-Crowne Social Desirability Scale (MCSDS), 159
Means-End Problem Solving (MEPS), 297–298, 301
Melatonin, 364
Mental Health Inventory (MHI), 238
Meta-construct model, 41–48
  in anxiety and depression, 45–48
  common features, 44–45, 47–48
  critical features, 44, 47–48
Methodology, 38–41, *see also* Research
Millon Clinical Multiaxial Inventory (MCMI), 147–148, 153, 161
Minnesota Multiphasic Personality Inventory, 140–141, *see also* MMPI-D Scale
MMPI-D Scale, 140–141, 161, 299, 301, 303, 433
Mood
  vs. mood disorder, 209–210
  ratings, 92
  self-reports, 7–12
Multidimensional Personality Questionnaire (MPQ), 14
Multiple Affect Adjective Check List (MAACL), 12, 148, 151–152, 191

N

Negative Affectivity (NA), 5, 9–22, 94, 109, 117, 123, 139, 162, 171–172, 183, 193–196, 217, 231–234, 257–259, 271, 277–278, 506, *see also* Affectivity
  and diagnosis, 21, 123, 506
  and DSM-III-R, 506
  heritability, 117
  measurement, 5, 14
  related to anxiety symptoms, 14–15, 94
  related to depression symptoms, 16, 94
Neuroticism, 5, 94, 109, *see also* Negative Affectivity

O

Observer drift, 91
Obsessive-compulsive disorder, 98, 328–329, 418, 423, 426–428

P

Panic disorder, 5–6, 57, 84, 87, 113, 116, 191, 193, 213, 403–404, 424–426, 497
  heritability, 5–6, 117
  pharmacological treatment, 118
  prevalence, 328–329
Peer Nomination Inventory of Depression (PNID), 182–183, 185
Personality Inventory for Children, 181, 186
Phase-shift hypothesis, 365
Phobias, 18, 64–65, 67, 87, 110, 113, 116, 415, 417, 418, 420–422
  prevalence, 328–329
  social phobia, 18, 418
Photochemical hypothesis, 365–366
Phototherapy, 352–359
  bright vs. dim light, 356, 359–360
  duration, 361
  light spectrum, 361–362
  neuroendocrine correlates, 367–368
  phase-shift hypothesis, 365
  photochemical hypothesis, 365–366
  physiological effects, 363–368
  side effects, 362–363
  time of day, 357–358, 360
Pleasant events, 433, 499–500
  in treatment of depression, 437
Pleasant Events Schedule (PES), 434
Positive Affectivity (PA), 9–12, *see also* Affectivity
  in assessment of anxiety and depression, 504–505
  and diagnosis, 21
  measurement, 14, 21–22
  related to anxiety symptoms, 14–15
  related to depression symptoms, 16
Positive and Negative Affect Schedule (PANAS), 14–17
Posttraumatic stress disorder (PTSD), 57, 418–419, 431–433
Preparedness, 66
Present State Examination (PSE), 102
Prevalence, 319, 326–330, *see also* Epidemiology
Prevention, 335
Problem solving, *see* Social problem-solving
Problem Solving Inventory (PSI), 299
Profile of Mood States (POMS), 150
Psychiatric Epidemiology Research Interview (PERI), 208, 213, 230, 233, 235, 239
Psychopharmacology, 6, 118, 190

R

Raskin Depression Scale, 93, 95
Reactive depression, 19, 107
Relapse, 401–402
Relationship between anxiety and depression, 83–84, 92–118, 121–123, 155–160, 494–497
  diagnostic, 98–99, 109–116
  genetics, 5–6, 117–118
  pharmacological response, 6, 118
  rating scales, 92–94
  self-report scales, 4–5, 155–160
  symptoms, 5, 102–109
Reliability, 39, 88–92, 136–137, 139
Research
  assessment implications, 503–505
  diagnostic implications, 505–507
  future directions, 501–503
Response prevention, 426–427
Revised Behavior Problem Checklist (RBPC), 181–182
Revised Children's Manifest Anxiety Scale (RCMAS), 179, 186–187
Risk factors
  age, 331
  family history, 333–334
  gender, 330–331
  marital status, 332
  race/ethnicity, 332
  social class, 331–332
  urban/rural residence, 332

S

Schedule for Affective Disorders and Schizophrenia (SADS), 89–91, 140, 433
Schedule for Affective Disorders and Schizophrenia for School-Aged Children (Kiddie-SADS), 182, 187

Schedule of Recent Experiences (SRE), 207
Schemata, 72, 382–383, 385, 388–390, 461–462, 466–467, *see also* Cognitive structures; Self-schema
School phobia, 175
Seasonal Affective Disorder (SAD), 341–369
  in animals, 349–350
  demographics, 344–345
  phototherapy, 352–359
  psychobiology, 363–368
  reverse SAD, 347
  seasonality, 347–349
  symptoms, 343–347
Seasonal Pattern Assessment Questionnaire (SPAQ), 343, 369
Seasonality
  in animals, 347–349
  energy conservation, 351–352
  in normals, 347–349
  in reproduction, 350
Secondary depression, 160
Self-control therapy for depression, 440–441
Self-focused attention, 29
Self-instructions, 402–403
Self-monitoring deficits, 436–437
Self-referent information, 387, 389
Self-report scales, 4–5, 131–163, 177–183, 207–208
Self-schema, 37, 47, *see also* Schemata
Social desirability, 158–159
Social interaction therapy, 438
Social problem-solving, 285–310, 496
  and anxiety, 305–310
  coping, 291–293
  deficits, 300
  and depression, 297–305
  process, 293–295
  therapy for depression, 302–305
Social Readjustment Rating Scale (SRRS), 207–208, 227
Social skills deficits, 434–436
Social skills training, 427–428
  for depression, 439–440
Social support
  and anxiety, 275–279
  and depression, 259–273
  individual differences, 257–259
  nature of, 254–259
  objective measures, 255–257, 269
  as stress buffer, 264–271
  subjective measures, 256–257, 269
Sociotropy/Autonomy Scale (SAS), 391
Specificity, 29, 32–38, 103–107, 211, 285, 307–310, 501–503
  in affective change process, 478–479
  cognitive-specificity hypothesis, 392–394
  control groups, 40
  critical vs. common features, 44–45, 47–48
  in depression, 17–19
  methodological issues, 38–41, 501–502
  treatment implications, 394–396
S-R Inventory of General Trait Anxiousness (S-R GTA), 147–148, 161
State-Trait Anxiety Inventory (STAI), 12, 144–145, 152, 215, 305–306, 431
State-Trait Anxiety Inventory for Children (STAIC), 13, 179–180, 183–188
Stress, 286–289, 308, *see also* Life events, 264–271
  and coping models, 67–68
  transactional model, 288–289
Stress inoculation training, 428–433
Suicide, 105, 211, 262
Symptom Checklist-90 (SCL-90), 149–150, 151, 153, 161
Systematic desensitization, 419–422, 427–428, 431

T

Taylor Manifest Anxiety Scale (TMAS), 142–143, 151, 161
Theory
  behavioral, 55–74
  cognitive factors in life events, 245
  cognitive factors in social support, 269
  cognitive-behavioral, 27–54, 56
  emotion, 3–22
  meta-construct model, 41–48
  specificity, 29
Treatment
  behavioral, 413–443
  cognitive therapy, 396–405
  cognitive-behavioral, 379–405
  pharmacological, 6, 118
  process of affective change, 455–486
  similarities/differences for anxiety/depression, 6, 441–443
Type A pattern, 287

V

Validity, 39, 93–97, 136–138, 150–155, 160–162, 184, 217, 259, 502
Vulnerability, 211, 265–267, 308, 348, 385–386, 390–392

Z

Zung Self-Rating Anxiety Scale, 143–144
Zung Self-Rating Depression Scale, 141

List of Previous Volumes

PERSONALITY AND PSYCHOPATHOLOGY
A Series of Monographs, Tests, and Treatises
David T. Lykken, Editor

1. The Anatomy of Achievement Motivation, *Heinz Heckhausen.**
2. Cues, Decisions, and Diagnoses: A Systems-Analytic Approach to the Diagnosis of Psychopathology, *Peter E. Nathan.**
3. Human Adaptation and Its Failures, *Leslie Phillips.**
4. Schizophrenia: Research and Theory, *William E. Broen, Jr.**
5. Fears and Phobias, *I. M. Marks.*
6. The Language of Emotion, *Joel R. Davitz.*
7. Feelings and Emotions, *Magda Arnold.*
8. Rhythms of Dialogue: The Loyola Symposium, *Joseph Jaffe* and *Stanley Feldstein.*
9. Character Structure and Impulsiveness, *David Kipnis.*
10. The Control of Aggression and Violence: Cognitive and Physiological Factors, *Jerome L. Singer* (Ed.).
11. The Attraction Paradigm, *Donn Byrne.*
12. Objective Personality Assessment: Changing Perspectives, *James N. Butcher* (Ed.).
13. Schizophrenia and Genetics, *Irving I. Gottesman* and *James Shields.**
14. Imagery and Daydream Methods in Psychotherapy and Behavior Modification, *Jerome L. Singer.*

*Titles initiated during the series editorship of Brendan Maher.

15. Experimental Approaches to Psychopathology, *Mitchell L. Kietzman, Samuel Sutton,* and *Joseph Zubin* (Eds.).
16. Coping and Defending: Processes of Self-Environment Organization, *Norma Haan.*
17. The Scientific Analysis of Personality and Motivation, *R. B. Cattell* and *P. Kline.*
18. The Determinants of Free Will: A Psychological Analysis of Responsible, Adjustive Behavior, *James A. Easterbrook.*
19. The Psychopath in Society, *Robert J. Smith.*
20. The Fears of Adolescents, *J. H. Bamber.*
21. Cognitive-Behavioral Interventions: Theory, Research, and Procedures, *Philip C. Kendall* and *Steven D. Hollon* (Eds.).
22. The Psychobiology of the Depressive Disorders: Implications for the Effects of Stress, *Richard A. Depue* (Ed.).
23. The Mental Health of Women, *Marcia Guttenberg, Susan Salasin,* and *Deborah Belle* (Eds.).
24. Assessment Strategies for Cognitive-Behavioral Interventions, *Philip C. Kendall* and *Steven D. Hollon* (Eds.).
25. Prolonged Psychosocial Effects of Disaster: A Study of Buffalo Creek, *Goldine C. Gleser, Bonnie L. Green,* and *Carolyn Winget.*
26. Adult Sexual Interest in Children, *Mark Cook* and *Kevin Howells* (Eds.).
27. Neurosis and the Social Environment, *A. S. Henderson, D. G. Byrne,* and *P. Duncan-Jones.*
28. Suicide and Self-Damaging Behavior: A Sociobiological Perspective, *Denys deCatanzaro.*
29. The Inheritance of Personality and Ability: Research Methods and Findings, *Raymond B. Cattell.*
30. The Abilities and Achievements of Orientals in North America, *Philip E. Vernon.*
31. Symptomatic Affective Disorders: A Study of Depression and Mania Associated with Physical Disease and Medication, *F. A. Whitlock.*
32. Physique and Delinquent Behavior: A Thirty-Year Follow-Up of William H. Sheldon's Varieties of Delinquent Youth, *Emil M. Hartl, Edward P. Monnelly,* and *Roland D. Elderkind.*
33. Gender and Psychopathology, *Ihsan Al-Issa* (Ed.).

PERSONALITY, PSYCHOPATHOLOGY, AND PSYCHOTHERAPY
A Series of Monographs, Texts, and Treatises
David T. Lykken and Philip C. Kendall, Editors

34. Obsessional Experience and Compulsive Behavior: A Cognitive-Structural Approach, *Graham F. Reed.*
35. Information Processing Approaches to Clinical Psychology, *Rick E. Ingram* (Ed.).
36. Treatment and Prevention of Alcohol Problems: A Resource Manual, *W. Miles Cox* (Ed.).
37. Psychopathology: An Interactional Perspective, *David Magnusson* and *Arne Öhman* (Eds.).
38. Inside Rational-Emotive Therapy: A Critical Appraisal of the Theory and Therapy of Albert Ellis, *Michael E. Bernard* and *Raymond DiGiuseppe* (Eds.).
39. Anxiety and Depression: Distinctive and Overlapping Features, *Philip C. Kendall* and *David Watson* (Eds.).